Food Plants of the Sonoran Desert

Food Plants of the Sonoran Desert

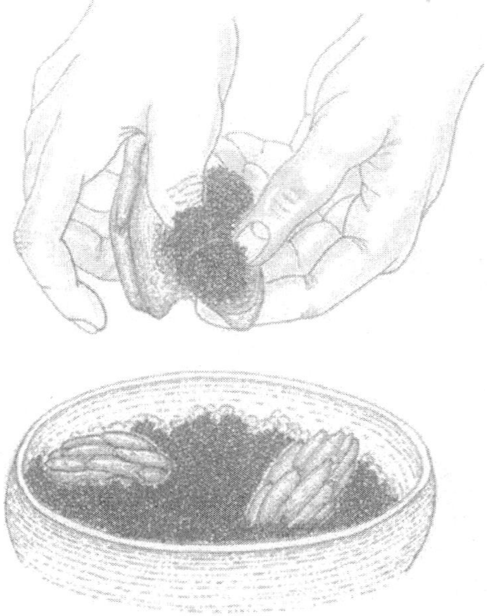

WENDY C. HODGSON

THE UNIVERSITY OF ARIZONA PRESS | TUCSON

The University of Arizona Press
www.uapress.arizona.edu

First paperback edition 2016

Printed in the United States of America
21 20 19 18 17 16 7 6 5 4 3 2

ISBN-13: 978-0-8165-2060-2 (cloth)
ISBN-13: 978-0-8165-3283-4 (paper)

Cover photograph, Saguaro fruit © David Burckhalter.
Cover illustrations by Wendy C. Hodgson
Original cover design by Sigrid Albert

Library of Congress Cataloging-in-Publication Data
Hodgson, Wendy C., 1951–
Food plants of the Sonoran Desert / Wendy C. Hodgson.
p. cm.
Includes bibliographical references and index.
ISBN 0-8165-2060-7 (acid-free paper)
1. Indians of North America—Ethnobotany—Southwest, New.
2. Indians of North America—Ethnobotany—Sonoran Desert.
3. Indians of North America—Food—Sonoran Desert.
4. Ethnobotany—Sonoran Desert. I. Title.
E78.57 H68 2000
581.6'32'0979—dc21
00-008564

British Library Cataloguing-in-Publication Data
A catalogue record for this book is available from the British Library.

♾ This paper meets the requirements of ANSI/NISO Z39.48-1992 (Permanence of Paper).

In memory of Rick, Rodney, and Joanne

CONTENTS

List of Illustrations ix
Preface xiii
Acknowledgments xv
Introduction 1

CATALOGUE OF FOOD PLANTS OF THE SONORAN DESERT

GYMNOSPERMS

Ephedraceae | Ephedra or Mormon-tea Family 11

ANGIOSPERMS: MONOCOTS

Agavaceae | Agave or Century-plant Family 13
Alismataceae | Water-plantain Family 51
Arecaceae | Palm Family 52
Commelinaceae | Spiderwort Family 56
Cyperaceae | Sedge Family 57
Dioscoreaceae | Yam Family 58
Liliaceae | Lily Family 58
Nolinaceae | Bear-grass Family 62
Poaceae | Grass Family 64
Typhaceae | Cattail Family 71
Zosteraceae | Eel-grass Family 72

ANGIOSPERMS: DICOTS

Acanthaceae | Acanthus Family 75
Aizoaceae | Aizoon, Mesem, or fig-marigold Family 75
Amaranthaceae | Amaranth Family 77
Anacardiaceae | Cashew or Sumac Family 81
Apocynaceae | Dogbane Family 84
Asclepiadaceae | Milkweed Family 84
Asteraceae | Aster Family 86
Bataceae | Saltwort Family 90
Begoniaceae | Begonia Family 90
Berberidaceae | Barberry Family 90
Bixaceae | Lipsticktree Family 91
Bombacaceae | Cottontree or Kapok-tree Family 95
Boraginaceae | Borage Family 97
Brassicaceae | Mustard Family 97
Burseraceae | Torchwood or Frankincense Family 100
Cactaceae | Cactus Family 100
Capparaceae | Caper Family 147
Caprifoliaceae | Honeysuckle Family 148
Celastraceae | Stafftree or Bittersweet Family 149
Chenopodiaceae | Goosefoot Family 149
Convolvulaceae | Morning-glory Family 153

Crassulaceae | Stonecrop Family 157
Cucurbitaceae | Gourd Family 157
Ebenaceae | Persimmon or Ebony Family 160
Euphorbiaceae | Spurge Family 160
Fabaceae | Pea or Legume Family 162
Fagaceae | Beech Family 189
Fouquieriaceae | Ocotillo Family 195
Geraniaceae | Geranium Family 196
Juglandaceae | Walnut Family 196
Koeberliniaceae | Junco Family 198
Lamiaceae | Mint Family 198
Lennoaceae | Lennoa Family 204
Loasaceae | Stickleaf or Blazing-star Family 207
Malpighiaceae | Malpighia or Barbados-cherry Family 209
Malvaceae | Mallow Family 209
Martyniaceae | Unicorn Family 209
Moraceae | Mulberry Family 212
Nyctaginaceae | Four-o'clock Family 214
Orobanchaceae | Broom-rape Family 215
Oxalidaceae | Woodsorrel Family 216
Passifloraceae | Passion-flower Family 216
Phytolaccaceae | Pokeberry or Pokeweed Family 217
Plantaginaceae | Plantain Family 218
Polygonaceae | Buckwheat Family 218
Portulacaceae | Purslane Family 221
Resedaceae | Mignonette Family 222
Rhamnaceae | Buckthorn Family 224
Rhizophoraceae | Red Mangrove Family 227
Rosaceae | Rose Family 227
Rubiaceae | Madder Family 229
Sapotaceae | Sapote or Sapodilla Family 230
Simmondsiaceae | Jojoba Family 232
Solanaceae | Nightshade or Potato Family 233
Sterculiaceae | Chocolate or Cacao Family 239
Theophrastaceae | Theophrasta Family 240
Ulmaceae | Elm Family 240
Verbenaceae | Vervain or Verbena Family 241
Viscaceae | Mistletoe or Christmas Mistletoe Family 243
Vitaceae | Grape Family 244

APPENDIX I. Plant Species and Parts Used 249
APPENDIX II. Fruiting Periods of Selected Species Providing Edible Fruit 265
APPENDIX III. Fruiting Periods of Selected Species Providing Edible Seeds 269
APPENDIX IV. Common Names (Non-English) 273
Literature Cited 281
Index 299

ILLUSTRATIONS

Note: The scale bar on pen-and-ink drawings depicts one centimeter.

1 Map of the Sonoran Desert and historic distribution of indigenous people ... 1
2 *Pennisetum ciliare* ... 4
3 Plants and People of the Sonoran Desert exhibit, Desert Botanical Garden ... 6
4 *Ephedra trifurca* ... 11
5 Roasted and sliced *cabezas* of an unknown agave ... 14
6 *Agave deserti* ... 15
7 *Agave chrysantha* ... 16
8 *Agave palmeri* ... 16
9 *Agave deserti* ... 20
10 Baja California groups and edible agaves ... 24
11 *Agave zebra* ... 29
12 *Agave vivipara* ... 30
13 María Beltran ... 31
14 *Agave* cf. *shrevei* ssp. *shrevei* ... 31
15 *Agave murpheyi* ... 35
16 *Agave murpheyi,* bulbils in inflorescence ... 35
17 *Agave murpheyi* ... 36
18 Close-up of turtleback scraper ... 36
19 *Agave delamateri* ... 37
20 *Agave delamateri,* close-up of plant ... 37
21 *Agave delamateri* ... 38
22 *Hesperoyucca whipplei* ... 43
23 *Yucca baccata* ... 46
24 *Yucca elata* ... 47
25 *Yucca arizonica* ... 48
26 *Yucca arizonica,* plant with immature fruits ... 48
27 *Yucca schottii,* plant with green fruits ... 48
28 *Yucca schottii,* plant with green fruits ... 48
29 *Yucca schidigera* ... 49
30 *Yucca schidigera,* close-up of fruits ... 49
31 *Sabal uresana,* close-up of greenish fruits ... 54
32 *Sabal uresana* ... 54
33 *Sabal uresana* ... 55
34 *Dioscorea remotiflora* ... 58
35 *Dichelostemma capitatum* ssp. *pauciflorum* ... 60
36 *Hesperocallis undulata,* close-up of corms ... 61
37 *Triteleiopsis palmeri,* corms and grasslike first leaves ... 61
38 *Dasylirion wheeleri* ... 62
39 *Dasylirion* sp. ... 63
40 *Panicum hirticaule* var. *miliaceum* ... 67

41 *Typha domingensis* 71
42 *Typha domingensis,* close-up of whitish rhizomes 71
43 *Trianthema portulacastrum* 76
44 *Amaranthus palmeri* 77
45 *Amaranthus palmeri* 79
46 *Rhus trilobata,* close-up of leaves and fruits 82
47 *Marsdenia edulis* 84
48 *Matelea* cf. *arizonica* or *M. producta,* vine in flower 85
49 *Sarcostemma cynanchoides,* close-up of submature fruits 85
50 *Sarcostemma cynanchoides,* close-up of flowers 86
51 *Helianthus niveus* 88
52 *Pectis papposa* 89
53 *Berberis haematocarpa,* branch with mature fruits 90
54 *Berberis harrisoniana,* branch with mature fruits 90
55 *Amoreuxia palmatifida,* close-up of flowers 91
56 *Amoreuxia palmatifida,* habit 91
57 *Amoreuxia palmatifida* 92
58 *Amoreuxia gonzalezii* 93
59 *Amoreuxia gonzalezii* 93
60 *Ceiba acuminata,* trunk with conical spines 95
61 *Ceiba acuminata,* young plant 95
62 *Ceiba acuminata,* close-up of green, immature fruits 96
63 *Ceiba acuminata* 96
64 *Carnegiea gigantea,* mature fruits 100
65 Juanita Ahill collecting saguaro fruit 103
66 Mrs. Noceo straining saguaro syrup 104
67 *Carnegiea gigantea* 104
68 Juanita Ahill straining saguaro fruit for syrup 105
69 Noceo family at summer camp 105
70 Saguaro fruit-gathering and fruit-processing camp exhibit 105
71 *Cylindropuntia acanthocarpa* 107
72 Gila River Pimas picking cholla buds 108
73 Lining cholla-bud baking pit with rocks 109
74 Carefully taking cooked cholla buds out of pit 110
75 Drying cholla buds on screens 110
76 Edna Jones winnowing cooked cholla buds 111
77 *Cylindropuntia versicolor* 113
78 *Cylindropuntia arbuscula* 113
79 *Cylindropuntia fulgida,* close-up of fruits 114
80 *Cylindropuntia leptocaulis* 115
81 *Echinocereus engelmannii* 116
82 *Echinocereus engelmannii,* mature fruits 116
83 *Ferocactus wislizeni, F. cylindraceus* spine cluster, *F. emoryi* spine cluster 119
84 *Ferocactus wislizeni,* habit with flowers and flower buds 119
85 *Myrtillocactus cochal* 124
86 *Opuntia engelmannii,* young pads 126

87 *Opuntia engelmannii,* mature fruit 127
88 *Opuntia engelmannii,* pads, fruits, and flowers 127
89 *Opuntia* sp. 130
90 *Pachycereus pecten-aboriginum* 131
91 *Pachycereus pringlei,* immature fruits 132
92 *Pachycereus pringlei* 132
93 *Pachycereus pringlei* 133
94 *Peniocereus greggii* var. *transmontanus* 135
95 *Peniocereus greggii* var. *transmontanus,* roots 135
96 *Stenocereus gummosus* 138
97 *Stenocereus thurberi* 140
98 *Stenocereus thurberi,* trunked 146
99 *Sambucus nigra* ssp. *canadensis,* branches and fruits 148
100 *Ipomoea arborescens* 154
101 *Merremia aurea* 155
102 *Apodanthera undulata* 157
103 *Cucurbita digitata,* leaves and immature fruit 158
104 Rosa Flores and José Astorga dig for the tuberlike roots of *Cnidoscolus palmeri* 161
105 Rosa Flores obtains the roots of *Cnidoscolus palmeri* 161
106 *Cercidium floridum,* immature pods 164
107 *Cercidium microphyllum,* mature pods 164
108 *Crotalaria pumila* 168
109 *Lysiloma candida* 169
110 *Olneya tesota,* habit with immature fruit 170
111 *Phaseolus acutifolius* var. *tenuifolius* and *P. filiformis* 172
112 *Phaseolus acutifolius* var. *latifolius,* habit and fruits 173
113 Five-pound bag of domesticated tepary beans 174
114 *Pithecellobium dulce,* seeds with edible aril 177
115 *Prosopis pubescens* 182
116 *Prosopis velutina* 184
117 *Prosopis velutina,* in flower and with mature pods 185
118 *Prosopis* sp., diagrammatic representation of fruit 188
119 *Quercus emoryi* 190
120 *Quercus emoryi* 191
121 *Juglans major* 197
122 *Salvia columbariae* 200
123 *Salvia columbariae,* habit 201
124 *Salvia carduacea,* habit and inflorescences 203
125 *Pholisma sonorae,* flattened disk with flowers 204
126 *Pholisma sonorae* 204
127 Gary Nabhan digging for underground stems of *Pholisma sonorae* 205
128 *Pholisma sonorae,* succulent underground stems 206
129 *Proboscidea parviflora* 210
130 *Proboscidea parviflora* 210
131 *Proboscidea althaeifolia* 211
132 *Proboscidea althaeifolia,* tuberlike roots 211

133 Tohono O'odham basket with fruit of *Proboscidea parviflora* var. *hohokamiana* ... 211
134 *Passiflora foetida* var. *arizonica* ... 216
135 *Antigonon leptopus* ... 219
136 *Rumex hymenosepalus*, habit with mature fruits and tuberlike root ... 220
137 *Condalia warnockii* var. *kearneyana* and *C. globosa* var. *pubescens* ... 224
138 *Karwinskia parvifolia* var. *pubescens* ... 225
139 *Zizyphus obtusifolius* var. *canescens*, branch with mature fruits and large seeds ... 226
140 *Randia echinocarpa*, branch with immature fruits ... 230
141 *Randia obcordata* and *R. echinocarpa* ... 230
142 *Sideroxylon occidentale* ... 231
143 *Simmondsia chinensis*, habit with mature fruit ... 232
144 *Capsicum annuum* var. *glabriusculum*, close-up of mature fruits ... 234
145 *Capsicum annuum* var. *glabriusculum* ... 235
146 *Lycium exsertum* ... 237
147 *Physalis crassifolia* ... 238
148 *Lantana horrida*, close-up of leaves, flowers, and mature fruits ... 241
149 *Lippia palmeri*, close-up of branches and subsessile inflorescence ... 242
150 *Lippia palmeri* and *L. berlandieri* ... 242
151 *Vitis* sp. ... 246

PREFACE

When I'm out with the Indian women, gathering roots and materials
for basket making, it's not that I expect to make baskets or drink their medicine,
it's the things you sort of soak up from the earth while you're with them,
it's the things that make women wise. I don't know if I can explain—
it's not as if they learned about the willows and the grasses in order to
make baskets, but as if they learned to make baskets by knowing willows.
I guess men used to learn that way once—learned to make bows
by knowing the junipers, the way the branches bend and spring back.
But now they try to do all their learning in their heads.

—*Mary Austin (1988:41)*

Since I first began studying Sonoran Desert edible plants nearly 25 years ago, I found a wealth of information that ranged from bare-bone statements without reference to specific plants used to clearly defined uses of documented plants, preparation methods, and their significance to native peoples. Popular publications on edible plants of various geographic regions include plants that grow in the Sonoran Desert. William Ebeling (1986) produced a valuable work on the useful plants of arid regions of North America. The first volume of the much-anticipated work regarding the useful plants of Texas has been published (Cheatham et al. 1995) and includes a wealth of information, including descriptions of methods actually tried by the authors. Readers must continue to be patient, however, because genera described are arranged alphabetically and the first volume covers *Abronia* to *Arundo*. David Moerman (1998) also provides information on many plants used by Native Americans.

This book is an expansion of previous work (Hodgson 1982). It provides information on the use of Sonoran Desert plants for food, based on current research, herbarium vouchers, ethnographies, personal narratives, and historic documents, and correlates this information with current taxonomy.

Although I have explored a number of sources and lived among and studied desert plants for 30 years, I still have not, nor will I ever, experience the intimacy shared by many whose roots were/are here in the Sonoran Desert and who interacted with its plants on a daily basis. Given that, however, it is my hope that botanists, ethnobotanists, and archaeologists will find this book a basis for (1) studying Sonoran Desert plant usage and its significance to cultures; and (2) conserving the more rare, useful plants, their habitat, and their folklore. For others, may their curiosity and appreciation of this magnificent desert be heightened beyond knowing what can be pulled from the ground or plucked from the bush.

ACKNOWLEDGMENTS

I am grateful to a number of people, close friends, and colleagues who have generously given me their time, talent, experiences, and encouragement over the years as I compiled this manuscript. My deepest thanks and appreciation are to Edward "Ted" Anderson, Vorsila Bohrer, Tony Burgess, Pat Comus, Richard Felger, Joe McAuliffe, Gary Nabhan, Donald Pinkava (who also first suggested this topic for study), and Amadeo Rea. They unselfishly gave a great deal of assistance, spent many hours reviewing the manuscript, and provided numerous thought-provoking discussions. A special thank you is given to Amy Prince, Julie Ramsden, Jon Rebman, and Liz Slauson for their encouragement, assistance, and good times in the field. I am also grateful to Karen Adams, Martha Burgess, Culver Cassa, Kevin Dahl, Yvonne Fortier, Robert Gasser, Ruth Greenhouse, Laura Jackson, Christine Mullen, Suzanne Nelson, and Bear. Sincere gratitude is expressed to the Desert Botanical Garden and the support of Robert Breunig and Carolyn O'Malley. Special thanks go to Jane Cole, former librarian at the garden. Diane Bean and Jennifer Orf continued to provide library assistance. Thanks also to Pat Smith, who provided the graphs in the appendixes. David Reichert, formerly with Dawson's Book Shop, Los Angeles, not only made me aware of publications available for study, but made me spend a lot of money.

I am indebted to the present and former directors, curators, and assistants at the following herbaria: Donald Pinkava and Les Landrum, Arizona State University (ASU); Charles Mason and Rebecca Wilson, University of Arizona (ARIZ); and Bruce Bartholemew, California Academy of Sciences (CAS). I also thank Tony Burgess for information on flowering and fruiting times of a number of edible Sonoran Desert plants. I am grateful to the curators at Arizona State Museum for the use of Helga Teiwes's fine photographs and Ché Puiche and Paula Liken of Mesa Museum for the use of some of my drawings.

I thank former and current staff at the University of Arizona Press, namely Barbara Beatty, Gregory McNamee, Alan Schroder, Jennifer Shopland, Marie Webner, and particularly Christine Szuter, director. I also thank Lisa DiDonato, copyeditor, for her care in reviewing the manuscript; also Linda Gregonis for providing the index. Thanks also to the Secretaria de Relaciones Exteriores, Mexico City, for permission to study and document *Agave* and *Amoreuxia* in northern Mexico.

I thank my mother and brothers and other friends who provided reassurance and encouragement throughout the completion of this book. Special appreciation and gratitude are extended to those who have passed on: Rick DeLamater, Rodney Engard, Howard S. Gentry, and Joanne "Jo" Winter, who enriched my own life as well as the lives of many. Finally, my sincerest thanks and gratitude to all those who have called the Sonoran Desert their home, whose intimate knowledge of plants and their environs might be better understood and appreciated by those who take the time to look, listen, and learn.

Food Plants of the Sonoran Desert

INTRODUCTION

The Sonoran Desert is defined according to Shreve (1964) and Wiggins (1964; for possible modifications, see McLaughlin 1989; Schmidt 1989). It comprises approximately 310,000 square kilometers and includes parts of Arizona, California, Baja California, and Sonora (fig. 1). Approximately 540 plants that grow in the Sonoran Desert are or may be considered edible and represent approximately one-fifth of the desert's flora (appendix 1). Nearly 10 percent of the edible plants are established exotics.

The borderlands region, which takes in the Sonoran Desert, is an area of rich natural and cultural diversity (fig. 1). In addition to the numerically dominant Hispanic and Anglo cultures of the borderlands, there are 73 other linguistically distinct indigenous cultures. More than 350,000 Native Americans live within the states along the U.S./Mexico border. There are approximately 75 Indian reservations in the states along the U.S. border and at least 25 *reservas indígenas* or other cultural enclaves for native Mexican peoples in northwestern Mexico. Native people have intimate, detailed knowledge about plants, including those useful, rare, or endangered plants that grow in the vicinity of their homes. Don Pedro Estrella Tánori's knowledge of the otherwise poorly known and very rare *saiya, Amoreuxia gonzalezii,* and Laura Kermen's fond memories of once harvesting stands of *Agave murpheyi* represent valuable information from indigenous people concerning rare plants that is often overlooked. Such oral histories remain the most important means of obtaining ethnobotanical information and can supplement or negate written historical documents, where facts may be distorted because of personal biases (see Nabhan et al. 1989a).

During the visitation and subsequent colonization by Europeans, personal narratives sometimes provided the first recorded observations of plant usage by indigenous peoples. Early accounts can provide a wealth of information. This is especially true for developing an understanding of Baja California and its indigenous inhabitants, who were exterminated throughout the southern two-thirds to three-fourths of the peninsula by the early 1800s. Fortunately, an increasing number of such accounts and documents are being translated into English, thereby making them more easily accessible. Baja California provides a unique opportunity for study in that most of its inhabitants south of 30°N

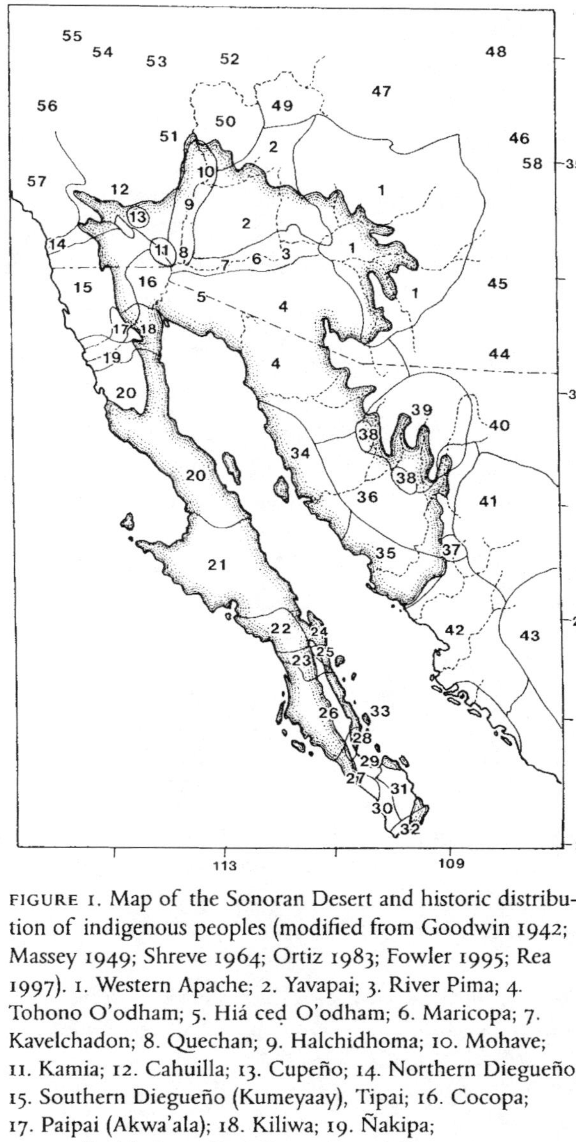

FIGURE 1. Map of the Sonoran Desert and historic distribution of indigenous peoples (modified from Goodwin 1942; Massey 1949; Shreve 1964; Ortiz 1983; Fowler 1995; Rea 1997). 1. Western Apache; 2. Yavapai; 3. River Pima; 4. Tohono O'odham; 5. Hiá cẹd O'odham; 6. Maricopa; 7. Kavelchadon; 8. Quechan; 9. Halchidhoma; 10. Mohave; 11. Kamia; 12. Cahuilla; 13. Cupeño; 14. Northern Diegueño; 15. Southern Diegueño (Kumeyaay), Tipai; 16. Cocopa; 17. Paipai (Akwa'ala); 18. Kiliwa; 19. Ñakipa; 20–25. Cochimí: 20. Borjeño; 21. Ignacieño; 22. Cadegomeño; 23. Laymon; 24. Didiu; 25. Monquí; 26. Guaicura; 27. Callejue; 28. Periúe; 29. Aripe; 30. Huchiti; 31. Cora; 32. Pericú; 33. Isleño; 34. Seri; 35. Yaqui (and Mayo combined under the name Cáhita); 36. Pima Bajo; 37. Guarihio; 38. Eudeve; 39. Ópata; 40. Mountain Pima; 41. Tarahumara; 42. Mayo; 43. Tepehuan; 44. Jano; 45. Chiricahua Apache; 46. Zuni; 47. Hopi; 48. Navajo; 49. Havasupai; 50. Hualapai; 51. Chemehuevi; 52. Shivwit; 53. Southern Paiute; 54. Timbisha Shoshone; 55. Panamint; 56. Kawaiisu; 57. Luiseño; 58. Tewa.

latitude did not produce pottery or exhibit other cultural traits characteristic of more-advanced groups but rather retained primitive traits long lost by other cultures. Much of this retained primitiveness is believed to be due to the isolation fostered by the characteristics of the peninsula itself. To help put this into perspective, natives of central and southern Baja California were being introduced to pottery and cooking vessels brought over by the Spaniards less than a century before Thomas Edison constructed the first central power station in New York City.

Other sources of information on how plants were used or perceived include ethnographies, which were based on information that may not be consistent throughout the group, and the ethnographer's interpretation of the information. However, by the time ethnographers arrived, indigenous peoples had often already undergone considerable acculturation, and their own aboriginal culture may have been lost or shifted. Even the more-isolated natives of Baja California were not immune to acculturation prior to the establishment of the missions on the peninsula. As Michael Mathes (1981) points out, the process of acculturation was well in place by the time the first mission was established in San Bruno in 1683, having begun nearly 150 years earlier. In 1535 Fernando Cortes arrived on the peninsula with soldiers, sheep, horses, hogs, and weapons (Mathes 1973). Explorers, pearl fishermen, pirates, and a few Jesuit missionaries continued to roam the southern end of the peninsula or its waters before the arrival of the Jesuit Frs. Kino, Salvatierra, Píccolo, Baegert, and del Barco, among others. Although far less scholarly than the careful observations and writings of Fr. Miguel del Barco in the mid 1700s, documents or reports on such early travels can provide important information in helping us understand the life and culture of the natives of Baja California.

Herbarium voucher specimens are a critical part of ethnobiological studies. They provide physical and permanent documentation for the scientific identity of the biological material about which observations and data are recorded and form the basis for review or reassessment of the original study (Bye 1986). Voucher specimens serve as the crucial link between folk knowledge and Western science; yet, despite their importance, they are not accepted or included in all disciplines. Although personal narratives are important sources of information, any reference to plant use or distribution is often difficult to understand because voucher specimens were not usually made. We can be grateful to Annetta Carter for her careful determinations and comments regarding Fr. del Barco's observations and descriptions of plants and their use. The works of J. N. Rose, Townsend Brandegee, and Edward Palmer in the late 1800s and early 1900s in Sonora, Sinaloa, Baja California, and Arizona are particularly important in that they included accounts of how vouchered, accurately identified (many previously undescribed) plants were used. Unfortunately, many of Palmer's notes were unpublished or lost (Bye 1972). Rogers McVaugh (1956), W. E. Safford, and Dr. W. A. Archer began sorting and processing his material (Bye 1972). Dr. Archer assembled Palmer's original notes, specimen records, and photos from various sources into the Safford-Palmer Ethnobotanical card file.

Later ethnographies tended to include the documentation of plants. Those studies with plant collections verified by a botanist are of greater value, particularly if specimens have been lost or destroyed. For example, Edward Gifford's (1932, 1936) studies on the Yavapai included plants whose determinations were made by J. Thomas Howell and Alice Eastwood. Plants discussed by Amadeo Rea in his already-classic work on the Gila River Pima (Rea 1997) were all vouchered and examined by experts of the taxa.

Our understanding of ethnobotany has continued to evolve since the term was first coined in 1895, although the discipline was practiced much earlier (Davis 1995). Rather than being simply defined as how people use/used plants, which stresses only utilitarian purposes, modern ethnobotany encompasses how people perceived and interacted with each and all of the plants within their environs. I think of ethnobotany as the study of the "cultural/natural ecosystem" (although we are a part of the natural ecosystem, whether we like to admit it or not). Modern ethnobotany is concerned with the "totality of the place of plants in a culture" (Ford 1978). Janis Alcorn (1995:24) describes it as "the study of plant-human interrelationships embedded in dynamic ecosystems of natural and social components"; it is the "study of contextualized plant use, shaped by history, physical and social environments and by inherent qualities of the plants themselves." E. Wade Davis (1995:43) reminds us that the emphasis in ethnobotany shifted from "the raw compilation of plant names and uses to an intellectual perspective that viewed the character of a people's relationship with the plant world as but one means of approaching an understanding of the cognitive foundations of a culture." Davis noted that modern ethnobotanists must record "not only lists of plant uses but a vision of life itself," which he conceded as a very difficult task. Davis (1995:44) continued: "[Ethnobotanists must] understand not just how a specific group of people use plants but how that group perceives them, how it interprets those perceptions, how those perceptions influence the activities of members of that society, and how those activities, in turn, influence the ambient vegetation and the ecosystem upon which the society depends."

Changes within Biological and Cultural Communities

The Sonoran Desert has been influenced by humans for all of its existence. To attempt to study so-called natural systems without including human presence is unrealistic, "the myth [that] there is a world out there without human influence" (Rea 1987). Just as certain plants or plant populations suffered from exploitation, harvesting practices benefited others. Harvesting underground rhizomes or roots of such plants as *Dichelostemma capitatum, Triteleiopsis palmeri, Amoreuxia palmatifida,* or *A. gonzalezii* may have encouraged their production and dispersal. Kay Fowler (1999) notes that Timbisha Shoshone women pinched off the ends of branches of piñon (*Pinus edulis* Engelm.) and *Quercus* sp., whereupon the number of cones and acorns increased. Intentionally set fires were an important resource-management tool for acquiring animal and plant foods (see Dobyns 1978, 1981; Bohrer 1992). Evidence suggests that pre-Columbian peoples collected the grain of native grasses that thrived on disturbed ground in La Ciudad, in the Salt River valley (Bohrer 1992). The manipulation of habitat or individual plants within the habitat by indigenous people is an exciting, although not well-understood, area of study. Undoubtedly, our understanding of a cultural/natural ecosystem will increase with the realization that habitat manipulation was probably a common agronomic tool.

However, the rate of change within biological communities has accelerated during the last 200 years, considerably so during the last 20 to 50 years (for an in-depth account of the demise of the Gila River, see Dobyns 1978; Rea 1983). In varying degrees, all desert communities in existence today are artifacts of decades of alteration (Rea 1983). Such changes have affected cultural communities as well. By the time serious floristic studies were done in New Mexico during the late 1880s and after the 1930s, plant distributions were much altered (Bohrer 1978). Vorsila Bohrer (1978:11) suggested that "our botanical understanding of the land could be historically nearsighted." The abundance of certain species has been reduced greatly, some to the point of local extirpation. These include food sources once important to indigenous Americans, such as *Mentzelia albicaulis,* nonweedy *Portulaca, Tradescantia occidentalis* (Bohrer 1978; Fowler 1999), and a number of cool-season grasses (Bohrer 1975). Grasses undoubtedly played a far greater role in the traditional subsistence patterns of various groups prior to domestic grazing. The Anglo's termination of Native American use of fires for hunting (Dobyns 1978) and production of plants for food and fiber, along with subsequent overgrazing of Anglo livestock, resulted in the increase of woody plant species at the expense of grasses and other useful herbaceous plants (Bohrer 1992; Fowler 1999).

The delineation of public and private lands, particularly "protected areas," interfered in native peoples having access to once-important plant populations. No longer could they encourage, tend, or harvest plants. Although acts to protect resources may have been well intended, the exclusion of Native Americans may not be the most sagacious course of action. Instead, the establishment of biosphere units, which usually do not deny access to people who once relied on the resources within the area, may be more appropriate. Careful monitoring of the impacts on resources, particularly rare taxa, should follow. In 1986–1987 Gary Nabhan and I initiated the FLORUTIL Conservation Project, a database that tracks historic and modern uses and management of useful rare plants within the borderlands region of the United States and northern Mexico, particularly national parks and monuments, and biosphere units (see Nabhan et al. 1988). Studies comparing "protected areas" in developed and developing countries that allow or discourage access to and use of the resources will assist us in understanding the effects (both negative and positive) on individual plants, plant communities, and cultural communities.

Such changes of plant-food availability and their effects on cultural communities are illustrated by the virtual disappearance of Sonoran panic grass *(Panicum hirticaule* var. *miliaceum)* and Palmer salt grass *(Distichlis palmeri)* to the Cocopa and the resulting disruption of the Cocopa's traditional harvesting of once-important food sources. Wild devil's claw *(Proboscidea parviflora)* became less available to the Tohono O'odham due to the impact of Anglo's cattle and the diversion of irri-

FIGURE 2. ***Pennisetum ciliare*** (L.) Link., or buffel grass, introduced for cattle forage. Native vegetation on thousands of acres here and elsewhere has been destroyed by the planting of buffel grass; note the one *Stenocereus thurberi* left standing. Approximately seven miles east of Navajoa, Sonora, November 1987.

gation water (Nabhan and Rea 1987). The impact of whites on Tohono O'odham resources was put into perspective by Indian Agent Elmer Howard in the late 1880s (Howard 1887:6):

> The country is fast filling up with cattlemen, whites, and now at almost every spring or well some white man has a herd of cattle, and the inevitable result follows, the Indian is forced to leave. I have traveled one hundred miles over a desert to secure an Indian the privilege of taking water from a well he had dug himself. The mesquite wood is rapidly being exhausted, being cut to supply mining camps and towns, thus depriving them of mesquite beans, which have always been one of their principal items of food.

The end result was that traditional subsistence patterns were significantly disrupted.

We are only beginning to understand the effects on the environment following the intentional or unintentional introduction of species not native to the Sonoran Desert. The preponderance of information in the literature on introduced plants used for food may reflect the fact that formerly important, accessible native food plants were reduced in number. Uses and folklore of some native plants had fallen out, due, perhaps, to their decrease in abundance and accessibility by the time serious ethnographic inquiries were made. With an increase in the abundance of related exotic edible plants, their use and documentation as food items also increased.

Such plant introductions can have more dramatic effects. Texas range-scientists introduced buffel grass, *Pennisetum ciliare* (L.) Link, to Sonorans for use as forage. Where there was once *Stenocereus thurberi*, *Pachycereus pecten-aboriginum*, *Ipomoea arborescens*, *Lophocereus schottii*, and *Cercidium praecox*, there is now a sea of buffel grass (fig. 2). The introduction of this and other nonnative plants continues in the United States as well.

Brassica tournefortii was inadvertently introduced to the New World and was first documented in Arizona in the 1950s (Felger et al. 1992). It has since become a dominant weedy plant in most of the Lower Colorado River valley of the Sonoran Desert and is now established as far north as the Grand Canyon and Colorado Plateau (Brian et al. 2000). Despite its ever-increasing abundance, obvious role in providing fuel for hotter summer fires in the desert, and probable competition with Palmer's blue sand-lily *(Triteleiopsis palmeri)*, *B. tournefortii* has received little attention by scientists.

The heavy use of herbicides and insecticides in the United States and Mexico has also affected the biological and cultural communities of the Sonoran Desert. For example, in 1988 the U.S. Department of Agriculture and American cotton growers initiated the Southwest Boll Weevil Eradication Program in central Arizona (E. Turcotte, pers. comm.). Fifty-four hundred gallons of malathion was allotted to treat 43,179 acres in central Arizona, and indiscriminate spraying was inevitable (Enos 1988). Edible plants along roads and agricultural fields are no longer safe to eat because of heavy herbicide and insecticide spraying. Salt River Pimas have complained about various sicknesses including headaches, sore throats, and nausea they believe were due to heavy spraying near agricultural fields and on their homes. Pesticides used include malathion, methyl parathion, lorsban, galecron, and phosdrin (Enos 1988). *Quelites* that once provided a nutritious, tasty, free traditional food are now used with hesitation. Unfortunately, the Pimas' complaints fell on deaf or denying ears.

The Importance of Traditional Foods to the O'odham

The importance of traditional foods to indigenous desert peoples and the preparation by traditional methods are becoming better understood. Aboriginal people living in both traditional and urban environments have two metabolic characteristics in common: high insulin responses and impaired glucose tolerance (O'Dea et al. 1982). These characteristics could have favored survival in a traditional environment by facilitating efficient fat deposition on an irregular, "feast-or-famine" food supply (Thornburn et al. 1987). In an early account of O'odham diet, the Jesuit missionary Fr. Pfefferkorn noted that a Tohono O'odham often had to go without food for two or three days, but that after such a fast he consumed large quantities of food in a short period of time (Treutlein 1949). The energy stored during food abundance could be used in times of food scarcity. Ethnic populations who resided in desert habitats for centuries may have had gastrointestinal and endocrine systems adapted to metabolizing the many slow-release complex carbohydrate foods available in arid zones (Brand et al. 1990). With a change in dietary habits and energy expenditure associated with urbanization, this "thrifty" metabolism promotes obesity and diabetes.

The River Pima of the Salt and Gila River valleys have the highest documented prevalence of adult-onset diabetes of any ethnic group in the world, with up to 35 percent of their population developing the disease and associated complications by adulthood (Knowler et al. 1978). Their diets today are considerably different from those before 1930, which were dominated by many wild and cultivated desert legumes (Nabhan et al. 1979) supplemented by various cacti (particularly *Opuntia* spp.) and small mucilaginous seeds, such as plants in the mustard and mint families. Donation of government-surplus commodities has led to the daily consumption of Western mainstays such as refined wheat flour, lard, sugar, coffee, and processed cereals (Calloway et al. 1974).

Slow digestion and absorption of starch in traditional foods may have been a factor that helped protect susceptible populations from developing adult-onset diabetes (Brand et al. 1990). Gila River Pima Joe Giff knew this. He remarked that, had they continued using their natural foods, *Se'ehe* would have provided rains that would have produced their desert foods and there would not be any diabetics (Rea 1997). Acorn, mesquite, tepary bean, lima bean, and mature corn meals exhibit low glycemic and insulin indices and slow starch digestibility, with acorns *(Quercus emoryi)* and mesquite *(Prosopis velutina)* pods having the lowest values, when prepared using traditional methods. Western staples such as immature corn, potatoes, bread, and other processed cereal products have rapid starch digestibility and produce high glycemic and insulin indices. Additionally, traditional methods used in preparing meals may also have contributed to the low indices of traditional foods (Brand et al. 1990). For example, acorns ground more coarsely than mesquite pods had a lower glycemic index.

It is also believed that the same hygroscopic mucilage that slows water-vapor loss in such desert plants as plantains (*Plantago* spp.), *chia (Salvia columbariae)*, and pepper-grass (*Lepidium* spp.), which are all Pima food plants, may also slow digestion and absorption in the diet and thus help control diabetes.

Because the Sonoran Desert knows no political boundaries, the conservation of biological and cultural communities requires an international commitment. Research on the useful threatened and endangered plants in the borderland states of the United States and Mexico is in progress. Not until 1989 was a list of plants at risk in the binational Sonoran Desert published (Nabhan et al. 1989c); this work benefited from the work of botanists working in institutions on both sides of the border together with indigenous people. The Desert Botanical Garden's landmark exhibit "Plants and People of the Sonoran Desert" (fig. 3), the brainchild of ethnobotanist Ruth Greenhouse (1986), helps foster an understanding of our area and its native inhabitants. We hope to appreciate and care for our biological and cultural communities now and in the future by having a better understanding of our resources and how they were used and perceived by desert peoples.

Plan of the Book

The catalogue represents those plants included in the flora of the Sonoran Desert based on Wiggins (1964) and Turner et al. (1995). Those plants whose distributions are marginal in geography or elevation are briefly mentioned. The majority of texts on edible plants include descriptions that are far too brief. Rather than follow this trend, I have omitted descriptions altogether. For plant descriptions, the reader can refer to Standley (1920–1926), Gentry (1942), White (1948), Kearney et al. (1960), Wiggins (1964, 1980), Felger (1980), Hickman (1993), Turner et al. (1995), and Martin et al. (1998). Nomenclature primarily follows Wiggins (1964), Lehr (1978), Lehr and Pinkava (1980, 1982), Kartesz and Meacham (1999), and recent revisions or treatments. Authors of scientific plant names were checked with Brummitt and Powell (1992) and Index Kewensis (1997). I have included synonyms ("syn."), in part, to assist the reader; hopefully any confusion with the acceptance of more appropriate, but perhaps unfamiliar, scientific names will be reduced. Herbarium acronyms follow Holmgren et al. (1990):

ARIZ	University of Arizona
ASU	Arizona State University
BCMEX	Universidad Autonoma de Baja California, Ensenada
CAS	California Academy of Sciences
DES	Desert Botanical Garden, Phoenix
NY	New York Botanical Garden
SD	San Diego Natural History Museum

FIGURE 3. Plants and People of the Sonoran Desert exhibit, Desert Botanical Garden, Phoenix, Arizona, August 1993. Photograph by John Nemerovsky, courtesy of Desert Botanical Garden.

English, Hispanic, and, more specifically, Sonoran and Baja Californian names (primarily Spanish) are included, with those names other than English obtained from Standley (1920–1926), White (1948), Gordon et al. (1972), Martinez (1979), Turner et al. (1995), Martin et al. (1998), and herbarium specimens. Local names are often used indiscriminately. The recorded name usually refers to the plant as it reflects Western taxonomy, rather than reflecting the more accurate folk taxonomy. Local names may refer not to the plant itself (as is so often recorded), but to a plant part useful to the culture, as noted and recorded by Fr. Miguel del Barco, a Jesuit missionary who lived among the Cochimí *(sensu lato)* for 30 years. Primarily, Spanish names are listed in appendix 4, with those names used exclusively in Sonora or Baja California shown in boldface type, although a few native names are also included.

Illustrations include plants that may or may not have been an important food plant or commonly encountered. Although documented specimens are invaluable and necessary to any research, few references on useful plants include specimen vouchers. Most of the illustrations have locality data and are vouchered by a herbarium specimen. Dates and condition of plants (presence of flowers, mature fruits, or absence of both) are included, thus offering information as to when plants and their parts can be used as a food.

Appendix 1 includes those food plants whose uses might be inferred but are as yet undocumented or their use is questioned. Those plants whose uses are not yet documented but are related to edible species may or may not have been used for food. Plants used for food but not included in the catalogue are cited with their respective references in appendix 1.

I have included uses of plants by non-Sonoran Desert peoples, although the primary focus is use by Sonoran Desert inhabitants. Including uses by those who live outside the Sonoran Desert may provide insight as to why a plant was or was not used by Sonoran Desert people. Questions that I consider include, Was a plant's use overlooked, never recorded, or never observed? Was there a mistaken identity of the plant? Would a plant's different life cycle or abundance in different regions reflect different use patterns? Why might linguistically and geographically distinct groups use the same plants or species within the same genus in similar manners? Could a plant have become locally extirpated prior to its use being recorded? Evidence suggests that pre-Columbian and historic diets have changed with the addition or deletion of certain foods over time (see Bohrer 1986). Plants may have fallen out of use for various reasons (see Bohrer 1978, 1986, 1991; Minnis 1991). Certain plants that were once important to indigenous peoples' diets may have become locally extirpated. The reverse situation may also arise, that is, the use of a particular plant was not recorded until recently, as exemplified by the Tohono O'odham use of the recently introduced mustard, *B. tournefortii,* as a *quelite.*

Appendices 2 and 3 depict fruiting periods based on specimens examined at ARIZ, ASU, CAS, DES, and data processed and made available by Tony Burgess. The condition of the plant was also recorded. In addition, a plant's locality, collector, date of collection, and collector's notes concerning the abundance and quality of fruits were noted. Only those plants collected within the Sonoran Desert were recorded. In particularly difficult groups, such as *Lycium,* only those specimens annotated by that group's specialist were noted. In appendices 2 and 3, continuous bars indicate the majority of recorded collections in the appropriate condition (i.e., mature fruit or immature fruit, state of fruit utilized). Noncontinuous bars indicate that time period in which the appropriate stage of fruit development is to be expected based on the flowering period; the fact that there were few, scattered collections with fruit; or the time of harvest as stated in the literature.

A number of questions can be addressed when interpreting the graphs in appendices 2 and 3. Were the fruits allowed to ripen after picking? What was the stage of ripening when used (e.g., *Rhus, Celtis,* and *Condalia* fruits were best eaten just as they ripened, prior to drying, and may not be obvious on the herbarium specimen nor mentioned on the label)? Were fruits from the previous season? Were the seeds and fruits still good? Could the harvest period be prolonged by collecting the seeds off the ground or from packrat nests? Does harvesting the fruit prolong flowering period? Are the fruits susceptible to consumption by animals? Are there significant variations in fruiting periods due to differences in elevation or latitude or population and individual variability? Is there any bias in the collections, particularly for those species whose flowering period is most or all of the year (e.g., a particular time of year may be favored for general collecting, such as spring rather than summer or winter, thus not giving a true picture of fruiting time)? Are the determinations correct, particularly in the more difficult groups? The considerations are many and the number of specimens examined and recorded could be expanded significantly to provide more substantial conclusions. However, it is hoped that these graphs illustrate some basic information on the availability of fruits and seeds of particular species.

From so much information there are often differences of opinion as to a plant's usage for food, its importance as a food source, and its palatability. The importance of a food plant to indigenous people can be better understood when considering certain interdependent factors. Such factors include the plant's dependability, availability, method of preparation, transportability to the site of preparation, palatability (including sense of feeling full), nutrient composition, storage characteristics, and a culture's taboos and beliefs. For example, the Cochimí did not eat jojoba fruit because it caused them to vomit, which they believed caused the loss of their souls. In addition, the reader should keep in mind that, although this book may identify similarities or differences *between* linguistic groups, it may not show the varied methods people might have practiced *within* a group.

Rules and suggestions that will aid in the safe use of plants for food are often included in edible plant books (see Harrington 1967; Kirk 1975; Kuhnlein 1985). There is not one safe general rule with respect to the degree of toxicity of a plant or the dosage tolerated by an individual. However, if one does not know what the plant is, how to render it edible, and how much can be eaten (some plants used for food can cause one's gastrointestinal tract to become upset), one should not eat the plant. Despite the large amount of nutritional information for desert plants, there is still much that we do not know about the use of native or established plants for food. We should approach plants with the respect that they deserve and attempt to understand them in their cultural and biological context. Finally, one should not harvest the more vulnerable or rare plants whose populations may suffer as a result; nor should one gather without permission plants protected by state, federal, or tribal law.

Information presented here is my responsibility. Any misinterpretation or errors I have made here are my responsibility alone.

Catalogue of Food Plants of the Sonoran Desert

GYMNOSPERMS

Ephedraceae | Ephedra or Mormon-tea Family

Ephedra | Mormon-tea, joint-fir

E. aspera **Engelmann ex S. Watson**
rough joint-fir, boundary ephedra, popotilla(o), pitamo real, hinimorreal, sanguinaria

E. californica **S. Watson**
California joint-fir, canutillo

E. fasciculata **A. Nelson**
Arizona joint-fir

E. nevadensis **S. Watson**
Nevada joint-fir, popotilla(o), tepopote

E. trifurca **Torrey**
long-leaf joint-fir, cañatilla, canutillo, popotilla(o), tepopote

E. viridis **Coville**
mountain joint-fir

Indigenous cultures who used joint-fir (fig. 4) valued it most for its medicinal qualities, but southwestern people also roasted and ate the relatively large seeds whole or ground them into flour. Although abundant in the northern third of the central desert region of Baja California, joint-firs are not mentioned in the early mission documents, undoubtedly due to the fact that this region was unknown when the earlier, more comprehensive descriptions of native peoples

FIGURE 4. ***Ephedra trifurca*** Torr. Pistillate plant. Mohawk Valley Dunes, Yuma County, Arizona, March 1984 (*Hodgson 2748*, DES).

were written (Aschmann 1997). However, Peveril Meigs (1939) mentioned that the Kiliwa of northern Baja California ate the seeds of *E. californica* as pinole. Despite their unpleasant taste, the seeds were eaten regularly because they were the first to ripen early in the summer (Aschmann 1959).

A number of groups made medicinal teas from *Ephedra*. Salt River Pimas, Santa Ysabel Dieguefios, and Hualapais made a medicinal tea from the green branches (Curtin 1949; Watahomigie et al. 1982; Hedges and Beresford 1986). Pimas collected the ends of fresh or dried branches, which they boiled and steeped (Curtin 1949; *Curtin 14A*, DES). Havasupais collected the stems, put them in a coffee pot filled with cold water, and boiled for two minutes, which prevented the tea from becoming bitter (Weber and Seaman 1985). One person believed that the tea tasted best when prepared during the fall months, although the reason for this belief is unknown. Hualapai elders related how their people gathered the stems during any time of the year, dried them, and made a tea (Phillips et al. 1994). The Hualapai regularly drink this tea, sweetened with sugar, as a remedy or preventative. They also inhale the steam from the tea to treat asthma.

ANGIOSPERMS: MONOCOTS

Agavaceae | Agave, or Century-plant Family

Agave | agave, century-plant, maguey

A. capensis **Gentry**
mesquilito

A. cerulata **Trelease**
mescal

A. chrysantha **Peebles**
golden-flowered agave

A. chrysoglossa **I. M. Johnston**

A. colorata **Gentry**
mescal ceniza

A. datylio **Simon ex Weber**
datiliyo, datilillo, mescaliyo, mescalillo

A. delamateri **Hodgson & Ecker**
Tonto Basin agave, Rick's agave

A. deserti **Engelmann**
amul

A. felgeri **Gentry**
Felger's agave

A. fortiflora **Gentry**

A. gigantensis **Gentry**

A. mckelveyana **Gentry**

A. moranii **Gentry**

A. murpheyi **Gibson**
Hohokam agave

A. palmeri **Engelmann**
Palmer's agave, lechuguilla

A. pelona **Gentry**
mescal pelón

A. shawii **Engelmann**
west coast mescal, else, amal

A. shrevei **Gentry**
lechuguilla, ceniza, totosali

A. sobria **Brandegee**
mescal pardo, pardo

A. subsimplex **Trelease**
mezcal

A. utahensis **Engelmann**
Utah agave, yamp

A. vivipara **Linnaeus (syn.,** *A. angustifolia* **Haworth)**
bacanora, lechuguilla

A. zebra **Gentry**
mescal lechuguilla

In the Southwest and Mexico, agave was (and still is in many areas of Mexico) used for food, alcoholic and nonalcoholic beverages, syrup, fiber, cordage, clothing, sandals, nets, blankets, lances, fire hearths, musical instruments, hedgerows (including boundary demarcations), soap, medicine, and ceremonial purposes. Pre-Columbian, historic, and present-day desert peoples highly valued agaves for their source of sweet, flavorful food; beverage; and fiber and often used the plants (cooked or uncooked) as an article of trade. The term "mescal" is a Native American name applied to agave plants, the cooked parts of agave, or, in northern Mexico, the distilled liquor made from the baked heart, or head (meristem), of the agave (Gentry 1982).

Most commonly the head (heart or caudex, often called *cabeza* or *corazón* in Mexico) of the flowering agave; its tender, young inflorescence; or base of the inflorescence was roasted or baked (fig. 5). There were many variations in the method of agave roasting, from baking the heads in large stone-lined pits to baking the heads without the use of pits. However, the majority of groups, including Baja Californians, baked the heads in large stone pits, a labored and complex process.

The inner, nonfibrous core was the most tender and sweetest part, being eaten immediately, whereas the outer, more fibrous part of the cooked head was usually dried and stored. Large heads were preferred. Although smaller plants such as *A. pelona, A. parviflora,* and *A. polianthiflora* are sweet and palatable, they were not used extensively because of their size (Gentry 1982). Additionally, those agaves having large amounts of sapogenins were generally not used for food because they were bitter tasting, but were used as cleansing agents or sources of fiber. An exception is the use of *A. cerulata* by Cochimí and Seri cultures for food.

Harvesting agave heads often required extensive travel over difficult terrain. An expedition to collect agaves and other plant foods could involve traveling from 16 to 26 kilometers (one way) and the usually heavy plant material had to be brought back to camp, where water was available. Cutting off agave leaves from the head was not only difficult due to their fibrous nature, but somewhat dangerous because they are

FIGURE 5. Roasted and sliced *cabezas* of an unknown agave, said to have come from Michoacan, Mexico. Note whole *cabeza* in left background. Corner stand in Obregon, Sonora, November 1987.

FIGURE 6. ***Agave deserti*** Engelm. Prior to emergence of flowering stalk; note splaying and shortening of innermost leaves. Organ Pipe Cactus National Monument, Pima County, Arizona, March 1987.

often spiny. In addition, many agaves, if not all, have caustic juice within their leaves that irritates (at the very least) one's skin. Once the harvested plants were brought back to camp, their baking required long preparations. For the indigenous cultures that used agave, such labor-intensive activities were worth the time and effort. So important were the plants that their harvest continued for centuries among many different and unrelated cultures.

An agave that is about to develop a noticeable flowering stalk contains large amounts of stored carbohydrates, which are necessary for the stalk's relatively rapid development. Baking converts much of the starch to sugars, thus making the heads sweet and palatable. Generally, the stage considered best for harvesting is just before the flowering stalk appears (fig. 6) or, if the stalk has developed, before it is one meter in height. Fr. Miguel del Barco, a Jesuit missionary who lived for 30 years among the Cochimí in south-central Baja California, was particularly observant of the natives' methods of harvesting agaves (and other plants) during the mid 1700s. He described in detail the proper stage when agaves were to be collected (del Barco 1980:225): "One is aware that they have reached this stage when the heart, which had been surrounded by closed and overlapping leaves, becomes open. The leaves, now opened and separated one from another, have each taken their place. At this stage the leaves that grew lastly are much smaller [becoming more bractlike] than the rest and, if the mezcal is not cut, a shoot gets ready to sprout out in the place where the heart was." In addition, the plant appears very swollen or bulbous at its base as compared to an agave that will not flower that season.

The ability to distinguish flowering agaves from nonflowering agaves and bitter species from nonbitter ones was (and still is) difficult and requires great skill on the part of the harvester. Agaves can vary greatly within a species, and such variability undoubtedly adds to the confusion. Homer Aschmann (1959:65–66) believed "that some Indians [in central Baja California] who used agaves as food did not know how to prepare some species," but he conceded that not all agaves were edible, regardless of their preparation. Aschmann added, "it is probably correct to conclude that some of the first and most useful facts a group of Indians [in the

FIGURE 7. (above) ***Agave chrysantha*** Peebles. Population at Superior, Pinal County, Arizona, November 1950. Photograph courtesy of H. S. Gentry.

FIGURE 8. (below) ***Agave palmeri*** Engelm. growing in same area *A. murpheyi* was said to have grown. Baboquivari Mountains, west side, Tohono O'odham Reservation, July 1988.

central desert region of Baja California] would learn about their territory was which species of agaves they could render edible and how each species should be treated."

Fr. Consag wrote in his diary how his "neophytes" (recently converted and baptized natives who lived at the missions), who accompanied him on his 1751 expedition "from the other side of the peninsula," tried to cook "some large agaves" that grew near the coast west of Santa Gertrudis (Ortega and Balthasar 1944:392). Being from another area, the natives were unfamiliar with these agaves. They apparently wasted a lot of time and effort in cooking these agave hearts, which turned out to be too bitter to eat. Peveril Meigs (1939) also noted how Kiliwas went to the trouble of baking agave heads on one occasion, but prepared bitter-tasting heads. Although some Kiliwas still struggled with distinguishing edible from inedible agaves, they noted that the "west coast Indians" (Diegueños) could make this distinction.

Agaves were the most important food plants to Western Apaches. So important were agaves that "long ago some Apaches would make the lengthy, arduous and sometimes dangerous trip on foot from the Payson area to Oraibi to trade their mescal to the Hopis for corn and blankets" (Gallagher 1976:51). Agaves were said to sustain life for weeks at a time "when other foods were not available" (Buskirk 1986:169). Those plants growing in the "lower country," below the Mogollon Rim, were preferred, although edible species *(A. parryi* var. *parryi)* grew at higher elevations. Northern and Southern Tontos would have had access to *A. chrysantha* (fig. 7), *A. delamateri* (see figs. 19–21), and *A. parryi* var. *parryi* (Hodgson 1999a). The San Carlos Apaches also would have had access to these agaves, particularly *A. chrysantha,* as well as *A. palmeri* (fig. 8) and remnant clones of *A. murpheyi* (see figs. 15–17). One person spoke of a "real good and big mescal" (possibly *A. delamateri*) that grew on Bylas Mountain, along the Gila River valley near Bylas (Buskirk 1986:169). Others related how the best mescal was "where the big cactus [saguaro] grows south of the Salt River." The southern slopes of the Pinaleno Mountains were favorite areas for agave collecting, providing food and an opportunity to escape from the more severe winter climate. The Mescal Mountains, which are located south of Globe and southeast of the Pinal Mountains in Gila County, was a favorite area for collecting agaves by the San Carlos group. Another favorite place to gather and process agaves in the spring was the southern slopes of the Graham (possibly Pinaleno) Mountains and on Turnbull Mountain in Graham County (Goodwin 1942). Here the White Mountain Apaches also had hidden camps from which to send raiding parties to Mexico. *Agave chrysantha* is common and abundant throughout this area. In addition, *A. delamateri, A. toumeyana, A. murpheyi, A. palmeri,* and *A. parryi* var. *parryi* (which usually grows at elevations above the Sonoran Desert proper) are also found as scattered populations or clones (Hodgson 1999a).

The amount of time Western Apaches generally spent traveling to, gathering, and processing agaves, mesquite beans, or saguaro fruit was from ten days to two weeks (Goodwin 1942) or longer (Buskirk 1986), customarily after the corn harvest (Buskirk 1986). If there was little to be had, they sought out more agaves to gather and prepare during the winter. However, the optimum time to gather and prepare agaves was in early spring, usually in April. This is generally immediately before the development of a noticeable stalk on any of the local agaves. Harvesters were able to gather enough plants to last through the summer or longer. Families from the Fort Apache Indian Reservation migrated south across the Black or Salt Rivers after the agricultural harvest in the fall and remained in areas with agaves until March or April. They camped at different places each year because the agaves would be exhausted in previously harvested areas (for an interesting account of the travels of a Cibecue family in the 1880s, see Buskirk 1986:163–164). Western Apaches harvested and prepared agaves upon reaching their winter camp, but relocated to a different one every 15 days or so. Agaves were also harvested just before people returned to their agricultural sites.

The Western Apache method of agave preparation was similar to that used by the Yavapai, Cocopa, Pima, Tohono O'odham, and Cahuilla, in that they baked the heads in a pit. Capt. John Bourke (1891:130) described them as "mescal pits made for all the world like a clambake." Agave harvesters were able to tell as early as the fall and winter which agaves were going to bloom late that following spring or early summer by examining the leaf bases and terminal shoot.

Agave harvesting and cooking involved both women and men. Usually groups of five to eight women searched and gathered agaves. They selected a roasting site in an area where there were numerous agaves, from where the women fanned out within a radius of one mile or more in search of plants. They used a wooden chisel with a wedge-shaped end to sever the crown or stem from the roots, by applying a blow to the tool's end with a rock. The leaves were trimmed with a mescal knife, a chert blade prior to the introduction of metal tools.

Western Apache women did not carry the agave heads to the roasting pit in baskets or nets. Rather, they carried a head in each hand by the leaf bases. Burden baskets were not usually used because the caustic juice from the plants would penetrate through a sack or basket "and cause the packer's body to swell and itch" (Buskirk 1986:170). In contrast, the Cochimí in central Baja California carried the heads in nets. Perhaps this difference in technique can be explained in part by the fact that the Cochimí had more limited access to extensive stands of agave and water, which often required one to travel greater distances to harvest the heads.

Generally, the men dug new roasting pits or cleaned out old ones. The pit measured from 1 to 3.5 meters in diameter and approximately 1 meter in depth. Oak was laid in a crisscross pattern; pine or other woods were not used because they spoiled the taste of the agave. The men laid round stones, preferably those of "vesicular lava," which were said to better retain the heat. After prayers were offered at sunrise, a man or woman who was "considered lucky" lit the fire using a drill (rather than matches) from the eastern, southern, western, and then northern sides. Among the Northern and Southern Tonto and White Mountain Apache, a person born in the summer lit the fire (Gifford 1940).

The fire was allowed to burn down and the fuel was consumed before green or wet vegetation was placed in layers over the hot stones (Buskirk 1986). The heads were placed on the vegetation and then covered with more layers of vegetation. This was then covered with earth. The heads baked two days and nights, or 48 hours. Surface fires were not usually built on top of the earth oven. Also, during the baking, sexual intercourse was forbidden, lest the agaves become undercooked and inedible.

The women took the cooked heads out of the pit two mornings after the fire lighting. They were able to recognize their own heads by various means, including placing the heads in a particular part of the pit, marking the heads with different kinds of grass or beargrass *(Nolina microcarpa),* or trimming the heads in a characteristic pattern.

The cooked agave was eaten both fresh and dried. Each person chewed a piece of cooked agave while preparing the cooked mass. They usually reserved the innermost portion of the heart, which was the sweetest part, for the children. The women pounded the cooked agave into sheets that were two to five centimeters thick and nearly a meter in diameter. They dried the sheets by a fire or placed them in the sun on drying racks overlaid with bear-grass or on stones. For storing, the women rolled the dried sheets into a bundle that they tied with bear-grass. Cooked agave thus stored was said to keep well for a year. When this food needed to be carried over some distance, the bundles were wrapped in grass. Two bundles were attached by yucca cordage across the back of a horse that carried four bundles. Western Apaches also baked the flower stalks for the juice.

Edward Castetter et al. (1938) provided a similar review of agave use by the Apache. They noted how Apaches sought populations of plants with developing flower stalks and recognized the difference between bitter, "man" plants (those that showed no signs of flowering) and potentially sweet agaves, or "woman" plants (those that showed signs of flowering). Apaches believed the "man" plants spoiled all the cooking agave heads because the "man" smoked and the smoke permeated all the mescal in the pit. The "man" plant changed into a "woman" plant when it flowered, then it dried up and was gone.

Pits were lined with flat rocks into which a hardwood fire was built. After the fire died down to coals, moist grasses and bear-grass (*Nolina microcarpa* S. Watson) were laid on the coals. Bear-grass leaves were preferred because they do not quickly burn and were readily available. (Other groups who may not have had access to bear-grass used plants such as *Suaeda* and cacti, which also provided green, moist material for steaming the agave heads.) As was found in other groups, the Apaches refrained from certain activities considered taboo, such as drinking and sexual intercourse, for fear of interfering with the baking process. When the heads were not thoroughly cooked, the problem was attributed to someone's disobedience and was usually blamed on the women.

Western Apaches often sprinkled unfermented mescal juice over the baked pulp before drying to help preserve it for future use, as practiced by the Yavapai and described by Gifford (1936). To prepare agave pulp for eating, the pulp was soaked and the water squeezed out. The leaf bases were thoroughly chewed soon after baking to retrieve the sweet juice. The masticated fiber, or "quids," were spat out. Western Apaches used baked agave heads in many food combinations, including juicy fruits, seeds, and greens such as species of *Amaranthus* and *Chenopodium*.

According to Marsha Gallagher (1976), her Tonto Apache friends said that agaves had not been collected and prepared in the vicinity of Mingus Mountain for some time and that many Apaches no longer used agaves due to the time and effort required. In addition, the Tonto Apache were not allowed to gather the plants as they had previously done, presumably due to state and federal (U.S. Forest Service) regulations. One woman told Gallagher that her mother used to cook her mescal in a pit near Payson, where she would have had access to *A. chrysantha* and *A. parryi*. Another woman related how her aunt maintained a mescal pit in the Fossil Creek area, where her family traditionally collected agave (presumably *A. chrysantha* or *A. parryi*). The Tonto Apache preferred plants whose flower stalks had just begun to appear and baked the agaves in a method similar to that described by other Apaches.

Agaves were also an important food to the Yavapai, and women played an important role in their harvesting and processing. Southeastern Yavapais had easy access to agaves, including populations of exceptionally large *A. chrysantha* and *A. toumeyana* plants in the Superstition Mountains, Maricopa County, particularly those on and near Fish Creek Hill. Northeastern Yavapais took agave expeditions into the mountains from Cordes, Yavapai County, and east to the mountains between the Agua Fria and Verde Rivers (Gifford 1936), where they would find *A. chrysantha, A. parryi,* and probably *A. delamateri* and *A. murpheyi*. They traveled to Granite Peak and Black Mesa, Yavapai County, where they could gather *A. chrysantha* and *A. parryi*. Western Yavapais traveled west to the Santa Maria River, where they would have encountered *A. mckelveyana, A. parryi,* and perhaps isolated populations of *A. utahensis* ssp. *utahensis,* the last being a representative of the Mohave and Painted Deserts.

Yavapais also traded baked agave with other groups. Northeastern Yavapais occasionally visited Navajo country, where they traded agave, among other items (Gifford 1936). Western Yavapais traded mescal with the Quechan, Mohave, and Tohono O'odham.

The Yavapai's method of collecting and preparing agaves was somewhat similar to that of Western Apaches. Jim Stacy, a Northeastern Yavapai, explained to Edward Gifford (1936:254) how his people harvested agave on a yearly basis. A party gathered agave in mid-November at a favored site approximately 40 miles east of Cordes (west of Cordes Junction) where there was a "red-earth hill with a saddle." The party remained here for three or four months preparing mescal, most of which was transported back to Cordes.

The women were responsible for cutting off the leaves with a knife. After trimming six or seven heads, the women carried them in burden baskets back to camp and then returned for more. One family usually gathered about a dozen heads, whereas a larger party might gather as many as 60 heads in a day. Women also assisted men in digging the pit using digging sticks. Such a pit was a little more than a meter deep and less than three or four meters in diameter. The Northeastern Yavapai used the branches of buckbrush (*Ceanothus greggii* A. Gray) and the deadwood of juniper (*Juniperus* spp.) as fuel sources. Stones saved from previous bakes were piled over the wood. The group chose a man, woman, or child born in summer, preferably in July or August, to light the fire. If a winter-born person lit the fire, it was believed the heads would cook white, instead of brown, and be underdone. The selected person lit the fire at a special hole left in one side of the pit. When the fire burned out, each woman in the group placed her gathered agave heads together in the pit on the hot stones, after having cut or poked holes in leaf stubs (leaf bases that remained on the head) to indicate ownership. A thick mat of grass was then placed over the heads, followed by soil dug from the pit. Grass, rather than brush, better prevented the earthen covering from sifting through. No surface fires were used to hasten the cooking process. The agaves were left to bake from "before noon to the dawn of the second thereafter" (Gifford 1936:259).

Taboos existed, including the abstinence from sexual relations, although a man and his wife could sleep together. Menstruating women or new mothers might help dig the pit, but could not scratch themselves with their fingers, lest the agave heads be bitter, white, or not thoroughly cooked. They were allowed to use wood to scratch themselves, however.

When Northeastern Yavapais removed the heads from the pit, they placed them on grass spread out on the ground. They pulled off the leaf stubs, peeled the heads, and threw any scraps in a basket. The women macerated the agave pulp on stone slabs using cobblestones with one sharp side or narrow stones that were used like a hammer. Leaf stubs and the heads were pounded to break down the fibers for drying and express the juice, which was saved in a small basket (Gifford 1932). Using a mescal brush, which was made from grass stems tied with soaptree yucca leaf fiber (*Y. elata* Engelm.), the women swabbed the juice over drying agave pulp (Gifford 1936). The resulting mass of pulp was about 20 millimeters thick, had an area of two-thirds of a square meter, and was "full of juice." Slabs of pounded, swabbed pulp were put on a litter made from two parallel agave flower stalks, overlaid with many stems of a relatively tall grass or stems of globemallow (*Sphaeralcea* sp.), and put out in the sun to dry for future use. The Northeastern Yavapai ate some of the cooked agave in the period of preparation and transported or cached the rest for later transport to more permanent camps. Women carried the first load, which consisted of six or seven slabs of cooked agave bundled together with agave cordage, and the men carried the remaining loads.

The Western and Southeastern Yavapai also baked agaves in a manner similar to that of the Northeastern Yavapai, but with notable differences. Western Yavapai women dug new or cleaned out old mescal pits while the men helped collect firewood (Gifford 1936). Women marked their agave heads by cutting the uppermost part of the head, or "stalk," in characteristic fashion, such as a point, diagonal angle, square angle, notch, or by stripping the outer epidermis down and tying it in a knot (Gifford 1932). After a young person born in the summer lit the fire, the women threw large stones onto the hot stones in the pit, which they raked over using a hooked piece of wood. They covered the heads with straw, which was then covered with earth. No surface fire was used. After removing the leaves, on flat rocks, women pounded the nonfibrous cooked agave core into slabs that measured one-half inch (12 millimeters) thick (Gifford 1936). They dried each side of the slab for one day, over the course of three or four days. Slabs were rolled separately, tied together with mescal rope, and carried on the backs of men to their homes. Women "carried other things in burden baskets, including circular cakes of second quality mescal about one foot in diameter" (Gifford 1936:260). Southeastern Yavapais used brush or grass to cover the baking heads before the earth was added. They stored dried mescal by putting the slabs on stick platforms in caves, which preserved but did not protect the mass against insects and rodents.

The River Pima highly valued agaves for food and fiber, but their use of the plants was limited due to their fear of Apache groups, who often raided agave gatherers (Russell 1908; Rea 1997). Traveling only one mile away from their territory put the Pima in danger of being attacked by the Apache. Numerous attacks occurred during forays to search for agaves (Rea 1997), some of which are described by Russell (1908).

Salt River Pimas would have had access to *A. chrysantha*, *A. toumeyana* var. *toumeyana*, and *A. murpheyi*. *Agave deserti* ssp. *simplex* (figs. 6, 9) was the only agave within easy reach of the Gila River Pima, being found only at the higher elevations of the Sierra Estrellas. This agave is considered among the more edible of the agaves (Gentry 1982). From April to May, people would move high into the Sierra Estrellas, set up camp, and gather and bake agaves as evidenced by numerous roasting pits (Rea 1997). Women also participated in the gathering of agave. In 1876 it was noted that "for a short time the Pimas were free from Apache attacks and they ventured into the mountains to gather mescal. While there, a race took place between a man and a woman, in which the woman won" (Russell 1908:55). In addition, the women gathered firewood for the pit fire. However, it was the men who gathered the agaves, using digging sticks found in the area. Thin-leaved agaves were not collected because they contained little nourishment and blistered the mouth. Pimas used two different kinds of roasting pits, a larger type for agaves and a smaller type for cholla. The agave heads were baked in a similar manner as that described for the Apache, and taboos were decreed, including the total abstinence from sexual relations until after the agaves were gathered and baked. Like the Tohono O'odham, Pimas enjoyed the sweet baked agave, especially when eaten with pinole.

The Pima's baked agave, syrup, and salt were later obtained by the Tohono O'odham, who used to come and cut wheat for the Gila River Pima each year in the summer (Rea 1997). One Pima related that in his youth the Hualapai brought roasted agave heads to Bapchule and Sacaton. Agaves that the Hualapai collected, baked, and traded were probably *A. utahensis* ssp. *utahensis, A. utahensis* ssp. *kaibabensis, A. mckelveyana* and possibly *A.*

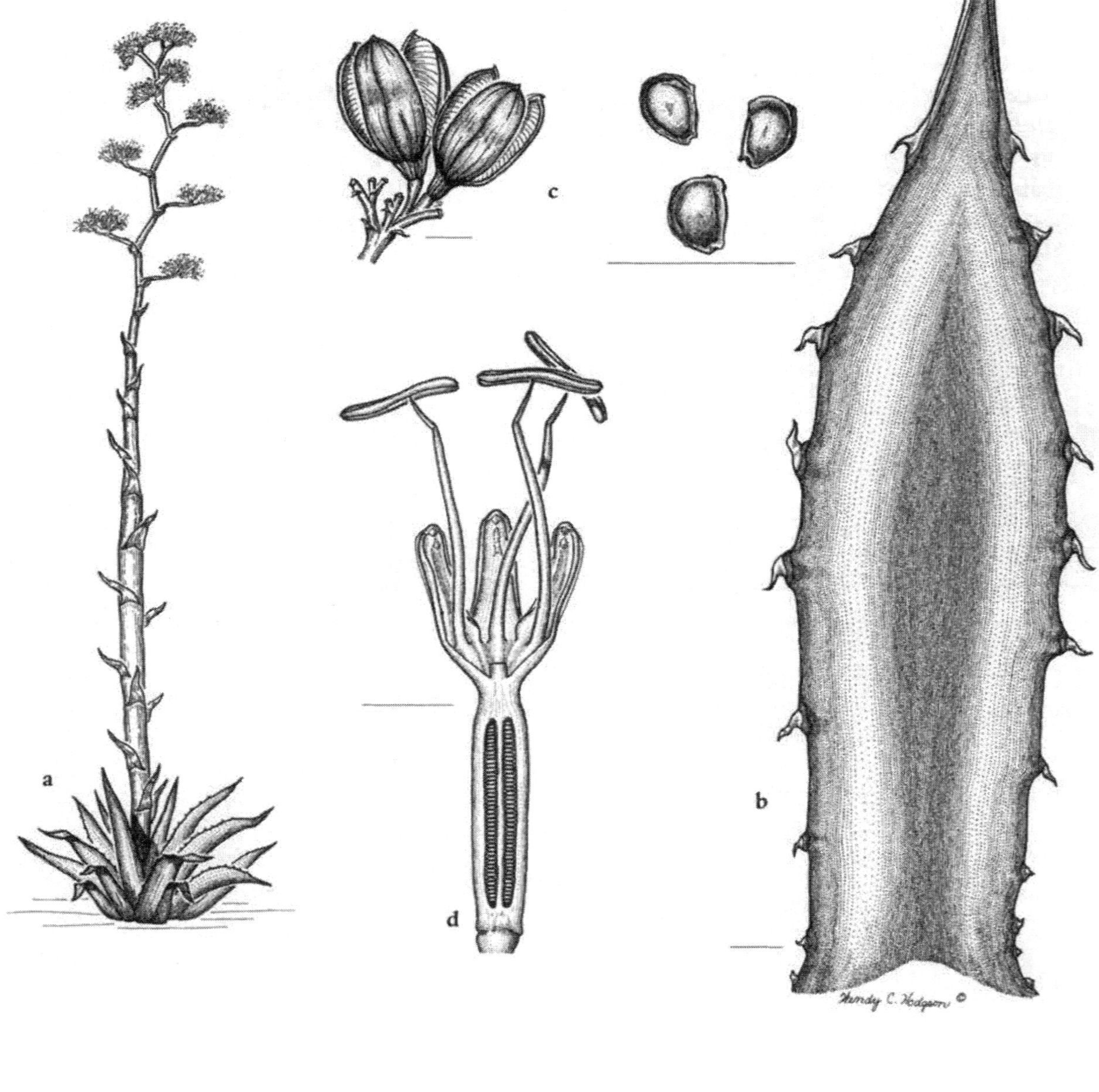

FIGURE 9. ***Agave deserti.*** **a.** Habit; **b.** leaf; **c.** capsules, seeds; **d.** flower, longitudinal section. The scale bar on this and later drawings depicts one centimeter.

deserti ssp. *simplex* (although collection of the last species would require traveling long distances). Agave flower stalks provided another food to the Gila River Pima, although not in the usual sense. A species of carpenter bee (*Xylocopa* sp.) deposits its eggs in the flower stalks, thus providing a wild source of honey for the Pima (Rea 1997).

Agaves were important to the Tohono O'odham living in Arizona and Sonora, who used *A. chrysantha, A. deserti* ssp. *simplex, A. murpheyi, A. palmeri,* and *A. parryi* as sources of food, beverages, and fiber. They commonly obtained agaves from such desert ranges as the Baboquivari, Santa Rosa, Santa Rita, and Santa Catalina Mountains and through trade (Castetter et al. 1938). Like the River Pima, the Tohono O'odham also feared Apache raids on agave-collecting trips. Laura Kermen related that the different villages were closely tied to one another, being "one big family" (W. Hodgson and G. P. Nabhan, unpubl. notes). The Tohono O'odham were no longer afraid of the Apaches after "the last Apache War," and different villages learned to live by themselves. The Tohono O'odham actively traded with the Gila River Pima in *maguey* products such as baked agave, agave syrup (made from boiling the baked agave with water and removing the juice), and fiber (Rea 1997).

Agave murpheyi is grown as an ornamental in some villages on the Tohono O'odham Reservation. In the summer of 1988, Laura Kermen, a Tohono O'odham, talked with Gary Nabhan, Rick DeLamater, and me about the special time of agave, or *a'uḍ*, harvesting. She reminisced about how her people harvested large stands of *A. murpheyi* in a canyon on the western side of the Baboquivari Mountains in the days of her grandfather. In her own yard she grows *A. murpheyi* and *A. schottii* Engelm., plants that, according to Kermen, came from this canyon.

During the winter months many people from different villages came to Sycamore Canyon (in the Baboquivari Mountains) to camp and harvest *a'uḍ*. Laura Kermen, her sister, and her brother assisted her father in collecting the agaves. Her father dug up the appropriate plants, cut off and discarded all the leaves, and rolled the agaves down the slope, where they were then piled up under certain trees. They piled the agave heads into the wagon one by one and took them home to bake. One or two families used the same pit during the baking process. The families used one or two large pits each year for baking the agaves. After the pit was dug and lined with rocks, they made a fire, which was allowed to burn down. The agave heads were then placed within the pit. The Kermen family covered the heads with up to two feet of soil and baked them. These baked heads were "the most fun to eat." Agaves were also dried and stored for future use. The family would pound slices of the cooked heads into tortilla-sized cakes. They partially dried the cakes on a low ramada, then folded the cakes and placed them in handmade earthen jars. Once the jar was full, they sealed the top with a mixture of adobe and wheat straw. When desired, they took the cakes out, sprinkled them with warm water, and wrapped them in deerskin until moist. Laura Kermen considered the best meal to be baked *a'uḍ* and cornmeal pinole.

Laura Kermen and other Tohono O'odham differentiated between agaves used for rope and those used for food. When gathering the agaves, they would say, "look for the rope-*a'uḍ* and food-*a'uḍ*." She thought that the rope-*a'uḍ* was the same agave, but with larger, thicker leaves. The agave used for rope may have been *A. palmeri,* which grows in the area. After they took out the baked heads of the food-*a'uḍ (A. murpheyi),* they put the leaves of the rope-*a'uḍ* into the pit on the still hot coals and rocks for a brief time. The leaves were then removed and scraped with a bone (usually from a deer) to separate out the fibers, washed in the stream, and hung to dry for use in making burden baskets. The Kermen family made three sizes of rope, a job Laura did not like. She rolled the fibers on her thighs with the palm of her hands and by the end of the day her legs itched badly (from the caustic substances in the leaf).

An *A. murpheyi* clone still exists at the San Luisito truck stop, which is near the site of an ancient O'odham village in Sonora. *Agave murpheyi* was also documented from another ancient village 20 kilometers away before much of it was bulldozed (Nabhan et al. 1988). In Quitovac, the Tohono O'odham call the plant *nonhakam,* or "it has eggs" or progeny. Here, they collected, roasted, and ate *A. murpheyi* as well as *A. deserti* ssp. *simplex* (Nabhan et al. 1982).

The Hiá ceḍ O'odham (Sand Papago) inhabiting Quitobaquito traveled to a mountain that "stands towards Sonoita from [Quitobaquito]" to gather century-plants *(A. deserti* ssp. *simplex),* called *a'ut* (Bell et al. 1980). Their method of baking agaves was very similar to that described by Laura Kermen, except that after the heads were baked, they were put in sacks.

The Mohave and possibly the Quechan used agaves, although the extent of such use is uncertain. According to Castetter et al. (1938), the Mohave's use was minimal because agaves did not grow in their immediate vicinity, and their only means of obtaining agaves was by barter with the Western Yavapai, Cocopa (Castetter et al. 1938), and the Hualapai (Stewart 1965). The Mohave would have had access to *A. deserti* ssp. *simplex* and *A. mckelveyana,* whereas the Quechan had access to *A. deserti* ssp. *simplex.* Unlike most groups, the Mohave did not roast agaves in an earthen oven, but put them in water, mashed them, and then drank the sweet liquid (Stewart 1965). Daryl Forde (1931:117) noted that even though the neighboring Kamia apparently ate mescal, the Quechan did not because they "disliked it."

Agave was the basic food staple of the Cahuilla (Barrows 1900; Bean and Saubel 1972; Gentry 1978). The southern Cahuilla used *A. deserti* ssp. *deserti* and probably *A. shawii* to a lesser extent. *Agave shawii,* although abundant north of the U.S.-Mexico border in 1896 (Benson and Darrow 1981), became nearly extirpated by 1935 due to economic exploitation and agricultural/urban development.

The numerous roasting pits found throughout the area, from steep mountain ridges to the broad valley floors (Hedges 1985), attest to the importance that agaves once had to the Cahuilla. The Cahuilla prized baked agave heads and emerging flower stalks (Barrows 1900; Bean and Saubel 1972). Large numbers of Mountain Cahuilla people migrated to the desert (Hedges 1985) to harvest agaves (probably *A. deserti*) in April (Barrows 1900). Lowell Bean and Katherine Saubel (1972) said that the prime time to collect agaves was November through December. *Agave deserti* flowers from April to July or August, whereas *A. shawii* flowers from February to June (Gentry 1982).

Certain gathering areas, which were located up to 16 miles away from their village (Hedges 1985), were claimed by specific lineages within the Cahuilla, although individual plants were not claimed (Bean and Saubel 1972; Hedges 1985). It is not known if the Cahuilla changed their claims annually if a particular year's harvest was poor. *Agave deserti*'s development of flower stalks is dependent on the number of wet days during the preceding two years. Years when few agaves flower in a given population tend to alternate with those when a high number of agaves flower (Nobel 1987).

As with other groups, harvesting agaves was a family affair for the Cahuilla, with people traveling in horse-drawn wagons (Bean and Saubel 1972). They baked the heads in large, rock-lined roasting pits dug in the sand (Barrows 1900) in a manner similar to that described for other groups. The Cahuilla also ate the emerging stalk after it attained a height of 1 to 1.5 meters (Bean and Saubel 1972). They detached the stalks from the plant base, roasted the stalks and leaves, and pounded them into cakes that were then dried and stored in sealed containers. Collecting the flower stalks for food was a practice that the Cahuilla believed would not interfere with an agave's ability to reproduce because plants produce small plants, or offsets, from their rhizomes. *Agave deserti* ssp. *simplex* is found north and northeast of the Colorado River delta and usually exists as a single plant, rarely producing one to three offsets (thus, the name *simplex*). However, *A. deserti* ssp. *deserti,* which is found west of the delta, produces numerous offsets. *Agave shawii* is single or can produce offsets.

The Santa Ysabel Diegueño, a Northern Diegueño group, used to travel to agave populations in the desert, usually in February, and gather and cook *A. deserti* ssp. *deserti* (Hedges and Beresford 1986). Their method of gathering and baking agave heads was similar to the methods used by other groups, although people referred to the heads as "roots." In addition, agave leaves, rather than other greens, were put on top of the baking agave heads in the roasting pit, although more recently burlap sacks were used. The Santa Ysabel Diegueño also cut out and roasted the developing stalk when it still formed a bud in the center of the plant and was less than 0.5 meter tall.

Delfina Cuero, a Diegueño from San Diego, related to Florence Shipek (1968:57) how her husband and others used to gather and bake agave *(A. deserti):* "Things began to grow in the spring [in April and May], Sebastian [her husband] and the other men would go [from San Diego] to the low mountains on the edge of the desert for about a week. They gathered agave, dug large pits, and roasted the agave in the pits. They used wooden shovels that they made from mesquite. Some Indians still do that, it is real good food."

Marshal South (1939:12) described baking agaves in a manner significantly different from that described for other groups. He believed it followed "very closely the method used by the Indians" in southern California. South believed that the agave was best used for roasting purposes when the flowering stalk first appeared. After digging out the agave, he cut off the top part of the stalk and trimmed its leaves. The heads were then ready to be roasted in a pit. He described the pits as being 12 feet in diameter, within which was a smaller, rock-bordered circle approximately 3 feet in diameter that served as the agave hearth. Within this smaller circle South dug a depression and lined it with rocks. He then brought in more rocks "from the outer ring and built them as a sort of coping around the edge of this circular hearth, leaving spaces between them where we are to lay the mescal hearts." After each of the openings between the rocks was filled with an agave head, a large fire was built over the hearth and agaves. The embers fell in on the shallow, stone-lined pit as the fire burned. When the fire burned down, the fire-charred heads "and the hot coping stones among which they have lain are tumbled into the shallow hearth-pit." Earth was then "generously" piled over this hot pile. The process was repeated with as many other pits as time (and agave availability) permitted. South "made the rounds," checking each pit after the heads baked from 36 to 48 hours.

Agaves were important food sources to those inhabiting Baja California, particularly people who lived inland and away from marine resources. The extensive use of agaves by the natives of Baja California is made apparent by the early missionaries' observations recorded in mission documents. Fr. Junipero Serra had just established his first mission at Vellicata (30°30'N) in north-central Baja California, where he patiently waited for three days until 12 new converts arrived with gifts (Watson 1934:61): "As a token of affection, I placed my hands over the heads of all, one by one. I filled their hands with dried figs, which at once they began to eat and, showing our great appreciation, we in turn received their offering which was a net filled with baked agaves, and four fine fish."

Agave shawii, A. moranii, A. deserti, and *A. cerulata* grow in this vicinity. At another time, Fr. Serra noted the importance of agaves to the natives (probably Diegueños) inhabiting the area around the newly founded mission at Puerto de San Diego (Watson 1934:53), where *A. shawii* once grew:

> Truly the heathen are very numerous all over the country and, the farther inland the territory, the more sterile we have found it and there is a great scarcity of food for the poor wretched heathens. The *maguey* plant is still the daily bread of the wretched people in this country. But even this is wanting in the greater part of the land, as far as I have been able to see with my own eyes, for which reason most of the savages are obliged to seek the coasts so as to subsist on what the sea yields.

Perhaps the natives traveled inland into the hills to harvest *A. deserti* in the late winter to early spring. Fr. del Barco (1980:23) was obviously impressed with agaves and their role in the subsistence patterns of the southern Cochimí as he declared: "The Author of Nature has so distributed His Gifts! These were well provided for with sufficient sustenance from the sea, and the miserable mountain dwellers, in order that they might survive, were given mezcales. This is their most ordinary food from October, inclusive, until April."

The Dominican missionary Fr. Luis Sales (1956:14–15) noted how "it is this [*maguey*] that serves to support the miserable Indians. It serves as food and drink and from it they get fiber and make serviceable cord." Fr. Linck was given gifts of cooked mescal by the northern Cochimí, specifically the Borjeños, on numerous occasions as he traveled north from San Borjas in the spring of 1766 (Burrus 1966).

One Jesuit missionary noted how the size and taste of agaves differed as one traveled north from the cape region of Baja California (Aschmann 1966), an observation that corresponds well with species complexes as outlined by Gentry (1978). In the more southern areas that the Pericú, Guaicura, Cora, Aripe, and Huichiti inhabited, the relatively large *A. aurea, A. capensis,* and *A. promontori* are found (fig. 10) as well as the more diminutive *A. datylio* var. *datylio.* Further north, at approximately 26°N, agaves "begin to change in size and come to be very small but sweet" (Aschmann 1966:54) and include the *A. sobria* complex, *A. gigantensis, A. datylio* var. *vexans* (Trelease) I. M. Johnston, *A. vizcainoensis,* and *A. aurea.* Near 29°N, agaves "again become large but most are bitter and inedible; or half of the head is sweet and the other half bitter" (Aschmann 1966:54), referring to the sapogenous *A. avellanidens* and *A. cerulata* ssp. *cerulata,* the latter whose leaves have a relatively high amount of sapogenins and are bitter but whose somewhat sapogenous heads are edible (Gentry 1982). This large area was the domain of the Cochimí *(sensu lato),* or more specifically, the Borjeño, Ignacieño, Cadegomeño, Laymon, Monquí, and Didiu, who inhabited that area between approximately 25°45' and 31°N (Massey 1949). The agaves that "become large between the Sierra [probably Sierra San Pedro Mártir and Sierra Juarez] and Pacific" are *A. shawii* ssp. *goldmaniana.* Those groups inhabiting the northern part of the peninsula included the Cocopa; Southern Diegueño, or Kumeyaay; Kamia; Tipai; Paipai; and Kiliwa (Massey 1949; Ortiz 1983), who had access to *A. deserti* ssp. *deserti, A. deserti* ssp. *pringlei, A. shawii,* and *A. moranii.*

If their stored food supply became exhausted, Cocopas searched for agaves *(A. deserti* ssp. *deserti,*

A. deserti ssp. *pringlei,* and possibly *A. deserti* ssp. *simplex)* in arroyos and mountains during March and April (Alvarez de Williams 1987). They stripped the leaves off and baked the heads in stone-lined pits. During the course of William Kelly's (1977) study of the Cocopa, he learned that all of those he spoke with considered agave as the most important desert food plant. The western Cocopa occasionally made food-gathering trips into Baja California. Some Cocopas who "knew how" would gather and cook the agave plant and "wild dates" (palm fruits), often with River Paipai, on their way to the Sierra Juarez to gather pine nuts. However, most agave and pine nuts were brought to the Cocopa by Paipai and Diegueño men to trade for agricultural products. Daniel MacDougal noted that in the early 1900s a favorite Cocopa camp and meeting place was at the mouth of Palomar Cañón, west of Agua de las Mujeres on the western slopes of the Cocopa Mountains and to the south of Laguna Maquata (MacDougal *in* Alvarez de Williams 1975). Getting to the camp necessitated a long and hazardous journey (Kelly 1977), but the camp was nevertheless popular. Its popularity was partly due to the presence of both water and the many agaves growing on the slopes from which the Cocopa baked and brewed mescal (MacDougal *in* Alvarez de Williams 1975).

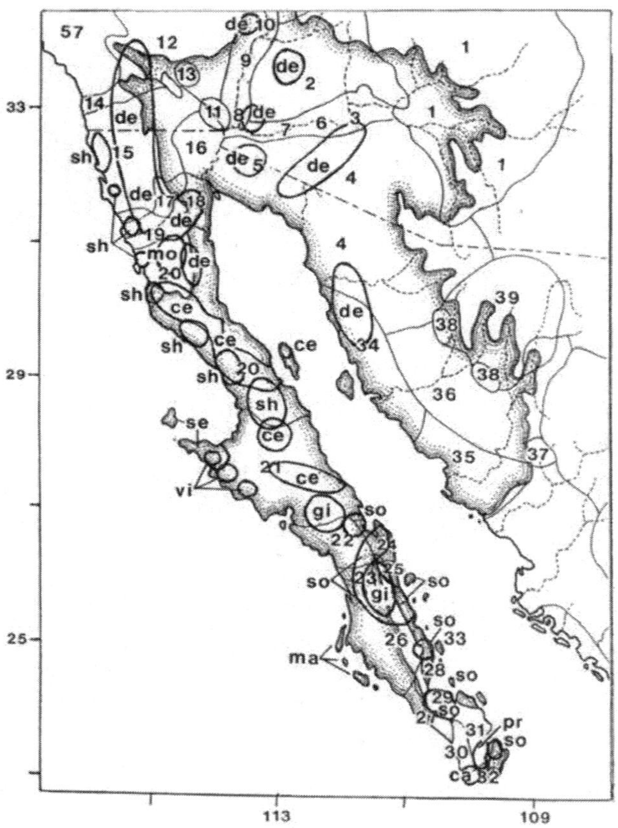

FIGURE 10. Baja California groups and edible or potentially edible agaves (see fig. 1 for key to group names).
Key: **ca:** *A. capensis;* **ce:** *A. cerulata* complex; **de:** *A. deserti* complex; **gi:** *A. gigantensis;* **ma:** *A. margaritae;* **mo:** *A. moranii;* **pr:** *A. promontori;* **sh:** *A. shwaii;* **so:** *A. sobria* complex; **vi:** *A. viscainoensis.*

Sam Spa, a Cocopa, recalled how they once baked agave (Kelly 1977). They put hot stones around and above the central stalk (possibly with the head), covered it with dirt, and built a fire on top. If the plants were large, they left the stalks in the large pit for three days. They then pounded the large stalks in a mortar and made them into cakes for trading purposes or for storage.

Agaves were important to the Southern Diegueño, or Kumeyaay (Hedges 1985), who had access to *A. deserti* ssp. *simplex, A. deserti* ssp. *deserti,* and *A. shawii.* On the mesas within their territory were an abundance of mescal, "the roasted hearts of which were another principal Indian food," being an important staple in the vicinity of missions San Vicente toward the coast and Santa Catalina on the slopes of the Sierra Juarez (Meigs 1939). People still gathered food even with good harvests of cultivated crops at Mission Rosario. Different parties were sent out after mescal and *pitahaya* fruit, rabbits and deer, or clams and mussels.

In the 1950s, Randall Henderson (1951:8) observed the Paipai (Akwa'ala) in Arroyo Agua Caliente, northern Baja California, still harvesting the young flower stalks, or "buds," of *A. deserti* (*A. moranii* also grows in this area). They "gouged the bud out of its rosette," using a sharpened stick. The edible part was the lower part of the flower stalk. These stalk bases were roasted in a pit, which was lined with rocks. The Paipai built a wood fire in the hole to heat the rocks. They tossed the "buds" into the bed of hot coals, piled more hot rocks on top, and then covered this with several inches of earth. The charred "buds" were removed after 12 hours of baking and had a color, consistency, and taste of "southern cooked yams." Jackrabbit, an 85-plus-year-old Paipai shaman, reminisced how "in the olden days young men had no money but [in 1920–1921] would pay a horse and food—especially mescal—to the bride's parents" (Gifford and Lowie 1928:341).

Agaves were unquestionably the most important food plant for the Kiliwa (Meigs 1939:22). The Kiliwa roasted and ate the heart of *A. deserti* ssp. *deserti,* their "chief plant food" (Meigs 1939:9, cited as *A. consociata*). Meigs also mentioned an agave with white leaves, called *mescal blanco,* whose hearts the Kiliwa also roasted and ate. This agave may possibly be the white-leaved form of *A. deserti* ssp. *pringlei* (Engelm. ex Baker) Gentry. *Agave deserti* is common throughout their territory. During his expeditions into Kiliwa territory toward the gulf, Lt. Gov. Arillaga noted the presence of numerous agaves, probably *A. deserti* ssp. *deserti* or *A. moranii,* on the eastern flanks of the Sierra Juarez and Sierra San Pedro Mártir. He observed how the natives on the eastern flank of these mountains "undoubtedly survived on mescal and other seeds in vicinity, but it is obvious that the Indians do not remain in this area long" (Tiscareno and Robinson 1969:29).

Peveril Meigs (1939:22) noted that, "according to the Indians, it [agave] can be gathered and prepared at any time of year," although they harvested the heads primarily in the spring. Agaves for harvesting were "especially abundant after a season of good rain, and for this reason, the people liked rain, otherwise there was just meat to eat." Kiliwas collected the heads when the plants were in the "prebudding stage," in March and April (Meigs 1939:25). They dug a pit, filled it with firewood, threw stones on the burning wood, and then piled the agave heads, trimmed of their leaves, on top of the hot stones. This was covered with the thick leaves and "mescal fiber to keep the food clean." They piled dirt onto this "protective layer," and built another fire on top of the pile. They left the agave heads to bake for three days and two nights and then removed them from the pit. Agaves that were not ready to produce a flower stalk that season were apparently also thrown in by mistake, as Meigs noted how Kiliwas discarded those baked heads that were bitter tasting. Meigs (1939:25) added that "the west-coast Indians [Diegueños] were able to distinguish between the good and bad heads of the large coastal variety of mescal before roasting." Kiliwas cleaned the "good heads" before drying them in the sun. The "dry crust which formed on the outside" of the baked mass could be kept for long periods. Kiliwas enjoyed eating the baked mescal heads, as evidenced by the fact that Emiliano, Meig's friend and source of information, did not know how long baked agave could keep because it "had always been eaten up by the end of fifteen or twenty days." Kiliwas were "said to grow fat on a few weeks' diet" of the very sweet, rich mescal food (Meigs 1939:22).

Among all the plants of Baja California, agaves were also the most useful to the Cochimí (del Barco 1980). Agaves provided sustenance during much of the year, but were the most common food from October to April. In May "they ceased to eat it because the time of ripening [of the head] is past or new shoots [flower stalks] are past and dry and will not start to ripen again until the beginning of autumn" (del Barco 1980:230). Agaves were the "daily bread of the Indians," their presence and abundance setting an "upper limit on population density as it was the most reliable staple" (Aschmann 1966:79). Agaves comprised up to 28 percent of the food consumed annually, but rose to 45 percent during times when other vegetable foods were scarce (Aschmann 1959).

The central desert inhabitants roasted both the flowering stalks and heads. Fr. Luis Sales (1956) noted how the young flower bud (just as the stalk emerged from the leaflike inner bracts) was cut off and roasted for a few hours on an open fire. Young flower stalks roasted on coals provided relatively quick food over an extended period of time. However, Homer Aschmann (1959:64–65) noted that "it is not always feasible to collect the stem and head at just the proper time, before the sugar is expended in growth, and the plant was also eaten when in its vegetative stage, after a more elaborate cooking procedure." Such a procedure involved baking the heads in piles of hot rocks covered with earth. In fact, rather than being in a "vegetative stage," the plants were in the early stages of flower stalk development. Apparently, agaves at this stage of development were preferred, as described by Fr. del Barco in his notes describing the Cochimí use of agave (del Barco 1980:226–230). His work remains one of the most valuable early ethnographic studies of any indigenous culture, in part due to his remarkable attention to detail.

Fr. del Barco (1980:224–225) differentiated between the native *mezcal* agaves and the much larger *magueys* (others made this distinction, such as Esteban Valenzuela [Mathes 1992], who in 1632 reported on Francisco Ortega's expedition). Del Barco considered the small *mezcal* agaves to have a delicately mild taste, whereas the *magueys* had a stronger taste. The larger *maguey* "is found in several parts of Europe ... and is not found in [Baja] California except [as] an occasional plant or two in some mission," having been transplanted there from New Spain, in central Mexico. The southern Cochimí only used agaves for eating and not for making beverages, unlike those who made *vino mezcal* in "some provinces of Guadalajara and Durango." Fr. Juan de Ugarte brought the large *magueys* to Baja California from central Mexico and planted them around the missions during the early 1700s. The plants produced so many offsets that he "used to give some of these large mezcales to his Indians on several occasions of the year" (del Barco 1980:226).

The women were responsible for the harvest of agaves. Three or more left their rancheria in the morning with a minimum of equipment. Each woman brought a carrying net; a small knife (those who were "more affluent" carried machetes); and a slab of hardwood in the form of a wide sword, but "without the point," thinned out at the end to cut out the agave heart. When they arrived at their destination, each woman separated to look for *mezcales* by herself. The women focused on those agaves that grew in clones, which are produced from vegetative offsetting. The agave heads were collected when the leaves began to separate from each other in the bud stage, just prior to the emergence of the stalk.

The Cochimí harvest is explained in detail by Fr. del Barco (1980:227):

> When one is found ready for harvesting, they take the little board in their hand and apply the thin end to the trunk of the plant which, by the time it has developed to this stage, has lost its leaves on the part nearest the ground. The trunk is therefore thinner here, but it has become hard, approaching the consistency of wood, and thus it is not edible. The higher part, which still has leaves, is thicker, juicier, and more tender; they call this part the head of the mezcal, and that is what is eaten.... They apply the beveled end of this wood to the trunk, where the leaves begin, and they hit the opposite end violently with a stone and, as with a chisel, it cuts the trunk off a little at a time.

With their knives, the women cut off the remaining leaves "that are close to the head, leaving undisturbed a small portion of these, that is, about two fingers." The leaves on this part of the head (bracts) had a thickness of "about a finger and a half, and for this reason they are frequently called *pencas* rather than leaves." The women then put the heads in their carrying nets and continued to search for more, carrying this load "sometimes one or two leagues, maybe adding on top of this some firewood for roasting." Each woman brought eight or nine *mezcales* back to a campsite near a water source, if not to their rancheria, by late afternoon (Aschmann 1959; del Barco 1980).

Near or at the rancheria, Cochimí women built a fire into which they threw moderate-sized stones (del Barco 1980). They spread the coals and red-hot stones with long sticks when the firewood "was consumed and the stones have become as red hot coals" (del Barco 1980:228). They placed the agave heads "in between the stones, arranged as seems as best for the purpose," a method that sounds similar to that described by Marshall South. The resulting mound of heads was covered with the surrounding hot dirt, thus keeping the heat concentrated in a way that it would not "dissipate for a long time." The women left the mass to bake for "at least 24 hours, and frequently, two nights and one day," although Homer Aschmann (1959) suggested that different species of agave required different amounts of cooking. They took out the "well cooked" heads, which were then left to cool. Fr. del Barco (1980) does not mention any type of activity that might suggest a ceremonial component of the baking process, such as abstaining from certain activities suggesting the recognition of taboos.

The heads provided enough food to last one family about three days, depending on the family size. The leaf bases, or *pencas,* were also chewed or sucked to extract the juice, which is "already sweet due to the cooking, and some large and hard fibers, which cannot be eaten." The quids, or *tacos de escopete* (shotgun wads), that were spit out were sometimes eaten by "old men and old women, who ... often picked these remains from the ground" (del Barco 1980:228). They ground the dried quids between two stones and ate the resulting powder. Some of the smaller, "delicate" native *mezcales* had little fiber in their leaf bases and quids were not formed upon ingestion. The agave heart was cut up into slices and the sweet mass consumed with gusto (del Barco 1980:227): "It is almost as sweet as preserves made with honey, though it may have a harsh taste in the mouth of those who have a delicate palate, and who may not be accustomed to eating it." Those not accustomed to eating baked agave sometimes suffered from diarrhea (Baegert 1952; Opler 1973). In addition, baked heads generally had some "fine threads," particularly in the lowest part of the head, that "when many of them were collected in the mouth, after their substance has been squeezed out, are left like coarse cloth and it is necessary to spit them out" (del Barco 1980:227). Some *mezcales* were more tender, "there exist in some territories some much more delicate *mezcales* that have few or none of these threads." The Cochimí stopped eating the *mezcales* in May "either because they cut them, or because they grew their stalk and dried up." Additionally, the "Californios themselves do not enjoy eating it in the warmest season, as mezcal is, of itself, a hot food, as is verified even by the first mouthful" (del Barco 1980:230). Apparently, the Cochimí did not store dried baked agave pulp.

The Cochimí *(sensu lato)* had access to *A. deserti* ssp. *deserti, A. cerulata, A. sobria, A. vizcainoensis, A. gigantensis, A. datylio* var. *vexans, A. shawii* (var. *shawii* and var. *goldmaniana*), and the more sapogenous agaves, *A. avellanidens* and *A. aurea.* The more northern groups of Cochimí ate the heads of *A. deserti* and *A. cerulata,* the latter a relatively sapogenous species generally considered to be not among the best for eating. While on an expedition toward the Colorado River delta, the Jesuit Fr. Linck noted that "a native chieftain and his entire settlement of Nuestra Señora de Guadelupe had prepared for us thousands of mescales, a food which is their daily bread and their favorite sustenance" (Burrus 1966:45). When Fr. Linck and his men crossed the southern end of the Sierra San Pedro Mártir, his "pagan friend" gave him ten loads of ground mescal, probably from *A. deserti* ssp. *deserti.*

There was confusion as to which agaves the Cochimí, or more specifically, the Laymon, used near the northern end of the Sierra de la Giganta. Here the area abutted with Guaicura territory. Howard S. Gentry (1982) did not believe Townsend Brandegee's (1889) statement that *A. sobria* was not used for making mescal (thus, the epithet *sobria,* for sober or not given to alcohol). Mescal is a distilled liquid made from baking the agave heart; if a plant was not used to make mescal, it would not have been used by the people for food either. Comondú inhabitants all agreed that *A. sobria* was good for making mescal when asked by Gentry (1982). Apparently, Brandegee confused *A. sobria* with *A. aurea* Gentry. *Agave aurea,* which grows in the vicinity and flowers in late winter into early spring, is not considered good for making mescal (Gentry 1978). Its leaves have a relatively high amount of sapogenins (Gentry 1982), the bitterness of which may explain why plants are not used. However, the heads of *A. aurea* may have lesser amounts of sapogenins, as was found for *A. cerulata.* Gentry's field assistant, Juan Arguelles, went with a guide into the Sierra de la Giganta to search for an agave called *lechuguilla* by Comondú informants (Gentry 1978). According to these informants, *lechuguilla* was the best for eating and distilling. After collecting specimens and receiving additional local information, Gentry (1982) concluded that the agaves to which Fr. del Barco was referring to were mainly *A. sobria* ssp. *sobria,* which flowers from March through early May, and *A. gigantensis,* which flowers from May through early August. It is not known if *A. vizcainoensis* was ever used for food.

What little is known indicates that agave was an important and useful plant to the Guaicura, Huichiti, and Pericú groups. Like other groups, whole villages may have been involved in harvesting agaves. In 1719, the intrepid explorer Fr. Clemente Guillén noted the absence of inhabitants in certain rancherias they cautiously passed in Guaicura territory (Mathes 1979:87): "We passed the rancherias of San Borja Cutoihui and San Andreas Tiguana, without finding their inhabitants in those places, for during these months [winter] they usually inhabit the mountains [Sierra de la Giganta] because they can find a food supply from the agave stands."

While he was attempting to find a route to Bahía Magdalena via the Sierra de la Giganta in 1684, friendly natives gave Adm. Isidro Atondo and his men "presents of fish and roasted mescal, in this season [late winter] their principal sustenance" (Bolton 1936:191). The Jesuit Fr. Johann Baegert noted how agaves were extensively used by the natives of this region (near 25°N), the plants being considered their "daily bread." An even earlier account is Esteban Valenzuela's report on Francisco de Ortega's expedition to San Bernabe and La Paz. Approximately "20 leagues" south of La Paz, soldiers found, among other plants, "very large stands of maguey [perhaps *A. aurea*] and many mezcal [*A. sobria*] where the Indians have much sustenance" (Mathes 1992:242). However, according to Fr. Baegert (1952:66), agaves were not as abundant in this area "as the Indians might wish." He noted that, "since drinking water is rarely to be found at the places where the aloes [sic] grow, they often have to be brought from another place two or three hours away." Baegert further noted that "many have to wait a long time to eat the mescal for the women have to carry it from many hours walk away and do not return until the next evening" (Baegert 1982:134). Based on known distributions, Guaicuras had limited access to *A. gigantensis* and *A. sobria,* except to the north and east in this mountain range rising above the Magdalena Plain.

Fr. Baegert (1952:69) described how the Guaicuras generally prepared foods, including agaves. Like their neighbors to the north, they spent little time preparing most foods:

> They know nothing about cooking, boiling, or roasting as it is understood in Europe, partly because they do not possess the necessary tools and knowledge

> [although they did parch small items of food, such as seeds, grains, and insects, in woven baskets or turtle shells].... They simply burn, singe, or roast in or on a fire everything which is not eaten raw. Meat, fish, birds, snakes, field mice, and bats are simply thrown in the middle of the fire or flames or on the glowing embers like a piece of wood, then left for about a quarter of an hour. Then the roast, which is charred on the outside, but raw and bloody within, is thrown on the ground or on the sand [to cool].

However, Fr. Baegert noted how agaves required more time and labor in their preparation. The inhabitants appeared to roast agave in a somewhat different manner, based on his brief description (Baegert 1952:69): "After cutting off the branches [leaves], the heads must be roasted in a strong fire for several hours. *Thereafter* [my emphasis], twelve to twenty of them are buried in the ground, covered well with heated stones, hot ashes, and earth. Finally, after twelve to fourteen hours, the 'dead' are dug out again. The aloe [sic] heads, which were white inside before, now appear golden yellow and are quite tender. They do not taste badly."

The Pericú, Cora, and Huichiti dependence and use of *mezcal* in the cape region of Baja California is briefly mentioned in various early accounts (Wagner 1929; Moriarty and Smith 1970; Mathes 1990, 1992). Wooden *tablas,* tools possibly once used to harvest agaves, were found in burial sites in the region (Molto and Fujita 1995). *Agave aurea, A. datylio* var. *datylio, A. promontori,* and *A. capensis* are found in this area. The sapogenin content of *A. aurea* is relatively high, whereas that of *A. promontori* and *A. capensis* appears to be relatively low. The sapogenin content of *A. datylio* is not known. *Agave promontori* is quite rare (Gentry 1982). *Agave capensis,* which is endemic to the Cabo San Lucas area, would be a significant food plant. Local inhabitants living north of Todos Santos called the plant *mescalito* and used it for making mescal (*Ecker 89* et al., DES). Around 1912, 20,000 liters of agave-based alcohol were produced each year in the vicinity of La Paz (Annals of the Missouri Botanical Garden, 22nd Report *in* Clavigero 1937:53).

Agaves and other native plants were important to the nonnatives as well. In 1720, Fr. Guillén realized that he and his men had too great a distance to travel en route to La Paz from south of Loreto and too few supplies remaining (Mathes 1979:70). They decided to continue for another 50 kilometers, around the southern end of the Sierra de la Giganta, over rugged terrain. With a bit of despair he wrote: "If the Sloop Triunjo de la Cruz [the ship Frs. Ugarte and Bravo were to be on] does not await our uncertain arrival, it is most certain that the return will have to be made on the basis of the horses we kill or the agave *[A. sobria]* or yucca [probably *Merremia aurea*] which we find."

Of interest is how the different groups prepared agave throughout the peninsula. It has been suggested that the level of cultural refinement of indigenous societies in Baja California decreased from north to south and that progenitors of the Cochimí *(sensu lato)* and more southern groups were more advanced than their successors (Taraval 1931; see Aschmann 1959, 1997). Prior to their missionization, the Cochimí and more southern groups did not use cooking utensils (except toasting trays), vessels, or ollas and apparently stored few foods. Yet, they spent considerable time and effort preparing agaves. A Jesuit missionary in southern Baja California stated that the most ingenious and valuable of the culinary techniques possessed by natives was the harvest and preparation of agave heads for eating (Aschmann 1959:64).

The elaborate and complex method of pit-baking agaves probably evolved from a simple procedure such as throwing the heads or stalks on top of a fire, which is similar to how the southern Baja California inhabitants cooked the flower stalks and most other foods. Foods processed this way would often be charred on the outside and remain uncooked within. Pit-baking foods ensured more thorough cooking and a better taste. Those groups inhabiting that area north of the southern end of Sierra San Pedro Mártir (30°N) pit-baked agaves, as evidenced by the presence of agave pits and historic and contemporary ethnographic accounts. It is unclear whether the Cochimí baked agave heads in pits. Fr. Miguel del Barco (1980), whose observations and notes were extremely keen, did not describe the preparation of a pit. Agave pits were thought to be absent south of the Sierra San Pedro Mártir. Below the southern end of this range is the Arroyo de El Rosario that "marks the boundary of the truly peninsular ethnological groups that populated the remaining 1400 km" (Mathes 1989:409).

This area also delineated a language division between the peninsular and California Yuman-speaking groups. When Fr. Fernando Consag made his voyage up the Gulf of California coast from Loreto to the Colorado River in 1746, he noted that for the first time he was barely able to converse in Cochimí at approximately 30°N (Krmpotic 1923). The distinction between the California and peninsular Yuman groups is more than linguistic. Ceremonial, religious, and cultural traits differed as well. Peninsular Yuman traits included the absence of pottery, sweat houses, and dogs (Massey 1966 *in* Mathes 1992) and the presence of a bizarre custom of swallowing meat tied to a string, only to retrieve it from within and pass to the next person.

Considering the distinction between the California and peninsular Yuman groups, Gentry (1982) assumed that groups south of the Sierra San Pedro Mártir did not bake agaves in pits. However, although the Guaicura or Pericú did little to prepare meats and roots, they do appear to have pit-baked agave heads, as suggested by Frs. Clavigero (1937), Baegert (1952, 1982), and Sales (1956). Homer Aschmann (1959) believed that the inhabitants of the central desert region of Baja California did indeed pit-bake agave hearts, although they preferred to cook the agave stalks on a surface fire. Aschmann further explained why there appeared to be only two sites where agave pits have been preserved. Several stone-lined pits, most likely designed for agave roasting, were found at the Missions Calamajue and Santa María. That only these pits were preserved was "explained by the fact that there never was an appreciable amount of agriculture at these sites, and until the missions were closed, agave roasting was important in their [missionaries'] economy as it was in that of the Indians" (Aschmann 1959:65). Additionally, the mission sites were not reoccupied by a non-Indian population when the missions closed. Thus, mescal pits would have been preserved at these sites. On neighboring islands in the Gulf of California, agave pits were found to be numerous (G. P. Nabhan, pers. comm.). Here the evidence of pits would also be better preserved, presumably because these pits experienced less impact.

Indigenous cultures of Baja California roasted agave stalks on coals, but baked agave heads. Although the Cochimí may not have pit-baked agaves in the sense of other groups such as the Apache, Pima, Yavapai, and even Pericú or Guaicura, they baked the heads using methods requiring considerable time, skill, and effort, nonetheless. The Cochimí method of roasting agave heads and other foods, "particularly heads of sheep and cows," as described by Fr. del Barco (1980:228), is somewhat more advanced than simply throwing the agave heads or stalks on a fire, but not so advanced as to involve pit-baking. However, the more southern groups appeared to have combined the two techniques by roasting the agave heads on a surface fire prior to baking them in an earth-covered pit, as noted by Fr. Baegert (1952). Annetta Carter (1970:30) imagined that the natives in the Sierra de la Giganta region (Guaicuras) prepared agaves "much as I have seen it done during the course of field trips" in this area. Here the local inhabitants baked the heads in pits "covered with coals and gravel and dirt, then built a second fire on top of the mound." They left the mescal heads to bake for two days before taking them out. It is of interest to note that Fr. del Barco believed that the Cochimí possessed a superior ability to the more southern groups, but conceded that the Pericú were ahead of the Cochimí in their knowledge of the properties of plants (see *Karwinskia*).

How did Baja Californians learn of baking agaves? Was it a practice learned long ago with the arrival of these cultures or long after their arrival, having been learned from the Californian Yuman peoples to the north or the Seri to the east? Perhaps Lower Colorado River groups shared such knowledge through transpeninsular trade, an idea proposed by W. Michael Mathes (1981:47). He described how the maize-growing Yumans of the Lower Colorado River "could have perhaps brought corn as food as well as rumors of the high culture areas of Arizona and New Mexico to southern Baja California."

Inhabitants of Sonora used agave, including five rare species, for food and more recently for making mescal. *Agave zebra* (fig. 11) is found only in the Cerro Quituni and Sierra del Viejo, where it is locally common and rarely produces offsets in the wild (Gentry 1982; pers. obs.). These plants were probably used in the past for food, but such use has never been recorded. According to Ricardo Tirado at Rancho Las Maravillas,

FIGURE 11. ***Agave zebra*** Gentry; most inflorescences of this agave were eaten by wildlife before maturation. Sierra del Viejo, north end, limestone ridge, May 1988.

Sonorans inhabiting the area about Sierra del Viejo made mescal from *A. zebra,* but have not done so since the 1950s (*Hodgson* et al. *5000,* DES).

Agave pelona is known from only a few locations, growing in the Sierra del Viejo, Sierra Seri, and the Sierrita de Lopez (Turner et al. 1995). The use of *A. pelona* for food is not well documented, although Felger and Moser (1970, 1985) noted that the Seri ate the cooked heads and leaf bases. *Agave pelona* was considered by one *mescalero* to be very sweet and suitable for making mescal, but its heads were too small for the labor involved in cutting and trimming (Gentry 1982). *Agave fortiflora,* or *lechuguilla,* is another rare agave that was good for pit-baking and eating, according to Howard Gentry's Tohono O'odham guide (Gentry 1982). *Agave colorata* is uncommon in the coastal and foothill areas of the Thorn Forest in Sonora and northern Sinaloa (Gentry 1982). According to Gentry, the natives considered the plants suitable for pit-baking.

Inhabitants living near Cerro Duranzo cultivated *A. murpheyi* for making mescal until about 40 years ago, having retrieved the plants from "someplace in the [nearby] mountains [Sierra Picu]" (pers. obs. with G. P. Nabhan). The Tohono O'odham and earlier inhabitants undoubtedly used this agave for food or fiber, as discussed below.

Seris gathered and pit-baked *A. vivipara* var. *vivipara* (fig. 12), *A. cerulata* ssp. *dentiens, A. chrysoglossa, A. pelona, A. colorata, A. subsimplex,* and possibly the sapogenous *A. felgeri* until the early 1980s (Felger and Moser 1970, 1985). Those Seri who lived in the interior of Tiburón Island gathered and cooked the highly sapogenous *A. chrysoglossa.* Seri methods of gathering, transporting, and cooking the agaves were similar to those previously described for other groups. However, to bake the heads of *A. chrysoglossa,* the Seri first heated the heads thoroughly in an open fire after they cut off all the leaves and leaf bases. They pierced the heads with a knife in different places, then pit-baked the heads in the usual manner. Although much of the bitter juice drained during the cooking process, the heads were still bitter.

Seris made flat cakes or patties from outer slices of the blackened heart (Felger and Moser 1970, 1985). When desired, the cake was dissolved in water and all

FIGURE 12. ***Agave vivipara*** L. and close-up of short, conical terminal spine. Located 6.3 miles east of El Coyote, west of Bacadehuachi, Sonora, July 1988.

FIGURE 13. María Beltran, a gracious and knowledgeable friend who is familiar with useful plants in the Guasabas area. Granados, Sonora, November 1987.

FIGURE 14. ***Agave* cf. *shrevei*** Gentry ssp. ***shrevei*** (plants appear to intergrade with *A. palmeri* in this area), with emerging inflorescence. Ten miles east of Guasabas, Sonora, July 1988.

was drunk, except the pieces of charred pulp. The inner portion of the baked agave head was usually cut and eaten with sea turtle fat or dipped in turtle oil.

Agaves sometimes played a crucial role as a famine food for Sonorans as recently as the 1940s, as suggested by Rosalio Moisés in his informative and interesting account of his life as a Yaqui (Moisés et al. 1971:217). Rosalio told of how he went out "into the brush" to gather wild foods when his girlfriend, Pancha, was very sick and they had no money or medicine: "Every night she prayed and prayed. There was so little I could do. I went out into the brush to gather wild foods. I gathered mescal hearts and baked them for twenty-four hours, buried in the ground. I could cook up to two dozen hearts at once. Lazaro liked eating the cactus [sic], and it kept us alive."

María Beltran (fig. 13), a friend who knew much about the plants in and around her home in Granados, northeastern Sonora, distinguished *A. shrevei* ssp. *shrevei* (fig. 14), or *lechuguilla,* from *A. vivipara,* or *bacanora* (Nabhan and Hodgson 1988). She explained that the larger heads and flowering stalks of *A. shrevei* were roasted and eaten, whereas the heads of *A. vivipara* were used locally and only for making an intoxicating beverage called *bacanora.* The Mountain Pima roasted the immature flower stalks of *A. shrevei* (probably ssp. *matapensis*) in May and June in a fire, then peeled and chewed them to extract the juice (Laferrière et al. 1991). The Tarahumara boiled or roasted the top foot of the flower stalk after cutting it down (Bye et al. 1975).

Southern Paiute groups, including the Chemehuevi, utilized agave (Kelly 1932–1934 *cited in* Fowler 1995), namely *A. deserti* ssp. *simplex, A. mckelveyana,* and *A. utahensis,* the last growing at the interface of the Sonoran and Mohave Deserts in and south of the Aquarius Mountains, Mohave County. So many people went after agave each year that Chemehuevi river camps were nearly deserted (Fowler 1995). One "could tell from great distances when people gathered mescal; could see fires on all mountains" (Kelly 1932–1934 *in* Fowler 1995:108).

Among Southern Paiutes, the spring harvest and cooking of agave was under the direction of a male or female specialist, the sex of the directors depending on the area. This person supervised the activities, sometimes lit the fire, and also offered special prayers for the success of the roast. (The Southern Paiute, like the Yavapai, believed that a person born in July should light the fire "in order that it burn nice and hot.") Prohibitions were also in effect. There is no evidence that agave-collecting areas were family owned.

Southern Paiutes gathered the plants in the spring when the flower stalks first emerged, using a chisel-shaped wooden wedge and a special knife (Kelly 1932–1934 *in* Fowler 1995). After cutting off the leaves, they carried the heads back to the central processing location using special pack frames. A pit was dug and a fire built. When the fire died down, rocks were added to the pit and each family placed its agave heads in one section. All other aspects of baking the heads were similar to those employed by other groups. After baking, each family removed and ate the dark mass and partly intact hearts fresh, then cooled, pounded, and formed the remaining portions into large, flat cakes for drying and storage.

Pug-a-roo, a Southern Paiute, related to her good friend Bradley Stuart (1945:79–81) how her people harvested *A. utahensis,* or *yamp,* while demonstrating her movements and activities with an imaginary plant. She described how they harvested the plant (which she referred to in the masculine) "when the bud was just about ready to open in the spring." Plants were gathered at other times as well, but this was the time when they were "fattest," or the rosette was the thickest. Such a spring harvest was a community affair and holiday for all.

The men could tell when the plant was ready. Men, women, and children would go to harvest the plants. Everyone collected wood and assisted in setting up camp. They dug out the plant and took his "clothes off," or trimmed off its leaves with a mescal knife. Pug-a-roo described how they quickly gathered many plants and carried the loads to where the fire was built to bake the heads. This pit was preheated, but not until the *yamp* was piled and ready to be placed. When the fire "was black" they put in the *yamp.* People who had *yamp* in the pit stood around it in a particular order. "You here, me here, other people here," she explained. People set their piles of *yamp* in particular sections of the pit. Each person then covered their *yamp* with rock. They covered the pile with dirt, built a large fire on top of the pile, and let it burn through the night and the next day. There was much gambling, dancing, and tending of the fire during this time. When the heads were black, they were taken out and carried home. Here they pounded the baked agave into thin sheets in a mortar with mesquite pod meal. Pug-a-roo credited the more traditional Indian food with their good health, rather than "white man flour," which made them "crazy." So important were agaves that indigenous groups were named after *yamp,* or *yampa,* including the Shoshonean bands Yapa, or Yamparika, the "*yampa* eaters."

Agave, or *viyal,* was important to the Hualapai, who had access to *A. utahensis* in and around the Grand Canyon (Phillips et al. 1994). Their method of preparing agave heads was similar to other methods described, but with noteworthy differences. Only plants that had leaves "with black stickers on them [which] must point upward" with a stalk two feet high were used because "incorrect" plants will be bitter. They put hardwood (oak or mesquite) into the pit and placed baseball-sized rocks and smaller rocks on top. The Hualapai made four "doors" at the cardinal directions and lit a fire through these doors (which is similar to the way the Western Yavapai lit the fire at a special hole left in one side of the pit). After the fire burned down, they put in barrel cactus (*Ferocactus cylindraceus* [Engelm.] Orcutt) and placed the agaves on this layer. They laid bear-grass (*Nolina* cf. *microcarpa* Wats.) and cattail (*Typha* spp.) leaves on top, then covered this with wet gunnysacks. Like other cultures, the Hualapai offered ceremonial prayers while they baked agave heads. After the baking was finished, they trimmed off the leaf bases and ate the nonfibrous cores immediately because they could not be stored (Mekeel 1935). They crushed the fibrous outer layers into a pulp on a metate and smeared it on a mat or other surface to dry in the sun. The dried slabs were then cut and folded and eaten or stored by being hung in caves or covered with skins. The Hualapai sometimes ate the pulp dry or boiled or soaked it in water. Cooked agave pulp was also stored in a vessel. In fact, researchers found a vessel in a Kingman cave that contained what appeared to be agave pulp, the lid of which was sealed with lac from the creosote bush lac insect, *Tachardiella larreae* (Euler and Jones 1956).

Fortunately, the Hualapai's relationship with agaves probably will not soon be lost. The "older people in their 80s and 90s" have shown others how to use agave at the Peach Springs school (Phillips et al. 1994). The practice continues to be taught periodically at the school and includes, if possible, a Hualapai elder to carry out its ceremonial component.

When boiled and seasoned, agave flowers can also provide food. The Western Apache gathered nectar by shaking the flowers into a basket or cup after a rain, usually in mid-June (Buskirk 1986), when all of the different types of agave within their area would be blooming. The nectar was added to tortillas or coffee or drunk as is. The Gila River Pima obtained the sweet nectar from the flowers of *A. deserti* ssp. *simplex* (Rea 1997). Edward Palmer (1878) noted that southern California inhabitants consumed the "honey-like nectar" that collected in the base (floral tube) of the flowers of *A. shawii*. The Cahuilla collected the flowers of *A. deserti* from April through August, parboiled them to remove their bitterness, and then ate them or dried them for future use (Barrows 1900; Bean and Saubel 1972). Inhabitants of Agua Caliente, Baja California, ate the good-tasting flowers of *A. moranii* (Gentry 1982). The Kiliwa used the flower nectar of an agave called "mescal west" as a sweetener (Meigs 1939:9). This "large mescal of the west-coast area" was undoubtedly *A. shawii*. The Cochimí collected the "honey" by holding each small cluster of flowers over a large bowl, emptying each flower of its nectar, and soon filling the bowl (del Barco 1980:230–231). This nectar was sweet, although "somewhat vexatious, but if boiled and the foam ... skimmed off" it became much better. Fr. Luis Sales (1956:15) also noted that the flowers of agaves were "covered with water, very sweet, like honey."

Tarahumaras gathered the unopened flowers of *A. shrevei* in times of food scarcity and removed the ovaries (Bye et al. 1975). They put the flowers, without ovaries, on the roof of the house overnight; in the morning they collected the flowers, which they said were then more sweet (why they were more sweet is not known). Tarahumaras thoroughly cooked and washed the flowers to remove any bitterness, then ground them with lime-cooked maize to be made into tortillas (Bye et al. 1975). They also collected the nectar of various agaves with a small tube.

A few groups used agave leaves as sources of food or moisture. The Cahuilla thought the leaves to be tender and edible almost any time of the year (Bean and Saubel 1972). The uppermost leaves, from where the flower stalk emerges, were baked and eaten or dried and stored (Barrows 1900; Bean and Saubel 1972). One Gila River Pima related how the leaves were also eaten after being roasted (Rea 1997). The Pima Bajo once baked the agave heads "with some of its leaves" (Pérez de Ribas 1968), although Mountain Pima only used the baked leaf bases of *A. shrevei* (Laferrière et al. 1991).

Agaves may also have supplied Baja Californians much needed water, a primary concern particularly for the inhabitants of the central desert region (Aschmann 1959; see *Stenocereus thurberi*). Although the native people did not use agave for making a beverage, agave leaves were chewed to obtain moisture (this could explain the rarely reported practice of other unrelated groups who "ate" agave leaves). Early reports related how people survived long periods by obtaining water only from agave leaves, stories that Aschmann (1959) had difficulty believing, but assumed to be true. Although fresh water can be found on Cedros Island (see Wagner 1929:219; Massey 1966), in the early 1700s survivors of disease epidemics were said to have lived primarily on agaves here (Venegas and Burriel 1966). Fr. Taravel sent his men to Cedros Island to bring the survivors back to San Ignacio. They became marooned on Natividad Island, which is devoid of any water (Brandegee 1900a), yet survived for three weeks only on the moisture from agaves. In fact, one woman is reported to have stayed there for three years! Cedros Island is the type locality for *A. sebastiana*, which also grows on the neighboring San Benito and Natividad Islands (Gentry 1978).

Fr. Luis Sales (1956:15) noted that the natives could live for a number of days on moisture obtained from partially roasted, crushed agave leaves: "The pulpy leaf of this *pitera*, or mescal half roasted is very succulent and supplies a drink. They go many days without tasting water by holding these leaves in their mouths." He added that the natives "move cautiously from one spot to another" and upon finding a camp "do not care whether there is water or not since they supply themselves from the leaves of the *piteras*."

Because the Cochimí made little use of containers for transporting water, the ability to extract moisture from agaves was particularly important if one was a hunter (Aschmann 1959). Roasting the leaves probably decreased the caustic nature of the leaves. Additionally, the natives inhabiting the northern part of the peninsula sometimes chewed the "tall mast, or stalk, when young and juicy ... for moisture as a substitute for water" (Meigs 1939:41).

The practice of extracting water from agave leaves was not limited to Baja Californians. Seris used cooked leaves of *A. cerulata* ssp. *dentiens* as an emergency source of water. After roasting pieces of leaves over a fire, they removed the charred portions, then cut up the remaining pieces to extract a sweet liquid (Felger and Moser 1985). One story related how some Seri individuals were marooned on San Esteban Island. Here they survived for four or five days on this liquid while building a makeshift balsa from agave flower stalks. Out of curiosity, I tasted the exceedingly copious amounts of juice from the leaves of *A. marmorata* Roezl. The otherwise caustic juice tasted very sweet and pleasant and did not blister my mouth.

John Rothrock (1878:52), in citing an analysis done by Dr. Loew, wrote that exposure to heat alone would cause the leaves "to yield grape-sugar in abundance." Additionally, "this also took place on application of cold water" and "it appeared impossible to separate the suspected new substance he had to deal with from the cellular tissue without simultaneous formation of grape-sugar." This "citrio-glucosid" could be separated "into grape-sugar [fructose] and citric acid" with "water alone." Rothrock continued to say that the immature ("green") flowering stalk was "much resorted to by Indians and travellers to alleviate the suffering caused by the parched mouth." The thirsty person took a section of the stalk, sucked out the "saccharine fluid," and afterward chewed the interior pith.

Agave "nectar" is being marketed as a sugar alternative for use as a natural sweetener with healthful benefits, such as its being highly soluble and easy to assimilate. However, others are concerned about agave nectar use because of its large amount of refined fructose. High fructose concentrations are believed to exacerbate the effects of copper deficiency, which is linked to coronary problems. They have also been linked with the potentially dangerous levels of triglycerides associated with heart disease (EWILHEL 1998). As with any foodstuff, use of agave nectar in moderation is recommended.

In Mesoamerica "man has chewed agave for at least 9,000 years" (Gentry 1982). Agaves have been and continue to be cultivated in Mexico as far north as Chihuahua (where I have observed Tarahumara cultivation of *A. vivipara*) and northern Sonora for food, fiber, or beverage. Yet, only within the last two decades has there developed strong evidence supporting the hypothesis that pre-Columbian peoples cultivated agaves north of Mexico (see Minnis and Plogg 1976; Fish 1984; Fish et al. 1985, 1990, 1992; Bohrer 1986, 1991; Gasser 1987; Hodgson et al. 1989; Rankin and Katzer 1989; Gasser and Kwiatkowski 1991a; Hodgson 1994a, 1994b; Hodgson and Slauson 1995). Extensive prehistoric agave cultivation in southern Arizona was deduced in the early 1980s from the strong association of roasting pits and mescal knives with rock-pile and check-dam features covering thousands of hectares of desert bajada slopes (Fish et al. 1985, 1990, 1992). Fragments from the Hohokam La Ciudad excavation in the Salt River valley have been tentatively identified as *A. murpheyi* (Bohrer 1986).

Agave murpheyi (figs. 15–17) was described from a clone (i.e., a group of plants with the same genetic makeup having originated from one "mother" plant by vegetative reproduction) growing on the hills between 2,000 and 2,500 feet near Queen Creek, just outside of Superior, Arizona (Gibson 1935). The only other clones known were from Paradise Valley, Arizona (a valley north of the present-day town of Paradise Valley), and Tonto Basin, an area well known for its impressive cliff dwellings and rich archaeobotanical remains (Hodgson et al. 1989). In the 1960s and early 1970s, additional clones were discovered along the Verde River, in modern gardens at Sells and Topawa on the Tohono O'odham Reservation, and at a truck stop in San Luisito, Sonora.

We have a better understanding of this disjunct distribution as a result of work by the late Rick DeLamater and my own reconnaissances. Nearly all of the 60 or so known clones are in pre-Columbian, historic and contemporary Indian fields and gardens or in modern Sonoran home gardens. At present, approximately 45 "wild" clones of *A. murpheyi* grow within the Bradshaw Mountains, New River and Agua Fria watersheds, and Tonto Basin. Clones do not exist in natural vegetation per se, but grow on pre-Columbian linear basalt cobble alignments (which were used to catch and direct water runoff), rock piles (which helped retain moisture and soil nutrients and perhaps discouraged damage to the plants by pocket gophers), and terraces. In the New River watershed, these features had been mapped by archaeologists a decade before without any reference to agave presence (Gumerman et al. 1975). Turtleback scrapers (sharp-edged rocks used to remove marginal teeth and leaf tissue; see fig. 18) and mescal knives (fig. 15) were also found in close association with living *A. murpheyi* clones. Agave remains, roasting pits, mescal knives, and suitable fields have all been located in the adjacent Agua Fria watershed (Green 1986; Rankin and Katzer 1989; A. Rankin, pers. comm.).

Agave murpheyi has many characteristics that may have contributed to its selection for cultivation for food and fiber by pre-Columbian cultures. Its large size and

FIGURE 15. ***Agave murpheyi*** Gibson. Gary Nabhan with mescal knife found within three meters of the clone; there is evidence of rock terraces and piles in the immediate area. New River foothills, Maricopa County, Arizona, April 1988 (*DeLamater 291*, DES).

FIGURE 16. ***Agave murpheyi*** bulbils in inflorescence. Author's home, South Mountain, Maricopa County, Arizona, September 1988.

cloning nature made it worthwhile and easier to process. Compared to most other larger agaves, plants were easier to handle. Its thin leaves are very easily cut and bear only small, straight, marginal teeth. Compared to other large agaves, *A. murpheyi* leaves do not have as caustic a juice. Its baked leaf bases and hearts have a very sweet taste. Additionally, its leaves have very fine fibers that are relatively resistant to rot (M. Yeatts, pers. comm.). Flowering in this species is nearly synchronous, that is, in a given year plants flower almost simultaneously. This was advantageous to groups who harvested and prepared agaves because such work was tedious, difficult, and time-consuming. It required a concerted effort by many people, thereby fostering family and social interaction and bonding. Because cooked agave pulp stored well, large quantities could be harvested at once.

Reproduction in *A. murpheyi* is almost exclusively by vegetative means. Small plants, called "pups" or "offsets," are produced from the rhizomes or leaf axils and transplant with little difficulty in desert soils. With supplemental water, plants can mature within 8 to 10 years, as compared to a maturation time of 20 to 50 years for most agaves without supplemental water. After the flowers are produced, fruits rarely develop in *A. murpheyi*. Instead, hundreds of small plantlets, called "bulbils," develop from shoots near where the flowers were borne (fig. 16). These bulbils may remain on the inflorescence for several months until they are shaken or blown down. Bulbils can root after being without water and nutrients for some time, although most will die on the flower stalk or on the ground if they are not planted or the soil is not disturbed. The ability to transport or trade hundreds of bulbils on one stalk was probably very beneficial to the Hohokam. Most of these characteristics do not favor the success and dispersal of a completely wild plant, but are very conducive for food use and cultivation.

The agave fields at Table Mesa in the New River Mountains provide the first record of pre-Columbian

FIGURE 17. (top) ***Agave murpheyi.*** Tonto Basin, Gila County, Arizona, June 1988.

FIGURE 18. (bottom) Close-up of turtleback scraper and Suzanne Fish demonstrating the use of this tool, which was found with *Agave murpheyi.* New River foothills, April 1988 (*DeLamater 291,* DES).

FIGURE 19. ***Agave delamateri*** Hodgson and Slauson. Agave found by Rick DeLamater, associated with ruins on this ridge; there was no evidence of capsules or bulbils. Tonto Basin, Gila County, Arizona, May 1988 (*DeLamater 302*, DES).

FIGURE 20. Close-up of ***Agave delamateri***. Note conduplicate (folded together lengthwise) habit (*DeLamater 302*, DES).

agave cultivation north of Mexico. These plants also represent the first documented confirmation that the Hohokam grew a particular agave for food and fiber, perhaps following someone's single or repeated selection of plants displaying desirable characteristics somehow developed (Hodgson et al. 1989). Offsets and bulbils were probably transported from northern Mexico through trade or cultural migration. The range of *A. murpheyi*'s cultivation in Arizona and Sonora is unknown. However, it was probably extensive and persists today among Hohokam- and Salado-engineered runoff systems and processing tools. Clones found today are remnants from plants grown centuries ago and have the same genotype (barring mutations) as their predecessors. In essence, clones of *A. murpheyi* are *living* archaeological assemblages preserved in their cultural landscape for more than five centuries after their presumed cultivation (Hodgson et al. 1989; Hodgson 1994a, 1994b; Hodgson and Slauson 1995).

Susan McKelvey was the first scientist to document *A. delamateri* (figs. 19–21), which she discovered in the late 1920s and early 1930s in the Sierra Anchas, Globe, and Coolidge Dam areas, Gila County, Arizona (Hodgson and Slauson 1995). Almost 60 years later, Rick DeLamater, for whom the plant is named, rediscovered this agave in Tonto Basin, Gila County. Since then, more than 90 clones have been documented in central Arizona within the Arizona Upland, often on alluvial terraces or ridges overlooking major drainages, such as Tonto Creek and the Salt, Gila, and Verde Rivers.

With little doubt, *A. delamateri* was grown for food or fiber by pre-Columbian cultures (Hohokam-Salado-Mogollon) inhabiting the area adjacent to, north of, and east of the Verde River but south of the Mogollon Rim (Hodgson and Slauson 1995). Like *A. murpheyi*, *A. delamateri* persists in or near indigenous cultural landscapes, rather than landscapes unmodified by past cultures. *Agave delamateri* also possesses characteristics that may have contributed to its selection for cultivation by pre-Columbian cultures. Plants clone freely and mature into relatively large individuals in a relatively short amount of time (a plant grown from a small pup in my yard in Phoenix, Arizona, received minimal watering and matured within nine years). Its leaves are extremely easy to cut and possess very fine, strong fibers (M. Yeatts, pers. comm.). Flowering is synchronous with the initiation of stalk production beginning in early May.

However, unlike *A. murpheyi, A. delamateri* is found with agave knives, pot sherds, and multiroom foundations above drainages where linear alignments and check dams are found (figs. 19, 21). It is probable that this difference in farming technique reflects the difference in topography and climate where the two agaves were grown (Hodgson and Slauson 1995). "Wild" clones of *A. murpheyi* grow in the Lower Colorado River valley and northern Arizona Upland subdivisions of the Sonoran Desert. The Lower Colorado River valley is characterized by gently sloping bajadas with an annual precipitation of only 80–250 millimeters. Here *A. murpheyi* is found on low-gradient slopes and benches in direct association with runoff features (such as linear rock alignments, rock piles, and check dams), which presumably were used to increase soil moisture and organic matter retention. In contrast, *A. delamateri* is primarily found in the northern part of the Arizona Upland subdivision of the Sonoran Desert, an area largely characterized by small mountains, hilly plains, and old dissected terraces. Annual precipitation ranges between 250 and 410 millimeters in Tonto Basin and the surrounding areas. In these habitats, *A. delamateri* is found only on top of the alluvial terraces overlooking drainages. Apparently there was little or no effort to construct runoff and channeling systems for the cultivation of *A. delamateri* due to the more favorable amounts of precipitation and the highly dissected nature of the terrain in this area. *Agave delmateri* required less moisture than the more drought-sensitive crops such as beans, maize, and squash that were grown with the aid of linear alignments and check dams within the drainages. Soils where check dams are found have high clay content, which has a high water-holding capability (J. McAuliffe, pers. comm.). When *A. delamateri* plantings were no longer cared for and left to grow "wild," they were probably harvested later for food or

FIGURE 21. ***Agave delamateri.*** Note mescal knife on rock, which was found within one meter of the clone. Tonto Basin, June 1988 (*DeLamater & Hodgson 104,* DES).

fiber by Apache and Yavapai peoples (Hodgson 1994a, 1994b).

Like *A. murpheyi, A. delamateri* may have originated in northern Sonora and was probably transported via migration or trade by indigenous peoples. Humans may have intentionally expanded the range of other agaves. Gentry (1982) suggested that *A. applanata* Koch ex Jacobi was disseminated from Veracruz and Puebla to as far north as Durango and Chihuahua "by man's hand in historic or prehistoric times." Sporadic localities in the northern part of *A. applanata's* range are found along the old Native American trail between central Mexico and Casas Grandes, Chihuahua. Near the bottom of the Grand Canyon is found another, as-yet-undescribed agave (Hodgson 1999b). These plants probably originated farther south and were planted and grown by historic or even pre-Columbian people who received the plants in trade. Three of the four known clones grow near or amid archaeological features in canyons inhabited and farmed by the Anasazi (R. Euler, pers. comm.) and possibly Southern Paiute (H. Fairly, pers. comm.).

Gary Nabhan (1985) suggested that pre-Columbian peoples in northern Baja California may have cultivated agaves. This was based on a document describing how Fr. Serra found agaves growing in lines with jojoba interspersed among them in the vicinity of San Telmo, in northern Baja California. Perhaps the missionaries, rather than the natives, planted these agaves. Cultivation of the large *magueys* at various missions by Jesuit missionaries was not an uncommon practice. When these agaves became plentiful, the missionaries gave them to others. San Telmo is in the region of interface between the peninsular Yuman Borjeños (northern Cochimí) and California Yuman groups. It is also just north of the area that Fr. Linck visited before the Jesuits were expelled from the peninsula. Additionally, it appears that at least the Cochimí did not use jojoba prior to their missionization (see *Simmondsia*). However, Europeans highly valued the shrub and may have cultivated it with the large *magueys.*

However, the possibility of pre-Columbian cultivation of agave in northern Baja California cannot be ruled out. As W. Michael Mathes (1981) points out, premissionization documents sometimes contradicted the more scholarly reports later produced by a few of the padres. According to Jesuit sources, the natives of central and southern Baja California knew nothing of agriculture or domestic plants. This may not have been the case. Mathes (1981) refers to Sebastián Vizcaíno's report that in 1596, upon bringing the natives corn, meat, and wine, they were shocked only at the Spaniards' speech, arms, and dress. In 1632 at La Paz, Diego de la Nava, the chaplain to Francisco de Ortega, stated that the natives recognized corn and made "it understood that there was a great deal of it inland, that those Indians inland brought it to trade for fish and salt that they took inland" (Mathes 1975a:58, 1992:226). Mathes (1981:47) suggests that although these and other reports contradict Jesuit accounts and contemporary work, they are worth considering. Mathes's proposal that a transpeninsular trade with the Lower Colorado River Yumans and southern Baja Californians may explain the possibility of corn agriculture. It may also help to explain Baja Californians' knowledge of agave processing and possible agave cultivation, if it did indeed occur, on the peninsula during premission times.

Many agaves used for food, fiber, or beverage in the Sonoran Desert have undoubtedly been reduced in numbers to local extirpation or, in one case, possible extinction. A number of factors may be responsible, including many years of exploitation.

For whatever reason, the tending of *A. murpheyi* plants (and possibly other agaves such as *A. americana* L.; Bohrer 1987) by the Hohokam ceased and agave fields were eventually abandoned. The Tohono O'odham, Northern Pima, and Sonorans may have harvested mature plants on sites that were accessible to them or brought live plants back to their homes to grow. "Wild" clones steadily decreased in numbers since their care by humans was, for the most part, terminated over the last three to five centuries. Remnants of clones that survived exploitation by historic peoples are still found north of the Gila River in the foothills and mountains of central Arizona. Here they are continually threatened by development or reservoir expansion. Clones that may have once grown in the Salt and Gila River valleys appear to have succumbed to exploitation and later extensive agricultural development. By 1915, farmers cultivated more than 250,000 acres of alfalfa, grain, citrus, cotton, and other crops in the Salt River valley (Luckingham 1989). Urban sprawl soon followed.

Agave delamateri may have suffered a similar demise, but one involving different cultures. With the possible fragmentation of Salado/Mogollon cultures, agave fields became feral and were probably harvested by Western Apaches or Yavapais (Hodgson and Slauson 1995). Today development and reservoir expansion threaten some clones.

I believe that overexploitation of *A. deserti* ssp. *simplex* by historic groups and livestock grazing in combination with the taxon's strict reproductive requirements contributed to its reduction in number of individuals. Plants reproduce primarily via sexual means and produce offsets from rhizomes infrequently (thus, the epithet *simplex,* or simple, referring to the single rosette). *Agave deserti* ssp. *deserti* can produce 65,000 seeds in a single inflorescence, yet seedlings are extremely rare in the wild (Turner et al. 1995). Although the establishment requirements of *A. deserti* ssp. *simplex* are not known, Park Nobel (1984) noted that *A. deserti* ssp. *deserti* seedlings require sheltered microhabitats, such as those provided by perennial grasses, to escape damage caused by high temperatures. In all but a few years, rainfall patterns do not favor the rapid growth necessary to reach the critical size for surviving droughts and most seedlings perish (Jordan and Nobel 1979).

Near the Salt and Gila River valleys *A. deserti* ssp. *simplex* is absent or restricted to the upper crests of desert mountains such as the Sierra Estrellas, where Curtin (1949) noted that plants were becoming rare. *Agave deserti* ssp. *simplex* is rare in the nearby White Tank Mountains. It is absent in South Mountain (formerly the Salt River Mountains) and in the Sacaton and San Tan Mountains (A. Rea and C. Cassa, pers. comm.), which are low, desert mountain ranges that experience high summer temperatures. At Table Top Mountain, south of Maricopa, Arizona, *A. deserti* ssp. *simplex* is rarely found at lower elevations, but is found with increasing abundance toward and at the summit. Perhaps the summit population represents vestiges of once larger populations that escaped the pressures of humans or the effects of overgrazing by livestock. Packrat midden, coprolite, or pollen analysis might be able to shed light on the plant's distributional patterns and abundance over the last 500 years if fibers, marginal teeth, terminal spines, or pollen can be determined to species.

Some of the more isolated and smaller populations of *A. chrysantha* may also have been greatly reduced in the past by local inhabitants. The Pima once gathered agave in the Picacho Mountains (Castetter et al. 1938). As far as is known, *A. chrysantha* grows only toward and at the very top of Newman Peak (photograph in Nelson and Nelson 1973; J. Weins, pers. comm.; pers. obs.) and possibly represents a vestige of a once larger population. In the Tucson Basin, archaeologists have found agave spines, numerous artifacts, and agricultural features associated with agave cultivation and processing (see Fish et al. 1985, 1990, 1992). No cultivated or wild agave is known to grow here or in the nearby Tortolita Mountains, a desert mountain range extending to 1,250 meters (4,100 feet) high.

It is believed that inhabitants of Baja California, particularly in the central desert region, overexploited agaves. Women sought out agave clones, which "might entail the complete destruction of a plant community [clones] that was the product of decades, perhaps centuries, of slow desert growth" (Aschmann 1959:79). Additionally, agaves had to be processed by a water source (it could take a minimum of four to five days to collect and bake the agaves). Homer Aschmann (1959:79) noted that "the hills nearest places of permanent water appear to have been scoured clean of agaves—the surviving stands were in places least accessible from waterholes." He believed that "in the driest times, when several bands were forced to congregate at each of the few enduring waterholes, the pressure on the nearby agaves may well have resulted in local extinction of the plant."

Missionaries did not discourage the collection and processing of agaves by their converts. Aschmann noted that plants were notably scarce, if not completely absent, in the immediate vicinity of missions: "Concentrating the entire population at a few spots must have placed such a strain on the local agave population that passage of a century and a half has not permitted it to recover completely" (Aschmann 1959:79). Fr. Baegert (1952) commented that the natives often had to travel 8–13 kilometers away to get agaves because the plants were rarely found where there was water. As noted by Homer Aschmann (1959), this comment may refer not so much to the plants' natural distribution as to their distribution resulting from exploitation by people. By 1783, Dominican missionaries complained that "their neophytes" had to travel great distances to get agaves.

Areas away from the missions may not have experienced such exploitation. This is suggested by the fact that agaves would not be able to come back with recurring dry periods (and thus the natives' increased reliance on the plants) if they were completely eradicated. Consequently, according to Aschmann (1959:80) "it seems reasonable to assume that through timely reductions of the human population or by deliberate protection of a few agave plants, that part of the flora was given an opportunity to survive and recover." Prior to their being deported to San Ignacio, survivors of disease epidemics on Cedros Island, who represented a small remnant of the original population, lived primarily on agaves in the early 1700s (Venegas and Burriel 1966). *Agave sebastiani,* which grows as a single plant or in large clones, has continued to maintain its populations on Cedros, San Benito, and Natividad Islands, being represented by 19 herbarium specimens collected from 1881 to 1975 (Gentry 1978). Additionally, in the mid 1800s "the few surviving Indians of San Borja could procure enough agaves in two days to feed everyone for 10 or 12 days" (Aschmann 1959:80).

Aschmann (1959) suggested that agaves are more abundant in *recent* times than they were more than 150 years ago in the peninsula's central desert region, when they were notably scarce or absent in areas near missions and waterholes. He believed that agave populations have since been recovering here, except in those areas where they were completely extirpated, and that the extirpation of the native peoples may have helped agaves maintain and even increase population densities. However, southern Baja California agaves, particularly from La Paz south, may not be recovering due to years of development and exploitation for alcoholic beverages. A reassessment of the status of agave populations in Baja California and Baja California Sur is needed. Liz Slauson's cursory observation of the infrequent occurrence and apparently common use of *A. capensis* for making mescal in the cape region of Baja California (*Ecker 89* et al., DES) demonstrates the need for such an assessment.

Agave colorata and *A. fortiflora* are uncommon Sonoran agaves. Howard Gentry (Gentry 1982:433) related how *A. colorata* "is uncommon in nature and on my very intensive travels through its area I do not recall it from any localities." He suggested that "it was formerly decimated as a sugar source by the Mayo and Yaqui Indians who occupied its area rather densely in precolonial times." *Agave fortiflora* is even more rare and may be extinct. If its populations were few and consisted of few individuals, exploitation for food may have been the most significant factor toward its extirpation from an area, if not its extinction.

Harvesting agaves in northeastern and northern Mexico for mescal, rather than for food, may have caused the decline and overexploitation of certain populations of agave. Gary Nabhan (1992) found little production of mescal west of the Nogales-Hermosillo highway. The northern limits of mescal production in eastern Sonora appear to be from Cucurpe to Arispe and Sinoquipe in the Río Sonora watershed to Fronteras in the Río Moctezuma watershed and Sonora-Chihuahua border. The southern limits are more difficult to define because mescal is produced in the Río Mayo watershed, where transplanted *Agave tequilana* plants are used.

Two major kinds of mescal are made: *mescal bacanora,* which is produced from wild populations of *A. vivipara,* and *lechuguilla,* which is produced from wild populations of *A. palmeri* and *A. shrevei* (Nabhan 1992). *Lechuguilla* is less flavorful in the areas where *A. vivipara, A. shrevei,* and *A. palmeri* exist because the mixture "bites the tongue" and varies in taste. However, some mescal makers still mix all three plants in the same ovens and same batches of brew. Local inhabitants who make mescal prefer it to commercial tequila made from *A. vivipara* ssp. *tequilana.*

If correct, the number of agaves harvested for *mescal bacanora* is staggering. Gary Nabhan (1985) estimated that one-half *million* plants are harvested from wild stands of agaves in Sonora each year. Most mescal makers, or *mescaleros,* claimed that about ten gallons of mescal could be produced from 50 to 60 heads, thus requiring them to make no more than four or five batches in a year (Nabhan 1992). Don Pedro Estrella Tánori's son-in-law showed Amadeo Rea a pit that contained 169 heads for the production of *mescal bacanora* (Rea 1997).

It would appear that such an operation would seriously deplete wild agave stands. However, according to Nabhan (1992) some Sonorans know how to manage the plant populations to favor regeneration. *Mescaleros* "castrate" agaves that will soon flower, the method similar to that practiced by the Tarahumara. Castrating the plant is said to encourage the production of offsets, thus resulting in an increase or stabilization in number of plants (Nabhan 1992), although the population's genetic variability is decreased. This castration causes the meristem, or heart, to become more sweet and massive as a result of the buildup of carbohydrates. Two months later, the *mescaleros* harvest the plants, but leave the offsets to regenerate the population. It is not known how populations of agaves respond to this practice. Only *A. vivipara* can produce numerous offsets from its rhizomes, whereas *A. shrevei* ssp. *shrevei* and *A. shrevei* ssp. *matapensis* Gentry, taxa that occur in this area (Gentry 1982), produce few offsets. Additionally, individuals of *A. palmeri* often do not produce offsets when wildlife or cattle consume the apical meristem. The frequency of and ability to offset in agaves may not only be specific to the species or population, but to the individual as well.

Mescaleros will move their still around to allow

agaves in an area to recover before being used again (Nabhan 1992). The availability of water and fuelwood may be a more limiting factor in some places than the number of agaves. Government-subsidized plantations of *A. vivipara* in Ónavas, Sonora, were not supporting much production of *mescal bacanora* in the early 1990s (Nabhan 1992, cited as *A. angustifolia*).

Some researchers believe that the overexploitation of agaves by indigenous peoples may lead to a reduction in both agave and bat populations (see Howell and Roth 1981; Howell 1985). Bats of the genus *Leptonycteris* feed on the floral nectar of *A. palmeri*, and Gentry (1982) postulated that they also feed on the nectar of other members of the Ditepalae, including *A. shrevei.* Nabhan (1992) argues that although mescal production could reduce the nectar resources available to migrating bat populations, it is not likely to reduce a migration corridor for the bats. In addition, the argument for a "coevolved mutualism of agaves and bats" is weak. Bats exploit other food sources, such as nectar and fruit from columnar cacti (Fleming et al. 1993). Even though characteristics of chiropterophily (pollination by bats) are exhibited by *A. palmeri* and *A. chrysantha*, a variety of diurnal pollinators appear to contribute significantly to pollination and fruit set in these plants (Slauson 1996). The variable seasonal and somewhat unreliable movements of *Leptonycteris* bats (Cochrum and Petryszyn 1991; Fleming et al. 1993) coupled with the phenology of *A. palmeri* seem unlikely to support a tight mutualistic relationship, but rather one that is more facultative (Slauson 1996). Studies like Slauson's are needed in areas within northeastern Sonora.

Habitat destruction in combination with collection has contributed greatly to the reduction of agave populations. Such activities are believed to account for the continuing extirpation of *A. murpheyi* in the Salt and Gila River valleys. Remnant clones in New River are threatened by development. The construction and continued expansion of Roosevelt, Bartlett, Horseshoe, and Lake Pleasant Reservoirs have destroyed not only clones, but their cultural context as well (Hodgson 1994a).

Unrestricted collecting and destruction of habitat has reduced *A. shawii* populations in southern California near the U.S.-Mexico border where, in 1896, the plant was abundant (Benson and Darrow 1981). It was believed that the plant was locally extirpated north of the border by 1935, although one population was known in 1937. Today *A. shawii* is only known from Border Fields State Park north of Tijuana. It has been introduced at Cabrillo National Monument, Torrey Pines, the national wildlife refuge headquarters in Imperial Beach, and other locales (Reiser 1994).

Agave shawii populations are continually being impacted south of the U.S.-Mexico border. There was a brief attempt to use the coarse fibers commercially during the 1950s. Howard S. Gentry (1978:93) observed plants that had been "bulldozed in piles for hauling to a decorticating machine," a project that was unsuccessful due to the poor quality of the short fibers. Gentry noted that "thousands of acres with large stands" had been destroyed for new agricultural lands, "made possible by modern well drilling" methods. Gentry (1978:92) predicted the future of this species. The "spread of urban growth along environs and beaches will continue to eliminate the wild agaves," and "when the human density in the *A. shawii* area reaches the dimension now existing in coastal southern California, *A. shawii* may be considered an 'endangered' species." His prediction is continuing to play out; because of relatively dense populations in Baja California, *A. shawii* does not have threatened- or endangered-species status in the United States, despite the fact that these populations in Baja California are also being continually impacted. Coastal populations of *A. shawii* were used for mescal production (Haiman 1974) and continue to be gathered, burned, and extensively cleared for development and agriculture.

Coastal populations of *A. shawii* may be more vulnerable to local extirpation than populations farther inland. Not only are they more vulnerable to being cleared for development/agriculture, but the species' reproductive characteristics may exacerbate its extirpation. Both subspecies of *A. shawii* reproduce sexually and asexually, the latter through the production of offsets from the branched stems. The degree of cloning within each taxon is variable (Turner et al. 1995). Southern coastal populations rely mostly on sexual reproduction because they are almost entirely composed of solitary plants. To the north there are populations that grow on granitic bajadas away from the coast; these produce numerous offsets and form tangled colonies.

Wildlife and livestock may negatively impact agave populations. Overgrazing can affect offset mortality directly due to trampling, herbivory, and loss of protective cover or indirectly due to stress, pathogens, and insects (see Martinez-Morales and Meyer 1985). Livestock regularly eat the emerging flower stalks of agaves, including *A. chrysantha, A. deserti, A. palmeri,* and

A. shawii, thereby affecting the plant populations' sexual reproductive success and genetic variability within populations. Near Torreon in the Tehuacan Valley, Mexico, ranchers have been observed to cut all tall flowering stalks of agaves on hillsides with machetes. They left the stalks in place, apparently providing forage for livestock (J. McAuliffe, pers. comm.).

Hesperoyucca | Our Lord's candle

H. whipplei **(Torrey) Trelease**
Our Lord's candle, lechuguilla

Hesperoyucca whipplei has been treated as *Yucca whipplei* by most authors. It is distinguished from yuccas by its bright green, capitate stigma; capsules that dehisce between the septae (loculicidal dehiscence); a tendency toward monocarpy (it flowers once, then dies); and self-incompatibility. Molecular analyses support a closer association with *Hesperaloe,* rather than *Yucca* (Bogler and Simpson 1995; Clary 1997), and suggest that it should be treated as a separate genus, *Hesperoyucca* (Bogler and Simpson 1995).

Hesperoyucca whipplei flowers primarily from February to June (Wiggins 1964; Turner et al. 1995, cited as *Y. whipplei*). Six to seven years are required before rosettes accumulate enough food and water reserves to produce the massive flower stalk and inflorescence (Wolf 1935, cited as *Y. whipplei*).

Its immense flower stalk, with thick base and numerous flowers (fig. 22), undoubtedly captured the attention of both pollinators and native peoples, who used these plant parts for food. *Hesperoyucca whipplei* plants that produce only a single rosette die after flowering and fruiting, as do agaves. This contrasts with *H. whipplei* plants that produce a number of offsets, in which only those plants, or rosettes, that flower within the clone die (see Turner et al. 1995:414–416, cited as *Y. whipplei*). People may have recognized the growth form of noncloning (noncaespitose) forms of *H. whipplei* as being similar to that of agaves and eaten the heads. Some of the ethnographic literature describes how groups roasted the head, or base of the flowering stalk, and the stalk itself. The Kaiwaiisu, who did not have access to agave, nonetheless treated the hearts of *H. whipplei* much like other groups treated agave with ceremony and prohibitions surrounding the pit-baking in the spring (Zigmond 1981, cited as *Y. whipplei* ssp. *whipplei*). They also roasted the split, green flower stalks. Kiliwas roasted the hearts of *H. whipplei,* the "mast sweet when young," in March and April (Meigs 1939:9, cited as *Y. whipplei*).

Tipais roasted the stalks over a fire, but baked the hearts, or "bases," of the plants in an earthen oven. They roasted the stalks by stacking them on a small fire built in a cleared space (Weiss 1994, cited as *Y. whipplei*). A larger fire was made over and around the stalks, which were periodically moved so that they cooked evenly. They removed the narrower, smaller stalks, which were roasted for about 20 minutes. The blackened outer portion was peeled and the inner tissue eaten. The Tipais allowed the larger stalk pieces to cook for ten additional minutes. The taste was described to be like a firm, fibrous sweet potato. To bake the hearts, or heads, Tipais dug a pit in the ground, into which they placed several heads. They put heated rocks around the hearts, then piled dirt over the heads. They baked the heads for one or two days before removing them. The Chumash, who inhabited an area in

FIGURE 22. Art Phillips III standing next to ***Hesperoyucca whipplei*** (Torr.) Trel. Single rosette form with massive flower stalk and dense inflorescence. Grand Canyon, Hualapai Indian Reservation, Colorado River mile 240.2, March 1995 (*Hodgson et al. 8915,* DES).

southern California far from the Sonoran Desert, roasted the young flower stalks and "the basal portion of the plant with leaves removed" (Timbrook 1990, cited as *Y. whipplei*).

However, much of the literature records only the use of the young flowering shoots of *H. whipplei,* with no mention of the plant base. Although *H. whipplei* plants were scarce in their territory, the Cahuilla nevertheless used them for food. They cut the stalk prior to its development of flowers, when "it was full of sap," and roasted it in sections in a fire pit (Barrows 1900, cited as *Y. whipplei*), which was covered with sand overnight (Bean and Saubel 1972, cited as *Y. whipplei*). They dried, ground, and mixed the cooked mass with water to form cakes or they sliced and parboiled the cooked mass. Cahuillas also related to Barrows (1900) how they gathered and baked the stalk *and* head of a small yucca or yuccalike plant having small spines, a plant thought by him to possibly represent a new species found on the northern slope of Torres Mountain in southern California.

Santa Ysabel Diegueños harvested the young stalks of *H. whipplei* in the spring, roasted them over a fire or in the ashes and coals, and peeled the stalks before eating them (Hedges and Beresford 1986, cited as *Y. whipplei*). They described the taste as sweet, similar to that of pineapple.

The use of *H. whipplei* by the Hualapai has never been documented, although they were emphatic about their use of young flowering stalks (and possibly the heads) of *A. utahensis* (Watahomigie et al. 1982; Phillips et al. 1994, cited as *Y. whipplei*). They probably also used *A. mckelveyana.* It would be of interest to closely study the use and perception of single-rosette and cloning forms of *H. whipplei* by native peoples.

The Cahuilla cooked the flowers of *H. whipplei* in water in an olla (Barrows 1900). The flowers were considered sweet when they began to open or when the plant "starts to flower" (Barrows 1900), but became bitter with age (Bean and Saubel 1972). The Cahuilla parboiled and ate the flowers—boiling the mature ones three times with salt—or dried and stored them. Similarly, the Santa Ysabel Diegueño picked the flowers of *H. whipplei* before they opened in the spring and boiled them twice to remove any bitterness; the taste was described as being similar to that of cabbage (Hedges and Beresford 1986, cited as *Y. whipplei*). Tipais harvested the flowers by carefully bending the stalk until it broke and then stripping the stalk of its flowers before putting them in a carrier. Sometimes they carried the whole stalk with flowers back home, although many flowers usually fell off the stalk. They washed the flowers thoroughly, then cooked them in water for approximately four hours. After cooling, draining, and chopping the flowers, Tipais fried them with onion, flour, salt, and pepper.

David Barrows (1900) reported that the Cahuilla ate uncooked, ripe fruits of *H. whipplei,* which were considered to be sweet and pleasant tasting. However, this is unlikely because the plant's mature fruits are dry capsules. Cahuillas interviewed in the 1960s by Bean and Saubel (1972) insisted that of the two yucca-type plants in their environment, they only ate the fruits of the Mohave yucca, *Yucca schidigera.*

Yucca | yucca, soapweed, Spanish bayonet, dátil, amole

Y. arizonica **McKelvey**
yuca, sota, dátil, palma criolla

Y. baccata **Torrey**
banana yucca, blue yucca, fleshy-fruited yucca

Y. brevifolia **Engelmann**
Joshua tree

Y. elata **(Engelmann) Engelmann**
soaptree yucca, Spanish bayonet, yuca, sota, dátil, solate, palmilla, palmito, cortadillo

Y. schidigera **Roezl ex Ortegies**
Mohave yucca, Spanish dagger

Y. schottii **Engelmann**
hoary yucca

Y. thornberi **McKelvey**
Thornber's yucca

Y. valida **Brandegee**
datilillo, dátil cimarrón

Yuccas were significant sources of food and fiber among indigenous peoples in the Southwest and northern Mexico, where the genus is well represented. Fruits of some fleshy-fruited, baccate species; the young flowering stalks (with or without their base); and flowers of most species of yucca were valuable additions to people's diets. The abundance and accessibility of flower stalks and fruits were major factors of their relative importance.

Yuccas that produce fleshy, baccate fruits in the

Sonoran Desert are *Y. arizonica, Y. baccata, Y. schidigera, Y. schottii* (growing at the margins of the Sonoran Desert), *Y. thornberi,* and *Y. valida.* As is the case with other yucca species, there is often confusion as to the identification of the fleshy-fruited yuccas because hybridization is a relatively common phenomenon. Indeed, *Y. thornberi* may have originated as a hybrid between *Y. baccata* and *Y. arizonica* (Webber 1953). Some populations in southern Arizona identified as *Y. baccata* may represent instead *Y. thornberi.* Yuccas having dry or corklike fruits are *Y. elata* and *Y. brevifolia.* Hybrids between *Y. elata* and the baccate species *Y. baccata* and *Y. schottii* have been documented (Brian et al. 2000).

To better understand and appreciate the use of yucca by indigenous cultures, particularly those that produce fleshy fruits or edible stalks, a brief discussion of their flowering and fruiting characteristics is presented. It is well known that the main (if not sole) pollinators of yucca species, including those used for food in the Sonoran Desert, are two moths, *Tegeticula yuccasella* and *T. maculata* (McKelvey 1947; Webber 1953; Turner et al. 1995). Following the oviposition of eggs by the female moth, the developing larvae feed only on the seeds, although the surrounding tissue becomes calloused.

A given plant within a population of *Y. arizonica* does not flower every year (McKelvey 1938; Gentry 1972) and entire populations may fail to flower following a year of drought (McKelvey 1938). Three years elapse between the production of flower stalks of *Y. baccata,* which is the period of time required to build up sufficient carbohydrate and water reserves (Wallen and Ludwig 1978; Turner et al. 1995). A similar requirement may also account for sporadic flowering in *Y. arizonica.* Western Apaches recognized that yuccas required time to flower and that flowering was sporadic. According to their understanding of *Y. baccata,* the plant reaches maturity in two to three years, with the "female" producing fruit every other year if sufficient moisture is present (Potter-Basso 1991). Peak flowering of *Y. arizonica* and *Y. baccata* is from March to May and April to June, respectively (Wiggins 1964; Turner et al. 1995). Fruits develop on *Y. baccata* ten weeks after flowers appear (Wallen and Ludwig 1978). Fruit production of *Y. arizonica* (McKelvey 1938) and *Y. baccata* (pers. obs.) may be poor even in years when the plants flower abundantly. Because these yuccas require pollen from another plant for fruit development (Webber 1953), the lack of pollinators could limit fruit production in some years.

Yucca schidigera flowers from February to June. Some plants flower every year in most populations, but only rarely do the majority flower in the same year (Beatley 1976). Flowering is sporadic and, like populations of *Y. baccata* and possibly *Y. arizonica,* may require similar conditions for flower stalk development (Turner et al. 1995). Fruit production is also variable from year to year (McKelvey 1938), which may be due to fluctuations in pollinating moth populations (Turner et al. 1995). *Yucca valida* flowers in April and May or September through November, with fruits of spring-flowering plants maturing in September and October (Turner et al. 1995).

The yucca most widely used in the Southwest was *Y. baccata* (fig. 23) because its extensive range made it accessible to many groups north of the Tohono O'odham area of occupation. The pleasant-tasting, sweet, and nutritious fruits were consumed when they were fully ripened from August through October. Immature fruits are extremely bitter and have a long-lasting aftertaste. Native peoples sometimes gathered the immature fruits to ripen in the sun because many fruits were lost due to herbivory by deer, birds, cattle, and insects (Bell and Castetter 1941). Fruits are a strong laxative, as noted by Edward Palmer (1871:418), who wrote that, "for some time neither salts nor castor-oil were needed from the medicine-chest, as this fruit proved to be a vigorous cathartic when dry." I can vouch for this, having suffered the effects of eating the fresh pulp of too many fruits in the Grand Canyon.

In the past Western Apaches considered the fruits of *Y. baccata* to be an important regular food, but today they consider the fruits a specialty item (Potter-Basso 1991). They ate the fruits fresh or more commonly dried and rehydrated. According to Edward Gifford (1940), Western Apaches peeled, split, and removed the seeds of the ripe fruit before eating the pulp fresh. If the fruit was not fully ripe, they roasted the fruit in ashes, immersed them in water, then peeled and removed the seeds. Western Apaches related to Winfred Buskirk (1986) that the fruits of *Y. baccata* had to be cooked before they were dried or else they would spoil. They roasted the fruit, removed the rows of seeds, then dried the fruit on bear-grass *(Nolina microcarpa).* Western Apaches stored the cooked pulp by wrapping it in bear-grass before caching it in a tree where they could keep it "indefinitely." When needed, they soaked the dried fruit pulp in water. Edward Palmer (1871:418) related that the cavalry troops in northern Arizona "captured a quantity of the dried fruit from the Apaches, and, being sweet, it was generally eaten." Marsha Gallagher (1976) had the impression that Tonto Apaches living in Clarkdale, Arizona, preferred ripe fruit, although they boiled and ate green, immature fruit as well. They collected and ate it in considerable quantities during September or October, before the fruit spoiled. During the 1970s, the Tonto Apache no longer split and dried the fruit for storage.

Northeastern Yavapais split the fruit of *Y. baccata* in four parts, removed the seeds, and roasted the fruit parts on coals (Gifford 1936). They ate the pulp after discarding the charred outer portion and sometimes dried the pulp in the sun for storing. When needed, dried pulp, which could keep up to five months, was boiled until the initially hard mass became soft. They drank the juice and ate the rehydrated pulp with meat.

Southeastern Yavapais also ate the fruit of *Y. baccata* (Gifford 1932). They often harvested immature fruit, which they placed in a fire and then immersed the fruit in water, "to hasten the ripening process," a step not necessary for fully mature fruit. They discarded the seeds, but ate the pulp with the outer "skin." They also stored the pulp after drying it in the sun for two or three days.

FIGURE 23. ***Yucca baccata*** Torr. **a.** Fruits and leaves; **b.** habit; **c.** flowers. Courtesy of the Mesa Southwest Museum.

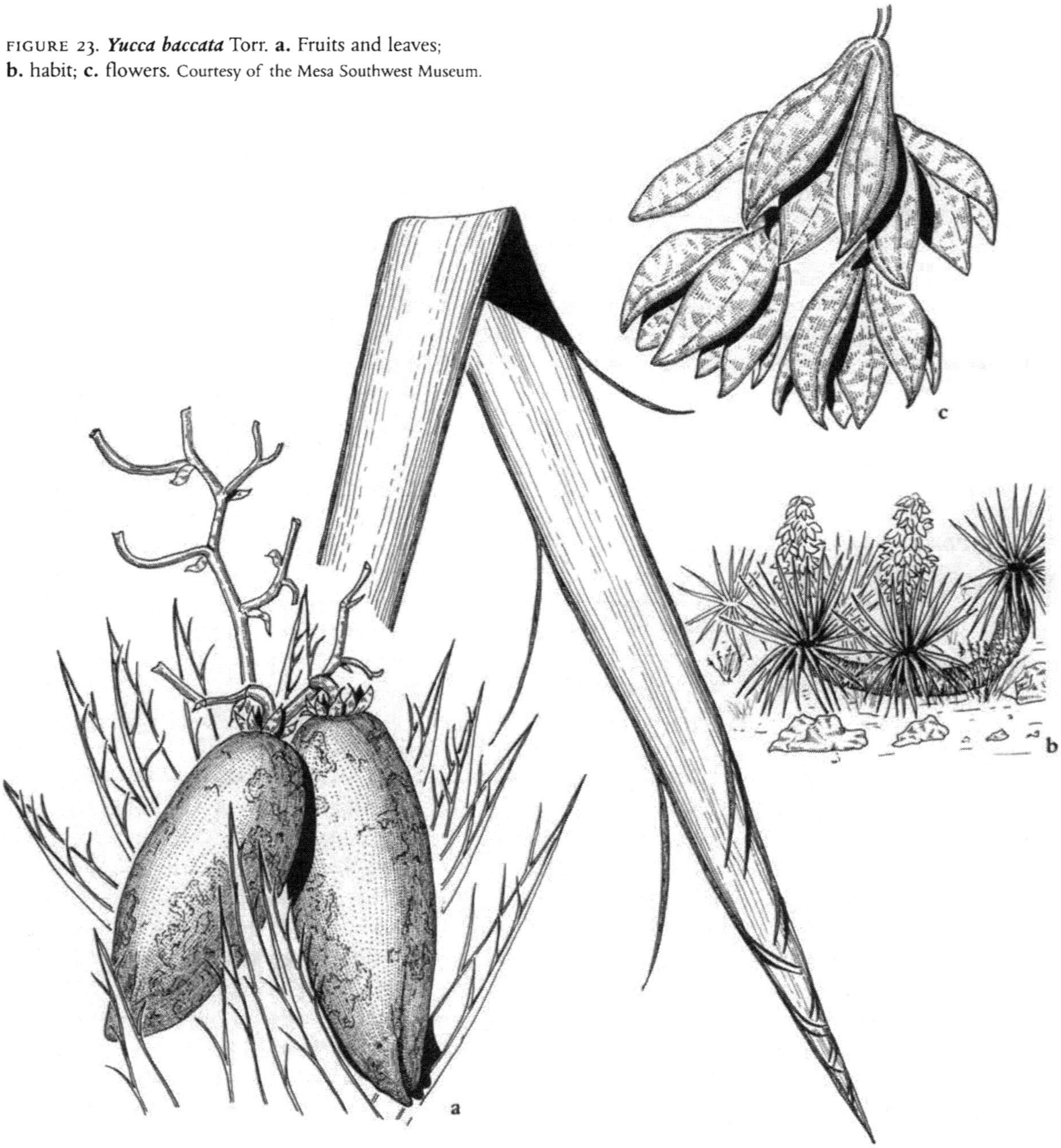

Five yuccas grow in the territory of the Tohono O'odham: *Y. elata* (fig. 24), *Y. arizonica* (figs. 25, 26), *Y. thornberi, Y. schottii* (figs. 27, 28), and possibly *Y. baccata*. The extent to which the Tohono O'odham used the fruits depended on the amount of fruit production and proximity of plants to their villages (Bell and Castetter 1941). They gathered and ate fully ripened fruits of *Y. arizonica* during expeditions to the mountains. Fruit sections were dried in the sun and carried home in baskets and stored. The Tohono O'odham also separated out the fruit pulp from the seeds and fiber in the field, spread the pulp on saguaro (*Carnegiea gigantea* Engelm.) ribs in the storehouse, then beat the pulp to remove any remaining fiber. In addition, they partially dried the pulp in the field by first scraping out the pulp with their fingers, making the pulp into cakes, then drying the cakes on a hot stone before taking them home. Partially dried cakes were spread out on their roofs at home to dry fully. The women also collected partially ripened fruits and placed them between layers of dry grass for further ripening. Juanita Norris, a Tohono O'odham at Ak Chiñ, told Amadeo Rea (1997) that to make the fruits sweeter, they pit-baked the fruits until the next morning. Seeds were stored in baskets and ground on a metate into a meal that was cooked with cornmeal (Castetter and Underhill 1935) or white flour (Hrdlička 1908) when needed.

FIGURE 24. ***Yucca elata*** Engelm. Photograph courtesy of H. S. Gentry.

River Pimas made expeditions into the hills to gather the fruits of *Y. baccata* (Bell and Castetter 1941) and received the preserved fruit of *Y. arizonica* and *Y. baccata* (and possibly *Y. thornberi*) in trade from the Tohono O'odham (Hrdlička 1908; Bell and Castetter 1941; Rea 1997). Salt River Pimas had access to *Y. baccata* 6 to 12 miles north and northeast of the river in the foothills of the Superstition, Mazatzal, and possibly Goldfield Mountains, which approaches Southeastern Yavapai territory. Where the Gila River Pima could have gathered any fleshy-fruited yucca is not known. Yuccas have never been documented from the nearby Sierra Estrellas, although the Pimas have inferred the existence of these plants (Rea 1997). A type of yucca was recently observed in the Sierra Estrellas, but never collected for identification purposes. Most of the banana yucca pulp the Gila River Pima ate was received through trade with the Tohono O'odham, at least until the beginning of the 20th century. Frank Russell (1908) described how the Gila River Pima boiled, dried, and ground the pulp on the mealing-stone then boiled the ground pulp with flour. Seris also harvested and ate the ripe fruits of *Y. arizonica* in early summer (Felger and Moser 1985).

Indigenous groups inhabiting areas outside the Sonoran Desert used *Y. baccata* as well. The Las Vegas Southern Paiute, whose areas of occupation extended into the southern Mohave Desert, also used the fruits of *Y. baccata* (Fowler 1995). They hastened the ripening of the fruit by partially breaking off the branch upon which the fruits were borne or by burying the fruit in a pit covered with earth (Kelly 1932–1934 *in* Fowler 1995), the latter method being similar to that described by the Tohono O'odham woman at Ak Chiñ. The Southern Paiute split the fruit, picked out the seeds, and dried the pulp in balls or pounded the pulp into flattened sheets. The dried pulp was carefully folded into sheets for storage and covered with bark for caching in rock shelters or juniper trees and was later retrieved and ground into flour for the preparation of mush or loaves or boiled and mashed.

Havasupais gathered the ripe fruits of *Y. baccata* at the end of September (Bell and Castetter 1941; Weber and Seaman 1985). The fruits were laid on a bed of dry sticks, partially cooked over a fire, and then removed and sprinkled with water (Weber and Seaman 1985). They separated the fleshy portions from the burned "rind," dried the pulp as a sheet that was folded and stored, and ground the seeds on a metate. The Havasupai broke off and ate the bits of dried pulp or

FIGURE 25. Rick DeLamater standing next to ***Yucca arizonica*** McKelvey. Near El Datil, Sonora, May 1988.

FIGURE 26. ***Yucca arizonica.*** Plant with immature fruits.

FIGURE 27. ***Yucca schottii*** Engelm. Plant with green fruits. Santa Catalina Mountains, Pima County, Arizona, barely extending into the Sonoran Desert here, July 1988 (*Hodgson 5074*, DES).

FIGURE 28. ***Yucca schottii.*** Plant with green fruits. Santa Catalina Mountains, Pima County, Arizona, barely extending into the Sonoran Desert here, July 1988 (*Hodgson 5074*, DES).

boiled the pieces in water and drank the liquid. Fresh pulp was also sun-dried and stored in a sack. Fruits chewed and allowed to ferment increased their sweetness (Cushing 1882). The Hualapai also gathered the fruits of *Y. baccata* (Bell and Castetter 1941; Watahomigie et al. 1982) in large quantities and prepared them in a manner similar to that of the Havasupai (Bell and Castetter 1941).

Although the Maricopa made expeditions northward to gather the fruit of *Y. schidigera* (figs. 29, 30), they generally said it was too far away to be important in their lives (Bell and Castetter 1941). The Mohave occasionally ate the peeled fruits.

The Cahuilla picked the fruits of *Y. schidigera* in April and May, when green and immature (fig. 30), and roasted them on coals (Barrows 1900:59, cited as *Y. mohavensis*). When cooked this way, the fruits had a "sweet, not unpleasant taste, slightly suggestive of roasted green apples." If fruits were gathered later, they became too bitter to eat (Bean and Saubel 1972).

Indigenous peoples of northern Baja California relied heavily on the fruits of *datile,* probably those of *Y. schidigera* (Meigs 1939). Tipais in northern Baja California ate the fruits of *Y. schidigera.* Doña Teodora Cuero and her daughter Cecilia, both Tipais, described how they harvested and ate the sweet banana-like yucca fruits in October (Weiss 1994). However, these yuccas are more important to these people for their use as cleaning agents. The leaves, stems, and roots contain saponins and are an important source of income for some Tipai, who gather plants to be sold in Ensenada or Tijuana for making shampoos and other hair products.

Joséfina Ochurte related that in the 1950s Paipais still collected the fruits of *Y. schidigera* as well as those of prickly-pears, piñons, and oaks, "at least occasionally when the field work was done" (Jöel 1976:58). Like fruits of *Y. baccata,* its fruits do not ripen all at once, but gradually. In addition, wildlife ate the ripe fruits. Paipais harvested both ripe and unripe fruits, collecting them "at various stages of ripeness during August and September." At this time they split open and dried the pulp of mature fruits. During the winter, they cooked the dried pulp in water and drank the juice. The Paipai also brought unripe fruits home, which they dumped into a pit and covered with branches. Fruits that ripened after three days were taken out, opened, and left covered in the sun to dry. They collected more unripe fruits and piled them into the pit. They continued doing so until all of the harvestable fruits were collected.

FIGURE 29. (top) ***Yucca schidigera*** Roezl. Large, caespitose (densely clumping), fruiting plants in large stand on outwash slopes of valley. Morongo Valley, California, July 1976. Photograph courtesy of H. S. Gentry.

FIGURE 30. (bottom) Close-up of ***Yucca schidigera*** fruits. Photograph courtesy of H. S. Gentry.

The Kiliwa highly prized the sweet, datelike fruits of the yucca, which ripened in July and August (Meigs 1939:25, cited questionably as *Y. baccata*). Peveril Meigs noted how fruits were especially plentiful following dry winters, such as that experienced in 1928. The Kiliwa used a hooked stick to pull down the fruit from tall plants. Meigs's photograph depicts plants suggestive of tall *Y. schidigera.* The northernmost populations of *Y. valida* grow 100 kilometers south of the Kiliwa's area of occupation. They had easier access to *Y. schidigera* populations, which grew in the western part of their territory.

The fleshy fruits of *Y. valida* were an important food item to the local inhabitants of central Baja California (Aschmann 1959), with their shape bearing "some resemblance" to that of the Barbary date, thus the common name *dátil* (Aschmann 1966). Plants bear fruit from September through November. The sweet fruit, if eaten in excess, was said to cause diarrhea, but it was considered "substantive because [the natives] got fat on it" (Aschmann 1966:33). One Jesuit missionary noted that when rain fell in an area where *Y. valida* populations were found, the local people were able to harvest much fruit. If rain did not fall, "a major part of the fruit is lost." Such loss of fruit was not because of inadequate moisture for the production of fruits, but because there was not enough drinking water for the people to stay for the harvest. Local inhabitants harvested the fruits at least until the 1800s, when it was noted how "poor people" roasted and ate the fruits "of a wild date" *(Y. valida)* in the vicinity of San Ignacio Mission (Aschmann 1959:89). Most people, with the exception of the Death Valley Shoshone, did not eat the spongy, corky mature fruit of *Y. brevifolia* (Fowler 1995).

The young flowering shoots, flowers, and inner stem tissues of most yuccas were also used as food (Gentry 1972). Western Apaches often charred the flowering stalk of *Y. elata* over a fire and ate it "like sugar cane" (Buskirk 1986), although they did not eat the flowering stalk of *Y. baccata.* A curing rite involved using a yucca stalk that the practitioner heated, chewed, and spit out fragments onto the sick person.

All groups living in or near Joshua tree habitat, including the Chemehuevi, used *Y. brevifolia* in a similar manner (Fowler 1995). The Panamints of southeastern California harvested the young terminal bud of rosettes in April, when the rosettes appeared swollen and were covered with young leaves (Coville 1892). They grasped four or five of the uppermost leaves together over the bud and, by using a twist and "a quick, sidewise bend," broke off the head. The older leaves and green tips of the rosette were discarded, thus leaving an "egg-shaped, solid, cream-like juicy mass" that was roasted on hot coals and then eaten (Coville 1892:355). The inner tissues of these young buds were considered very sweet because they were full of sugar and other carbohydrates.

Yucca flowers were usually boiled and eaten as a vegetable or combined with other foods (Gentry 1972). Their taste varies, although the flowers of *Y. elata* are considered the best. The more sapogenous species, such as *Y. arizonica* and *Y. brevifolia,* have a bitter-tasting pistil that was usually removed. Western Apaches boiled the flowers of *Y. elata* with a "small black seed" or with fat or bones (Buskirk 1986:182). Flowers were said to be bitter "unless picked by a lucky person who knew the proper time to collect them." Western Apaches dried the cooked flowers for later use. Juanita Norris, a Tohono O'odham, related to Amadeo Rea (1997) how they cooked and ate the flowers of *Y. elata,* although contemporary Pima are unfamiliar with this food. Southern Paiutes and Shoshones who harvested the rosettes of *Y. brevifolia* left some to develop a flower stalk and returned later to harvest and roast the developing flowers (Fowler 1995).

The seeds of most yuccas were generally not consumed, although some groups gathered, ground, and ate the seeds of *Y. arizonica* and *Y. brevifolia* (Bell and Castetter 1941; Palmer 1878). Seeds may have been important to Baja California natives. In 1709, English privateer-pirates Edward Cooke and Woodes Rogers noted that the Pericú ate the fruits and seeds of a plant that may have been a yucca (Andrews 1979:42): "Sort of Fruit growing in Cods, like our Flower-de-Lucas before they are blown; the outwart Part is green, and peels off, and within, upon a stalk, are many flat seeds, much like the Head of a Clove, which the Natives also eat, and it tastes and smells like green Pease." Annetta Carter (*in* Andrews 1979) suggested that the plant was *Y. valida,* which grows in the area where they visited, namely, the Cabo San Lucas–Cabo Falso vicinity. *Yucca capensis* Lenz (Lenz 1998) also grows in this general area, but outside the boundaries of the Sonoran Desert.

There is some confusion as to whether yucca roots were used for food. Hernando de Alarcón, in his explorations of the Lower Colorado River region in 1540, noted that the natives (probably Cocopa) "brought with them certain conies and yucas" (Hakluyt 1904:301; Mathes 1992:117). Albert Elsasser (1980:23) suggested that "conies" referred to jackrabbits, but he made no mention of what "yucas" might be. Alarcón's *"yuca"* may have been the fruits of *Y. schidigera,* which grows no less than 50 kilometers west of the delta, or even the succulent rhizomes of *Pholisma sonorae* (see *Pholisma*). Fr. Salvatierra wrote of "the stately mescales, the large yuccas and other roots, and fruit trees" in the lands of San Francisco Javier de Biggé Bianundo, west of Loreto, in the Sierra de la Giganta (Burrus 1971:160). He was probably referring to *Y. valida* when writing about yuccas, and his writing does not necessarily infer that their roots were used for food (see *Merremia*).

Other Jesuit missionaries referred to a plant called "yucca" or *"yuca,"* its roots considered the "daily bread" of the inhabitants of south-central and southern Baja California and Sonora (Bolton 1948; Baegert 1952; Píccolo 1967; Nentvig 1980). Although thought by some to be possibly a yucca (Pradeau and Rasmussen *in* Nentvig 1980), the plant providing edible roots and referred to as "yucca" or *"yuca"* was probably *Manihot chlorosticta* Standley and Goldman (see *Manihot*), *Amoreuxia* sp. (see *Amoreuxia*), or in Baja California, *Merremia aurea* (Kellogg) O'Donell (see *Merremia*). Fr. del Barco (1980: 231) did not confuse *yuca* with yucca as he described a plant *(M. aurea)* whose "stalk intertwines itself into and climbs on any thicket." No other information regarding the use of yucca roots for food is known.

Alismataceae | Water-plantain Family

Sagittaria | arrowhead

S. latifolia **Willdenow**
wapato, duckpotato

Arrowhead tubers of all Sonoran Desert species may be used as a food source if they are of sufficient size. Other desert arrowheads are *S. cuneata* Sheldon (arum-leaf arrowhead) and *S. longiloba* Engelm. (including *S. greggii* J. Smith; long-barb arrowhead). However, indigenous people having access to the plants primarily ate the tubers of *S. latifolia* by boiling or roasting them like potatoes. The Mohave dug up the tubers as soon as the flow of the Colorado River subsided in the spring (Castetter and Bell 1951). Edward Palmer observed Cocopas using the tubers for food near Colonia Lerdo, Sonora (Vasey and Rose 1890b, cited as *S. variabilis*). The tubers served as a famine food when agricultural products and the fruits of grass and weedy plants were maturing (Kelly 1977).

Arrowhead matured in late summer, whereupon Cocopa men dug up the tubers with a stick (Kelly 1977). They baked the tubers in coals, rubbed the "skin" off, and ate them whole or mashed (Castetter and Bell 1951; Kelly 1977). Opinions varied as to the taste, which was described variously as "exceedingly farinaceous and palatable" eaten raw or cooked with other foodstuffs (Palmer 1878) or "not very tasty" (Kelly 1977). Because tubers could not be stored, large quantities were not gathered (Kelly 1977; Alvarez de Williams 1987). Researchers have indicated that arrowhead tubers may be a good source of carbohydrates (King 1984) and may have medicinal properties (Neumann et al. 1989).

Following dramatic changes within riparian communities of the Southwest, populations of arrowhead decreased significantly during the twentieth century, as noted by Castetter and Bell (1951). The genus has been completely extirpated from the Gila River Reservation since being documented in the early 1930s (Rea 1997). Use of arrowhead tubers by Sonoran Desert peoples is not well documented, although undoubtedly its importance as a food has been diminished with a decreased abundance of arrowhead plants.

Arecaceae | Palm Family

Erythea | hesper palm

E. armata S. Watson
blue fan palm, palma blanca, palma ceniza

E. brandegeei Purpus
red palm, palma coloradas, la pamilla, palmilla de taco, palma negra, palmilla

E. elegans Franceschi ex Beccari
babiso

The abundant fruits of *Erythea* spp. are round; drupelike; brown, black, or purplish black; 15–24 millimeters long; and have a somewhat fleshy pericarp (fruit wall) at maturity, which provides a food source. For indigenous peoples, harvesting the fruits of *Erythea* was more advantageous than harvesting the fruits of *Washingtonia.* A single spathe may produce as much as 40 pounds of fruit, whereas that of *Washingtonia* may produce only about 2 pounds (Aschmann 1959). Additionally, Charles Orcutt (1885) noted that *W. filifera* (Lindl.) Wendl. fruits ripen a year after they bloom, whereas fruits of *E. armata* mature soon after plants flower.

Erythea armata is endemic to the northern half of Baja California. Cocopas ate the relatively large fruits of *E. armata* fresh or dried them for future use (Gifford 1933). They also pit-roasted the seeds to remove any bitterness before eating them (Felger and Moser 1985). The Seri, however, considered the seeds inedible (Felger and Moser 1985, cited as *Brahea armata*). During the 1880s, Charles Orcutt (1885) observed that Diegueños and Kiliwas sought out and eagerly ate the abundant fruit in June. Some Tipais still enjoy the fruit, which they consider very sweet (Weiss 1994). Fr. Consag noted that in a mountain valley between Santa Gertrudis and San Borja, the inhabitants (Borjeños) tied sticks to palm tree trunks to facilitate climbing and gathering the fruit, of which they were very fond (Krmpotic 1923).

The fleshy fruits of *E. brandegeei,* an endemic of the southern half of Baja California, are called *tacos* by the native inhabitants (Moran 1977, cited as *Brahea brandegeei*). They develop soon after plants flower in the spring and are black when mature. When immature and yellow, however, the fruits are good to eat, having a taste similar to that of dates.

Erythea elegans grows as scattered populations in east-central Sonora (Municipio Yécora), central Sonora (Municipio Ures), and on the coast near Guaymas and in the Sierra Libre (Joyal 1996). The inhabitants in and around Ures consider the fruits of *E. elegans* to be edible and to have a good taste (Joyal 1996), whereas the Seri consider the fruits inedible (Felger and Moser 1985). It is not known whether the thin-fleshed, hard fruits of *E. roezlii* (Lindl.) Becc. were eaten.

The young leaves in bud, or "hearts," of *Erythea* were also eaten. Many Cocopas left the hot Colorado River delta during August and traveled west to the canyons where *E. armata* grew with *Washingtonia filifera* and gathered the young shoots to eat (Gifford 1933; Alvarez de Williams 1987). Inhabitants of the cape region of Baja California knew *E. brandegeei* as *la palmia.* Here Townsend Brandegee (1904) noted that, at the turn of the century, people still cut out and ate the young leaf buds. The taste was compared to that of a raw turnip. However, prior to the natives' uprising in 1734–1735, inhabitants of southern Baja California did not appear to use palms, which were quite abundant, to a great degree. In 1721, Fr. Nápoli commented on the abundance of palms in Cora territory on the southeastern coast of the peninsula (Moriarty and Smith 1970). Although not one to carefully record natives' uses of plants, Fr. Nápoli did note that Cora women wore skirts made of palm leaves.

Fr. del Barco (1980), who arrived on the peninsula in 1738, noted that the natives used the straight, tall "trunks" for roof timbers, "even in the churches." However, they did not always eat the "hearts" of palms. He described how the local inhabitants soon learned to use palm hearts to the point of destroying magnificent palm groves (del Barco 1980:108–109):

> When the missions of the South were founded there were many and frequent palm groves, because the Indians took absolutely no advantage of these large palms. With the occasion of the uprising of the year 1734, people from the province of Sinaloa came to that part of California in order to participate in its pacification. These people began to cut the hearts of the palms, which they called *palmito,* in order to eat them. The Indians learned to eat *palmito* from these or from others a short time before, because prior to that they did not know that it could be eaten. They liked it so much that in a short time

> they finished several beautiful palm groves. This occurred because the palm tree dries up when its heart is cut away, since it does not produce shoots in another place as is the case with other trees.

Palmito harvesters cut down the whole palm and pried out the heart while the tree lay on the ground. They also climbed up the tall trunks to the top and cut out the *palmito,* a method feared by both harvesters and onlookers alike, as described by Fr. del Barco (1980: 108–109):

> This fear [of climbing up the palm trees] is necessary and often extreme in those who must go up to the heights of the palm in order to cut the palmito. This is because these palms are very tall ... [with] no leaves except ... near the tip or heart .... And so, in addition to the difficulty of climbing so high on a trunk which has no place to grab onto [did they not make a ladder?], the climber reaches the top and while he is cutting the palmito, the palm is swinging, going to and fro, from one side to the other, seeming to want to shake from itself the person who is going to take its life, and frightening even those who are only looking up from the ground .... This effect is much more pronounced if there is some wind.

The extent of the natives' exploitation of palm hearts is further described by Fr. del Barco (1980:109): "In four or five years those great palm groves of their territories were left dry and without a single leaf. The resulting dead palms resembled a great multitude of giant and extinguished candles." Palms harvested in this manner rotted easily as "the carved-out tips" filled with rainwater. Inhabitants of the area further impacted the palm groves (del Barco 1980:109): "There remained intact, about halfway between Santiago and La Paz, a great many other palm groves of the territories, until then untouched. However, as mines began to be worked in this area, their operators and wood choppers are finishing even these, as they cut down the palms with axes in order to eat the palmito. As the palms grow usually in the beds of arroyos, once they are cut down they are carried downstream to the sea." In what seems to be empathy, Fr. del Barco added that "truly speaking, the palmito is a very delicious and estimable thing in salads, and in those places where it can be had, the Spaniards eat it as a real treat."

It is not clear whether del Barco was referring to *E. brandegeei* or *Washingtonia robusta* H. Wendl. *Palma blanca,* the type that had white "wood," may be *W. robusta* (Carter *in* del Barco 1980). Fr. del Barco seemed especially knowledgeable and interested in those plants on the mainland, particularly those that grew near Guaymas; he often compared them with the same or close relatives on the peninsula. Guaymas was often the port from which the boats set sail, so he and others would have been more familiar with plants and their uses in this region. *Washingtonia robusta* grows near Guaymas. The Baja California inhabitants probably used the young shoots of both *W. robusta* and *E. brandegeei,* and populations of both palm species were undoubtedly severely impacted by such a practice. *Washingtonia robusta* grows faster than *E. brandegeei* (Brandegee 1904) and buds from young, short plants could be harvested more easily and quickly. However, *W. robusta* was not preferred for construction because of its inferior quality when compared with *palma rubra,* or *E. brandegeei* (del Barco 1980).

Clear-cutting for the development of mission settlements also impacted native palms. In Cora territory, dense stands of palm groves grew near permanent water, the most favored sites for the founding of missions. At Las Palmas Bay and its surrounding area, Fr. Nápoli found vast, extensive, and numerous palm groves, which "resemble thick woods" (Moriarty and Smith 1970:65–66). At one particularly favorable site, "our soldiers now began to clear the little hill and to fell palm-trees, in order to build a house [chapel] with all speed." More than two centuries later, Liberty H. Bailey (1937) commented that wild populations of *E. brandegeei* were declining as a result of floods and timber cutting.

Sabal | sabal, palmetto, palma, palma del suelo

S. uresana Trelease

Sabal uresana occupies the most xeric habitat of any of the 16 species of *Sabal* (Joyal 1995), with Sonoran Desert populations being concentrated in and around Ures, between Batuc and Hermosillo, in Guaymas (Wiggins 1964; Joyal 1995), and in Ónavas, Sonora (Joyal 1995). Plants flower primarily from March to June, with fruits commonly ripening from August to October (Joyal 1996). Fruits of plants growing in the deserts ripen one or two months earlier than those from plants in the sierras (fig. 31). Many told Elaine Joyal that

FIGURE 31. (left) ***Sabal uresana*** Trel. Close-up of greenish fruits from beneath crown; note the absence of prickles on petioles of fronds. Located 24 miles southwest of Moctezuma on the way to Masocahui, Sonora, July 1988.

FIGURE 32. (above) Young ***Sabal uresana.*** Located 12 miles south of Moctezuma on the way to Masocahui, Sonora, July 1988.

fruiting was not always abundant and that there were "good and bad years." Low fruit production was thought to be caused by cold temperatures, extremes in rainfall, or wind.

Yaquis (Alvarez de Williams n.d.), Río San Miguel inhabitants (Felger et al. 1976), and Seris (Felger and Moser 1985) formerly ate the fresh fruits of sabal palm. Not everyone thought that sabal palm fruits were edible. The fruits are eaten in Buena Vista and Ónavas, which are located in subtropical thornscrub, but considered unpalatable in the more arid area of Ures (Joyal 1996). Fruits of plants growing in the vicinity of Ures are small, brown, and often bitter at maturity in late summer. Fruits from plants growing in the more mesic thornscrub can be larger, sweeter, and black at maturity in the fall. This difference may be a result of the lack of precipitation in the desert, which may inhibit sugar development and thus complete ripening of the fruit (Joyal 1996).

The young buds, or "palm hearts," were also used for food. Fr. Nentvig (1980) described how the palm heart was harvested and prepared (he wrote of two kinds of palms and it is not clear to which he was referring when he described the use of the hearts). The hearts were the size of a "sugar loaf" and could feed four to six people. They were eaten either raw or slightly cooked. The Guarijío ate the hearts of young palms raw or roasted (Gentry 1942; fig. 32). Ónavas Pimas pit-baked the hearts in the same manner as that described for agave heads (Pennington 1980). Local inhabitants told Joyal (1995, 1996) they knew that palm hearts were edible, but no one had firsthand experience or knew anyone who had eaten them.

Sabal uresana is important economically. Its leaves are used for weaving, thatching, and making brooms and the trunks for construction of corrals (fig. 33) and as house crossbeams (Joyal 1996).

FIGURE 33. ***Sabal uresana.*** Corrals in the area are commonly made from the trunks of the sabal palm. Located 10.5 miles south of Rayon, Sonora, September 1988.

Washingtonia | fan palm

W. filifera **(Lindlen) H. Wendland**
California fan palm, palmilla

W. robusta **H. Wendland**
skyduster fan palm, Washington fan palm, palma de castilla, palma, palma colorada, palma blanca, palma rubra

The genus *Washingtonia* was once widespread from the Mohave Desert to the Pacific Coast during the Tertiary, but has since been eliminated across much of its range by climatic and geologic changes (Axelrod 1950). Populations became restricted to the western Sonoran Desert, particularly along the shores of the former Lake Cahuilla, what we call now Salton Basin (Axelrod 1950), where most populations are still found (Turner et al. 1995). No native stand is now known west of the Mohave Desert, but apparently one persisted until recently (Moran 1977). In 1893, while exploring Valle de las Palmas, which is 25 miles southeast of Tijuana, Charles Orcutt thought the area was devoid of palms until he and his group found them in a large canyon (Moran 1977:11). However, he found more trees lying dead on the ground than were growing erect. The ex-governor of the region was at the time harvesting the palms for his own roof and "apparently ... completed his work."

Outlier populations in western Arizona and northwestern Baja California (Moran 1977) may be relics, may have arisen via long-distance seed dispersal, or may have been planted by Native Americans (Moran 1979). Much of the *W. filifera* cultivated in California at the turn of the century probably came from seed collected along the western edge of the Sonoran Desert in southwestern Arizona, southeastern California, and near Campo in northern Baja California (Brandegee 1904).

Plants flower in the spring and occasionally in the summer (Turner et al. 1995). *Washingtonia*'s fruits are edible; the seed is enveloped by sweet flesh that tastes like a domestic date (Bean and Saubel 1972). Gila River Pima children gathered and ate the fruits as a snack food from trees planted "here and there" on the reservation (Rea 1997). The Cocopa collected the palm's fruits during August while also collecting the young shoots of *Erythea armata* (Alvarez de Williams n.d.).

Washingtonia filifera was very important to the Cahuilla, whose permanent village sites and smaller campsites were palm oases (Moran 1977). They considered the fruit of *W. filifera,* which was gathered from June through early November, a dependable and important source of food (Bean and Saubel 1972; Moran 1977). Each tree could produce numerous fruit clusters, each weighing from 5 to 20 pounds (Bean and Saubel 1972). The Cahuilla sometimes lassoed and retrieved the clusters, but more commonly used long willow poles with a notch at the end to collect the fruits. More recently, tin-can tops were attached to the pole's end to disengage the fruit clusters. Fruits were eaten fresh or dried in the sun for later use (Bean and Saubel 1972; Moran 1977). They made flour from ground dried fruits (including the seeds) and mixed it with other flours and water to form a mush.

The Cahuilla periodically burned the palm oasis to increase fruit yield by killing the insects that ate the fruit (Bean and Saubel 1972). They later abandoned this practice, as inferred by a Cahuilla informant who said that the medicine men (who burned the trees) all passed on and that worms were eating the flowers and fruits. The U.S. Department of Agriculture later confirmed that periodic burns are the most effective way to rid the palms of insect pests (Bean and Saubel 1972; Nabhan 1985). Fires kill the beetle *Dinapate wrightii,* which tunnels close to the trunk's exterior and weakens or kills the palms (Cornett 1984). Periodic burning reduces parasitism and competition for moisture, nutrients, and sunlight, thereby increasing fruit production (Cornett and Stewart 1986).

Over the years fire suppression, urban development, and agriculture have contributed to the demise of the palms and their habitat, with less than 400 hectares of native palm oasis habitat left (Cornett 1984). Many of the palms in the three groves at Thousand Palms, California, have been saved only by an irrigation system. Arroyo downcutting and severe lowering of the water table have drastically impacted Powell Palms, the smallest of the fan palm groves.

Washingtonia robusta flowers from late spring to early summer and produces somewhat fleshy fruits. Inhabitants at San Carlos Bay, Sonora, used the seeds for food (Watson 1889, cited as *W. sonorae*), whereas the Seri ate the fruits (Felger and Moser 1985).

The young buds were also used for food. Inhabitants at San José del Cabo recognized two forms of *W. robusta* as *palma blanca* and *palma rubra,* according to the color of the "wood," or inner tissue (Brandegee 1904, cited as *W. sonorae*). Fr. del Barco also observed the same differentiation by southern Baja Californians of two palms according to the color of the "wood," some 150 years prior. Here, the native inhabitants learned from people living in "the province of Sinaloa" (probably Yaquis) how to roast and eat the young buds of either this palm or *Erythea brandegeei* (del Barco 1980; see *Erythea*). Harvesting the "hearts" provided a short-term source of food, but killed the tree. It is not certain which palm del Barco was referring to when he noted that the inhabitants destroyed numerous palm groves (see *Erythea*). Populations of *W. robusta* may have been extirpated in this and other areas. Populations were once found at Mazatlan and along the coast of the cape region of Baja California at the turn of the century (Brandegee 1904), localities that have not been cited in more recent works (Wiggins 1964, 1980; Moran 1977).

Commelinaceae | Spiderwort Family

Tradescantia | spiderwort, wandering-jew

***T. occidentalis* (Britton) Smyth**
prairie spiderwort

Tradescantia occidentalis is an attractive herbaceous perennial when in flower from April through September. Use of spiderwort by Sonoran Desert people is not known, although Navajo and Hopi people ate its tender shoots raw or cooked like spinach (Hough 1898; Swank 1932; Castetter 1935; Bailey 1940). However, people's use of the plant gradually discontinued. This is suggested by the lack of any record of use by the Hopi in the late 1930s (Whiting 1939) or in the Río Grande valley, where the plant may have become locally extirpated before its uses were recorded (Bohrer 1978). Cattle, which are fond of the young shoots of spiderwort, undoubtedly reduced the plant's range and abundance. It is probable that such a phenomenon occurred within the Sonoran Desert, which has suffered years of severe overgrazing. Spiderwort may have been part of the diets of Sonoran Desert inhabitants when plants were more abundant prior to the impact of cattle, but before its uses were recorded. By the time later ethnographic studies were pursued, the plant may have fallen out of disuse due to its scarcity.

Cyperaceae | Sedge Family

Cyperus | flat-sedge, tule

C. erythrorhizos **Muhlenberg**
red-root flat-sedge

C. esculentus **Linnaeus**
yellow nut-sedge, yellow nut-grass, chufa, peonia, tulillo

C. odoratus **Linnaeus**
rusty flat-sedge, cuentas de Santa Elena

C. rotundus **Linnaeus**
purple flat-sedge, purple nut-sedge, purple nut-grass, coquito

The inner base of the young stems of all species of *Cyperus* may be used for food. The stems stripped of leaves and sheaths expose tissue "laden with a very palatable sugary juice" (Coville 1892; Chamberlain 1911, cited as *C. utriculata*).

Gila River Pimas primarily collected the small rhizomatous tubers of *C. esculentus,* although those of *C. erythrorhizos, C. odoratus,* and *C. rotundus* apparently were also collected (Rea 1997). They ate these tubers fresh or dried as a snack, with the taste being described as slightly sweet or sour-sweet (Curtin 1949; Rea 1997). Mountain Pima children of northeastern Sonora occasionally ate the tubers, primarily during the planting season when the tubers were pushed up by the plows (Laferrière et al. 1991). The children easily gathered them and ate them raw with a minimal of cleaning. The "sweet" tubers are too small to constitute a major food source. Tubers contain 44 percent carbohydrates, 17 percent lipid, and 4.4 percent protein by dry weight (Mokady and Dolev 1970). Pimas also used the tubers of *C. esculentus* and possibly *C. rotundus* as medicines to treat colds and, in some cases, snake bites (Curtin 1949; *Curtin II,* DES).

Sedges grow primarily in moist or wet areas and are usually very abundant. Pimas looked upon these plants with favor, whereas white settlers in Scottsdale, Arizona, considered them as noxious weeds (Curtin 1949). The Gila River Pima referred to the plant as *vashai s-uuv,* and the Pima name for Scottsdale was *Vashai S-uuvak* (Curtin 1949; *Curtin II,* DES; Rea 1997) because sedge was so common. However, as with so many riparian plants within the Sonoran Desert, its habitat and abundance has decreased dramatically in the last half of this century.

Schoenoplectus | club-rush

S. acutus **(Muhlenberg ex Bigelow) A. & D. Love (syn.,** *Scirpus acutus* **Muhlenberg)**
hard-stem club-rush

S. americanus **(Persoon) Volkart ex Schinz & R. Keller (syn.,** *Scirpus americanus* **Persoon)**
chairmaker's club-rush

S. maritimus **(Linnaeus) Lye (syn.,** *Scirpus maritimus* **Linnaeus var.** *paludosus* **[A. Nelson] Kukenthal)**
salt-marsh club-rush, tule

S. tabernaemontani **(K. Gmelin) Palla (syn.,** *Scirpus validus* **Vahl,** *Schoenoplectus validus* **[Vahl] A. & D. Love)**
soft-stem club-rush, tule

Like cattails (*Typha* spp.), club-rushes and bulrushes were plants for all seasons, with different plant parts used at different times of the year. However, little is known of Sonoran Desert peoples' use of *Schoenoplectus* and *Scirpus.* When Amadeo Rea asked a Gila River Pima friend if he used bulrushes for anything, he was told they were "just decoration for the creeks" (Rea 1997:104, cited as *Scirpus* spp.). Ruth Giff related to Amadeo that they used to chew the small, tasteless, underground "tubers" (rhizomes) of *Schoenoplectus americanus,* or *vak,* gathered from the waters of the Lower Santa Cruz River (Rea 1997, cited as *Scirpus americanus*). The Cocopa, "before starting on a journey procure some of these roots [sic] to chew as a preventative of thirst, and at the same time to afford them nourishment" (Palmer 1871:408, cited as *Scirpus lacustris*). Inhabitants outside the realm of the Sonoran Desert ate the sweet bulrush rhizomes (Densmore 1928, cited as *Scirpus* sp.) or pounded the baked or dried rhizomes into flour (Saunders 1948, cited as *Scirpus* sp.).

The rhizomes of *Schoenoplectus tabernaemontani* also provided a food source to people, although their use is not well known. California natives not only ate the rhizomes raw or made a bread from the rhizome flour, they also made bread from its pollen (Palmer 1878, cited as *Scirpus validus*).

Bulrush fruits were consistently found in small quantities in coprolites from a site located on the northern shores of what was Lake Cahuilla prior to ca. A.D.

1500, when the Salton Sea formed (Sutton 1993). Following their harvest of cattail pollen, the people living around Lake Cahuilla may have eaten bulrush fruits with fish from May through August. In Myoma Dunes, the fruits formed a major constituent in some coprolites.

Club-rushes and bulrushes are primarily herbaceous perennials that grow in moist or mesic habitats. Like other riparian plants, their habitat within the Sonoran Desert has decreased. Amadeo Rea recently collected *Schoenoplectus maritimus* along the Lower Salt River and at the Salt-Gila River confluence (Rea 1997, cited as *Scirpus maritimus* var. *paludosus*). He has not seen *S. acutus* or *S. tabernaemontani* on the Gila River Pima Reservation or the Lower Salt River since 1979 (Rea 1997, cited as *Scirpus acutus* and *Scirpus validus*).

Dioscoreaceae | Yam Family

Dioscorea | yam

D. remotiflora Kunth
chichiwo

Dioscorea remotiflora is a twining perennial vine that has large, fleshy roots (fig. 34). The plant produces leaves and yellow flowers from July through August (Martin et al. 1998). The "Guarijío, Mayo, and Mexicans" ate the long tuberous roots of *chichiwo* raw or roasted, especially in the summer months, when it produces leaves (Gentry 1942, *Gentry 1634, 2328*, ARIZ; Altschul 1973; cited in all as *D. convolvulacea* ssp. *grandiflora*). Howard Gentry added, "it is the yam of the Río Mayo, and an important food in the diet of the Guarijío, especially in times of scarcity of corn during late spring and early summer" (Gentry 1942:98).

FIGURE 34. ***Dioscorea remotiflora*** Kunth. Note the large roots. Morelos, Mexico. Photograph courtesy of H. S. Gentry.

Liliaceae | Lily Family

Allium | onion, garlic, wild leek, cebolla, ajo

A. acuminatum Hooker
taper-tip onion

A. bisceptrum S. Watson var. *palmeri* (S. Watson) Cronquist (syn., *A. palmeri* S. Watson)
aspen onion

A. fimbriatum S. Watson
fringed onion

A. haematochiton S. Watson
red-skin onion

A. macropetalum Rydberg
large-petal onion

A. parishii S. Watson
Parish's onion

Native Americans ate the bulbs of various species of onion raw, cooked, or used as a seasoning for other foods (Chestnut 1902; Sparkman 1908; Chamberlain 1911; Robbins et al. 1916; Castetter 1935; Castetter and Underhill 1935; Castetter and Opler 1936; Saunders 1948; Gentry 1963; Bean and Saubel 1972; Hedrick 1972; Altschul 1973; Bye 1976; Bell 1980; Zigmond 1981; Watahomigie

1982; Felger and Moser 1985). However, the Havasupai experienced headaches after eating wild onions and thus ate them only when very hungry (Weber and Seaman 1985, cited as *A. palmeri*).

Gila River Pimas once used wild onions and traveled a long distance to collect them (Rea 1997). No aboriginal Gila River Pima name for them survives, although *A. macropetalum* has been collected about 20 miles east along the Gila River within foraging and hunting ranges. Wild onions have not been documented within White Tank Mountains Regional Park (Keil 1970) or Sierra Estrella Regional Park (Sundell 1974), although the latter study encompassed only the northern foothills of the rugged Sierra Estrellas. However, Gila River Pimas described a type of "wild" onion that originated locally or from the foothills of Table Top Mountain (south of Interstate 8 and Maricopa) and Baboquivari Mountains in Tohono O'odham country (Rea 1997). It is not known if Salt River Pimas used or had access to wild onions. Within the nearby Superstition Mountain Wilderness Area *A. bisceptrum* var. *palmeri* and *A. macropetalum* have been documented from only a few localities at elevations above the desert (Rice 1994).

In the summer, Tohono O'odhams collected the bulbs of a wild onion that supposedly grew only on Baboquivari Peak and then used them in trade (Castetter and Underhill 1935, cited as *A. unifolium*). Wild onions were significant to the Hiá ceḍ O'odham. Fernando Flores, a Hiá ceḍ O'odham, described a type of onion that grew in desert hills or mountains and that was especially plentiful in the Ajo Mountains, Organ Pipe Cactus National Monument (Bell 1980). The only wild onion documented within Organ Pipe Cactus National Monument is *A. macropetalum,* which was collected from a site in the Puerto Blanco Mountains (Bowers 1980). The Cahuilla and Hualapai gathered onions in the spring, prior to flowering (Bean and Saubel 1972; Watahomigie et al. 1982).

Because cattle are fond of the emerging green shoots, overgrazing is believed to be responsible for the local extirpation or greatly reduced numbers of *A. macropetalum* in desert grasslands (Bohrer 1978) and possibly *A. bisceptrum* as well. That the Ramah Navajo formerly gathered enough bulbs to store for winter use (Vestal 1952) suggests an abundance of plants; today the species is rarely found with such abundance, except in refugias that have escaped continuous years of severe overgrazing (Bohrer 1978).

Calochortus | mariposa, mariposa-lily, butterfly-tulip, sego-lily

***C. ambiguus* (M. E. Jones) Ownbey**
doubting mariposa-lily

***C. concolor* (Baker) Purdy**
golden-bowl mariposa-lily

***C. flexuosus* S. Watson**
winding mariposa-lily, straggling mariposa

***C. kennedyi* Porter**
desert mariposa, red mariposa-lily

Western Native Americans considered the corms of mariposa-lilies to be a good, potato-like food (Coville 1892; Havard 1895; Fewkes 1896; Hough 1897, 1898; Chestnut 1902; Sparkman 1908; Chamberlain 1911; Castetter 1935; Saunders 1948; Vestal 1952; Balls 1970; Bean and Saubel 1972; Hedrick 1972; Weber and Seaman 1985). People generally steamed or roasted the corms, then stored and pressed the mass into cakes that were dried in the sun (Saunders 1948). The corms were also eaten raw or boiled. Sonoran Desert peoples' use of mariposa-lily is not well documented. The Cahuilla gathered and cooked mariposa-lily corms from May through August (Bean and Saubel 1972). Havasupais ate the baked corms of *C. nuttallii* Torrey & A. Gray (and possibly *C. flexuosus*) with bread and cooked agave pulp (Weber and Seaman 1985).

Other mariposa-lilies that grow as "stragglers" in the Sonoran Desert from southern California south into northern Baja California are *C. dunnii* Purdy, *C. plummerae* Greene, and *C. weedii* Wood (Wiggins 1964).

Dichelostemma | snake-lily

***D. capitatum* (Bentham) Wood ssp. *pauciflorum* (Torrey) G. Keator (syn., *D. pulchellum* [Salisbury] Heller var. *pauciflorum* [Torrey] Hoover)**
bluedicks, coquito de tierra, covena, coveria

Dichelostemma capitatum ssp. *pauciflorum,* or *covena* (fig. 35), is an herbaceous perennial from an underground corm that produces purplish blue flowers primarily from February to May. San Carlos Apaches ate the flowers raw (Hrdlička 1908). Numerous accounts mention that southwestern groups gathered the small corms

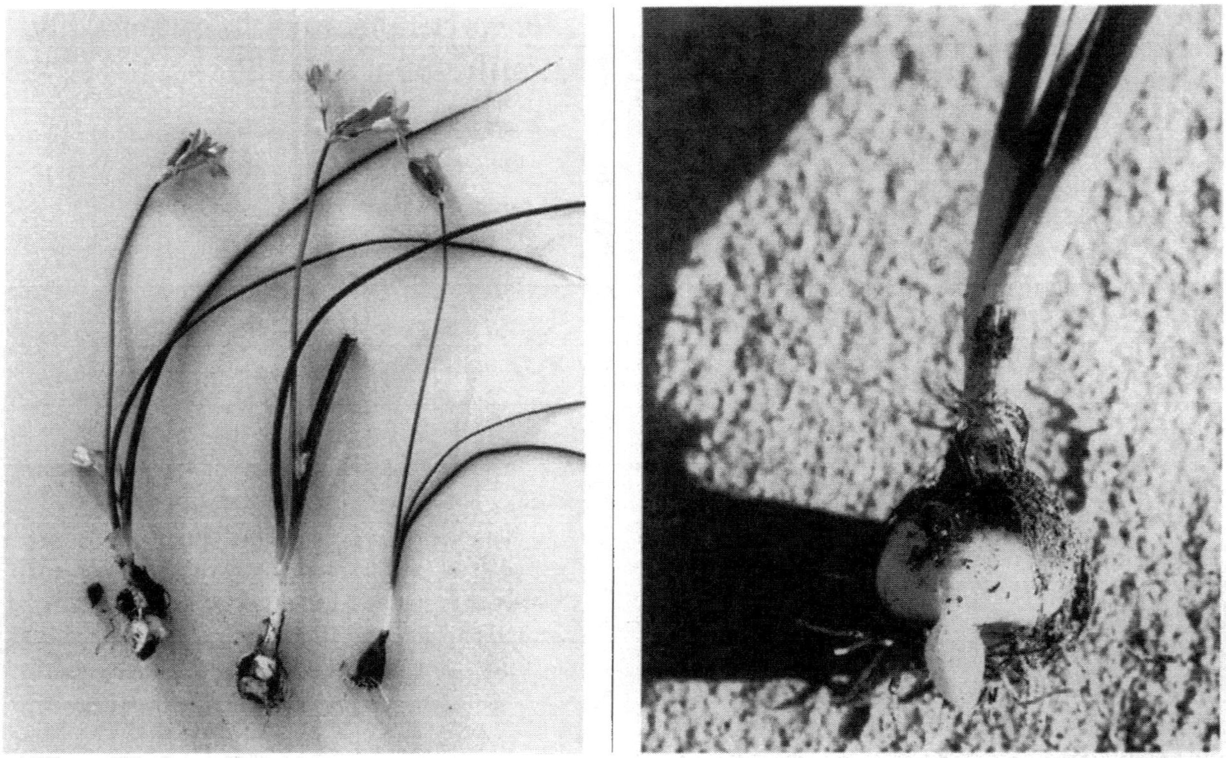

FIGURE 35. ***Dichelostemma capitatum*** (Benth.) Wood ssp. ***pauciflorum*** (Torr.) Keator. Habit, corm, and flowers; close-up of corms. Just west of Bacadehuachi, Sonora, February 1988 (*Hodgson 4918*, DES).

extensively (unless otherwise noted, all cited as *D. pulchellum;* Palmer 1878, cited as *Milla capitata;* Havard 1895; Chestnut 1902; Hrdlička 1908; Sparkman 1908; Castetter and Underhill 1935; Gifford 1936; Saunders 1948, cited as *Brodiea capitata;* Bean and Saubel 1972; Bell 1980; Rea 1997). Opinions varied as to its palatability, although people described the taste as mucilaginous and flat. Although people often ate the corms raw, the taste was greatly improved if boiled or roasted.

At the turn of the century, San Carlos Apaches apparently knew little of most underground plant parts, such as bulbs or roots, for use as food (Hrdlička 1908). However, everyone ate the raw or cooked corms of *covena* in the spring. Aleš Hrdlička (1908:258), having cooked the corms with salt and butter, found them to be "agreeable to the taste and also, apparently, quite nutritious and without unpleasant after effects," although they were somewhat glutinous.

Edward Gifford (1936) noted how Northeastern and Western Yavapais collected and ate the "roots of a purple-flowered plant" after its shoots appeared in the spring. The Tohono O'odham collected the corms in the spring and ate them raw, despite the unpleasant taste (Castetter and Underhill 1935). Gila River Pimas mention its use as a "tasteless" food eaten raw by the children and possibly the adults (Rea 1997). The Hiá ceḍ O'odham ate the sweet-potato-tasting corms raw after removing the outer epidermis (Bell 1980).

The Cahuilla only kept the large corms for food and planted the smaller corms to ensure a crop the following year (Bean and Saubel 1972). Seris did not have much knowledge of *covena* (Felger and Moser 1985).

Hesperocallis | desert-lily

H. undulata **A. Gray**
ajo-lily, desert-lily, ajo

Hesperocallis undulata (fig. 36) is an herbaceous perennial that grows from a relatively large bulb and flowers from February to May. Desert people who had access to this beautiful plant ate the bulbs (fig. 36) raw, roasted, or boiled (Palmer 1878; Havard 1895; Castetter and Bell 1951; Bean and Saubel 1972; Hedrick 1972). Gila River Pimas did not know of its use as a food and only on the western end of the reservation were they even familiar with the plant (Rea 1997). One Pima re-

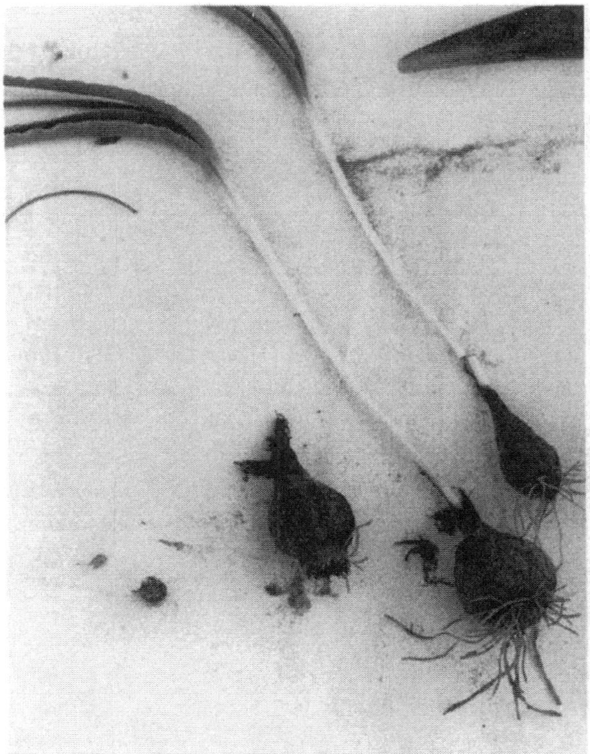

FIGURE 36. ***Hesperocallis undulata*** A. Gray. Close-up of corms. Sand dunes at Yusmex, Yuma County, Arizona, April 1987.

lated that it is eaten raw, like onions, by those living on the Lower Gila River, that is, the Hiá ceḍ O'odham. Ajo-lily reaches its northeastern range on the Gila River Reservation. It once grew in sand dunes located south of Laveen along 51st Avenue on the reservation, but has since disappeared due to its habitat being converted to fields and roads (Rea 1997). Ajo-lily exists on a few stationary dunes in the area and has been documented in Sierra Estrella Regional Park, where it was said to be uncommon (Sundell 1974).

Triteleiopsis | baja-lily

T. palmeri **(S. Watson) Hoover**
Palmer-lily, blue sand-lily, Palmer's baja-lily, Palmer's blue sand-lily

Triteleiopsis palmeri is also an herbaceous perennial that produces small, white corms. Its attractive blue flowers are produced from February through May. The single corms or clusters of small cormlets (fig. 37) have a sweet taste when eaten raw, but its use by Sonoran Desert

FIGURE 37. ***Triteleiopsis palmeri*** (S. Wats.) Hoover. (top) Corms and grasslike first leaves, Pinta Sands, Yuma County, Arizona, April 1987; (bottom) close-up of corms, in deep sand dunes at Yusmex, Yuma County, Arizona, April 1987 (*Hodgson 4494*, DES).

peoples is not well documented. Inhabitants in the Gran Desierto region of northwestern Sonora may have eaten the cormlets (Felger 1980). The Seri name translates as "companion-child-what-he-eats" (Felger and Moser 1985). "Companion-child" refers to a young child of a pregnant mother, who is often undernourished because of the insufficient amount of milk provided (the inability to nurse a previous baby or young child by a pregnant mother was described by María Chona, a Tohono O'odham; Underhill 1936). The Seri companion-child ate the corms, which were cooked in water until soft, as a survival food. The cooked corms were one of the soft foods fed to young children when they started to eat solid food. Children enjoyed the corms so much that mature plants were difficult to find. In the early 1980s, girls and women at El Desemboque dug up whole plants and transplanted them to their gardens (Felger and Moser 1985).

Palmer-lily corms could be located when there was no growth above ground (winter or spring) if one returned to an area where plants were previously found (Felger and Moser 1985). However, the plant's growth, reproduction, and abundance appear to be greatly influenced by precipitation (pers. obs.). Palmer-lily was known in the United States by a few collections and was considered rare prior to 1983. With sufficient winter precipitation, however, Palmer-lily can become abundant and cover the dunes with hundreds or thousands of plants. Despite its potential for becoming very abundant, it is, like most sand-dune species, vulnerable and sensitive to disturbance by off-road vehicles in unprotected areas and possible competition by exotic plants such as the mustard *Brassica tournefortii* Gouan.

Nolinaceae | Bear-grass Family

Dasylirion | sotol

D. wheeleri S. Watson
desert-spoon, sotol, sawo

Dasylirion wheeleri (fig. 38) generally grows at elevations above 1,000 meters from central and southern Arizona to western Texas and northern Sonora and Chihuahua (Kearney et al. 1960; Wiggins 1964), but is absent in Baja California. Plants flower from May to August.

The Tohono O'odham (Castetter et al. 1938), Apache (Castetter and Opler 1936; Gifford 1940; Buskirk 1986), and Tarahumara (Pennington 1963) sometimes used sotol for food, primarily by baking the emerging flowering stalks in a manner similar to that of baking agave heads (Standley 1912). Edward Gifford (1940) also stated that San Carlos Apaches ate the flowers, whereas Northern and Southern Tontos ate the seeds of *D. wheeleri*. Winfred Buskirk (1986) assumed that the Western Apaches did not use the "mescal with thorns" when "other mescal" was available. Whether his Western Apache informants were actually referring to *Dasylirion* when they spoke of the "mescal with thorns" is uncertain.

Outside the Sonoran Desert, Tepehuans supposedly used the roots (which was apparently distinguished from the crown, or head, of plants) in times of food shortage (Pennington 1969). They pit-baked the roots

FIGURE 38. ***Dasylirion wheeleri*** S. Wats., Santa Catalina Mountains, Pima County, Arizona, July 1988.

for several days, then ate the nonfibrous portion of the root immediately or sliced and dried the edible portions for later use. Sotol roots are thick and fusiform, or spindle shaped (Bogler in press). Young plants usually have two to three large fusiform roots the size and shape of carrots.

Southwestern groups valued the plant more for its use in making bed matting, cradle mats, back mats (for the carrying frame), headbands, and baskets (Castetter and Underhill 1935). An example of such a basket was used for straining juice from saguaro pulp (Crosswhite 1980).

A somewhat different type of sotol (fig. 39) grows in the Sierra Jojoba and foothills of the Sierra del Viejo in northwestern Sonora. It has a more strict, cloning habit; deep yellow green leaves; and smaller fruits than *D. wheeleri* and grows at an elevation of 500–850 meters (*Hodgson 4992, 4998*, DES). Whether it deserves species or varietal rank is not yet known (Bogler in press). Ricardo Flores Tirado, a caretaker at Rancho las Maravillas near Sierra del Viejo, said that people in the area used the sotol for making a winelike drink (*Hodgson 4992, 4998*, DES). According to him, the drink affects you "differently, but positively, like no other liquor." Señor Tirado said he never drank the wine.

FIGURE 39. ***Dasylirion*** sp. This specimen is seemingly distinct from *D. wheeleri* because it has a strict habit, yellowish olive green leaves (not at all glaucous), and small fruits. Sierra del Viejo, Sonora, common on north-facing slopes here and in the Sierra Jojoba, May 1988 (*Hodgson 4998 & DeLamater*, DES).

Nolina | bear-grass

N. beldingii **Brandegee**

N. bigelovii **(Torrey) S. Watson**
Bigelow's bear-grass

N. microcarpa **S. Watson**
bear-grass, sacahuista

Western Apaches cut the young flowering stalks of *N. microcarpa* when they were approximately 70 centimeters high in May and June (Buskirk 1986). They cooked the flowering stalks by placing them on a fire for about 30 minutes, then peeled and ate the stalks. Edward Gifford (1940) noted that San Carlos Apaches also ate the fruits, White Mountain Apaches ate the seeds, and Southern Tontos ate the flowers.

According to Lowell Bean and Katherine Saubel (1972), the Cahuilla baked the flower stalks of *N. bigelovii* overnight in stone-lined pits that were covered with sand. Bean and Saubel believed that plants described by David Barrows (1900) as being a different type of small yucca with slender spines may have been this nolina. However, plants representing *N. bigelovii* have large rosettes and its leaves are spineless. It has also been reported that flowering stalks of *N. beldingii* var. *deserticola* were roasted and eaten (Hake 1980, 1983).

Poaceae | Grass Family

John Doebley (1984) provides an overview of grasses used by southwestern groups. Southwestern indigenous cultures used primarily the fruits, or grains (often referred to as "seed"), for food, although the rootstocks, shoots, and sap of *Phragmites australis* (Cav.) Trin. ex Steud. provided food. Collecting adequate amounts of grains for food required both large enough numbers of plants and a tremendous amount of time. Evidence suggests that the Hohokam burned large tracts of desert to promote grasses and cool-season annuals that were important to them (Bohrer 1987, 1991). Bohrer (1991) proposed that in the Queen Creek area (Pinal County) the Hohokam used fire as an agricultural practice in the desert surrounding their villages. This practice in conjunction with the introduction and encouragement/cultivation of barley (*Hordeum pusillum* Nutt.), agave, cholla, *crucillo* (*Condalia warnockii* Johnst. var. *kearneyana* Johnst.), and a variety of cool-season annuals was beneficial. The Hohokam could extend their growing season and enhance the yield of a wide range of native and introduced species. The recovery of naked (without the bracts adhering to the grain), or "free-threshing" barley grains from La Ciudad (Phoenix) and other sites in the Salt and Gila River valleys suggests selection and cultivation of *H. pusilum* by the Hohokam (Bohrer 1987, 1991). The Tohono O'odham burned groups of plants to separate and gather small seeds or grains (Castetter and Underhill 1935), a practice that may also have encouraged growth and reproduction of useful annual plants.

People usually gathered, winnowed, toasted, and ground the grains. They often combined this meal with other ground meal to add variety to the usual fare of mesquite- and cornmeal-based breads and mushes (Niethammer 1974). Sonoran Desert people also used various species of grass in the process of pit-baking foods such as *maguey* (*Agave* spp.), *Yucca* spp., and bulb- or corm-producing plants in Liliaceae. Additionally, the O'odham brushed off the spines and glochids (very small, barbed spines) of prickly-pears (*Opuntia* spp.) using the stems, or culms, of grasses such as alkali sacaton, *Sporobolus airoides* (Torrey) Torrey.

Documentation on the use of southwestern desert grasses by indigenous people is relatively limited and sometimes ambiguous. Ethnographic voucher specimens, if made at all, were often inadequate; this made species determination difficult and possibly erroneous, further clouding the picture of how people used grasses. Because of land-use practices such as the construction of dams, rechanneling of watercourses, groundwater pumping, overgrazing, and the introduction of nonnative species, many native grass species are far less common than over a century ago. Between 1870 and 1939, overgrazing impacted many cool-season grasses that were food plants for humans (Bohrer 1975).

Species growing in the Sonoran Desert documented as a food source are listed in appendix 1. Four genera are discussed here, two of which played important roles in the subsistence patterns of those who lived in the Colorado River delta and vicinity and in Sonora, Mexico. *Panicum hirticaule* var. *miliaceum* and *Distichlis palmeri* illustrate how the disruption of traditional, desert-adapted land and plant management practices negatively affected both the plants and the people who relied on them.

Distichlis | salt grass

D. palmeri (Torrey) Rydberg

Palmer salt grass, zacate salado, trigo gentil

Ethnobotanist Edward Palmer observed the Cocopa of the Colorado River delta use this grass, which grew "abundantly on the tidal lands," as a principal food (Vasey and Rose 1891b, cited as *Uniola palmeri*). Called *nypa* by the Cocopa, its grain was the first sizeable food crop that could be obtained in sufficient quantities (Kelly 1977). So abundant was *D. palmeri* that in 1863, Jacobo Blanco, a Mexican mapmaker, described fields of this grass as lands covered with a salt grass, which formed "prairies extending beyond eyesight" (Alvarez de Williams 1987:26). Edward Palmer provided the most complete information on the Cocopa's use from an Anglo's point of view. He saw the Cocopa nearly up to their knees in soft, adhesive clay as they cut off the fruiting heads into baskets (Vasey and Rose 1891b; Castetter and Bell 1951; cited in both as *Uniola palmeri*). Later they dried the seed heads near fires, threshed them with sticks, and then trod on them to free the grains. Ethnobotanist and botanist Anita Alvarez de Williams (1989:17, 19) also wrote of *nypa* use and abundance:

> In spring entire families took to the [Colorado] river on large tule rafts, open air houseboats, and headed south to the mouth of the river where extensive stands of wild wheat awaited harvest. A hundred years ago these wild wheat fields extended from one to 20 miles out from the sides of the lower Colorado River along the southernmost 15 miles of its course to the gulf. Known to the Cucapa as *nypa* … this nutritious plant … requires only 24 hours of fresh water to germinate, provided seasonally by the river's flooding. From then on, it thrives on saltwater irrigation from the gulf tides …. The Cucapa harvested the wild wheat, threshed it out on clay floors near the river, and carried the surplus home on the houserafts, poling or paddling, or hauling the craft upriver with long willow ropes.

The Seri or their ancestors may have learned to harvest the grains of Palmer salt grass from the Cocopa, with whom some Seri had contact (Felger and Moser 1985). This grass and eel-grass (*Zostera marina* L.) are the only well-documented cases of seed plants growing with ocean water that have been used as major food resources (Castetter and Bell 1951; Felger and Nabhan 1978; Felger and Moser 1985). The procedures for harvesting both are similar (Felger and Moser 1985). Another salt grass, *D. spicata* (L.) Greene, may also have been eaten, as evidenced by its grains and fibers being frequently found in coprolites from Lovelock Cave, Nevada (Napton 1969).

During the first half of the 1900s, rechanneling, damming, and tamarisk (*Tamarix* spp.) invasion drastically altered salt grass and other plants' habitat (Alvarez de Williams 1987). By the 1950s, the Cocopa had seen the last of the great stands of native delta vegetation. Remnant stands of *D. palmeri* were rediscovered in the Colorado River channels (Nabhan 1983; Alvarez de Williams 1987). In addition, Palmer salt grass was found to be relatively common in the San Felipe and Puerto Peñasco estuaries following extensive plant surveys (Yensen et al. 1983). Nicolas Yensen and others hypothesized that *D. palmeri* is derived from *D. spicata* populations in the vicinity of the mouth of the Colorado River (Yensen et al. 1983, cited as *D. spicata* ssp. *stricta*). The cultivation and harvest of *D. palmeri* by the Cocopa in the river delta area may have assisted in its differentiation from *D. spicata*.

Distichlis hybrids have the greatest potential for putting some of the world's 3.8 billion acres of salinized land into crop production (Yensen et al. 1988). Because halophytes grow much better on salinized farmland than on full-strength seawater, development of such a crop need not threaten estuaries or other coastal habitats. For example, *D. palmeri* can grow in fresh water as well as saline water up to 40 parts per thousand. It is believed that it would be far more economical to put billions of acres of salinized farms back into production than to attempt the farming of salt flats or coastal habitats using seawater. Furthermore, "the development of a useful halophytic crop from a nearly extinct plant would … demonstrate the urgency of protecting virgin saline habitats and their native floras and faunas" (Yensen et al. 1988:820).

When compared to wheat and barley, grains of *D. palmeri* are relatively low in protein, high in fiber and carbohydrate content, and low in ash (Yensen et al. 1988). Hybridization of *D. palmeri* with another species of *Distichlis* has successfully produced a large-grained hybrid that results in yields many times that of the original plants.

Cereal made from the grains of *D. palmeri* may be a good wheat substitute for people allergic to gluten (Nabhan 1983; Alvarez de Williams 1987). Its flour has a sweet taste and its consistency is favorable for making tortillas, breads, atole, and biscuits.

Hordeum | barley

H. pusillum **Nuttall**
little barley

Hordeum pusillum is an annual, cool-season grass that is commonly found throughout the United States in disturbed areas. In the southwestern deserts, plants reach maturity before the summer months and provide an edible grain for harvest during late spring and early summer (Bohrer 1987). These and other cool-season grasses played an important role in the people's diets in the Southwest, particularly if summer crops did not provide sufficient food until the next harvest (Bohrer 1984). *Hordeum pusillum's* grains were undoubtedly parched and ground into multipurpose flours (Gasser 1982). Additionally, little barley "became one of a variety of grasses and herbaceous plants gathered to generate steam for roasting in the pit ovens" (Bohrer 1987:87).

Vorsila Bohrer and others have unveiled evidence that strongly supports the view that the Hohokam not only cultivated little barley, they domesticated the grass. Many of the wild barleys have adhering bracts (lemmas and palea), and the bractless, or "naked," form is characteristic of domesticated forms (Harlan 1968). The importance of having bracts that adhere to the grain becomes evident when one understands the plant's reproductive strategy, as described by Bohrer (1984:249):

> In wild barley, the three spikelets containing the central fertile grain disarticulate as a unit, and the sharp tip functions as a self-planting mechanism. Normally, the tight adherence of the bracts to the fertile grains assures that the grain will not slip from the attached planting case. When a grain is not cemented to the bracts, it might disengage itself from the self-planting mechanism. Lost grain in the wild would be exposed to the high temperatures of the ground surface for an extended period of time and be placed at a reproductive disadvantage. However, if man were to plant naked barley, he would assure himself of an easily threshable annual grain crop.

Naked grains, or grains that lost the usually adhering lemmas and palea, were found at numerous sites in the Southwest and central United States (Bohrer 1987). The naked condition of the grain is believed to have arisen from domestication, rather than as a result of deterioration, carbonization, or parching. This is advantageous for people who rely on the grains for food because harvesting naked grains would be far less laborious and time-consuming. The plant would not need the bracts for increasing the chance of a successful germination during the brief period when conditions may be favorable, because the grains would be intentionally planted and cared for. In addition, Bohrer (1987) suggested that the Hohokam did not harvest the disarticulating spikelets using a seed beater into a basket, but rather harvested the entire heads. They may also have stored the barley unthreshed.

This quickly maturing cool-season crop could extend the "limits of agriculture" in "more arid regions where early maturity during the cooler part of the year makes maximum use of limited available moisture" (Bohrer 1984:252). Barley was found to grow along the edges of the Sahara Desert and other desert regions on less rainfall than any other desert cereal (Harlan 1972 *in* Bohrer 1984). Little barley appears to have played a more important role in the subsistence patterns of the Sonoran Desert's Hohokam than was ever thought. With the continuing work of Vorsila Bohrer and others, this Hohokam mystery will be better understood.

Panicum | panic grass

P. hirticaule **Presl var.** ***miliaceum*** **(Vasey) Beetle (syn.,** ***P. sonorum*** **Beal)**
Sonoran panic grass, Mexican panic grass, sagui, sauwi

The grains of the majority of *Panicum* species were sometimes used for food. Species include *P. capillare* L. (common panic grass), *P. hirticaule* var. *miliaceum* (fig. 40), *P. obtusum* Kunth (blunt panic grass, *zacate gramilla*), and *P. urvilleanum* Kunth (desert panic grass). Grains thought possibly to be *Urochloa fasciculatum* (Sw.) R. Webster were identified from Snaketown (Bohrer 1970, cited as *Panicum fasciculatum*) and were also found in a bowl with *Chenopodium* seed in an adult male burial site at Tumacacori, Arizona (Nabhan and DeWet 1984, cited as *Panicum fasciculatum*).

Fruits of Sonoran panic grass were formerly used as a grain food for humans and forage for livestock. This panic grass may represent one of the earliest important New World cultivates (Gentry 1963, cited as *P. sonorum*). Fruit production per plant is prolific, up to 2500 grains per plant (Nabhan 1984b, cited as *P. sonorum*), and thus provides an abundant food source. Adapted to flood or runoff soil disturbance, Sonoran panic grass usually germinated with summer rains at or near high flood lines on deltas or alluvial fans on the Colorado River and near its confluence with the Gila River following the seasonal flooding of these rivers. Various native inhabitants, including the Colorado River Yuman people and Cocopa, harvested wild Sonoran panic grass stands and planted the grains. Edward Palmer (1871:419, cited as *P. sonorum*) described the close relationship between Colorado River groups and the Sonoran panic grass:

> It grows on the bars and moist sides of the Colorado River, in Arizona. After the June rise in the river has subsided, the plant rapidly perfects its seeds, which the Indians collect with much care, cleaning them by means of the wind, and store them for winter use. After the seeds are ground into flour, water is added and the mass is kneaded into hard cakes, which, when dried in the sun, are ready for use. Gruel and mush are likewise made of the flour. Sometimes the Indians plant this grass near their homes, to avoid the trouble of hunting it, by blowing them from their mouths, and a crop is the result, which for them is equal to wheat.

Edward Gifford (1931:267, cited as *P. sonorum*) offers this sketch: "*Heschmícha,* grain resembling wheat. Among Yuma grew wild, scattered along river. Planting by men; away from wives 4 nights, no food taboo. Continence to make plants grow without weeds and molestation by birds. Each man had his own patch, marked by sticks laid on the ground. Harvested by planter or his delegate. Harvest shared with relatives."

William Kelly (1977:38, cited as *P. sonorum*) described a very organized panic grass planting:

> Panic grass was planted by Cocopa in the sandy mud flats along the main channel where the flood had caved the river banks and carried away all vegetation. One such area was described by Sam Spa as being five miles long and up to 500 yards wide, planted in five plots by five different men. Every effort was made to plant the seed as soon as the water stopped running; the planters always waded in deep mud and water, and frequently carried a pole under one arm for support in bad spots. Seed was carried in a gourd hung with a strap around the neck and planting was done by blowing the seed from the mouth, preferably on a winter day. Spa described some fields as being so large as to require six days for one man to plant; the work, of course, was very slow in the deep mud. Once a field was planted, no further attention was given it until harvest time.

FIGURE 40. ***Panicum hirticaule*** Presl var. ***miliaceum*** (Vasey) Beetle. Gentry Agroecology Project, Desert Botanical Garden, Phoenix, Arizona, October 1988.

The Guarijío planted the grains of Sonoran panic grass, which were valued in the making of pinole (Gentry 1963). They recognized two kinds of grains: those that were white and those that were hard and black, the latter of which they picked out of the fields and did not resow because they were relatively tasteless (Gentry 1942, cited as *P. sonorum*). The Guarijío harvested the inflorescences with the white grain type in October or November and placed them on woven mats to dry. They rubbed or rolled the dried inflorescences over with a smooth-sided stone and separated out the chaff by winnowing. Some grains were saved for future planting, whereas the remaining grain was ground into flour and used in making tortillas, tamales, and atole. The Guarijío made a nourishing drink by mixing the flour with salt, sugar, and milk. As recent as the 1960s, however, Gentry (1963:88) noted that "while generally known to both the Guarijío and the barrancan Mexicans, [Sonoran panic grass] appears to be quite scarce and its culture is being lost." The cultivation of Sonoran panic grass has persisted longer in the remote southeastern Sonora and southwestern Chihuahua barranca country (Nabhan and DeWet 1984, cited as *P. sonorum*). However, because of gradual acculturation and the abandonment of other small-seeded crops, panic grass cultivation by the Guarijío is declining. Alan Beetle, a grass expert, suspects that "while it seems doubtful that ground was cultivated for this species alone, apparently when land was disturbed for other purposes, such as a corn field, Sonoran panic grass was a welcome and aggressive weed" (Beetle 1981:32).

Sonoran panic grass was once common on the Colorado River delta and at the convergence of the Gila and Colorado Rivers. Not since 1940, when a Yuman Reservation resident gave grains of the grass to ethnographers Edward Castetter and William Bell, have native populations been documented in the United States (Nabhan and DeWet 1984). Its historic range included the type locality, which is approximately 50 miles south of the delta, north to the Yuma and Parker-Needles area south from the Río Mayo watershed in Sonora to Oaxaca along the west coast of Mexico.

Although Sonoran panic grass has been found from Sonora and Chihuahua south to Tobasco and Chiapas, it has decreased to a point of possible extirpation north of Mexico due to habitat loss. Because panic grass is adapted to flood or runoff soil disturbances (Nabhan 1984b, cited as *P. sonorum*), seasonal flooding within the Colorado River delta and confluence of the Colorado and Gila Rivers helped in the persistence of spontaneous stands (Nabhan and DeWet 1984). Destruction of panic grass's habitat began in 1901 with the diversion of the Colorado River into Imperial Valley. The river's flow was permanently redirected following the break of the Colorado River's western banks in 1905 and the 1909 construction of the Laguna diversion dam. This diversion forced the Cocopa to abandon their panic grass agriculture for the most part (Nabhan 1984b), as implied by a Cocopa who said that only about one family in five living near the river bothered with harvesting and planting this crop (Kelly 1977). The floodplains continued to dry up as a result of droughts and the construction of Vacanora Canal and Hoover and Parker Dams in 1935 and 1938, respectively (Nabhan 1984b). With diminished soil disturbance and available water, panic grass was outcompeted by tamarisk, which invaded the Colorado and Gila River watersheds in the 1920s and 1930s.

Inhabitants near Alamos, Sonora, still use and grow Sonoran panic grass in much the same way as did those inhabiting the Colorado River delta. At the Tucson Botanical Garden, Native Seeds/SEARCH staff and volunteers successfully grew and used Sonoran panic grass (Nabhan 1984a). The Colorado River Tribe was provided access to this plant due to the efforts of Native Seeds/SEARCH and Anita Alvarez de Williams. Sonoran panic grass has never appeared on any state or federal list of rare, threatened or endangered plants, despite its extremely rare status and major role as a food source for pre-Columbian and historic Native Americans.

Phragmites | reed

***P. australis* (Cavanilles) Trinius ex Steudel (syn., *P. communis* Trinius)**
common reed, carrizo, cane, tule

Phragmites australis is a tall, coarse perennial grass that grows in marshes or wet ground. The practice of eating the sweet exudate found on its leaves may have been centered among the Paiute groups (Woodward 1938). However, Baja California and Colorado River people collected the sweet substance and ate it whole or mixed with water (Palmer 1878; Coville 1892; Clavigero 1937; Jones 1945; Bolton 1948; Píccolo 1967; Bye 1972; del Barco 1980).

Gathering was a family or band activity, at least among the Paiutes, who set up camp for a short time to collect the exudate, a job usually performed by women and children (Woodward 1938). People who used this exudate for food commonly cut the leaves, allowed them to dry in the sun, then beat or threshed them "to shake off the tiny sweet droplets, these gathered and pressed into balls or cakes" (Heizer 1949:140). The Panamints of southern California sifted out the flour from the dried, ground stems, then set the sticky mass by a fire until it swelled and browned (Coville 1892). Southern Paiutes stored the balls in leaves, which they placed in baskets (Woodward 1938).

There is frequent mention of a sweet pasty food that was known to Baja California inhabitants and adopted by the Jesuit missionaries (Jones 1945). In 1702, Fr. Píccolo (1967:61) wrote in his *informe* to King Philip V that "heaven provides sugar in quantity during the months of April, May, and June in the dew which falls during this period on the broad leaves of the reed grasses, were it coagulates and hardens." The natives gathered large quantities of this sweet mass, which Fr. Píccolo tasted, describing it as being as sweet as sugar, differing only in its darker color. (Fr. Kino also wrote of this reed, exactly as Fr. Píccolo had [Bolton 1948:II:56], but he was in Pimería Alta during this time.) Reeds were not uncommon in parts of Baja California, and Jesuit missionaries and explorers often noted their dense stands. A rancheria named *Kada kaaman,* northwest of Mulegé, was named for the *carrizo*-bordered pools and stream found here, the "arroyo of the carrizal" (Massey 1949:299; Burrus 1984:114). Fr. Píccolo visited this area and the natives living there in 1716, paving the way for the later founding of Mission San Ignacio de Kada kaaman, in 1728, by Juan Bautista Luyando (Weber 1968). In 1721, Fr. Nápoli found that in Cora territory the "many flowing streams have numerous beds of thick reeds, the first that I have found or seen in the unhappy land of California" (Moriarty and Smith 1970:45). Fr. del Barco (1980:136), however, noted that the exudate was not found "in all the reed thickets, but only in certain places." Use of the sweet exudate ended with the availability of refined sugar. Edward Palmer described how the locals near Santa Rosalia used *P. australis* for various purposes, including material for weaving, roofs, and door screens, but did not mention its use for food (Vasey and Rose 1890b).

This sweet exudate was highly prized, considering the time and energy exerted to gather it. Arthur Woodward (1938:180) noted that in aboriginal times concentrated saccharine foods were rare in North America outside the maple sugar region. Plants providing sweet-tasting products were "eagerly exploited, often at great labor," when present. Woodward knew of no recorded use of "honey-dew" by any group inhabiting the Gila and Salt River drainages, who would have had access to agaves. Yavapais and Cocopas procured a sweet exudate from willows *(Salix)* and other plants (Woodward 1938) including agaves. Their efforts to secure a sweet food from agaves are legendary. In contrast, the Kiliwa of northern Baja California derived most of their sugar from *Rhus ovata,* according to Charles Orcutt (1887:46; see *Rhus*), as well as agaves, although they sometimes had difficulty in determining which species were edible (see *Agave*).

The origin of the exudate long remained a mystery. Fr. Venegas (Venegas and Burriel 1966:I:50–51) explained that "The good father [Píccolo] talks according to the common opinion [of the other missionaries] as if the manna dropped from the sky. But botanists [and Cochimí] are agreed, that it is a juice exudating from the plants themselves in the same manner as gums, incense, balsams, resins, etc." Fr. del Barco (1980:136) added: "It seems that the old Californios were already convinced of this fact when they called the *manna,* found in their country, by the name of *cadece,* which means 'juice of reed.' The Cochimies still use this name, and have even extended it to include sugar and *panocha,* which is dark sugar, because when they first saw and tasted these new types, finding them very similar in sweetness to their *cadece,* they applied the same name to them." Although both were incorrect, the Cochimí (and botanists) were closer in determining the origin of the sticky substance.

John Bidwell, a pioneer in the Humboldt Sink area in 1841, related how "honey-dew was produced on tules by a pediculous-looking insect" (Woodward 1938:177). Early pioneers traded for and relished the substance at first, "but upon learning its source and that insect bodies are in it, they no longer relish it." It was later determined that the "pediculous-looking insect" that excreted this substance was an aphid (Palmer 1878; Bye 1972). Not until 1927 was the identity of the mysterious aphid discovered. Dr. M. Gilmore of the Museum of the American Indian in New York obtained specimens of both insect and plant material from the Paiutes of Moapa, Nevada (Woodward 1938:177–178). He determined the plant as *"Phragmites communis,"* but sent the insects to Dr. P. W. Mason, then associate entomologist for the Bureau of Entomology at the U.S. Department of Agriculture. In a letter to Gilmore, Mason identified the insect as *Hyalopterus arundinis,* the "mealy plum aphis." This aphid usually passes the winter on *Prunus* spp. and migrates to various reeds and grasses, including *Phragmites,* in the summer. It was believed that this aphid could pass through the winter on the summer host, *P. australis,* in warm climates.

It was suggested that the terms *"tule,"* "reed," "cane," and *"carrizo"* referred to *P. australis* when discussing the sweet exudate, or "honey-dew" (Woodward 1938, cited as *P. communis*), although this was not always the case. Early Jesuit missionaries distinguished between populations of large and small reeds in Baja California. For example, Fr. del Barco (1980:136–137) apparently differentiated between the introduced reed brought over from the mainland (*Arundo donax* L.), and the native reed *(P. australis):*

> The reeds are thin and small in the whole Peninsula. If in some place there is a reed that is thick and long like the Spanish one *[Arundo donax]*, then such has been brought over from the coast across the gulf, and has been transplanted in [Baja] California where it grows as well as in any other site. The proper reed grass of California is commonly no thicker than the fingers of one's hand, excepting the thumb, as it would be rare to find a reed so thick.

Carrizo refers to *A. donax* in the vicinity of Loreto and San Javier (Carter *in* del Barco 1980). Here are located the missions of Nuestra Señora de Loreto and San Francisco Javier, which were founded in 1697 and 1699, respectively. Apparently, the Jesuits also found a new home for the introduced reed. Or was the plant introduced into this region prior to the arrival of the Spaniards? The reader is encouraged to read an interesting account by Fr. Venegas (Venegas and Burriel 1966:I:50–51) and later reproduced by Fr. del Barco (1980:136–137) that describes studies done on the exudate produced by *A. donax* as a source for medicine in Spain.

Loss of habitat and possible competition with the introduced reed *A. donax* have impacted populations of *P. australis*. The presence of permanent water, where reeds were often found, was an important factor in selecting a site for the establishment of a mission in Baja California. Dense stands of reed (and native palms) were cleared away, particularly in those more fertile and mesic areas in the cape region of Baja California. Fr. Nápoli described a potential site for the founding of a mission in Cora territory (Moriarity and Smith 1970:59): "Below the palm grove there is good land which is moist without irrigation. Here it will be possible to make an excellent garden, and when the large reed bed is cleared away, there will be a space for a field of maize."

Few Gila River Pimas knew that *carrizo*, which they apparently did not distinguish from the giant reed *A. donax*, was once common along the banks of the Gila and Lower Santa Cruz Rivers (Rea 1997). Loss of *carrizo* populations was noted as far back as the early 1900s, when the plants were not as available for use in making mats due to seasonal drought (Russell 1908), diversion of rivers' headwaters (Kissell 1916), and groundwater pumping (Curtin 1949). People living on the western end of the Gila River Pima Reservation remember *carrizo* because, due to the area's geological peculiarities, the Gila River did not dry up until much later (Rea 1997). To date, no specimen from the reservation exists.

Sporobolus | dropseed

S. airoides **(Torrey) Torrey**
alkali sacaton, cresta de gallo, zacaton alkalino

S. contractus **Hitchcock**
narrow-spike dropseed, zacate alkalino espigado, zacaton de arena

S. cryptandrus **(Torrey) A. Gray**
sand dropseed, zacaton des granador, zacate encubierto, zacaton de arena

Because these species were considered healthful, nutritious, and good tasting, native peoples once gathered the grains of *S. airoides* and *S. cryptandrus* in great quantities (Palmer 1878). The Tohono O'odham collected and winnowed the grains of *S. airoides*, tasks that took a great amount of time (Castetter and Underhill 1935). They pulled the plants up whole, laid them on a mat made of fiber, then beat out the grains with a stick. Another method of separating out the grains (or small seeds in general) was to burn the group of plants, then sweep the grains off the ground. This practice may also have encouraged growth and reproduction of the plants. As with all seeds, the Tohono O'odham parched and sun-dried the grains prior to storing them. When desired, they ground the grains into a flour, which they ate dry or used to make bread or mush. The Seri, however, did not eat the grains of *S. airoides*, although the children did enjoy eating the newly emerging shoots of *S. virginicus* (L.) Kunth (seashore dropseed; Felger and Moser 1985).

Typhaceae | Cattail Family

Typha | cattail

T. domingensis **Persoon**
southern cattail, espadilla, cola de gato, hueizacat

T. latifolia **Linnaeus**
broad-leaf cattail, espadilla, cola de gato, hueizacat

Native Americans depended on cattails (fig. 41) to meet many of their needs (Morton 1975). The young shoots, bases of stems, flowers, pollen, and achenes furnished food to the Western Apache, Maricopa, Mohave, Cocopa, Kamia, Quechan, Paipai, Pima, and other southwestern peoples (Palmer 1878; Coville 1892; Chestnut 1902; Chamberlain 1911; Castetter 1935; Gifford 1940; Saunders 1948; Curtin 1949; Balls 1970; Bean and Saubel 1972; Kelly 1977; Watahomigie et al. 1982; Alvarez de Williams 1987). Desert peoples ate the emerging flower stalks, without the sheaths, raw, boiled, or made into soup (Palmer 1878; Morton 1975; Nabhan et al. 1982; Watahomigie et al. 1982; Alvarez de Williams 1987). *Typha* also provided an important basketry material.

According to a Pima man born in 1860, River Pimas gathered the tender young white cattail rootstocks (fig. 42) year-round and ate them raw (Curtin 1949; Rea 1997). The Mohave, Quechan, and Maricopa gathered the rootstocks by digging them out with a pole (Castetter and Bell 1951). Usually they ate them without preparation, but occasionally they dried, stored, and later pounded broken pieces of rootstock into flour, which they boiled with fish. The Cahuilla gathered the rootstocks in June and July (Bean and Saubel 1972) and in the autumn and winter, after the inflorescence turned brown (Coville 1892). Although the Cocopa considered cattail rootstocks relatively unpopular, it was for them a never-failing food source (Kelly 1977). They gathered, dried, and pounded the rootstocks on a metate to extract the dry powdery pulp. Cocopas ate the roots of young plants raw "like green onion."

FIGURE 41. ***Typha domingensis*** Pers. habit. Plants and People of the Sonoran Desert exhibit, Desert Botanical Garden, Phoenix, Arizona, June 1988.

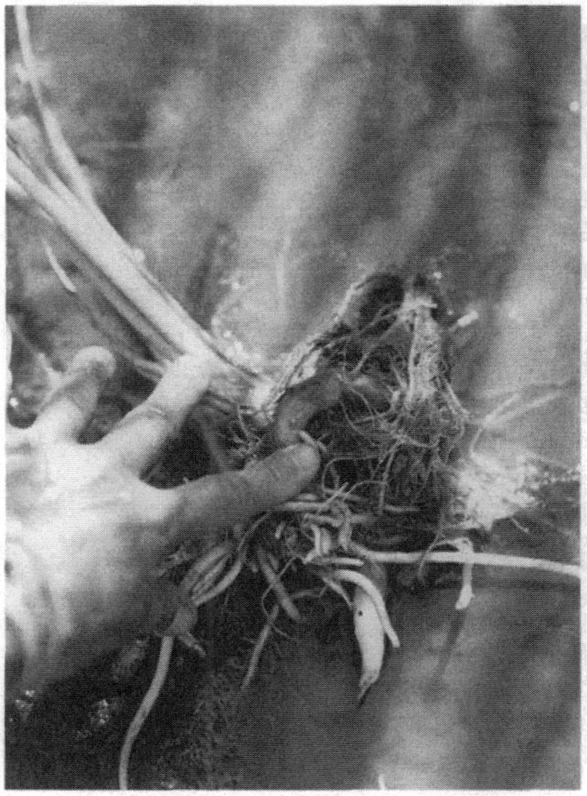

FIGURE 42. ***Typha domingensis.*** Close-up of whitish rhizomes.

Pollen provided an especially good food to desert peoples, although its collection and preparation required much time and care. Mary Manuel, a Maricopa woman, related to Leonora Curtin (1949:64–65) how they prepared pollen for food:

> The buds were picked [in the spring] with great care, and placed in baskets, and as the pollen is very fine, it must be winnowed into an olla. Mary Manuel, who said, "we go to collect this every day, as we are crazy about this food," gave two recipes for its preparation: a fire is built, and after it has burned down, the ashes are pushed aside; cold water is sprinkled on this cleared spot and a layer of powder spread upon it. The process is repeated until an entire basketful of pollen is used. The top layer is then wet down, the whole covered with hot ashes and allowed to bake until considered done. When removed, it resembles a biscuit, and the color has changed to a brownish shade. "You'd swear it contained sugar, but that is its natural sweetness," said Mary. The other method: for every two handfuls of powder, add one of ground wheat, then stir into boiling water to form a gruel. "I use no salt, because I like it sweet," Mary concluded.

Lower Colorado River inhabitants also collected and prepared pollen from the staminate inflorescences. Those living around Lake Cahuilla prior to its desiccation (ca. A.D. 1500) heavily exploited cattail pollen for food in the spring. This was suggested by data from coprolite studies in the Salton Basin (Sutton 1993) in areas where the Cahuilla probably occupied, at least when Lake Cahuilla started to disappear some 500 years ago (Wilke 1978). Pollen appears to have been consumed largely alone and formed the bulk of the diet, with other resources, including fish, being of secondary importance.

Cocopas harvested the pollen heads (staminate inflorescences) in large quantities and brought them back to camp to dry before they extracted the pollen (Kelly 1977). They found this job to be tedious, considering the amount of pollen secured. After the pollen heads were dry, the Cocopa held them over a pottery dish. They knocked the pollen into this dish by striking the head against the rim or by striking the heads with a stick. According to Castetter and Bell (1951), the Cocopa dug a small pit in the ground, fenced it with arrow-weed (*Pluchea sericea* [Nutt.] Coville), and then placed a cloth over the hole supported by the twigs. They tapped the inflorescences with a stick over the pit to shake out and gather the pollen, and sifted the pollen through a willow-twig strainer. Sometimes Cocopas simply tapped the dried inflorescences over a pottery vessel. They ate the pollen raw or boiled it in water to form a thin gruel. This sweet gruel was highly prized and was added to other foods to impart more flavor (Castetter and Bell 1951; Kelly 1977; Alvarez de Williams 1987). Pollen was also placed in a hollow pumpkin stem and baked for about ten minutes in coals, the result described as being "just like candy" (Kelly 1977). During the time of Kelly's (1977) fieldwork, pollen was still gathered in large quantities, but only for use as a very potent medicine.

Access to cattail populations in desert environments is often more difficult today due to the alteration of its habitat. However, not all riparian areas have experienced a decrease in cattail abundance. This is suggested by the recent development of lush cattail marshes in the backwaters and eddy return channels along the Colorado River through the Grand Canyon, where marshes had not previously existed during the predam period (Carothers and Brown 1991). However, the use of cattails may only be a memory; Hualapai elders have related that *T. domingensis* is not used today (*Hodgson 8551 & Phillips*, DES).

Zosteraceae | Eel-grass Family

Zostera | eel-grass, seawrack

Z. marina Linnaeus

eel-grass, seawrack, zacate del mar, trigo del mar

Zostera marina is a submerged aquatic perennial that grows on muddy bottoms in bays and estuaries along the Atlantic and Pacific Coasts of North America and Eurasia (Wiggins 1980; Felger and Moser 1985). To the Seri, eel-grass seed was one of the most important foods and was seasonally harvested until the 1980s. Coastal Yaqui and Mayo may also have used the plants (Felger and Moser 1985).

The Seri harvested the mature fruits in April or early May, when an abundance of seeds could be had at one time. Prior to its harvest, plants underwent rapid rhizome and shoot growth through the winter. In the warm waters of the Gulf of California, all of the shoots can form an inflorescence. When the fruit matures, the inflorescences break off, float to the surface, and wash ashore. The Seri waded into the water to pull in the long strands of these inflorescences, which they dried on the beach. After they removed any debris, they threshed the eel-grass with wooden clubs on sheets of cloth, plastic, or other material and collected the fallen fruit. The fruit was winnowed in a shallow basket and then toasted. The Seri pounded the toasted fruits to release the seeds, which were again winnowed to rid the seeds of chaff. They then ground the seeds on a metate, put the resulting flour in a basket, and tapped the basket from beneath to remove any remaining chaff. The flour was cooked into a bland-tasting gruel and often eaten with sea turtle oil. They also ground eel-grass seeds with those of cardón (*Pachycereus pringlei* [S. Watson] Britton & Rose).

Eel-grass provides an excellent example of how different cultures in different climates or regions did not employ the same use patterns. This may reflect the plant's reproductive strategy, as summarized by Felger and Moser (1985). The Seri did not use the fleshy roots and leaf bases for food, although more northern groups did. Within the range of the species, there is an increase in the percentage of sexually reproductive shoots from the colder waters of the northern latitudes to the warmer waters of the south, with 100 percent of the shoots becoming reproductive in the Seri region. The colder waters may favor vegetative reproduction by rootstocks, whereas the warmer waters favor sexual reproduction by flower and fruit development. Groups in the Pacific Northwest use only rootstocks of eel-grass for food (Turner and Bell 1973), whereas the Seri and possibly other groups farther south use only the seeds. In addition, because its fruits must be dried quickly, the combination of high seed productivity and warm, drying winds contribute to the importance of eel-grass as a food source (Felger and Moser 1985).

ANGIOSPERMS: DICOTS

Acanthaceae | Acanthus Family

Justicia | water-willow

J. californica **(Bentham) D. Gibson (syn., *Beloperone californica* Bentham)**
hummingbird-bush, chuparosa, coomeme

The nectar-laden flowers of *J. californica* are produced throughout the year. They once provided food to the Tohono O'odham and Diegueño, who sucked out the nectar (Standley 1923; Kearney et al. 1960; Bean and Saubel 1972). Although the nectar provides a good source of food for hummingbirds, it is a negligible source for humans.

Aizoaceae | Aizoon, Mesem, or Fig-marigold Family

Carpobrotus | Hottentot-fig, sun-rose

C. chilensis **(Molina) N. Britton (syn., *Mesembryanthemum chilense* Molina)**
sea-fig, baby sun-rose, flor de sol, rocio

Carpobrotus chilense is a perennial leaf succulent introduced from Chile. Little is known of how Sonoran Desert inhabitants used these plants. Ice plants were probably less abundant a century ago, although Palmer (1878) remarked that an ice plant (cited as *M. acinaiciforme* L.) was one of the most common plants along the sea coast of southern California growing on sand beaches. Inhabitants here, including "Indians, Mexicans, and other Whites" (Palmer 1878), ate the abundant, pleasant-tasting fruits of *M. chilense* at the turn of the century (Sparkman 1908; Hedrick 1972, cited as *M. aequilaterale* Haw.). This may be the species that Charles Parry referred to in the mid 1800s as having an edible, juicy fruit (Hedrick 1972).

Mesembryanthemum | ice plant, sea-fig

M. crystallinum **Linnaeus**
common ice plant, pig's-face

As with *Carpobrotus chilensis,* little is known regarding the use of this plant, which was introduced from the Cape of Good Hope. Inhabitants along the California coast ate the fruits and slightly acidic-tasting fleshy herbage raw (Morton 1963; Medsger 1966). Populations of *M. crystallinum* are a common sight growing on sand dunes along the coast and inland in northern and central Baja California.

Trianthema | horse-purslane

T. portulacastrum **Linnaeus**
desert horse-purslane, horse-purslane, pigweed, verdolagas, verdolagas de cochi, verdolaga blanca, verdolaga del sapo

Trianthema portulacastrum (fig. 43) is an exotic, somewhat succulent, herbaceous perennial frequently found on disturbed sites. There appears to be conflicting evidence of the importance of *T. portulacastrum* in the diets of native peoples. Fr. del Barco (1980) described how the Cochimí used only the seed of this plant and only when there was an abundance because when there were few plants, they paid no attention. They collected the mature, tiny seed by pulling up the plants and releasing the seed on their basket trays. Annetta Carter (*in* del Barco 1980) noted that it is still relished as a green by Baja Californians and that it was *T. portulacastrum,* and not *Portulaca* spp., that Homer Aschmann (1959) was referring to when he noted that *verdolagas* provided edible seeds and leaves to the indigenous people. According to Aschmann, *verdolagas* generally referred to *Portulaca* spp. (Aschmann 1959, 1966).

Amadeo Rea tells an amusing story relating that *T. portulacastrum* is *not* eaten by southwestern peoples (Rea 1997). He and a friend gathered two grocery bags full of what they thought was the edible green *ku'ukpalk (Portulaca oleracea)* for their friend Sally Pablo. After presenting the greens to Sally, she informed him that they had picked the wrong plant and promptly threw the greens into the garbage. Rather than picking *ku'ukpalk,* they instead had picked *T. portulacastrum,* a weed considered useless by the Pima. Indeed, the two plants look very similar when not in flower.

It is thought that Leonora Curtin and others may have confused *T. portulacastrum* with *verdolaga,* or *P. oleracea* (Rea 1997). Curtin noted that the Salt River Pimas cooked *T. portulacastrum* as greens in the summer (Curtin 1949, *Curtin 21,* DES). At Quitovac, Sonora, the Tohono O'odham cooked these plants as greens (Nabhan et al. 1982); a village patriarch told Amadeo Rea and Gary Nabhan that the local people ate *T. portulacastrum,* called *kashvan,* in the past (Rea 1997). Rea wondered if this information should be trusted coming from a man, because the subject is generally considered the domain of women. Additionally, in and around Ónavas, Sonora, the Pimas were said to have cooked the herbage of *T. portulacastrum* as a potherb (Pennington 1980). While at Ónavas, Amadeo Rea asked his Piman friend Don Pedro Estrella Tánori about *T. portulacastrum* (Rea 1997). Señor Estrella Tánori could not remember the Pima name, but said it was called *verdolagas.* Upon hearing this, his daughter María shook her head and said that the useless plant was *not* edible. Her name for it was *verdolaga del sapo,* "the *toad's* verdolagas." Twelve years later María Estrella confirmed this, telling Amadeo and me that the pink-flowered *verdolaga del sapo* is not eaten.

FIGURE 43. ***Trianthema portulacastrum*** L. prior to flowering. South Mountain Community College, September 1988.

Amaranthaceae | Amaranth Family

Amaranthus | amaranth, pigweed, tumbleweed, quelite, bledo

***A. albus* Linnaeus (syn., *A. graecizans* Linnaeus)**
tumbleweed, cochino, quelite manchado

***A. caudatus* Linnaeus**
love-lies-bleeding, quelite

***A. fimbriatus* (Torrey) Bentham ex S. Watson**
fringed amaranth

***A. hybridus* Linnaeus**
grain amaranth, smooth amaranth, spleen amaranth, quelite morado

***A. lepturus* Blake**

***A. obcordatus* (A. Gray) Standley**
trans-Pecos amaranth

***A. palmeri* S. Watson**
carelessweed, redroot, Palmer's amaranth

***A. retroflexus* Linnaeus**
rough pigweed, red-root amaranth

***A. venulosus* S. Watson**
baja amaranth

***A. watsonii* Standley**
Watson's amaranth

Amaranths, particularly *A. palmeri, A. albus, A. retroflexus,* and cultivated forms of *A. hybridus,* were important food plants in the western United States and northern Mexico and provided indigenous groups edible greens and seeds.

Amaranthus palmeri is one of the most abundant plants ("weed" to some) in disturbed habitats. Farmers on Tohono O'odham lands harvest the highly competitive amaranth both for human and livestock food (Nabhan and Teiwes 1983). In addition, amaranth may also serve to reduce insect damage to tepary bean crop (*Phaseolus acutifolius* A. Gray) in their fields (Nabhan and Teiwes 1983) because amaranth foliage is preferred to bean vines by black cutworms, a widespread crop pest (Genung 1959).

The young herbage of amaranth (fig. 44) supplied an important edible green. Western Apaches soaked, beat, and then added baked agave pulp to amaranth or goosefoot *(Chenopodium)* greens (Palmer 1890). Northeastern Yavapais usually boiled the leaves for greens

FIGURE 44. Young herbage of ***Amaranthus palmeri*** S. Wats. Salt River Project right-of-way, South Mountain area, Maricopa County, Arizona, June 1988.

and mixed the herbage with dried agave pulp (Gifford 1936). The Tohono O'odham collected the greens when only 20 centimeters in height, roughly a hand's breadth, and cooked the young greens in water (Nabhan et al. 1982; Nabhan 1985). One Tohono O'odham woman described how she and her family still enjoyed amaranth even though she lived in an urban setting in Long Beach, California (Marsh 1969). Her brother supplied her an abundant amount of young amaranth collected in the spring from a nursery where he worked. She cut off the roots and smaller stems of each plant and boiled the remaining leaves and stems in salted water for 20 to 30 minutes. She then added chopped onion and tomato to the drained cooked greens and fried the whole mass in vegetable oil.

River Pimas valued *A. palmeri* as a *quelite* with high regard. "Of the various greens available to the Pima, this one is the most widely used and I suppose will be the last one forgotten." (Rea 1997:200). They picked and boiled the tender leaves and whole tips of stems. Young growth of this summer annual is available for gathering from late spring to early summer. On the Salt

River Reservation, Pimas boiled and ate the leaves of *A. palmeri* with pinole (Curtin 1949). According to Aleš Hrdlička (1908), the Pima gathered leaves of this amaranth in the fall for use as a *quelite,* usually cooked like spinach. Frank Russell (1908) commented on how the Pima gathered the leaves in the spring and sometimes baked them in tortillas.

The Cahuilla, Mohave, Quechan, and Cocopa boiled and ate leaves of amaranth (Castetter and Bell 1951; Bean and Saubel 1972; Kelly 1977). Some also rolled the cooked greens into balls that they baked on hot coals (Castetter and Bell 1951).

Amaranth greens were second only to Palmer salt grass *(Distichlis palmeri)* in terms of quantity for the Cocopa (Kelly 1977). The greens were gathered and prepared by groups of older girls, "one of their few subsistence responsibilities." They gathered the leaves of *A. palmeri* and *A. caudatus* as a choice green vegetable soon after floodwaters receded and after summer rains (Alvarez de Williams 1987). Fewer plants were available when there was little flooding, but this may not have been a concern to the already reduced populations of Cocopa in the late 1800s (Kelly 1977). They laid a thick layer of amaranth leaves over a bed of hot coals, mashed the leaves down, and packed the mass with their feet. Green *quelite* plants and dry weeds and branches were placed on this mass and set on fire. The mashed leaves were allowed to bake from one to three hours; the resulting "cakes" were removed, cut into chunks, and divided among families. The Cocopa also boiled the leaves in water for three minutes, then molded the greens into round balls and stored them for later use.

The Spanish term *bledo* was used to include other edible greens such as *Chenopodium* spp. in Baja California (and elsewhere), which may have obscured the actual frequency of the use of amaranth (Aschmann 1959). The Cochimí collected amaranth only when plants were abundant (del Barco 1980:196). For use as greens, they cut off and ate the tips of plants "less than a handbreadth in height." According to Fr. del Barco (1980:196), sometimes they did not bother to gather the plants by hand, but just "nipped" off the plants' tops with their mouths, appearing to "graze like beasts." He must have realized how absurd this sounded, for he added, "I know very well that in former times they used to do it in this manner, and I have seen it myself many years ago, though I am convinced that they, at least the most polished ones, no longer eat amaranth in this animal fashion."

Peoples outside of the Sonoran Desert also used amaranth greens extensively. The Guarijío cooked the young leaves and stem tips of *A. palmeri* and other species as potherbs (Gentry 1963). Tarahumaras used amaranth, including *A. retroflexus,* to a large extent (Pennington 1963; Bye 1976, 1981). They relied heavily on sprouting amaranths and other *quelites* from April through July (Bye 1976, 1981). One hundred grams of edible seedlings of *A. retroflexus,* which was considered a daily serving for a Tarahumara adult, could be harvested in May and early June from a four-square-meter plot. Regeneration of amaranth seedlings is relatively fast and occurs in a week. The Tarahumara cooked the greens slightly in warm water, rinsed the greens in cold water two or three times, and ate them with a little salt and tortillas or pinole.

Young amaranth plants are nutritious, especially when cooked soon after they are gathered. The Tarahumara practice of using warm water to cook amaranth greens minimizes loss of nutrients (Bye 1976, 1981). When compared to other wild greens that are high in nutrients, such as lambsquarter (*Chenopodium* spp.) and wild purslane (*Portulaca oleracea* L.), uncooked *A. palmeri* greens are exceptionally rich in iron, calcium, and niacin and have similar amounts of vitamins A and C (Meals for Millions Foundation 1980).

Some amaranths have been found to be high in oxalic acid (Gontzea and Sutzescu 1968; Greenhouse 1979), although the amount may vary according to agricultural conditions and plant maturity (Greenhouse 1979). Calcium combines with oxalic acid to form insoluble compounds that may not be absorbed by humans. The actual extent to which oxalic acid may limit the utilization of calcium has not been established, but the problem is considered insignificant. In fact, oxalate levels in desert amaranths are relatively low when compared to other leafy vegetables (Nabhan 1985). In addition, as noted by Nabhan (1985:99): "Vulnerability to oxalates is serious only in diets that are extremely low in calcium to begin with. [Tohono O'odham], Yaqui, and Pima populations in the Sonoran Desert had access to many calcium-rich foods, including beans, cholla buds, prickly-pear fruit, and mescal."

There is some concern about amaranth's ability to absorb potentially dangerous levels of nitrates from the soil. Nitrate poisoning from amaranth in livestock may result from an animal's consuming enough of the plant to equal 2 percent of its total weight. It is highly doubtful that humans could eat an equivalent number of servings. Additionally, *A. palmeri* has a lower nitrate content than other amaranths and commonly used leafy vegetables (Ehleringer 1983). With increasing drought, the nitrogen content in the herbage *decreased* as nitrogen was transported from the foliage into the developing seeds. Amaranth harvesters need to be more concerned with lead poisoning from automobile emissions and herbicide spraying than with oxalic acid or nitrates (fig. 45). Plants growing alongside major highways have as much as 15 times more lead in their tissues than plants growing in Tohono O'odham fields (R. Bye, pers. comm.).

The seeds of amaranth were also valued as a food item. Women generally gathered the small, black seeds of *A. palmeri* from late summer through fall. Pimas mixed the ground seeds with meal or squash or ate the seeds parched, ground, and dry (Russell 1908). Sometimes the seeds were dried and ground; one or two handfuls of the meal was cooked in a pint of boiling water with a teaspoon of salt (Curtin 1949).

The Cahuilla gathered the seeds of *A. fimbriatus* in late summer, which they then threshed, parched, and ground (Bean and Saubel 1972). Cocopas collected, threshed, winnowed, and ground the seeds of *A. palmeri* and *A. caudatus*. Kelly (1977) provides the most descriptive account of the gathering and preparation of amaranth seed by the Cocopa. The women harvested the corn and bean crops first, then collected the amaranth. On occasion whole families moved to a good harvesting area, where they would camp for a week. Two methods of collecting were employed. The first involved breaking off the inflorescences into a basket that was carried to a collecting/threshing area. Women also pulled the plants down over a basket and rubbed the seeds off between their hands. Some threshing and cleaning of seed was done in the field. At camp they piled the inflorescences outside against the house, then covered them with arrow-weed (*Pluchea sericea*) or willow (*Salix* sp.). Women beat the inflorescences with a stick, then pounded the material in a mortar with a pestle. They poured, winnowed, or blew on the material to separate out the chaff. Cleaned seed was stored in mud/straw ollas, whereas the unthreshed seeds were kept in a pile and used as needed because they stored well. The Cocopa ground the seeds into a meal, which they either ate uncooked or added to boiling, salted water to make a mush. This mush was eaten alone or mixed with corn or beans. The Cocopa also made cakes by mixing the flour with water and baking them in hot ashes. The cakes were approximately 2.5 to 5.0 centimeters thick and 17 to 25 centimeters in diameter.

Amaranth seeds played an important role in the diet of those people inhabiting Baja California. Good yields of these seeds followed heavy rains. Following drought a good yield came only from "deep valleys permanently wet by ground water" (del Barco 1980:196). Fr. del Barco noted that the Cochimí women collected amaranth seeds in October, but only if there were many other kinds of plants from which seed could be easily collected. The women spent considerable time filling their wooden bowls with the tiny seed and separating out the seed from the spiny chaff with their hands (the bracts of *A. palmeri* are spinelike and subtend the fruits). Even though their hands "accustomed to work, are hard ... they feel the extreme harshness of such thorns, and only the necessity of getting something to eat makes them put up with this special inconvenience" (del Barco 1980:196). Edward Cooke and Woodes Rogers noted that "a very small black Seed they grind upon Stones they have for that Purpose, and then eat it by Handfuls; my Men us'd to thicken their Broth with it, and said it serv'd as well as Flower [sic]" (Andrews 1979:42). It was suggested that

FIGURE 45. ***Amaranthus palmeri.*** Roadside plant with submature pistillate inflorescence; less than one day later this and other plants in the area were heavily sprayed with an unknown herbicide. Baseline Road near 24th Street, South Mountain, Maricopa County, Arizona, August 1988.

the seeds were those of *Amaranthus,* of which three types grow in the cape region of Baja California (Carter *in* Andrews 1979:42). It is also possible the plants described were *Oligomeris linifolia* (Vahl) Macbr. (see *Oligomeris*).

The Seri gently rolled the branches of *A. fimbriatus* and *A. watsonii* in their hands to free the seeds and chaff onto a cloth (Felger and Moser 1976, 1985). They separated the chaff from the seeds by winnowing, then toasted and ground the seeds. This flour was sometimes mixed with sea turtle oil. Near the turn of the century, Sonoran inhabitants living near Guaymas gathered and sold the seeds of *A. palmeri* in the markets for making bread and atole (Watson 1889). Rosalio Moisés, a Yaqui, remembered that in the 1930s they ate the young leaves and later the "tiny brown" seeds of a plant he called *hue-e* (possibly *A. palmeri*) during especially difficult times (Moisés et al. 1971:158). The Yaqui parched and made the seeds into a type of pinole or boiled, ground, and made the flour into masa for tortillas and tamales. According to Moisés, the flavor left something to be desired—he remembered the tortillas as looking and tasting like dirt. The common name *hue-e* is similar to *weywi,* a name given to the cultivated form of *A. hybridus* by the Guarijío (Gentry 1963). Perhaps Rosalio and others did not distinguish between the cultivated and wild species, the name *hue-e,* having once applied to *A. hybridus,* more recently encompasses both.

Amaranthus hybridus, a species widely introduced throughout much of the United States and northern Mexico, was in the past an important food. A form of this grain amaranth is believed to have been cultivated extensively throughout the Southwest (Bohrer 1991) as far north as the Salado (Sauer 1967) and Hohokam territory (Gasser and Kwiatkowski 1991a). Seeds from the cultivated form recovered from archaeological remains differ from those of *A. palmeri* in that they are larger, have a different morphology due to the larger embryos (Miksicek 1983), and are often pale in color (Rea 1997).

The small amount of evidence that the Gila River Pima cultivated grain amaranth is provided by Frank Russell (1908; see Rea 1997). Russell (1908) referred to a plant the Pimas called *ki'ak,* and described its harvest and preparation. His description provided the only clues as to whether the River Pima ever cultivated grain amaranth because there is "no longer any tradition among living Gila [River] Pima that they once cultivated any species of amaranth for seed" (Rea 1997:307). They may have remembered *ki'ak* only as a plant from their past, because their cultivation of grain amaranth ending during the "stress years of the 1870s and 1880s when watershed deterioration and drought reduced the Gila flow and Anglos and Mexicans upstream cut off what remained." Someone early in this century still remembered the robust cultivar of *A. hybridus* and applied the name, loosely or in error, to the large, wild *A. palmeri.*

Amaranth plants continued to be cultivated in northern Mexico. By the mid 1900s, the Northern Tepehuan still grew the domesticated amaranth (Pennington 1963), and Gentry (1963) collected the pale seeds of this cultivar from the Guarijío. Perhaps by the 1930s some Yaqui, including Rosalio Moisés, did not differentiate between the cultivar and *A. palmeri* and *hue-e,* if it did pertain to *Amaranthus,* was used for both species.

Encouragement and cultivation of native amaranth have also been documented. The Chemehuevi increased the abundance of the edible greens by sowing seed they had previously collected (Nabhan 1979c). They collected the seeds by harvesting mature plants and by drying them upside down with a bag attached to the inflorescence. When dry, they shook the seeds to the bottom of the bag and sowed them. More recently, Sonoran mestizos commercially harvested the greens of *A. palmeri* several times in one season from dense stands found along the highway between Nogales and Imuris (Nabhan 1979c). Such dense stands were produced from seeds gathered the previous autumn and later sown. The Tohono O'odham also sow seeds to a limited extent as well as protect and harvest *A. palmeri* plants that come up on their own. It is also believed that the red stems of *Amaranthus* protect fields from evil spirits, thus providing another incentive to protect or not disturb these plants (R. Bye, pers. comm.).

Anacardiaceae | Cashew or Sumac Family

Cyrtocarpa | plum-tree

***C. edulis* (Brandegee) Standley**
plum-tree, plum, ciruelo

Cyrtocarpa edulis is a narrow endemic restricted to Baja California Sur and adjacent islands extending as far north as 26°N (Turner et al. 1995), but is more common to 25°N (Carter *in* del Barco 1980). Its fruits are fleshy drupes called *ciruelo* (Brandegee 1900b, cited as *Tapirira edulis;* Rose 1900; del Barco 1980). When mature they are approximately two centimeters long, clear yellow, have a thin exocarp (outer layer of fruit wall), fleshy mesocarp (middle layer of fruit wall), and a bony endocarp (inner layer of fruit wall; Turner et al. 1995). Fruits are available for harvest throughout the summer and into the fall. The slightly acidic-tasting mature fruits were usually considered very pleasant, although some trees always produced bitter fruits (Brandegee 1891a, 1891b, cited as *C. procera;* Goldman 1916, cited as *Tapirira edulis*).

Fruits were highly esteemed by Guaicuras, Coras, Huichitis, and Pericus, and later Baja California inhabitants in the early 1900s (Brandegee 1900b; Goldman 1916; Standley 1923; Coyle and Roberts 1975). In 1596, while attempting to establish a permanent camp he named San Felipe at 24°N, Sebastián Vizcaíno received these fruits from the Coras, a peaceful group of the southeastern coast below La Paz (Mathes 1992:136): "That day [September 3] the Indians brought me some presents of the fruits of the land which were pitahaya and some small, round fruit of the texture and size of white plums of Castile, with a rough skin like a peach and of good flavor, the seeds of which had a center of the same flavor as Castilian walnuts and they brought us many of these in the eight days that we were there."

Fr. Ignacio Nápoli noted that the Cora gathered seeds, fish, *pitahayas,* and the fruits of *ciruelo* (Moriarty and Smith 1970:53): "A very excellent and palatable fruit, which they call a plum and which, though a wild fruit, is very delicious and refreshing. In form and flavor it is like an apricot, and I see no difference between the two. This fruit when ripe falls to the ground and the Indians harvest it in great quantities. It is better than the almond or the pinon."

Fr. Ascensión, who accompanied Vizcaíno in 1602, noted that near Bahía San Bernabe (at the southern tip of Baja California) there was an "infinity of plum trees." He was not able to taste the fruits because "they were little and green," although "those who have been in the Californias say that they are very good, and of good flavor" (del Barco 1980:110; see also Wagner 1929:193). Edward Cooke, an English officer to privateer Woodes Rogers, described a fruit eaten by the Pericú (Cooke 1712:321; Andrews 1979:41–42): "[The fruit is] Sort of like a Curan, has a white pulp, and eats tartish, having a large stone within which looks like a Bird's eye, and has a Kernel, that may also be eaten. The Taste of it is pleasant enough, and I believe much esteem'd by the Natives."

Cyrtocarpa edulis does not grow north of the Mission Guadalupe area and thus was of no significance to the Cochimí in most of the central desert region (Aschmann 1959). In Fr. del Barco's mind the Cochimí would not have missed anything because he thought the taste left much to be desired (del Barco 1980:112): "Their fruit or plums can taste good only to those who do not have a delicate palate, such as Indians, sailors of those seas ... and for people of even medium appreciation, they [fruits] are not worthy of regard. But, anyway, the Indians eat them willingly."

The most valuable part of the fruit was the seed within the pit, the "kernal or almond within their seeds" (del Barco 1980:112). Jesuit missionaries compared the flavor of the seeds to hazelnuts or almonds. Even Fr. del Barco thought the seeds had good flavor. They were also appreciated by the Spaniards who bought them from the local inhabitants. So important were the fruits that it was suggested that the plants "be exploited and commercialized" (Huerta 1988:42).

Malosma | laurel-sumac

***M. laurina* (Nuttall) Nuttall ex Abrams**
laurel-sumac, lantisco

Fr. del Barco (1980:111) commented that Fr. Ascensión had erred in reporting that *lantiscos,* or laurel-sumac, grew in the vicinity of San Bernabe (southern Baja California) or anywhere in Baja California, that being "the Christianized California up to a latitude of 31 degrees." The name *lantisco* is also applied to *Pistacia mexicana* Kunth and *Rhus virens* Lindh. ex A. Gray in mainland Mexico (Carter *in* del Barco 1980). In Fr. del Barco's frame of reference, he was correct. However, *lantisco* currently refers to *M. laurina,* a common evergreen shrub in southern California and northern Baja California that also grows sporadically in the mountains and along watercourses of the cape region. Fr. del Barco (1980:111) noted the presence of this plant he "mistook" for sumac: "However, there are certain bushes or bundle of sticks in one bush by way of sumac, which plant they also resemble in the shape of their leaves. It turns out that even I, when I had recently arrived in [Baja] California, mistook them for sumac or I had my doubts about their identity, until I was made aware later on." In all probability del Barco was describing *M. laurina,* whose small, white drupes are produced from spring to autumn and may be edible.

Rhus | sumac

R. integrifolia **(Nuttall) Bentham & Hooker f. ex Brewer & S. Watson**
lemonade sumac

R. kearneyi **Barkley**
Kearney's sumac

R. ovata **S. Watson**
sugar sumac

R. trilobata **Nuttall**
skunkbush, ill-scented sumac, squawbush, squawberry, lemonade-berry, saladito, sidra, agrillo, lemita, lambrisco

Rhus trilobata is a common shrub of the Southwest and northern Mexico that flowers from February to August. Its fruits are small, red drupes, which are seven millimeters long (fig. 46). Southwestern and northern Mexican indigenous women gathered the fruits in the summer months. They used the berries fresh or dried and ground (Palmer 1878; Hough 1898; Barrows 1900; Chestnut 1902; Hrdlička 1908; Sparkman 1908; Chamberlain 1911; Robbins et al. 1916; Standley 1923; Gifford 1932, 1936; Castetter 1935; Kroeber 1935; Whiting 1939; Steggerda and Eckardt 1941; Elmore 1943; Nequatewa 1943; Saunders 1948; Fernald and Kinsey 1958; Balls 1970; Bean and Saubel 1972; Coyle and Roberts 1975; Weight 1977; Watahomigie et al. 1982; Weber and Seaman 1985; Phillips et al. 1994).

The pubescence on the fruits contains malic acid, which renders a pleasant acidic taste when prepared as a drink. Marsha Gallagher (1976) provides an excellent description of Clarkdale Apache use of *R. trilobata* fruits, which is representative of how other groups processed the fruits. Apaches were very fond of the berries and made a drink from them. Among Clarkdale Apaches, this drink was jokingly referred to as "Apache lemonade" or "Apache Kool-Aid" (Gallagher 1976:58). Several families still made this beverage during the early 1970s, "traveling long distances to collect quantities of the berries" (Gallagher 1976:59). Women picked only the ripened, red berries in mid to late June, because too many green fruits spoiled the flavor. They washed the berries thoroughly, thereby removing the sour taste. Although people used the berries fresh, they were more often sun-dried and stored, to be later used for making the beverage. To make the drink, the berries were ground on a stone metate or, more recently, a food grinder. Some Clarkdale Apache still preferred using the metate and maintained that it produced a "better-tasting product" (Gallagher 1976:60). Water was sprinkled on dried berries to facilitate their grinding. They soaked the berries in water (approximately

FIGURE 46. ***Rhus trilobata*** Nutt. Close-up of leaves and fruits. Photograph courtesy of Robert Gasser.

one quart of water for each pint of berries) for a few minutes, then stirred, and strained the mixture into a container, separating the seeds and "skin." Sugar was added to sweeten the drink. Traditionally, the Apache sweetened the drink by first soaking slices of dried mescal in water for a brief period, then discarding the pieces. The ground berries were added to the sweetened water, soaked, stirred, and strained.

Yavapai women gathered and prepared the fruits in a similar manner, also using pounded agave pulp to sweeten the liquid. Berries ripened "in the dark of the moon," in early May (Gifford 1932:211) or June (Gifford 1936). Favorite places for Western Yavapais to gather the fruits were in the Bradshaw and Kofa Mountains. Northeastern Yavapais often gathered squawberries near Cleator in the Bradshaw Mountains, whereas the Southeastern Yavapai favored the Pinal Mountains for gathering the fruit.

Hualapais either made a drink with the fruits, which they called "Indian Kool-Aid," or dried the fruit in the sun (Phillips et al. 1994). Dried, stored berries were ground and soaked when desired. To make the drink, the Hualapai crushed the fruits on a grinding stone and soaked them in water two or more times. They too drank the liquid as is or sweetened it with sugar or pieces of baked agave (Weber and Seaman 1985).

Rhus ovata descends into the Sonoran Desert along desert washes, but is absent in the low desert mountain ranges along the Colorado River (Turner et al. 1995). Because some plants are dioecious, that is, the staminate and pistillate flowers are on different plants (pers. obs.), not all develop fruits. Fruits are produced in the summer. They are coated with a thin, waxlike exudate that tasted like refined sugar (Havard 1896). However, the fruit's pulp has an acidic taste. According to a rancher who lived in the mountains of northern Baja California, "the Indians obtained their main source of sweetener" from a shrub identified as *R. ovata* (Orcutt 1887:46). The "white oily substance on the berries hardened into many delicate white waxy curls." The "curls" were sweet and easily collected from the berries and rolled together in the palms of the hand into little balls that "looked like white bees wax." However, Southeastern Yavapais (Gifford 1932) and Hualapais (Kroeber 1935) washed the fruits to remove the "salty" or "bitter" taste. Women mashed the fruits on a metate and added water (and frequently cooked agave pulp) to the mixture, then removed any solid matter and drank the liquid (Gifford 1932). The berries were also soaked in water to make a "good-tasting lemonade" (Havard 1896; Standley 1923; Saunders 1948; Balls 1970). The Cahuilla cooked the flowers of *R. ovata* in water for food (Barrows 1900; Standley 1923).

Edward Palmer described the fresh red fruits of *R. integrifolia* as having a white, acidic-tasting coating; these fruits were used in making a cool drink when prepared like *R. ovata* (Watson et al. 1880). An "old Spanish lady" related to Charles Orcutt (1887) how she and others used to gather, dry, roast, and grind the berries like coffee beans. They could then store the fruits for use in making a lemonade-like beverage when the fresh fruit was not available.

Rhus kearneyi ssp. *kearneyi* fruits are pleasantly acidic tasting and were probably eaten, although there is no specific reference to their use. The restricted range of the species in a few mountain ranges of extreme southwestern Arizona and northwestern Sonora (see Moran 1969) and its tendency toward dioecism (pers. obs.) undoubtedly limited its use as a food plant. Baja Californians probably ate the fruits of *R. kearneyi* ssp. *borjaensis* Moran and *R. kearneyi* ssp. *virginum* Moran.

It is not known if the fruits of *R. lentii* Kellogg or *R. tepatate* Standley & Barkley were used. Although listed in Wiggins (1964, 1980), *R. microphylla* Engelm. ex A. Gray does not grow in Baja California or elsewhere in the Sonoran Desert; specimens from Baja California were misidentified as *Pachycormus discolor* (Bentham) Coville var. *veatchiana* (Kellogg) Gentry (Young 1975).

Apocynaceae | Dogbane Family

Vallesia | pearlberry

V. glabra (Cavanilles) Link
pearlberry, sitavaro, otatave, huelatave, frutilla, uclatave, sitevase, huitatove

Vallesia glabra is widespread in the tropics and subtropics of the New World and reaches its northern limit in the Sonoran Desert. Here it grows as widely scattered populations from central to southern Baja California and Sonora, with a disjunct population growing in northern Sonora near Tajitos (Turner et al. 1995). The Seri had access to populations and ate the small white fruits fresh (Felger and Moser 1976, 1985). Mexican children also ate the fruits (Watson 1889, cited as *V. dichotoma;* Standley 1924). Edward Palmer thought the taste to be like that of litchi nuts (*Nephelium litchi* Cambess.). Inhabitants of the cape region of Baja California ate the fruits of a type of *Vallesia* (Brandegee 1891a), which may have been *V. glabra* or the more pubescent *V. laciniata* Brandeg. I know of no other documentation on the possible use of *V. laciniata* or *V. baileyana* Woodson.

Asclepiadaceae | Milkweed Family

Marsdenia | netvine

M. edulis S. Watson
batanene blanco, talayote, marrube, tonchi, cuaguayote

Marsdenia edulis is a woody vine of northwestern Sonora and Sinaloa that produces flowers sporadically following summer rains (Wiggins 1964) from June to August (Gentry 1942). The Seri (Felger and Moser 1976, 1985), Guarijío (Gentry 1942, 1963, *Gentry 1588*, ARIZ), and inhabitants near Guaymas (Watson 1889) ate the young green fruits from late summer to early fall as the fruits mature in late fall (Gentry 1942). Seris also cooked the mature fruits (fig. 47), peeled and ate the inner white "skin" but not the seeds (Felger and Moser 1976, 1985).

FIGURE 47. ***Marsdenia edulis*** S. Wats. habit and fruits growing among *Acacia constricta.* Two miles east of Presa de la Angustura, Sonora, February 1988 (*Hodgson 4944*, DES).

Matelea | milkvine

M. caudata (A. Gray) Woodson

M. cordifolia (A. Gray) Woodson
Sonoran milkvine, talayote, comot

M. parvifolia (Torrey) Woodson
spearleaf, talayote

M. petiolaris (A. Gray) Woodson

M. pringlei (A. Gray) Woodson

Plants in the genus *Matelea* are primarily perennial vines (fig. 48), although a few species are herbaceous or shrublike, such as *M. caudata.* Fruits of all species are smooth, warty, or winged follicles.

Inhabitants of San José del Cabo and Miraflores in the cape region of Baja California ate the young fruits of *M. cordifolia* raw (Brandegee 1891a) in early to late fall. Sonorans ate the immature green fruits of *M. caudata* raw or roasted in the fall (Gentry 1963, *Gentry 1628*, ARIZ, cited as *Vincetoxicum caudatum;* Pennington 1980). Guarijios toasted and ate the young fruits of *M. petiolaris* (A. Gray) Woodson, which Howard Gentry originally identified as *M. tristeflorum* (*Gentry 1626* ARIZ) and *M. cordifolia* (*Gentry 1626a* ARIZ; Martin et al. 1998). *Matelea tristeflorum* and *M. cordifolia* grow in the Sonoran Desert, whereas *M. petiolaris* grows near the desert's edge in Río Mayo country, extending into Chihuahua and Sinaloa.

Seris toasted and ate the fruits of *M. pringlei* and *M.*

FIGURE 48. ***Matelea*** cf. ***arizonica*** (A. Gray) Shinners or ***M. producta*** (Torr.) Woods. Vine in flower. Esperero Canyon, Santa Catalina Mountains, Pima County, Arizona, August 1988.

cordifolia, but distinguished those of *M. pringlei* from the latter by the presence of small spines (Felger and Moser 1985). Seris ate young and tender fruits whole, but ate only the exocarp (skin) of mature fruits.

It is not certain if Sonoran Desert inhabitants used the leaves for food. Tarahumaras boiled, drained, and ate the salted leaves of *Matelea* spp. (Bennett and Zingg 1935, cited as *Vincetoxicum* spp.; Pennington 1963). Robert Bye (1976) mentioned a type of *Matelea* used for food, but the species and part used were not known.

It is not known if the fruits or leaves of other species of *Matelea,* including *M. producta* (Torr.) Woodson (Texas milkvine), *M. arizonica* (A. Gray) Shinners (Arizona milkvine), *M. altatensis* (Brandeg.) Woodson, *M. umbellata* (Brandeg.) Woodson, *M. fruticosa* (Brandeg.) Woodson, and *M. chrysantha* (Greenm.) Woodson, were used for food. Taxonomic confusion and difficulty in species determination may have contributed to possible misinformation or lack of information with regard to which species were used for food.

FIGURE 49. ***Sarcostemma cynanchoides*** Decne. Close-up of submature fruits. Salt River Project right-of-way, along bike path, South Mountain, Maricopa County, Arizona, June 1988.

Sarcostemma | climbing milkweed

S. cynanchoides **Decaisne (syn.,** ***Funastrum cynanchoides*** **[Decaisne] Schlechter)**
climbing milkweed, huirote, sandia de la pasion

S. pannosum **Decaisne**
talayote

The Pima and Tohono O'odham in Arizona and Sonora made a chewing gum from *S. cynanchoides* (Curtin 1949, cited as *Funastrum heterophyllum, Curtin 39,* DES; Nabhan et al. 1982; Rea 1997). Gila River Pimas, particularly children, primarily collected the immature fruit (fig. 49), but used the tender shoots in its absence (Rea 1997). They opened the fruits or shoots and collected the white latex that exuded from the damaged part, drop by drop, into the stem (petiole) of a squash leaf. They cooked the latex-filled petiole in the hot ashes of a small fire, then ate the soon-to-harden gum. Salt River Pimas and Hiá ceḍ O'odhams also boiled the sap in a bowl to make a type of chewing gum (Curtin 1949, *Curtin 39,* DES; Felger et al. 1992). Seris ate the fresh flowers of *S. cynanchoides* (fig. 50; Felger and Moser 1985).

FIGURE 50. ***Sarcostemma cynanchoides.*** Close-up of flowers.

Fr. Nentvig (1980:42) may have provided the only known reference to the use of *S. pannosum* for food. He described a small plant with fruit "about the size of a hen's egg" with a "rough, course rind on the order of the shell of a snail." He noted that the fruits had to be eaten at a certain time, "in the latter part of August when the skin is green and tender" or else "it hardens and dries, and the meat becomes soft, white and cottony as the meat of *[pochote]*." The roots of *S. pannosum* were said to be poisonous to animals.

It is not known if people used the fruits or flowers of *S. arenarium* Decne., *S. clausum* (Jacq.) Sch., *S. crispum* Benth., or *S. hirtellum* (A. Gray) Holm. for food.

Asteraceae | Aster Family

Ambrosia | ragweed, bursage

A. confertiflora **de Candolle**
slim-leaf bursage, weak-leaf burr-ragweed

Ambrosia confertiflora is a frequently encountered herbaceous perennial that flowers from April to October. The only use of this plant for food is that reported by Castetter and Underhill (1935, cited as *Franseria tenuifolia*). The Tohono O'odham gathered and cooked the young herbage in the summer as greens. They did not dry and store the plants for future use. In addition, whole villages collected the roots with digging sticks along the flood plains in the fall, providing them a staple food.

Slim-leaf bursage is commonly parasitized by *Orobanche cooper* (A. Gray) Heller and is called *mo'otaḍk jeej*, or "broom-rape's mother," by the Gila River Pima (C. Cassa, pers. comm.; Rea 1997).

Bidens | bur-marigold, beggar-ticks

B. pilosa **Linnaeus**
Spanish needles, sticktights, hairy beggar-ticks, railway-daisy, blackjack, sactilla

Use of Spanish needles by Sonoran Desert inhabitants is not known. However, Julia Morton (1962) considered it a valuable wild food source and described the cooked young herbage as having a taste like pine needles or spinach. Tarahumaras harvested these important *quelites* following germination and ate the young herbage raw or cooked (Bye 1976). Before cooking, they washed and pounded the plants on a smooth rock surface. They then set the greens in the sun for a brief period, a practice that was said to tenderize the older leaves and increase the flavor. After briefly cooking the herbage in a small amount of water, they drained the liquid, then rinsed the herbage in cold water. Greens were eaten without further preparation, fried with or without lard and seasonings, or mixed whole or ground with maize and bean dishes.

Dicoria | twinbugs

D. canescens **A. Gray**
desert dicoria, desert twinbugs

The use of *Dicoria* is rarely documented in ethnobotanical accounts, although the Hopi were said to have eaten the achenes and flowers of *D. canescens* ssp. *brandegeei* (A. Gray) Karte (Hough 1897; Whiting 1966, cited as *D. brandegei*). Archaeological evidence suggests that the achenes of *D. canescens* (probably *D. canescens* ssp. *clarkiae* [Kennedy] Keck) provided an important food to those inhabiting the Coachella Valley in the late prehistoric period, with their use extending into historic times (Wilke et al. 1979). Achenes were present in a large number of human coprolites at a site that once overlooked Lake Cahuilla. Additionally, achenes were also found in a basket in the Last Chance Mountains, southeastern California. The achenes of dicoria were available in the winter and provided a particularly important food item to people who had to rely on and subsequently deplete stored food reserves.

Dicoria canescens flowers from May to December and produces a large quantity of fruits. Plants are usually locally abundant where found, particularly along flood plains and bottoms of major river channels, such as the Salt and Gila Rivers in Arizona.

Helianthus | sunflower

H. annuus **Linnaeus**
common sunflower, giganton, girasol, lampote, maiz de Texas

H. niveus **(Bentham) Brandegee**
showy sunflower

H. petiolaris **Nuttall**
prairie sunflower

Helianthus annuus is a common roadside annual that is probably native to the Southwest, but spreads to the east as weeds and domesticates (Heiser 1976); this species flowers from March to October (Wiggins 1964). The Mohave used and perhaps cultivated *Helianthus,* but the Maricopa, Cocopa (Castetter and Bell 1951), and River Pima (Rea 1997) apparently never ate the achenes. However, its achenes have been an important, nutritious food source to many North American peoples since pre-Columbian times. A 100-gram portion of achenes contains 24 grams protein, 47 grams fat, 20 grams carbohydrate, 120 milligrams calcium, and 7 milligrams iron (Watt and Merrill 1963).

Generally, women broke off the inflorescences ("heads") in the fall. After drying and beating the heads with sticks, thereby releasing the achenes, people winnowed, parched, and ground the achenes into a paste that had the consistency of peanut butter. This oily meal was often mixed with cornmeal to make a mush, gruel, or bread or used as a thickener for soup (Palmer 1878, cited as *H. lenticularis;* Havard 1895; Chamberlain 1911; Castetter and Opler 1936; Saunders 1948; Castetter and Bell 1951).

Sunflower fruits were important to the Western Apache. Groups established ownership of a stand of wild sunflowers by tying the immature heads together (Buskirk 1986:184). They picked the achenes in the fall when "birds began to flock around the ripened heads." They used a stick two feet in length with an oval-shaped basket-head on the end to beat the achenes into a basket hung over their shoulder. The Western Apache also collected the whole heads and sun-dried them, then shook the achenes loose. The San Carlos group dried the heads over a fire before they shook out the achenes (Gifford 1940). Clarkdale Apache (probably Northern Tonto) would not gather the fruits until the "petals" had withered and dropped (Gallagher 1976:34). They smacked the dry heads "sharply against their hands to discharge the seeds into their palms."

Western Apache women parched the achenes in a basket tray, then ate the achenes as is or with salt (Gallagher 1976) or ground the achenes twice into a fine meal (Buskirk 1986). This meal was mixed with cornmeal, put into hot water, then eaten as a "pasty bread" without salt (Buskirk 1986). They also ground the achenes with corn into flour (Gallagher 1976; Buskirk 1986). Parched achenes were also ground with baked agave, the mixture said to taste like candy. Wives of "army scouts" ground about 25 pounds of the achenes for rations to be taken on an expedition. Children were not allowed to play or laugh while eating whole sunflower seeds for fear they would choke on them. Clarkdale Apache women no longer collected the fruits in 1971, although they still enjoyed eating them as a snack food purchased from a grocery store (Gallagher 1976).

Yavapai women collected the achenes in October by breaking off the heads. They tied the heads in bundles with yucca fiber and sun-dried them. Using their hands, the women rubbed out the achenes into a burden basket, then carried the lot home. Here they parched, ground, and winnowed the achenes. Unlike "the cultivated sunflowers," these achenes had "no shells" (suggesting *H. petiolaris*). The meal was "very greasy and the nutritive value was evidently high, for this meal was carried on war parties" (Gifford 1932: 212). Cultivated sunflower achenes were parched, pounded in bedrock mortars, and winnowed.

Northeastern Yavapai women usually pulled up whole plants in October (achenes ripened in September), dried them, and then struck the heads over the edge of the burden basket to cause the achenes to fall (some women did this with the plant still in the ground). They also beat the heads piled onto buckskin to separate out the achenes. The achenes were then parched, ground on a metate, and eaten dry or moistened (Gifford 1936).

The Havasupai prepared the achenes in a different

manner, by first toasting them in live coals in an earth-covered basket tray and then grinding the achenes into a meal that was formed into cakes (Cushing 1965). They baked the cakes slightly in ashes before eating them with other foods, but often replaced meat with the cakes in the summer. Like other groups, the Havasupai made seed butter by adding a small amount of water to the parched and ground achenes (Nabhan 1979b, 1985).

Helianthus petiolaris also flowers from March to October. This species produces achenes that were used in a manner similar to that described for *H. annuus*, except that their "shells" were not removed (Kelly 1964; Harrington 1967; Bye 1972; Weber and Seaman 1985).

The flower buds of *H. annuus* are also edible and have a good taste when boiled in water (Hedrick 1972), although its taste may be affected by a sticky, foul-smelling resin associated with the plant (Harrington 1967).

FIGURE 51. ***Helianthus niveus*** (Benth.) Brandegee. Pinta Sands, Yuma County, Arizona, April 1987 (*Hodgson 4503*, DES).

Helianthus niveus ssp. *canescens* (A. Gray) Heiser (fig. 51) is perhaps the most heat-adapted sunflower known. This species inhabits the xeric, sandy habitats of the southwestern United States and northwestern Mexico. It may have potential for increasing the drought and temperature tolerance, polyunsaturated oil seed quality, and insect resistance of cultivated sunflowers if successfully crossbred (G. P. Nabhan, pers. comm.).

Lasthenia | goldfields

L. californica **de Candolle ex Lindley**
California goldfields

Lasthenia californica is an attractive annual when in flower from March to May. The Cahuilla of southern California collected and ground its small achenes into a fine flour, which they ate dry (Barrows 1900).

Pectis | cinchweed

P. angustifolia **Torrey**
lemon-scented pectis

P. papposa **Harvey & A. Gray**
chinchweed, foetid-marigold, many-bristle cinchweed, kapo, limoncillo

Pectis angustifolia barely extends into the Sonoran Desert and flowers from July to October, whereas *P. papposa* (fig. 52) is found throughout much of the Sonoran Desert and flowers from June to October (Wiggins 1964).

The highly aromatic herbage and inflorescence of *P. papposa* were used as a seasoning, adding a pungent flavor to foods. However, little, if anything, is known about Sonoran Desert peoples' use of the plants. Alfred Whiting was told that Havasupais dipped freshly collected plants in salted water before eating them with mush or cornmeal as a condiment (Weber and Seaman 1985). However, other Havasupai made no reference to its use as a food or condiment.

The use of *P. angustifolia* and *P. papposa* is better documented among those who lived in New Mexico and northeastern Arizona. The Zuni gathered and hung *P. papposa* in the house to dry for winter use (Stevenson 1915; Castetter 1935). They used the flowers as a seasoning by crushing them in their hands and sprinkling the pieces onto their stew meat. The Zuni also ate the plants fresh or dried and as greens boiled with salt, corn, or mutton (Bohrer 1957). Leslie White (1942:52) obtained this recipe using what may have been *P. papposa* in Santa Ana Pueblo, New Mexico: "A quantity of leaves and flowers of a plant called *kapo (Pectis;* Span. *limoncillo)* are gathered, then washed carefully. The plant fragments are dried, then ground into flour. This flour is mixed with a little corn or wheat flour and salt. After a thick dough is made, little cakes were molded, each of these then wrapped in two corn husks, then baked in an oven."

The Hopi and possibly Havasupai usually ate the leaves of *P. angustifolia* uncooked or dried and stored the leaves for future use (Hough 1897; Standley 1912; Spier 1928; Castetter 1935; Whiting 1939; Nequatewa 1943). For storing, they tied the plants in bunches to dry after the summer rains (Nequatewa 1943). The Hopi rarely, if ever, boiled the greens, but did eat them with fresh, green, roasted corn; dried, parched corn; or as a seasoning with corn dumplings in salted water.

FIGURE 52. ***Pectis papposa*** Harv. & A. Gray. Gentry Agroecology Project, Desert Botanical Garden, Phoenix, Arizona, June 1988.

Sonchus | sow-thistle, prickly sow-thistle

***S. asper* (Linnaeus) Hill**
spiny-leaf sow-thistle, alchicoria dulce, chinita

***S. oleraceus* Linnaeus**
annual sow-thistle, common sow-thistle, tlamatsalin, alchicoria dulce, chinita

***S. tenerrimus* Linnaeus**
slender sow-thistle

River Pimas recognized and differentiated among the sow-thistles. Pimas ate the young stems of *S. oleraceus* raw or cooked (Rea 1997). Pimas also ate the young, peeled stems of the introduced *S. asper* raw, in the manner of celery (Rea 1997). Leonora Curtin (1949, *Curtin 63*, DES) was told that Pimas ate the greens of both *S. asper* and *S. oleraceus* either after they were rubbed between the palms of their hands or cooked. The sweet juice from freshly peeled stems was said to quench one's thirst if eaten raw. Frank Russell (1908) noted that Pimas ate the leaves of *S. asper* raw or boiled.

The Mohave considered *S. asper* as a starvation food and occasionally roasted the young shoots on hot ashes (Castetter and Bell 1951). Tarahumaras cooked and ate its leaves as greens with pinole (Bennett and Zingg 1935).

According to Hedrick (1972), *S. tenerrimus* can be eaten raw or cooked. However, Sylvester Matthias had no Pima name for *S. tenerrimus* when shown a specimen by Amadeo Rea (1997).

Bataceae | Saltwort Family

Batis | turtleweed

B. maritima Linnaeus
saltwort, beachwort, turtleweed, vidrillo

Saltwort is a mat-forming or low-growing shrub found commonly on mudflats or salt marshes or less commonly on beaches of the Gulf of California, Pacific Ocean, and Gulf of Mexico. The plants often root at the nodes of the branches. The Seri collected a large quantity of these roots, which they crushed and cooked in water to make a sweet beverage (Felger and Moser 1976, 1985). They also chewed and sucked out the juice from the roots or added peeled roots to their coffee as a sweetener. The succulent leaves have a salty flavor when eaten raw (Standley 1922) or pickled (Hedrick 1972).

Nicolas Yensen and others believe that saltwort holds much promise as a salt-tolerant edible crop (Yensen et al. 1983). At Puerto Peñasco, Sonora, the plant grows extremely well as a groundcover and is watered by drip irrigation using seawater.

Begoniaceae | Begonia Family

Begonia | begonia

B. gracilis Kunth var. *nervipilosa* A. de Candolle
caña aigre

Begonia gracilis var. *nervipilosa* is a somewhat succulent perennial that grows in shaded canyons and seepy areas in Sonora and southward (Wiggins 1964). Mountain Pima children ate the juicy, mucilaginous, and pleasantly acidic stalks (leaf petioles?) of *caña aigre* (Laferrière et al. 1991). *Caña aigre* also refers to *Rumex hymenosepalus* Torrey, whose leaf petiole ("stalks") were also eaten by local inhabitants.

Berberidaceae | Barberry Family

Berberis | barberry, mahonia

B. haematocarpa Wooton
red-holly-grape, barberry, mahonia, algerita, palo amarillo

B. harrisoniana Kearney and Peebles
Harrison's barberry

The use of *Berberis* spp. for food by Sonoran Desert people is not well documented. Opinions varied with regard to the taste of the juicy berries, it being described as pleasantly acid (Castetter 1935) or too acidic to be enjoyed (Laferrière et al. 1991). The bittersweet, bright red fruits of *B. haematocarpa* (fig. 53) are available primarily from late spring to early summer. Those who encountered *B. harrisoniana* (fig. 54) probably ate its large, bluish black fruits.

Barberry fruits contain compounds that limit their use for food in large quantities (Laferrière et al. 1991), with a few of the many alkaloids found in root bark also found in the fruits (Brazdovicova et al. 1980 *cited in* Laferrière et al. 1991).

FIGURE 53. (far left) ***Berberis haematocarpa*** Woot. branch with mature fruits. Camp Verde, Yavapai County, Arizona, June 1970 (*Aitchison s.n.*, DES).

FIGURE 54. (left) ***Berberis harrisoniana*** Kearney and Peebles branch with mature fruits. Kofa Mountains, La Paz County, Arizona, March 1985 (*Milke & Priebe s.n.*, DES).

Bixaceae | Lipsticktree Family

Amoreuxia | yellowshow

A. gonzalezii **Sprague and Riley**
Santa Rita Mountain yellowshow, saiya

A. palmatifida **Sessé & Moçiño ex de Candolle**
Mexican yellowshow, saiya, sairya, saya, temaqui

Plants within the genus *Amoreuxia* are some of the better kept secrets of the southwestern plant world, with their beauty and usefulness being known to relatively few, fortunate people. All parts of *A. gonzalezii* (figs. 58–59) and *A. palmatifida* (figs. 55–57) were formerly used as food items, including the tuberous roots, young leaves, flowers, fruits, and seeds (Hodgson 1989, 1993). Howard S. Gentry (1959) recognized and eloquently described special qualities of *A. palmatifida,* or *saiya,* during the 1950s:

> Saiya has all the appearance of a plant that would fit well into man's garden. Its tuberous roots contain much starch and other unassayed nutritional constituents. They have long been a wild source of food among the indigenous peoples of Sonora, Chihuahua, and Sinaloa. They are still eaten by the poor people and I observed where they had been dug up near Navajoa [Sonora] only last week. The young tender green fruits containing the large tender, white, kidney-shaped seeds may be plucked and eaten out of hand. Their piquant fresh vegetable flavor is acceptable even to the touchy North American palate and add a racey agreeable flavor when cut up and added to green salads. I once cultivated them for this purpose in my Culiacan garden. As the fruits mature they lose their succulence and eventually dry brown and papery, splitting open to show a white tissue-paper-like inner lining with the seeds eventually rattling out through it. The seeds turn from white to reddish and are still chewly edible. At maturity they are a dark fuzzy brown with a rather loose seed coat. When this is rubbed off a shiny black seed appears.

Edward Palmer (1878:601) related how *A. palmatifida* provided edible roots (fig. 57) to the Arizona groups, who roasted or baked the roots in hot ashes. He described the taste as being "quite palatable, with a

FIGURE 55. (left) ***Amoreuxia palmatifida*** Sessé & Moçiño ex DC. Close-up of flowers; note dark spots at base of petals and dark lower anthers. Located 7.3 miles north of El Coyote, on the way to Huachinera, Sonora, July 1988 (*Hodgson 5116,* DES).

FIGURE 56. (right) ***Amoreuxia palmatifida*** habit. Located 7.3 miles north of El Coyote, on the way to Huachinera, Sonora, July 1988 (*Hodgson 5116,* DES).

slightly bitter tang." The River Pima know *saiya* even though the plant's northern limit of distribution is in Tohono O'odham country south of their territory (Rea 1997:42). Sylvester Matthias related to Amadeo Rea how someone from a northern Tohono O'odham village used to bring "about half a burlap sack" of the plant's roots to his father as a trade item. He thought the roots were rather bland tasting. (I find that the pleasant taste of uncooked roots is similar to raw white potatoes.) Plants were collected as far north as Santa Rosa, Arizona, on the Tohono O'odham Reservation (Palmer 1878; Havard 1895). *Saiya* harvesters were careful to not confuse it with *Jatropha macrorhiza* Benth. var. *septemfida* Engelm., of the Euphorbia family. Those who inadvertently did suffered for days from diarrhea (G. P. Nabhan, pers. comm.).

Amoreuxia palmatifida was accessible to and used by the Hiá ceḍ O'odham, with the plants found "in Sonoran sand on the southwest side" and north of Ajo (Bell 1980). The only known population in Hiá ceḍ O'odham territory is in a sandy wash south of Three Points, Pima County, just east of the present-day Tohono O'odham Reservation western boundary (pers. obs.).

FIGURE 57. ***Amoreuxia palmatifida*. a.** Habit, root; **b.** fruit, near Ruby, Santa Cruz County, Arizona, August 1986 (*Hodgson 4381*, DES).

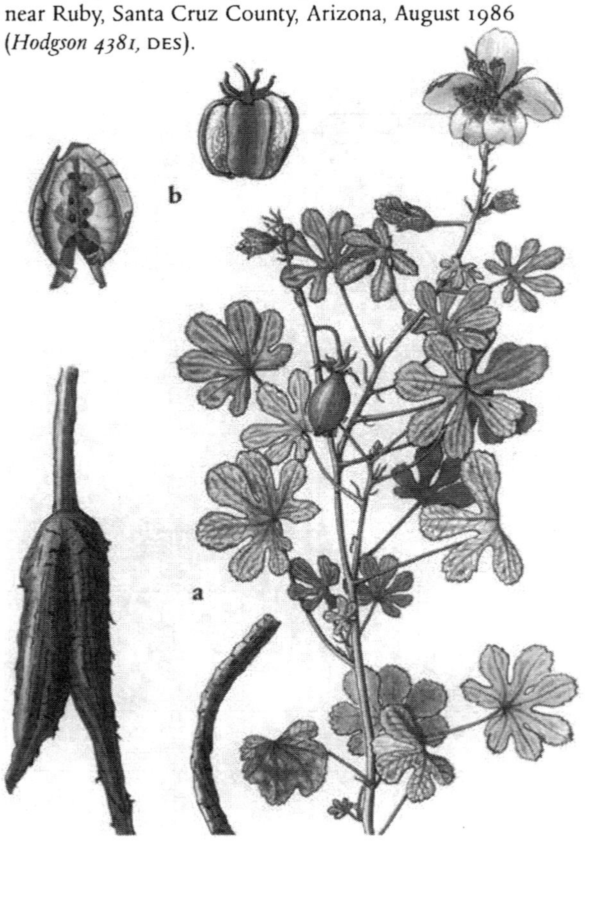

Amoreuxia palmatifida may have played an important role as a food plant for Baja California inhabitants. Homer Aschmann (1959) suggested that the plant providing an edible root in the central desert region of Baja California was *zaya*, rather than *Manihot chlorosticta* Standl. & Goldm., whose distribution is much farther south (see *Manihot* account). Aschmann (1959:88–89) noted that the inhabitants still used *saiya* in the mid 1900s:

> The roots of this plant are still collected from the clayey soils, often mixed with rock fragments, which form on high, relatively level basalt surfaces in the mountainous central part of the peninsula as far north as San Borja, though the plants are much more abundant near Mission Guadalupe. The plant sprouts after summer rains and dies back in the fall. The edible tubers can be collected at any time through the following spring, and the modern inhabitants of isolated mountain *ranchos* are very adept at finding the tubers when only a bit of dry stalk can be seen. The tubers are about the size, shape, and texture of a small parsnip. They are commonly boiled or roasted, though they can be eaten raw. Today each mountain family eats several pounds per year, gathering the tubers from a few special plots, some in quite remote spots visited in connection with herding or hunting activities. A traveler along a burro trail will recognize such plots, and will often dismount and dig in the stony clay until he has collected a pound or two of roots.

At least during the 1960s, people living in Comondú, Baja California, used *saiya* roots in soup, baked, or dried and ground into flour for tortillas (Gentry 1963). Indeed, *A. palmatifida* is common in the Sierra San Francisco, where the locals knew and continued to use it in the 1990s (*Hodgson 9572 & Rebman*, DES). In all probability, *A. gonzalezii* also grows in Baja California and was once used for food by those who had access to the plants. It is a rare plant known from less than a dozen sites in Arizona, Sonora, and northern Sinaloa (Hodgson 1989, 1993). Ira Wiggins (1964, 1980) does not list it as growing in Baja California. *Amoreuxia gonzalezii* is similar in appearance to the more common *saiya*, *A. palmatifida*, from which it differs by its silky, pubescent ovary; long, football-shaped fruits; and globose seeds (Hodgson 1993). Townsend Brandegee described a plant he collected in the vicinity of San José del Cabo, Baja California Sur, in 1890, which he identified as *A. wrightii* A. Gray, a Chihuahuan Desert

FIGURE 58. (left) ***Amoreuxia gonzalezii*** Sprague & Riley in flower. Note pale spots at base of petals, light colored anthers, and relatively wide spatulate leaf lobes. Located 7.5 miles north of Masocahui, on the way to Moctezuma, Sonora, July 1988. Site revisited in early September and just a few plants, in fruit, were found; this plant and many others not relocated (*Hodgson 5130*, DES).

FIGURE 59. (right) ***Amoreuxia gonzalezii*** with immature, green, ellipsoidal fruit. Santa Rita Mountains, Santa Cruz County, Arizona, late August 1988 (*Hodgson 5142, DeLamater & Zimmerman*, DES).

saiya. He described it as having capsules that were "much more acuminate" than those of *A. wrightii* and seeds that were globose, rather than oblong. These characteristics match *A. gonzalezii,* which was described 32 years later.

The roots of *A. palmatifida* were especially important to a Seri band inhabiting Tiburón Island (Felger and Moser 1976, 1985). They dug the tuberous root with a stick, then ate the roots raw, boiled with mule deer meat, or toasted lightly in the fire savored with honey or turtle fat. The outer "bark" of the root was cooked like beans with fat. The band often strung thin slices of the root as necklaces. A mother sometimes gave slices of the strung, dried root to her child to eat while walking in the desert.

The Ópata made tortillas, atole, and pozole from the roots of *temaquí,* or *A. palmatifida* (Nentvig 1980). Edward Palmer noted that Yaquis also ate the roots, which he described as having a taste like parsnip or carrot (Watson 1889). Yaqui survivors of the 1890s battle with the Mexican government sought refuge in the Sierra Bacatete, where they survived largely on *saiya* roots (Beals 1945). Ónavas Pimas boiled and ate the roots of *A. gonzalezii* (Pennington 1980; figs. 58–59). Don Pedro Estrella Tánori related how he and others of his community of Ónavas used to frequently harvest *A. gonzalezii* roots from a graphite mine site, but more recently (1960s–1970s) harvested them only incidentally (A. Rea, pers. comm.). Guarijios peeled and ate the fleshy roots of both *saiyas* boiled or, preferably, roasted (Gentry 1963). At San Bernardo, Sonora, people roasted and ate the roots of *A. gonzalezii* (*Gentry 2280*, ARIZ). Milk was added to the cooked roots for enhanced flavor (Martin et al. 1998). María Beltran related that *temaquí (A. palmatifida)* roots were still eaten about her community and Guasabas as recently as 1988 (Nabhan and Hodgson 1988).

The young fruits and mature seeds of both *saiyas* were also used for food (figs. 57, 59). Inhabitants living at Comondú, Baja California, ate the young green pods and used the mature seeds of *A. palmatifida* (fig. 57) as a coffee substitute (Gentry 1963). *Saiya* seeds were still used as a "Nescafe substitute" by goat ranchers near Mulegé in the 1980s (G. P. Nabhan, pers. comm.). Seris cooked the tender young fruit with deer fat and bones (Felger and Moser 1976, 1985). In the vicinity of San Bernardo, the natives ate the young tender pods of *A. gonzalezii* raw. Howard Gentry described the immature fruits as having "an unusual pungent, and not unpleasant flavor" (*Gentry 2280,* ARIZ; Martin et al. 1998). Ónavas Pimas boiled and ate the fruits of *A. gonzalezii* (Pennington 1980).

In addition, Río Mayo natives boiled and ate the herbage as a green vegetable (Martin et al. 1998). Seris (Felger and Moser 1976, 1985) and Ópatas (Nentvig 1980) also ate the flowers of *A. palmatifida* (figs. 55–57), which are produced from July to September.

Amoreuxia palmatifida has potential as an economically significant crop, as noted by Gentry (1959): "Approximately 50 fruits or a median of 5 plants yielded 1 pound of seed. Transposing this to an acre estimate, with approximately 10000 plants per acre with a 3 by 1.5 foot spacing, a considerable yield of seed, 2000 pounds is indicated. With other potential products represented in the fruits and the tuberous roots, *saiya* appears to represent a subject well worth the investigation [as a new crop]." However, *saiya* is difficult to cultivate, as further noted by Gentry (1959): "I have planted the seeds of this plant several times, but have never observed any germination. The people at Comondú in Baja California once told me that they also could never get any plants to grow from seeds. The ones I have cultured came from transplanted root crowns with their tuberous roots." Homer Aschmann (1959:89) also commented on the difficulty in propagating *saiya* from seed and suggested that regular exploitation of the roots and subsequent disturbance of the soil increased yield: "Several ranch families told me that they had tried to grow *zaya* from seeds in their gardens on the arroyo bottoms without success. The soil of the most regularly visited plots looks as though it had been plowed, and these places prove to be the most productive. Since regular disturbance of the soil seems to increase the production of *zaya* roots, when the larger aboriginal population exploited more regularly the flats where they grow, a larger yield of roots may have been maintained."

Considering the difficulty in germinating the seeds, one wonders how either *saiya* species is so successful in the wild. Good production of flowers and fruits appear dependent on adequate summer rains. With little precipitation, few fruits are produced from very depauperate plants (pers. obs.). In determining the agronomic potential of *saiya,* Gentry determined that wild plants in "good seasonable years" (with adequate summer rainfall) produce fruits freely. In one population near Navajoa, Sonora, he found that plants produced from 8 to 24 fruits (Gentry 1959). However, plant and fruit development is also influenced by other factors. Flowers and fruits are often subjected to insect and ungulate herbivory. Don Pedro Estrella Tánori told Amadeo Rea that the cattle ate the fruits of the very rare *A. gonzalezii* near Ónavas, Sonora. Even on moderate to lightly grazed areas, livestock, which relish the tender, juicy, immature fruits and seeds, consume the majority of fruits, thereby decreasing potential seed set. I have located populations of both *saiya* species in flower in southern Arizona and northeastern Sonora. Upon revisiting these same populations three weeks later, few, if any, plants, let alone fruits, were found.

Additional research on *saiya's* seed germination requirements, nutritional composition, and potential as an important crop is encouraged. Additionally, more intensive fieldwork with complete herbarium specimens of *Amoreuxia* is needed. At the University of Sonora, research is being conducted to study *saiya's* usefulness as an economic food plant. Both the Desert Botanical Garden and the CICTUS research branch of the University of Sonora are maintaining germ plasm of these species in seed banks so that their gene pools can be at least partially conserved (Hodgson 1989).

Bombacaceae | Cottontree or Kapok-tree Family

Ceiba | kapok-tree

C. acuminata **(S. Watson) Rose**
cottontree, kapok, ceiba, pochote, hadmunig

Ceiba acuminata (figs. 60–63) enters the Sonoran Desert in central Sonora and grows infrequently on plains, hillsides, and canyons in Sinaloan thornscrub (Wiggins 1964). Although it is said to grow in southern Baja California (Wiggins 1964, 1980), no specimen has been found (Turner et al. 1995). Plants flower while they are leafless, primarily in the spring from March through May, but occasionally as late as July (Krizman 1972). Fruits begin to develop from late spring through summer, become mature through the winter and spring, and dehisce and disperse seeds with silky fibers, or *kapok,* when the tree is leafless (fig. 63). This brief surge of leaf production and presence of tuberous roots suggest that plants experience a high photosynthetic rate and carbohydrate buildup in the roots. These reserves are diminished when the flowers and fruits mature (Turner et al. 1995).

Yaquis, Ónavas Pimas, Tarahumaras, Guarijíos, and Tepehuans ate the well-developed roots raw or roasted as a source of food or moisture (Gentry 1963; Pennington 1963, 1969, 1980; Alvarez de Williams n.d.). They were aware that young roots were not only better to eat than older, more mature roots, but were also better at different times of the year. Howard S. Gentry (1963) noted that young plants formed a large, white, spindle-shaped, soft, and juicy "corm" (fig. 61). The Guarijío collected these succulent roots at the end of the summer rainy season, then roasted the roots in hot coals. At this time, plants leafed out and their fruits began to develop. Tarahumaras peeled and ate the tender roots raw (Bennett and Zingg 1935) "when the kapok fruits began to develop," but would add the peeled, mashed roots to pinole "at other times" (Pennington 1963), when plants were leafless. Tepehuans ate the roots raw "in the green stage" (perhaps it was the fruits that were green and immature, not the roots), but baked the "more mature roots" whole or crushed (Pennington 1969:141). Young plants of *C. acuminata* are a potential root crop, with their roots considered better tasting and probably more nutritious than those of mature plants (Nabhan and Felger 1985).

Yaquis and Tarahumaras collected and split the immature fruits of *C. acuminata* (fig. 62), then removed,

FIGURE 60. ***Ceiba acuminata*** (S. Wats.) Rose trunk with characteristic conical spines.

FIGURE 61. Young ***Ceiba acuminata;*** note enlarged tuberlike root. Gentry Agroecology Project, Desert Botanical Garden, Phoenix, Arizona, June 1988.

roasted, and ate the seeds (Pennington 1963; Alvarez de Williams n.d.; fig. 63). The Tarahumara also ground the seeds and added them to green corn to make an atole called *oliki* (Bennett and Zingg 1935; Pennington 1963). Tarahumara guides continue to eat mature seeds along the trails in the Barranca del Cobre area. The Guarijío collected and ate the seeds, which Howard S. Gentry noted as being rich in oil and having a nutlike flavor (Gentry 1942, 1963; *Gentry 1451,* ARIZ). One ton of uncleaned *kapok* contains about 40 to 50 percent seeds that yield 12 percent oil (Martinez 1936).

Not only are the roots and fruits edible, but its young leaves, large flower petals, and seedlings are edible as well (Nabhan and Felger 1985).

FIGURE 62. ***Ceiba acuminata.*** Close-up of green, immature fruits; this is a common plant in the area. Five miles south of Masocahui, Sonora, early September 1988 (*Hodgson 5171 & Slater,* DES).

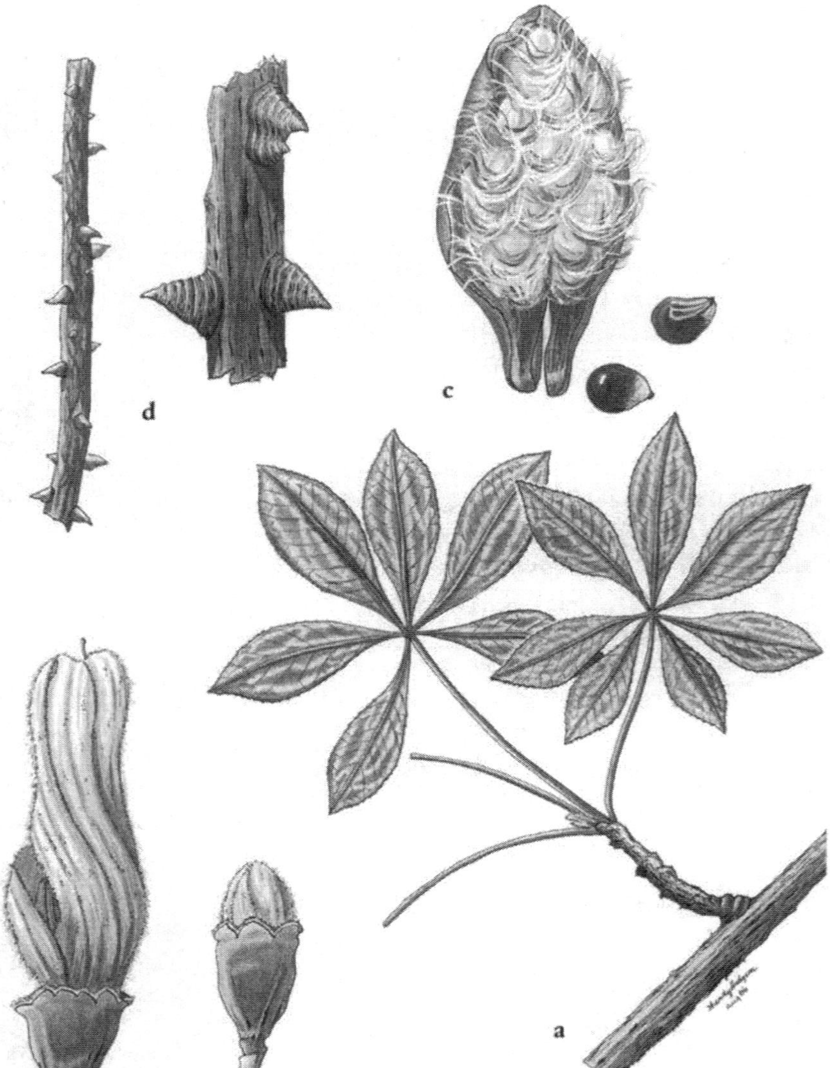

FIGURE 63. ***Ceiba acuminata.*** **a.** Branch and leaves, near Alamos, Sonora, May 1984 (*Hodgson 2932,* DES); **b.** flowers and flower buds, east of Guasabas, Sonora, June 1971 (*Gentry 22934,* ARIZ); **c.** mature fruit showing *kapok* and seeds, Alamos, February 1953 (*Blakely 1654,* DES); **d.** young and older stems showing spines (*Blakely 1654*).

Boraginaceae | Borage Family

Bourreria | strongbark

B. sonorae S. Watson

Bourreria sonorae is a small tree that flowers in the winter and produces a black drupe that is six to ten millimeters in diameter. It grows from Bahía de la Concepcion south to the cape region in Baja California, on Gulf of California islands, and in the vicinity of Guaymas, Sonora (Wiggins 1964, 1980). Edward Palmer collected this plant in early February 1890 in La Paz and noted that the fruit was edible, having a "taste of hawthorn," or *Crataegus* (Vasey and Rose 1890c:73). Perhaps it is this fruit that the English officer Edward Cooke was referring to while traveling near Cabo San Lucas in 1709 (Cooke 1712:321; Andrews 1979:41): "Here is a Sort of round Berries the Natives gather off the Trees, in Bigness and Shape resembling our Ivy-Berries. These they dry at the Fire; and when bit, the Skin peels off, and the Inside looks and eats somewhat like our parch'd Pease."

Brassicaceae | Mustard Family

Brassica | wild mustard

B. juncea (Linnaeus) Czernajew
Chinese mustard

B. nigra (Linnaeus) W. Koch
black mustard, mostaza negra, mostaza

B. rapa Linnaeus (syn., *B. campestris* Linnaeus)
rape, mostaza, flor de nabo, nabo de canario

B. tournefortii Gouan
Asian mustard

All members of the genus *Brassica* have been introduced to the New World. Native peoples were probably quick to accept wild mustards following the successful establishment of the plants and used the seeds and herbage for food. Seeds were easily gathered from the dried mature fruits and added to foods for flavoring or ground into a powder or meal. The sharp taste that is characteristic of mustard preparations is derived from mustard oils, which is found in greatest concentration in the seeds (Kingsbury 1964). The oil exists as a glycosidic compound, which is freed upon enzymatic breakdown. The glycosidic precursor is nonirritating; the oil derived from it, however, is capable of serious injury to animal tissue if consumed in large amounts.

Mustard leaves were used as greens (Chestnut 1902; Sparkman 1908; Yanovsky 1936; Bye 1979a, 1981), although their use by Sonoran Desert cultures is not well documented. They are nutritious, having high amounts of vitamins A and C, calcium, phosphorus, thiamine, niacin, and riboflavin (Leung 1961).

Brassica tournefortii is a relatively recent addition to the Sonoran Desert, having been first documented in 1950 near Yuma (Felger et al. 1992). It has since become a well established and often dominant species in the Sonoran Desert and has established itself as far north as Marble Canyon, Coconino County (Brian et al. 2000). The Tohono O'odham living at Quitovac, Sonora, accepted this plant as a food source and prepared and ate the young plants as greens during the 1970s (Nabhan et al. 1982). This mustard is being investigated for its role in Sonoran Desert fires and its effects on rare plant populations, such as Palmer-lily (*Triteleiopsis palmeri*).

Some Tipais of northern Baja California still enjoy eating the young leaves of wild mustard cooked in water, then fried with onions and a small amount of flour (Weiss 1994). A woman in one Tipai community gathers and sows seed of an unknown mustard in her *huerta,* or house garden, so that she can always have a supply of these greens. According to María Beltran, some people in the Granados-Guasabas area of northeastern Sonora still use *mostaza silvestre* (an unknown wild *Brassica*) as a *quelite* (Nabhan and Hodgson 1988). Tarahumaras considered *B. rapa* to be an important *quelite* in the 1970s and often preferred it to *Amaranthus* and *Chenopodium* (Bye 1979a, cited as *B. campestris*). They usually selected immature plants, but used more mature plants only if the flowers had not opened because older stems are fibrous and flowers are bitter. When they gathered the mustard, Tarahumaras pulled off the roots to expose the whitish hypocotyls and leafy bases. The leaves and hypocotyls were rinsed in cold water, placed in the sun until the leaves became limp, and then cooked in warm water. After the leaves were again rinsed in cold water they could be eaten as is or mixed with other foods such as beans, tortillas, or other *quelites*. Tarahumaras also sun-dried and stored the leaves for later use during the winter months.

So important were mustards to the Tarahumara that they cultivated the plants, due in part to the scarcity of fertile land; greater amount of leafy vegetable that can be harvested in a short amount of time; and mustard's ability to withstand early, light frosts (Bye 1979a). *Brassica rapa* also exhibits allelopathy (the ability to inhibit root growth of other plants, thereby reducing competition), a characteristic recognized by the Tarahumara, who used the plant to control weeds.

Descurainia | tansy-mustard, pamita

D. obtusa **(Greene) O. E. Schulz**
blunt tansy-mustard

D. pinnata **(Walter) N. Britton ssp. *halictorum* (Cockerell) Detling**
western tansy-mustard, pamita

Probably all species of *Descurainia* provided edible greens and seeds. Mohaves and Quechans baked the young growth for use as greens in a pit lined with hot stones (Castetter and Bell 1951). They piled alternating layers of greens and hot stones, covered the top with earth, and steam-cooked the greens for approximately 30 minutes, after which they ate the greens at once or dried and stored them.

Tansy-mustard seeds were an important food source to indigenous cultures. Seeds must have been used during pre-Columbian times because they were found in an olla recovered from a Hohokam site (Bohrer et al. 1969) and from a pottery vessel at Snaketown (Bohrer 1970). It is possible that *Descurainia* was cultivated by the Hohokam (Bohrer 1986). Historically, its seeds continued to be used for both food and medicine. River Pimas beat the seeds into baskets then parched, ground, and mixed the meal with cold or hot water and ate it as an atole (Hrdlička 1908; Russell 1908; Castetter 1935; Curtin 1949). Care was taken to gather the seeds, lest they be lost upon dehiscence of the capsules (Curtin 1949). George Kyyitan related to Amadeo Rea (1997) that the mixture of roasted, ground seeds and water had a good, albeit greasy, taste.

Tansy-mustard seeds were considered to be the most commonly used of the seed crops by the Tohono O'odham (Castetter and Underhill 1935). After beating the seeds out from the plants on a mat, they winnowed and then parched the seeds in a flat basket with a few hot embers or stirred the seeds on a piece of broken pottery held over the embers. The parched seeds were spread out to dry before being stored. The Tohono O'odham also put ground seeds in cold water with sugar added, which provided a cooling drink in the summer (Hrdlička 1908).

David Barrows (1900:65) was especially fond of the tansy-mustards, describing its seeds as "the most beautiful little seed of all." The Cahuilla ground the seeds, cooked the meal in a large amount of water, and ate it with a little salt. Mohaves and Quechans ate the seeds of *D. obtusa* and *D. pinnata* (Castetter and Bell 1951). Maricopas also used the seeds of *D. pinnata* by parching and grinding the seeds in a manner similar to other small seeds.

While studying the uses of plants throughout Mexico in 1897, J. N. Rose described a "most refreshing" beverage prepared from the seeds of *D. pinnata* (Rose 1900, cited as *Sisymbrium canescens*). A person mixed a small amount of seed with water in a glass, added a small amount of lime juice, then mixed the drink again. Blackberry brandy was added, the mixture again stirred, water was added, and the mixture was finally drunk.

Tansy-mustard seeds were valued more for their medicinal properties than as a food item in some areas. Seeds were collected in "great quantities" around Altar and sold at Guaymas, Sonora (Rose 1900). People living in San Bernardo, Sonora, once collected the seeds, which they sold to druggists in Alamos and Navajoa (Gentry 1963, *Gentry 1303*, ARIZ). The seeds were mixed with sugar and water and drunk as a "hepatic remedy" (with or without the brandy?). Those living in the Guasabas-Granados area of northeastern Sonora used the seeds of *pamita cimarrón*, an unknown species of *Descurainia*, as a medicine for the stomach (Nabhan and Hodgson 1988). Tansy-mustard seed coats produce a mucilaginous substance when moistened, a characteristic shared by *Salvia columbariae*, *Lepidium*, and *Plantago* seeds. These mucilaginous seed coats may be viscous enough to slow digestion and absorption in the human digestive system, thereby helping control the development of diabetes (Brand et al. 1990). It is also of interest that the Seri used seeds of *Lepidium* for "sore eyes" (Felger and Moser 1985) and River Pimas used the seeds of *Descurainia, Salvia columbariae,* and *Plantago* spp. to extract foreign objects from the eye.

Lepidium | pepper-grass, pepperwort

L. flavum **Torrey**
yellow pepperwort

L. fremontii **S. Watson**
bush pepperwort

L. lasiocarpum **Nuttall ex Torrey & A. Gray**
hairy-pod pepperwort, lipasote, pazote, epazote

L. nitidum **Nuttall ex Torrey & A. Gray**
shining pepperwort

L. oblongum **Small**
veiny pepperwort

L. thurberi **Wooton**
Thurber's pepperwort

L. virginicum **Linnaeus var.** ***medium*** **(Greene) C. Hitchcock**
poorman's pepperwort

Pepper-grass supplied both seeds and edible greens, although their use by Sonoran Desert cultures is rarely recorded in the ethnographic literature. The Seri used the whole, spicy-tasting plant or inflorescence of *L. lasiocarpum* fresh and dried as a flavoring for meat (Felger and Moser 1985). The Luiseño used the seeds of *L. nitidum* for food (Sparkman 1908). Seeds of *L. fremontii* and *L. virginicum* were ground with other seeds for flavor and cooked into bread and gruel, eaten separately, or used in soups (Palmer 1878). Like those of *Descurainia, Salvia columbariae,* and *Plantago,* the seed coats of *Lepidium* produce a mucilaginous substance. Consumption of its seeds for food or medicine may contribute toward controlling diabetes in genetically susceptible people (Brand et al. 1990).

Lepidium virginicum greens were a favorite food of the Tarahumara (Bennett and Zingg 1935; Pennington 1963; Bye 1976), who collected the leaves from March to June (Bye 1976). Women sowed the seeds in the fall when the fresh *quelites* (except *Brassica*) were lacking. They collected the dried fruiting inflorescences along the margins of fields, then stored and later beat out the seeds over corrals around the fields. Plants germinated within two months, and the leafy rosettes with the white hypocotyls were collected, cooked briefly in water, and eaten. In such plots, pepper-grass was found to be quite productive, producing nearly 1,120 servings, 100 grams each, in a 25-square-meter plot (Bye 1976).

Rorippa | yellowcress

R. nasturtium-aquaticum **(Linnaeus) Hayek**
watercress, berro

R. palustris **(Linnaeus) Besser var.** ***hispida*** **(Desvaux) Rydberg**
bog yellowcress

Watercress is a water-loving herbaceous perennial well known for its use in salads. Audrey Weiss (1994:211) was told by her Tipai friends that *berro* was "good for diabetes" when eaten raw or cooked. They prefer to eat young plants that have not flowered as a salad, because plants with flowers are considered "too spicy." Older, flowering plants are eaten after being cooked, which reduces the amount of greens to be had. Some simply discard the flowers and roots and eat the uncooked greens as a salad with lemon juice and a bit of salt.

Little is known on the use of bog yellowcress, although the leaves are edible (Chestnut 1902; Harrington 1967; Hedrick 1972).

Burseraceae | Torchwood or Frankincense Family

Bursera | gumbo-limbo, bursera, copal

B. fagaroides **(Kunth) Engler var.** ***elongata*** **McVaugh & Rzedowski**
fragrant elephant-tree, copal, torote, torote blanco

B. microphylla **A. Gray**
elephant-tree, copal, torote, torote colorado

Bursera fagaroides var. *elongata* grows as an isolated population in southern Arizona, becoming more abundant south into Nayarit and east into Chihuahua. *Bursera microphylla* is found throughout most of Baja California and central Sonora, reaching its northern limits in south-central Arizona (Turner et al. 1995). The thin arils surrounding the seeds are said to have an agreeable flavor (Rzedowski and Kruse 1979). Pima Bajo children ate the fruits of *B. fagaroides* var. *elongata* (Pennington 1980). Homer Asch-mann (1959) noted that inhabitants of the central desert region of Baja California ate the seeds (most likely the arils) of *B. microphylla* only in times of hunger.

Cactaceae | Cactus Family

Carnegiea | saguaro, giant cactus

C. gigantea **(Engelmann) Britton & Rose**
saguaro, giant cactus

The fruits and seeds of *C. gigantea* (figs. 64, 67) provided a dependable and important food for those who had reasonable access to the plants, such as the River Pima, Tohono O'odham, and Hiá ceḍ O'odham (for an extensive annotated bibliography on the ethnobotany of the saguaro, see Fontana 1980). Saguaros require warm temperatures and moisture for germination and establishment and produce copious amounts of fruit and seed prior to the summer monsoon, from the end of May through July (Steenbergh and Lowe 1977). Fruit production and maturation varies with latitude and elevation, a phenomenon understood by indigenous people, who migrated with the progression of saguaro fruit development. Saguaros have the capacity to produce numerous fruits in a single season. A saguaro reaches sexual maturity at 30 to 35 years, when it only produces a few fruits. By the time the cactus produces its first branches, when it is four to five meters tall and 50 to 70 years old, it can produce as many as 100 fruits per year (Turner et al. 1995). The number of fruits on a given plant increases dramatically with the development of each new branch. In the more arid habitats (such as those near and along the Colorado River), saguaros may completely fail to flower (Brum 1973).

FIGURE 64. Mature fruits of ***Carnegiea gigantea*** (Engelm.) Britton & Rose split open to expose red pulp and black seeds.

Saguaro fruit preserves (without the seeds or added sugar) are high in reducing sugars (62 percent) and the seeds contain significant amounts of protein and fat. An average serving consisting of five fruits contributes four grams of protein, five grams of fat, and 167 calories (Greenhouse 1979). The fruit of the saguaro is very sweet; with the seeds, they have a nutlike flavor.

However, not all Sonoran Desert peoples relied heavily on the plants for food. According to Buskirk (1986), saguaro fruit was a relatively unimportant food to the Western Apache. Harvesting the fruits required them to leave their cooler, higher camps and travel to the hot desert lowlands. The Aravaipa bands allowed White Mountain Apaches to collect fruit within their territory. San Carlos people stayed two or three months at saguaro sites until they gathered all of the matured fruits. Western Apaches generally used a long pole made from saguaro ribs with a crosspiece tied at one end to remove the fruits with a push-pull action. They often ate the fruit raw, but women usually prepared the pulp and seeds. They drank any juice expressed from the pulp, then made cakes from pulp dried on a rock, with the cakes storing fairly well for a year. Sometimes women made a preserve by boiling the fruit pulp. They washed, dried, parched, and ground the seeds that had been separated from the pulp.

Of all the cacti, Southeastern Yavapais especially liked the fruit of the saguaro. The northern band visited "Superstition Mountain" in July to collect the fruit. Men "watched from the heights for enemies while the women gathered [the fruit] in the desert lowland" (Gifford 1932:180). The Pinal group sometimes ventured south for the saguaro fruit, but "had to watch for the hostile Chiricahua Apache." They used a hooked pole to dislodge the fruit off the plants; after peeling the fruit, they took them home in a watertight basket. Once home, the Pinal Yavapai first drank the juice, sometimes diluted with water, and squeezed out additional juices from the fruits with their hands. They dried the fruit pulp on sticks and grass on the ground for one day, then placed the dried pulp in burden baskets to be stored in pottery ollas. These ollas were closed by setting a small pot right-side-up on top of the larger pot filled with dried pulp; the junction of the two pots was then sealed with clay.

Southeastern Yavapais preferred ripe saguaro fruit that had fallen naturally to the ground (Gifford 1932). They sometimes treated these fruits separately, by pressing the pulp with their hands into a cake. They often pressed the pulp in the sun for further softening; any juice expressed from the pulp was drunk. The pressed pulp was made into large cakes, which were dried and stored in pits lined with straw or walled with flat stone. Cakes stored well "for years," unless they were exposed to moisture and developed mold. When needed, the Southeastern Yavapai broke off pieces of dried cake that they then soaked in water. Juice was sucked, but fibrous matter and seeds were spat out. The seeds were not discarded, however. They collected, dried, parched, and stored the seeds in sacks made of fawn skin. To test whether the seeds were adequately parched, they ground a few. If the meal was white, they continued to parch the seeds. If the meal was brown, the seeds were adequately parched and the remaining seeds were ground and pressed into a solid cake.

Northeastern Yavapais traveled to the lower elevations of the Bradshaw Mountains, Yavapai County, and as far south as Cave Creek, Maricopa County, in mid-June to gather saguaro fruit (Gifford 1936). They traveled according to the ripening of various types of fruit and finally harvested fruits from saguaros near Cleator, Yavapai County. Here saguaros are near their most northern range and flower later than those at lower elevations and latitudes. Because saguaro fruits ripened quickly, a man was sent to check on their condition. People stayed only two weeks at Cave Creek because the fruits ripened so quickly. Men collected the fruits of saguaro, while women collected seeds of paloverde (*Cercidium* spp.). Northeastern Yavapais also used a pole made from saguaro ribs, with the hook made from forked branches of jojoba (*Simmondsia chinensis* [Link] Schneid.) that was attached at different heights. A jojoba branch attached toward the top dislodged fruits from tall stems, whereas those attached at lower levels dislodged fruits from shorter stems. Whole fruits were placed in burden baskets and split fruits were placed on sticks over a watertight basket so that juice would be saved and drunk. People immediately ate the fruits raw or, more often, mixed the fruit in water, which they then drank. The seeds settled to the bottom of the container and were collected, washed, dried, parched (in a basket), and ground. They formed this pasty meal into cakes and ate or stored the cakes for later use.

The fruit pulp was the most esteemed part of the fruit to Northeastern Yavapais. They opened the whole fruit with both hands and with thumbs together and flattened the pulp into layers. These layers were laid on a litter of globemallow branches *(Sphaeralcea ambigua)* to dry for two days. Fresh juice was applied to these slabs, which were usually an inch thick because thicker slabs tended to spoil. Pulp from fruits that were already split open were dried and pressed into thick bricklike cakes. When needed, they broke off and soaked in water pieces from this slab. Seeds that settled to the bottom were collected and prepared.

Western Yavapais also traveled to such places as the Kofa Mountains, La Paz and Yuma Counties, to gather saguaro fruit. They collected the fruit in burden baskets made partially watertight by "smearing it inside with gummy Indian 'wheat' [possibly seeds of *Plantago* spp.] ground on a metate" (Gifford 1936:260). A small, coiled basket was tied below the larger burden basket and held between the burden basket and the person's back. This allowed the capture of any saguaro juice that dripped. The fruits and pulp were prepared in a manner similar to that of the Northeastern Yavapai.

Saguaros were important to the River Pima, who started their calendar year with its harvest in the "saguaro harvest moon" around June (Rea 1997). The "short planting moon" in August was a critical point in the year for Gila River Pimas, who had to plant their crops by August 15 to avoid the first winter frosts in November.

Saguaro fruits provided a rich food resource because they came after the spring crops were planted and before the winter wheat was harvested (Rea 1997). Pimas ate the fruit fresh or dried, with the seeds. At the turn of the century Pimas told Frank Russell (1908) that the Gila River failed to flow in midwinter every five years, thus requiring them to go "far afield" in search of saguaro and mesquite in the summer. Sylvester Matthias suggested that fruit production varied. He said that few fruit would be available following a wet spring, but they would be abundant in another year (Rea 1997). Gila River Pimas once gathered saguaro fruit just west of 51st Avenue, in an area now supporting acres of cotton. Numerous saguaros grew on South Mountain and Sierra Estrella and provided the Pimas ample fruits. They would "just go anywhere to pick" saguaro fruit, although some individuals had their own favorite places to collect an abundant amount of saguaro fruit.

The Gila River Pimas' method of collecting the fruit was similar to that of the Tohono O'odham—they ate the fruits raw or cooked (Rea 1997). Gila River Pimas also made a nonalcoholic drink from water and pulp. Saguaro syrup was an important staple among many River Pima families. They broke fresh or dried fruit pulp in water, strained out the seeds, then boiled the mixture to the desired thickness. They stored saguaro syrup in ollas sealed with unfired clay.

Gila River Pimas considered the seeds as an important food. Ruth Giff related that seeds a Tohono O'odham woman normally would have discarded were saved for her (Rea 1997). In the past, the Northern Pima practiced the infamous "second harvest," or the removal and consumption of undigested seeds from fecal material (Russell 1908). Amadeo Rea (1997:257) inquired about this practice, and "needless to say, no vestige or even knowledge of this particular custom seems to have persisted into the generations" with which he worked.

Gila River Pimas mixed ground saguaro seeds with ground whole-wheat grains and made a "delicious" breakfast that some people very much missed (Rea 1997). They also made a type of gravy using saguaro seed meal and an atole of ground wheat with saguaro seeds to induce lactation in nursing mothers. They have virtually abandoned the harvest of saguaro fruit during the last half of this century, despite having access to dense stands of saguaro in the Sierra Estrella bajada and elsewhere on the reservation.

Saguaros were very important to the Hiá cẹd O'odham as well. Candalaria Orozco emphasized the importance of saguaros and other native foods in their once healthier diet (Bell et al. 1980:85): "Years ago we worked hard to preserve our food. We gather cholla buds, saguaro cactus fruit. This is why we live longer lives .... The old people are strong. Now the young people get old fast because they eat soft food." Miguel Velasco echoed this sentiment (Bell et al. 1980:64–65): "We drank the desert fruit juices in harvest time. The desert food is meant for the Indians to eat. The reason so many die young is because they don't eat their desert food."

Important cactus gathering camps for the Hiá cẹd O'odham included Ajo, Bates Well, Quijotoa Mountains, and Santa Rosa in Arizona and Quitovac and Sonoita in Sonora (Bell et al. 1980). With the exception of Santa Rosa, these camps were probably used for *pitahaya dulce* (*Stenocereus thurberi* [Engelm.] Buxbaum) as well. Maricopas traveled down the Gila River annually to gather saguaro fruit in the vicinity of Gila Bend (Kroeber 1980).

The saguaro was especially important to the Tohono O'odham, whose utilization of cacti in general was considered the most highly developed (Euler and Jones 1956). Edward Castetter and Willis Bell (1937) and Frank Crosswhite (1980) described in detail the uses of saguaro by the Tohono O'odham. Of interest is how the Tohono O'odham's own cycle of life and death reflected or paralleled that of the saguaro, as described by Frank Crosswhite (1980).

For the Tohono O'odham, the saguaro provided life. Their own life cycles were strongly linked to the saguaro as a resource and their respect of it is "undoubtedly based on their historic dependence on it" (Crosswhite 1980:7).

Saguaros provided the Tohono O'odham a fresh, moist, sweet food during June and July, which was a time of food scarcity. They processed the fruits into syrup, jam, dehydrated pulp, chicken feed, seed flour, oil, pinole, atole, snack foods, soft drinks, wine, and vinegar. None of the fruit was wasted, and even the outer "husk" (fruit wall and old calyx of flower) was discarded in a way that the split portion faced the sky to hasten rain. Also, the Tohono O'odham relied on bacterial necrosis to help facilitate the decomposition of saguaro tissue, enabling them to use the ribs or "boots" more quickly than if necrosis did not occur (Crosswhite 1980; Rea 1997).

The new year of the River Pima and Tohono O'odham calendar begins in June and early July with a saguaro fruit harvest leading into the wine-making and wine-drinking *nawait* ceremony, the rain-making event that allows crops to be planted. Traditionally, planting was not allowed until after the wine-drinking ceremony (Underhill 1946).

Each month of the Tohono O'odham calendar is based on the phenology of the saguaro and progression of the seasons, rather than on the sun and its equinoxes (Crosswhite 1980). The Tohono O'odham performed a ceremony in March that marked the beginning of spring (a time of renewal) and sang songs to ensure a good saguaro harvest. Such renewal rituals continued into April and May (Lumholtz 1912). The peak of fruit ripening occurred during the last week of June and the first two weeks of July, which is *haashañ mashad,* or saguaro harvest month (Crosswhite 1980). Like the Yavapai, the Tohono O'odham understood that fruit maturation varied depending on elevation and latitude; therefore, they may have moved with the progression of the season to pick fruit (G. P. Nabhan, pers. comm.).

The Tohono O'odham had a winter home, summer home, and a cactus camp (Crosswhite 1980; figs. 65, 66, 68–70). Winter homes, called "the well," were in the desert mountains where the Tohono O'odham had access to reliable water sources. Summer homes, called "the fields," were located in the valleys, which were provided with water from summer thunderstorms, and farmed (Castetter and Bell 1937). When the Tohono O'odham moved from their winter well site to the summer field site, their families annually camped in large groves of saguaros to which they had a "more or less" hereditary right to harvest and prepare the fruits (Underhill 1946). The availability of commercial jams or syrups has contributed to the abandonment of activities associated with cactus fruit collecting. However, some families continue to set up camp and process the fruit (Crosswhite 1980).

Traditionally, setting up a cactus camp meant hauling in much equipment, food, and water on foot. Such work was made much easier by the later use of horse and wagon and eventually the pickup truck (Crosswhite 1980). Cactus camps may have once consisted of nothing more than four mesquite or paloverde poles with a ramada of thatch, a water jar, and perhaps a metate and a cooking camp (Castetter and Underhill 1935). Families may not stay overnight anymore, but simply leave their blanket rolls, pots, groceries, and water jugs.

FIGURE 65. Juanita Ahill collecting saguaro fruit. West of Saguaro National Monument West, July 1970. Photograph by Helga Teiwes, courtesy of Arizona State Museum, University of Arizona.

FIGURE 66. (left) Mrs. Noceo straining saguaro syrup. Four miles southwest of Sil Nakya, Tohono O'odham Reservation, July 1968. Photograph by Helga Teiwes, courtesy of Arizona State Museum, University of Arizona.

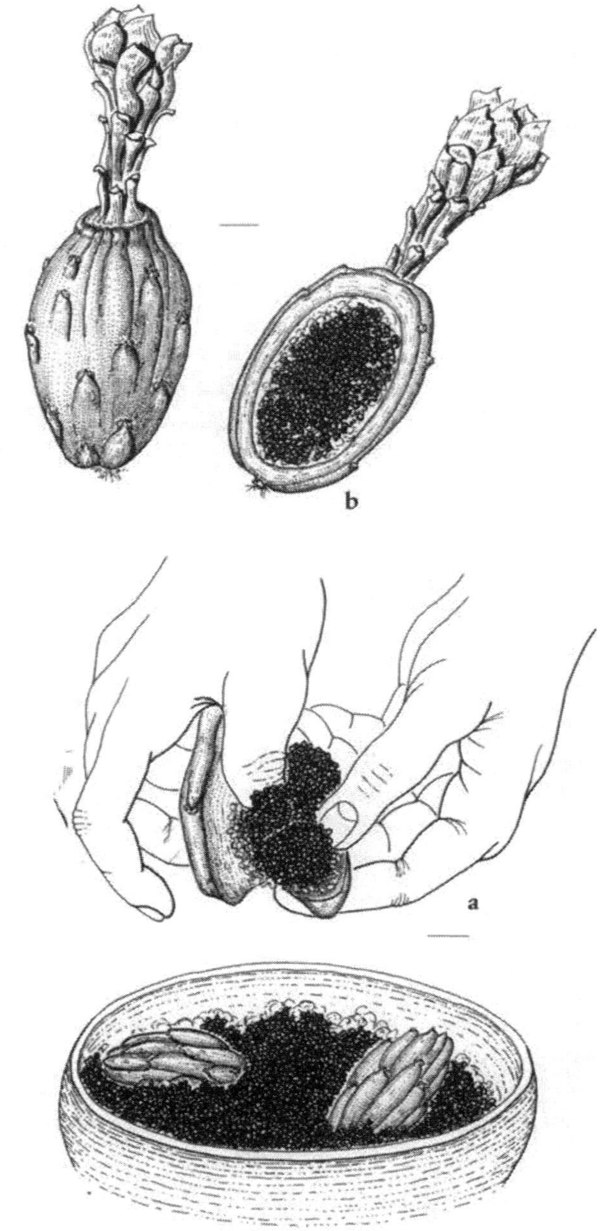

FIGURE 67. (right) ***Carnegiea gigantea*. a.** Separating pulp; **b.** fruit with old perianth. Courtesy of the Mesa Southwest Museum.

The fruit-picking season lasted two to four weeks or more (Lumholtz 1912; Castetter and Underhill 1935; Underhill 1946; Waddell 1973). Tohono O'odham women collected the fruits while the men took care of the horses and camp (Crosswhite 1980). Harvesting poles made out of two long ribs of a dead saguaro and a crosspiece attached at its top were used to "hook" off the ripe fruits on top of the saguaro stems. Women usually worked in pairs (Herbert 1969; Niethammer 1974). They collected the fruits in the early morning, when the air was cooler and before the birds ate many of the fruits (Castetter and Underhill 1935), although the Tohono O'odham were told to share the fruit with the birds, according to a saguaro legend (Enos 1945). They usually made two trips per day to an area of approximately a half square mile, and visited every plant once in three or four days to gather the fruit (Castetter and Underhill 1935).

Women used the fruit's dried calyx or their long thumbnail to split the fruit open (Thackery and Leding 1929; fig. 67). They extracted the pulp by using their thumb and thumbnail and put the pulp in the basket. They carefully discarded the outer fruit wall and calyx ("husk") in such a manner that these parts faced upward so as to encourage rain (Castetter and Underhill 1935). They continually filled smaller baskets with fruits that they emptied into a larger basket, which was hidden in a bush to keep ants out (Underhill 1951). They returned to camp quickly to process the fruits because they spoiled quickly. One large basket full of fruit pulp weighed approximately 40 kilograms (Herbert 1955) and held 12.6 liters (Thackery and Leding 1929).

The amount of fruit harvested primarily depended on the quantity of fruits available and the number of people who assisted. If two women from each family collected two basketfuls per day, it was calculated that half of the 1,200 families could collect 990,000 kilograms of fruit pulp, or 1,650 kilograms per family in three weeks of harvest (Crosswhite 1980). Each family could produce from 3 to 37 liters of syrup and 7.4 liters of jam, as well as a sack full of dried fruit and roasted seed (Herbert 1955).

It was the grandmothers who processed the fruit in the afternoon (Crosswhite 1980). They placed the cleaned pulp immediately in water, soaked it for two to three hours, and cooked the pulp before fermentation began. They mashed, mixed by hand, and then cooked the mixture further. The cooked mixture was strained through a basket (fig. 68) and set on top of a large olla, metal pot, or wash tub (Crosswhite 1980). The straining basket was once made from desert spoon *(Dasylirion wheeleri),* but more recently from screen wire, flour sacks, or burlap bags. They retrieved the pulp and seed mixture and spread this out to dry (fig. 69). They continued to cook the cleaned and strained juice further until it was a thick, reddish brown syrup. Excess syrup could be traded or sold, with the cost ranging from 50 cents per quart in 1929 (Thackery and Leding 1929) to 7 to 10 dollars per pint in the 1980s (G. P. Nabhan, pers. comm.).

The women drained off a portion of juice and boiled the remaining moist pulp until it was a sweet, sticky, jamlike mass (Castetter and Underhill 1935). They also mixed the dried seedless pulp with water, which they boiled into syrup in an olla. When the mixture formed a "gelatin-like mass," they transferred it to a large mixing olla and beat it vigorously for 30 minutes. The interval between boiling and sealing the pulp or syrup could not be long or else it began to spoil.

FIGURE 68. (top) Juanita Ahill straining saguaro fruit for syrup after first boiling. West of Saguaro National Monument West, July 1970. Photograph by Helga Teiwes, courtesy of Arizona State Museum, University of Arizona.

FIGURE 69. (center) Noceo family's summer camp; spread out seeds are in the foreground, ramada and camp in background. Four miles southwest of Sil Nakya, July 1968. Photograph by Helga Teiwes, courtesy of Arizona State Museum, University of Arizona.

FIGURE 70. (bottom) Saguaro fruit-gathering and fruit-processing camp exhibit. Plants and People of the Sonoran Desert exhibit, Desert Botanical Garden, Phoenix, Arizona, June 1988.

Thus, it was believed that such processing was systematic, in that one load of fruit was processed entirely and then sealed before another was gathered (Thackery and Leding 1929).

That cactus utilization was most highly developed among the Tohono O'odham is reflected in how they stored not only saguaro, but organ pipe *(Stenocereus thurberi)* and prickly-pear *(Opuntia engelmannii)* fruits as well. These fruits are highly perishable and seasonal in nature. Most groups simply sun-dried the pulp, a process that usually resulted in the loss of fresh flavor and possibly nutrients (Euler and Jones 1956). By cooking the syrup, the Tohono O'odham practiced pasteurization, a process by which foods could be stored for long periods of time while retaining nutrients and taste. Boiled syrup and pulp were stored in pottery vessels covered with potsherds, leaves, cornhusks, or tin sealed in place (Thackery and Leding 1929; Bowen 1939; Euler and Jones 1956). If properly sealed, the syrup or jam could last more than a year. The Tohono O'odham sealed the vessels with either adobe mud mixed with grass or gum of lac produced by a scale insect and gathered from *Coursetia glandulosa* A. Gray (Thackery and Leding 1929). Melted beeswax was also used to seal ollas of jam (Stone 1943). They also stored jam in small, earthen jars hermetically sealed one or two feet below the ground (Whittemore 1893). At Quitovac, saguaro fruit was still used for making jam in the 1970s (Nabhan et al. 1982) and is considered by some to be a luxury fruit (R. Felger, pers. comm.).

The Tohono O'odham also used the seeds of saguaro fruit. The women dried the previously separated pulp and seeds in the sun for one day, then rubbed the mass between their hands and separated out the seeds (Castetter and Underhill 1935). They further dried the pulp on top of houses and beat out any remaining seeds with a stick. They also separated the seeds by soaking the pulp in water and skimming off the seeds that floated to the surface (Keasey 1975). They collected any remaining seeds by dipping an ocotillo branch in and out of the water. Pulp stuck to the spines and left many seeds in the water. Dried pulp could be stored and used later, when women simply broke off and boiled chunks of pulp in water to make syrup or jam. They used dried, parched, and stored seeds for meal cake or chicken feed (Castetter and Underhill 1935). By mixing seed meal with water, they made pinole; by boiling seed meal with salt and water, they made atole. Parched seeds were ground with water to yield a small amount of oil. As mentioned above, the Tohono O'odham may also have practiced the "second harvest" of the seeds in the past.

Seris collected the fruits with a gathering pole similar to the one that the Tohono O'odham and northern Pima used (Felger and Moser 1976, 1985). They prepared the fruits of saguaro much the same way as those of *pitahaya dulce (Stenocereus thurberi)* and of *cardón (Pachycereus pringlei).*

Cylindropuntia | cholla

C. acanthocarpa **(Engelmann & Bigelow) Knuth**
buckhorn cholla, tesajo

C. arbuscula **(Engelmann) Knuth**
pencil cholla, tesajo

C. bigelovii **(Engelmann) Knuth**
teddy-bear cholla, cholla del oso, cholla güerra, ciribe

C. echinocarpa **(Engelmann and Bigelow) Knuth**
silver cholla, golden cholla

C. fulgida **(Engelmann) Knuth**
chain-fruit cholla, cholla de coyote, velas de coyote

C. x *kelvinensis* **(Grant and Grant) Heath**
Gila cholla

C. leptocaulis **(de Candolle) Knuth**
desert Christmas cactus, tesajillo

C. ramosissima **(Engelmann) Knuth**
diamond cholla

C. spinosior **(Engelmann) Knuth**
cane cholla

C. thurberi **(Engelmann) Knuth**

C. versicolor **(Engelmann ex Coulter) Knuth**
staghorn cholla, tesajo, morada cholla

C. whipplei **(Engelmann and Bigelow) Knuth**
Whipple's cholla

Cylindropuntia is one of 13 genera now recognized within the subfamily Opuntioideae (Anderson 1999), which includes 33 species (Anderson 2001). Until recently, the genus *Cylindropuntia* remained taxonomically confusing, but with the work of Bruce Parfitt, Mark Baker (*in* Hickman 1993), Jon Rebman (1995a), Donald Pinkava (1999), and others its status is better understood.

Chollas played an important role in the lives of many southwestern peoples. Cholla flower buds supplied an important and nutritious green vegetable to those who knew how to prepare them for food. Those chollas that develop fleshy fruits also supplied an edible green, whereas joints were eaten only in times of food scarcity. Although potentially all have edible flower buds, only a few, in particular *C. acanthocarpa* (fig. 71), were considered an important food source. Small flowering species, such as *C. leptocaulis* and *C. ramosissima,* were generally not used.

Baked, dried buds of *C. acanthocarpa* have moderate amounts of iron, but high amounts of calcium (Greenhouse 1979; this and all of the literature citations that follow recognized chollas as being within the genus *Opuntia*). A 100-gram serving, or approximately 50 freshly baked buds, provides 1.4 milligrams of iron and 650 milligrams of calcium, or 14 percent of the recommended iron allowance and 81 percent of the recommended calcium allowance for adult males. Stone-ground ingredients of an atole, made with ground cholla buds, dry white corn, and saguaro seeds, yield an iron content five times that of cooked cholla buds alone and a calcium content three and a half times that of corn.

White Mountain and Cibecue Apaches apparently pit-baked flower buds of chollas (Buskirk 1986). Chollas providing edible flower buds within the range of the Western Apache may have included *C. acanthocarpa, C. bigelovii,* and *O. fulgida.* Other chollas include

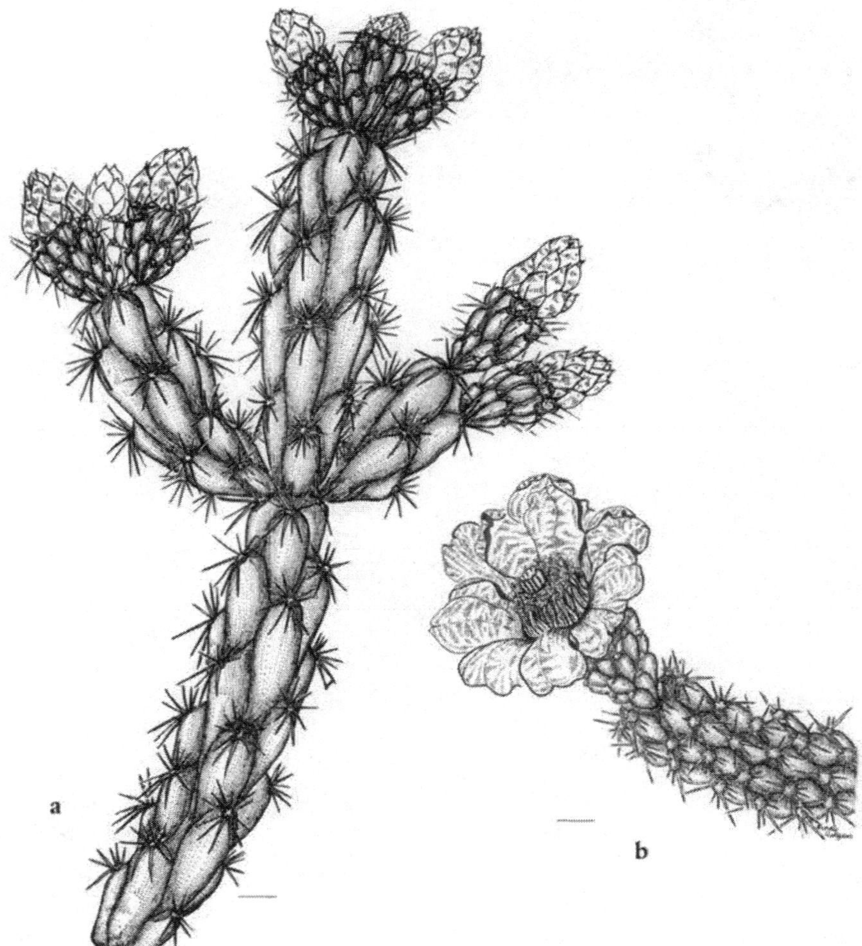

FIGURE 71. ***Cylindropuntia acanthocarpa*** (Engelm. & Bigel.) Knuth. **a.** Stems with flower buds; **b.** stem with flower.

FIGURE 72. Resident of the Gila River Pima Reservation picking cholla buds (1977). Photograph courtesy of Ruth Greenhouse.

C. spinosior and *C. whipplei.* Curiously, Edward Gifford (1932) noted that Southeastern Yavapais did not use chollas for food, despite having easy access to a number of chollas, including *C. acanthocarpa.* However, Northeastern and Western Yavapais ate the buds of *C. echinocarpa* by squeezing the boiled buds between their fingers until the inner portion of the bud "popped" into their mouths (Gifford 1936). Perhaps they also ate the flower buds of other chollas, including *C. acanthocarpa* and *C. bigelovii.*

Cylindropuntia acanthocarpa, or *hannam,* was one of the most important plant foods for the River Pima, and its use (and the use of other chollas) is better understood as a result of the work by Greenhouse (1979), Greenhouse et al. (1981), and Rea (1997). As saguaro utilization was so highly developed among the Tohono O'odham, cholla utilization was most highly developed among the River Pima. So important were cholla buds to the Gila River Pima that, except for the collecting of annual greens (or *quelites*), they are the only other wild plant that is still gathered by these people (Greenhouse 1979; Rea 1997). *Cylindropuntia acanthocarpa* flowers from April to May. In Gila River Pima territory, buds begin to emerge as soon as the weather warms, particularly after good winter rains (Rea 1997). Pima women say that cholla buds were always collected around Holy Week. They claim that if Easter is early in the spring, the flower buds develop early, and if it is later in the spring, the flower buds develop later. The number of cholla buds varies from one year to the next, their production being dependent on winter rains. Sites having the largest population of chollas in bud were selected, but gathering sites could be changed from year to year (Greenhouse et al. 1981).

There was a division of labor among the River Pima when harvesting cholla flower buds (Rea 1997). Women were the principle collectors of cholla buds, although the men sometimes participated in the collecting as well. They gathered unopened flower buds because opened flowers, although edible, were not as desirable (Greenhouse et al. 1981; Rea 1997). Carmelita Raphael described how flower buds that were beginning to open the morning of collecting were not desirable because they fell apart during the roasting (Rea 1997). Stem shoots were used if there were too few flower buds to collect because the new shoots tasted like flower buds. Pimas did not discriminate between the various colored forms of *C. acanthocarpa.*

Pima women pulled off the flower buds with a lateral twist of metal or wooden tongs (Greenhouse et al. 1981; Rea 1997), with the mature buds detaching easily (fig. 72). Before the use of metal or wooden tongs, bud pickers were made from a piece of willow branch that was split for most of its length (Rea 1997). Cholla buds could be gathered quickly if the supply was good.

As recently as the 1930s, people often processed cholla buds in the field (Castetter and Underhill 1935; Underhill 1936), but in later years processed them in the villages (Greenhouse et al. 1981; Rea 1997). Prior to the availability of pickup trucks, Pima women probably chose to roast their buds up on the bajadas rather than carry uncooked buds back to the village (Rea 1997).

The men were primarily responsible for excavating or redigging the pit, gathering the mesquite wood, and firing the pit, although women also participated in these activities (Rea 1997). The roasting pit (fig. 73) was usually dug into sandy, disturbed soil and basalt river cobbles were placed on the bottom of the pit and up

FIGURE 73. A Gila River Pima lining a cholla-bud baking pit with rocks. Photograph courtesy of Ruth Greenhouse.

the sides (Greenhouse et al. 1981). Cholla roasting pits were sometimes reused the following year, but were abandoned when it was easier to make a new pit. Pimas either filled in the abandoned pit, sometimes with trash, or let the pit fill in naturally.

Cholla roasting pits varied somewhat in size, but most were approximately 1 meter in diameter and 0.5 meter in depth and could hold 25 to 30 gallons of packed buds (Rea 1997). Women covered the very hot rocks on the bottom and sides of the pit with the somewhat succulent-leaved seepweed, *Suaeda moquinii* (Torr.) Greene, after the mesquite wood was allowed to completely burn down (Greenhouse et al. 1981; Rea 1997). They poured the cholla buds into the pit and then covered the buds with more seepweed. Pima women continued to collect, dry, and store seepweed for use with cholla bud roasting into the 1980s (Greenhouse et al. 1981).

The amount of seepweed added and the degree to which the pit was heated were important. If the layer of seepweed was too thin, the buds nearest the outside of the pile might burn or become too mushy and have to be discarded (Rea 1997). If the pit was not hot enough, the buds would be undercooked and require several additional hours. In one instance, Carmelita Raphael wanted to postpone cooking the buds because it was too windy and the heat would dissipate. A hide, canvas, or, more recently, a piece of corrugated metal roofing, was put on top of the plant material. This was then covered with soil to trap the steam produced by the buds and seepweed inside. This mass of buds was allowed to cook overnight, for approximately 12 hours. Unlike agave roasting, cholla bud roasting involved no sexual abstinence. However, there is a saying among the Gila River Pima that no one should experience any flatulence over or around the pit while the buds were baking or else the buds will not cook thoroughly (Rea 1997).

There are varying opinions regarding the best time to remove the spines from the buds. Some women removed the spines prior to baking (Thackery and Leding 1929; Curtin 1949). Most of the people with whom Amadeo Rea picked buds removed the spines from uncooked buds (Rea 1997). They put a few quarts of buds into a shallow box with a hardware cloth bottom, which acted as a sieve, although a special despining basket made out of willow twigs was once used. Women raked the buds back and forth with a

piece of saguaro rib, knocking off spines and glochids. Others roasted and dried the buds first, then removed the spines in the screened box. Ruth Greenhouse et al. (1981) observed that the women carefully removed the spines from the soft buds after 18 hours of roasting (fig. 74). Ruth Giff did not like to dry the buds first, but preferred to let them stand one day after picking before knocking off the spines and glochids (Rea 1997).

On the morning after baking, they opened the pit and tested the buds. If the buds were not thoroughly cooked, they were left in the pit until the evening. Care was taken not to overcook the buds—they should have the consistency of asparagus and not be mushy (Rea 1997). Some of the thoroughly cooked buds were eaten fresh from the pit and the rest were spread on mats, grates, or screens (fig. 75) to dry for a week (Greenhouse et al. 1981; Rea 1997). They removed any remaining spines or glochids by first rubbing the dried buds on the screens with sticks or by stirring the buds in a basket, then winnowed the buds further by their own breath (fig. 76) or by the wind.

Gila River Pima women stored the dried buds indefinitely. They rehydrated the buds when needed and cooked them for three hours with onions, seepweed or canned spinach, and chiles (Rea 1997). Others cooked them with young shoots of Wright's saltbush (*Atriplex*

FIGURE 74. (top) A Gila River Pima carefully taking cooked cholla buds out of the pit. Photograph courtesy of Ruth Greenhouse.

FIGURE 75. (bottom) Gila River Pimas drying cholla buds on screens. Photograph courtesy of Ruth Greenhouse.

wrightii Wats.; Greenhouse 1979; Greenhouse et al. 1981; Rea 1997). A more traditional and nutritious Pima food was porridge made with ground buds, dry white corn, and saguaro seeds (Greenhouse 1979). Ruth Giff remembered how people sometimes made this atole using whole-wheat flour, rather than dry white corn, to help stimulate milk flow in a new mother (Rea 1997). The meal mixture was slowly sprinkled into a quart of boiling water, cooked until it reached the consistency of a thick porridge, and then salted.

Other chollas supplying edible buds to the River Pima include *C. arbuscula, C. versicolor, C.* x *kelvinensis,* and perhaps *C. echinocarpa.* The smaller flowers of *C. arbuscula* are produced from May to June, thereby providing a food source if the spring crop of *C. acanthocarpa* was poor or missed (Rea 1997). However, plants of *C. arbuscula* are generally less numerous than those of *C. acanthocarpa* and its flowers (and fruits) are more difficult to reach. Baked flower buds of *C. arbuscula* have been described as being different than *C. acanthocarpa* and somewhat sour in taste.

Cylindropuntia versicolor is common in Tohono O'odham territory and may have once extended into Gila River Pima country near Sacaton and Casa Grande. Gila River Pimas knew the plants as a trade item from the Tohono O'odham, who came north to work in the Pima wheat harvest until the early 20th century (Rea 1997). River Pimas prepared the flower buds as they did for *C. acanthocarpa,* although most were not familiar with the plant. The taste of the cooked flower buds was considered as being different from that of *C. acanthocarpa* cooked buds.

River Pima probably did not use *C. echinocarpa* flower buds for food. The distribution of *C. echinocarpa* is outside of River Pima territory; the easternmost known population grows just south of Morristown, northwest of the White Tank Mountains in northwestern Maricopa County (Pinkava 1999). The flower buds of *C. leptocaulis* were not used for food (Rea 1997), probably because of their small size.

The Tohono O'odham prepared cholla buds in a manner similar to that of the Pima. They gathered then pit-baked or boiled the buds of *C. acanthocarpa* and *C. fulgida* in May (Castetter and Underhill 1935; Nabhan et al. 1982). Again, the women were responsible for collecting and baking the buds (Castetter and Underhill 1935). After the buds were collected, the women brought them in coiled baskets to a central point where "an old woman" directed the baking (which is different from the Pima method). María

FIGURE 76. Edna Jones winnowing (by blowing on) cooked cholla buds. Photograph courtesy of Ruth Greenhouse.

Chona described how the buds and joints were collected and prepared (Underhill 1936:8):

> When its buds were green we all went and stayed for many days picking them up in the hills. [The women] broke off the new stems with tongs and rolled them around on the ground to get the thorns off, and then baked them all night in a big pit. When the big pit was roasting slowly in the night, the women threw green cholla stems on the campfire ashes to cook. We pulled them [stems and buds] out, knocked off the thorns, and ate them hot. Ah, good, good food! We ate nothing else for those three weeks.

The women carried home the roasted portions of cholla and continued to go out for more until a large area surrounding the village was picked over.

Tom Childs (1954:35) briefly described some of the native plant foods eaten by his Hiá ceḍ O'odham friends and in-laws, with whom he lived for most of his life. Of the cholla, he writes:

> There is another flower they dry and eat. It is taken from a tall cholla cactus. The bud when in flower is pinkish to yellow. When they gather this flower they let it shrink some [a practice similar to that described by Gila River Pima Ruth Giff], and then beat the stickers off with a light stick, then roast it to get all the stickers off it. But they still leave enough on them that it makes it hard for me to eat them, although they are slightly sourish and rather nice tasting. They are called *'chi'odima'*.

Betty Melvion Childs remembered how important desert foods such as the cholla were to her and lamented that the practice of gathering these foods has all but died out. She described how her people gathered the cholla buds and baked them (Bell et al. 1980:100):

> We come back here [perhaps Dome or Wellton] when the saguaro cactus fruit and cholla buds are ready for picking [probably on separate trips]. My grandmother told me after gathering the cholla buds, they build a big fire. When the fire turned to coals, they spread the cholla buds on the coals. On top of the cholla buds they spread a cloth or sack. It is covered securely. This method ripens the cholla buds and makes the stickers come off easier. Sometime when the cholla buds dried, my grandmother ground the cholla buds and made atole to drink. They also cooked the cholla buds and fried them with onions.

Her friend Angie Puffer still collected and cooked cholla buds; however, when offered some of Angie's collection, Betty did not want any because they were full of spines.

According to Edward Castetter and Willis Bell (1951), the Lower Colorado River groups made no use of cholla buds, despite the fact that *C. acanthocarpa, C. bigelovii,* and *C. echinocarpa* were available to them. However, Maricopas gathered the buds of *C. acanthocarpa* var. *major* (Engelmann) Pinkava (cited as *O. acanthocarpa* var. *ramosa*) in May. Cahuillas collected and steamed the buds of *C. bigelovii* in a pit (Barrows 1900; Bean and Saubel 1972), in a manner similar to that previously described, then ate the buds immediately or dried them for future use.

William Kelly (1977:40) had no information on the Cocopa use of cactus for food, "although these plants were unquestionably important to the Western Cocopa, who made occasional food-gathering and visiting trips into Baja California." The Cocopa would have had access to *C. bigelovii, C. echinocarpa,* and *C. munzii* (Wolf) Backenberg.

Although chollas are well represented in Baja California, there has been little, if anything, written on their use for food by indigenous cultures. Whether chollas that produced flower buds of sufficient size were ever eaten is not known. Flowering periods vary within each species, but many flower from March through May into August. *Cylindropuntia cholla* (Weber) Knuth (chain-link cholla, *cholla pelona*) flowers from February through October (Rebman 1995a) and thus would have provided a source of food for a relatively long period of time. The Southern Diegueño and Kamia had access to *C. bigelovii, C. californica* (Torrey & A. Gray) Knuth (California cholla), *C. echinocarpa,* and *C. munzii.* Paipais, Tipais, and Kiliwas had access to many chollas, including *C. alcahes* (Weber) Knuth *(clavellina, cholla brincadora), C. bigelovii, C. californica, C. munzii, C. prolifera* (Engelm.) Knuth (coastal cholla), *C. tesajo* (Engelm.) Knuth *(tesajo),* and possibly *C. cholla* and *C. molesta* (Brandegee) Knuth (*agujilla,* cholla).

Fr. del Barco (1980) spent most of his 30 years at the mission of San Francisco Javier, which is located about 50 kilometers southwest of Loreto, where he worked among the Cochimí (Léon-Portilla *in* del Barco 1980). Despite the probable presence of six species in the area, del Barco described only two types of chollas, both with fleshy, spineless fruit. He did not mention any use of chollas by the native inhabitants and described the chollas as being "totally useless and harmful" (del Barco 1980:175).

Chollas that produce fleshy fruits could all be potentially edible. Juicy, spineless fruits were probably preferred, gathered and prepared in a manner similar to that described for preparing flower buds or eaten raw. Chollas with fleshy, spineless fruits are *C. arbuscula, C. fulgida, C.* x *kelvinensis, C. leptocaulis, C. versicolor, C. prolifera, C. thurberi* (Engelm.) Knuth (Thurber's cholla), *C. alcahes, C. cholla,* and *C. molesta* (Rebman 1995a). Fleshy-fruited species, with or without spines, include *C. calmalliana* (Coulter) Knuth. Those producing moderately fleshy fruits are *C.* x *tetracantha* (Toumey) Knuth, *C. spinosior,* and *C. bigelovii.*

A White Mountain Apache woman related that they gathered the yellow cholla fruit (probably fruit of *C. spinosior*) "during a certain limited season" (Buskirk

FIGURE 77. ***Cylindropuntia versicolor*** (Engelm. ex Coulter) Knuth. Plant with numerous fruits. Esperero trailhead, Santa Catalina Mountains, Pima County, Arizona, August 1988.

FIGURE 78. ***Cylindropuntia arbuscula*** (Engelm.) Knuth. Stems with fruits. Desert Botanical Garden, Phoenix, Arizona, June 1988.

1986:180). They steamed and pit-baked the fruits for one day, then dried and stored these fruits to be later boiled, with their seeds, in fat or soup. A Cibecue Apache said that fruits were picked when ripe and yellow in the fall. They cooked the fruits in a fire, then dried and "cracked" them to remove the seeds. Seeds were not discarded, but roasted and ground with corn. Aleš Hrdlička (1908:257) noted that San Carlos Apaches parched, ground, and boiled the seeds of a "high-branching opuntia" (possibly *C. arbuscula, C. fulgida,* or *C. versicolor*) into a mush or ate the flour made from ground seeds.

Edward Gifford (1936) noted that the Northeastern and Western Yavapai collected the fruits of *C. echinocarpa,* brushed off the spines with branches of rabbitbrush (*Chrysothamnus* spp.) or buckwheat (*Eriogonum* spp.), and boiled the fruits. *Cylindropuntia echinocarpa* fruits are dry and spiny at maturity. Gifford also described how some Western Yavapais stirred the fruits of a cactus, possibly a cholla (or prickly-pear, *Opuntia engelmannii*), in a burden basket to remove the spines before eating the fruits. Chollas having fleshy or somewhat fleshy fruits accessible to these Yavapai groups include *C. bigelovii, C. leptocaulis, C. spinosior* (at the plant's northwestern range), and *C. whipplei.*

Frank Russell (1908) described how the River Pima collected and ate the fruit of *C. versicolor* (fig. 77) raw or, more often, baked in a manner similar to how they baked the flower buds of *C. acanthocarpa.* Leonora Curtin (1949) also noted that the River Pima gathered the fruit of both *C. arbuscula* and *C. versicolor* in the spring and placed them in a basket to remove the spines (possibly glochids). George Webb, a River Pima, related how his people picked and dried the fruits before storing them or boiled the green, fresh fruit with saltbush (*Atriplex* sp.), the taste being more sour than that of the cooked flower buds of *C. acanthocarpa.* Mature fruits of *C. arbuscula* (fig. 78) develop in the summer and, although green and tinged with purple, they are spineless and possess only glochids. Fruits of *C. versicolor* are also spineless and develop during the summer and early fall, although they will persist through the winter, sometimes proliferating and forming small chains. However, *C. versicolor* does not grow as far north as the Gila River Reservation (Pinkava 1999). Gila River Pimas knew *C. versicolor* only as a trade item and received *C. versicolor* buds and flowers from the Tohono O'odham (Rea 1997).

Gila River Pimas had easier access to populations of *C. spinosior* on the eastern end of their reservation, where they gathered the spineless, yellow, fleshy fruits (Rea 1997). George Kyyitan thought that the taste was not bitter and compared favorably with that of cooked flower buds of *C. acanthocarpa.* He also said that the plants once grew in the Gila riverbed toward Snaketown, but were washed away by floods.

Cylindropuntia x *kelvinensis* is a hybrid between *C. spinosior* and *C. fulgida* that produces spineless fruits in small chains. Plants once grew from Florence to Casa Blanca, or Bapchule (Kearney et al. 1960), the latter locality noted by George Kyyitan (Rea 1997). Lyman Benson (1969) cited an individual as growing along the Gila River near Sacaton. By the 1980s, plants became more restricted in this region due to flooding and agriculture. Their present location on the reservation is on unfarmed flats between Sacaton Flats and Blackwater (Rea 1997), although a number of individuals grow east of the reservation within southern Gila, extreme eastern Maricopa, Pinal, and northern Pima Counties (Pinkava 1999). The Gila River Pima ate the fruits of *kokavi hannam,* a name that includes both *C. spinosior* and *C.* x *kelvinensis* (Rea 1997). They described the taste as being good and not bitter.

No Gila River Pima knew that the fruits of "white cholla," or *C. fulgida,* could be eaten (Rea 1997). However, they may have once eaten the fruits, at least in starvation times, because the species is mentioned in one version of the Creation Story. Chain-fruit cholla fruit provided a food source year-round and was significant as a famine food, because most cholla buds were available for only a few weeks.

The River Pima, Tohono O'odham, and Seri also ate the mature, red fruits of *C. leptocaulis* (fig. 80), which were available year-round (Curtin 1949; Nabhan et al. 1982; Felger and Moser 1985; Rea 1997). Gila River Pimas no longer eat the fruits, although some remembered eating them as children (Rea 1997). Aleš Hrdlička (1908) observed that, to a limited extent, Gila River Pimas ate the fruits raw, without the seeds, at the turn of the century. Leonora Curtin (1949) noted that River Pimas still gathered the fruits in baskets, nearly 40 years later. They brushed off most of the glochids with a branch and removed the spines (this is questionable because fruits of *C. leptocaulis* have no spines) with a cloth before eating the fruits raw.

Gila River Pimas did not use the fruits of *C. bigelovii* for food, but plants were nonetheless important to them (Rea 1997). The heavily spined cholla was formerly used as a barricade against "night marauders" in the fields because it was "recognized as the most effectually armed of the many cacti and is the symbol in Pima lore of impenetrability" (Russell 1908:92).

The Tohono O'odham and Ónavas Pima dried, boiled, and then ate the fruits of *C. fulgida* (fig. 79; Castetter and Underhill 1935; Curtin 1949; Nabhan et al. 1982; Rea 1997). The Seri extensively used the fruits (but not the flower buds) of *C. fulgida* as recently as the 1980s (Felger and Moser 1985). Larger-than-average fruits (up to 13 centimeters in length) were selected from specific stands and from plants that consistently produced larger fruits (Nabhan and Felger 1985; Felger and Moser 1985). The Seri removed the fruits by carefully twisting them with their fingers or by knocking them off with a stick (Felger and Moser 1985). Seris removed most of the glochids by sweeping the fruits

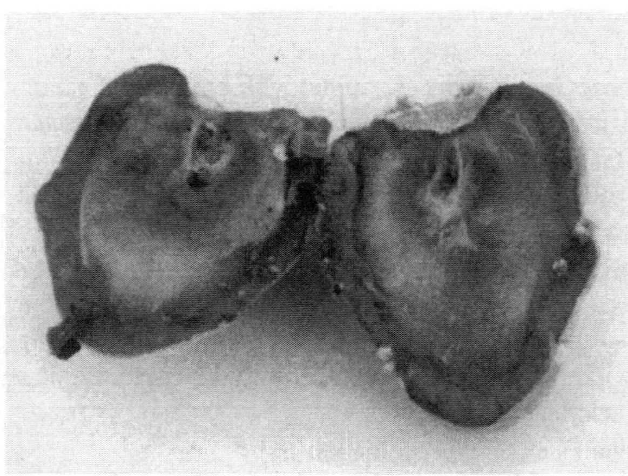

FIGURE 79. ***Cylindropuntia fulgida*** (Engelm.) Knuth and close-up of fruits. One-half mile north of Organ Pipe Cactus National Monument, Pima County, Arizona, March 1988.

with branches of creosote bush, wiping the fruit with a wet cloth, or by rolling the fruit in sand. Back at camp, they soaked the fruits in water to remove any remaining spines. Harvesters sliced away the skin or peeled it off with their fingernails or knives, leaving the fleshy, green inner part of the fruit and seeds for them to eat fresh, with or without the addition of salt. Seris also briefly roasted the flesh in hot coals. They also relished an edible gum that was exuded on the branches where they dislodged the fruit. Seris ate the gum as is; boiled it with sugar or honey; or toasted, ground, and mixed it with water or with the juice of cooked *Agave subsimplex.*

The Cahuilla ate the fruits of a "very furry cactus with round jointed stems two to three feet high," according to David Barrows (1900:68). He further described the plant as being "brown in color and grows in communities … to the exclusion of almost everything else." Plants "throw off extremely disagreeable balls of spines … its fruit [which he never saw] is said to be very good." Based on his brief description, Barrows may have been referring to *C. bigelovii,* or possibly *C. alcahes.* According to Bean and Saubel (1972), Cahuillas also ate the fruits and stems of *C. ramosissima.* If not for the fact that this is the only pencil-type cholla in southern California, the use of its fruits for food would be doubted, due to their exceedingly spiny nature.

What little is written on the use of chollas for food by Baja California inhabitants requires clarification. Any of the fleshy-fruited chollas could have provided a food source to local inhabitants. It was said that Baja Californians ate the fruits of *C. imbricata* (Haw.) Knuth and *C. tesajo* raw (Hake 1980, 1983). However, *C. imbricata* is a Chihuahuan Desert species, found far from the peninsula or neighboring islands (Pinkava 1999), and fruits of *C. tesajo* are dry at maturity. The Kiliwa collected and ate the seeds of two chollas, which were identified as *C. bigelovii* and *C. cholla,* in July (Meigs 1939). Chollas in their territory include *C. bigelovii, C. munzii, C. ramosissima,* and *C. tesajo* (Rebman 1995a).

Fr. del Barco (1980:174) noted that the small plant he called *tesajo* produced a type of fruit, or *tuna,* that "never quite ripens so that it could be eaten." Cholla species that the Cochimí may have encountered all produce fleshy fruits. Del Barco did not look upon these plants with favor as he wrote, "there is a great abundance of this useless and even harmful plant in all [Baja] California." However, he did concede that "because of the great lack of firewood [in the more northern missions], one is forced to make use of dry tasajo to supply part of this need, and for this reason it has this small usefulness there." It is interesting that groups inhabiting central and southern Baja California may not have used the numerous chollas available to them for food, considering that they roasted and pit-baked agaves.

As with agaves and other taxa, it is probable that Hohokam and later cultures cultivated chollas around their homes. Cultivation of a plant for food increased an otherwise limited resource for use or trade and decreased the need to make dangerous forays into surrounding areas. Chollas may have been cultivated in areas where the demand was high relative to the abundance of chollas in larger, more permanent sites, as suggested by the high concentration of cholla pollen (Fish 1984). This contrasted with the relatively low amount of cholla pollen found with seasonally occupied sites adjacent to dense cholla stands, where there would be no impetus to increase this resource. The Hohokam may have cultivated cholla at La Ciudad (in the vicinity of Phoenix) because cholla pollen was found in

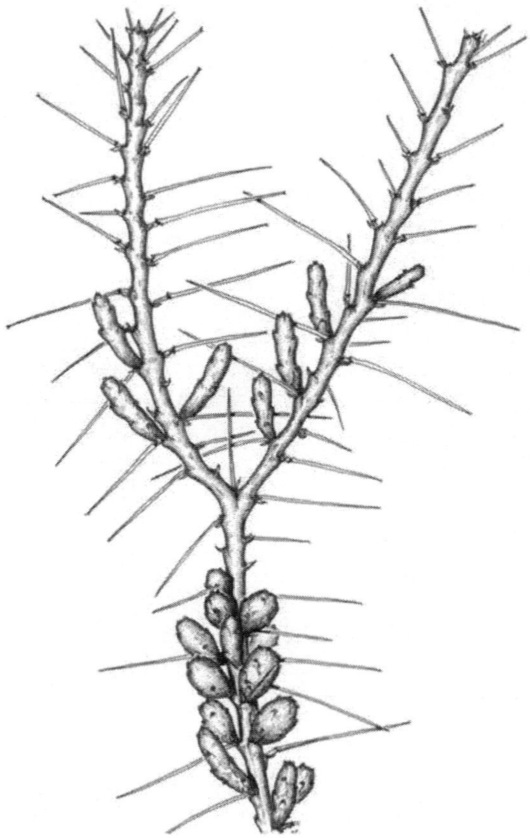

FIGURE 80. ***Cylindropuntia leptocaulis*** (DC.) Knuth. Plant with mature, red fruits. Desert Botanical Garden, Phoenix, Arizona, August 1988.

every house and trash pit (Bohrer 1987; Gish 1987), whereas saguaro and hedgehog cactus seeds were rarely recovered (Bohrer 1991). Vorsila Bohrer (1991) suggested that cultivation of cholla would make sense, given that a large number of people inhabiting the Salt River valley were competing for the relatively scarce and limited cholla buds from the bajadas.

Exceptionally large and selectively picked fruits of *C. fulgida* can be grown from the variable wild populations and exhibit traits that render them exceptionally good-tasting and prolific (Nabhan and Felger 1985). Traits such as thinner ovary walls and smaller seeds can be selected. Such selection and cultivation has been suggested for numerous taxa, including a cholla that has arisen through the hybridization of *C.* x *viridiflora* (Britton & Rose) Knuth and *C. imbricata* (see Housely 1975). Human activity, such as the use of chollas in ceremonies and as food sources, may have played a major role in their distribution and hybridization.

Echinocactus | barrel cactus, cottontop cactus, devil's pincushion, bisnaga meloncillo, biznaga de dulce, bisnaga

E. polycephalus **Engelmann & Bigelow var.** ***polycephalus***
many-headed barrel cactus, cottontop cactus, devil's-head

Echinocactus polycephalus var. *polycephalus* grows sporadically throughout the Mohave Desert and in the Sonoran Desert of southwestern Arizona and northern Sonora (Chamberland 1991). A "watery juice" was said to have been procured from the pulp, which was also used to make a type of cactus candy in a manner similar to that described for *Ferocactus* (Coville 1892; Standley 1924; Morton 1963; Balls 1970; Hedrick 1972; Zepeda 1985). In 1983, Beatrice Melvin, a Hiá ceḍ O'odham, related to Ofelia Zepeda (1985:49) how her people used to gather the devil barrel cactus. They cut the "skin off," sliced its "meat," or pulp, and cooked it, usually by boiling or sometimes roasted "inside a pit, ... and then more recently ... made candy out of it, the cactus candy." They added sugar to the boiling pulp or sometimes even chocolate. Mrs. Melvin considered the cooked pulp very good tasting.

The Panamints of southern California pried the seeds from the fruits of *E. polycephalus* var. *polycephalus* and ate them fresh or dried them to be later parched and ground for meal (Coville 1892). They considered the seeds especially good because they remained fresh and edible until spring, when foods were scarce. Havasupais also ate the seeds of *E. polycephalus* var. *xeranthemoides* Coulter fresh or dried and parched (Weber and Seaman 1985). Both varieties flower in July. Their fruits mature about one month after flowering and may persist on the plant for several months (Chamberland 1991). The small seeds tend to remain wedged together until the fruit is torn open. The Cahuilla gathered and ate the flower buds of *E. polycephalus* var. *polycephalus* in May and June (Bean and Saubel 1972).

Echinocactus horizonthalonius Lemaire var. *nicholii* L. Benson is a rare cactus that is federally listed as an endangered species by the U.S. Fish and Wildlife Service. It grows in only a few populations in southern Arizona and northwestern Sonora. The distinction of this variety from *E. horizonthalonius* var. *horizonthalonius*, a common Chihuahuan Desert cactus, is questioned. Chamberland (1995) believes the Sonoran Desert populations are simply disjunct populations of the more wide-ranging Chihuahuan Desert species. It is not known if its Arizona and Sonoran populations were ever used for food.

Echinocereus | hedgehog cactus

E. brandegeei **(Coulter) Schumann**

E. englemanni **(Parry) Lemaire**
Engelmann's hedgehog, strawberry cactus, saint's cactus, sinita barbona

E. fasciculatus **(Engelmann ex B. Jackson) L. Benson (syn.,** ***E. fendleri*** **[Engelmann] F. Seitz var.** ***fasciculatus*** **[Engelmann ex B. Jackson] N. Taylor)**

E. nicholii **(L. Benson) Parfitt**
Nichol's hedgehog

Echinocereus is represented within the Sonoran Desert by 13 species, of which 8 are endemic to the Baja California mainland and adjacent gulf and Pacific islands (Taylor 1985). The juicy fruits of most, if not all, hedgehog species are probably edible and are eaten either raw or preserved.

Echinocereus engelmannii (fig. 81), *E. fasciculatus*, and

FIGURE 81. (above) ***Echinocereus engelmannii*** (Parry) Lemaire. Desert Botanical Garden, Phoenix, Arizona, June 1988.

FIGURE 82. (right) Mature fruits of ***Echinocereus engelmannii.*** Note fallen spine clusters. South Mountain, Maricopa County, Arizona, May 1988.

E. nicholii flower from March through May and soon develop juicy fruits. *Echinocereus brandegeei,* a stout-spined hedgehog that inhabits the driest region of Mexico in the Vizcaíno and Magdalena Deserts of Baja California, flowers from July through October and produces relatively large, juicy fruits in late summer and early fall (Wiggins 1964; Taylor 1985).

The pulp of mature *E. engelmannii* fruits (figs. 81, 82) is pink or white and is sweet and pleasant tasting. The pulp is rich in sugar and the seeds are high in fat (Benson 1969). Spines fall from the mature fruit, making the tasty food even more desirable to wildlife, which quickly consume the pulp and seeds. Ruth Giff, a Gila River Pima, said that one had to be quick to get the fruits or else the animals discovered them first (Rea 1997). River Pimas ate hedgehog fruits at the turn of the century (Russell 1908) and mid 1900s (Curtin 1949). Its use as a food is still remembered by some within the past decade, although hedgehog cacti are not known by the present generation of Gila River Pima (Rea 1997). They ate the fruits raw, as soon as they collected them, or sometimes ate dried fruits. The more mature the fruits, the sweeter they become. Even some Anglos appreciated the fruits of *E. engelmannii.* John Dobbs described how "the Indians prepare them with cream and sugar and no white hostess ever served a more delicious drink" (Dobbs 1933:42).

The use of hedgehog fruits by riverine inhabitants in the Salt and Gila River valleys can be traced back to the Hohokam. Excavations, particularly at a site called Los Hornos located in the floodplain just southwest of Twin Butte in Tempe, were rich in hedgehog seeds. Seeds were found at levels higher than expected

(Gasser 1982), suggesting that plants may have been cultivated by the Hohokam for use as a trade item (Gasser and Kwiatkowski 1991a, 1991b). However, *E. engelmannii* var. *acicularis* L. Benson habitat includes the floodplain as well as desert bajadas and hills. Plants are still commonly found along the Gila River floodplain in areas not yet converted to agricultural fields or sand and gravel operations (A. Rea, pers. comm.)

According to Hiá ceḍ O'odham Chico Shuni, his people ate the fruits of both *E. fasciculatus* and *E. nicholii.* The taste of *E. fasciculatus* fruits was described as being like that of cantaloupe (Nabhan 1989b). I find the fruits of *E. nicholii* to be even sweeter and somewhat better in taste. Hiá ceḍ O'odhams distinguished *E. fasciculatus* fruits, called *moihindam'i:svig,* from those of *E. nicholii,* called *'i:svig.* That *E. fasciculatus* fruits are a marked folk taxon and those of *E. nicholii* are not suggests that the fruits of *E. nicholii* were used more or longer by the Hiá ceḍ O'odham.

Tohono O'odham continued to eat the fruits of *E. fasciculatus* var. *fasciculatus* in the 1970s at Quitovac, Sonora (Nabhan et al. 1982). Seris ate hedgehog fruit fresh as a snack because fruits were never abundant (Felger and Moser 1976, 1985, cited as *E. fendleri*).

Little has been written on the use of the smaller cacti in Baja California. Inhabitants of central and southern Baja California ate the fruits of *E. brandegeei* (Hake 1980, 1983). Audrey Weiss (1994) was told that Tipais enjoyed the sweet fruits of *E. engelmannii,* which to them tasted like strawberries.

Ferocactus | biznaga, barrel cactus

F. cylindraceus **(Engelmann) Orcutt (syn., *F. acanthodes* [Lemaire] Britton & Rose)**
California barrel cactus, biznaga

F. emoryi **(Engelmann) Orcutt (syn., *F. covillei* Britton & Rose)**
Emory's barrel cactus, biznaga

F. herrarae **Ortega**
biznaga

F. viridescens **(Torrey & A. Gray) Britton & Rose**
biznaga

F. wislizeni **(Engelmann) Britton & Rose**
compass barrel, biznaga de agua

Of the 15 species and 22 taxa currently recognized as growing within the Sonoran Desert, only six species and seven taxa grow on the mainland of Mexico and the United States. The remaining nine species and 15 taxa are endemic to Baja California and the adjacent islands (Wiggins 1964; Lindsay et al. 1996; Anderson 2001; J. Rebman, pers. comm.). Interspecific hybridization is a common phenomenon on the peninsula and has contributed to not only taxonomic confusion, but ethnographic confusion as well. Such confusion is not as great for the mainland species.

The literature abounds with accounts of drinking stem pulp juice of barrel cactus as a thirst-quencher, although it is often unclear as to which cactus is preferred. Obtaining any measurable amount of liquid is difficult, and its taste varies from intolerable to barely tolerable. Early descriptions of how one obtained the so-called thirst-saving juice were often deceptively ambiguous (or exemplified the dire situation one was experiencing). The thirsty person simply cut off the top of the cactus and mashed the pulp with a hatchet or club to obtain "a clear, pleasant-tasting liquid" (Palmer 1871; Havard 1896; Castetter 1935; Saunders 1948). Edward Palmer (1871:417) offered this: "Travelers in passing through the cactus wastes often resort to this plant to quench their thirst, its interior containing a soft white watery substance, of slightly acid taste, which is rather pleasant when chewed. It is a common sight to see on each side of the road these plants with a large perforation made by the thirsty traveler." Lt. William Emory (1848:65) was quite intrigued with a type of barrel cactus *(F. wislizeni):* "I found what was to us a very great vegetable curiosity, a cactus, 18 inches high, and 18 inches in its greatest diameter, containing 20 vertical volutes, armed with strong spines. When the traveler is parched with thirst, one of these split open, will give sufficient liquid to afford relief."

Frederick Coville (1903:503) was especially interested in certain desert plants that were used as sources of water. He noted that the Seri and Tohono O'odham "betake themselves to the water stored in cactuses," in particular *F. emoryi* and *F. wislizeni* (figs. 83, 84), their juice being "sweet and palatable." While seeking a location for a desert botanical laboratory for the Carnegie Institution in February 1903, Coville and D. T. MacDougal had an opportunity to observe the extraction of juice from the *biznaga,* approximately 12 kilometers west of the railroad station of Torres, Sonora:

> The plant selected was about 1 meter high and .5 meter in diameter. Its top was first sliced off, exposing the white interior. It was evident that this was

> saturated with water, but the structure of the tissue was such that the water did not exude of its own accord. The Indian cut a stake of palo verde (*Parkinsonia microphylla* [sic]) about 7.5 centimeters in diameter at the larger and blunt end, and with this proceeded to mash the white flesh of the cactus into a pulp. As the churning progressed a bowl was formed in the top of the cactus, and when a suitable quantity of pulp had accumulated in it the Indian, taking this up handful by handful, squeezed out the water into the bowl, throwing the rejected pulp upon the ground.
>
> From the upper 20 centimeters of the cactus about 3 liters of water was obtained. Its flavor may be described as very slightly salty and somewhat herbaceous. Any really thirsty traveler would have drunk it without hesitation, and our Papago, although he had had plenty of water from the supply we carried, drank the cactus juice with evident pleasure.

Coville was told that there was "no deleterious effect through drinking a quantity of the water, unless one subjects himself immediately afterwards to violent physical exercise." Coville added that the natives used the cactus juice, "if need be, for mixing bread, and evidently it could be devoted to any camp use."

Likewise, John Dobbs (1933:42) generously conferred laurels to the cactus:

> Along the dreary way, at frequent intervals, in lieu of streams or fountains, Nature has posted relays of food and water in many grotesque green barrels, a foot across and nearly ten feet high—the barrel cactus *(Echinocactus covillei)* [sic], from which abundance of refreshing water is obtained by cutting off the top of the plant and crushing the fleshy part within to a pulp with a convenient stick or stone. The water is cool and invigorating after fatigue as well as ample in each plant for the necessities of one person for one day.

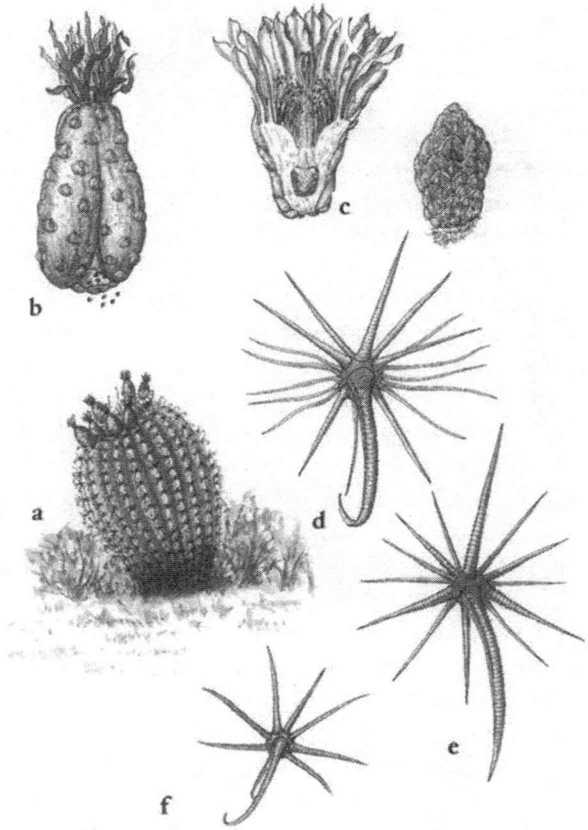

FIGURE 83. (top) ***Ferocactus wislizeni*** (Engelm.) Britton & Rose. **a.** Habit; **b.** mature fruit; **c.** flower and flower bud; **d.** spine cluster, author's home, South Mountain area, Maricopa County, Arizona; **e.** ***F. cylindraceus*** (Engelm.) Orcutt spine cluster; **f.** ***F. emoryi*** (Engelm.) Orcutt spine cluster.

FIGURE 84. (bottom) ***Ferocactus wislizeni*** habit with flowers and flower buds. Santa Rita Mountains, Santa Cruz County, Arizona, August 1988.

To obtain liquid from the pulp requires one to slice through the thick spines. Bighorn sheep, who appear to rely heavily on barrel cactus for moisture during drought, spend considerable time pawing and butting individual *F. cylindraceus* to obtain the liquid (Warrick and Krausman 1989).

Western Apaches cut and pounded the pulp of *F. cylindraceus* to obtain water (Buskirk 1986), the San Carlos group doing so only when "extremely thirsty" (Hrdlička 1908). River Pimas were well aware of the use of the barrel cactus as an emergency supply of water (Russell 1908; Curtin 1949; Rea 1997). George Webb described the taste of the liquid as being neither sweet, sour, nor bitter (Curtin 1949). The Cahuilla valued *F. cylindraceus* for its thirst-quenching character, which, according to various tales, frequently saved lives (Barrows 1900, cited as *Echinocactus cylindraceus*). However, Bean and Saubel (1972, cited as *E. acanthodes*) made no reference to its use for liquid.

Not all barrel cacti produce a potable liquid, and biochemical analyses and a comparison of species might explain the differences. The presence of oxalic acid in the juice may make it bitter and cause some people to become nauseated. To the Seri, the juice of *F. cylindraceus* is not potable; if they eat the pulp, they will develop a headache (Felger and Moser 1976, 1985, cited as *F. acanthodes*). The Seri also considered the liquid extracted from *F. emoryi* to be too strong and dangerous and to cause upset stomach, diarrhea, aching muscles, and inability to walk (Felger and Moser 1976, 1985, cited as *F. covillei*).

However, the Seri collected the pulp juice from *F. wislizeni* as a substitute for fresh water (Felger and Moser 1976, 1985). The juice was especially important to them during the hot, dry months of late spring and early summer. They believed that a leaning barrel cactus contained more liquid than an erect plant; this may be a way to distinguish *F. wislizeni,* which is barrel-shaped and often leans to the southwest (figs. 83, 84), from the tall, erect *F. cylindraceus.* The Seri first burned off the spines to get potable water from *F. wislizeni.* They uprooted the cactus or severed the plant just above its roots, chopped the plant open, then scraped out the juicy pulp. They also obtained liquid from the pulp by poking the pulp with sticks until the pulp was mashed and then squeezed out the liquid from the pieces of pulp into a container.

Coville (1903:504) noted that the juice from different *biznagas* had a different taste: "A bisnaga of approximately spherical form (perhaps *F. wislizeni*) furnishes a more palatable water than the cylindrical specimens many years older [possibly *F. cylindraceus*], and care is taken to use for a masher a wood which has no bitter, resinous, or poisonous qualities."

Although obtaining water was a primary concern for the native inhabitants of the central desert region of Baja California, there was only very "casual" mention of obtaining moisture from *biznaga* (Sales 1956; Venegas and Burriel 1966). Fr. del Barco did not mention any native's use of the pulp for water.

The stem pulp of barrel cacti was often used for food as well. Edward Palmer (1871:417) described an important meal prepared by Western Apaches and Yavapais:

> An Indian, when traveling and wishing to make a meal, selects a large plant, three feet or more long and two in diameter, cuts it down and hollows it out so as to form a trough; into this he throws the soft portions of the pulpy substance which surrounds the central woody axis, and adds meat, roots, seeds, meal, fruits, or any edible thing on hand; water is added, and the whole mixed and, as they cool, are taken out, licked clean, reheated, and returned to the cooking vessel, until the mixture is thoroughly boiled.

Two generations ago, River Pimas cut the pulp of *F. wislizeni* into strips that they boiled all day (Hrdlička 1908; Russell 1908; Curtin 1949; Rea 1997). They often cooked the strips with alternating layers of mesquite beans in a cooking olla and occasionally boiled the pulp with sugar (Russell 1908). When asked what it tasted like, Gila River Pima Sylvester Matthias told Amadeo Rea (1997) that it was something like a green casaba, although apparently he had never eaten the pulp.

Cooked strips of barrel cactus were popular among the early settlers. They obtained the pulp from the Tohono O'odham, who pared off the "rind" (epidermis) and spines of large plants and let the pulp remain several days "to bleed" (Palmer 1871). They then cut the pulp into pieces, boiled the pieces in either saguaro or *pitahaya dulce (Stenocereus thurberi)* fruit syrup, separated the pulp from the syrup, and dried the pulp. Edward Palmer (1871) noted that the pieces of pulp resembled and tasted as good as candied citron. Hiá ceḍ O'odhams roasted the pulp of the stem of *F. cylindraceus* or *F. wislizeni* in a pit and sliced and ate the "meat" (Zepeda 1985). The Seri ate the pulp only as a survival food (Felger and Moser 1976, 1985). Fr. del Barco (1980:163) noted that the tender, juicy pulp of *biznaga* is made into a very good preserve in "various parts of New Spain," but not in Baja California. However, Tipais still consider the pulp of young, small plants of *F. cylindraceus* to be a delicious food when cut into pieces and preserved with honey, sugar, or brown sugar (Weiss 1994). Howard Gentry noted that the native people ate the "meat," or pulp of *F. herrarae* (Gentry 1942, cited as *F. wislizeni;* Martin et al. 1998).

The pulp of barrel-cactus stems was made into a type of candy that was sold in the United States and Mexico. The great demand for this novelty item made the business profitable, particularly in the 1920s and 1930s. Sylvester Matthias remembered that the candy was sold in Mexican markets, from homes, or by peddlers to anyone camping in the 1920s (Rea 1997). William Bright (1935:20) angrily noted how barrel cactus was used and impacted in California for the purpose of making cactus candy during the 1930s: "There are those, here in Los Angeles, who make it a business to dispatch a truck, every few weeks, to the deserts some hundred or more miles out, and there cut down the largest and finest specimens of *Ferocactus [cylindraceus],* or Barrel Cactus. These plants are brought to town, their spines burned off, the outside cut off with a hatchet and the body cut up into little squares, boiled with sugar and then offered to the public as 'Cactus Candy.'" So many plants had been vandalized and hauled away that, according to Bright (1935:20), there was no *biznaga* left in Los Angeles County. Cactus candy has little taste, as pointed out by Bright, who exclaimed that "candy made from gelatine has more body and as much flavor." People made and bought the candy because "they think it is clever to send a box of cactus candy back East to friends," even though most people did not care much for it.

The flowers and flower buds (figs. 83, 84) provided food to native peoples and their harvest was not so destructive. The Cahuilla usually parboiled the flower buds of *F. cylindraceus* to remove any bitterness or fried the flower buds with or without chiles (Bean and Saubel 1972, cited as *Echinocactus acanthodes*). They considered the opened flowers to be more bitter than flower buds, but cooked them nonetheless. *Ferocactus cylindraceus* flowers from spring to early summer.

The Cocopa favored the buds of a barrel cactus (Alvarez de Williams 1987, cited as *F. peninsulae*); the group had access to *F. cylindraceus. Ferocactus peninsulae* (Engelm. ex Weber) Britton & Rose grows in central and south-central Baja California (Wiggins 1964, 1980; Lindsay et al. 1996). Cocopas blanched the flower buds in two or three changes of water and then either cooked the buds in oil, steamed the buds, or added the buds to meat or fish dishes (Alvarez de Williams 1987). Peveril Meigs (1939, cited as *Ferocactus*) noted that in June the Kiliwa collected and boiled the flower buds of *F. cylindraceus* with salt or fried the buds. He described the flower buds as having "a delicious, delicate flavor." Tipais continue to eat the flower buds of *F. cylindraceus.* They boil the buds in water, then cook them with tomatoes, onion, and garlic (Weiss 1994, cited as *F. acanthodes*). In the town of Sierra San Francisco in south-central Baja California, inhabitants also collect and cook the flower buds of *F. emoryi* var. *rectispinus* (Engelm.) Taylor in late summer (*Hodgson 9615 and Rebman,* DES).

The relatively large yellow fruits of barrel cacti are also edible (fig. 83) and supply some moisture. The taste of the fruit is lemony and sour, but not unpleasant. Southeastern Yavapais boiled and ate the fruits of *F. cylindraceus.* In contrast, River Pimas "seldom if ever" eat them, but frequently grow the plants in their yards as ornamentals (Rea 1997). Townsend Brandegee noted that Baja Californians did *not* eat the acidic fruits of a particular barrel cactus, despite its "not unpleasant" and "acidic" taste (Brandegee 1889:161, cited as *Echinocactus wislizeni*). The barrel cactus described by Brandegee may have been *F. peninsulae* (F. Weber) Britton and Rose or *F. cylindraceus* (*F. wislizeni* does not grow on the peninsula). However, Tipais eat the fruits of *F. cylindraceus* fresh, fried, or stewed (Weiss 1994). Fr. Consag implied that the fruits of a barrel cactus were eaten whole by northern Cochimí populations in the mid 1700s (Krmpotic 1923), as is occasionally done by local inhabitants. Barrel cacti within the range of the northern Cochimí include *F. townsendianus* Britton and Rose, *F. fordii* (Orcutt) Britton and Rose, *F. gracilis* H. Gates, and possibly *F. peninsulae* (based on Lindsay et al. 1996; Anderson 2001). Seri children ate the fruit of *F. cylindraceus* despite its sour taste (Felger and Moser 1976, 1985).

The seeds of any barrel cactus can be eaten. San Carlos Apaches, Seris, Baja Californians, Sonorans, and Guarijios ground and ate the seeds parched or unparched. They used the seed meal to make bread or tortillas or cooked the seeds in water as gruel (Palmer 1871; Hrdlička 1908; Clavigero 1937; Aschmann 1959; Gentry 1963; Felger and Moser 1976, 1985; del Barco 1980). Kiliwas ate the seeds of *F. cylindraceus* (Meigs 1939). Fr. del Barco (1980:162) described how the central desert inhabitants of Baja California extracted the seeds of *biznaga,* which they spread in the sun so "that the phlegm [pulp] will be consumed or dried up," then toasted the seeds in their trays and ate them ground. Inhabitants in the Río Mayo area ate the seeds of *F. herrarae* (Gentry 1942, cited as *F. wislizeni;* Martin et al. 1998).

Mention is made of the Hualapai use of *F. cylindraceus.* The buds and flowers were used for food, eaten raw, or mixed with other foods; additionally, the Hualapai occasionally ate the fruits dried and pounded (Phillips et al. 1994). However, the plant was more important for its use in the baking of agave, with the stem pulp slices used in place of grass or prickly-pear pads to provide the steam.

Barrel cacti populations have not escaped the pressures of humans; they have been impacted by the loss of habitat through development and collection by candy makers and cactus fanciers. Coastal populations of *F. viridescens* (Torrey and A. Gray) Britton and Rose var. *littoralis* Lindsay and *F. fordii* are being severely impacted by development (Anderson 2001; J. Rebman, pers. comm.). *Ferocactus chrysacanthus* (Orcutt) Britton & Rose ssp. *chrysacanthus,* which is endemic to Cedros and San Benito Islands, has been greatly impacted by illegal collecting. *Ferocactus cylindraceus* var. *cylindraceus* and *F. viridescens* var. *viridescens* are considered uncommon and threatened by collecting in southern California (Hickman 1993). *Ferocactus diguetii* (Weber) Britton & Rose, a spectacular cactus that grows to four meters in height, is only found on Carmen Island. It was once reported to grow on Isla Coronados near Loreto, having been documented by Ivan Johnston in 1921 (J. Cota *in* Lindsay et al. 1996). George Lindsay failed to find the plant there in 1938 and 1952. Loreto inhabitants told Lindsay that in years of drought they collected the *biznagas* from Isla Coronados and Carmen Island for use as stock food, a practice that may have eliminated the plants on Isla Coronados.

William Bright's (1935) reference to the extirpation of barrel cacti in Los Angeles County is of interest. Assuming he was correct in the location and name of the county, his statement infers that barrel cacti were once relatively common there. Driving "100 or more miles" into the deserts would impact populations in the Mohave and Sonoran Desert, the latter in the vicinity of Indio, Riverside County. No collection in Los Angeles County is known, although potential habitat for *F. cylindraceus* is found in the northeastern part of the county in the Mohave Desert (Hickman 1993). The closest known documented population to Los Angeles County is in the Barstow Mountains, San Bernardino County, 40–50 miles northeast of the county line. Did collecting and urban sprawl decimate the populations west of the Barstow Mountains, perhaps on the foothills of the San Gabriel Mountains? It is difficult to know for certain, but accounts such as Bright's may provide clues.

Lophocereus | senita, sina, garambullo

L. schottii **(Engelmann) Britton & Rose (syn., *Pachycereus schottii* [Engelmann] D. Hunt)**
barbon, cabeza del viejo, hombre viejo, pitahaya barbona, sina, tuna barbona, garambullo, musaro, pitayita

Lophocereus schottii usually flowers from April to August (Wiggins 1964). Many small fruits are produced, with an Arizona *senita* producing an average of 100 fruits per year (Parker 1989). Fruits develop and ripen from July to October (Humphrey 1975), but generally in early summer before the more highly favored fruits of *pitahaya dulce* (*Stenocereus thurberi;* Aschmann 1959; Felger and Moser 1974, 1985; del Barco 1980). However, one Jesuit missionary (probably south of Cochimí territory in southern Baja California) observed that the fruits of *senita* developed after the "true fruit," or *pitahaya dulce* (Aschmann 1966). *Senita* plants near the center of Tiburón Island and near Punta Sargenta, Sonora, flower and fruit twice a year (Felger and Moser 1974, 1985). I have observed *senita* flowers and green and red fruits in early December on the Pinacate lava flow (*Hodgson 5350 et al.,* DES). The presumably immature green fruits had mature, black seeds embedded in the sweetish pulp. Seeds and pulp of the red fruits were totally consumed by various frugivores.

Use of the abundant fruits of *L. schottii* for food was limited. Fruits were eaten fresh or made into syrup or preserves by the River Pima (Rea 1997), Tohono O'odham (Nabhan et al. 1982; Rea 1997), Hiá ceḍ O'odham (Felger et al. 1992), Seri (Felger and Moser 1974, 1985), Eudeve (Pennington 1982), and possibly the Cochimí (Aschmann 1966; del Barco 1980). Some Gila River Pimas still remember receiving homemade syrup and preserves of *senita* (and organ pipe) cactus from their Tohono O'odham friends or relatives (Rea 1997). Otherwise, they would have had no access to plants, except for one very old colony being tended at

Sacaton. The Cochimí of central Baja California valued *senita* more for its stems, which they used as a fish poison. Tipais also valued the plant they call *garambullo* for the treatment of diabetes; they prepared the stems (assuming this is the plant part used) as one prepared prickly-pear pads (Weiss 1994).

Mammillaria | fishhook pincushion, pincushion cactus, chollita, cabeza del viejo

M. thornberi Orcutt
Thornber's fishhook cactus

Of the 40 to 50 species of *Mammillaria* found in the Sonoran Desert (Wiggins 1964), 26 to 32 are endemic to Baja California (Wiggins 1980; J. Rebman, pers. comm.). *Mammillaria* species described in the ethnobotanical literature as having edible fruits include *M. grahamii* Engelm. var. *grahamii* (Castetter and Opler 1936; Gentry 1942; Felger and Moser 1976, 1985, cited as *M. microcarpa*), *M. grahamii* var. *oliveiae* (Orcutt) Benson (Castetter and Opler 1936; Pennington 1980), *M. mainiae* K. Brand. (Castetter and Opler 1936), *M. heyderi* (Engelm.) Benson (Yanovsky 1936), *M. roseana* K. Brand. (Rose 1892), *M. thornberi* Orcutt (Nabhan et al. 1986, 1988, 1991), *M. tetrancistra* Engelm. (Kelly 1964), *M. sheldonii* (Britton & Rose) Boed. (Felger and Moser 1976, 1985; Pennington 1980), *M. goodridgei* Scheer (Brandegee 1891a), and *M. dioica* K. Brand. (Coyle and Roberts 1975; Hedges and Beresford 1986). People generally ate the small, rather dry fruits as a raw snack.

Special mention is made of Thornber's fishhook cactus, *M. thornberi*. These plants grow in patches over a 1,600-square-kilometer range as scattered populations in Pinal and Pima Counties in Arizona and northern Sonora near the Arizona-Sonora border (Reichenbacher 1984; Nabhan et al. 1986; Ecker 1990). Major Arizona populations are located in Avra Valley and on the Tohono O'odham Reservation. Smaller populations exist on lands of Organ Pipe Cactus National Monument, Saguaro National Park (West Unit), the Gila River Indian Community, the Bureau of Land Management (BLM), and the Bureau of Reclamation (Reichenbacher 1984; Nabhan et al. 1988, 1991). Plants usually grow in sandy or gravelly soils on gentle slopes dominated by saguaro, cholla, creosote, and paloverde (*Cercidium microphyllum* Torr.), but at their more northern range they grow in the sandy or silty loam soils of the Gila River valley in an *Atriplex-Lycium* community (Rea 1997). The species was considered rare enough and as having impending threats to existing populations to be listed as a threatened species (U.S. Department of the Interior 1985).

The Tohono O'odham contrasted the plants' small astringent fruits with the larger, sweeter ones of *Echinocereus engelmannii* (Nabhan et al. 1988, 1991). They casually ate the fruits despite the bitter taste, which they say is due to the coyote's spoiling of the fruits. *Mammillaria thornberi* is humorously tolerated and occasionally protected or cultivated by Tohono O'odham families. One clump found near a family's saguaro fruit gathering camp was carefully transplanted to the edge of a backyard religious shrine at the family's home. The Hiá ceḍ O'odham also ate the fruits (Nabhan 1989b).

Mammillaria thornberi was probably common in the Gila River valley during early historic times, where the Pima once farmed and had their villages (Rea 1997). Wholesale leasing for agriculture has converted the *Atriplex-Lycium* communities the plants occupy. The northernmost record for the plant is in Komatke on the Gila River Pima Reservation (Nabhan et al. 1988; Rea 1997). Some Gila River Pima distinguished between this and the more common pincushion, *M. grahamii*. Sylvester Matthias was probably referring to *M. thornberi* when he told Amadeo Rea (1997) that the relatively dry fruits were not good for eating when compared to those of hedgehog (*Echinocereus* spp.) and saguaro *(Carnegiea gigantea)*.

The core of its range west of Tucson has been increasingly converted to irrigated farms, trailer parks, and suburban ranchettes (Nabhan et al. 1986). The Central Arizona Project (CAP) aqueduct cut through the densest populations of *M. thornberi* (Nabhan et al. 1986; Ecker 1990). Recent Bureau of Reclamation surveys along the CAP route found the plant to be more abundant than had been previously thought (Nabhan et al. 1986, 1991) and the species was downlisted from the U.S. Fish and Wildlife's proposed threatened status. Many of these recently discovered populations were removed from their habitat before they were destroyed by the aqueduct and transported to the Desert Botanical Garden (Ecker 1990), then transplanted to the Bureau of Reclamation preserve area, which is located within one mile from the aqueduct (L. Slauson, pers. comm.). Populations may have also declined in Organ

Pipe Cactus National Monument and Saguaro National Park, due primarily to suburban sprawl and illicit poaching by tourists (Nabhan et al. 1988, 1991).

Myrtillocactus | cochal

M. cochal **(Orcutt) Britton & Rose**
cochal

Myrtillocactus cochal (fig. 85) is found nearly throughout the length of Baja California, where it is locally common on hillsides and mesas (Turner et al. 1995). Plants flower throughout the year (Wiggins 1964). Its mature fruits are medium-sized, globose, red, juicy, and

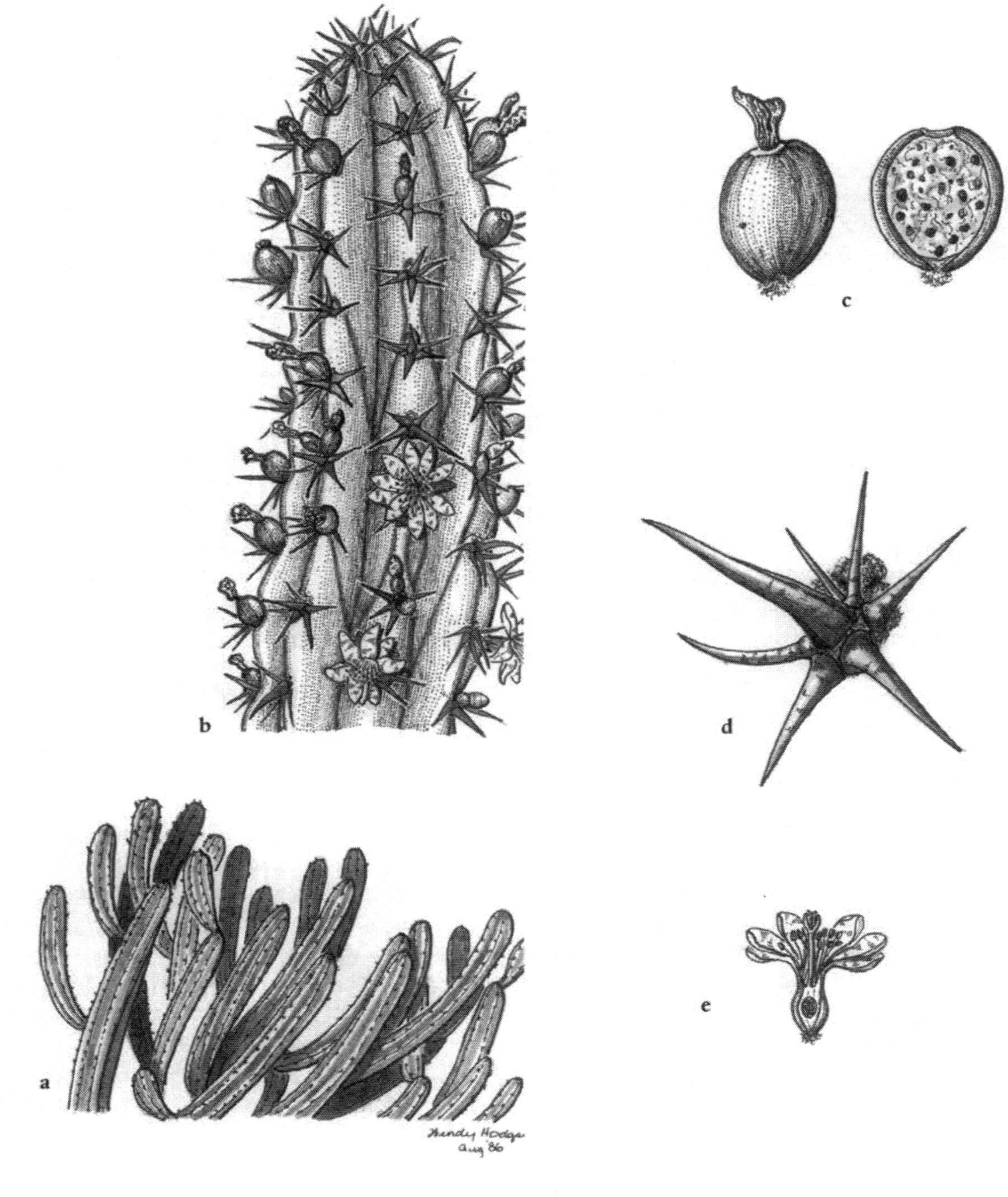

FIGURE 85. ***Myrtillocactus cochal*** (Orcutt) Britton & Rose. **a.** Habit, south of San Vicente, Baja California, June 1971 (*Pinkava 8771,* DES); **b.** stem with flowers and fruits (*Pinkava 8771,* DES); **c.** fruits (*Pinkava 8771,* DES); **d.** spine cluster, near El Rosario, Baja California, June 1971 (*Pinkava 8814,* DES); **e.** flower, Desert Botanical Garden, Phoenix, Arizona.

slightly acidic tasting and were eaten by the inhabitants of Baja California (Standley 1924; Martinez 1936; Castetter and Bell 1937; Wiggins 1964; Coyle and Roberts 1975). Baja Californians usually collected the fruits in the morning. They relished the cool and refreshing taste, which was much appreciated on hot days. Any reference by early missionaries to the use of cochal by the native inhabitants is not known.

Opuntia | prickly-pear

O. basilaris **Engelmann & Bigelow var.** ***basilaris***
beavertail cactus

O. bravoana **E. Baxter**

O. chlorotica **Engelmann & Bigelow**
pancake prickly-pear, clockface prickly-pear, nopal

O. engelmannii **Salm-Dyck ex Engelmann**
Engelmann prickly-pear, cactus-apple, nopal, tuna

O. ficus-indica **(Linnaeus) Miller (including "*O. megacantha* Salm-Dyck," the spiny form of the species)**
Indian-fig

O. gosseliniana **Weber**
violet prickly-pear

O. littoralis **(Engelmann) Cockerell**
coastal prickly-pear

O. macrocentra **Engelmann**
purple prickly-pear, nopal

O. oricola **R. Philbrick**
chaparral prickly-pear, nopal

O. phaeacantha **Engelmann**
tulip prickly-pear, nopal

O. polyacantha **Haworth**
plains prickly-pear

O. pycnantha **Engelmann**

O. santa-rita **(Griffiths & Hare) Rose (syn., *O. violacea* Engelmann)**
purple prickly-pear, Santa Rita prickly-pear, nopal morado, tuna

O. tapona **Engelmann**

Approximately 18 different species of prickly-pear are now recognized within the Sonoran Desert, although their taxonomy is not well understood in Sonora. Several of the prickly-pears provide edible young pads, called *nopales,* and juicy, calcium-rich fruits, called *tunas.*

Nutritional data on prickly-pear pads are incomplete. Homer Aschmann (1959) considered the food value of prickly-pear pads to be low, but pads may have added useful bulk to the otherwise "concentrated" Cochimí diet. Prickly-pear pads' high calcium content is largely due to the plants' ability to accumulate insoluble calcium oxalate (Laferrière et al. 1991). Much of the calcium is unavailable for absorption by humans. The calcium may be bound as insoluble calcium oxalate or bound by soluble mucilage. As a result, the amount of calcium available for digestion may vary according to the time of day. However, prickly-pear pads appear to have hypoglycemic effects. Daily meals of pads fed to healthy, obese, and diabetic individuals significantly lowered total cholesterol and glycemia in all groups (Frati-Munari et al. 1983). Evidence suggested that the soluble fibers, such as the viscous mucilages in prickly-pear pads, have hypoglycemic effects due to an inhibition of the absorption of simple carbohydrates (Frati-Munari et al. 1988). The viscous fibers may form a physical barrier between other carbohydrates eaten at the same meal and the digestive enzymes that break down those carbohydrates. Thus, the carbohydrates are digested and converted into sugars more slowly. Additionally, prickly-pear pads may have high levels of amylose, a starch that breaks down into simple sugars much more slowly than does amylopectin, the form of food starch commonly found in white bread and potatoes. Even today, Tipais of northern Baja California recognize *nopal* as a remedy for diabetes and eat the young pads raw or soaked in water (Weiss 1994). Some Tipais believe that eating cooked *nopales* did not work for treating diabetes because cooking the pads destroyed their chemical substances.

Western Apaches and Yavapais may not have used prickly-pear pads for food; if they did, their use was minimal. River Pimas sliced, cooked, and seasoned the young pads of *O. engelmannii* (fig. 86; Curtin 1949), although Frank Russell (1908) made no mention of their use of *nopales.* Gila River Pimas did not use the pads of *O. engelmannii* for food, but did start eating the young pads of *O. ficus-indica* after learning of its use from the Hispanics, who introduced the plants into the area (Rea 1997). However, they were aware of the use of wild prickly-pear pads by other neighboring groups, such as the Tohono O'odham, who at Quitovac ate the young pads of *O. engelmannii* with chiles (Nabhan et al. 1982).

FIGURE 86. ***Opuntia engelmannii*** Salm-Dyck ex. Engelm. Note young, edible pads. South Mountain, Maricopa County, Arizona, April 1988.

Southern Diegueños cleaned, chopped, and boiled the young pads of *O. engelmannii* and *O. ficus-indica* with tomatoes, onions, and peppers (Hedges and Beresford 1986). Cahuillas and Panamints especially liked the young pads of *O. basilaris* var. *basilaris* (Coville 1892; Barrows 1900; Saunders 1948; Bean and Saubel 1972), despite the presence of an exceptionally large number of glochids. They collected the pads in May or early June, then carefully rubbed the many glochids off with grass and spread them in the sun to dry. The thoroughly dried pads could be stored indefinitely, then boiled and eaten with salt when needed. The Cahuilla also steamed the pads in stone-lined pits similar to those used for cholla bud roasting (Barrows 1900; Bean and Saubel 1972). It is not known if the Kiliwa, Paipai, Kamia, or Cocopa used pads for food, although it is probable. Tipais are still especially fond of *O. ficus-indica,* whose pads are available for harvest from March to June (Weiss 1994). They scrape off the spines or glochids, wash and dice the pads, then cook the pieces in water for approximately 20 minutes. The cooked pieces are eaten as a salad or fried with onions, garlic, cilantro, and tomatoes or with scrambled eggs. Tipais also consume *nopal* raw, usually as a *licuado,* for treating diabetes.

The Cochimí of the central desert region of Baja California ate the young pads, "the leaves, when tender, ... eaten after stewing and cooking," making a "tasty vegetable dish" (del Barco 1980:170). Possible species used were *O. chlorotica, O. engelmannii, O. tapona,* or *O. ficus-indica* (both spineless and spiny forms grow throughout the peninsula, having been brought over from the mainland by priests who planted them near their missions). Fr. Salvatierra wrote from Loreto in 1709 that he and his party were suffering "greatly from hunger" in February and March, and "were reduced to eating nopales [presumably the young pads and not the fruits] and other wild roots given to them by the natives" (Burrus 1971:225).

The juicy fruits of many prickly-pears were and continue to be used for food. Prickly-pear fruits are an excellent source of water and calcium. With the exception of *O. basilaris,* all of the approximately 18 species of prickly-pear in the Sonoran Desert produce relatively fleshy fruits. These include *O. chlorotica, O. engelmannii, O. macrocentra, O. phaeacantha, O. santa-rita,* the introduced *O. ficus-indica* (including "*O. megacantha* Salm-Dyck," the spiny-form of the species), *O. littoralis, O. oricola, O. bravoana, O. pycnantha, O. tapona,* and *O. gosseliniana.* The prickly-pear most commonly used was *O. engelmannii* (figs. 94, 95) because its fruits are relatively large and juicy throughout (figs. 87, 88).

Western Apaches ate the fruits of *O. engelmannii* and traveled long distances to gather them. Women gathered the fruit with tongs of split sticks, removed the glochids with branches or grass or rolled the fruit on the ground, then packed the fruits in a burden basket (Buskirk 1986). They ate the fruit peeled and raw, although a "sweet variety" was made into a kind of butter (Reagan 1930). Western Apaches generally ate the seeds with the fruits, although children experienced intestinal problems upon ingesting them. Seeds were generally not ground, although the Southern Tonto ground and mixed the seeds with acorn meal (Gifford 1940). Fruits were sun-dried and stored (Buskirk 1986).

Southeastern Yavapais harvested the fruits of *O. engelmannii* when ripe in September, frequenting "a place near Tortilla Flat" (Gifford 1932:180) along the Apache Trail, Maricopa County. They collected the fruits with tongs made of ash (*Fraxinus* sp.), then placed them in burden baskets. They emptied the fruits on a

FIGURE 87. (right) ***Opuntia engelmannii*** with large, juicy fruits. Foothills of Baboquivari Mountains, Tohono O'odham Reservation, July 1988.

FIGURE 88. (below) ***Opuntia engelmannii*** habit, pads, fruits, and flowers. Courtesy of the Mesa Southwest Museum.

cleared area on the ground, then rid the fruits of glochids by brushing them with plant material. They swept away all glochids from the fruits and ground before putting all of the fruits back into their burden baskets to be taken home. Peeled fruits were eaten raw without the seeds, because the seeds caused "abdominal swelling and constipation" if eaten. They opened the fruits, removed the seeds, and sun-dried the fruit pulps with outer "skin" on grass or sticks. They then packed the dried fruits into a solid mass and stored it in caves in pits lined with straw or stones. Seeds were not usually saved, but were sometimes parched and ground, the resulting flour considered sweet in taste and not a cause of constipation.

The Northeastern Yavapai collected the fruits of a prickly-pear, probably *O. engelmannii,* from September through November (Gifford 1936). Fruits from plants growing at higher elevations, such as those found on Granite Peak, Yavapai County, were collected later in the year. They transported the fruits to camp, where they peeled them, removed the seeds, and ate the pulp. They sometimes dried the pulp after squeezing out and drinking the juice. Fruits were also ground, with the meal then stored for long periods. Edward Gifford (1936, cited as *O. erinacea*) also said that Northeastern Yavapais ate the very spiny and rather dry fruits of *O. polyacantha* Haw. var. *erinacea* (Engelm.) Parfitt raw. Additionally, the Northeastern and Western Yavapai ate the "exceptionally sweet" fruits of *O. chlorotica* raw after the numerous glochids were brushed off.

Gila River Pimas also collected the fruits of *O. engelmannii,* rolled them in the sand to remove the glochids, discarded the seeds, and ate the pulp raw (Russell 1908; Rea 1997).

The Tohono O'odham piled the fruits of *O. engelmannii* on the ground and brushed them with creosote branches to rid them of the glochids (Castetter and Underhill 1935). They ate large quantities of fresh fruits, then carried the remaining lot home. Unused fruits were dried or made into syrup. To dry the fruits, the Tohono O'odham removed the seeds, spread the pulp on grass, then sun-dried the pulp for two days. After the fruits were dried, the pulp was stored in a sealed jar. They made syrup by mashing the pulp in a basket with a stick, then squeezed out and strained the juice.

The Cahuilla used "about a dozen" prickly-pears for their edible fruits, according to David Barrows (1900: 67), who could identify only a few species. The fruits of the spineless and spiny forms of *O. ficus-indica* were an important contribution to the Cahuilla diet (Barrows 1900; Bean and Saubel 1972, cited as *O. megacantha*). The Cahuilla sometimes obtained the fruit from other groups because plants did not grow on their reservation (Barrows 1900:67). Surprisingly, the only other prickly-pear David Barrows could identify, whose fruits were used by the Cahuilla for food, was *O. basilaris.* Fruits of *O. basilaris* are dry at maturity and possess many glochids. Despite this, Barrows considered the plant to be "an especially valuable cactus" to the Cahuilla, who gathered its young fruits in summer when they were "full of sweetness." They collected the "buds" in a basket, brushed off the glochids with grass or twigs, and then cooked or steamed the fruits with hot stones in a pit for 12 hours or more. The Panamints also pit-steamed the fruits (Coville 1892). The Santa Ysabel Diegueño ate the dried, cleaned fruits of *O. basilaris* and children once sold dried fruits in small sacks for ten cents (Hedges and Beresford 1986). (Out of curiosity, I once carefully ate the immature fruits of *O. basilaris.* I found the flesh to be tart and edible and the many glochids that filled my mouth to have a nutty flavor.)

Barrows (1900:68) described another type of prickly-pear that had "flat, ugly jointed stems," the "flat joints about the size of one's palm crowded along their edges with buds [fruits] as big as the last joint of a man's thumb." Cahuilla women gathered large quantities of the fruits, which they brushed, dried, and stored for future use. When needed for food, they boiled the dried fruits in water with salt and lard. They often let the fruits mature to harvest the seeds. After the fruits (or "figs") were dried, women sat down beside their piles of fruits and threshed out the seeds by "flailing" them with palm fronds. After further winnowing the seeds, the women stored them. For use as a food, the seeds were pounded into meal and cooked into an atole. Seeds were obtained this way from "several species of cactus." It is not certain as to what species this prickly-pear with small pads belongs.

David Barrows (1900:68) also spoke of two prickly-pears that grew on the slopes of Torres Mountain that produced "luscious fruit in large quantities." He described one type as resembling a "neglected and stunted" *O. ficus-indica* (suggesting *O. oricola,* which has a treelike habit). The other he described as having a low-growing habit with "exceptionally long spines, two to three inches," suggesting *O. phaeacantha* or possibly *O.* x *curvospina* Griffiths (D. Pinkava, pers. comm.).

The importance of prickly-pear fruits as a food item

to past Baja California cultures is uncertain, although prickly-pears are important to the Tipai today. Homer Aschmann (1959:82) commented that "of the several opuntias native to the Central Desert [region of Baja California], the interest in the fruit or tunas as a food source seems to have been concentrated on [the] platyopuntias." Peveril Meigs (1935:33, 101) noted that inhabitants of northern Baja California lived on the mescal, *pitahaya, datile,* and "the seeds of *tunas.*" They ate the fruits of a prickly-pear when ripe in August (Meigs 1939), possibly being those of *O. engelmannii.* Yet, prickly-pear fruits were generally not held in especially high esteem. The "Spaniards definitely, and the Indians apparently," considered prickly-pear fruits as an inferior food, although Fr. Baegert (1952:34) considered the fruits to be tasty, "and with a little sugar," made "an excellent addition to a meal of field fare." Prickly-pear fruits extended the cactus fruit season because they ripened earlier than those of *Stenocereus thurberi,* or *pitahaya dulce* (Baegert 1952; Venegas and Burriel 1966). However, according to Fr. Baegert (1952), fruits were not very plentiful in south-central Baja California, were produced only for three to four weeks, and would keep but a few days.

Fr. del Barco (1980) recognized different kinds of prickly-pears as being smaller than those found in "New Spain," and all produced red fruits that matured "around September." He noted that the local inhabitants cleaned off the small glochids, called *ahuates,* by rubbing the fruits with other plants. The natives did not remove the thick "skin" because it was tender, juicy, and not bitter. The only part of the fruit they removed was the "little depression," or umbilicus. Although he thought the fruits to be without flavor, "it is a tasty thing to the Indians, and they esteem tunas a little less than pitahayas" (del Barco 1980:171). Undoubtedly fruits were esteemed for their source of moisture as well as for food. Of interest is the Cochimí name for the fruits, the single letter *"A."*

Fr. del Barco (1980) referred to another tall, native prickly-pear (possibly *O. bravoana*) that produced fruits so sour that they could not be eaten alone, but instead were often mixed with baked agave. These fruits were not highly favored by the inhabitants, who often ignored them during their travels.

Missionaries brought *O. ficus-indica* from New Spain to the peninsula and planted the cacti around the missions. Here the plants did well and produced very good-tasting fruit, although they required some watering (del Barco 1980). These imported prickly-pears, "their great consistency in weathering these droughts notwithstanding," did not produce abundant fruit following dry periods, as did the *pitahaya.* With the exception of the tall, sour-fruited prickly-pear, even the other native, smaller prickly-pears did not do as well as the "imported ones," or *O. ficus-indica,* as described by Fr. del Barco (1980:170): "The little tuna-bearing nopales, native to [Baja] California, feel the lack of water the same way and even more acutely, if there is nothing in the months mentioned to water them with except what comes from the clouds. Because this often occurs late ... the poor little nopales spend some part of the year in difficult and anguished life, but they do not die and they even bear fruit." Fruits of *O. bravoana, O. tapona,* and even *O. basilaris* were eaten raw or cooked by more contemporary Baja Californians (Hake 1980, 1983). Audrey Weiss (1994:210) found that the fruit of prickly-pears, particularly those of *O. ficus-indica,* are still a "highly prized and richly enjoyed treat" to the Tipais. They collect the fruits in July, remove the glochids and "skin," then eat them raw.

Joséfina Ochurte, a Paipai, related to Judith Jöel (1976:180) how a type of prickly-pear, possibly *O. engelmannii* or *O. littoralis,* was abundant on the eastern flanks of the Sierra Juarez. Here Paipais gathered its fruits, usually in September. They brought the fruits home, where they opened them with a knife. They drank the juice expressed from the fruits or cooked and stored it in a clay jar. They dried and pounded the pulp (possibly with the seeds) to make a pinole that they also stored in clay jars. This pinole was mixed with water and drunk during the winter.

When Campbell Pennington worked with Ónavas Pimas from 1968 to 1971, they knew three types of prickly-pear fruits. They harvested the fruits in August and boiled them with sugar to make a crude marmalade (Pennington 1980). Additional research is needed to determine what species of prickly-pears the Ónavas used and if they still use the plants today. Prickly-pear fruits were one of the few wild food plants eaten by the Cáhita in the early to mid 1900s (Beals 1945). During the summer, the Guarijío gathered and ate the fruits, with seeds, of several prickly-pears raw or boiled and peeled (Gentry 1942). María Beltran spoke of *nopal grueso,* whose fruits were still eaten in the vicinity of Guasabas during the 1980s (Nabhan and Hodgson 1988). Whether she was referring to a common, unidentified prickly-pear with shiny, dark green pads and red, juicy fruits (fig. 89) is unknown.

Eating prickly-pear fruit sometimes caused problems

FIGURE 89. ***Opuntia*** sp. Common in Guasabas-Moctezuma-Bacadehuachi area, Sonora; characterized by shiny, dark green pads and red, obovoid juicy fruits. Located 6.4 miles east of El Coyote, on the way to Bacadehuachi, Sonora, July 1988.

for some individuals. According to Capt. John Bourke (1895:44), "the Apaches say that the use of [prickly-pear fruit] must be attended with some precautions, as it predisposes to fevers." The Tohono O'odham differentiated between prickly-pears that produced chills and nausea and those that were safe to eat without any ill effects (Castetter and Underhill 1935). Frank Russell (1908) noted that those who got fever were those not accustomed to eating the fruits. The Gila River Pimas (Curtin 1949; Rea 1997) and Ópatas in Sonora (Nentvig 1980) also made such a distinction. Leonora Curtin (1949) was told that eating too many fruits or eating the dark purple fruits gave one chills. Eating more than two or three fruits was considered by some to be too many (Rea 1997). One person claimed that taller plants produce fruits that cause chills and the low-growing types produce good, very dark maroon fruits (which is the opposite of what George Webb told Leonora Curtin). It is possible that they were differentiating the green, somewhat dry fruits of *O. phaeacantha* var. *major* Engelm. (which is not within the range of the River Pima) from the very juicy fruits of *O. engelmannii*. Such a distinction may reflect fruits of *O. engelmannii* parasitized by an insect, *Asphondylia opuntiae*. Fruits develop abnormally after the insect lays her eggs in the ovary and become relatively elongated, reddish orange (not dark purple or maroon), and fleshy but not juicy.

However, perhaps it is not the type of prickly-pear, an insect parasite, or the number of fruits eaten that matters, but how the plant is addressed. Rosalio Moisés, a Yaqui, remembered how he and his girlfriend found it necessary to collect *nopal* fruit and other wild foods during especially hard times in the mid 1930s. Neither of them liked the fruit and he knew of the fruits' propensity to cause illness (Moisés et al. 1971:159): "It is very bad to eat the red tuna from the nopal, unless you know just what to do, because you can get a fever called *ta-he-hue-chi-a na-bom*. If you know how to yell at the nopal to scare it, you can eat the tunas without getting the fever."

There is evidence of encouragement or cultivation of native prickly-pears. Some of the plants found on the flats on the Gila River Pima Reservation have exceptionally large pads, having originated from pads brought down from the top of South Mountain, in the vicinity of the radio towers (Rea 1997). A prickly-pear having small seeds was said to have been "brought north to the Cibeque area from the Salt River Valley and to have obtained its start from seeds expectorated by people eating the fruit" (Buskirk 1986:180). Populations of *O. engelmannii* producing large pads and fruits and red flowers are also found in many of the larger side canyons within the Grand Canyon, possibly having been grown and cultivated by the Southern Paiute or earlier inhabitants (Hodgson 1999b).

Pachycereus | cardón

***P. pecten-aboriginum* (Engelmann) Britton & Rose**
cardón, cardón hecho, cardón barbón, cardón espinoso, hecho, tutus

***P. pringlei* (S. Watson) Britton & Rose**
cardón, cardón pelón, saguesa, saguera, sahueso, organo

Pachycereus pecten-aboriginum is characteristic of Sinaloan thornscrub and extends into the southernmost part of the Sonoran Desert in Sonora (Turner et al. 1995). Its bristly gold-colored fruits (fig. 90) ripen in June and July (Krizman 1972) and were sought not only for use as a food, but for hairbrushes (Goldman 1916; Standley 1924; Bennett and Zingg 1935; Castetter and Bell 1937; Gentry 1963; Pennington 1963). A Jesuit missionary described the fruits as being like a "chestnut ball" and having a very small amount of reddish or white flesh, with seeds having the flavor of poppy seeds (Aschmann 1966). Carl Lumholtz (1902:188–189) stated that "*cardon hecho* has the best wild fruit growing in the north-western part of Mexico, and the Indians from all around had come to gather it." He described the fruit as being as large as an egg and having soft, sweet, and nourishing flesh, which tasted better when picked at dawn rather than later in the day. A "tree-like cactus known in Mexico as *pitahyd*" was second only to agave in importance to the Tarahumara (Bennett and Zingg 1935). They picked the immature green fruits in mid-May by knocking them off with long poles to which a fork had been attached with agave cordage (Pennington 1963). Birds were also attracted to the fruit, thus providing a signal to Tarahumaras that the fruits were ready.

Ónavas Pimas gathered the fruits in May and June, using a pole made from stems of *Arundinaria longifolia* Fourn. or *Arundo donax* L., with a twisted wire hook or long thorn attached at one end to get fruits high up on the stem (Pennington 1980). They attached a piece of wood shaped like a small cross below the hook or thorn. Fruits were either speared or hooked from the plant and carried home in large baskets. They removed the seeds and boiled the pulp into a thick, sweet mass called *dulce,* which could be stored in an olla for several weeks. The Guarijío ate the fruits raw or cooked. They boiled the pulp in water, separated the seeds, and ground and boiled the seeds again to produce a thick, nourishing oily paste (Gentry 1963). They cooked the pulp of the inner "rind" into a jelly or jam, known as

FIGURE 90. ***Pachycereus pecten-aboriginum*** (Engelm.) Britton & Rose. Small plant with old, persistent fruit; note long spines on fruit. Five miles south of Masocahui, Sonora, early September 1988.

miel de hecho. Yaquis also collected the fruit and scraped out the pulp and seeds to eat (Beals 1945).

Pachycereus pringlei is widespread throughout most of Baja California south of 31.2°N, the gulf islands, and within 50–75 kilometers of the coast in Sonora south to Nayarit (Turner et al. 1995). The ripe fruits of *P. pringlei* split open in the summer (Moran 1968) or as early as May in the southern part of its distribution (Turner et al. 1995). Fruits contain a richly colored, thick, sweet pulp that envelops numerous small, black seeds (fig. 91). The fruits provided a food source to Baja California groups, the Seri, Pima Bajo, Eudeve, Yaqui, Mayo, and Guarijío. *Cardón* seeds are nutritious, being high in protein, fat, carbohydrates, and fiber.

Pachycereus pringlei fruits are considered an "unfailing resource" in periods of extended drought (Felger and Nabhan 1976). Their use by Baja California inhabitants, which included the "second harvest" of the seeds (see *Stenocereus thurberi*), is mentioned by Clavigero (1937), Meigs (1939), Baegert (1952, 1982), and del Barco (1980). Kiliwas used the stalk of an agave to retrieve the ripe fruits of *cardón* in June in the San

FIGURE 91. ***Pachycereus pringlei*** (S. Wats.) Britton & Rose. Immature fruits with light green pulp and mature seeds exposed.

FIGURE 92. ***Pachycereus pringlei.*** Massive stems with submature fruits; note confluent areoles on stem and short spines on fruit. Desert Botanical Garden, Phoenix, Arizona, June 1988.

Felipe Desert region, then ate the pulp raw (Meigs 1939). Fr. del Barco (1980) thought *cardón* fruit pulp, or "viscous humor," was too meager to make it important. Birds consumed most of this limited fruit pulp (Aschmann 1959). Fr. Baegert never tried the fruits, but considered them to be "nothing special" (Baegert 1982). In addition, the fruits were often high up on the massive stems (figs. 92, 93) and thus out of reach. Fr. Baegert seemed more impressed with the massive size of *cardón* than the taste of its fruits. In one of his more interesting descriptions of plants found in the region, he wrote of how some Guaicuras actually climbed these immense cacti (Baegert 1952:32): "This terrifying scaffold in the shape of a plant is scaled by the natives either to pick the tasteless fruit which grows out of the sides of those beams [branches] or to survey the country in search of game, heedless of the fact that the whole structure shakes and bends from side to side because its substance is so weak and the roots no more than two spans long." This show of athleticism was made possible by the fact that spines are absent on the trunks and older parts of stems, as noted by Fr. Baegert (1952). Supposedly, the Guaicuras climbed the tall stems only when the *pitahaya* crop failed (Aschmann 1959).

The Pericú, Guaicura, and Cochimí apparently valued *cardón* seeds more than the pulp. The Cochimí saved them for future use, according to Fr. del Barco (1980:157): "These seeds are very black and they have a high luster. With the help of fire and sun they clean the fibers that the seeds have and toast them to keep them from spoiling and so preserve them for the winter when there is greater lack of food. These seeds of the cardón are very much esteemed by the Indians."

Homer Aschmann (1959) believed that *cardón* fruits may have been of minor importance to the inhabitants of the central desert region, south of 28°N, because of the competition with *pitahaya dulce* for use as food. In contrast, the harvest of *cardón* seeds and fruits was an important, major event north of 27.5°N, where *cardón* is common and *pitahaya dulce* is not.

Richard Felger and Mary Moser (1974, 1985) presented the most detailed information on the use of *cardón. Cardón* fruit was one of the most important traditional foods in Seri culture and was still harvested in the 1970s. Seris harvested the ripe fruits in June and July in the morning. They did not collect fruits that had already fallen to the ground because all of the pulp and seeds would have been eaten by animals. Like other cultures, the Seri used a fruit-gathering pole made specifically for *cardón* and saguaro from a saguaro rib with two crosspieces of creosote bush stems. Seris either pushed up or pulled down on the pole to dislodge the fruit. They opened each fruit with a bone awl or knife, squeezed the pulp into a basket, and threw away the "peel," or epidermis. Individual *cardones* that consistently produced large fruits each year were sought. Seris distinguished three kinds of *cardón* according to

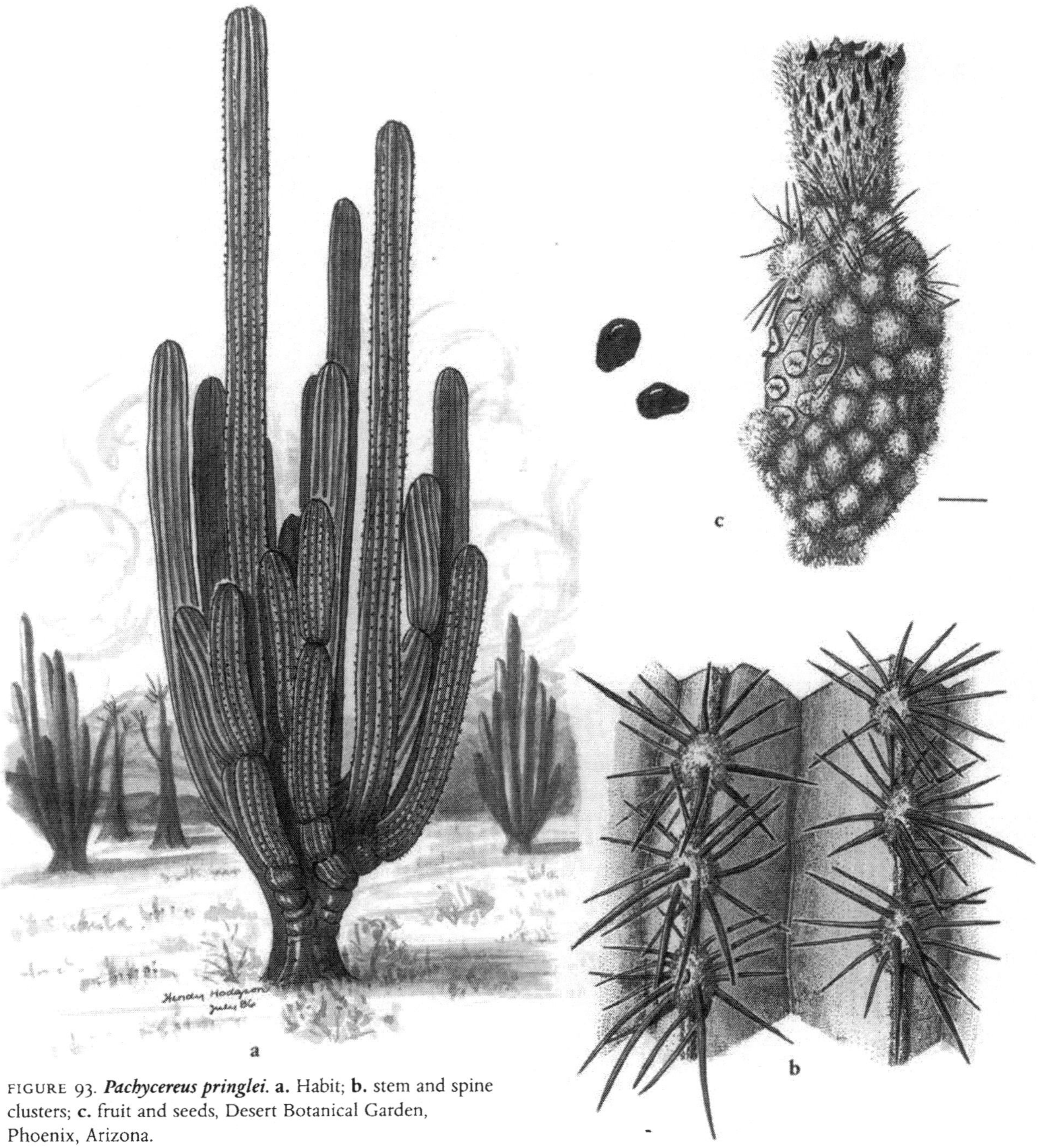

FIGURE 93. ***Pachycereus pringlei*. a.** Habit; **b.** stem and spine clusters; **c.** fruit and seeds, Desert Botanical Garden, Phoenix, Arizona.

their fruits. The first kind had spineless fruits that were always red, bitter, and seldom eaten. The second kind produced spiny fruits with pulp of various colors (white, light yellow orange, pinkish white, or red) and were good to eat. The third type produced fruits that were spineless, of "normal" size, variable in color, and good to eat. Seris ate the fruit pulp fresh or preserved, mixing the pulp from ripe fruit with unripe fruit. This mixture was mashed and kneaded, the juice poured into an olla, then the pulp was patted into flat, round cakes that were left overnight to dry. The next morning they broke up the dried mass into pieces that they stored. Seris cooked and mashed the dried pulp with water to eat.

Seris considered *cardón* seeds to be an important stored food source, and prepared the seeds in a variety of ways. After separating the seeds from the pulp by using a strainer, they cooked the seeds in water, then mashed and salted them. Seeds thus prepared did not taste good and were eaten only when other food was scarce. Seris also toasted and ground *cardón* seeds with salt into a sticky paste, which they rolled into balls. The taste of this paste was described as being better than that of sesame butter. Seris also mixed *cardón* seeds with those of eel-grass *(Zostera marina)*. In the past, they practiced the "second harvest," of *cardón* seeds only. After leaving their fecal material on a flat rock in the sun to dry, they returned to glean the seeds from the matter, then thoroughly cleaned and cooked the seeds to be prepared for food or stored in pottery vessels. The Seri also made a wine from the fruit pulp and occasionally ate the flowers.

The Seri may have introduced the *cardón* to the Sierra Libre, a low mountain range located between Hermosillo and Guaymas (Yetman and Burquez 1996). Some Seris retreated to the Sierra Libre in the 1750s to evade possible genocide by the Spaniards and remained there for 20 years before hunger forced them to surrender. *Cardón* may have sprouted from seeds that were randomly scattered, germinated in fecal matter, or (less likely) deliberately planted because these refugees anticipated an extended stay.

The Yaqui may also have had access to *Pachycereus* near the coast. Rosalio Moisés, a Yaqui, reminisced how the red *ahuesoim* fruit was thought to be very good when ripe (Moisés et al. 1971:158). He added that the *ahuesoim* did not grow in the Yaqui Valley, but that "there are lots of plants scattered between the low hills near the sea at Guaymas," an area where *P. pringlei* grows.

One interesting (if not amusing) medicinal use of *cardón* is mentioned. A Jesuit missionary noted how the natives would "half roast" a piece of stem and apply it to an aching tooth (Aschmann 1966:51). The stem brought immediate relief "but it does cause the teeth to fall out."

Peniocereus | night-blooming cereus

P. greggii **(Engelmann) Britton & Rose var.** ***transmontanus*** **(Engelmann) Backeberg**
night-blooming cereus, queen-of-the-night, deerhorn cactus, reina de la noche, huevos de venado, saramatraca

P. striatus **(Brandegee) Buxbaum (syn.,** ***Wilcoxia striata*** **[Brandegee] Britton & Rose,** ***Neoevansia striata*** **[Brandegee] Sanchez-Mejorada)**
pitahayita, pitahita, jacamatraca, jarrmatraca, sacamatraca, tracamatraca

Both species of *Peniocereus* are unusual plants in that from their large, tuberlike roots they develop wandlike stems. The roots can weigh as much as 40 kilograms in *P. greggii*, but usually weigh between 2 and 7 kilograms (Rea 1997).

Peniocerus greggii var. *transmontanus* often grows under trees or shrubs such as ironwood (*Olneya tesota* A. Gray) or creosote (*Larrea divaricata* Cav.), with the stems being inconspicuous among the branches (fig. 94). It is protected by the Convention for the International Trade of Endangered Species. Despite its low numbers in any given locality, the queen-of-the-night is distinguished from other cacti in the folk taxonomies of desert peoples, from the Ópata descendants in the area of the Río Bavispe, Sonora, to the Gila River Pima in Arizona (Nabhan et al. 1988, 1991).

Desert dwellers regularly noted this cryptic plant and used its flowers, fruit, and roots. Its fruits (fig. 94) are produced in the summer and are scarlet, juicy throughout, and sweet. Despite their edibility, there exists little documentation on the use of fruits for food, although Aleš Hrdlička (1905) noted that the San Carlos Apache ate the fruits and flowers.

The distinction between a plant part used for food or for medicine can often be a fine line. Such is the case with the use of the roots of the night-blooming cereus. The Tohono O'odham consistently referred to the use of the often massive roots (fig. 95) for food and medicine. They ate the "shoots" as greens to some extent, and chewed the tuberous roots to quench their thirst

(Castetter and Underhill 1935). They also baked the whole roots in ashes, then peeled and ate them. The Tohono O'odham boiled pieces of root and drank the liquid for use as a medicine, because it had long been considered an aid to digestion and respiratory ailments and headaches (Nabhan et al. 1991).

Chico Shuni, a Hiá ceḍ O'odham, related that his people dug up and boiled the roots, gave the liquid to children to drink, or put the roots on the soft spot of a child's head to treat dehydration and fallen fontanel (Nabhan 1989b). They also ate pieces of root to aid digestion and to treat respiratory ailments and headaches.

The use of the roots for controlling Type II diabetes has become increasingly important in this century because the frequency of this disease has rapidly increased among the Pima, Tohono O'odham, other desert Native Americans, and Mexican-Americans (Nabhan et al. 1988, 1991). Historically, Type II diabetes was far less common before these groups began to include a large proportion of store-bought foods in their diets. Traditional Pima foods were digested much more slowly than Western staples such as bread, potatoes, and corn (Brand et al. 1990). Ingesting traditional foods protected desert peoples who were genetically predisposed to developing Type II diabetes—their

FIGURE 94. ***Peniocereus greggii*** (Engelm.) Britton & Rose var. ***transmontanus*** (Engelm.) Backeberg. **a.** (top left) Stems with flower bud growing among creosote bush, Desert Botanical Garden, Phoenix, Arizona, June 1988; **b.** (top right) submature fruit, Desert Botanical Garden, August 1988.

FIGURE 95. (bottom) ***Peniocereus greggii*** var. ***transmontanus***. These roots weighed 135 pounds. Photograph by Rodney Engard, courtesy of Desert Botanical Garden, Phoenix, Arizona.

digestive and endocrine systems having evolved in a "feast-or-famine" environment. Although there is no reference regarding the use of the night-blooming cereus roots to control diabetes in Mexican herbals, it seems likely that the Tohono O'odham learned of the plant's benefits for this purpose from Mexicans who paid them to gather the roots for market (Rea 1997). Amadeo Rea suggested that the River Pima's use of queen-of-the-night in controlling the disease may have been learned more recently from surrounding cultures, including the Tohono O'odham and Arizona Yaqui.

Specialty collectors of *P. greggii* had depleted populations in the Gila River region by 1930, and commercial use had apparently waned (Nabhan et al. 1991). Since that time, conversion of land for modern agriculture and housing subdivisions has had a more extensive and lasting impact on the plant populations in the region (Nabhan et al. 1988, 1991). Several Tohono O'odham families cultivate the plant in dooryard gardens for its historic significance and for the quality of its floral fragrance. The plant is exceedingly rare on the Gila River Pima Reservation, but is occasionally found growing in Pima yards because of its flowers (Rea 1997). Here, the community protects this species and other desert plants with an ordinance, which prohibits their destruction or removal by outsiders, and a committee must approve any collection. This is the first native plant law of its kind enacted by a reservation community.

Peniocereus striatus grows inconspicuously in sandy or alluvial soils (Wiggins 1964; Pinkava 1995) at very low densities. Plants are usually hidden under trees or shrubs, with their thin, weak, dead-looking stems arising from tuberous roots. They mimic the form of more common, often unpalatable "nurse plants," such as the long-lived creosote bush and ironwood, and thus escape herbivores while receiving physical support (Suzan et al. 1994).

The Tohono and Hiá ceḍ O'odham distinguish between *P. greggii* and *P. striatus,* considering the latter more useful for medicinal purposes than for food (Nabhan 1989b). Hiá ceḍ O'odham women cook up pieces of *pitahayita* root in water and drink it for controlling diabetes and cholesterol. The Seri also considered the plants more useful for medicinal purposes (Felger and Moser 1985).

The conspicuously large, scarlet, and moderately juicy fruits of *pitahayita* mature from August though September and early October. Seris ate these fruits fresh and considered the taste to be not as sweet as the fruits of *pitahaya dulce* (Felger and Moser 1985, cited as *Neoevansia striata*). Townsend Brandegee (1891b) noted that the inhabitants of the cape region of Baja California thought the flowers and fruits, the latter of which he considered insipid in taste, to resemble those of *Stenocereus gummosus* (Engelm.) Britton & Rose.

Pitahayita populations grow at low densities within a narrow geographic range and are thus particularly vulnerable to extirpation by human activities (Nabhan et al. 1991). Activities that are threatening this already rare plant include the clearing of areas for ranching and agriculture and the selective depletion of legume trees, such as ironwood, which is used for carvings, firewood, and charcoal (Mellink et al. 1991). The selective harvest of ironwoods is especially significant in the more northern populations, where they are more vulnerable to frost and heat and therefore more dependent on the protective canopy of these trees (Suzan et al. 1994). *Pitahayita* grows near Bahía Kino, and finding a mature ironwood requires traveling a great distance from the town. One depauperate plant was found outside of town within an area of five to ten square hectares, growing more or less in the open under a similarly depauperate *Melochia tomentosa* L. (*Hodgson et al. 5741,* DES).

Local pesticide spraying near populations at the U.S.-Mexico border adjacent to Organ Pipe Cactus National Monument may also reduce *pitahayita* reproduction (Suzan et al. 1994). Sphingid moths pollinate *pitahayita* flowers. Periodic spraying of pesticides from June to September to control sphingid moth larvae in adjacent cotton fields in Mexico seemed to affect pollination of *pitahayita* flowers on both sides of the border. Few moths were present and fruit and seed set of *pitahayita* was low. However, sacred datura (*Datura* spp.), which grows at the edges of nearby agricultural fields, is also pollinated by sphingid moths. Hopefully, its flowers may attract and encourage the incidental pollination of *pitahayita.*

Stenocereus

S. alamosensis **(Coulter) Gibson & Horak (syn., *Rathbunia alamosensis* [Coulter] Britton & Rose)**
octopus cactus, sina, sinita

S. eruca **(Brandegee) Gibson & Horak (syn., *Machaerocereus eruca* [Brandegee] Britton & Rose)**
creeping-devil, chilenola, chirinola

S. *gummosus* (Engelmann) Gibson & Horak (syn., *Machaerocereus gummosus* [Engelmann] Britton & Rose)
bittersweet pitahaya, pitahaya agria, pitahaya agridulce, pitahaya, pitayo agrio

***S. thurberi* (Engelmann) Buxbaum**
organ pipe cactus, pitahaya dulce, pitahaya, mehuelé, mevuelé

Stenocereus alamosensis grows in alluvial or sandy soil on plains and bajadas in central and southern Sonora below 800 meters elevation (Turner et al. 1995). Plants enter the periphery of the Seri region in the vicinity of Bahía San Carlos, northwest of Guaymas and between Hermosillo and Bahía Kino. Seris ate the small fruits, but considered them bitter in taste (Felger and Moser 1974, 1985). In the Río Mayo region, people eagerly gathered and ate the fruits raw (Martin et al. 1998). I agree with Marshall and Bock (1941), who described the fruit pulp as being sweet and edible.

Stenocereus eruca has a very limited distribution, being confined to the Magdalena Plain of central Baja California Sur, where it is locally common on silty or sandy flats close to the Pacific Coast. It is found "creeping along the coastal lands and over the fine drifted sands of the seashore like countless thousands of caterpillars crawling over the ground, worming their way slowly across the sandy plains to the sea" (Thornber and Bonker 1932:2). Jesuit missionaries appear to not have made any reference to this plant or its use, perhaps because of its relatively restricted distribution. However, Paul Standley (1924) noted that the spiny fruits were edible when immature, whereas John Thornber and Francis Bonker (1932:3, 19) considered the mature fruits to be "delicious and relished by Indians and Mexicans, both as a salad and as a preserve." Townsend Brandegee (1891b) described the fruit as dull red when ripe and having a pleasant, acidic taste, being more acidic than those of *S. gummosus.*

Populations of *S. gummosus* (fig. 96) are locally abundant from the north-central Pacific Coast of Baja California and Isla Ángel de la Guarda south throughout much of Baja California Sur and adjacent islands (Turner et al. 1995). Baja California inhabitants greatly prized the fruits of *S. gummosus,* or *pitahaya agria.* Sebastián Vizcaíno, a pearl fisherman and explorer, provided what may be the earliest reference to the use of *pitahaya.* He had just named and proclaimed the settlement of San Felipe and the port of San Sebastián, at the southern tip of the peninsula on September 3, 1596. He wrote of how on this day, "the Indians [probably Coras or Aripes] brought me some presents of the land which were pitahaya" (Mathes 1992:136). The *pitahaya* was probably *S. gummosus* because its fruits would have been mature at that time. Fr. Kino observed that natives along the coast brought many "tamales" of dried *pitahayas* and some little boxes of fresh *pitahayas* (Bolton 1948).

Kiliwas traveled to the west coast to harvest the fruits, which they ate raw (Meigs 1939). Because the fruits are very juicy, they provided "a food and drink at the same time, therefore those who eat a lot of it need little to drink," although one was shocked initially to see his or her urine turn red (del Barco 1980:153). Even the Jesuit missionaries, such as Frs. Taravel, Linck, and Baegert liked the fruits. Fr. Baegert (1952:36) noted how "sprinkled with sugar, this fruit deserves to be set on a princely table." In a letter to his brother George, Fr. Baegert (1982:132) described *pitahaya agria* and its use by the Guaicuras of south-central Baja California:

> I shall only tell about two [plants] because they bear fruit which one would not be ashamed to be eaten and seen at European and aristocratic dinners. The worst is that they do not last the whole year, for then I and the Indians would be well off. Just imagine how it looks, several of them partly creeping on the soil, one and a half yards long; partly they swing up one or two yards high, sprouting out into green branches three or four inches long or an arm thick on which grow some dozen of cilia. Out of this "desperate morning star" grows a fruit, also green, covered with numerous little thorns on the shells, big as the egg of a duck. If one cleans the thorns from the shell and opens it, the round fruit [pulp] rolls out, some purple, others dark red, mixed with thousands of black little grains.

In the land of the Guaicuras, the fruits ripened in "early November and December" (Baegert 1982:132). To the north, fruits ripened from early September through October or November, and "in some places [rarely] ripens as late as the end of December" (del Barco 1980:153–154). *Pitahaya agria* fruits extended the harvest period of *pitahaya* and cactus fruits in general because they matured "when the sweet ones *[pitahaya dulce]* are gone" (Baegert 1952:36).

The fruits of *pitahaya agria* are relatively large, being "as large as oranges" (del Barco 1980:153; fig. 96). According to the German Jesuit missionary Fr. Linck, each fruit weighed "as much as two pounds" (Burrus

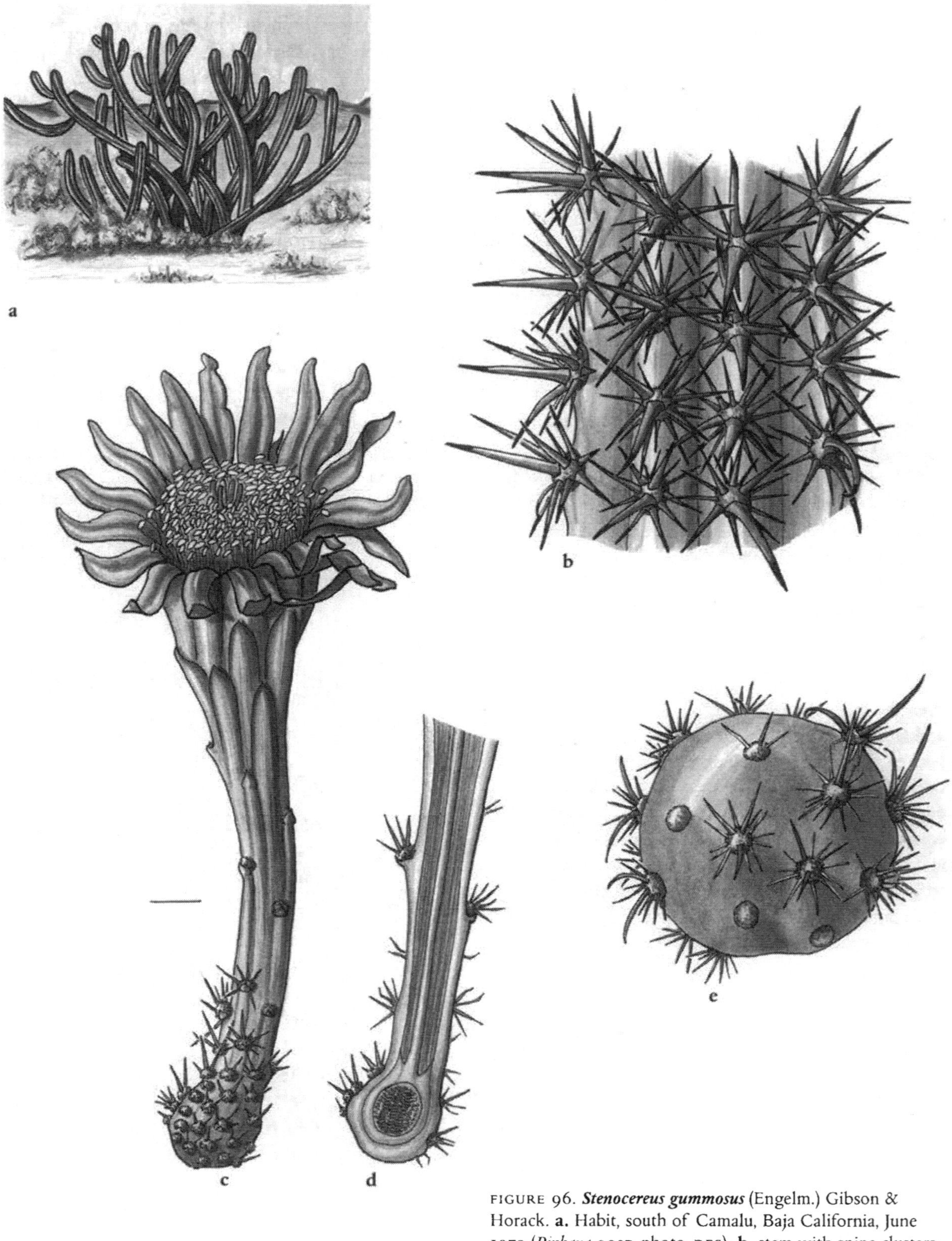

FIGURE 96. ***Stenocereus gummosus*** (Engelm.) Gibson & Horack. **a.** Habit, south of Camalu, Baja California, June 1972 (*Pinkava 9037*, photo, DES); **b.** stem with spine clusters; *Pinkava 9037*, DES); **c–d.** flower, south of San Vicente, Baja California, August 1972 (*McGill 500*, DES); **e.** fruit.

1967:68). Fr. Baegert (1952:35) considered one as being "more than enough" when he ate it as dessert. Despite the relatively large size of the fruits of *pitahaya agria,* the amount of fruit one could collect was small, being much less than that of *pitahaya dulce.* Fr. Baegert commented on how "of the many plants in the central part of peninsula" with their numerous stems, "not one in a hundred bears fruit" (Baegert 1952:35) and "it is a lot if you find on one plant three [fruits]" (Baegert 1982:132). However, on "both coasts they [fruits] are more plentiful." Fr. del Barco (1980:154–155) also noted that *pitahaya agria* was more plentiful on the coasts: "There is an abundance of these fruit-bearing plants only in the territories near the beaches of both coasts. Once upon the mountains and in the midlands between the coasts, it is a rare occurrence to come upon one of these plants, and the few that exist do not give fruit." Additionally, birds ate many of the fruits as they ripened, making a significantly important food source less so (Aschmann 1959).

People took great care in the collection of any fruits remaining, which was a very tedious task fraught with difficulty. Fr. Baegert (1952) lamented that "there is often so many of these spreading, spiny plants [they grow in dense patches] that make it difficult to collect fruits." Fr. del Barco (1980) noted how the spiny stems were often too thick and tangled to collect fruits, even at arm's length. Contrary to what Fr. Clavigero (1937) stated, collecting the fruits did not require a tool with a "hook" at the end, like that used for collecting *cardón* or *pitahaya dulce* fruit. According to Fr. del Barco (1980:154) "one cannot penetrate it to collect the pitahayas that are in the middle, because of the many and strong thorns with which everything is covered and which close access unless some clearing is found through which one can get in." Fr. Baegert also noted that the fruits in the middle of the spiny stems were often ignored because it was too difficult to secure them without tearing one's flesh (Baegert 1982). The numerous fierce spines were extracted from the flesh with "great difficulty or, if it should break, it cannot come out except by incising the affected part . . . or left inside until it grows pus" (del Barco 1980:152).

Cochimí women braved these spines and collected the likewise spiny fruit in "great quantities," by picking "the fruit with one's hand, putting aside the thorns or dumping the pitahayas to the ground first" (del Barco 1980:154). After peeling the fruit, the women mixed and kneaded all of the pulp. They later covered this "great ball of dough" with corn husks "or some other thing." Thus stored, the dried pulp could "be preserved for a long time" without it spoiling and losing its flavor, being an "exquisite treat among those Indians" (del Barco 1980:154). The tiny seeds embedded in the pulp were not removed, but eaten "without being conscious of it" (Aschmann 1966:88). Seeds of *pitahaya agria* and *pitahaya dulce* were removed from fecal material and prepared, a process the missionaries called the "second harvest."

Pitahaya agria fruits were commonly preferred to those of *pitahaya dulce,* "particularly when they are quite ripe or fully mature" because the juicy pulp was "delicate, and no less delicious than the sweet ones" (del Barco 1980:153). Fruit "skin" and pulp varies from being light red to dark red, although Fr. Baegert (1952:36) heard of "a few yellow ones found in the northern part of [Baja] California." Fruits that were red did not necessarily mean they were ripe, as described by del Barco (1980:13): "Even though they attained a deep red color, which is [usually] the signal that they have ripened, the sourness dominates more than what is agreeable, a property not shared by fruits of *pitahaya dulce* [which] when they have this fleshy red color, are all in their prime ripeness."

Fr. Baegert also noted that *pitahaya agria* fruits tasted better than sweet ones, being "as good as any European fruit known to me" (Baegert 1982:132), although the sour taste "sets the teeth on edge" (Baegert 1952:36). He observed that "the native inhabitants paid no attention to this bitterness or don't notice it as they never eat bread after it." Townsend Brandegee (1891b) commented that the flavor is soon lost after the fruits are collected. Inhabitants on Carmen Island made preserves and jams from the fruits near the turn of the century (Rose 1892, cited as *Cereus "gamosus"*).

The Spaniards were especially interested in *pitahaya agria* fruit because "its most valuable quality is its being a specific against the *distemper de Loanda,*" or scurvy (Venegas and Burriel 1966:43; del Barco 1980). For the coastal inhabitants, however, the stems were probably more important for their use as a fish poison, which may have yielded "more food than the fruit" (Aschmann 1959:81).

Stenocereus gummosus is also found in a small area on the Sonoran coast and on Tiburón Island. David Yetman and Alberto Burquez (1996) suggested that the Sonoran populations appear to grow only near current or former Seri habitations and along routes that were historically well traveled. Seris ate the fruits fresh and dried them, if plentiful, for future use. These harvests continued until the 1980s (Felger and Moser 1985). The Seri pierced the fruits with a pole having a pointed stick of creosote or oregano (*Lippia palmeri* Wats.) inserted at the end, then with a twisting motion pulled them off the plant's stem. The Seris also knew of plants that produced yellowish fruits in the vicinity of El Desemboque, Sonora.

Populations of *S. thurberi* (fig. 97) are extensive on the mainland south of 32°N in northern Sonora, but northern populations are small and separated by several kilometers (Turner et al. 1995). Plants are absent in Baja California until south of 28'15°N and become more abundant south of 26'30°N. This species shows dependence on fairly predictable warm-season rain

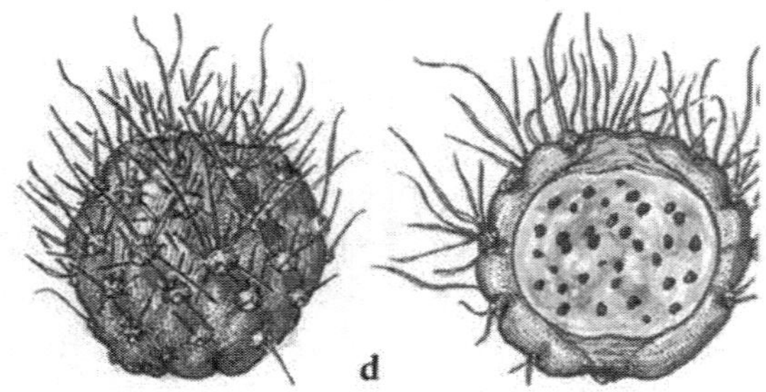

FIGURE 97. ***Stenocereus thurberi*** (Engelm.) Buxbaum.
a. Habit, Ajo, Pima County, Arizona, 1939 (*Lindsay s.n.,* photo, DES); **b.** stem cross-section showing ribs and spine clusters, south of Alamos, Sonora, May 1984 (*Hodgson 2994,* DES); **c.** stem and spine clusters, Desert Botanical Garden, Phoenix, Arizona; **d.** fruit, Desert Botanical Garden.

throughout its range. In the late 1700s, Fr. Linck noted the relationship between the plant's distribution and precipitation. He observed that "in areas between 29 and 31°N plants were rarely seen because it rains so little or not at all" and were "found only in the area were it rains at least once a year in June or July" (Burrus 1967:68).

Fruits of *S. thurberi,* or *pitahaya dulce* (fig. 97), were a favorite food to those who accessed them through collection or trade. Groups included the Pericú, Cora, Huichiti, Guaicura, Cochimí *(sensu lato),* Hiá ceḍ O'odham, Tohono O'odham, Gila River Pima, Seri, Yaqui, Pima Bajo, and other neighboring groups such as the Mayo, Ópata, and Tarahumara.

Fruits mature from June through August, although the time varies. Fr. del Barco (1980) observed that fruits ripened from the beginning of June through the end of August in south-central Baja California. Elsewhere in Baja California fruits began to mature "around Saint John's Day" (June 24) or later, and continued through mid-August. Fruits ripened later in "the more northerly missions," becoming most abundant for harvesting in August. Even though fruit production was relatively dependable and prolific, it seemed to be affected by previous amounts of precipitation. The crop failed completely in wet summers (Clavigero 1937; Sales 1956). Luis Sales, a Dominican missionary, observed that "when it rains much [of] the fruit drops or does not hold its sweetness" (Sales 1956:16). Fr. del Barco (1980: 151) observed that "overripe" (dried) and maturing *pitahaya* fruits were lost if it rained toward the end of the season. He added that there were "so few *pitahayas* that one can even say 'none'" in some years. While comparing the ability of the prickly-pears to stand such drought with that of the *pitahayas,* del Barco (1980: 172) noted that *pitahaya* fruits were numerous following dry periods, but were few following moist periods:

> Their [prickly-pears'] great consistency in weathering these droughts notwithstanding, they do not equal in this respect that of the striated plants *[cardón, pitahaya agria, pitahaya dulce]* which, even in the most severe dry spells, maintain themselves serene and with the same greenness as always, and without the least alteration. Rather, during years preceded by greater dryness, *pitahayas* give their fruit more abundantly. In the winter of 1739–1740 it rained there several times, and so much on one occasion, many arroyos swelled up and ran swiftly, an event that I witnessed only this time in the thirty years that I was there ... but the *pitahayas* did not bear fruit that year of 1740. It seems they complained of having had so much moisture.

In contrast, Fr. Sistiaga noted the opposite (Burrus 1984:115): "When spring has been dry—a frequent occurrence—there is little or no fruit [*pitahayas* and prickly-pears] to be had, inasmuch as in Lower California it usually rains very little except in the southern tip where regular rain falls."

When the Sinaloan governor, Adm. Isidro de Atondo, and Fr. Eusebio Kino were attempting to cross the peninsula in 1684, it was noted that the natives were very sad. It had not rained, "and, because they had nothing to eat as the fields were dry and there would be no pitahayas, they asked if we would make it rain" (Mathes 1969:39). Another story relates that, after engaging in a first fruit ceremony, certain chiefs told soldiers at San Isidro that their people worshipped a god "who gave them their food, coming down from heaven when it rained to give them pitahayas and medesé [medesá; *Cercidium microphyllum*]" (Bolton 1936:177).

Edward Palmer (1871) and Valery Havard (1895, 1896) noted that the fruits of *S. thurberi* were of better quality than those of the saguaro and were used for the same purposes by the inhabitants of Arizona and Sonora. Plants were not abundant enough to be an important food for the Gila River Pima, who did, however, receive syrup from the Tohono O'odham (Rea 1997). The Tohono O'odham prized the fruits of *pitahaya dulce* as much as those of saguaro (Castetter and Underhill 1935). Jam made from the fruit sold for as much as 12 dollars (U.S. currency) for a 20-ounce jar in 1989 at Quitovac, Sonora (G. P. Nabhan, pers. comm.). *Pitahaya dulce* continued to be a major wild crop for those living at Quitovac, who harvested 1,200 kilograms of its fruit for making jam, drying, and eating fresh in the summer of 1991 (Felger et al. 1992).

Stenocereus thurberi was important to the Hiá ceḍ O'odham. Tom Childs (1954) said that they made a jam from the *pitalla.* Ramon Anita related that the Hiá ceḍ O'odham dried and stored the pulp in sealed ollas, which they then buried in the sand (Thomas 1963). They put a long stick over each cache to make sure they could find the ollas if sand drifted over the spot. Individuals found and dug out the stored food, which they lived on through the winter months.

Pitahaya dulce was extremely important to Baja California inhabitants who had reasonable access to the plants. The plant was "held in the highest regard"

(Aschmann 1966) and provided both food and water. The Spaniards called the fruit *pitahaya* as well, but to the Cochimí the plants were *ambia* and the fruits *dammia,* or *tammia* (del Barco 1981). The "summer solstice and two months thereafter" was a great time for celebration to the natives, who consumed large quantities of the usually plentiful fruits. At this time the "heaven hangs full of violins and the good Indian thinks paradise has flown to California" (Baegert 1982:133). Fr. Baegert (1952:35) called this period "the carnival season for the California Indians; after that the nine months of misery begins again." Fr. del Barco (1981:51) also noted that the *pitahaya* season was a time of great joy and happiness for the natives:

> The season of pitahaya harvest was like vintage time for them. They were merrier and more cheerful at this time than in all the rest of the year. The three months of pitahaya (venerable Fr. Salvatierra has reported), are celebrated like the three carnival days before Ash Wednesday in some European countries, when to a great degree people go out of their senses. These Indians also go out of their senses, dedicating themselves completely to their feasting, dancing, invitations to parties of distant rancherias, and their peculiar type of merrymaking.

So important was *pitahaya dulce* that "not even the pozole [boiled corn, a favorite food of the neophytes] of the missionaries could keep them at the mission, or stop them from participating. Day after day old and young disappeared, until the Fathers to their sorrow found themselves alone" (Engelhardt 1908:83). This displeased the padres, of course, because time away from the mission meant loss of work and religious lessons. Fr. Baegert (1952:124) seemed even more annoyed than usual: "I once asked a California woman who understood Spanish, why she did not perform the penance imposed at the last confession, which consisted in the recital of the rosaries. I received this reply in good Spanish: 'de puro comer,' which is to say, merely on account of eating [the *pitahayas*]." However, it was not wise for the padres, particularly early Jesuits such as Salvatierra, Píccolo, and Ugarte, to discourage the natives from going out into the desert to gather *pitahayas.* They found themselves having to rely on these and other desert plants for food when supplies were low and not replenished and when efforts to cultivate plant foods were relatively fruitless.

Pitahaya dulce served the Cochimí, Pericú, and probably Guaicura as their time calendar, "for to live in adultery one *ambia* is as much as 12 months and three *ambia* is as much as three years" (Baegert 1982:133). Fr. del Barco (1981:31–32) described how the Cochimí divided the year into six parts, some of which reflected a time of plenty because of the availability of the *pitahayas* and other foods:

> The first part is called *meyibo,* which is the season of pitahayas. Because of the abundance of this delicious fruit, this is for them the happiest time and most appreciated time. It lasts part of June, all of July, and part of August. The second part is called *amada-appi,* and includes all of September and part of both August and October. This is when the land, after it has rained, is dressed in green, and it is the season of prickly pears and bittersweet pitahayas *[S. gummosus].* It is therefore a much esteemed time for the Californios, and no less because they also gather other seeds during this time.

Fr. del Barco (1981:32) continued to say that the final sixth season, called *meyijben-maayi,* included part of April, all of May, and part of June. The suffix meant "a bad thing," as this season was "when they experience the greatest hunger." It was during this period that "there was no mezcal to eat and there was the common scarcity of other food," so much that "the Indians can barely find enough in the field to sustain life." Again, the importance of the *pitahayas* is realized, as understood by del Barco: "The following season is greatly esteemed by itself, because of the abundance and goodness of the sweet pitahayas, but even more so because it brings them out of their preceding misery."

The plant's importance undoubtedly is due to the fact that large quantities of fresh, sweet, juicy fruit could be harvested, providing them not only a tasty food, but also an adequate supply of water. Available water was always a concern for the inhabitants of the central desert region of Baja California. According to Homer Aschmann (1959:59), of great significance "was the ability to survive for considerable periods on the water contained in succulent plant tissues." Fr. Baegert (1952) commented that "at the time of the *pitahayas,* the California Indians can go for several days without water," a statement believed to be both conservative and accurate by Aschmann (1959). The juicy fruits of *pitahaya dulce* also allowed groups at their time of harvest to travel "to any place where the *pitahayas* grow in order to exploit other resources, even though no other water supply existed in the vicinity" (Aschmann 1959:59). This was important because the local inhabitants made little use of containers for carrying water. The equivalent of two or three quarts of water was carried at other times, but only "able-bodied individuals could carry turtle bladder containers of water over an extended [at least one-day] journey [and] family groups could not" (Aschmann 1959:59). Esteban C. de Valenzuela, in his report on Francisco de Ortega's exploratory trip to La Paz in 1632, described not only the friendliness and thoughtfulness of the natives, but the water containers they used (Mathes 1992:229): "And the friendship which they demonstrated toward us was such that they carried water for us from the freshwater lake in our jugs, because that which they drink is kept in fish stomachs like bladders and smells of seafood."

Small groups of both men and women traveled about in search of the *pitahaya*. Whole rancherias commonly traveled to a common meeting place "scores of miles" away to collect the fruits (del Barco 1981:59). Pregnant women, accompanied by other women, sometimes went to the field in the morning "to gather cactus or some other things and while busy at this endeavor the labor of childbirth begins" (del Barco 1981:59).

The fruits were described as having a red or yellow "skin" and pulp whose color closely corresponded to the color of the "skin" (del Barco 1980). Plants producing yellow fruits were apparently not uncommon in Baja California. The fruit pulp was considered "juicy, delicate, and very tasty ... worthy of the table of the greatest monarchs" (del Barco 1980:149). Even Fr. Baegert enjoyed the fruit when he added wine and sugar to the pulp, which to him was like "eating strawberries or even something better" (Baegert 1982:133). Pericus and Huichitis probably ate the small fruits of the dwarf form, *S. thurberi* var. *littoralis* K. Brandegee. Ann Zwinger (1983) described the grape-sized fruits as being delicious.

Mature fruits of *S. thurberi* would splatter if knocked on the ground and could not be caught by hand due to their spiny nature. Therefore, Cochimí women or men used a long, thin pole (sometimes from reedgrass, probably *Phragmites australis*) to which was firmly attached a thin, pointed bone "three or four fingers in length," which formed the "hook" at the top, or used a stiff, pointed stick to collect the fruits (del Barco 1980). *Pitahaya* hooks dating to 100 B.C., which "implied a gathering aspect" of the Comondú culture, were found in the Sierra de la Giganta (Massey 1966:50–51). These hooks were made by "lashing pointed hardwood pieces at an acute angle to cane shafts" and used for gathering *pitahaya* fruits. The Comondú was a common culture of central Baja California that was both prehistoric and historic (Massey 1966). The hooks were a "peninsular counterpart" (Massey 1966:50) of the saguaro hooks used in Arizona (Driver and Massey 1957).

The harvesters set off in search of *pitahayas* armed with this pole and net. The harvester hooked the ripe fruit and brought it down, taking care that the fruit did not drop on the ground, but instead fell into the net. If a fruit "puts up a resistance," the harvester impaled it with the pointed end and then pulled it down (del Barco 1980:51). Fruit was also picked by hand or by using short sticks, if obtainable. During a period of food shortage or if "particularly delectable morsels were sought, the Indians would risk severe scratches" (Aschmann 1959:62). They easily removed the spines (if fruits were ripe) with "any little stick" (del Barco 1980:150) or by brushing the fruits off with leaves (Aschmann 1959). They ate their fill of fruits immediately, with the spines removed, then collected the remaining ripe fruit, which they threw into their net (or "knapsack") to take back home "either for their children, or for themselves when their digestion has left some empty space" (del Barco 1980:150, 1981).

Much fruit could be eaten at one time. Fr. Baegert (1952:283) related how, because of "the meager supply of food the rest of the year and no refrigeration, they [Guaicura, Huichiti, or Pericú groups] gorged themselves, much to the disapproval of the missionaries." He further noted that "they eat their fill without time and labor, whenever they desire." They ate so much, in fact, that Baegert could not recognize some of the inhabitants when they returned from the field where they spent three to four weeks, because their "whole bodies, especially the face [was] so filled out and bloated" (Baegert 1952:35).

As important as *pitahaya dulce* was, the Baja California natives had relatively little time to enjoy its fruits, which provided them food for only two months. The natives of central and southern Baja California apparently did not dry the pulp for future use (Baegert 1952; Aschmann 1959; del Barco 1980), although they did store sun-dried pulp of *S. gummosus* for long periods (del Barco 1980). Fr. del Barco (1980:150) noted that the fruits of *pitahaya dulce* must be used the same day "because the following day they are already tending to sour, because of spoilage, particularly those that have opened." However, if left on the plant, "the more they ripen, the sweeter they become." The pulp of *pitahaya dulce* would spoil more quickly than the more tart pulp of *pitahaya agria* because of its higher sugar content, unless the pulp was boiled down into a syrup or jelly. Because the Cochimí and more southern groups did not have vessels or ollas prior to Spanish contact, they could not boil and thus store the pulp.

Uncollected fruit dried and fell to the ground toward the end of the *pitahaya* season if it had not rained. These fruits were collected from the ground and brought home to be saved "for a later time, if they have no need for them then" (del Barco 1980:151), which suggests minimal storage. In this case, the only edible part was the "skin," which when collected fresh had a sour taste. The "skin" of older fruit became sweeter over time because it had absorbed some of the sweet pulp, thus making it "edible and even palatable to the Californios."

All of the Baja California groups who utilized both types of *pitahaya* fruits practiced a second type of harvest "but collecting it from the tree only once" (del Barco 1981:76). This practice again illustrates the resourcefulness of using an important, but limited, food resource, although it was a subject of much amusement and some disgust among the missionaries. Flour made from seeds saved from the "second harvest" may have even aided the people in their survival during May and June (Aschmann 1997). Early missionary documents often mentioned this "second harvest," but Fr. del Barco (1981:75–76) described it in illuminating detail:

> When fruits are eaten, [they are] so full of seeds not perceived or bothered with. It appears that [the Indians] lamented the fact that the seeds of this delicious fruit escaped without their being able to enjoy their particular flavor. So, during *pitahaya* season, when they generally did not eat anything else, each family got a spot near their dwelling ready where they could evacuate their bowels. For greater cleanliness they lay flat rocks or dry, broadleaf plants or similar things on the designated spot. This assured that the excrement will not mix up with dust or sand. After it was well dried up, the women put it in their trays, and they would break up to a powder with their hands all the superfluous matter that was not *pitahaya* seeds. This operation caused them no more concern than if their hands had been in flowers. In order to separate the smelly powder from the seeds, they moved the tray as is normally done when one cleans any grain.

The women then prepared the seeds like any other. They toasted the seeds by throwing hot coals onto them in a tray. Such toasting emitted an "intense fetid odor" that pervaded the air "over a wide area" (del Barco 1981:74). They ground the toasted seeds and ate the resulting flour. One amusing story related how this "delicious treat" was offered to "Fr. Francisco María Píccolo as a present during a visit which he made to the unconverted natives" (del Barco 1981:77). Fr. Píccolo was unaware of what this present of food was or how it was prepared. To show his appreciation, he ate the flour (whether he liked or pretended to like the flour is uncertain). This incident was "made known among the other priests and it was sometimes a subject of amusement whenever they talked with Fr. Píccolo." Even the natives were apparently sometimes amused while engaging in this practice. Fr. Baegert (1952:68) told how after gleaning, grinding, and roasting the seeds, they ate them "with much joking." This "second harvest" did not contribute toward gastrointestinal disorders or other illnesses because seeds were thoroughly cleaned and dried (Aschmann 1959). This practice was eventually abandoned, even during Fr. del Barco's stay.

Pitahaya dulce harvests also affected the social framework of these people. The fruits probably contributed little to maintaining or increasing the population, but enabled people to congregate, support, and enforce the social and religious structure of their society (Aschmann 1959). In a letter to José M. Villaisan, attorney general of the *Audencia* of Guadalajara, Fr. Salvatierra wrote that he and the soldiers aboard the *San Javier* were near death because of famine. They were also under threat of attack by some hostile Monquis (a Cochimí group living north of Loreto), who, having always hated the Spaniards, used the *pitahaya* harvest to their advantage (Burrus 1971:211):

> At the very time we're half famished, we were in peril of being attacked. A young soldier, Jose Perez, married an Indian girl from the mountains. At the time of the *pitahaya* harvest, the other natives enticed her to participate in their evil practices on the occasion. The soldier set out secretly, against the orders of the captain, in search of his wife. He killed an old Indian because the man opposed the girl's return. The natives then slew the soldier and called for concerted attack against all of us. Many of the natives agreed to such an action; but others refused to take part, and thus we were spared.

Many Monquis were very friendly to the Spaniards for various reasons. Fr. Salvatierra wrote that the Monquí eagerly assisted him and his company and carried their supplies of maize, flour, and other items to Londó, early in the summer of 1699 (Burrus 1971:165–166). Here many Cochimí rancherias were said to exist. This was the time of the *pitahaya* harvest, and near Londó there was an abundant supply of the fruits. Salvatierra suspected that the Monquis hoped to gain access to the *pitahayas,* under the pretext of assisting him and his group. Rather, the natives hoped to make peace with the Cochimí in Londó and join them in their feasting and dancing.

Harvesting the *pitahayas* precipitated another documented encounter. In an account written to a fellow missionary, Fr. Píccolo described how Yejui, a certain chieftain of the Ignacieño northwest of Mulegé, was to be summoned by his tribal members and meet with Fr. Píccolo on the padre's arrival. Yejui explained to Píccolo that he could not because he was detained by other, more aggressive natives, translated as such (Burrus 1984:84): "They informed me, but I could not come immediately because I was with my people along the shore and slopes of the Rio de Kaelmet de Los Angeles, where I went to eat pitahayas. And as the Indians there wanted to keep us from the fruit, I had to fight. When I saw the captain of Los Angeles, I told him to leave the place as I did not want to fight him. He left, and the people fought; some of them got hurt."

Besides instigating fights, *S. thurberi* also served to warn others of impending attack. While returning from La Paz to San Juan Malibut (south of Loreto), Fr. Guillén and his entourage passed through friendly Huichiti-speaking natives into Guaicura territory. The Guaicuras were always considered "bellicose, finicky," and generally disagreeable to natives and foreigners alike (although their ill temperament was said to have been exacerbated by the Anglo pearl fishermen's mistreatment). As they left Aripité, they saw a strange sight (Mathes 1979:85): "Upon leaving this rancheria [Aripité], at about a stone's throw, we saw a pitahaya plant, completely destroyed, broken to bits, and some of the larger pieces pinned to the ground with stakes or sharpened branches; this was interpreted by our Indian friends and experienced Spaniards to be an act of declaring us to be enemies and of opening war upon us."

Pitahaya also served to protect the Spaniards from attack by acting as a physical barrier. Fearing that the settlement of La Paz may have come under attack during his absence, Sebastián Vizcaíno returned only to find the people at peace "and the camp well-fortified with a trench around it that Captain Figueroa [the captain in charge in Vizcaíno's absence] had made from trees cut into stakes and branches from the pines and pitahayas, as wide and high as a pike and on which all had worked more than could be desired" (Mathes 1992:141).

Pitahaya dulce was a valuable food for the Seri (Felger and Moser 1974, 1985). They harvested the fruits in early summer, using a special pole about four meters long, with a spatula-shaped piece of mesquite wood (*Prosopis* spp.) fastened at the end. A wire or sharp, pointed strip of metal (a piece of creosote bush was used traditionally) extended beyond the pole that speared the fruit. Pulp that was not fully red was considered to be the best tasting. They ate the "skin" and seeds with the pulp. The Seri also dried the pieces of fruit by laying them on *pitahaya dulce* ribs placed on the ground after peeling and slicing the fruits into thin sections. They would then turn the pieces over several times while the fruit slices dried. Water was added to the fruit, which was then eaten raw or cooked. Seri bands living on the mainland also made two kinds of wine from *pitahaya dulce* fruit, but those living on Tiburón Island, where the plant is common, did not (Kroeber 1931).

Stenocereus thurberi is represented by very tall plants possessing definite trunks in the Sinaloan thornscrub in central and southern Sonora, with the branches produced being three to four meters or more above the ground (fig. 98). Ónavas Pimas gathered and ate its fruits (Pennington 1980). Perhaps it was these plants that Fr. del Barco (1980:154) noted, being made aware of a "very different variety" of bittersweet *pitahaya* that grew in New Spain: "[the cactus was] not only a tree, but a very large one, a tree larger than that of the sweet pitahaya, and also because the fruit of that tree is little esteemed in those territories where they grow, whereas if they were like the ones in California, they would certainly be greatly esteemed."

Ralph Beals (1945) described how the Cáhita used a long cane spear with a point of heartwood attached to collect the fruits from the tall, arborescent, trunked plants. After spearing the fruit, they placed them in a special container made of cane splints twined with mesquite bark and carried it over their shoulders. When land was cleared for farming, the Mayo, and less frequently the Yaqui, usually left some of the larger individuals of *pitahaya dulce.*

Rosalio Moisés, a Yaqui, remembered how he and others collected *pitahya dulce* during the mid 1930s, while living in Torim, a Yaqui settlement in Sonora (Moisés et al. 1971):

> During June, July, and August everyone goes out to gather pitahaya. With a long, sharpened carrizo cane you spear the fruit, which may grow fifteen or twenty feet above the ground. At home the fruit is peeled, put in an *olla* without water, and cooked. The women decide when it has reached the jelly stage by dropping a little in a cup of water. The sweet pitahaya jelly, which we call *sitoim,* can be kept a long time. This sort of jelly can be made from other cacti, but that made from pitahaya is the best.

Fr. Nentvig (1980:36) was probably referring to the tall *pitahaya dulce,* when he wrote of its fruits as being "foremost among the wild fruits of Sonora, equally relished by Spaniards and *gente de razon.*" The translators, Pradeau and Rasmussen, "corrected" him saying it was the saguaro (*Carnegiea gigantea*) to which he was referring. On the contrary, Nentvig was correct to distinguish this tall *S. thurberi* type from the saguaro. He described the plants as having a definite trunk, white or purplish flowers, and fruits "the size of a hen's egg" that were covered with spines. Spines were removed and the rind opened, exposing the edible pulp. The "thinner the rind, the more savory the fruit [pulp]."

FIGURE 98. A very large, trunked ***Stenocereus thurberi,*** which is characteristic in the area around Ónavas, Sonora, November 1987.

Andrés Pérez de Ribas wrote that the Névome of Sinaloa enjoyed the *pitahaya* fruit for "the longest period" during the mid 1600s (Pérez de Ribas 1968:6). He described it as a tree with branches "several inches in diameter, and of the nature of thorny green striated wax tapers extending as much as thirty feet in height." Its fruit was softer and more delicate than that of the fig and varied in color from white, red, or yellow. Like the Baja California missionaries, Pérez de Ribas (1968:7) also noted that fruits were particularly more appealing when harvested before the rains came in summer. Plants were not only tall, but they were abundant, as evidenced by his comment that "one may often travel among them for a distance of 10 or 20 miles."

Howard S. Gentry (1963) described how the Guarijío and Mexicans collected the highly valued fruits. In the very early morning, they searched for the most choice "trees and fruits," carrying long, hooked poles of *Arundinaria longifolia* to reach and knock down the fruits. Fruits that were not eaten were immediately carried home in baskets to be eaten later, dried, or cooked into jam. Gentry also noted the presence of a yellow-fruited variety growing in the area of the Guarijío.

People still collect and process the fruits in north-central Sonora. María Beltran told how she and others living in and around Granados still eat the fruits of *pitahaya dulce* regularly by boiling them down into a syrup (Nabhan and Hodgson 1988). She obtained "as much as two bucketfuls of syrup a day if it is a good season," whereas only "one bucketful of syrup is obtained during a poor season."

The greatest impact on *S. thurberi* is the complete eradication of it and other plants for the introduction of buffel grass (*Pennisetum ciliare*; fig. 2), an unfortunately common activity in northern Mexico.

Capparaceae | Caper Family

Cleome | spiderflower, beeplant

C. isomeris Greene (syn., *Isomeris arborea* Nuttall)
bladderpod

C. lutea Hooker var. *jonesii* J. F. Macbride
yellow spiderwort, yellow beeplant

C. serrulata Pursh
Rocky Mountain beeplant, guaco

Cleome lutea is native to central and south-central Arizona and northern Baja California, whereas *C. serrulata* has been introduced in the Mohave Desert and is expected to be found in the northwestern part of the Sonoran Desert (Wiggins 1964).

Cleome isomeris is restricted to the deserts of California, although it has been documented along the Salt River, Tempe, Maricopa County, where it has undoubtedly escaped cultivation (*Hodgson 1688,* DES). Plants flower throughout the year.

Use of *Cleome* by Sonoran Desert inhabitants is not well documented, probably due to the plants' limited distribution or recent naturalization in the Sonoran Desert. The Carrizo and Cibecue bands of the Western Apache used the leaves and whole young plant of *C. serrulata* as greens (Buskirk 1986). Plants may have been brought to Cibecue before 1900 "by Indian Cooley, who obtained seeds from the Carrizo and threw them on a sandy place near Lower Cibecue Mission" (Buskirk 1986:192). The plant spread along the roads, but was not abundant in the 1940s. Winfred Buskirk saw "scattered stands on the road between McNary and Whiteriver" during this time, where he believes it may have been recently introduced.

Other groups in New Mexico and northeastern Arizona used Rocky Mountain beeplant leaves and flowers for food (Fewkes 1896; Hough 1897; Standley 1912; Stevenson 1915; Robbins et al. 1916; Castetter 1935). People primarily used beeplant as a potherb. They cooked the tender young shoots and leaves with charred rock, later substituted with charcoal or metal, to lessen the apparently bitter taste of the greens. The amount of time to cook the greens was from 2 to 12 hours, a practical method only if there was plenty of water available. They removed the stems and further boiled the liquid down to a thick, blackish residue that was dried on a board. The hardened cakes could be stored indefinitely. This dried mass was soaked in hot water for use as paint or dye or soaked and then fried in grease for use as food. However, Western Apaches did not use the plants for dyes or any other purpose, other than for edible greens (Buskirk 1986).

The pods and seeds of *C. serrulata* also provided a food source, but information is limited to those groups from areas outside the Sonoran Desert. Plants generally flower from June to September. Some New Mexican groups observed a taboo against eating beeplant (Curtin 1947). Their lore includes a story of a great drought in which their ancestors would have starved had they not resorted to tortillas made from the ground seeds of this plant. Although not very palatable, the seeds were said to have saved many lives. At Ojo Caliente, Coahuila, on the south banks of the Río Grande, local inhabitants encouraged the plants to grow in their fields in the late 1980s (G. P. Nabhan, pers. comm.).

Little is known about the use of *C. isomeris* for food by Sonoran Desert peoples. However, the Tipai of northern Baja California enjoy eating the plants as a *quelite* (Weiss 1994, cited as *Isomeris arborea*), and their method of preparation is of interest. Unlike most *quelites,* whose young herbage is preferred, Tipais prefer mature flowering plants. They gather and boil the yellow flowers with the leaves from three to four hours to remove the bitter compounds present in the flowers. Audrey Weiss (1994:240) was served the leaves and flowers of bladderpod, which were cooked together in water for three hours, with water added when needed as it evaporated in the cooking process. She described the food as "similar in texture to any greens like spinach, very deeply green in color from the leaves, which overpowered the yellow of the flowers" (she did not comment on its taste).

Bladderpod was a common plant throughout Cahuilla territory. The Cahuilla cooked the "small" (probably immature) capsules in a small hole in the ground with hot stones (Barrows 1900, cited as *I. arborea*). The use of bladderpod had been "entirely forgotten" by the 1960s (if not earlier), due perhaps to the accessibility of other, probably more tasty and less foul-smelling foods, such as cacti, other *quelites,* and agricultural products (Bean and Saubel 1972:79–80, cited as *I. arborea*).

Forchammeria | forchammeria

F. watsoni **Rose**
palo San Juan, San Juanico, jito, palo jito

Forchammeria watsoni is an attractive, dark-green-leaved tree that flowers from March to April and produces orange to purple, dryish drupes. This plant appears to have been erroneously reported as providing edible flowers and fruits to the Tipai, who were said to have cooked the flowers with tomatoes, onion, and garlic, according to Audrey Weiss (1994:236). She apparently did not see the plant, as she noted, "I have yet to have anyone suggest we go gathering *Palo San Juan;* it does not seem to enjoy the urgency of popularity of some of the other food plants." *Forchammeria watsoni* grows well south of Tipai territory, being found south of 26'30°N in Baja California (Turner et al. 1995). Another species called *palo San Juan* and not easily accessible to the Tipai is *Jacquinia macrocarpa* Cav., which grows in coastal Sonora (see *Jacquinia*). Unfortunately, a specimen of the Tipai's *palo San Juan* was not obtained and its identity remains a mystery.

However, there is evidence that the drupes of *F. watsoni* are edible. Rosalio Moisés (Moisés et al. 1971: 159), a Yaqui, remembered eating the fruit, recalling that "the tiny red fruit from the *jito* tree (called *San Juanico* in Spanish) can be cooked like beans." In the Río Mayo region, "natives boil the fruits with sugar and pronounce the stew as tasty" (Martin et al. 1998:285).

Caprifoliaceae | Honeysuckle Family

Sambucus | elderberry, elder

S. nigra **Linnaeus ssp.** *canadensis* **(Linnaeus) R. Bolli (syn.,** *S. mexicana* **Presl ex de Candolle)**
elderberry, black elder, Mexican elderberry, tapiro, sauco, condumbo, bixhumi

Mature fruits of Mexican elderberry, or *tapiro* (fig. 99), have a whitish covering and are blue black, juicy, very good tasting, and generally safe to eat. They can be easily collected and dried on flat trays in the sun, then stewed with sugar or lemon and served as a sauce. Elderberries contain substances that are purgative if taken in moderate to excessive amounts.

The Northeastern Yavapai, River Pima, Tohono O'odham, Hiá ceḍ O'odham, and Cahuilla ate the fruits of *tapiro* (Gifford 1936; Curtin 1949; Thomas 1963; Nabhan et al. 1982). *Tapiro* fruits were one of the "old" foods of the Salt River Pima, who made the fruits into jams and jellies during the late 1940s (Curtin 1949, *Curtin 42,* DES; cited as *S. mexicana*). Folklore regarding *tapiro* also disappeared among the Northern Pima (Rea 1997, cited as *S. mexicana*). Although the Pima were aware of using the flowers for medicinal purposes, they were not aware of using the fruits for food (Rea 1997). Frank Russell (1908, cited as *S. mexicana*) did not mention *tapiro* as an edible or medicinal plant, perhaps because it was becoming rare in the Sacaton area where he studied, an area on the reservation first impacted by watershed and riparian destruction (Rea 1997).

FIGURE 99. ***Sambucus nigra*** L. ssp. ***canadensis*** (L.) Bolli branches and fruits. Tonto National Monument, Gila County, Arizona, May 1961 (*Strong 103,* ASU).

The Tohono O'odham still ate *tapiro* fruits in the 1980s at Quitovac, Sonora (Nabhan et al. 1982, cited as *S. mexicana*). Additionally, *tapiro* provides both food and shade to the Tohono O'odham, who often grow this tree in their faucet-watered yards or along ditches running to their fields from floodwater reservoirs (G. P. Nabhan, pers. comm.). The Cahuilla gathered the "relished" fruits in great quantities throughout July and August (Barrows 1900:70, cited as *S. mexicana*). According to Barrows, *tapiro* was enjoyed so much that families would frequently "live for weeks on little else." They cooked dried fruits into a "rich sauce that did not need sweetening."

Wine was, and still is, made from elderberry fruits by Anglos and Native Americans alike. The German Jesuit Fr. Nentvig (1980:41, cited as *S. mexicana*) noted that the Pima "make a beverage so potent that those who drink it to excess get so drunk that it takes two or three days to sober up." The missionaries, believing that such drunkenness was "the cause of many evils," unsuccessfully tried to stop the natives from making the wine. Nentvig went on to say that of all their intoxicating beverages made of corn, mezcal, wheat, and Indian-figs (*Opuntia* sp.), the wine made from *tapiro* was the worst "because of its lasting effects" (Nentvig 1980:61). Sylvester Matthias and other Gila River Pima did not know that wine could be made from the fruits (Rea 1997).

Although widely distributed, *tapiro* is not common in the deserts north of Mexico due to extensive groundwater pumping, dams, water diversion projects, and agricultural and residential development.

Celastraceae | Stafftree or Bittersweet Family

Maytenus | mayten

***M. phyllanthoides* Bentham (syn., *Tricerma phyllanthoides* [Bentham] Lundell)**
Florida mayten, mangle dulce, mangle, palo blanco, aguabola, mangle aguabola, granadilla

Maytenus phyllanthoides is mainly a coastal plant, although it grows inland near saline lakes (Wiggins 1964). It is one of the most widely distributed species above the intertidal zone in Sonoran Desert salt marshes (Yensen et al. 1983). Plants produce red capsules with seeds enclosed by a fleshy, red aril. Seris ate these arils, which they considered sweet when dark and fully ripe (Felger and Moser 1976, 1985). The Seri often raided packrat nests to get the arils that the animals tightly cached.

Schaefferia | desert-yaupon

***S. shrevei* Lundell**
desert-yaupon

Campbell Pennington (1980) stated that Ónavas Pimas ate the drupes of *Schaefferia cuneifolia* in July. This is doubtful as this plant occurs in central Baja California and Texas south to Tamaulipas (Turner et al. 1995). It produces fruits as late as November and December. However, *S. shrevei* occurs in central Sonora and central Baja California, and produces its fruits from September to November. The orange drupes of both are small and have little pulp.

Chenopodiaceae | Goosefoot Family

Allenrolfea | pickleweed, iodinebush

***A. occidentalis* (S. Watson) Kuntze**
pickleweed, iodinebush, chico, hierba del burro

Allenrolfea occidentalis is a dominant succulent shrub along tide lines in many Sonoran Desert salt marshes (Yensen et al. 1983). The minute seeds were primarily a famine food, being used mostly during periods of food shortage.

River Pimas gathered the ripened seeds in baskets during the summer (Curtin 1949, *Curtin 80*, DES). They winnowed the seeds, roasted them in a special pot, and ground them on a metate, then added water and cooked the flour. Frank Russell (1908) described how the River Pima pounded the inflorescences in a mortar before winnowing and washing the seeds. They spread the seeds out to dry and then parched them in a piece of olla before grinding them on a metate, the flour then eaten as pinole. Plants have a more limited distribution on the western end of the reservation and were probably more abundant in the past (Rea 1997).

The Mohave, Quechan, and Maricopa gathered the seeds in December, preferably after a frost, then parched and ground them (Castetter and Bell 1951). The Cahuilla ground the seeds into a powder, which they mixed with water to make a drink or gruel (Bean and Saubel 1972). They also made "cookies" by dampening the flour, then shaping and drying the mass. Seris also toasted, ground, and ate the seeds with turtle oil or cooked the seeds as gruel (Felger and Moser 1976, 1985).

Atriplex | saltbush, orache, chamizo

A. californica **Moquin-Tandon**
California saltbush

A. elegans **(Moquin-Tandon) D. Dietrich**
wheel-scale saltbush, chamizo cenizo

A. lentiformis **(Torrey) S. Watson**
quailbush, lens-scale, chamizo, saladillo

A. polycarpa **(Torrey) S. Watson**
cattle-spinach, saladillo, chamizo cenizo

A. wrightii **S. Watson**
Wright's saltbush

Of the 14 or so species of *Atriplex* that grow in the Sonoran Desert, those listed above were used for food, supplying edible seeds and herbage. *Atriplex* seeds were used by many groups, generally as a famine food. The seeds were ground into meal, mixed with water, and drunk or mixed with some other meal and used as flour. Edward Palmer (1878) noted how people having access to *A. californica* parched and ground its seeds into flour, from which they made a gruel or bread, or ground the seeds without parching.

River Pimas steam-baked the cleaned seeds by placing them on the inner papery bark of cottonwood (*Populus* sp.) with iodinebush *(Suaeda moquinii)* in a heated hole in the ground, which they covered with additional vegetation, and then baked the mass for one or two days (Hrdlička 1908; Russell 1908). They dried, parched, and stored the seeds. When needed, the River Pima made gruel by cooking the seeds with water, sometimes with salt added (Hrdlička 1908). The Mohave, Quechan, and Cocopa collected the fruits of *A. lentiformis* by beating its branches to dislodge the fruits into baskets (Castetter and Bell 1951). Further pounding separated the seeds from the bracts. They steam-baked the seeds in pits to remove the salty taste, then parched and ground the seeds. The meal could be moistened and eaten or boiled into gruel.

The Cahuilla ground and cooked the seeds of *A. lentiformis* with salted water (Barrows 1900). The Cocopa also toasted and ate its seeds although they were not particularly fond of this food (Alvarez de Williams 1987). Despite this, the Cocopa took much time and care in preparing the seeds for a meal (Kelly 1977:39): "The seeds were beaten off the plant into a basket with a stick and were then winnowed. To prepare these seeds for eating, a small hole was dug and lined with hot coals. The seeds were poured on top of these coals and covered with another bed of coals, and then everything was covered with dirt and allowed to cook for about three hours. When removed, the seeds were ground on a metate and eaten dry, or boiled in water to make mush."

The Mohave also gathered the seeds of *A. lentiformis,* with their laborious method of preparation being described in minute detail by Stewart (1965:49):

> They would put the seeds in the sun to dry. Then they pounded them in the mortar. Then they would put them on a little basketry tray of willow and sifted them. The women would blow the seed away all day and get the little seeds. Then the seeds were ground on the metate. Then they were sifted again. Then they'd put them in a pan of water. It would foam, and they would scrape off the foam for a long time. They'd stir it right along until the foam stopped. Then they'd put it on a little plate. While it was still damp, they'd put it on the metate and grind some more. Then they would put it in the water again and stir some more. This made it like a dough. Then they'd build a fire in a pit, with mesquite or screwbea[n] wood. They'd put a doughpat in the hole where the fire was. They'd put ashes on that, and then build another fire on top. This takes all day. By this time it was late in the afternoon. Then they'd build the fire two or three times and leave it over night. In the morning they'd clear away the cold ashes. They'd get arrowweeds and use them like a broom. Then it was ready to eat.

Much of the ethnographic literature describes the seeds of *Atriplex* as being salty, and the addition of salt appears perplexing. Leonora Curtin (1949, cited as *A. polycarpa*) described the seeds of *A. lentiformis* as still being salty in taste, despite the Pima's intensive effort to winnow the seeds from the chaff. However, halophytic plants such as *Atriplex* do not accumulate salts in their seeds, even under saline conditions (O'Leary 1988; Yensen et al. 1988). Less sodium and chloride reaches the fruits and seeds than reaches the leaves. In addition, more sodium and chloride is taken up by the fruiting bracts ("chaff") that surround the seeds than by the seeds themselves. The Cahuilla added salt to ground seeds, which suggests that their grinding and winnowing techniques resulted in a mixture having very little remaining chaff.

The seeds of *A. lentiformis* and possibly *A. polycarpa* appear to have been used only as famine foods by the Hohokam along the Salt River valley (Bohrer 1985). *Atriplex* fruiting bracts were recovered in a series of levels in two ovens, thus suggesting food processing. Seeds were parched or were used as a packing material when steam-roasting other foods.

The leaves and young shoots of *Atriplex* were also used as edible greens, imparting a salty taste when added to other foods. *Atriplex elegans* was formerly used by the River Pima, who boiled the young herbage with other foods (Kearney et al. 1960), such as wheat, or used the herbage as a stuffing for roasted rabbit (Russell 1908). By the 1940s, Leonora Curtin (1949) noted that the only *Atriplex* the River Pima used for greens was *A. wrightii*. *Atriplex elegans* was apparently never "the saltbush of choice," being used only when other greens were unavailable (Rea 1997:201). *Atriplex wrightii* was essentially the only species used well into the 1980s by River Pima who still enjoyed these greens.

Atriplex wrightii was ready to harvest in March or April, when only 30–37 centimeters high (Rea 1997). The uppermost leaves and stem tips were picked so that new leaves would develop for later harvesting. River Pimas boiled the young herbage in water before frying it or cooked the greens with cholla buds, thus providing steam and flavor while keeping the buds from charring (Curtin 1949). Aleš Hrdlička (1908) noted that the River Pima cooked the leaves without seasoning, then pressed out the water. The cooked leaves were sometimes mixed with roasted and ground teparies and maize or eaten with pinole or cholla buds.

The Tohono O'odham also collected and cooked the uppermost leaves and young stem tips of *A. wrightii* alone or with cholla buds, the greens being harvested from April through September (Meals for Millions Foundation 1980; Nabhan et al. 1982). They spread the greens on screens or hung them in the shade to dry, prior to their being stored in ollas.

More northern groups, such as the Hopi, Navajo, and Zuni, added ashes of *Atriplex* to corn and other foods. A significant gain of minerals resulted from this practice (Calloway et al. 1974). Corn cooked in the ash solution has more potassium and calcium and is somewhat higher in magnesium and phosphorous than corn cooked in deionized water (Greenhouse 1979).

Chenopodium | goosefoot, quelite, pigweed, lamb's-quarter

C. album **Linnaeus**
lamb's-quarter

C. ambrosioides **Linnaeus**
Mexican-tea, Spanish-tea, pazote, epazote, epazote de comer

C. berlandieri **Moquin-Tandon**
common lamb's-quarter, pit-seed goosefoot, quelite salado, quelite cenizo, ashecani, huauzontle, chual, cual

C. californicum **(S. Watson) S. Watson**
California goosefoot

C. fremontii **S. Watson (including** ***C. incanum*** **S. Watson)**
Fremont's goosefoot

C. leptophyllum **(Moquin) Nuttall ex S. Watson**
slimleaf goosefoot, quenopodia, chual, cual

C. murale **Linnaeus**
nettle-leaf goosefoot, quelite de puerco, quelite de perro

C. neomexicanum **Standley var.** ***palmeri*** **(Standley) T. Walters (syn.,** ***C. palmeri*** **Standley)**
New Mexico goosefoot

The young herbage and mature seeds of *Chenopodium* provided a food source to desert peoples, with *C. berlandieri* and *C. fremontii* probably being the most important. The introduced goosefoot, *C. album*, is uncommon in the desert region of the Southwest, but is often erroneously cited as a food source, being confused with *C. berlandieri* (see Rea 1997:202–203). Like most *quelites*, the young herbage was gathered and boiled alone or with other foods (Palmer 1871; Bennett and Zingg 1935; Nequatewa 1943; Curtin 1949; Meals for Millions Foundation 1980). *Chenopodium berlandieri* greens are high in calcium (258 milligrams per 100-

gram edible portion) and vitamin A (9700 I.U., cooked and drained; Greenhouse 1979, cited as *C. album*). These amounts compare favorably with one cup of milk and one serving of spinach (100-gram edible portion), which have 288 milligrams of calcium and 8100 I.U. of vitamin A, respectively.

Winfred Buskirk (1986) believed that *Chenopodium* was the plant Aleš Hrdlička mentioned as being used by the San Carlos Apache. They called the plants *i-tan* and ate the leaves raw or chopped and mixed with fat and salt, then boiled (Hrdlička 1908). Western Apaches sowed the seeds of *C. leptophyllum* or *C. fremontii* var. *incanum* (Wats.) Heller around their camps for easier access to many plants (Buskirk 1986). They widely used *Chenopodium* on Fort Apache Indian Reservation in the 1940s. In the summer, Northeastern Yavapais collected a handful of plant material, "picked off morsels with fingers of other hand," then boiled the young herbage (Gifford 1936:156). After draining the leaves they mashed them with mescal juice for sweetening.

Chenopodium is not well known on the River Pima reservations. In the 1940s, Leonora Curtin (1949) noted that River Pimas boiled the leaves of a goosefoot, presumably *C. album,* in salted water, drained them, and then fried the leaves in grease. The Tohono O'odham sometimes washed the greens of *C. berlandieri, C. murale,* and *C. fremontii* before cooking (Castetter and Underhill 1935; Nabhan et al. 1982), thereby removing the salty taste (Meals for Millions Foundation 1980). The Mohave and Cocopa also boiled the young shoots of *C. murale* and *C. fremontii* (Castetter and Bell 1951).

Chenopodium was probably used as a *quelite* by Baja Californians, at least those living in the northern part of the peninsula. Tipais still gather and eat young plants or new growth of more mature *Chenopodium* species. They cook the greens in water for approximately 15 minutes or fry the greens with meats or onions after boiling them (Weiss 1994).

Certain goosefoots are considered potentially toxic. *Chenopodium album* contains relatively high concentrations of nitrates (Kingsbury 1964). The Tarahumara understood that certain goosefoots might be potentially toxic because they carefully processed and ate the herbage of *C. ambrosioides* and *C. album* (Pennington 1963). They only processed a few fresh leaves or a small amount of dried leaves of *C. ambrosioides* to use as a condiment in beans. They collected only young herbage for use as a *quelite,* cooking it with two or more changes of water (Bye 1976).

The seeds of various goosefoots also were eaten after being parched and ground into flour. Edward Palmer (1871) described the flour made from ground seeds of an unidentified goosefoot as having a peculiar gray color that gave the bread a very "dirty look." However, it was quite nutritious and had a taste and appearance similar to buckwheat.

Northeastern and Western Yavapais, as well as Anglos, gathered the seeds of *Chenopodium* in the fall (Gifford 1936). They collected the inflorescences with mature seeds in conical burden baskets, then spread these inflorescences on a flat surface and beat them with a stick. The winnowed seeds were parched with coals in a basket, then ground, boiled, and eaten.

River Pimas gathered the seed of *C. berlandieri* early in the summer, then parched and ground the seeds, with the resulting flour eaten as pinole or combined with other meal (Russell 1908). *Chenopodium berlandieri* ssp. *nuttalliae* (Safford) Wilson & Heiser was formerly cultivated for its numerous, edible seeds, but its cultivation ended during the drought years of the 1870s (Rea 1997).

The Cahuilla gathered the seeds of *C. fremontii,* which commonly grew in the canyons, and ground them into flour (Barrows 1900). After a good harvest, the granaries along the canyon fringes were said to have been full of *Chenopodium* seeds. The nearby Luiseño ate the seeds of the perennial *C. californicum* (Sparkman 1908).

Cycloloma | winged-pigweed

C. atriplicifolium **(Sprengel) Coulter**
winged-pigweed

Although this plant grows in more northern and eastern areas and was not listed by Wiggins (1964), *C. atriplicifolium* has been collected near Tempe, Arizona, possibly from seeds carried down the Salt River (Kearney et al. 1960). Little has been written on the use of this plant for food. The Zunis made gruel or cakes from its ground seeds (Stevenson 1915).

Monolepis | poverty-weed

M. nuttalliana **(Schultes) Greene**
Indian-spinach, Nuttall's poverty-weed, patata, patota

Monolepis nuttallianum, or *patota,* is a widely distributed succulent annual that grows throughout the Sonoran Desert and produces both perfect and imperfect flowers from February to October. *Patota* was an important food source to the O'odham, supplying them with edible greens and seeds. Like amaranths, the iron and calcium content of the herbage is quite high. A 100-gram portion of young plants contributes almost 50 percent of the recommended daily allowance of iron while supplying 10 to 15 percent of the recommended daily allowance of calcium for an adult male (Greenhouse 1979).

Of all the cooked greens, *patota* is still the favorite among the River Pima, who recognize and pick herbage when it is very young and tender, usually in January and February or occasionally March (Rea 1997). They wash the young plants thoroughly, boil them briefly, and then drain the plants. The cooked greens are eaten as is or salted and fried with oil or lard. Such recently recorded preparation (Greenhouse 1979) differs little from that described a half a century ago (Curtin 1949, *Curtin 22,* DES) or nearly a century ago (Hrdlička 1908; Russell 1908). The Tohono O'odham usually harvested *patota* in February and March, providing an especially esteemed wild green during the cool-weather season, although plants appear from October to April (G. P. Nabhan, pers. comm.).

People also harvested the top portions of more mature plants and the slightly sweet-tasting roots (Greenhouse 1979). Aleš Hrdlička (1908) noted that the plant tips of more mature plants were eaten raw or boiled and drained when cooled, mixed with lard and occasionally with salt, and then eaten with tortillas. Frank Russell (1908) observed how the River Pima washed and boiled the roots in an olla, then cooled them in a basket. After squeezing out the water, they cooked the roots in the olla with some fat or lard and salt, then served them with tortillas. River Pimas also once boiled, partially dried, parched, and then ground the numerous, tiny seeds on a metate and ate the meal as pinole.

Salicornia | glasswort, saltwort, pickleweed

S. europea **Linnaeus**
pickleweed, saltwort

S. pacifica **Standley**
pickleweed

Both *Salicornia* species are succulents, but *S. europea* is an annual whose distribution in the Sonoran Desert is limited to near Puerto Peñasco, Sonora, whereas *S. pacifica,* a perennial, is more widely distributed among the salt marshes (Wiggins 1964).

Little has been written on the use of *Salicornia* for food by Sonoran Desert people, although its seeds are edible. David Barrows (1900:57) noted that this "queer little plant" grew abundantly around "Indian Wells" and that the Cahuilla finely crushed its seeds into an edible meal. *Salicornia* species may be a potential halophytic oilseed crop for human consumption (O'Leary 1988). Seed oil is high in unsaturated fatty acids, thus ranking it as a highly desirable vegetable oil. As with other halophytes, the salt content is not higher than seeds of non-salt-tolerant plants.

Convolvulaceae | Morning-glory Family

Ipomoea | morning-glory

I. arborescens **(Humboldt & Bonpland) G. Don**
tree morning-glory, palo blanco, palo santo, palo bobo, palo santo amarillo, palo del muerto, casahuate, casahuate blanco, ozote, palo cabra

I. bracteata **Cavanilles (syn.,** ***Exogonium bracteatum*** **[Cavanilles] Choisy)**
jicama, zicana, cocanatain, bejuco de la candlai

I. jicama **Brandegee**
jicama

I. purpurea **(Linnaeus) Roth**

Ipomoea arborescens (fig. 100) is a strikingly beautiful and conspicuous tree when it produces flowers during the winter and spring, before the emergence of its leaves (Turner et al. 1995). Its use as a food item was minimal, however. Yaquis once ate its roots (Alvarez de Williams n.d.), whereas Tarahumaras ate the "small, tender," but leathery fruits (Bennett and Zingg 1935).

Ipomoea bracteata is a perennial vine found in southern Baja California and mainland Mexico that produces large, juicy roots, which are considered to be as sweet

FIGURE 100. ***Ipomoea arborescens*** (Humb. & Bonpl.) G. Don. Magnificent trees in leafy condition. Located 7.5 miles northeast of Mesocahui, on the way to Moctezuma, Sonora, July 1988.

as yams (Standley 1923; Gentry 1963, cited as *Exogonium bracteatum*). The inhabitants of Baja California knew little about the use of this plant, despite it being common in the cape region.

However, the plants were better known on the mainland. Edward Palmer noted that the large "sweet-potato-like" roots were eaten by Sonorans (Vasey and Rose 1891b). From December to May, Tarahumaras collected, peeled, and ate the roots raw, before the plants produced flowers (Bennett and Zingg 1935; Pennington 1963, cited as *E. bracteatum*). They also ate the pounded, heated roots with pinole or atole (Pennington 1963). Guarijios baked the sweet roots in hot ashes or ate them raw (Gentry 1963, cited as *E. bracteatum*). Río Mayo inhabitants held the roots in high regard as an edible food, but the roots grew deep into the ground and were difficult to collect (Gentry 1942). Pimas at Ónavas, Sonora (Pennington 1980, cited as *E. bracteatum*), and Tepehuans (Pennington 1969, cited as *E. bracteatum*) also baked the roots in ashes or on hot coals.

Ipomoea jicama may have been a significant and favored food for those who had access to it in south-central and southern Baja California. While exploring the cape region in 1709, Edward Cooke (1712:322; Andrews 1979:42–43; Mathes 1992:297) may have been referring to *I. jicama* when he described a plant the Pericú used as being "a sort of root that has three round knobs, looks and eats very much like the Yams in the West Indies." However, *I. bracteata, Merremia aurea,* and *Manihot chlorosticta* also grow in this region. Fr. Miguel del Barco (1980:232) described the attributes of a plant called *jicama,* whose roots were used by the natives: "The second root is *jicama,* which has the shape of a good-sized turnip, but not long, almost round instead, or a little longer than thick. Some people say that they taste better than those of Mexico, although they are smaller in size. They are found in the lands near the beaches of both seas. They are well suited to quench one's thirst, because they are full of a watery juice." Unfortunately, Fr. del Barco did not provide his usual careful description of the plant itself, although Annetta Carter believed he was referring to *I. jicama* (Carter 1970; Carter *in* del Barco 1980).

Neither *I. bracteata* nor *I. jicama* should be confused with *Pachyrhizus erosus* (L.) Urban (Fabaceae), or *jicama.* This legume is widely cultivated for its edible, juicy roots and has become naturalized in Sinaloa and other states of Mexico (McVaugh 1987). The historian Fr. Clavigero confused these plants. He described a plant called *xicama,* whose "roots were the shape and size of an onion, white, succulent, savory, and cooling; and it is always eaten raw" (Clavigero 1937:53). The roots of *I. jicama* were considered better tasting than the roots of *P. erosus,* which is found on the mainland of Mexico. Fr. Clavigero wrote that "the *xicama* of Mexico *[P. erosus]* is ordinary; but that of California, although smaller, is better in the opinion of many." He described the *xicama* as a leguminous plant having leaves arranged in threes, purple flowers, and seeds like lentils enclosed in black pods. This is a good description of *P. erosus,* but not *I. jicama.* Fr. Clavigero relied on Fr. del Barco's writings on the natural history of the peninsula for his own work, but Fr. del Barco never described *jicama* as being a legume with purple flowers. Clavigero admitted, "it is very easy for the one who writes the history of a country in which he has never been to make a mistake" (Clavigero 1937:5).

Townsend Brandegee (1889:118–119) considered *jicama* to be one of the more interesting plants in the vicinity of San Gregorio (26°N). He described the attributes and use of its roots:

> [*Ipomoea jicama* is] a woody species climbing about other plants, and rarely producing large white flowers. Its roots bear tubers that are much sought for on account of their fine flavor and watery juice. One weighing six pounds is said to have been found, and traditions of a ten-pounder are extant, but the largest seen weighed two or three pounds, and they are usually much smaller. These tubers must grow very fast during the rainy and Spring season, for their location, often three feet or more from the base of the stems, is discovered by the growth cracking the soil. New stems never spring from them, and their use to the parent plant is uncertain. Perhaps it is to store up moisture to be drawn upon during the dry season. These round tubers or *jicamas* are always eaten raw, and resemble in taste a very tender turnip somewhat sweetened. Wherever the plant grows near habitations or along trails, numerous little holes may be seen around the plant at distances varying from two to four feet, showing the places from which the tubers have been dug.

It seems that juicy roots that were eaten raw were generally referred to as *jicama,* whereas roots that required cooking were referred to as *camotes* or sometimes *yuca.*

Few references allude to or mention the use of *I. purpurea* for food. However, Tarahumaras gathered the leaves from June to July (Bye 1976) and boiled and ate them as a *quelite* (Bennett and Zingg 1935). They also occasionally used the flowers as a *quelite* from December through February (Bye 1976).

Merremia | wood-rose

M. aurea (Kellogg) O'Donell
yuca

Merremia aurea (fig. 101) is an attractive, yellow-flowered vine that is endemic to southern Baja California. Its large, tuberous roots are edible and provided a food source to the Pericú, Guaicura, and undoubtedly other groups who had access to the plants. However, as with other Baja California plants bearing edible roots, reference to the use of *M. aurea* is confusing.

Explorers, historians, and missionaries, including Frs. Salvatierra (Burrus 1971), Venegas (Venegas and Burriel 1966), Baegert (1952, 1982), Kino (Bolton 1948), and Clavigero (1937), mentioned a plant called

FIGURE 101. Cultivated ***Merremia aurea*** (Kell.) O'Donell. Desert Botanical Garden, Phoenix, Arizona, August 1988.

"yucca," "yuca," or "guacamote of the sweet type," whose roots were considered to be "the daily bread" of the native people. *Yuca* is also a common name for certain species of *Yucca* (see *Yucca*). Fr. Salvatierra learned of the edible roots in a rather unusual way in 1697. He wrote of the discovery of "*yucca* in this area; from its root manioc [sic] is made, the sustenance of many realms in the Americas" (Burrus 1971:140–141). Salvatierra and his small entourage of soldiers had just successfully defended their stored supplies of maize and other items from being raided by Monquis and other groups. Those natives who did not take part in the battle joined the padres and soldiers, who in the meantime had assumed that the ship was lost (it returned ten days later with Fr. Píccolo) and were content to remain there, despite the grim outlook. One of the natives arrived, insisting that he had not fought against them, but rather "had gone to the mountains to gather roots to eat." Fr. Salvatierra continued (Burrus 1971:121): "And as proof, he had brought us a very large root which he showed us. At first we were puzzled by the root, but finally all of us recognized it as yucca. Afterwards, the Peruvians from the galliot [sloop, or ship] confirmed our conjecture. Yucca tastes very good. It furnishes manioc, a sort of bread consumed in so many American regions."

Fr. Venegas (Venegas and Burriel 1966:44) wrote of three kinds of plants having an edible root, all of them "frequent in New Spain." One of these was "yuca, a large thick root, which they cut into slices and express the juice, afterwards it is made into broad thin cakes, and eaten instead of bread." Fr. Baegert appeared to have confused yuccas, of the genus *Yucca,* with herbaceous perennials with edible roots, specifically *M. aurea.* Responding to Fr. Venegas's writings, Fr. Baegert (1982:179) was emphatic in pointing out that the preparation of yucca, as described by Fr. Venegas, would be "too much work, when they have yucca, they dig it out and throw it directly on the fire or on hot embers." He added, "yucca takes the place of bread, meat, cheese, soup, salad, boeuf a la mode, and everything else." Fr. Baegert (1982:66) also wrote that yucca "provides the daily bread for many American Indians and not a few Spaniards on the island of Cuba." He added, "in other places a kind of bread or cake is made from the ground roots of the yucca," but "in Baja California the yucca is not plentiful." The only yuccas in southern Baja California are *Y. valida,* called *dátil cimarrón* or *datilillo* by the inhabitants, and *Y. capensis.* The roots of both of these species, like those of other yuccas, are bitter, not enlarged, and inedible. In addition, *Y. valida* is not found between 26'30° and 24°N (which includes Loreto and vicinity), except for populations far to the west (Turner et al. 1995). *Manihot chlorosticta* Standl. & Goldm. grows well south of Loreto (Rogers and Appan 1973).

At La Paz in 1596, Coras or Aripes presented Sebastián Vizcaíno with "some thick white roots as large as an arm and of reasonable flavor, which is the ordinary bread from whey they sustain themselves" (Mathes 1992:137). Edward Cooke (1712:322; Andrews 1979:42–43; Mathes 1992:297) described "a Sort of Root that has three round Knobs, looks and eats very much like the Yams in the West Indies." Fr. Nápoli noted that the inhabitants of southeastern Baja California (Coras or Guaicuras) ate seeds, *pitahayas,* plums, fish, and "the roots of plants" (Moriarty and Smith 1970:53). Fr. Guillén realized that he and his party might have to rely on the horses they killed, the mescal, or *yuca* on their return trip from La Paz in 1720, should their ship and supplies not await them at the port (Mathes 1979).

Fr. del Barco (1980:231–232) carefully described a plant called *yuca,* or *ujuí,* as the Cochimí called it, whose roots provided food to those living in the vicinity of Loreto:

> There are three kinds of roots proper to this land of which the natives avail themselves to eat, and which also occur frequently in New Spain [*M. aurea* is endemic to southern Baja California]. The first one is *yuca,* a root which the Cochimies call *ujuí,* which after the rains grows or sprouts a stalk complete with leaves, and this stalk intertwines itself into and climbs on any thicket that is near. When the Indians become aware that the root of this stalk is ready for harvest, they make a small hole at its foot [presumably, of its stalk] and they dig it out. This root is from six to eight fingers in length, sometimes more, sometimes less. Its thickness does not reach three fingers put together, but perhaps a few may get that large. These roots are earth color or brown on the outside. Inside, however, they are white. Roasted before they are eaten, they have a good flavor but are stringy.

Despite the apparently common use of the roots for food by the local inhabitants, Fr. del Barco did not agree with Venegas and others. It was his opinion that "they are found with sufficient frequency, but not so much that they can be called the daily bread of the

Californios, as some individuals have written." Annetta Carter identified the plants Edward Cooke and Fr. del Barco referred to as being *M. aurea* (Carter *in* Andrews 1979; del Barco 1980), and not *M. chlorosticta* or *Amoreuxia palmatifida,* the latter suggested by Homer Aschmann (1959). Frs. Nápoli and Guillén were also probably referring to the roots of *M. aurea. Merremia aurea* flowers year-round (Wiggins 1980) and thus would have been located without problem any time of year. More recently, ranchers spoke of the roots of *M. aurea* as being edible (Carter *in* del Barco 1980). However, *M. chlorosticta* provides edible roots as well (see *Manihot*).

Crassulaceae | Stonecrop Family

Dudleya | live-forever

D. arizonica Rose (syn., *D. pulverulenta* [Nuttall] Britton & Rose ssp. *arizonica* [Rose] Horan)
Arizona live-forever

D. attenuata (S. Watson) Moran
taper-tip live-forever

D. pulverulenta (Nuttall) Britton & Rose
chalk live-forever

D. saxosa (M. E. Jones) Britton & Rose
rock-echeveria, live-forever

According to Edward Palmer (1878), native people of southern California collected the tender leaves of various dudleyas in the spring and ate them raw. The Cahuilla considered young dudleyas a delicacy, with their flowering stems being delicious and sweet (Bean and Saubel 1972). The Cahuilla may have had access to *D. arizonica, D. pulverulenta,* and *D. saxosa* var. *aloides* (Rose) Moran. Delfina Cuero, a San Diego Diegueño, reminisced that as a young girl she and her family often spent the whole day obtaining food. Besides eating shellfish, rabbits, and cactus, she also ate dudleya leaves (Shipek 1968).

Baja California inhabitants chewed the flowering stems of *D. attenuata* and the leaves and flowering stems of *D. pulverulenta* fresh and raw for food (Weiss 1994) and moisture (Meigs 1939). *Dudleya attenuata* flowers from May to June, whereas *D. pulverulenta* flowers from May to August (Wiggins 1964).

Cucurbitaceae | Gourd Family

Apodanthera | melon loco

A. palmeri S. Watson
melon loco, Palmer's melon loco

A. undulata A. Gray
melon de coyote, melon loco

Opinions vary with regard to the edibility of *Apodanthera.* As suggested by the common name, *melon de coyote,* the fruits of *A. undulata* (fig. 102) are extremely bitter and foul smelling. Ónavas Pimas ate the fruits only during times of great food shortage (Pennington 1980). Gary Nabhan and I asked María Beltran of Granados, Sonora, whether she or others ate the fruits of *melon de coyote.* She replied with an emphatic "No!" and exclaimed, "no one in their right mind would eat it!" However, Edward Palmer, who collected *A. palmeri* in the vicinity of Guaymas in 1887, said that its fruits were edible when ripe in the early fall, having a taste "nearly of muskmelon" (Watson 1889:511, cited as *Apodanthera? palmeri*).

Campbell Pennington (1969) suggested that seeds of *A. undulata* found in a cave in Tepehuan habitat may have been used for food. However, seeds found in several pre-Columbian sites in the United States may have been a result of rodent, rather than human, activity (Cutler and Whitaker 1961).

FIGURE 102. ***Apodanthera undulata*** A. Gray vine with immature, green fruit. Santa Rita Mountains, Santa Cruz County, Arizona, August 1988.

Cucurbita | gourd, calabaza

C. digitata A. Gray
finger-leaved gourd, coyote gourd, calabacilla, chichi coyote

C. foetidissima Kunth
buffalo gourd, Missouri gourd, calabazilla, calabazilla loco, calabaza de coyote, calabaza amargosa

C. palmata S. Watson
coyote melon

The common name *chichi coyote* ("coyote's breasts") refers to several species of wild gourds. Sonoran Desert cultures called wild relatives of gourd crops what would translate to "Coyote's plants," which they considered inferior (Nabhan 1982). According to folklore, Coyote defecated on wild gourds making once-sweet pulp extremely bitter. In fact, women slit the fruits and rubbed the pulp on their breast to wean their babies (Merrick and Nabhan 1984). The foul-smelling substance responsible for the bitterness is a triterpenoid glycoside called cucurbitacin that is found in all parts of the plants except the seeds (Berry et al. 1976). Accidental consumption could cause nausea, cramps, and diarrhea.

FIGURE 103. ***Cucurbita digitata*** A. Gray leaves and immature fruit. Photograph courtesy of Desert Botanical Garden, Phoenix, Arizona.

Seeds of wild gourds were used for food. They were roasted or boiled and eaten or ground finely into a meal (Palmer 1878; Russell 1908; Gifford 1936; Cutler and Whitaker 1961). The oil from seeds of most species of *Cucurbita* is generally edible (Jacks et al. 1971) and nutritious. Seeds of *C. foetidissima* contain from 22 to 35 percent protein (Berry et al. 1976), a nutritive value comparable to that of legumes (Thompson et al. 1978). In addition, its seeds contain from 25 to 42 percent oil or fat, and a low percentage of carbohydrates (Berry et al. 1976).

Today, use of the seeds for food appears to be minimal at best. Gila River Pimas denied any knowledge of the seeds being eaten (Rea 1997). *Cucurbita digitata* (fig. 103) is uncommon on their reservation, although Amadeo Rea frequently encountered the plants there 25 years ago. However, some Chihuahuan Desert inhabitants still eat the seeds of *C. digitata* and *C. foetidissima,* which are soaked in calcium-bicarbonated water before being consumed (G. P. Nabhan, pers. comm.; pers. obs.). Seeds of *C. foetidissima* can be collected in September and October when the fruits are still green, whereas those of *C. digitata* can be collected later in the year (Niethammer 1974).

The roots and fruits are well known for their medicinal and cleansing properties, respectively. There is some evidence that the young fruits and roots provided an edible food despite the presence of cucurbitacin. The Zuni once prepared the immature, green fruits of *C. foetidissima* by boiling them to a paste, mixing the paste with "rancid suet," then frying the mixture on hot stones (Standley 1912; Cushing 1920). Hugh Cutler and Thomas Whitaker (1961:470–471) also mentioned the use of the fruits and roots as a food source:

> The wild species with the widest distribution and the one most frequently seen in collection from living Indians or from archaeological sites is *Cucurbita foetidissima* . . . . All parts of this plant usually are so bitter and obnoxious to taste and smell that some form of treatment is required before they can be eaten. The seeds were gathered by many Indian groups and roasted or boiled, the young fruits are reported to have been boiled repeatedly, often with some ashes, before being consumed, and the pulp of the fruits was used as a detergent for cleaning

> and scouring. Pieces of the large starchy roots of wild *Cucurbita* found in Tularosa Cave suggest the roots were also used for food [or medicine].

Wild gourds may be another example of plants whose use for food or medicine is not differentiated.

The potential of xerophytic wild gourds, such as *C. digitata, C. foetidissima,* and *C. palmata,* as a food source has been recognized for some time, despite the varying opinions as to the plants' edibility. Indeed, selection for the oily seeds of *Cucurbita* may have preceded selection for the sweet flesh of melons (Rea 1997). Because the quality of cucurbit oil compares favorably with commercial cooking oils, breeding work has been directed toward increased seed productivity and oil content (Bemis et al. 1967). Oils from these xerophytic gourds are highly unsaturated as compared to the more mesic-adapted domesticated and wild species. The production of hybrids having seed oil higher in polyunsaturates than that found in the domesticated gourds is feasible (Gathman and Bemis 1983).

The potential to develop *C. foetidissima* as a root crop has also been shown (Curtis 1979). Although containing low percentages of protein and oil or fat, roots contain 56 percent starch (Berry et al. 1975). The starch is similar to that of tapioca (*Manihot esculenta* Crantz) and cornstarch, but has additional properties that make it superior to other commercially available starches (Drehrer and Berry 1983). However, to render the starch edible, extraction of the bitter principles is necessary.

Cucurbita plants can be very productive. High-yielding plants of *C. foetidissima* produced numerous, large roots and approximately 300 seeds per fruit (Felger and Nabhan 1976). It was estimated that wild populations of *C. foetidissima, C. digitata,* and *C. palmata* produced from 500 to 3,000 pounds of seeds per acre (Curtis 1946; Bolley et al. 1950; Shahani et al. 1951). These yields are comparable to those of commercially grown oil seeds, such as cottonseed, sunflower, and peanut (Jacks et al. 1971).

Despite its promise as an important food crop, commercial growers are hesitant to grow *C. foetidissima* (Nabhan 1985). However, they may focus on the plants' ability to control pests (Metcalf et al. 1982). Cucurbitacin usually discourages herbivory, but for beetles in the tribe Luperini, the cucurbitacin-rich tissues provide a food source. These beetles include the corn rootworm and cucumber beetle, two major agricultural pests. Planting trap crops of wild gourds near vulnerable commercial crops may attract the beetles away from crop plants that would otherwise be attacked.

Tumamoca | Tumamoc-globeberry

T. macdougalii **Rose**
Tumamoc-globeberry

The Seri described a plant that produced a large underground root, leaves like a watermelon plant, and red fruits, which they ate fresh (Felger and Moser 1985). Richard Felger and Frank Reichenbacher later confirmed that the plant to which the Seri referred was the Tumamoc globeberry. Its fruits normally mature from August through October (Olwell 1986). Fruits quickly turn from being dark green, malodorous, and dry within to becoming red and juicy. The ripe fruits are soon devoured by birds and insects (pers. obs.).

Tumamoc globeberry is not a common plant, being represented by approximately 60 populations in Arizona and Sonora (Olwell 1986). Sixty percent of the populations in Arizona are located on nonfederal land, where modification of habitat could result in their destruction or damage. Existing and potential major impacts on the globeberry, its nurse plants, and its habitat include agriculture and housing developments, the CAP aqueduct, BLM land transfers, reseeding and land imprinting programs, and chaining woody perennials for increased production of nonnative grass species.

Ebenaceae | Persimmon or Ebony Family

Diospyros | persimmon

D. californica (Brandegee) I. M. Johnston
guayparin

D. sonorae Standley
guayparin, persimonio

Diospyros californica is endemic to southern Baja California, whereas *D. sonorae* grows from southern Sonora into Sinaloa (Wiggins 1964). After flowering from July to August, both species produce edible drupes. Townsend Brandegee (1894, cited as *D. texana*) considered the mature, black fruits of *D. californica* to be very pleasant tasting. Fruits were eaten raw or cooked into syrup (Hake 1980, 1983). The insipid-tasting fruits of *D. sonorae* were collected in June and October in Alamos, Sonora, where natives ate them "eagerly, either raw or cooked with panoche" during the 1940s (*Gentry 2263, 4777,* ARIZ). Additionally, Mayos boiled the fruits in milk and toasted and ground the seeds for tortillas or atole (Martin et al. 1998).

Euphorbiaceae | Spurge Family

Cnidoscolus | bull-nettle, tread softly

C. maculatus Pax & K. Hoffmann
ortiga, caribe

C. palmeri (S. Watson) Rose
mala mujer, ortiguilla

Cnidoscolus maculatus is endemic to the southern part of Baja California, and *C. palmeri* grows in central Baja California to the cape region, on many islands in the Gulf of California, and near Guaymas, Sonora. Seeds and roots were once significant food sources. It is not known if people ate the seeds of *C. angustidens* Torrey.

Inhabitants of south-central Baja California consumed the large seeds of *C. maculatus* (Carter *in* del Barco 1980:189), which are rich in proteins and oils (Nabhan and Felger 1985). Fr. Miguel del Barco (1980:198) described a type of plant, called *ortiga,* that grew following summer rains. It had fine thorns that were "meaner and of a greater sharpness" than the "European variety of ortiga ... so that where they sting a blister is formed." The natives of southern Baja California called this plant *tedegua,* or "that which causes pain." Its seeds were "like almonds ... although narrower," and had a good flavor. The "Indians eat them although, because there is not a lot of this seed, they do not gather a harvest from it to keep." However, Fr. del Barco noted that there were more plants in the southern part of the peninsula, thus enabling the natives to collect much more seed. This is undoubtedly the species to which Fr. Clavigero (1937) and Homer Aschmann (1959) referred in describing this "malvaceous plant with hairy leaves" and edible seed. Fr. Clavigero's reasoning was probably based on his misinterpretation of Fr. del Barco's notes, which described its leaves as being large "as those of mallows" (del Barco 1980:198).

Cnidoscolus palmeri, or *mala mujer,* produces numerous large, fleshy, tuberlike, edible roots that contain 82 percent starch and 7.5 percent protein, which compares favorably with the potato (Nabhan and Felger 1985). Because they are available year-round, Seris once considered these plants to be an important food source (Felger and Moser 1985). They dug the roots out with a digging stick, shovel, or crowbar (figs. 104, 105), a task that required much care and time. One woman worked almost an hour to obtain 14 roots from a single plant. Small roots had a better taste, although roots were generally considered bland tasting, despite their crisp and succulent nature when eaten raw. Seris collected and then brought back to camp whole roots, which they prepared by peeling away the outer brown layer before eating them raw or stored them for a considerable length of time. They also roasted the roots whole over coals, then removed the blackened outer portion and ate the inside mass, often with honey.

Cnidoscolus offers a great range of agronomic possibilities (Nabhan and Felger 1985). Of the 60 species, 9 are known to have edible leaves, protein- and oil-rich seeds, and potato-like roots. The hybridization potential is unknown. The presence of stinging hairs inhib-

FIGURE 104. Rosa Flores and José Astorga dig for the tuberlike roots of ***Cnidoscolus palmeri*** (S. Wats.) Rose with a shovel. Rosa Flores went directly to this population after not having visited it for more than 30 years. Photograph courtesy of Robert Gasser.

FIGURE 105. After a great deal of time and patience, Rosa Flores obtains the roots of ***Cnidoscolus palmeri.*** Photograph courtesy of Robert Gasser.

its harvesting to some extent. Domesticated forms lacking stinging hairs have been cultivated for their edible leaves in central Mexico and used in *licuados* and as a vegetable (G. P. Nabhan, pers. comm.).

Manihot | manihot

M. chlorosticta **Standley & Goldman**
yuca, cuadrado

Manihot chlorosticta produce tuberlike roots that were used for food. However, there is confusion regarding which plants provided edible roots, particularly to natives of Baja California.

Esteban Valenzuela, in his report of Francisco de Ortega's voyage to the cape region of Baja California, described how the peaceful Coras had to defend some fisheries and "a place where much tobacco and camote, a root like sweet potatoes of Spain, are fathered," just south of La Paz (Mathes 1992:241). While exploring the cape region in 1709, Edward Cooke (1712:322; Mathes 1992:297) described a plant the Pericú used as being "a sort of root that has three round knobs, looks and eats very much like the Yams in the West Indies." Fr. Salvatierra said that *guacamote,* which was found in the vicinity of Loreto, was the same as the *casabe* of the Indies, a species of *Manihot* (Aschmann 1959). *Yuca,* or *guacamote* "of the sweet type" was mentioned by Clavigero (1937), Baegert (1952, 1982), Venegas and Burriel (1966), Nentvig (1980), and others as being the "daily bread of the Indians" (see *Merremia*). Fr. Baegert mentioned that the roots of *yuca* provided food to "not a few Spaniards on the island of Cuba," although he confused it with *Yucca* (Baegert 1982:66). However, *M. chlorosticta* does not grow as far north as Loreto, but is restricted to that area between Santiago and Cabo San Lucas (Rogers and Appan 1973). *Yucca,* or *yuca,* may have referred in some cases to *Amoreuxia* spp. (see *Amoreuxia*) or *Merremia aurea* (see *Merremia*). Based on Fr. del Barco's detailed description, which was later cited by Fr. Clavigero, *yuca,* or *ujuí* (as the Cochimí called it), referred to *M. aurea.*

Fr. Nentvig (1980:39) discussed how *maqui,* or what appears to have been *M. chlorosticta,* provided the "everyday bread for the Jovas." He noted that the roots were poisonous if eaten raw, "causing death to the partaker," but if "boiled two or three times, each time in different water until it ceases to froth, it can be eaten safely." These roots were "similar to the cassava of Puerto Rico, Campeche, and Cuba." Fr. Nentvig further described how "after two or three boilings it is pounded and boiled again until a sort of dough settles at the bottom." This mass was kneaded into loaves, tamales, or tortillas and cooked on *cajetes,* or flattened clay bowls. After being mashed by pounding, the mass was left to rot "a little." It was then spread on mats, dried in the sun, and stored for future use. When needed, the Jova boiled the mass again and ate it with pinole. People enjoyed this plant despite the time and labor required to make its root edible.

Fabaceae | Pea or Legume Family

Acacia | acacia, catclaw, wattle

A. brandegeana **I. M. Johnston**
vinorama, asigandú

A. cochliacantha **Willdenow**
boat-thorn acacia, spoon-thorn acacia, espino, huinole, guinolo, guinora, chiroui, cucharillo, cubata, quisache costeño, vinolo

A. greggii **A. Gray**
catclaw acacia, long-flower catclaw, devil's claw, uña de gato, tésota, algarroba, gatuno, tepame

A. pennatula **(Chamisso & Schlechtendal) Bentham**
tepamo, tepame, algarrobo, chirahui, palo garrobo, yepouchecha, huizache

Certain Sonoran Desert acacias provided edible seeds to *indigenes.* Except for one Sonoran population, *A. brandegeana* is endemic to southern Baja California and reaches both coasts (Turner et al. 1995). It is abundant in the Sierra de la Giganta, especially near San Javier, but sparse in the cape region (Carter *in* del Barco 1980). Its fruits mature during the summer rains from late May to early June. Early missionaries referred to the plant as *asigandú* (Clavigero 1937; Aschmann 1959); in the vicinity of San Javier and Loreto, *A. brandegeana* was known as *vinorama* (Carter *in* del Barco 1980). *Acacia brandegeana* is not to be confused with *A. farnesiana* (L.) Willdenow, which was also called *vinorama* in the cape region of Baja California, whose seeds were "good for nothing" and were not even eaten by the natives (del Barco 1980:137). Seeds of *A. brandegeana* were not a preferred food source, but were of some importance because they matured in May and June, a time of great scarcity of plant foods as described by Fr. del Barco (1980:134): "As it is the season of the entire year when those poor Indians are most in need of sustenance, they take advantage of those grains or seed [of *A. brandegeana*], for lack of something better, to alleviate their want. They toast them, grind them by hand between two stones, and eat them as a coarse flour, as they do with their other seeds." It became quite obvious when someone had eaten the toasted seeds, as further explained by Fr. del Barco (1980:134): "When they toast them, they give out a slight smell, noticeable also in the breath of those who have eaten them. When many Indians gather in a room at this time, for instance during church holidays, and if a non-Indian comes in after they have been there a while, he can scarcely bear the smell which originates from the aforementioned cause."

Acacia cochliacantha is a disturbance-adapted shrub found near Magdalena, Sonora, south into Sinaloa (Turner et al. 1995). It also grows as disjunct, perhaps recently introduced, populations in the cape region of Baja California. The seeds of *A. cochliacantha* also provided an edible food to those who had access to the plants. Guarijios roasted, ground, and ate the seeds in the form of atole or used the ground seeds to make tortillas (Gentry 1963, cited as *A. cymbispina*). This acacia was a major wild food plant for those inhabiting the

Río San Miguel watershed in northern Sonora, particularly in pre-Columbian times (Felger et al. 1976). Additionally, Tarahumaras gathered the ripe pods, ground them, and then added the meal to ground corn to prepare a mixture called *esquiate* (Pennington 1963).

Acacia greggii grows throughout much of the Southwest into Baja California and Sonora, but is absent in the arid regions just west of the Colorado River and north of the Gulf of California (Turner et al. 1995). Its fruits ripen and fall at the onset of summer rains. Few groups used the pods or seeds. Those who did generally pounded the seeds into a coarse, nutritious meal that they made into atole or cakes (Barrows 1900; Castetter 1935; Bean and Saubel 1972). Clarkdale Apaches roasted and ground the fruits, then sifted the resulting meal to remove the seeds (Gallagher 1976). They used the meal in a manner similar to that of mesquite meal. At least by the 1970s, the Clarkdale Apache no longer used the fruits because their preparation was tedious. River Pimas once ate the beans "in primitive times," but no one by the turn of the century knew how the fruits were prepared (Russell 1908:76). None of the contemporary Gila River Pima know about the use of the seeds for food (Rea 1997).

The Cahuilla did not consider the catclaw seeds a favorite food because of the sometimes-bitter taste. They ate the pods fresh or dried and ground them into flour, from which they prepared mush or cakes (Bean and Saubel 1972). If pods were too bitter, they "parboiled" the pods to remove the bitterness.

Catclaw acacia seeds produce cyanogenetic glycosides in the herbage and seeds (Kingsbury 1964). It is probable that its seeds also contain antinutritional factors that interfere in protein digestion, unless the seeds are properly cooked.

Acacia pennatula reaches its northern limits along the eastern edge of the Sonoran Desert from the vicinity of Cumpas, Sonora (near 30'55°N), southward (Turner et al. 1995). Its fruits begin to develop in June, but do not reach maturity until the next dry period. Little is known about the use of *A. pennatula* for food by groups living in or near the Sonoran Desert. Guarijios ate its seeds (Gentry 1942, 1963) during times of winter famine in the 1930s (Altschul 1973).

Caesalpinia | holdback, nicker

C. platyloba **S. Watson**
palo colorado, hueilaqui

C. pulcherrima **(Linnaeus) Swartz**
Barbados flower, pride of Barbados, bird-of-paradise, barba del sol, flor de San Francisco, chacmol, flor de guacamaya, flor del camarón, poinciana enana, tetezo, tavachín, talcapache, tabaquín, matachín

Caesalpinia platyloba is a small tree that is widely distributed in Mexico, but restricted to the arroyos within the Sonoran Desert in southern Sonora (Turner et al. 1995). Its fruits develop and persist into winter. Guarijios collected its seeds in November and December, then roasted, ground, and ate the meal in the form of an atole (Gentry 1942, 1963).

Caesalpinia pulcherrima is widely cultivated in the tropics and subtropics and is naturalized throughout the warmer parts of Mexico (Standley 1922; Wiggins 1964), but not in Arizona (Turner et al. 1995). Its seeds mature in the winter and are edible, but they never constituted a significant food. Guarijios collected the immature pods in August and September and ate the seeds raw (Gentry 1963). Mexican muleteers grabbed the pods on trailside plants, split the pods, and nibbled the seeds as they went by (Gentry 1942). The seeds were described as "sweet as a tender pea," but the seed coat was first removed. Ónavas Pimas also collected the fruits, called *ejotes,* and, like the Guarijío, removed the unpalatable seed coat (Pennington 1980). The Yaqui, who called the plant *matachín,* likewise ate the immature, green, sweet-tasting seeds (Alvarez de Williams n.d.).

A large number of seeds can usually be obtained from the pods, although some plants produce few seeds per pod (Turner et al. 1995). The pods contain tannins and are used for tanning and dyeing. *Caesalpinia pulcherrima* should not be confused with *C. gillesii* (Hooker) Wallich ex D. Dietrich, a shrub that can produce severe irritation in the digestive tract following consumption of the immature pods (Kingsbury 1964). *Caesalpinia gillesii* grows in the Sonoran Desert as an escaped cultivar. It differs from *C. pulcherrima* by having clear yellow petals (as compared to orange) and heavily glandular-dotted inflorescences and pods.

Cercidium | paloverde

C. floridum **Bentham ex A. Gray ssp.** ***floridum*** **(syn.,** ***Parkinsonia florida*** **[Bentham ex A. Gray] S. Watson)**
paloverde, blue paloverde

C. microphyllum **(Torrey) I. M. Johnston (syn.,** ***Parkinsonia microphylla*** **Torrey)**
paloverde, littleleaf paloverde, yellow paloverde, foothill paloverde, dipúgo, dipúa, medesá, medezá

Cercidium floridum ssp. *floridum* grows throughout the arid regions of southern California, Arizona, and south into Sinaloa, whereas *C. microphyllum* grows in the arid regions of southwestern Arizona, Sonora, and throughout much of Baja California (Turner et al. 1995). Both develop fruits soon after they flower in the spring, prior to the onset of monsoon rains.

Their pods and seeds provided an edible food to many desert groups, although those of *C. microphyllum* were often preferred. One can easily differentiate between the fruits and seeds of the two paloverdes. *Cercidium floridum* has broader pods with minimal constriction between the few flat, thin, and hard seeds (fig. 106). *Cercidium microphyllum* has narrow pods with conspicuous constrictions between the more numerous, relatively plump, chewable seeds (fig. 107).

Edward Gifford (1932, cited as *C. torreyana*) simply noted that the Southeastern Yavapai ate the seeds of *C. floridum*. However, he provided more information on the Northeastern Yavapai use of *C. floridum* (Gifford 1936, cited as *C. torreyanum*). They traveled to the lower elevations in mid-June to collect both saguaro and paloverde seeds. As the season progressed, they moved up to the higher elevations, such as the area near Cleator, to harvest the later-maturing fruits. While the men gathered saguaro fruit, the women gathered paloverde seeds. They collected the mature pods (presumably) in a basket, then beat or stirred them to release their seeds. Seeds were parched with live coals in a basket, with the seeds and coals "thrown in air" to prevent the basket from becoming burned. They cleaned the parched seeds by rotating and shaking the basket, which brought the coals to the surface. Seeds

FIGURE 106. Cultivated ***Cercidium floridum*** Benth. ex A. Gray. Immature pods, with developing seeds. South Mountain area, Maricopa County, Arizona, May 1988.

FIGURE 107. ***Cercidium microphyllum*** (Torr.) I. M. Johnston mature pods; note constrictions between the seeds. South Mountain Park, Maricopa County, Arizona, June 1988.

were then ground on a metate, with the meal being slightly dampened or sometimes mixed with ground saguaro seed before being eaten.

River Pimas, Tohono O'odham, and Hiá ceḍ O'odham differentiated between *C. floridum,* called *ko'okmaḍkĭ,* and *C. microphyllum,* called *kuk chehedagĭ* (Rea 1997). Frank Russell (1908, cited as *Parkinsonia microphylla* and *P. torreyana*) noted that River Pimas ate the seeds of both paloverdes fresh or after being pounded in a mortar, sometimes mixed with mesquite meal. They also ground the seeds with ironwood and used this mixture in pinole (Nabhan et al. 1979). Gila River Pima George Webb related to Leonora Curtin (1949, *Curtin 10,* DES) that they gathered the green pods of *C. microphyllum* (mistaken for *C. floridum*) in the summer. Ruth Giff reminisced that "when picking wheat in the field, someone would go out on horseback and gather a bunch" of *C. microphyllum* pods (Rea 1997:164). They ate only the "very young" seeds raw.

Tohono O'odhams gathered the pods of *C. microphyllum* in August, then dried and beat them to separate out the seeds (Castetter 1935, cited as *Parkinsonia microphylla*). They parched and stored or ground the seeds, the meal being mixed with mesquite meal. A Tohono O'odham friend told Amadeo Rea (1997) that they usually would not eat the mature seeds of *kuk chehedagĭ,* although they once pounded the seeds in rock mortars and drank the meal mixed with water. However, the Tohono O'odham still enjoy eating its young seeds raw or, if seeds are more mature but still green, boiled like garden peas. People collected and roasted the mature seeds of *C. floridum,* but generally avoided its immature, bitter-tasting pods and seeds. A simple taste test explains the differential selection of the paloverdes. The immature seeds of *C. microphyllum* are usually sweet and tender (although I have found their taste to be variable even when collected from the same tree at the same stage of development). Its immature pods are likewise sweet and edible. Mature seeds are not extremely hard or bitter tasting. On the contrary, immature pods and seeds of *C. floridum* are extremely bitter and the mature seeds are extremely hard.

Hiá ceḍ O'odhams also ate the seeds of both paloverdes. They parched and ground the seeds of *C. microphyllum* into flour that they ate as gruel or atole (Felger et al. 1992). Fernando Flores, a Hiá ceḍ O'odham, described how seeds of paloverde were gathered in large quantities, shelled, ground on stone, mixed with deer fat and water, and baked in the ground to form a breadlike mass (Bell 1980).

The Cahuilla collected the pods of *C. floridum* from July to August, then ground the "beans" (presumably mature seeds) into a flour that they ate as an atole or used in mush or cakes (Barrows 1900, cited as *Parkinsonia torreyana;* Bean and Saubel 1972).

Paloverdes appear to have been an important food to Baja California *indigenes.* Cocopas made seasonal trips south to the eastern flanks of the Sierra Juarez to gather seeds, including those of *C. microphyllum.* In September 1796, Lt. Gov. Arillaga observed such a trip (Tiscareno and Robinson 1969:58): "The Indians from the Colorado [delta] came to this dance, where they no doubt live at certain seasons, during the seed of the *medesa* tree [*C. microphyllum*] which is found in great quantity in this vicinity [one of the tributaries of the Arroyo Agua Caliente]."

Paloverde was also important to native people who once lived in the central desert region of Baja California. They distinguished between three different kinds of paloverde and only now can one associate the local names with the species. Local names given were *dipúa* or *medesá, palo brea,* and *palo verde.* Paloverdes that grow in Baja California are *C. microphyllum, C. praecox* (Ruiz and Pavon) Harms, *C.* x *sonorae* Rose and Johnston, and *C. floridum* ssp. *peninsulare* (Rose) Carter (Carter 1974; Wiggins 1980). *Cercidium microphyllum* grows within the areas of the Kiliwa, Cochimí (*sensu* Massey 1949; including Borjeño, Ignacieño, Monquí, and Didiu), and northern Guaicura. *Cercidium floridum* ssp. *peninsulare* and *C. praecox* grow in areas formerly occupied by the southern Cochimí (including the Laymon, Cadegomeño, Monquí, and Didiu), Guaicura, Huichiti, and Pericú.

Most of the mission accounts mention *dipúa* or *medesá,* whose seeds were eaten, and *palo brea.* The use of the names *dipúa* or *medesá* may reflect regional differences because the southern Cochimí called the seed *medesá,* whereas those "speaking the Loreto language" to the north called them *dipúa* (del Barco 1980:178). Local inhabitants insisted that they could distinguish between *dipúa* or *medesá* and *palo brea.* Fr. del Barco (1980:129) mentioned a "third type of tree with a green bark ... from which the least benefit is obtained." This tree offered the inhabitants nothing in the way of wood or edible seed, but had value in providing good shade when it reached maturity. Annetta Carter (*in* del Barco 1980:129) believed that Fr. del Barco was referring to *C. floridum* ssp. *peninsulare.* By the mid 1900s, only *dipúa* and *palo brea* were names commonly used in Baja California for the green-barked trees.

Palo brea means "tar tree," referring to the waxy substance or resin that exudes from the bark of *C. praecox,* which became pliable when heated (Aschmann 1959; del Barco 1980). This resin was used to glue together the shafts of arrows (Clavigero 1937) or mixed with suet for use on canoes and boats or as a sealant on the missionaries' jars (del Barco 1980). No mention was made of *palo brea's* use for food by people, although its young branches supplied abundant fodder to livestock. I have found mature and immature fruits and seeds from Sonoran populations of *C. praecox* to be unpleasant tasting.

Thus, it appears that the only paloverde used for food by Baja California inhabitants was *C. microphyllum,* and that *dipúa* and *medesá* refer to this species because seeds of *C. floridum* ssp. *peninsulare* and *C. praecox* were not edible or used. *Dipúa* or *medesá* "was the leguminous tree of greatest importance in the Indian food supply" (Aschmann 1959:84). Mature pods were easily shelled and the seeds toasted and ground. So many fruits were produced that, according to Fr. Píccolo, one tree produced enough seeds to feed a family. Seeds were one of the few foods stored by the Cochimí (and more southern groups). They saved the seeds for the winter "as they have pitahayas and other fruits at the same time [early summer] that they gather these seeds" (del Barco 1980:127–128). The Cochimí esteemed the seeds of *medesá* "only a little less than corn" because they provided "good flavor and nourishment" (del Barco 1980:129). So highly esteemed were the seeds that their harvest and preparation were not only important, but probably annoying to anyone who wished for peace and quiet, as explained by Fr. Ducrue (Aschmann 1959: 84, 1966:52): "When there is an abundance of these seeds it is not possible to remain in the rancherias because of the noise which the natives make, by day and even more so at night, breaking and grinding these seeds with stones. There appears to be an arrangement among the Indians whereby scarcely have some begun to crack the seeds whereupon others are ready to continue the noise."

In southern Cochimí territory, Fr. del Barco (1980:128–129) described that around July "whole rancherias go gather this [mature] fruit wherever it happens to be. They are busy at this project for several weeks." Eating too many of these highly esteemed seeds was apparently risky. According to Fr. Ducrue, "these seeds actually cost many Indians their lives when, because of their eagerness to eat them, they gather them before they are well ripened, and eaten in that state they cause a fatal diarrhea" (Aschmann 1959: 84, 1966:52–53).

Fr. del Barco's (1981:74) description of how the Cochimí toasted seeds is both interesting and significant:

> They first toast all the seeds they eat, whether they be from trees or grasses. They eat them while they are still hot but, more frequently, they grind them up between two stones after they toast them. Having reduced them to a coarse flour, they eat it dry. The delicate flavor that toasting the seeds gives this flour is for them a special and delightful relish. All this is the responsibility of the women, who toast the seeds in the following manner. They put in their wooden tray three or four handfuls of seeds. On top of them they put hot charcoals, then they move everything continuously so that all the seeds can partake of the heat without burning either the seeds or the tray. When they recognize that the seeds have been done, they remove the charcoals with their hands. They clean the seed of every foreign object and particularly of the small pieces of charcoal left. Then they put aside the seeds that are finished, they put new seed in the tray with new hot charcoal, and they continue the operation until they finish.

The presence of unretrieved charcoal was not bothersome to the Cochimí, as del Barco (1981:74) described further their toasting of seeds: "No matter how careful they are, it is inevitable that with this method of toasting the seeds some particles of charcoal become stuck to the seeds, as has been experienced by those who are not accustomed to this food. When they taste it, they sense right away the noise which the charcoal makes between the teeth. However, our Californios, who are not so particular, eat it with pleasure without stopping to think about these petty details."

Cercidium microphyllum seeds played an important role in what was believed to be a "first fruit ceremony," as observed of the Didiu (a southern Cochimí group) by soldiers of the Atondo–Kino expedition in November 1684 (Engelhardt 1908; Bolton 1936; Clavigero 1937; Mathes 1974). A figurine the size of a newborn baby was carried by "the last Indian in the procession" to "a place where they had nailed up a branch of pitahaya" (Mathes 1974:101). Here, the natives placed the "bust" under a cover of *torote* (*Bursera* sp.) branches "a little above the ground at the foot of a great pile of seeds which they call *medese.*" At sunset, after two days and nights of dancing, "wailing," and shouting, the natives "sat in a circle in several places and began to pass out the said *medese* seed which they had piled up in front of said bust." Mathes (1974) believed this ceremony to be a funereal ceremony, rather than one that appealed for rain and thus fruit, as previously believed (possibly it was for both purposes). He argued that the distribution of food (among other practices), in this case *medesá* seed, was a common funereal practice among native Baja Californians. However, Mathes (1974:106) was incorrect in suggesting that *medesá* seeds might be those of *ciruelo (Cyrtocarpa edulis)* or *mezquite dulce* (cited as *Prosopis juliflora*). Of note is that the ceremony was observed in November, months after *medesá* seeds developed and matured, which thus supports del Barco's observation that the natives stored the seeds. Perhaps it was this ceremony that Lt. Gov. Arillaga witnessed that September day in Cocopa territory.

The Seri traditionally gathered the pods of *C. microphyllum* from packrat nests (Felger and Moser 1976, 1985). They rubbed handfuls of these pods together in a cloth to free the seeds after the pods dried under the sun. The seeds were toasted and ground. The resulting flour, which was frequently stored for future use, was mixed in water. This gruel was an important traditional food to which honey, mesquite flour, or sea turtle oil might be added. Those who inhabited the interior of Tiburón and San Esteban Islands ate substantial quantities of these seeds. Immature pods were also collected and cooked with meat, eaten raw, or dried and ground into a meal that was prepared as gruel. The Seri also utilized the seeds of *C. floridum*. They dried, toasted, and ground the seeds into flour, then mixed the meal with water and ate it with honey. Seris also ate the flowers of *C. microphyllum* fresh or first cooked them in water, squeezed the juice from the flowers, then mixed them with turtle oil or honey (Felger and Moser 1976, 1985).

Flowering and fruiting of *Cercidium* species appear to be strongly influenced by previous amounts of precipitation, which influenced the plants' use as a food item. *Cercidium microphyllum* flowers from late April to late May. Seeds ripen and fall approximately six weeks after the end of the flowering period (Turner et al. 1995). This species is absent south of 25°N (Turner et al. 1995), where rain falls primarily in the summer (Wiggins 1980). Early summer fruiting is characteristic in years when the winter rains have been good in Arizona and Sonora (Shreve 1964). When the fruits ripened in late spring—early summer in central Baja California, "it afforded an especially welcome addition to the food supply because this was often a season of acute want" (Aschmann 1959:85). Flowering of *C. microphyllum* may fail altogether following dry winters (Shreve 1964). Fr. del Barco (1980:128) noted that "in the vicinity of the Gulf it [*C. microphyllum*] bears good fruit some years but in others it produces nothing, and the years when it rests are more numerous than the years when it bears fruit."

In addition, bruchid beetles, soil fungi, and termites attack the fruits of *Cercidium* (Kingsolver et al. 1977; Siemens et al. 1992). Infestation has variable degrees and effects, but it can devastate fruit yield. *Cercidium floridum* and *C. microphyllum* have evolved different strategies to reduce seed loss to bruchid beetles. Seeds of *C. floridum* are more resistant to herbivore (including bruchid) attack, due to the presence of unidentified chemicals in their seed coat (Siemens et al. 1992). However, *C. microphyllum* escapes significant seed predation by dropping its pods early, prior to seed infestation by bruchid predators. The different strategies exhibited by the paloverdes also help explain the difference in exploitation of their fruits by humans. Bruchids may still develop in cached seeds of *C. microphyllum* that have not germinated. Fr. del Barco (1980:127) described how "they [Cochimis] clean it [seeds], and then they toast it so that it will not grow worms [sic]. Without this precaution, the worms soon take it over. This is done also to keep it from sprouting in case it gets wet by accident."

Paloverdes are now more useful for their use as livestock fodder than as food for humans in Baja California (Carter *in* del Barco 1980).

Crotalaria | rattlebox

C. incana **Linnaeus**
shakeshake, ajonjoli

C. pumila **Ortega**
low rattlebox, jojolino, chipil

Crotalaria incana and *C. pumila* (fig. 108) are weedy annuals that grow from the southern United States south into South America and other distant areas (Wiggins 1964; Kearney et al. 1960). They flower from June to October. Howard Gentry noted that Guarijios once ate the seeds of *C. incana* (Gentry 1942). Including *C. pumila* as a food source depends entirely on one noteworthy reference. George Hinton collected the plant in Mexico in 1932, noting that "it [presumably the seed] was edible, boiled with ripeseed" (*Hinton 1636,* NY; von

FIGURE 108. ***Crotalaria pumila*** Ort. in flower with submature fruit. On dirt road to Cabachi, 10.4 miles northeast of main road to La Colorada, Sonora, September 1988 (*Hodgson et al. 5179,* DES).

Reis and Lipp 1982). Gentry (1963) also observed that the Guarijío ground the seeds of an unidentified kind of *Crotalaria* before eating them as pinole.

Hoffmanseggia | rush-pea

H. glauca **(Ortega) Eifert**
hog-potato, rat-potato, waxy rush-pea, camote de ratón, coquito

Hoffmanseggia glauca forms long, creeping roots with tuberlike thickenings at their ends, which develop to 0.5 meter in depth and at least 0.5 meter away from the parent plant. These thickened roots are edible and were collected and eaten raw, boiled, or preferably roasted, like the common potato (Standley 1912; Castetter 1935, cited as *H. densiflora;* Rea 1997; *D. Francis 71,* DES). Eating too many of the tuberlike roots raw could cause an upset stomach (Hrdlička 1908).

River Pimas know the plant well, its use having persisted at least in memory (Rea 1997). They once collected the roots with a stick (which would be very difficult in the often-clayey soils), although by the 1940s they opted for a shovel (Curtin 1949, cited as *H. densiflora*). Ruth Giff told Amadeo Rea that women went into the fields in January to collect the little "potatoes" (Rea 1997). She remembered that they had to make very large holes to collect the tuberlike roots, which the women then carried home and boiled. The roots were tough, but considered sweet, although Ruth Giff thought they were tasteless. Sylvester Matthias reminisced that, as a youngster, he and other children would follow the plow to collect the roots, sometimes raiding pocket gopher caches of the roots (Rea 1997). Girls were prohibited to eat these cached tubers, although older, menopausal women were not.

Hoffmanseggia glauca commonly formed large colonies in flooded areas along the Lower Colorado River and may have been the *camote de ratón* collected and eaten by Cocopas, Mohaves, and Quechans (Castetter and Bell 1951). Tarahumaras may also have eaten its tuberlike roots in a similar fashion. Among the several unidentified edible roots, they ate one kind referred to as *camote* (Bennett and Zingg 1935). However, *camote* referred to a number of edible, starchy root foods.

Lysiloma | feathertree, false-tamarind

L. candida **Brandegee**
palo blanco

L. microphyllum **Bentham (syn.,** *L. divaricata* **[Jacquin] J. F. Macbride)**
mauto, quiebra hacha, saji, tepemezquite

L. watsonii **Rose (syn.,** *L. microphylla* **Bentham var.** *thornberi* **[Britton & Rose] Isely,** *L. microphyllum* **Bentham ssp.** *thornberi* **[Britton & Rose] E. Murray,** *L. thornberi* **Britton & Rose [in part])**
little-leaf false-tamarind, tepeguaje, machauhui

The seeds of *Lysiloma* provided a food source to peoples of northern Mexico. *Lysiloma candida* (fig. 109) is endemic to Baja California except for an isolated stand at Ensenada Grande north of Guaymas, Sonora (Turner et al. 1995; Carter *in* del Barco 1980). Its seeds ripened from September through November (Aschmann 1959; del Barco 1980). Fruits were normally

FIGURE 109. ***Lysiloma candida*** Brandegee. Comondú, Baja California, on lava rocks. Photograph courtesy of H. S. Gentry.

scarce and provided little seed for the women to roast, grind, and eat (del Barco 1980).

Lysiloma microphyllum grows in the Sonoran Desert in central Sonora and in the cape region and Sierra de la Giganta of southern Baja California (Turner et al. 1995). *Lysiloma watsonii* enters the Sonoran Desert in the Rincon Mountains, Pima County. These species' fruits mature from late fall to winter and late summer or fall, respectively. The Guarijío collected, roasted, ground, and ate the seeds of *L. microphyllum* and *L. watsonii* in the form of an atole (Gentry 1963).

Other uses of *L. candida* are of interest. The Cochimí called the plant *gokio,* but the Spanish called it *palo blanco,* in reference to the white color of the trunk and branches (del Barco 1980). However, according to one source, *palo blanco* referred to the white, transparent, and sweet gum exuded from the leaves and branches in May (Aschmann 1966). Fr. Ducrue observed that in the month of May, the "Indians also ate a gum scraped from the bark of a tree that was called *palo blanco.* There is no other reference to this practice" (Aschmann 1959:84). This "sweet gum" was "regarded by the Indians as a delicacy for some other effect which is not understood" (Aschmann 1966:53).

Lysiloma candida "has probably suffered more from modern exploitation than any other tree" (Martinez 1947:130), due to the excellent tanning properties of its bark. The Cochimí knew of its tanning virtues (del Barco 1980:125): "Extracted from the tree and bark, the juice is good to cure hides and soles, in such a way that these obtain the color that they usually have ... it is usually mixed with a softer one of another tree in order to moderate it and correct its strength." Annetta Carter (*in* del Barco 1980:123) noted that "it is said that the plain south of La Paz was forested with *palo blanco* but that the trees were killed by the bark being stripped for tanning." Townsend Brandegee (1889) remarked that *palo blanco* was well known from Purísima and Comondú southward. Most of the wine in that region was made in hides conditioned with tannins from the bark during the 1800s, giving the wine a somewhat disagreeable flavor.

The Cochimí also used ground bark of *palo blanco* to treat "any type of sore" (del Barco 1980:125), similar to the Guarijío's use of *L. watsonii* bark to treat ailing teeth and gums (Gentry 1963). This is a common application of plant parts rich in tannins.

Olneya | desert ironwood

O. tesota A. Gray
ironwood, desert ironwood, olneya, arbol de hierro, palo fierro, tésota, uña de gato

The distribution of ironwood corresponds well with the Sonoran Desert. Its fruits begin to ripen in May or June (fig. 110) and fall four to eight weeks later (Shreve 1964). Southwestern groups ate the seeds using various preparation methods (Palmer 1871; Russell 1908; Forde 1931; Gifford 1932, 1933, 1936; Castetter 1935; Curtin 1949, *Curtin 73*, DES; Felger and Moser 1976, 1985; Alvarez de Williams 1987). Seeds have low amounts of amino acids and high levels of canavanine, an antinutrient (Becker 1982), although they are considered a good protein source (see *Phaseolus, Prosopis*). As a result, ironwood seeds have a low protein efficiency ratio. Cooked seeds have a protein efficiency ratio three times higher than that of uncooked seeds, which compares favorably with that of raw soybean flour.

FIGURE 110. ***Olneya tesota*** A. Gray with immature fruit. South Mountain Park, Maricopa County, Arizona, June 1988.

Southeastern Yavapais ate the seeds after extensive preparation, as described by Edward Gifford (1932:211):

> The pods were laid on hard, smooth ground and the seeds beaten out with a stick. The seeds were soaked in water for two or three days and then boiled three or four times to remove the bitter taste. After drying they were parched with coals in a basket. Then followed the cracking of the hulls on a metate, winnowing to remove the hulls, and further soaking of the seeds in cold water to remove any lingering bitterness. The meats become whitish in color. After thorough drying in the sun, they were parched until brown. Then they were ground on a metate and the meal made into cakes, which were very greasy.

Western Yavapais traveled to "White Tank, on the north side of Gila River, near Mohawk" to harvest ironwood seeds (Gifford 1936:258). They boiled the seeds in a pot or stone-boiled them in a basket three or four times "to leach out bitterness." Cooked seeds were then dried, parched, and ground on a metate. The resulting meal, which was "very greasy," was eaten dry.

Ruth Giff, a Gila River Pima, gathers the pods from the ground and beats them to release the seeds with a stick (Rea 1997). River Pimas generally parched or roasted the seeds, then ate them without further preparation (Russell 1908) or ground and mixed the meal with water to make pinole (Curtin 1949). The flavor resembled that of acorns or peanuts. Most people considered the seeds to be bitter, thus it was generally the custom to leach the seeds in some manner. Aleš Hrdlička (1908) described how, almost a century ago, Pimas put the seeds into deep baskets that they hung overnight in a swift current in the river. In the morning they dried and preserved the seeds for future use. When desired, they roasted and ground the seeds into a coarse meal. A second method involved grinding the seeds coarsely, then putting the meal into a hole in the sand near the river that washed away the bitterness. Ruth Giff described how they used to soak the seeds in water (for what reason she did not know because she did not think that the seeds were bitter), dry them, then roast and eat the seeds (Rea 1997). She preferred toasting the seeds on top of the stove using a parching pan made of clay, rather than a frying pan, because the seeds tended to burn in the latter. Sylvester Matthias described another method of leaching (Rea 1997). They dug a hole in the fine, dampened sand, put the seeds into the hole, then covered them overnight. They uncovered the seeds the next day, then dried and roasted them. One grandmother put the seeds in a gunnysack before putting them in the Santa Cruz River overnight (Rea 1997). Another method practiced during the 1930s involved roasting the seeds whole, breaking them on a metate, and then packing the meal into an earthen pit kept full of water to leach out the bitterness. They changed the water every other day for a week. The meal was then spread out to dry before being used.

For the Tohono O'odham, ironwood and littleleaf paloverde followed mesquite as important wild protein sources (Nabhan et al. 1979). One elderly Tohono O'odham recalled that they ate so much of it as children, they dislike the taste or smell today (G. P. Nabhan, pers. comm.). At Quitovac, Sonora, however, ironwood was more important for the wood it provided than for its seeds (Nabhan et al. 1982).

Kiliwas collected the fruits of ironwood in the San Felipe Desert, then ate the seeds as pinole (Meigs 1939). Despite the fact that ironwood is common along the gulf half of Baja California (Turner et al. 1995), ironwood seeds appear to not have been used for food by *indigenes* living in the central and southern part of the peninsula because they were considered inedible (Clavigero 1937; del Barco 1980). Perhaps they were unaware of how to soak the seeds in water to make them more palatable. The scarcity of water may have also limited the use of ironwood seeds by inhabitants living in the more arid parts of the peninsula, particularly the central desert region.

Cooked ironwood seeds tasted like peanut butter to the Seri (Felger and Moser 1976, 1985). They cooked the seeds in two changes of water until soft to remove the unpleasant smell. The outer seed coat was discarded. They ate the seeds as is, ground and salted, or sometimes boiled with meat. Rodents collect the fruits at night, crack the pods open to get the seeds (Shreve 1964), and carry them back to their caches. Seris often raided these caches to gather the pods and seeds.

Ironwood seeds have become a personal favorite. After soaking the seeds overnight, I dry them thoroughly, then toast them with salt in either a parching pan or frying pan on the stove. The seeds will pop like popcorn and once cooked have a very good taste. I have also found raw, uncooked seeds not soaked in water to be pleasant-tasting and not bitter. However, people probably once ate a substantial amount of ironwood seeds, thus necessitating them to leach the seeds that would otherwise irritate their intestinal tract (A. Rea, pers. comm.).

Ironwood and its habitat face many threats. Probably the most severe impact is the conversion of ironwood habitat to agricultural lands and suburban development. Woodcutting for charcoal production, fuelwood, and the ironwood carving industry (the machine-assisted mass production of carvings by Mexican communities) has impacted ironwood populations (Arizona-Sonora Desert Museum 2000). Overgrazing and competition by buffelgrass, *Pennisetum ciliare*, which fuels hot wildfires, also threaten ironwood. Ironwood can receive a level of protection within Mexico, which protects plants under laws and regulations that are, unfortunately, difficult to enforce. In June 2000, President Clinton proclaimed the designation of Ironwood Forest National Monument in southern Arizona.

Parkinsonia | Jerusalem thorn

P. aculeata **Linnaeus**

Mexican paloverde, retama, bacapore, junco, junco marino, bagota, guacóporo, guachigelle

Parkinsonia aculeata is indigenous to the Sonoran Desert throughout much of Sonora and Baja California and may be indigenous in southern Arizona south of 32°N (Turner et al. 1985). It is notably absent in that area surrounding the Gulf of California and San Felipe Desert.

The seeds of Mexican palo verde were not an important food, probably owing to the bitter qualities of the seed coats. Lack of its use in the northern regions of the Sonoran Desert may also be due to its relatively recent occurrence as a disturbance-adapted plant. However, further south, Guarijios ate the seeds raw, when green and tender in late spring (Gentry 1942, 1963). They considered the seeds to be as sweet and tender as peas after the seed coats were removed.

Bioassays conducted on this plant suggest that its seeds (probably seed coats) contain toxic compounds that would quickly affect mammals that consume them (Nabhan et al. 1979). *Parkinsonia* fruits are eaten by bruchid species of the genus *Mimosestes* (Kingsolver et al. 1977). Because bruchids feed on seed tissue, the outer, bitter seed coats may not affect them.

Phaseolus | bean

P. acutifolius A. Gray
tepary bean, tépari, frijolillo, tépari del monte, escomite, garboncillo bolando, yori muni, pavi

P. filiformis Bentham
slimjim bean, frijillo, frijol

P. ritensis M. E. Jones
Santa Rita Mountain bean

FIGURE 111. **a.** ***Phaseolus acutifolius*** A. Gray var. ***tenuifolius*** A. Gray dehisced pod and mature seed, Baboquivari Mountains, Pima County, Arizona, September 1982 (*Mittleman 522,* DES); **b.** ***P. filiformis*** Benth. leaves and pod, Verde River, two miles below Bartlett Dam, Maricopa County, Arizona, May 1975 (*Engard 459,* DES).

Most of the wild *P. acutifolius* are represented by var. *tenuifolius* A. Gray and var. *latifolius* Freeman. They usually grow on the semi-arid margins of the Chihuahuan and Sonoran Deserts, including the Sierra la Laguna and Tiburón Island, where it was documented nearly three decades ago. Arizona populations grow as isolated patches in Santa Cruz and Pima Counties. Wild teparies flower with the summer rains in late August (Nabhan and Felger 1978) and the pods ripen primarily in October, during the fall dry season (Gentry 1942). Both varieties tend to have outer seed covering colors that match the background colors of the particular soil on which they grow, even though they are not associated with any particular soil type (Nabhan 1978a). Their shapes and disruptive color camouflage them from seed predators, including humans, when scattered on the ground.

The two varieties tend to occupy different microclimates that reflect their different morphology and habit. *Phaseolus acutifolius* var. *tenuifolius* occupies more open, nutrient-deficient sites on slopes or benches above floodplains and is a low climber over grasses and shrubs (Nabhan 1978a). It has narrower leaflets and smaller, more numerous seeds per pod (fig. 111a), which are probable adaptations to a more unpredictable, xeric habitat. *Phaseolus acutifolius* var. *latifolius* is often restricted to more mesic, shaded spots on streambanks and floodplains, growing in high density patches with the vines climbing relatively high into trees and shrubs. Its leaflets are broader and the seeds are larger and fewer per pod (fig. 112). In its habitat, moisture is not so limiting; with broader leaflets, it can compete more efficiently for sunlight in the dense canopies characteristic of streambanks. In addition, *P. acutifolius* var. *latifolius* more frequently colonizes flood- and human-disturbed habitats than does *P. acutifolius* var. *tenuifolius* due to its larger leaflets, which may help the variety compete for light in lush, weedy locations in early successional stages where competition among seedlings is high. Thus, *P. acutifolius* var. *latifolius* may have been "preadapted" to colonizing floodplain fields that pre-Columbian farmers developed for planting (Pratt and Nabhan 1988). This may be an example of why one variety was domesticated, while another was not.

Wild and cultivated forms of *P. acutifolius* have been a high-protein food source for more than 5,000 years in the Americas (Nabhan 1975; Felger and Nabhan 1978; Pratt and Nabhan 1988). Although based on limited seed stocks, research indicates that teparies compare favorably with common beans and other legumes in quantity and quality of proteins, vegetable oils, starches, and riboflavin and have higher calcium and niacin contents (Scheerens et al. 1983). A 100-gram portion of dry, white tepary beans contains 24 grams protein, 144 milligrams calcium, 405 milligrams phosphorus, and 1,653 milligrams potassium (Calloway et al. 1974). In addition, teparies have a significantly higher protein content when grown in traditional O'odham floodwater fields (Nabhan 1979a).

Teparies were important to the River Pima throughout historic times (Nabhan et al. 1979), but more recently, Gila River Pimas know only the cultivated varieties that they produced in abundance until their rivers went dry (Rea 1997). It is not known if they ever knew about wild teparies or if the Tohono O'odham ever brought wild teparies to trade during the wheat harvest. The Gila River Pimas' cultivation of teparies may have been extensive. J. Ross Browne (1869:110–111) noted that in 1858, the Gila River Pima produced "a large quantity of beans called *taperis* [sic] and a vast quantity of pumpkins, squash, and melons." Three years later, Pimas sold 20,000 pounds of what is assumed to have been tepary beans to the California Column.

The Tohono O'odham were long ago called the *Babavi* (or *Pabavi*) O'odham, or the "Tepary Bean People." In 1914, the most productive site for the harvest of wild teparies by the Tohono O'odham was along a wash in the Santa Rosa Mountains, Pima County (Freeman 1912; Nabhan and Felger 1978). In 1976, Gary Nabhan and Richard Felger sampled a site near Rosemont, Pima County. The plants here yielded 191 grams of dry seed from 250 plants in a 100-square-meter plot, which is the equivalent of 20 kilograms per hectare (Nabhan and Felger 1978). Beans were reputedly sold at trading posts. The Tohono O'odham continued to harvest wild teparies at least until after World War II.

The seeds of wild *P. acutifolius* were also a major food source to the Seri inhabiting Tiburón Island (Felger and Moser 1976) and their harvest persisted until the middle of this century (Felger and Moser 1985). Rosa Flores, a Seri, located the tepary population at a traditional gathering place on the island after not having visited the area for 34 years (Nabhan and Felger 1978; Felger and Moser 1985). According to Flores, the fruits ripened at the end of the summer monsoon. The women gathered the mature pods in the early morning. Pods gathered later in the day dried quickly and dehisced, thus scattering the seeds. Women carried the pods back to camp in their skirts and rubbed them between their hands over blankets or deerskin to free the seeds. The seeds were often boiled alone or cooked with deer meat or bones, if available. According to another Seri woman, Sara Villalobos, teparies were boiled like regular beans (*P. vulgaris* L.).

Gary Nabhan and Richard Felger (1978) presented an overview of tepary cultivation from pre-Columbian times to the present and illustrated the importance of this bean when grown and harvested in the appropriate context. The reader is also referred to Rea (1997) for an informative account of Gila River Pima cultivation of teparies.

As early as 1716, Fr. Luis Velarde commented that the principal harvest of Papagos west of the Santa Cruz River was the "beans called *papavi*" (Wyllys 1931). It was suggested that teparies were surpassed only by maize in terms of relative abundance under cultivation in the Sonoran Desert (Castetter and Bell 1942, 1951). Tepary bean production far surpassed corn production, with the Tohono O'odham producing 816,690 kilograms

FIGURE 112. ***Phaseolus acutifolius*** var. ***latifolius*** habit and fruits.

of teparies and 136,111 kilograms of corn (McDowell 1920).

Interest in tepary as an important drought-tolerant crop able to produce high yields under minimal irrigation developed in the early 1900s (Nabhan and Felger 1978). Non-Indian farmers in Arizona, New Mexico, California, and elsewhere were turning marginally productive land over to tepary cultivation by 1915, and soon these beans became available in markets throughout the country. However, teparies were not well accepted. The small, relatively unattractive beans have a strong flavor and odor and may produce flatulence. In addition, the introduction of gasoline-powered pumps into Arizona in 1902 allowed access to groundwater, thus resulting in the irrigation of lands that could previously only have been dry-farmed. The rapid expansion of groundwater-irrigated agriculture (U.S. Department of Agriculture Soil Conservation Service 1950) soon after the beginning of the tepary boom probably contributed to the decline of tepary dry-farming because drought-tolerant crops were no longer critical to the existence of agriculture in arid lands (Nabhan and Felger 1978). Ironically, tepary production is once again increasing, following a period when modern irrigated agriculture permitted drought-intolerant crops to be grown in semi-arid zones.

The change from dry-farming to groundwater-based agriculture occurred more slowly for the Indians of the Southwest and northern Mexico (Nabhan and Felger 1978). They worked for wages in cotton fields or other industries, which caused them to abandon their own fields. A traditional barter and gift economy was almost entirely replaced by the cash economy among the Tohono O'odham and others (Dobyns 1949). Only those who did not get jobs and buy all their food from stores continued the very limited dry-farming of teparies.

Tepary cultivation has persisted to the present in northern Mexico, despite the Spanish introduction of many other grains and legumes that often took the place of Indian crops (Felger and Nabhan 1978). Although larger-scale irrigation systems have replaced the dry-farming techniques, some Sonoran farmers continue to use *acequia* and *temporal* dry-farming.

Considerable loss of genetic variability in tepary crops was an important consequence of the abandonment of traditional subsistence farming (Pratt and Nabhan 1988). In addition, overgrazing at the turn of the century by Anglos' cattle caused the loss of wild tepary gene pools due to direct habitat degradation and to habitat elimination from subsequent arroyo cutting. Other negative impacts on wild populations have included fire suppression, fuelwood overharvesting, vegetation conversion, urbanization, and land clearing for agriculture. Documentation of wild tepary populations, particularly those in southern Arizona—where they reach their most northern limit of distribution—would be valuable for determining the range of variability in vegetative and reproductive characteristics, including seed size and morphology (G. P. Nabhan, pers. comm.).

Two types of tepary beans continue to be sold commercially in Sonora and on or near Indian reservations (Pratt and Nabhan 1988). The larger-scale farmers grow teparies mostly for sale to merchants (Bouscaren et al. 1983), who sell them in markets and *aborrotes* in an area between Phoenix, Arizona, and Hermosillo and Agua Prieta, Sonora (Nabhan and Felger 1978; fig. 112). The smaller-scale farmers grow teparies in small, irrigated fields for domestic use and sell them only when there is a surplus (Bouscaren et al. 1983). A few Sonoran farmers are known to smuggle truckloads of teparies to the Tohono O'odham Indian Reservation, where the beans are sold for a high price (Nabhan and Felger

FIGURE 113. A five-pound bag of domesticated tepary beans that sold for 1.09 dollars per pound, Hermosillo, Sonora, 1988.

1978). Teparies were sold wholesale for 20 dollars per 45 kilograms and marketed retail in trading posts for 50 cents to 1.38 dollars per 0.4 kilogram in Arizona in 1975. Teparies were sold for about 30 cents per 0.4 kilogram in 1987 (G. P. Nabhan, pers. comm.; fig. 113). They were sold at Sacaton and Casa Blanca markets, on the Gila River Pima Reservation in July 1997 (A. Rea, pers. comm.).

Despite its early failure, interest in continuing to farm teparies as a cash crop is primarily due to the plant's adaptations to drought and heat and its high yields in arid lands. Teparies are extremely productive in climates with less than 50 centimeters of rain annually and withstand high evaporation rates. They are productive on sandy or alkaline soils and respond well when additional moisture is available. By dropping most of their leaves, teparies can even withstand periods of extreme drought when other crops die out (Freeman 1912). Plants put out new leaves, flowers, and fruits following the addition of moisture. Traditional tepary crop harvest was relatively dependable, with four of five years yielding good harvests when grown in floodwater-fed fields (Nabhan et al. 1979). Teparies can be harvested 60 to 75 days after planting and are seldom damaged by insects or disease (Nabhan and Felger 1978).

Tepary genes have already proved useful for another bean crop. Tepary's resistance to *Xanthosoma phaseoli*, the agent of common bean blight, has been bred into the Great Northern cultivar, *P. vulgaris* (Honma 1956). Desert-adapted agroecosystems might incorporate these drought-tolerant plants into multiple cropping systems in the future (Duke and Terrell 1974).

The "rediscovery" of teparies appears to be moving slowly. In a survey of tepary-growing localities in Sonora, Sonorans ate the teparies in stews, broths, and soups, but only once a week to once a month, whereas pinto beans were eaten three times a day (Bouscaren et al. 1983). Only at one location visited did people eat boiled teparies as is or mash them for refried beans. If tepary is used little, then why should one grow the plant? The answer may be in the fact that most people visited knew that tepary has been around a very long time and that it was connected with the pre-Columbian inhabitants of the area (Bouscaren et al. 1983). Could tepary, like the wild chiltepines (see *Capsicum*), provide Sonorans a boost of cultural identity? Perhaps for this reason Sonorans would rather spend the time and energy to grow this native crop, rather than to see it and its folklore die out.

Lack of tepary use by the Tohono O'odham is especially ironic, considering how important this legume once was to them. An average daily consumption of tepary beans was approximately 300 grams per person during the 1940s (Ross 1944). More recently, teparies have been prepared infrequently, except for special family occasions when they are eaten with wheat tortillas and chile (Nabhan and Teiwes 1983). At large community feasts, pinto beans have replaced tepary beans. Tepary prices were often two or three times that of pinto beans at trading posts where many Tohono O'odham families buy their beans.

The O'odham's diet and health have changed drastically in recent years. The extremely high rate of adult-onset diabetes (Type II diabetes) among the Tohono O'odham and River Pima is as much as 15 times that of the national average and is partly the result of their vastly altered diet (Nabhan 1985). Teparies and other O'odham traditional foods may protect these people from dangerously rapid rises in blood glucose levels after meals (Brand et al. 1990) and control these levels enough to reduce the need for insulin shots. The glycemic and insulin indices of teparies are low, 29 and 38 percent, respectively, as compared to the much higher indices for such Western staples as potatoes, bread, and other processed cereals (e.g., commercial sweet corn has a glycemic index of 59 percent). Teparies have a relatively low percent starch digestibility, from 26 to 33 percent digested after four hours, as compared to 55 percent starch digested for bread. The potential value of teparies to the O'odham diet is increasingly appreciated. At present, O'odham tepary seed sources are available and programs have been initiated to provide encouragement and impart the skills for these people to once again grow their own teparies (Nabhan and Teiwes 1983).

Although considered a good source of protein, teparies have a low protein digestibility when compared to other cultivated legumes, but values are comparable to those found for some common bean varieties (Scheerens et al. 1983). Poor levels of protein digestibility associated with certain legumes may be caused by a variety of factors. These include the effect of incomplete starch or carbohydrate digestion, the presence of antinutritional factors that inhibit the function of digestive tract enzymes (protease inhibitors) or intestinal absorption, and the effects of processing or preparation and cooking. Uncooked tepary starches are digested slowly relative to other processed cereal grains (Brand et al. 1990); they could inhibit protein digestion, as do starches of other protein-rich vegetables. However, tepary starch is probably readily digestible after cooking (Scheerens et al. 1983). Additionally, teparies contain antinutritional factors similar to those of the common bean. However, their antinutritional qualities can be largely inactivated with proper cooking because these molecules are heat-sensitive (Pratt and Nabhan 1988), thus making an otherwise undigestible starch readily digestible (Scheerens et al. 1983). Starch digestibility and its effects on protein availability, which is in turn dependent on the activities of various protease inhibitors, is complex and not well documented for teparies (see Scheerens et al. 1983).

The same characteristics of teparies (and some other traditional foods) that helped control rapid elevation of blood sucrose levels (e.g., high fiber content, slow digestibility, low glycemic and insulin indices) may also affect protein availability—all of which are affected by how the food is prepared (Nabhan et al. 1979). The Tohono O'odham and River Pima appear to have achieved this physiological balance only if a number of resources were available. According to Nabhan et al. (1979), people were apparently protected from serious nutritional problems as long as a number of varied protein- and carbohydrate-rich foods and fuelwood were available. However, Nabhan et al. (1979) raised several questions. Assuming that mesquite was the primary fuel source, did early O'odham or their ancestors always thoroughly cook teparies? This could have impacted mesquite populations and even tepary populations. Did these people partially cook teparies, thus sacrificing potential proteins but supplementing their diet with other foods rich in available proteins? Were harvest and preparation of tepary (and other foods) cyclic, with the patterns depending upon availability of fuelwood (and water)? Because teparies are storable, the available seeds need not have been cooked all at once. However, bruchid beetles attacked teparies unless the seeds were stored in the form of dried cakes. The significance of escalating habitat degradation and resource competition (in this case, mesquite wood) early in this century between Anglos and O'odham becomes apparent (Nabhan et al. 1979). If people's main source of fuel was wood, the availability of fuelwood can be seen as a limiting factor for their use of tepary beans.

Tepary has also been considered for introduction to other cultures. However, prior to introducing nontraditional crops to other cultures, efforts should be made to understand the culture's traditional foods, diet constraints and problems, and available resources (Nabhan et al. 1979). For example, the introduction of a crop such as tepary is not appropriate for people who have a protein-deficient diet and a limited primary fuel source. Fuelwood is characteristically in short supply in underdeveloped areas. Introduction of teparies into fuel-poor areas may contribute to additional nutritional problems in people's diets because these beans require long cooking time to improve the availability of their protein (Scheerens et al. 1983). This can result in a greater impact on already limited resources.

Mention is made of two other native beans used for food. *Phaseolus filiformis* (fig. 111b) is one of the most, if not the most, xerophytic of wild beans growing from south-central Arizona southward at least to southern Sonora and the cape region of Baja California. The protein content of *P. filiformis* seeds is relatively high, approximately 26 percent (Ariffin 1984). Its significance to cultures is ancient, as caches of seeds were discovered from prepottery archaeological sites in southern Arizona that are at least 2,000 years old (Nabhan and Felger 1985). It flowers during any month if the precipitation is adequate (Wiggins 1964). The flowers, mature seeds, and immature pods were still eaten by the Hiá ceḍ O'odham and others who lived in the Pinacate region of northern Sonora in the late 1970s and early 1980s (Nabhan 1985). The pods and seeds are similar to lentils and the flowers have a pleasant, nutty flavor. The Hiá ceḍ O'odham refer to the plant as *ban bawi*, or "coyote bean" ("that which the coyote has spoiled"), but some no longer remember it as a food (Nabhan et al. 1989a). Wild beans persisting at Agua Dulce Springs, which were formerly planted there by the Hiá ceḍ O'odham (Fontana 1974), may represent *P. filiformis* (Nabhan et al. 1989a). This bean has resistance to bean golden mosaic virus, but efforts to cross it with *P. vulgaris* have been unsuccessful.

Phaseolus ritensis grows as a straggler in the Sonoran Desert in southern Arizona, mainly at higher elevations. It is easily distinguished from other beans by its coarse perennial habit; tuberlike root; and large, scabrous leaflets. The pods are produced from July through mid-October. The mature seeds, which are quick to fall from ripened pods, are large and may be prepared and eaten like teparies. I find the green, immature seeds to have a pleasant taste when eaten raw.

The pods and seeds of the "*P. metcalfei* group" (as defined by Nabhan et al. [1980], which included *P. ritensis*; *P. metcalfei* is considered a synonym of *P.*

maculatus Scheele) have been eaten by humans for a long period of time (Nabhan et al. 1980). Western Apache probably collected and ate the seeds fresh or stored the seeds of the closely related *P. maculatus* for later use. Dr. H. Rusby (1906:452) noted that the tuberous-rooted bean "*P. retusus*" (plants of the *P. metcalfei* group, sensu Nabhan et al. 1980) was "especially abundant in central Arizona." He added that the beans appeared to have been extensively collected and eaten by native groups. Rusby described the immature seeds as tender and agreeable and noted that "even after ripening, their toughness does not prevent the Indian from gathering them in large quantities for winter use." More recent ethnobotanical work does not mention the use of *P. metcalfei* or *P. ritensis* pods or seeds for food. This was probably due to the drastic shift in Apache lifestyle when their migratory subsistence patterns were terminated. In addition, the lack of more recent information on the use of these plants may reflect their more rare occurrence due to livestock grazing (Nabhan et al. 1980, cited as *P. metcalfei*). Grazing pressure drastically reduced the abundance of certain wild species that were important food items to people in pre-Columbian or early historic times (Bohrer 1978). *Phaseolus ritensis* and *P. maculatus* are not common plants today, and their relative rarity may be a result of past grazing practices.

Pithecellobium | blackbead

P. confine **Standley**
palo fierro, ejotón, ojotón

P. dulce **(Roxburgh) Bentham**
monkeypod, guamúchil, chucum blanco

P. leucospermum **Brandegee**
cucharo, palo fierro, palo eba, palo ebano

Little is known about the use of *P. confine* for food. It is limited to the coast of Sonora, islands in the Gulf of California and Natividad Island, and the southern half of Baja California (Turner et al. 1995), where they are common in the cape region and Sierra de la Giganta (Carter *in* del Barco 1980). Here the plant is called *ejotón* or *ojotón* by the local inhabitants, who use its seeds as a coffee substitute, presumably after they are toasted and ground.

Pithecellobium dulce was introduced from the East Indies and has been planted in Baja California, Sonora, Chihuahua, and south into South America (Wiggins

FIGURE 114. ***Pithecellobium dulce*** (Roxb.) Benth. seeds with edible aril. At home of Ramon Valenzuela, near Urique, Cañón de Higuera, Chihuahua, July 1997.

1964). The fruits ripen toward the end of the dry season, from the end of May through July. Although people cooked and ate the young pods, they favored the mature fruits for use as a food. "Mexicans and Indians" alike considered the white, fleshy aril (expanded portion of the funicle, or place of attachment of ovule to placenta, that envelops the seed) of the mature seed of *P. dulce* to be a favorite spring food (Gentry 1963:94; fig. 114). People commonly ate the arils raw or used them in the preparation of a beverage similar to lemonade (Rose 1900; Goldman 1916; Standley 1922; Gentry 1963, *Gentry 1224*, ARIZ). In Mexicali, Baja California, people grow *guamuchil* in their yards because the tree provides shade, fruits with edible arils, and seeds that they use as a vermifuge (C. Gorena, pers. comm.). The taste of the aril of the mature seed is sweet and quite pleasant when eaten raw.

Howard S. Gentry (1963:94) noted that Guarijío women and children traveled "along the streamways seeking the trees with sweeter pods." These gathering trips appeared to provide pleasurable times to the families. They "go equipped with baskets and long poles affixed with a hooking prong, thong-bound at the end." Children climbed the trees and gathered fruits that were not reachable from the ground. They often gorged themselves to the point of becoming sick. What was not eaten was carried home in baskets to dry in the sun. At San Bernardo, Sonora, naturalized trees on private lands were regarded as the personal property of the man in possession and were respected by the wild fruit gatherers as if they were in a cultivated orchard (Gentry 1942, 1963). A single tree can be very productive; it was estimated that many bushels of fruit could be produced (Rose 1900). Mature fruits were sold in the streets or, more commonly, in the markets (Rose

1900), such as those in Alamos and Navajoa (Gentry 1942).

Tarahumaras gathered the fruits of *P. dulce* in June and July, then mashed and mixed the arils with corn for tortillas (Bennett and Zingg 1935; Pennington 1963). They still gathered the fruits in July 1997 using a long pole made of *Arundinaria longifolia* and ate the aril raw. Ónavas Pimas also collected the fruits in June and sometimes sold them to Anglos (Pennington 1980).

Pithecellobium leucospermum grows along the Río Yaqui valley in southeastern Sonora and the cape region of Baja California, where it is nowhere abundant (Turner et al. 1995). The Guarijío gathered, roasted, ground, and ate the seeds of *P. leucospermum* raw or made into tortillas (Gentry 1942, 1963, cited as *P. undulatum*). Ónavas Pimas collected the fruits (seeds?) in the fall, then toasted and added them to pinole (Pennington 1980, cited as *P. undulatum*).

Prosopis | mesquite

> *P. glandulosa* **Torrey var.** *torreyana* **(L. Benson) M. C. Johnston**
> honey mesquite, western honey mesquite, mezquite, mezquite amarillo, mezquite blanco, mezquite colorado, mezquite chino, péchita
>
> *P. pubescens* **Bentham**
> screwbean mesquite, tornillo
>
> *P. velutina* **Wooton**
> velvet mesquite, mezquite, péchita

Mesquite was one of the most widespread and useful wild food plants in the desert regions of North America. Ethnographic work often referred to mesquite in the generic sense and did not note specific taxa. There is some confusion concerning which species or variety was used, particularly in Baja California, where four taxa grow. *Prosopis juliflora* (Swartz) de Candolle is frequently cited as the mesquite used in the Sonoran Desert. Because the species does not extend into the United States, this misapplied name referred to either *P. glandulosa* var. *torreyana* or *P. velutina*. Marshall Johnston's (1962a) monograph of *Prosopis* sect. *Algarobia* and Burkart and Simpson's (1977:201–255) illustrated key to *Prosopis* are useful in determining distribution and identification.

Prosopis glandulosa var. *torreyana*, or honey mesquite, is found from southeastern California south throughout much of Baja California into western Sonora and north along the Colorado, Gila, and Bill Williams Rivers in Arizona (Johnston 1962a). Honey mesquite fruits were considered the "staple of life" to the Mohave, Quechan, Cocopa, and Cahuilla and extensively used by the Havasupai, Diegueño, Hiá ceḍ O'odham, Seri, Cáhita (contemporary Yaqui and Mayo), Pima Bajo, and Eudeve.

The Mohave regularly included mesquite pods in their diet, which also helped alleviate starvation during seasons of low or no flooding of the Colorado River. A man had a claim to the yield of any mesquite trees that grew on his land, and no one could collect beans from them without his permission (Stewart 1965). If the trees were not on "private property," a person might hang a bundle of arrow-weeds *(Pluchea sericea)* on a tree to claim the beans. Most beans were collected in the summer, although green beans were sometimes eaten directly from the trees. In September, dry beans were collected off the ground or shaken from the trees with a long pole. Women carried the beans home in carrying nets on their backs, supported by tumplines across their foreheads. The green fruits were eaten by individuals who were "young and still with teeth" (Stewart 1965:48) to chew the pods. Young mesquite beans were sometimes roasted in ashes and eaten and were considered tender. The Mohave spread the remaining beans on the ground or on rooftops, dried them for one or two weeks, then stored the pods through the winter in giant basket granaries. Dried pods were pounded in a wooden mortar and the meal made into a kind of cake as described by Stewart (1965:48):

> They pounded the mesquite beans to a powder, then added a little water to make a ball. A fire was built, and when it burned to ashes they scraped off the sand. They put the ball of mesquite powder there and left it out in the sun until it got hard. They'd put mesquite bean seed over it to cover it. When it gets hard, it binds in and holds it together. Then they would break off little chunks and eat it when they wanted to. They would also put in water and drink it. If there were plenty of mesquite cakes a family might put them in piles and share them with others for a dance and feast.

Honey and screwbean mesquites were also very important foods to the Quechan and insured against starvation in years of irregular floods (Forde 1931:116). Plants were not owned exclusively, but families made it a habit of collecting beans "from the same districts every year." Women and children gathered mesquite pods, which ripened from late June to early July, turning over their planting duties to the men, if necessary (Bee 1989). They stored pods in permanent storage bins on or near their houses and near the "foot of a mesa in the vicinity of the most abundant food supply" (Forde 1931:116). Bins were erected on cottonwood poles on platforms 1.5 meters above the ground. The Quechan built bird's-nest-type burden baskets upon the platform, into which they tightly packed broken pods. The bins were filled, covered with arrow-weed, and sealed with damp mud, which hardened upon drying under the sun. They pounded the pods with stone pestles in wooden mortars, dampened and kneaded the meal into lumps, then dried these cakes.

Mesquite was an important food not only to the Mohave and Quechan, but Anglos as well, as they also exploited the beans. While a captive of the Mohave, Olive Oatman relied on the fruits, but it was much to her dismay. She lamented that "nothing but starvation could be expected" for her, her sister Mary Ann, and their Mohave captors, following a particularly dry spring and poor harvest in 1852 (Stratton 1857:185). Pods overlooked the previous year were even gathered by the women. She did not look forward to the reliance on mesquite meal: "They ground their seed between stones, and with water made a mush, and we spent many mournful hours of conversation over our gloomy state as we saw the supply of this tasteless, nauseating 'musquite mush' failing, and that the season of our almost sole dependence upon it was yet but begun." As the mesquite supply diminished, Miss Oatman and her captors relied on a shrub called *taneta* that produced "berries" called *oth-to-toa*, necessitating a perilous journey of 60 miles to obtain "this 'life-preserver'" (Stratton 1857:188). The shortage of food was too great, however. Mohave children and Mary Ann later starved to death.

The Quechan suffered great food shortages and heavy casualties during the early 1850s, to the point of near extinction, according to Kroeber (1980). A military expedition was sent in the fall of 1850 against the Quechan, who fled their homes. When the troops departed in late October, Anglos living at the junction of the Gila and Colorado Rivers continued to consume the Quechan's food supply, including the local supply of mesquite pods. In November, a small garrison of U.S. soldiers arrived at Yuma Crossing and also began harvesting mesquite. Thus, the Quechan lost much of what would have been a good harvest of pods. Some Quechans moved north along the Colorado River, where they subsisted on mesquite and screwbean pods (Sitgreaves 1853).

Honey and screwbean mesquite was "certainly a determining factor in site location" for the Cahuilla (Hedges 1985:6). Clans owned designated mesquite groves and, as with oaks, families owned individual trees. Cahuillas gathered, dried, and packed large quantities of honey mesquite fruits in granaries as well (Barrows 1900). They pounded the pods in a wooden mortar, placed the resulting meal in earthenware, and soaked it thoroughly. The meal was either eaten in this form or allowed to ferment, to improve the taste. Sometimes they rolled the mass into compact balls that they carried for food on a journey. Like the River Pima, who traded velvet mesquite with the Tohono O'odham, a Cahuilla group who had limited amounts of mesquite in their area traded their acorn (*Quercus*) and piñon (*Pinus*) crops for mesquite from their desert neighbors who had access to larger groves (Bean and Saubel 1972). Thus, at its geographic limits, mesquite was used as an item of commerce (Felger 1977).

Honey and screwbean mesquite may have been a determining factor in site location for the Kumeyaay, or Southern Diegueño, villages (Hedges 1985). Delfina Cuero, a Kumeyaay, reminisced that they "went down into the desert near Mexicali every year to get mesquite beans" (Shipek 1968:58) of either *P. glandulosa* var. *torreyana* or *P. pubescens*. She noted that mesquite beans made good flour for bread and could be soaked in water to make a "good cool drink." Santa Ysabel Diegueños also used the pods of *P. glandulosa* by pounding them in a mortar or grinding them on a metate into a meal that they made into mush (Hedges and Beresford 1986).

The first ethnographic reference to mesquite use in North America may be that of the Spanish explorer Hernando de Alarcón. In 1540 he was presented "some cakes of maize and a loaf of *mizquiqui*," thought to be bread made from the meal of *P. glandulosa* var. *torreyana* pods in the vicinity of the Colorado River delta (Elsasser 1980:14; Mathes 1992:100). Cocopas considered honey and screwbean mesquites, which were common in their area, to be very important because of the many uses. Women and older girls gathered the ripened pods of honey mesquite during the planting season (Kelly 1977). Unlike the Cahuilla, no one owned particular trees, thus allowing the women to carefully select the sweetest pods. They tested the pods by breaking and tasting them and then pulled down the higher branches to collect the pods using a long, hooked pole. Only enough mesquite was harvested to supply immediate wants because the pods ripened when all available help was needed for planting their crops. In late July and August, women carefully selected and picked large quantities of dried pods off the ground for winter storage. The men helped the women carry the pods to camp. Sometimes they robbed caches of pods in packrat nests, probably during years when the harvest was poor. Dried, broken pods were tightly packed into bird's-nest-type baskets and stored.

Cocopa women and sometimes men pounded the pods to remove the seeds and coarse fiber (Kelly 1977). Further shaking and winnowing separated out the larger pieces to leave the mesquite meal. The Cocopa made a drink by adding water to the meal, ate the meal washed down with water, or formed the meal into cakes that they stored. The cake was built by adding more and more meal while sprinkling it with water. Once shaped into the desired form, dried meal was sprinkled over it and the mass was left overnight. More recently, the Cocopa shaped the cake in a cloth, thereby keeping the cake moist. Usually only four or five cakes were made at one time. Pieces of stored cake were broken off when needed and used as one would use loose meal. Cocopas generally neither liked nor disliked mesquite meal, although Sam Spa, William Kelly's main source of information, was of the opinion that cake meal was sweeter than freshly ground pods. However, the meal did supply a bulky food that filled the stomach, often for an extended period of time (Kelly 1977). The Cocopa did not generally eat the seeds or fiber, but occasionally ground the hard seeds into a coarse meal (Alvarez de Williams 1987). In contrast, Peveril Meigs (1939) noted that Kiliwas ate the seed of *P. glandulosa* as pinole, the fruits being ripe in August.

There are few references to the use of mesquite by the inhabitants of Baja California south of Diegueño, Cocopa, and Kiliwa territory, despite its frequency and ample supply of pods. This apparent lack of use can be explained by comparing mission documents and the distribution of species on the peninsula. Of the four mesquites that grow in Baja California, only *P. glandulosa* var. *torreyana* and *P. pubescens* provided edible pods. Fr. Baegert (1952) noted that few of the mesquites supplied edible beans. Fr. Clavigero (1937) stated that two varieties of mesquite trees grew on the peninsula, one being a large, native tree producing bitter beans and the other being an introduced, smaller tree with sweet pods that were eaten by the local inhabitants.

The native inhabitants did not use the fruits of *P. articulata* S. Wats. and *P. palmeri* S. Wats. for food (del Barco 1980). Only the bitter mesquites, that is, *P. articulata* and *P. palmeri*, rather than *mezquite dulce*, were found in southern Cochimí and Guaicura areas of occupation prior to European contact. After "the conquest had begun," *mezquite dulce* became available, as described by Fr. del Barco (1980:122):

> In Yaqui and other parts of that coast these seeds [of mesquite] have a good flavor, and the people eat them. But in [Lower] California they are all bitter, and that is why only beasts eat them. In Loreto and in one or another mission some sweet mesquites can be found, but these came originally from the area of the Yaquis, or from that coast. They were taken from there to [Lower] California either as seed or when they were very small and grew there fairly well. This transplant was made after the conquest had begun, because before there was not a single one which was not bitter.

The *mezquite dulce* to which Fr. del Barco was referring was probably *P. glandulosa* var. *torreyana* (Carter *in* del Barco 1980, cited as *P. juliflora* var. *torreyana*). These plants are common in and around Guaymas, Sonora (Turner et al. 1995), near where Yaquis and Seris live.

Very large *mezquite dulce* trees were still standing in Loreto; one tree in front of the church in Loreto was believed to have been more than 100 years old and brought to Loreto by the Jesuits (Carter *in* del Barco 1980:121). *Prosopis glandulosa* var. *torreyana* is not common from central to southern Baja California, but becomes more common in the northern part of the peninsula, where it is undoubtedly native. A preliminary analysis of middens from Cataviña in north-central Baja California indicates that it became common after chaparral plant species disappeared (Turner et al. 1995).

Franciscan and Dominican missionaries established missions approximately north of 30°N from the 1760s through 1770s. With few exceptions, these missionaries did not make careful observations and documentation of aboriginal life, including the use of plants by native peoples. This contrasts with the skills and priorities of the Jesuits who were "given a free hand in establishing Spanish control in Baja California" from 1697 to 1767, and as a result, provided a well-documented record of native life and groups (Massey 1949:272). Put another way, "it may be assumed that the Jesuits, as skilled propagandists, recognized that accuracy in detail made the most effective message"

(Aschmann 1986:238). The Jesuits, such as Frs. del Barco, Baegert, and Linck, "were notably acute in recording tribal and linguistic information since it was fundamental to their success" (Massey 1949:273). This difference in priority among the clergy of different orders and the probable increase of *P. glandulosa* var. *torreyana* to other areas in Baja California Sur following its introduction in Loreto, may help explain the lack of recorded use of mesquite for food by central and southern Baja California inhabitants. However, Diego de la Nava, chaplain to Francisco de Ortega, made a curious reference to the use of mesquite by southern Baja California natives (probably Coras) at La Paz in 1632 (Mathes 1992:400). He testified that "the sustenance of these people is mesquite bean, fish, and other types of maize." As Mathes (1981) points out, premissionization documents sometimes contradicted the more scholarly reports later produced by the Jesuits and should be carefully interpreted.

Despite the fact that it has not been used in recent times, honey mesquite was formerly one of the most important native resources for the Seri (Felger and Moser 1971, 1985; see also Felger 1977). In 1709, Fr. Salvatierra noted that Seris lived on mesquite beans that were "a very healthy food for them inasmuch as it is somewhat laxative" (Burrus 1971:60). The Seri named and used eight stages of fruit growth, ranging from pods less than one inch long to mature pods that had fallen to the ground (Felger and Moser 1971, 1985). They collected and tied young pods into small bundles and cooked them with meat. The older, but still green pods picked from the tree were mashed in a mortar formed in bedrock or hard earth and cooked in a pot. Fallen pods were most easily harvested and used. Seris sometimes pounded the pods in the mortar, chewed the pod fragments, swallowed the juice, and discarded the pulp. However, they usually toasted the pods before pounding, using a rather creative and involved method. They first piled the dry pods on a cleared area of ground that was previously burned over. Four piles of sand were placed around the area and fires were burned on each pile to heat the sand. They sprinkled the pods with the hot sand, thereby toasting the pods and probably killing or displacing the larvae of seed-eating beetles (Bruchidae). This time of year (approximately July) is known as "the moon to sprinkle [sand]" and is the beginning of the new year for the Seri. Women pounded the toasted pods, then put the pulp in a basket to be winnowed gently, separating out the flour from the seeds and fiber. They placed the flour in a jug after winnowing it again. Rolls and round cakes were made from flour placed into a large basket, mixed with water, and kneaded into dough that was immediately dried. Seris also used the seeds and fiber separated from the pulp, pounding and winnowing the seeds to obtain a flour which they mixed with water and drank. They also chewed the sweet-tasting fibers.

Mention is made of the use of *P. glandulosa* var. *torreyana* by Southern Paiute and Shoshone peoples in the Mohave Desert, which illustrate similarities with other groups inhabiting the Sonoran Desert. The Timbisha Shoshone pit-roasted immature green pods (before the seeds formed) on a layer of hot stones (Fowler 1995). They and some Southern Paiute groups ate the green pods raw at a slightly later stage, when the seeds formed. The Southern Paiute collected green, ripened pods from the trees, then pounded them into a pulp in stone mortars with stone pestles, and made a drink from the pulp. The Timbisha and Panamint Shoshone collected slightly more mature yellow pods, pounded the pods in large tree-stump mortars with stone pestles, and made a juice. Older people could drink as much of this sweet juice as they wanted, but young people were warned that too much would make them drowsy.

Shoshones and Southern Paiutes made use of mesquite pod meal from fully ripened fruit (Fowler 1995). They first laid out all of the pods to dry, then pounded the pods into a fine powder in stone mortars with stone pestles. Mesquite seeds are extremely hard, thus allowing for the use of stone mortars and pestles. In contrast, acorns are more fragile and require the use of stone against wood (K. Fowler, pers. comm.). The meal was sifted in a tray to remove the fiber and seeds, which the Timbisha Shoshone later used to prepare large meal cakes for storage. To make their cakes, the Timbisha lined a winnowing tray with this fiber, then formed the meal into a cake on the tray and sprinkled water between the layers to help them pack it more tightly. This cake could be as much as a foot or more in height. It was covered with an additional layer of fiber and wet to form a crust. The Timbisha sun-dried this cake and cached it in a grass-lined pit. A cake was left in the house to supply a ready food that was eaten without further preparation.

Of interest are Kay Fowler's (1999) observations and information Timbisha women provided her. In Death Valley, prior to its establishment as a national monument, Timbisha women used to trim the lower branches of mesquite for use as fuel and to keep the area clear and free of litter. This allowed easier access to the pods and provided an area for camping. Such practices benefited the health of individual plants and the population. Trimming the branches allowed sand to blow through under the canopy, which aided in the scarification of the seeds. Mesquite seedlings require light for better establishment. Women were not allowed to visit and tend their mesquite (or any other plant) after monument designation. Thus mesquites are partially buried in sand hummocks and produce smaller fruit. However, their dream of being able to return to areas within the monument to tend and harvest plants using traditional methods is becoming a reality.

Moapa Southern Paiutes made their cakes in either conical burden baskets or in a small hole dug to shape and lined with mesquite pod pulp (Fowler 1995). These cakes could be as much as two feet thick. The cakes were dried thoroughly and stored in grass- or bark-lined pits in rock shelters, caves, or underground pits. Like the Timbisha, the Moapa kept a cone or cake in the house and people ate pieces without further preparation or added them to water for juice. The Moapa also combined dried mesquite meal with cooked agave *(Agave utahensis)* and made the mixture into small cakes that provided meals suitable for the trail or in camp.

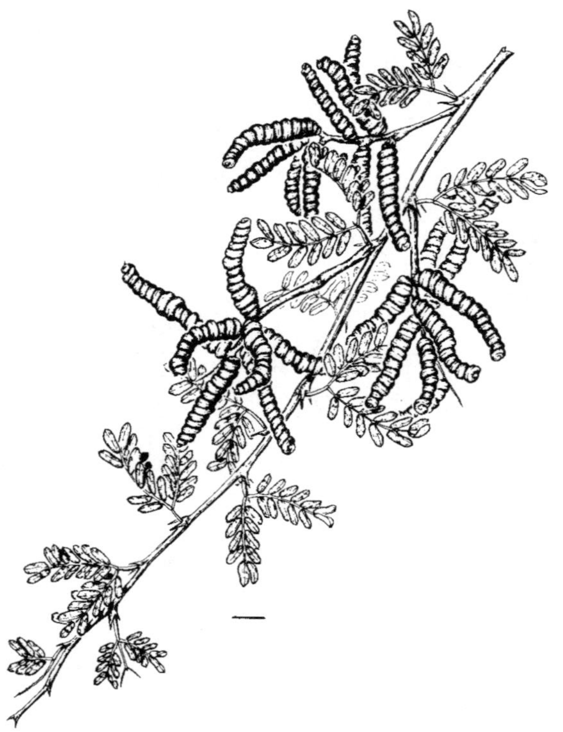

FIGURE 115. ***Prosopis pubescens*** Benth.

Dried pods were often stored and processed later, despite the possibility of bruchid larvae damage. The Timbisha cached the pods in pits lined with arrow-weed *(Pluchea sericea)* and covered them with earth. In the fall, the beans were uncovered and processed before the larvae emerged, thus allowing the larvae to be eaten as well.

Prosopis pubescens, or screwbean mesquite (fig. 115), has a more restricted distribution than *P. glandulosa.* It grows along the major waterways in southeastern California; along the Colorado, Gila, and Bill Williams Rivers; and south into northern Baja California and Sonora. Despite its more restricted range, screwbean mesquite was used extensively by people who had access to dense stands. These trees were important to the Western Yavapai, Quechan, Cocopa, Hiá ceḍ O'odham, Mohave, and River Pima (Barrows 1900; Gifford 1936; Bell and Castetter 1937; Castetter and Bell 1951; Stewart 1965; Kelly 1977; Alvarez de Williams 1987; Nabhan et al. 1989a; Rea 1997).

Screwbean pods generally are bitter when immature and fresh. However, ripe, dried pods were considered sweeter than those of the honey or velvet mesquites (Barrows 1900; Bell and Castetter 1937). Screwbean pods were used in much the same way as the other mesquites, except for the fact that the Western Yavapai, Maricopa, Pima, Mohave, and Quechan "cooked" them in the ground (Gifford 1936; Castetter and Bell 1937), which hastened their maturation. Western Yavapais dried screwbean pods under ashes, then ground them into a fine meal. This was not necessary for "mesquite" pods (probably *P. velutina*). They soaked the pods of both types of mesquite in water to make a drink or sucked the sweet liquid from a handful of wet meal, spitting out the solid matter. They did not store the pods in baskets.

Frank Russell (1908) described the process of pit-"cooking" the pods by the River Pima. They placed the pods in alternating layers with cocklebur (*Xanthium* sp.) leaves in pits lined with arrow-weed. This mass was then covered with earth and left to stand for three or four days, after which the pods were removed and dried for use or for storage in arrow-weed basket bins on top of the houses. Pimas pounded the dried pods in a mortar, then ate the fine flour as pinole. The "coarser portion is taken up in the hands with water, the juice sucked through the fingers, and the remainder rejected" (Russell 1908:75). This method of preparation has fallen out of use, as contemporary River Pima did not know of pit-"cooking" screwbean pods (Rea

1997). Screwbean is rare along the Gila River, where it was formerly abundant. Amadeo Rea (1997) found it occasionally on terraces of the Gila River between Komatke and Coop Colony. He never encountered it on the middle or eastern reservation portions of the Gila, along the Lower Santa Cruz River, or on the Lower Salt River, although older Pimas told him it was once common throughout these areas.

The Mohave gathered young screwbean pods and honey mesquite pods at the same time (Stewart 1965). Each woman claimed a section of a large pit lined with arrow-weed and then placed the bitter, young screwbean pods into this section. They covered the beans with more arrow-weed, sprinkled water over the pit, and then covered it all with soil. The pods remained here for one month, until they became red. They dried the cooked pods on the ground for four to five days, then pounded them into flour, which was made into a drink with the addition of water.

Screwbean mesquite pods did not ripen until after the Cocopa planting season, in August. Their method of harvesting was similar to that of honey mesquite, except that the pods were almost always harvested from the ground (Kelly 1977). Like the Mohave, the Cocopa also developed a special ripening process to bring out the full sweetness of the mesquite pods. They sometimes packed the pods in a large pit lined with arrow-weed and then covered the pods with dirt and left them for approximately six weeks. The formerly yellow pods turned dark brown, thus signaling that they were ready to store. The same pit was usually used for storing the pods until spring. Another method to ripen the pods involved cooking them quickly over a fire. They built a fire in the bottom of the pit, then lined the pit with arrow-weed. Pods were packed into the pit and often sprinkled with water, then covered with dirt, brush, and another fire. They left the pods to cook for approximately three weeks.

A coarse, sweet meal was obtained by grinding the dry pods (Castetter and Bell 1937). Bread was made using coarse meal that was reground; the resulting finer meal was mixed with water, kneaded, and baked in the sun. However, Cocopas did not make screwbean meal into cakes because the ground pulp did not stick together like honey mesquite meal (Kelly 1977). This characteristic assisted in separating out the pulp from the fiber and seed when immersed in water. One obtained a thick, good-tasting syrup, by boiling the coarse meal with water.

For the Southern Paiute and Shoshone, two groups that inhabited the Mohave Desert, screwbean mesquite was very important. Like the Mohave and Cocopa, the Southern Paiute used a pit to further ripen the pods (Fowler 1995). The screwbean pods were placed in a pit lined with arrow-weed, with water sprinkled between the layers. A man tamped down the pods and covered them with more arrow-weed and clay soil. This sat for about a month, thus allowing the pods to perhaps ripen quicker or improve their flavor. The pods changed from tan to red; it was at this stage that they were removed and placed in storage granaries or processed into meal using a stone mortar. They removed the especially hard, small seeds from the ground mixture by tapping the edge of a winnowing tray, to where the seeds migrated. Seeds were collected and ground on a metate. This meal was eaten as a drink or made into dried cakes. Ripened screwbeans were widely traded.

Prosopis velutina, or velvet mesquite (figs. 116, 117), grows as a dominant plant in the Arizona Uplands from central Arizona to central Sonora, but becomes rare in the Lower Colorado Desert. Velvet mesquite has been extensively used from early pre-Columbian times to the present (Felger and Nabhan 1976). Its pods may have more mesocarp within than those of *P. glandulosa* (A. Rea, pers. comm.).

Western Apaches esteemed the pods of *P. velutina* for food, but plants grew at lower elevations along the Gila and Salt Rivers (Buskirk 1986). However, they still ate mesquite pods in the 1930s (Opler 1973). Some plants grew at old campsites at Cibecue, having germinated from expectorated seed originally from fruits of plants growing near the Salt River (Buskirk 1986). Parties traveled to these rivers in the fall to gather the pods and brought them back to their homes. The Western Apache either pounded the fresh pods with the seeds on a metate or in a stone mortar or dried and stored the pods before pounding, with the seeds discarded. Cakes were made by mixing this fine flour with water and then baking them in ashes or drying them in the sun. Western Apaches often drank the juice from the pounded pulp and discarded the fiber. Stored, dried pods were chewed or pounded into flour that was eaten or mixed into a mush. They also mixed this flour with warm (not hot) water to make a drink. Cakes were made by moistening the flour and allowing it to harden. White Mountain Apaches made a hole in the center of the cakes and strung them on a cord.

Except for one woman, Clarkdale Apaches no longer used the pods in the 1970s (Gallagher 1976). However, the woman described how she dug and lined

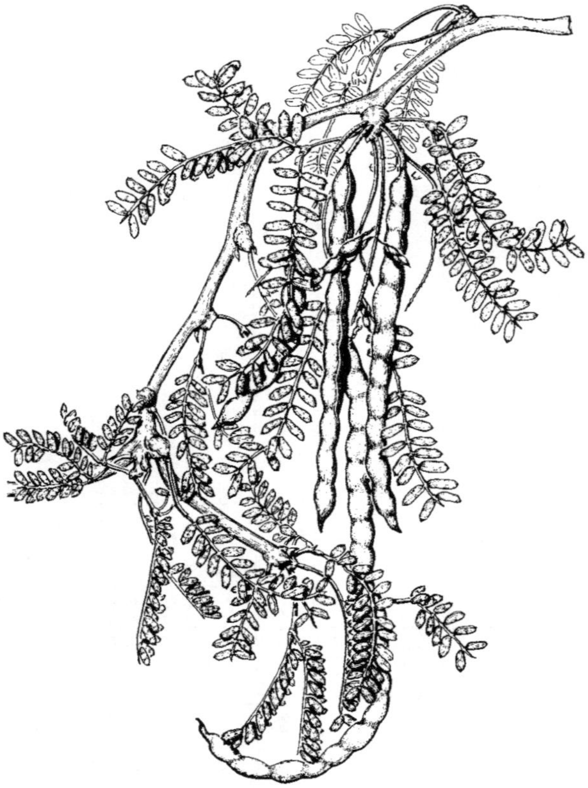

FIGURE 116. ***Prosopis velutina*** Woot. Courtesy of the Mesa Southwest Museum.

a hole in dry ground with canvas. The ripe, dry pods were placed in the hole, then pounded with a stone to make fine flour. A sweet-tasting gruel or beverage was made by mixing the meal with water and straining the mixture to remove the seeds. She also sifted the meal to remove the seeds, then mixed it with water to make dough. Cakes were formed from the dough and eaten fresh or dried. The cakes stored well and were once thought of as a "fine food for traveling" (Gallagher 1976:41). Some people told Gallagher that fresh, ripe pods when boiled had a sweeter taste.

Southeastern Yavapais collected the ripe pods of *P. velutina* in burden baskets during the latter part of July (Gifford 1932). A favorite place to collect them was "at a place near Tortilla Flat" (Gifford 1932:180), presumably off the Apache Trail in the northern end of the Superstition Mountains, Maricopa County. They pounded the pods in a bedrock mortar with a stone (not wooden) pestle, then moistened the mass in a watertight basket. They expressed the juice from this mass using their hands and then drank the juice. Juice was also obtained by one's sucking on a portion of this moistened meal and expelling the solid material.

Northeastern Yavapais pounded the pods of mesquite in a bedrock mortar, then made the meal into cakes for easy transport (Gifford 1936). The Verde Valley and Black Canyon regions, where *P. velutina* is commonly found, were principal sources for gathering the pods. Western Yavapais gathered the pods of "mesquite" and screwbean in July. They would have had access to mainly *P. velutina,* although *P. glandulosa* var. *torreyana* may have been encountered. Pods were pounded in a bedrock mortar, with a stone pestle found in the immediate area, or in a cottonwood mortar, with a stone pestle. They did not store pods in baskets.

Velvet mesquite was the tree of life, the principal food to the River Pima. So important was mesquite, that two months in the Pima calendar refer to the life cycle of it: "mesquite leaves moon" and "mesquite flowers moon" (Rea 1997). They recognize five stages of the plant's life cycle, from when it leafs out to when its fruits are ready for harvest. Trees were once so abundant and fruited so prolifically that people could selectively collect the thickest, sweetest pods from the ground. Dried, fallen pods have the highest carbohydrate content (Felger 1977).

River Pima recognized two harvest periods. The first summer harvest began on San Juan Day, June 24, or "anytime in the 20s" (Rea 1997:184–185). The second harvest was in October, when the pods were fewer but very sweet, according to Joseph Giff. Such a brief spurt of new pod development is in response to late summer rains (Nabhan et al. 1979). According to Sylvester Matthias both crops were important.

Men and women gathered huge quantities of ripened pods in the summer (Rea 1997). George Matthias remembered how families would go together and collect two wagon loads of mesquite pods in a day. George Kyyitan related to Amadeo Rea how he and his family would camp for a week to collect the pods in gunnysacks that they brought home and stored. Then they would go out again for another week to pick more pods. Mesquite groves were not claimed and families would "just go where they can find [the pods]" (Rea 1997:185).

Two kinds of bins were used by the Pima to store their massive amounts of pods (Rea 1997). The pods were most often stored in bins made of arrow-weed and willow (*Salix* sp.) branches, their shape reminding observers of a huge bird's nest. The second type of bins were jug-shaped baskets used to store mesquite flour in a storage shed. These baskets could be six feet tall and were made of wheat straw bound with strips of bark.

FIGURE 117. ***Prosopis velutina*** Woot. in flower and with mature pods. Salt River Project canal right-of-way, South Mountain, Maricopa County, Arizona, June 1988.

According to Frank Russell (1908), River Pimas separated the seeds from the pods, then parched and ground the seeds. All of Amadeo Rea's friends said that the seeds were discarded and not used (Rea 1997). Even 90-year-old Adolph Juan, who lived before the time of Russell's work, said that the seeds were not used.

Mesquite flour was a staple to the Pima. Ruth Giff demonstrated how she made flour by pounding the mesocarp to a pulp, using a mesquite log or mortar and an oblong stone (Rea 1997). She sifted the material in a special basket to remove the fibrous portion and the seeds to obtain the flour or meal. To make a loaf or cake, she placed a cloth in a basket, then added dry meal sprinkled with water. She continued to add layers until she formed a loaf six inches high and thick. Dried, unbaked cakes stored indefinitely and were resistant to insect attack. The cakes were so hard, however, that a stone was required to break off a piece.

The River Pima also made a pudding, which tasted like carob, by cooking the mesquite flour with whole-wheat flour (Rea 1997). After they squeezed out the water, they molded the remaining pulpy substance into cakes, then baked them in hot ashes. They also boiled dried mesquite pods until very soft, cooled the pods, and then mashed and strained the pulp. The juice was saved, but the fibers and seeds were discarded. Whole-wheat dumplings were dropped into the juice and cooked until the dish thickened. River Pimas prepared another kind of "dumpling." They boiled the pods in water until soft, cooled them, then pressed the water out of the pods with their hands (Curtin 1949, *Curtin 30*, DES). The remaining liquid with pods was again boiled and small wheat-flour tortillas were added. They boiled this until all of the liquid disappeared. This is similar to a dish prepared with thick wheat tortillas, alternately layered with dried mesquite pods, as described by Ruth Giff (Rea 1997). They covered the layers with water, then slowly cooked them for several hours, until almost dry. The pods were discarded and the mushy pulp eaten or dried for use in travel. Toasted, ground wheat flour was sweetened with mesquite flour as well. The River Pima also made a sweet drink by soaking crushed mesquite pods in cold water, then taking the mixture in their hand and sucking out the juice. This drink is no longer made, despite the fact that it was much esteemed.

Tohono O'odhams sometimes received mesquite beans and meal in trade with the Northern Pima (Castetter and Bell 1937). When crops failed, the fruits of the saguaro and mesquite were the most abundant and accessible food. Hiá ceḍ O'odhams had access to all three mesquites. Fernando Flores recalled that the pods of mesquites were eaten fresh or dried for later use (Bell 1980). They ground the pods into a fine powder using stone grinders. They removed the seeds, which were later cooked with meat, then shaped the meal into cakes that they stored to be eaten later as a gruel or as a sweetener with wheat gruel.

Tom Childs (1954:34–45) also described the Hiá ceḍ O'odham's use of bedrock mortars to pound mesquite pods: "On the southwest side [of the Pinacates] there's a large rock tank where they [Hiá ceḍ O'odham] undoubtedly lived for centuries. They've pounded holes into a large number of them [large rocks] that nearly drove through the rock then turned them over and some more was pounded almost through the reverse side. The Indians gathered the beans from the mesquite trees when ripe, and pounded them in those holes that were in those rocks."

In the Pinacate area of northwestern Sonora, unique grinding tools called gyratory crushers have been found. The crushers resemble a perforated mortar, with a projection of the pestle extending through the perforation in the mortar base. The pestle was gyrated to grind and separate the seeds easily (Hayden 1967; Felger and Nabhan 1976; Felger 1977; Felger and Moser 1985). Seeds of velvet mesquite were seldom used for food because of the difficulty in separating them from the inedible, hard endocarp. The gyrating crushers also served to separate seed from endocarp. With these crushers, the extensive use of mesquite seeds seems to have been achieved by the Amargosan-Pinacateño people who occupied the Pinacate lava fields (Hayden 1967, 1969). Such use apparently ceased there about A.D. 1100–1200. Cocopas made extensive use of both the metate and mano and the mortar and pestle (Kelly 1977). Metates were formed from natural boulders with "a minimum of pecking to shape a crude grinding surface." In a photograph of W. J. McGee standing next to a young Cocopa man (Kelly 1977:55), one can see part of a wooden pestle with a long tip, which is suggestive of that type used with the gyratory crusher. Cocopas occasionally ground the seeds into a coarse meal.

Prosopis velutina is common throughout much of Sonora. The Pima Bajo gathered only from trees that produced the largest and thickest pods. Pods that had red streaks were considered the best tasting (Felger 1977). Rural people in north-central Sonora distinguished between mesquite trees yielding bitter-tasting pods and those with sweet, edible pods. Trees with sweet pods were thought to be far more common than trees with bitter pods and were distinguished from each other only by taste. Ónavas Pimas gathered, washed, cooked, and strained the sweet pods through a woven basket or metal strainer, then ground the pod pulp on metates (Pennington 1980). They placed the resulting meal back in the basket or strainer, poured water through it, then cooked it as an atole.

In the mid 18th century, Sonorans enjoyed making a pinole and atole from mesquite pods, called *péchita* (Treutlein 1949; Nentvig 1980). Ópatas harvested mesquite twice a year (Nentvig 1980:40, cited as *P. juliflora*). In April they gathered, boiled, and dried the "tender" (young) pods for later use in their stews. In June the "ripened" pods, or *péchitas,* were collected; some were eaten "at the time of picking," but most were "saved to make atole and other dishes." Fr. Pérez de Ribas (1968:6) noted that the "principal form of sustenance in its season [May–June] is the pod of a tree which is called mesquite. These pods, when ground, they drink, being somewhat sweet, is to these people what chocolate is to the Spaniards." In contrast, the Cáhita used mesquite only in an emergency situation because it was considered an inferior food (Beals 1945). Rosalio Moisés, a Yaqui, remembered chewing pods "all day" while chopping wood or tending his watermelons (Moisés et al. 1971:180, 185).

In the mid 1950s, Ópatas still made mesquite bean gruel, *atole de péchita,* in Tepupa, which is 70 miles east of Hermosillo. Thomas Hinton (1956) described how children gathered the pods off of the trees, then set them aside in the kitchen for six weeks until the pods were thoroughly dried. The pods were soaked in water overnight until soft, then mashed in a wooden bowl. The pods were squeezed numerous times to extract the juice and pulp until the water became thick and discolored. They threw out the fibers and seeds and strained the remaining mixture. This liquid was poured into a clay olla, except for a cupful that was set aside, then cooked until it became syrup. Wheat flour or pinole was mixed with the cupful of liquid, then added to the olla and the contents stirred. They added cinnamon and ground cloves and drank the resulting atole or served it as a hot or cold thick broth or thin gruel. This favored atole and made up a significant part of the diet.

The use of mesquite pods or meal for food does have two major drawbacks: the production of flatulence, in that "apparently [the pods produce] even more flatulence than do beans" (Rea 1997:188), and the infestation of bruchids. Apparently, the larvae and beetles did not seem to bother the Gila River Pima, who called them a name that translates to "mesquite pod babies" (Rea 1997:187), or other groups of Native Americans (Felger 1977). However, today the presence of so many larvae and beetles is no longer accepted. Bruchid-containing food has become unpalatable to the River Pima (Felger 1977; Rea 1997), Cahuilla (Bean and Saubel 1972), and doubtless other groups, in part, because of changing food prejudices.

Mesquite is considered to be a perennial crop that can be depended on to produce large crops year after year independent of short-term climatic conditions (Felger 1977). However, mesquite populations may fail to produce substantial pod crops as frequently as once every five years (Nabhan et al. 1979). Sam Spa, a Cocopa, remembered a particular time when the mesquite crop was poor (Kelly 1977). High winds and cold weather injured the flowers that had just begun to develop, thus greatly reducing the amount of fruits one could harvest.

Rather than being an "unfailing" plant, mesquite appears to be primarily a "facultative producer," and harvest of its pods depends on a spatially and temporally flexible subsistence pattern by indigenous people (Nabhan et al. 1979). Also, within populations, there is great variability in pod production per tree.

Production of fruit also varies temporally from year to year in the same populations. Pod development may begin as early as April or as late as July in the same population in different years (Glendening and Paulsen 1975). In another study, pod development peaked in late June and early July in 1972, but not until August and September in 1973 (Solbrig and Cantino 1976). Brief spurts of new pod development can occur into October in response to late summer rains (Nabhan et al. 1979), thus providing pods for the second period of harvest, as experienced by the Gila River Pima. Joe and Ruth Giff offered Amadeo Rea (1997:184–185) another explanation similar to that related to William Kelly by Sam Spa. Strong winds "when [the] young pods are setting at the end of flowering," rather than the lack of water, caused the pods to not develop by interfering with pollination.

An opportunistic group of the O'odham probably shifted harvesting areas from year to year, depending on where there grew a bumper crop (Nabhan et al. 1979). Indeed, when asked if the River Pima go to certain areas to harvest the pods, Sylvester Matthias answered that they "just go where they can find [the pods]" (Rea 1997:185). Such flexibility would be advantageous for those groups who did not lay claim to certain mesquite groves.

Flexibility of harvesting patterns may also have been influenced by variations in bruchid beetle infestation (Nabhan et al. 1979) because the beetle's association with mesquite may influence fruit availability. A brief discussion of bruchid biology is presented.

Members of the bruchid family are by far the most numerous and most specialized insects that utilize *Prosopis* fruits (Kingsolver et al. 1977). Larvae of most of the estimated 1,000 species of bruchid beetles develop in the pods of many legumes. Generally, the female lays her eggs singly or in clusters on the pod surface (Kingsolver et al. 1977). The larvae hatching from the eggs burrow into the fruit and subsequently feed on the tissue of the seed and/or endocarp. The bruchids pupate inside the fruit within a feeding chamber in the seed after a succession of molts.

In response to bruchid infestation, various species of legumes seem to produce either toxic seeds or so many seeds that the insect population cannot consume all of them (Janzen 1969; Siemens et al. 1992). Mesquites produce large quantities of nontoxic fruits, which is advantageous for the indigenous cultures who relied on them for food, although seeds of *P. chilensis* (Mol.) Stuntz contains cyanogens (Becker 1982). Mesquites have also developed more specialized adaptations in response to bruchid infestation. Mesquite pods may have bare, smooth surfaces; have pubescence (such as those of *P. velutina*), which hinders gluing of eggs on the surface by the female; or produce a gum that is released when the pod is pierced by the female, thus pushing off the eggs. However, many seeds are still destroyed by bruchids, despite these adaptations. From 14 to 75 percent of all velvet mesquite seeds were destroyed during one season in central Arizona (Kingsolver et al. 1977).

How is it that so much seed is still destroyed? The answer may be explained partly by the ability of bruchid species to coexist on one tree by filling different ecological niches. Four species of bruchids coexist on

P. velutina in central Arizona. They include bruchids that attach to pods at different times during the season, oviposit at different sites on the pod, infest pods at different levels of heights on the tree, and use hosts other than mesquite (Kingsolver et al. 1977). The most common bruchid on velvet mesquite, *Alarobius prosopis*, uses the pods at different stages of development, from when the pods are green and immature to when they are hard and dry. The female deposits her eggs in cracks on the surface of pods, usually in the upper canopy of the tree. Three generations are produced in one season. The rare bruchid *Mimosestes protractus* is confined to the lower canopy of the tree and produces only one generation per year.

In addition, other species of insect larvae use the seeds and pulp of mesquite fruit for food, feeding on the pods from the outside or from the inside, with feeding behavior dependent on the age of the fruit (Kingsolver et al. 1977). One common external feeder on young pods of *P. velutina* in south-central Arizona is the leaf-footed bug, *Mozena obtusa*. This insect damaged an estimated 50 percent of the potential fruit production of honey mesquite in Texas (Swenson 1969). A number of small species of Lepidoptera feed inside the pods of *Prosopis* in the Southwest, consuming both the seed and mesocarp (Kingsolver et al. 1977).

The preparation of mesquite flour was well worth the time, effort, and probable infestation of bruchids. Mesquite pods can be gathered at a rate of 3.0 kilograms per hour (dry weight; Doelle 1980); of this, 0.9 kilogram, or 30 percent of the weight of the unprocessed pods, can be converted into edible flour through traditional processing techniques (Doelle 1976). The gross energy yield rate, based on the caloric value of mesquite flour, was very high, supplying 3,150 kilocalories per hour (Ross 1944).

In addition, mesquite fruits, with seeds, are good sources of sugars and protein. Seeds from one screwbean tree had a protein content of 26 percent, whereas those of velvet mesquite had reported protein contents of 29 percent (Becker 1982) and 39.9 percent (Jones and Earle 1966). Whole pods of velvet mesquite contain 12 percent protein and 19 to 22 percent sugar, and the mesocarp contains 32 percent sugars (mostly sucrose) and only 7 percent protein (Becker 1982).

Ruth Greenhouse (1979) calculated that the fresh pod material (100-gram edible portion) of *P. velutina* contains 12.4 percent water, 6.7 grams protein, 1.5 grams fat, 47.9 grams carbohydrates, 33.1 grams fiber, and 232 calories, values that are somewhat lower than those reported by Ross (1944). The embryos of the seeds (100-gram edible portion) contain 6.6 percent water, 65.2 grams protein, 6.8 grams fat, 11.6 grams carbohydrates, 1.9 grams fiber, and 368 calories. Mesquite pods (100-gram edible portion) contain 469 grams calcium (Ross 1944).

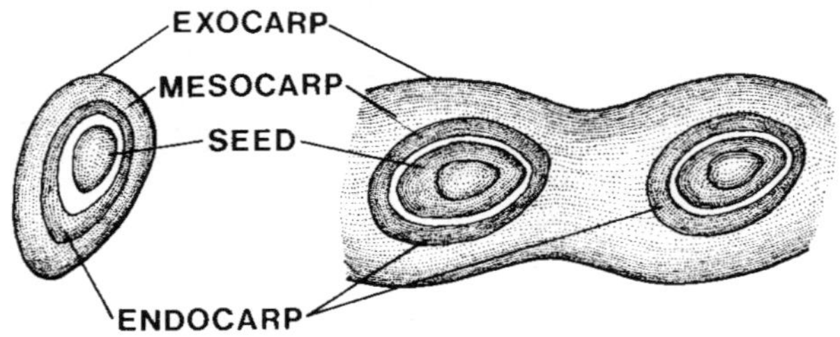

FIGURE 118. Diagrammatic representation of ***Prosopis*** sp. fruit (adapted from Kingsolver et al. 1977:111).

The composition of *P. glandulosa* pods during different stages of maturation has been studied. Carbohydrates accumulate primarily in the pericarp, which consists of the exocarp; the thick, sweet mesocarp; and the hard endocarp (fig. 118). Mature pods contain approximately 80 percent total carbohydrate, as compared to 63 percent found in very immature pods (Harden and Zolfaghari 1988). The amount of moisture and protein in *P. glandulosa* pods decreases considerably as pods mature, from 78 to 9 percent and 28 to 12 percent, respectively. Seeds contain 82 percent of the total pod protein, but the pericarp protein has a relatively better essential amino acid pattern than the seed protein. Fat content of the pod increases slightly with maturation.

Seeds of mesquite also contain a fibrous gum, galactomannin, which has similar properties to guar and carob gum (see Becker 1982). Galactomannin gums are thought to be potentially useful in the dietary treatment of diabetes by controlling blood sugar increases after eating (Brand et al. 1990). These gums were found to lower glycemic responses, the glycemic index being 25 percent, as compared to 59 percent in sweet corn (Brand et al. 1990). In addition, mesquite meal is digested much more slowly than other meals. There are heat-sensitive protease inhibitors (molecules that interfere with the enzyme breakdown of proteins, which makes the proteins available for use) in the fruits of velvet mesquite (Becker 1982). Cooking the pods inactivates these inhibitors, but may also cause the galactomannin gums to interfere with nitrogen absorption. However, because of the quality and quantity of proteins in velvet mesquite, cooked pods, with seeds, are still an excellent source of protein. This is not the case for screwbean, which loses nitrogen when cooked.

Other parts of the mesquite were used for food, although incidentally. Some River Pima could not wait for the fruits to develop and ate the sweet flowers of velvet mesquite (fig. 117) by stripping them from the inflorescence (Russell 1908; Rea 1997) or sucking the inflorescence (Curtin 1949). Sylvester Matthias described another, albeit starvation, food, using velvet mesquite flowers mixed with a certain kind of clay found "only when the river is high" (Rea 1997:184). Adding clay to a food or soaking the food in wet mud (or perhaps cooking foods in clay pots) is a form of detoxification, called geophagy, whereby earth or clay binds to plant toxins before being ingested (Johns 1990). A number of groups ate specific types of clay to a point where this practice took on important ceremonial meanings (see Bourke 1888). Cocopas also used mesquite flowers as a "sweet tidbit, but often as a welcome addition to the food supply in the perennially hungry weeks of April and May" (Kelly 1977:34). Women and girls gathered only the sweetest flowers, which they threw into a pan or bowl of water. They mashed the flowers gently and consumed the sweetened liquid. The flowers are also a source of excellent honey, which is considered the best in Arizona (Kearney et al. 1960; Niethammer 1974), where it has become a multimillion dollar industry (Nabhan et al. 1985).

River Pimas also chewed the amber-colored resin exuded from cuts in the trunk as a "candy." Ruth Giff remembered eating the sap of screwbean after collecting it on a stick until large balls were made (Rea 1997), although the exudate from velvet mesquite was used more often (A. Rea, pers. comm.). A white exudate formed from branches wounded by the long-horned beetle, or mesquite girdler *(Oncideres rodostricta)*, was also sweet. The Cocopa chewed bits of mesquite sap as chewing gum (Alvarez de Williams 1987). Seri children chewed the rather bitter gum of honey mesquite, then spit it out and drank some water, which was made sweeter by the chewed gum (Felger and Moser 1971, 1985).

Mesquite is considered by some to be a serious pest in overgrazed grasslands, where its numbers increase rapidly. However, destruction of habitat, through mesquite eradication programs; urban, commercial, and agricultural development; dam construction; groundwater pumping; and extensive use of mesquite as a fuelwood (including mesquite charcoal for our barbecues) have impacted mesquite populations. If its importance as a potential economic resource is realized, mesquite could be better managed, as exemplified by the Colorado River Indian Tribe and described by Nabhan et al. (1985). A recommendation was made to the tribe that its members consider developing its mesquite wood resources, but only for specialty products that would allow selective cutting of trees rather than clearcutting wildlife habitat. The honey resource would also be retained. In addition, it was recommended that fuelwood cutting by tribal members be restricted to an area where wildlife would suffer least.

Fagaceae | Beech Family

Quercus | oak

Q. agrifolia Née
coast live oak

Q. chrysolepis Liebmann
canyon live oak

Q. dumosa Nuttall
scrub oak, coastal sage—scrub oak

Q. emoryi Torrey
Emory's oak, bellota, encino negro, encino prieto

Q. engelmannii Greene
Engelmann's oak

Q. grisea Liebmann (syn., *Q. arizonica* Sargent)
gray oak, Arizona oak

Q. kelloggii Newberry
California black oak

Q. oblongifolia Torrey
Mexican blue oak, encino, bellota

Q. palmeri Engelmann
encino roble

Q. peninsularis Trelease

Q. turbinella Greene
scrub live oak

Evidence suggests that acorns have been used for food for many thousands of years. Acorn use as a food has diminished significantly in recent years, and only a few groups still gather acorns (Weiss

FIGURE 119. ***Quercus emoryi*** Torr. This plant is common in southern Arizona and northern Sonora. Foothills of Patagonia Mountains, Santa Cruz County, Arizona, August 1988.

1994). At least 30 different kinds of oaks are or have been used within the United States for food and for the rich oil (Bainbridge 1985). Most oaks in the southwestern United States and northern Mexico, with the exception of *Q. turbinella* and *Q. palmeri,* grow in the middle to higher elevations near or above the Sonoran Desert limits.

Acorns contribute much fiber and fat to the diet. They are rich in protein, carbohydrates, fats, and essential vitamins and minerals (Weiss 1994). In addition, the acorns of *Q. emoryi* and probably other species may protect people from dangerously high increases in blood-glucose levels after meals. Acorn meal has the slowest rate of digestion, having 8 percent starch digestibility as compared to the 55 percent digestibility of white bread (Brand et al. 1990). In addition, acorn meal was found to have the lowest glycemic response. Like mesquite and tepary beans, this contrasts with the rapid and high glycemic responses of such foods as potatoes, bread, and other processed cereal products.

Acorns are selected according to oil richness and sweet taste, which is due to a relatively low tannin content. The "white oaks" of the subgenus *Quercus,* including *Q. grisea,* and the "live oaks," such as *Q. oblongifolia, Q. dumosa, Q. turbinella* (Landrum 1993), and *Q. engelmannii,* have fruits that mature the first season and are the sweetest and most palatable. The "red oaks" of the subgenus *Erythrobalanus,* including *Q. emoryi* (fig. 131), produce acorns that mature in the second season. The "intermediate oaks," or "black oaks," of the subgenus *Protobalanus* produce acorns biennially, with the exception of *Q. agrifolia,* and were usually used to a lesser extent. Other black oaks include *Q. palmeri, Q. kelloggii,* and *Q. chrysolepis.*

The degree of bitterness depends on the amount of tannic acid present in acorns. People rendered the more bitter acorns palatable by such processing methods as grinding, pounding, grating, and leaching. Grinding breaks down the tissues of the cell walls, thereby exposing more surface area to water action, which improves the leaching process and removal of tannic acid (Weiss 1994). Grinding also provides increased surface area for digestive enzymes to act, thus making nutrients more readily available (Johns 1990). The acorns of *Q. emoryi* (figs. 119, 120) have a relatively low tannin content, as was alluded to by Harold Driver and William Massey (1957), who determined what leaching methods were used to prepare acorns in North America. In areas that correspond to the distributions of *Q. emoryi* and *Q. oblongifolia,* the acorns were eaten without preparation.

The time of harvest was critical because rainfall affects the harvest and processing of useable, mature acorns. For example, acorns of *Q. agrifolia* mature primarily from November to December and were harvested from October to November, before the onset of winter rains. Acorns of *Q. emoryi* mature from late July to September and were usually harvested prior to summer monsoon rains, in mid-July. Immature acorns that have fallen to the ground will not develop further, but instead turn black and rot. In addition, rain or overcast skies impeded the drying and subsequent grinding of acorns (Weiss 1994).

At least to some groups, the place of processing was also important. Peveril Meigs (1939:101) described the discovery of bedrock mortars atop a ridge overlooking two rancherias south of San Diego in Diegueño territory. People gathered *chia* seeds and acorns on the lower slopes and valleys, but ground them in these mortars on the ridges "or other commanding points" where they liked to camp while away from home. People collected acorns from the ground or knocked

FIGURE 120. ***Quercus emoryi.*** (left) Branch, Payson, Gila County, Arizona, July 1986 (*Landrum 5123,* DES); (above) bag of acorns bought at Hermosillo, Sonora, for 500 pesos (2,100 pesos per U.S. dollar), November 1987. In Nogales ten months later a bag of approximately the same size sold for 1,000 pesos.

them from the tree using a flexible pole in such a way that they did not harm the plant. Kay Fowler (1999) noted that Timbisha Shoshone women always used the long branches of willow (*Salix exigua* Nuttall) to "whip" the trees, even when metal poles became available. In addition, by pinching off the ends of branches, they encouraged the plants to produce more acorns the next season. I am not aware of Sonoran Desert people doing this, but would not be surprised if some actually did.

Acorns were very important to Western Apaches, who harvested them primarily in late July and August. By the late 1940s, it was the one crop still harvested by the Western Apache to any extent because distant trips requiring overnight camping were generally no longer made (Buskirk 1986). Many families at Cibecue continued to travel to Pleasant Valley, Gila County, in 1947–1948 and remained there a week to gather acorns. Clarkdale Apaches enjoyed the acorns of *Q. palmeri* and continued to collect the fruits in the 1970s. However, Marsha Gallagher (1976:42) suggested that "it may be that actual knowledge of and experience in the preparation of acorns is limited to the older generations." When available, they collected the brown acorns from the ground or less often from the tree, usually in late summer. The acorns were ground or lightly pounded and the shells separated. They ground the "meats" into a fine meal, which they stored. The meal was mixed with water to form a paste and gradually added to stews or soups as a thickening agent.

Grenville Goodwin noted that a favorite area to collect "Emmory's [sic] oak" was between and in the Graham (possibly Pinaleno) and Santa Teresa Mountains, Graham County (Goodwin 1942:13, 157). Another favorite site for acorn collecting was in the vicinity of Oracle, on the northern slopes of the Santa Catalina Mountains, Pinal County. Goodwin further described how large parties, including a number of families, traveled to these sites in late July. As many as 75 families still loosely congregated at Ash Flat, south of Safford, Graham County, to harvest acorns in the 1930s. The harvest lasted for four weeks or more. When families gathered all that they needed, they returned to their farming sites individually or remained until all were ready to go home. Southern Tontos utilized the acorns of *Q. gambelii, Q. emoryi, Q. turbinella,* and another, "unidentified type of oak" (probably *Q. chrysolepis*). The San Carlos ate the acorns of *Q. grisea* (Gifford 1940, cited as *Q. arizonica*), but did not like "the blue oak" (possibly *Q. palmeri*).

Western Apaches frequently reserved those trees with promising crops by marking them (Buskirk 1986). They usually used straight, long poles to dislodge the acorns, although some climbed the trees and shook the acorns to the ground. Women and children usually gathered and transported the acorns back to camp. They stored them, with or without the "shell," in baskets, sacks, gourds, or pottery vessels. Acorns were also cached in rock shelters, rather than in the ground, where they would rot. Some preferred to store dried, unshelled acorns because shelled acorns developed a bad taste. Drying the unshelled acorns in the sun for three to seven days prevented them from becoming "wormy" (Buskirk 1986:175).

Western Apaches usually ground acorns on a sandstone (rather than vesicular lava) metate, but they also ate them whole and raw (Buskirk 1986). Southern Tontos used stone mortars (Gifford 1940). They ate the meal dry or moistened, pounded into meats, and sprinkled on foods (Buskirk 1986). Southern and Northern Tontos boiled acorn meal in soups (Gifford 1940), although other Western Apache groups did not because boiling produced a disagreeable taste (Buskirk 1986). However, they would mix ground acorn meal with soups. Western Apaches did not usually parch or roast acorns. They made a type of bread, using one part acorn meal with five parts wheat flour (Reagan 1930). Western Apaches often added uncooked acorn meal to a meat stew, a food that remained a favorite to some in the 1940s. Ground, cooked meat and acorn meal was also popular (Buskirk 1986).

The Yavapai, in general, used only sweet acorns and avoided bitter ones (Gifford 1936). They apparently "knew nothing of the leaching of bitter acorn meal as practiced by their congeners, the Diegueño, and other Californians," despite their relative closeness to California (Gifford 1936:254). Southeastern Yavapais traveled far to gather acorns, their principal gathering areas being the Mazatzal (probably the western flanks; Maricopa, Gila, and Yavapai Counties), Superstition (Maricopa and Pinal Counties), Pinal, Mescal, and Dripping Springs Mountains (Gila County; Gifford 1932). They primarily used *Q. emoryi* acorns, but would also have had access to *Q. turbinella* and *Q. grisea.* Based on Les Landrum's (1993) Arizona oak treatment, unless the Southeastern Yavapai traveled over the Mazatzal divide into Apache territory, they probably did not have access to *Q. chrysolepis.* They sampled fallen acorns until they found a tree that produced sweet ones. Trees bearing edible acorns "were often tall," and both men and women "pounded the trunk with a stone," or the men "climbed up the tree and knocked down the acorns using a stick" (Gifford 1932:208). Women collected the acorns from the ground. Rather than picking up each acorn, they sometimes swept up the acorns with a branch into a flat basket, then winnowed the mass to rid it of debris. Green acorns were bitter, but might become sweeter with further ripening. They shelled the acorns by cracking them with their teeth or by "rubbing them with a muller on a metate and then winnowing them on a coiled basketry tray with the aid of the wind" (Gifford 1932:208). Shelled acorns were pounded on a metate. They did not use a bedrock mortar as they did when they pounded mesquite pods and hard seeds. Acorn meal was not a staple food, but was cooked with meat. They made a gravy by stirring the acorn meal into a meat broth, then pouring it into the main pot with the meat.

Even though Southeastern Yavapais had access to *Q. grisea,* its acorns, although larger than those of *Q. emoryi,* were usually considered bitter (Gifford 1932: 208, cited as *Q. arizonica;* identified by Alice Eastwood, CAS). Acorns of *Q. grisea* "would have proved a valuable source of easily accessible food," had they known how to leach acorn meal. It is interesting to note, however, that they leached the seeds of ironwood.

Northeastern Yavapais enjoyed the sweet acorns of *Q. emoryi.* They collected and prepared the acorns and meal using methods similar to those practiced by the Southeastern Yavapai. They also stored shelled acorns by placing them in burden baskets that were set in the ground "to prevent capsizing" (Gifford 1936:257). They covered the baskets with stones, then hid them under bear-grass *(Nolina microcarpa).* One favorite place for Verde Valley Yavapais to gather *Q. emoryi* acorns was the Granite Peak region, Yavapai County, during August and September. Edward Gifford (1936:254) described another type of oak whose acorns were used, but were "scarcely larger than piñon nuts, bitten in half, shelled and eaten raw." He thought the oak might be *Q. arizonica* (under synonymy with *Q. grisea*), but the description of small acorns suggests a small-fruited *Q. turbinella* or possible hybrid.

River Pimas received acorns in trade from the Tohono O'odham, because they had no easy access to the plants. Ruth Giff recalled that "Papago children brought the acorns to school" (Rea 1997:320). Contemporary Pimas think that acorns were once shelled, ground, and made into a gravy. Not everyone liked the taste of the acorns. Ruth Giff said she and others did not eat the fruits at all.

The Tohono O'odham went on long camping excursions to collect *Q. emoryi* (Castetter and Underhill 1935) and *Q. oblongifolia.* They continue to go to areas in southern Arizona such as Arivaca and Fort Huachuca. Here, with White Mountain Apache and Hispanic families, they set up temporary camps to collect acorns during the summer (Rea 1997; G. P. Nabhan, pers. comm.; pers. obs.)

Native peoples of southern California and northern Baja California relied heavily on acorns, particularly those of *Q. agrifolia.* The Cahuilla primarily used the acorns of *Q. kelloggii, Q. dumosa, Q. chrysolepis, Q. dumosa,* and *Q. agrifolia.* According to David Barrows (1900), however, *Q. agrifolia* was apparently rare within the habitat of the Cahuilla and its acorn was not of great importance at the turn of the century. Cahuillas gathered the acorns of *Q. dumosa* in considerable quantities by the turn of the century. Valery Havard (1895) noted that sand mixed with acorn meal had a "decided effect" on the teeth, wearing the crowns down even to the gum line. Barrows (1900) never noticed such effects on the teeth, despite the Cahuilla's constant use of the "sand basket" (presumably the indentation made in sand used to leach acorn meal when leaching baskets were not used).

Lowell Bean and Katherine Saubel (1961, 1972) provided an in-depth account of acorn use among the Cahuilla following years of fieldwork in the 1960s. The Cahuilla favored the acorns of *Q. kelloggii,* which had an outstanding flavor and the most gelatin-like consistency when cooked, which is "a prerequisite for good acorn mush." Although often far away from villages, trees were abundant and produced heavy yields of fruits dependably. *Quercus chrysolepis* and *Q. agrifolia* were of secondary importance. *Quercus dumosa* was the least favored of the oaks, being used primarily as an additive to other types of acorn meal when there was a shortage of the more preferred types.

How important acorns were to the Cahuilla depended on where the people lived. Acorns were not the most important food source of the Cahuilla groups in the Colorado Desert, who exploited the least favorable acorn-gathering sites (Bean and Saubel 1972). In contrast, the mountain groups of Cahuilla relied heavily on oaks and possessed the best oak groves. Lineages owned oak groves and families within a lineage owned individual trees. Areas with the most complex social groupings were those with many oak groves, suggesting a tie between acorn use and the complexity of the group's social structure.

The Cahuilla harvested acorns from October to November, before the arrival of the first winter rains (Bean and Saubel 1972). If rainfall came earlier or at "the wrong time of year," the acorns would split and rot on the tree. Those who visited the groves notified the village when the acorns were ready for harvest. Much ceremony was associated with the harvest and preparation of the acorns. Each Cahuilla woman had her own gathering and processing equipment. They used portable mortars and bedrock mortars for grinding. After they ground the acorns, they placed the meal in a loosely woven leaching basket or an indentation in the sand, with a layer of fibrous vegetation at the bottom to prevent loss of the meal. Warm or cold water was poured through the meal several times. The Cahuilla used a fine acorn meal to make bread, which was replaced by the Mexican tortilla. Coarse meal was used to make mush. Bean and Saubel (1972:129) noted that "the skill, sophistication, and care exhibited by a woman in grinding, leaching, preparing, and cooking acorn served to enhance her status." A "skilled cook knew how to vary the taste of acorn meal by mixing in different proportions of any of the four types of acorns" and "might add her own special flavorings, such as wheat, chia seed, berries, or meat." The reader is encouraged to refer to Bean and Saubel's (1961, 1972) in-depth discussion of Cahuilla gathering and preparation of acorns.

Acorns were a major food to the Diegueño. The Santa Ysabel Diegueño utilized six types of oaks, but preferred the acorns of *Q. kelloggii,* with those of *Q. agrifolia* closely behind (Hedges and Beresford 1986). Acorns of *Q. dumosa, Q. turbinella,* and *Q. chrysolepis* were used if the other oaks produced a poor crop of acorns. Meal from *Q. dumosa* was coarse and, when cooked, the atole was "heavy rather than creamy and smooth." Thus, *Q. dumosa* meal was best mixed with other types of acorn meal. Acorns of *Q. chrysolepis* were hard to grind, but were not oily.

Within the Santa Ysabel Diegueño, groups of a few families traveled to the mountains in the fall, where they established a camp, complete with shelter for the women and children (Hedges and Beresford 1986). They gathered fallen acorns from the ground; if they picked acorns from the trees, the acorns became watery when pounded. They stored the acorns whole and unshelled and discarded worm-infested ones. Care was taken to not place too many acorns in storage until they were completely dry. Also, acorns had to be dry before being shelled. The Santa Ysabel Diegueño cracked the acorn with a "hammerstone" and removed the shell by hand. They lightly pounded the acorns to remove the papery skin. After winnowing, they pounded the acorn meats in a portable or bedrock mortar, then further winnowed this coarse meal before grinding it again on the mortar with a small amount of water added to reduce the "oiliness." This was repeated until all of the meal became fine flour.

Diegueños leached the acorn flour by spreading it in a cloth-covered leaching basket at a thickness of 10–12 millimeters (Hedges and Beresford 1986). They poured warm water through their fingers (to slow the force of the water) into the basket to wash out the bitterness. They added enough water to fill the basket, all the time testing the flour to determine how much more leaching was required. After leaching, they picked up the cloth and squeezed the wet flour into a lump. Enough water was added to the flour to make it "slightly fluid." This was poured into another pot of hot water and boiled for ten or more minutes, while being constantly stirred. They considered the mush done if a small amount dropped in cold water floated to the surface. The nutty-tasting mush was eaten with milk and sugar, honey, or with meat.

Leslie Spier (1923) described how the Southern Diegueño processed acorns. Women gathered the acorns in the fall and dumped them into storage baskets, which were set on posts and woven so tightly that rodents could not get to the fruits. They stored them in these bins until February, when the acorns were dry. Women and "old men" cracked the acorns to remove the shells, ground the meats on bedrock or boulder mortars, then sifted the meal by tossing it in a flat coiled basket in such a manner that the larger fragments were shaken over the near edge and under the right arm. The sifted meal was put in a shallow basket with cold water and then warm water was strained through. After approximately one-half hour, the thick doughy meal was removed by the handful, stirred into cold water, and set on the fire.

Delfina Cuero, a Diegueño woman, pounded acorns to remove the shell, then sifted and pounded them again into fine flour. The Diegueño leached this flour with water to remove the bitterness. They usually used a special basket to leach the flour, but as told to Delfina by her grandfather, they did not always have this basket (Shipek 1968:30–31): "A long time ago when they didn't have the *nyipu'n* [special leaching basket] to leach the *w tut* [acorn meal], they would fix a place in the sand and pack all the acorn meal in there real thick and then put more on top; then soak it and soak it. Then they would scrape off the top meal to cook it to eat."

The Cocopa also used acorns, sometimes receiving them in trade from the Diegueño (Castetter and Bell 1951). They also made trips into the Sierra Juarez, northern Baja California, to gather acorns and piñon nuts. Here they would have had access to *Q. peninsularis, Q. chrysolepis, Q. dunnii, Q. turbinella,* and possibly *Q. engelmannii.*

Joséfina Ochurte, a Paipai, related how they collected and processed *Q. agrifolia* acorns (which they still did in the late 1950s). They traveled to groves and gathered the acorns in December, then brought them back home to process (Jöel 1976:68–69). They pounded the acorns on a metate, then put them out in the sun all day. They removed the shells and, the next day, spread the acorns out in the sun to dry further. When the acorns were dried, they placed them in a sack, then ground them "completely." Acorns of *A. agrifolia* are bitter and the meal was therefore leached. Paipais stretched a sack over a basin made in the ground, into which they placed the acorn meal. They poured water through repeatedly until the bitterness was removed. Any moisture was squeezed out through the canvas. They ground the meal on a metate, then placed it in a clay jar; in this form it was ready to be eaten as mush. Hot acorn mush was described as being watery, whereas cold mush was hard. Joséfina remembered that her ancestors ate large quantities of acorn meal when acorns were available, being more abundant then than now.

The Kiliwa of northern Baja California obtained acorns from the San Pedro Mártir foothills. They would have had access to those oaks accessible to the Cocopa, as well as *Q. agrifolia* and *Q. dumosa.*

Audrey Weiss (1994) described the significance and use of acorns by the Tipai of northern Baja California. She was especially surprised to find some of these people still using acorns for food, although the use of acorns is diminishing. In fact, she "found that Mexican women living in the [Indian] community typically did not have any knowledge of acorns, and referred me to their Indian companions" (Weiss 1994:174). Those people whose income allows them to buy food for their families do not spend the considerable time required to collect and process acorns. However, as explained by Weiss (1994:176), others in a community valued the acorns: "The less-well-to-do and/or those who are not engaged in wage labor place a higher value on the nutritious nuts, and feel the impact in those times when acorns are not abundant or when they are for some reason restricted from gathering them."

Additionally, those living in one community that "follows a more 'traditional' bent" held acorns in high esteem. Acorns of *Q. agrifolia,* which mature from November to December, are "by far the most consistently favored by the *indigenes* of this region" (Weiss 1994:153). Acorns of *Q. chrysolepis* mature in September. They are sweeter, do not require leaching, and are cracked between the teeth and eaten raw. Those of *Q. dumosa* were generally not used.

Tipais apparently collected acorns off the ground and from the tree. An elderly matron explained that acorns should be dried with the shell on, then pounded to remove the shell and skin, then ground, with the meal then washed with water (Weiss 1994). Acorns are dry when their cupules, or "caps," become tan-colored and are then easy to crack. After cracking the acorns, Weiss was told to leave the acorns to dry further so that the skin would easily detach. Others simply used a metal sledgehammer to crack the undried acorns. Weiss found that using the nail file on her pocketknife worked well to extract the meat, but she still could not keep up with those who had far more experience. The Tipai dried the acorns for several days before grinding and cooking them. Weather affected not only the collecting of acorns, but also the drying because most of it was done outdoors. Grinding could not be done if the acorns were moist.

After grinding the shelled, dried acorns, Tipais leached the meal by using a special apparatus. Audrey Weiss had the opportunity to watch one grandmother leach the meal. A cloth was attached to a frame, the meal was put into the cloth, and hot water mixed with cold water was poured over the meal. She had to pour water over it four or five times. The leached meal was put into a large pan with water and cooked, while being stirred constantly, until it came to a boil. Leaching methods varied. For example, another grandmother used only cold water to leach the meal. Salt is not usually added, and the cooked meal is eaten as is or served with sugar, milk, or made into breads or cookies.

Fr. del Barco mentioned no use of oaks by early *indigenes* of south-central Baja California, although he noted the occurrence of the plants, particularly in parts of the Sierra de la Giganta. *Quercus brandegeei,* a Baja California endemic in the low mountains of the cape region, has edible acorns (Carter *in* del Barco 1980). *Quercus oblongifolia* grows as scattered populations farther north in southern Baja California. The Cochimí and other southern Baja Californians probably did not know of leaching acorn meal; even if they had, the scarcity of water would have precluded such a practice.

In Sonora, the Pima Bajo (Pennington 1980) and Tarahumara (Pennington 1963) utilized the acorns of *Quercus* including those of *Q. emoryi,* which were toasted and eaten without being leached. Acorns of *Q. emoryi* continued to play a major role in the diet of those living in northern Sonora in the early 1970s (Felger et al. 1976).

Fouquieriaceae | Ocotillo Family

Fouquieria | ocotillo, candlewood

F. burragei **Rose**
palo adán, ocotillo blanco, pichilinge

F. diguetii **(Van Tieghem) I. M. Johnston**
palo adán, ocotillo

F. macdougalii **Nash**
tree ocotillo, paloverde, ocotillo macho, torote verde, torote prieto, torote espinosa, torote jabonsillo, chimulí

F. splendens **Engelmann**
ocotillo, coachwhip

The bright red flowers of *F. splendens, F. diguetii,* and *F. macdougalii* produce relatively abundant nectar at the base of their ovaries. The Northeastern Yavapai, Tohono and Hiá ceḍ O'odham, Cahuilla, and Seri ate the flowers or nectar of *F. splendens* (Barrows 1900; Standley 1923; Gifford 1936; Felger and Moser 1985; Felger et al. 1992). Ónavas Pimas ate the flowers of *F. macdougalii* (Pennington 1980).

The Cahuilla parched, ground, and ate the seeds of *F. splendens* as a protein-rich flour for use in making mush or cakes (Standley 1923; Bean and Saubel 1972). Early Baja California inhabitants were said to have gathered the seeds of an ocotillo from the end of May to the beginning of June; they toasted, ground, and ate the resulting meal (Hake 1980, 1983; Piña Puente 1983). When they toasted the seeds a faint odor was given off, and those who ate the seeds had similar-smelling breath, which is like an experience described by Fr. del Barco by those who ate *Acacia brandegeana* seeds. No other reference suggesting the use of ocotillo seeds for food by early Baja California *indigenes* appears to have been made.

Geraniaceae | Geranium Family

Erodium | filaree, heron's-bill, stork's-bill, crane's-bill, alfilaria

E. cicutarium **(Linnaeus) L'Heritier de Brutelle ex Aiton**
filaree, heron's-bill, red-stem stork's-bill, aguja del pastor, agujitas, peine de bruja

E. texanum **A. Gray**
large-flowered stork's-bill, Texas stork's-bill

Erodium cicutarium is a common winter and spring annual in the Sonoran Desert that was introduced from Europe. In contrast, *E. texanum* is native to the Southwest and northern Mexico and occupies lower elevations. *Erodium cicutarium* has often been cited in the literature for its use as an edible food, with the young herbage eaten raw or cooked as greens (Palmer 1871; Kephart 1921; Harrington 1967; Hedrick 1972). Such reports have probably overshadowed the historic and possible pre-Columbian use of *E. texanum,* which is rarely mentioned in the ethnographic literature, despite the ease in distinguishing between it and *E. cicutarium.* Fruits of a type of filaree were discovered in archaeological samples from the New River Mountains (Bohrer 1984), 30 miles north of Phoenix. Because *E. cicutarium* was introduced much later by livestock, the New River fruits were presumably those of *E. texanum.* The introduced filaree appears to establish itself in old and recently disturbed areas as well as undisturbed desert and occupies a wide elevational range. *Erodium texanum* only occupies old disturbed areas and undisturbed desert (Conrad 1981). Both species were most likely used for food following the introduction of *E. cicutarium.* However, the extensive documentation of its use by later ethnographers relative to that of the native filaree may be an example of how a once-used native food plant fell out of use at the expense of a successfully established, introduced species.

Juglandaceae | Walnut Family

Juglans | walnut

J. major **(Torrey) Heller**
Arizona walnut, nogal, nogal silvestre

The fruits of *J. major* (fig. 121) were used as a food source, although their use among Sonoran Desert dwellers was minimal or not well known. Western Apaches collected walnuts in September (Castetter and Opler 1936), often from the ground because as the fallen fruits were considered better-tasting (Buskirk 1986), or by occasionally climbing the trees and shaking the walnuts down (Gifford 1940). They pounded the fruits to remove the "hulls," then washed them in a basket in a running stream. The walnut meats (embryos) were further pounded and the meal was mixed with juice from roasted mescal. Corn bread was often dipped into this mixture, which tasted like "sweetened milk" (Buskirk 1986:187). Western Apaches also parched and ground the walnuts with corn, then ate this pinole. They generally did not boil walnuts, although it was reported that they pounded the walnut hulls and meats into a fine meal, boiled the meal in water, then filtered and drank the liquid (Reagan 1930). Clarkdale Apaches simply cracked the fruits open and ate the meats (Gallagher 1976). They also once made a beverage from walnuts and mescal. They removed the outer "hull," then pounded the meats with dried slices of baked agave. Water was added to this mixture, which was stirred and strained. They drank this liquid or, more often, poured it over pieces of ash bread that they ate.

Edward Gifford (1932) provided a detailed account of walnut preparation by the Southeastern Yavapai.

FIGURE 121. ***Juglans major*** (Torr.) Heller. **a.** Branch; **b.** details of fruit, Tonto Creek Road, Gila County, Arizona, July 1974 (*Reeves 517*, ASU).

After collecting the walnuts from the ground into burden baskets, they placed them in a hole near a stream. They pounded the fruits with a cobblestone to mash the outer covering (the involucre or hull), then washed the remaining fruit part in a stream. The hull-less walnuts were pounded on a metate to break the shells (fruit walls), then shaken in a coiled basket to separate the "meat" from the shells. They also laid walnut meats on a dried slice of baked agave, which they folded over the meats and hammered with a muller. Any juice expressed during this process was saved. They placed the macerated slice of agave pulp and walnut meat in a watertight basket or pottery jar, then added water. After stirring the mixture, they sucked on the slices to obtain a sweet juice.

Northeastern Yavapais collected walnuts from the ground in August and piled them under a tree (Gifford 1936). Walnuts were abundant in the "Turkey Creek Cave area" (probably the lower eastern slopes of the Bradshaw Mountains, north of Cleator) and many large walnut trees were found "on Black, or Crown King Mountain" (Bradshaw Mountains, Yavapai County). They cleaned off the hull with their fingers after pounding the fruits, but sometimes submerged the walnuts in a creek. Walnuts were then cracked on a metate with a muller. The Northeastern Yavapai also pounded the meat in mescal syrup and drank the mixture. They stored whole walnuts in burden baskets inside their homes.

River Pimas are more familiar with the fruits of walnut, rather than the plant, because they live outside the natural range of the plant, based on historical distributions (Rea 1997). However, native walnuts commonly wash down the Salt and Gila Rivers with periodic floods (and may even occasionally sprout and become established, like *Rhus ovata,* along the Lower Salt River in Tempe). Curiously, River Pimas did not use these fruits for food. Rather, women put the fruits in their mouths and played with them, making a clicking sound with their teeth on the walnut. By using the walnuts in this fashion, one did not get thirsty (Rea 1997).

María Beltran of Granados, Sonora, related to Gary Nabhan and me (Nabhan and Hodgson 1988) that walnuts of *nogal* used with *mescal bacanora* was good as a tonic and as a flavoring for wine.

Koeberliniaceae | Junco Family

Koeberlinia | all-thorn

K. spinosa Zuccarini
all-thorn, crucifixion-thorn, corona de Cristo, junco

What little that has been written on this crucifixion-thorn, the genus of which is placed by some within the Capparaceae, is confusing and in need of clarification. Winfred Buskirk (1986:191) noted that Western Apaches ate the "berries of *Canotia holacantha.*" Fruits of *K. spinosa* are globose, dark greenish red berries that average five millimeters in diameter (Wiggins 1964). Fruits of *C. holacantha* are inedible dry capsules. Buskirk probably was referring to *K. spinosa* var. *spinosa,* whose distribution includes territory once inhabited by Southern Tontos and San Carlos Apaches (Turner et al. 1995). Malcom Rogers corresponded with Edward Castetter and Willis Bell in 1948 regarding the occasional use of the fruits of crucifixion-thorn, *Castela emoryi,* for food by Lower Colorado River people (Castetter and Bell 1951, cited as *Holacantha emoryi*). *Castela emoryi* fruits are dry, inedible drupes. In addition, David Brown, a Gila River Pima, told Amadeo Rea (1997) that a tea made from the seeds of *C. emoryi* was even more bitter than creosote tea (which is very bitter). Rogers may have been referring to the berries of *Koeberlinia spinosa* var. *tenuispina* Kearney and Peebles.

Lamiaceae | Mint Family

Hyptis | bush mint, salvia

H. suaveolens **(Linnaeus) Poiteau**
pignut, conivari, cham, confiturilla, confitura, chia grande, chia gorde

Hyptis suaveolens is a disturbance-adapted plant that grows in the Sonoran Desert in southern Sonora and flowers from September to January (Wiggins 1964). While on expeditions into Sonora and Colima in 1890 and 1891, Edward Palmer noted that locals collected the seeds of *conivari* in considerable quantities and sold them in the markets (Rose 1895). When the seeds were soaked in water, a refreshing drink was made that was much used by the sick. Maximino Martinez (1936) noted that Tepic inhabitants made a drink, called *bate,* by mixing the toasted, ground seeds of *conivari* with brown sugar. Edward Palmer (1891:141–142) noted that people in Colima, Mexico, gathered the seeds "in large quantities from wild plants as well as those cultivated as a crop ... and they are used in the same manner as the seeds of Salvia, developing apparently even a greater quantity of musilage when wetted." They made an atole or gruel, called *bate,* by mixing it with corn, over which they sprinkled sugar syrup. Women sold this drink and atole in markets, keeping it in large gourds covered with banana leaves. When a woman gave a customer the drink or food, she used a small gourd as a dipper and added water when the atole became too thick.

Howard S. Gentry (1963, *Gentry 1842,* ARIZ; Martin et al. 1998) observed Guarijío (and Mayo) families planting *conivari* in their *milpas* during the 1930s. Guarijios mixed unground and uncooked seeds with sweetened water or milk and drank the mixture as gruel. They "regarded the seeds not only as good food but [as a] curative for fevers and sluggish bowels." Seeds are aromatic and the source of the fragrance is primarily in the calices of the flower and fruits. Roasted seeds have no fragrance, probably due to the loss of chaff. Guarijios and Mayos still cultivated and used *conivari* from their gardens during the 1980s (G. P. Nabhan, pers. comm.). *Hyptis suaveolens* may not be native to the Río Mayo area because wild plants were not observed for some distance south, away from homes (G. P. Nabhan, pers. comm.).

Conivari may also have been introduced to Baja California, but is not listed by Wiggins (1980). Townsend Brandegee (1894) noted a shrubby hyptis growing abundantly near a ranch at La Mesa (in the cape region of the peninsula), where he thought it was probably introduced. It should be noted that *conivari* is a moderately branched annual that can grow to more than two meters tall. In 1890, Brandegee collected and later described the perennial shrub *H. collina,* which the inhabitants called "Salvia por la Mesa" (Brandegee 1891a:164). I assume that Brandegee was able to distinguish between this and *H. suaveolens.*

Conivari seeds have 21 percent protein, 33 percent oil, and are very high in fiber, comparing favorably with *Salvia carduacea, S. columbariae,* and *S. hispanica* L. (Weber et al. 1991). The seeds dissolve in water to form a high-fiber gel and are "as effective as psyllium [*Plantago* sp.] seeds on the digestive system" (Martin et al. 1998:376). As with so many other seeds that produce a gel upon soaking, after mixing the seeds with saliva Guarijios inserted the seeds into the eye to remove foreign objects (Gentry 1942, 1963).

Salvia | salvia, sage

S. apiana **Jepson**
California white sage

S. carduacea **Bentham**
thistle sage, chia, cardo

S. columbariae **Bentham**
California sage, chia

In his botanical travels throughout Mexico, Edward Palmer (1891) found that several plants of the mint family were called *chia* and were commonly used as food and drink. Linguistic evidence suggests that *chia,* a Nahuatl term carried north by the Spanish, was an oily and greasy seed that, in the opinion of the Spanish, provided a flavorful oil (Truman n.d.).

Chia seeds are nutritious. One teaspoon of *S. columbariae* seed "was sufficient to keep an Indian going for 24 hours on a forced march" (Palmer 1891: 140). One tablespoon of *S. columbariae* seed furnishes approximately 20 percent protein and 31.5–34.0 percent oil (Earle and Jones 1962; Weber et al. 1991). Its seeds are a good source of calcium (Ross 1944). Seeds of *S. carduacea* have 26.5 percent protein and 32 percent oil (Weber et al. 1991). Seeds of *S. apiana* are composed of only 7.9 percent protein and 6.9 percent oil (Earle and Jones 1962). Seeds of *S. columbariae* and *S. carduacea* provide approximately 536 kilocalories per 100 grams (Weber et al. 1991). Seeds of *S. columbariae* are also high in certain constituents often found to have hypoglycemic effects, such as high amounts of fiber, mucilaginous substances, and polysaccharides (Winkleman 1992). Indigenous peoples often soaked the seeds in water. By so doing, the seeds form mucilaginous polysaccharides, which are thought to be potentially useful in treating diabetes and diabetes complications.

Edward Palmer (1891) noted that *S. columbariae* (figs. 122, 123) grew so abundantly in some localities in southern California and northern Mexico that it could be cut, threshed, and cleaned like grain. *Chia* seed was the basis of one of the most popular drinks "used by Mexican, Indian, and many Americans" (Palmer 1891: 140). *Chia* harvesters usually gathered the seeds by bending the inflorescences over a bowl or finely woven basket, then beating the fruits with a paddle or fan to separate out the seeds. They dropped the uncooked and unground seeds into water, where the seeds expanded to several times their bulk and produced a thick, soothing, fragrant drink. The seeds are not aromatic; instead the bracts and calices of the inflorescence and flowers have the aromatic, volatile oils, which are destroyed upon cooking.

John Rothrock (1878:48), surgeon and botanist of Lt. Wheeler's expeditions of 1873–1875, described how the seeds were used for food, a description later reiterated by Palmer (1891):

> During the summer of 1875 my attention was called, while in Southern California, to a mealy preparation in popular use among the Indians, Mexicans, and prospectors. On inquiry, I found it was called "Chia." Further examination proved that it was furnished by the seeds of *Salvia columbariae* Benth. The seeds are collected, roasted, and ground, in the native way, between two stones. This puts it in the condition in which I first saw it. It is used as a food by mixing it with water and enough sugar to suit the taste. It soon develops into a copious mucilaginous mass, several times the original bulk. The taste is somewhat suggestive of linseed meal. One soon acquires a fondness for it, and eats it rather in the way of a luxury than with any reference to the fact that it is exceedingly nutritious besides.

FIGURE 122. ***Salvia columbariae*** Benth. In fruit, herbage dried, and close-up of fruiting inflorescence and seeds. South Mountain Park, Maricopa County, Arizona, April 1988.

Edward Palmer (1891:140) considered the pinole to be "one of the best relished and most nutritive foods while traveling over the deserts; the ground meal mixed with sugar being very portable and easy to prepare while journeying."

San Carlos, Cibecue, and White Mountain Apaches parched the seeds of a plant called *chia* in a basket. It "was eaten dry by all the Western Apache," although the Cibecue apparently ate the seeds wet (Gifford 1940:14). It is presumed that the *chia* was *S. columbariae* and that its seeds were ground after being parched.

Edward Gifford's (1932) relatively short list of food plants used by Southeastern Yavapais does not include *chia*. His later work on the Northeastern and Western Yavapai (Gifford 1936) includes a number of edible plants, including *chia*. In June, Northeastern Yavapais commonly collected and ate this plant while staying near Cleator (Bradshaw Mountains, Yavapai County) before traveling to lower elevations to gather saguaro fruits and mesquite pods.

River Pimas were said to be especially fond of atole made from parched, ground *chia* seeds (Palmer 1891). Uncooked *chia* seed meal was also mixed with roasted cornmeal or other grains to make pinole. Pimas born 30 years after Palmer's work are mostly unfamiliar with the plant and its use (Rea 1997).

Hiá ceḍ O'odhams made a beverage from *S. columbariae* seeds (Felger et al. 1992). Chia was well known to the Mohave, Hualapai, Chemehuevi, Quechan, and Paiute. The Mohave thought the seeds to be like those of *Atriplex*, but "soapy-like" (probably in reference to the mucilaginous qualities when soaked in water, rather than its taste); they gathered the seeds on "sandbars" in the summer months (Stewart 1965). Harrison Doyle, one of *chia's* most ardent supporters, was once a long-distance runner and often ran with Mohave boys when he was young. One Mohave friend told him that Indian runners ran to the California coast from Needles, using two routes, carrying trade items such as turquoise, gourd shells filled with water, and *chia* seed to sustain them (Doyle 1963:19). He remembered that *chia* plants were common all along the "Old Mohave Trail," where "the greatest of all prehistoric Indian turquoise diggings were also found" (Doyle 1973:10).

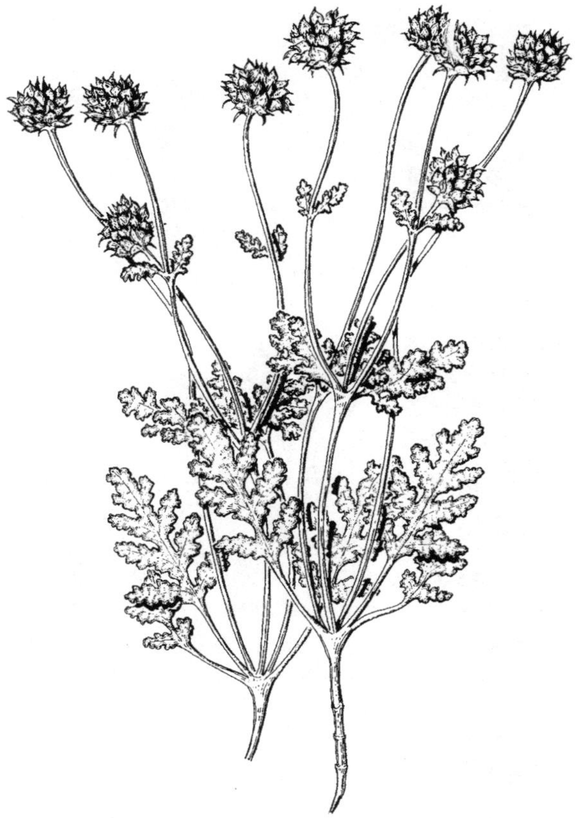

FIGURE 123. ***Salvia columbariae*** habit. One mile south of Alamo State Park, Yuma County, Arizona, March 1973 (*Pinkava 10327 et al.*, ASU). Courtesy of the Mesa Southwest Museum.

Salvia columbariae was especially important to the Cahuilla, who filled their ollas with stored *chia* seeds in the summer (Barrows 1900):

> The seeds are gathered by the Coahuillas [sic] with the seed fan and flat basket, and are parched and ground. The meal is then mixed with about three times as much wheat flour and the whole pounded up together. It makes a dark looking meal. This is "pinole," called by the Coahuillas *to-at.* It is an old and famous preparation. . . . Pinole, by the Coahuillas, is sometimes baked into little cakes or biscuits. Either way chia is used, it is very good; has a pleasant, nutty flavor, and is exceedingly wholesome. Moreover, it grows in considerable quantity through the mountain ranges of the Coahuillas, and in the early summer ollas stored with these seeds stand in every home, and throughout the cooler hours of the day and evening there is ever a woman grinding at her mill.

Many desert travelers carried a small amount of *chia* meal with them (Palmer 1891; Barrows 1900) for energy and to relieve ones' thirst. Rothrock (1878:48–49) noted that *chia* seed was a favorite among travelers: "[*Chia* seed] is in great demand among the knowing ones who have a desert to cross, or who expect to encounter a scarcity of water, and what there is, of bad quality. By preparing it so thin that it can be used as a drink, it seems to assuage thirst, to improve the taste of the water, and, in addition, to lessen the quantity of water taken, which in hot countries is often so excessive as to produce serious illness."

The Cahuilla added a few teaspoons of the seed meal to a quart of potable but alkaline water to make a nutritious and less-alkaline drink (Barrows 1900). Santa Ysabel Diegueños chewed a handful of seed over long journeys for added strength (Hedges and Beresford 1986).

Undoubtedly those people living in the northern half of Baja California once used *chia.* Sebastián Vizcaíno had just established a new port named San Diego in 1602 (Mathes 1992:162). He and a few of his men were taken to an Indian rancheria, where they found women "making their threshing pile of a seed like that of flax." Such seed may have been *chia, S. carduacea,* or more likely, *S. columbariae.* Southern Diegueños gathered a "wild flaxseed" for food (Spier 1923), which may also have been *S. columbariae.*

Hernando Alarcón, while exploring the Lower Colorado River area in 1540, described the natives of the region wearing small bags that contained powder from an herb (Hakluyt 1904:101; Elsasser 1980:15; Mathes 1992:101): "They carry also certaine little long bagges about an hand broade tyed to their left arme, which serve them also in stead of brasers [wrist guards] for their bowes, full of the powder of a certaine herbe, whereof they make a certaine beverage." I agree with Castetter and Bell (1951), who suggested that the "powder" was meal made from *S. columbariae* seeds, rather than tobacco, as suggested by Hakluyt (1904).

Tipais once used *chia* seeds as a food, but no longer do so. They highly valued the "delicious and nutritious" drink they made by soaking the ground seeds in water (Weiss 1994:215). As with acorns, Tipais did not mention *chia* seeds as being "good for" treating diabetes, although seeds have constituents often found to assist in controlling blood sugar. Of interest is the distinction they made between two types of *chia. Salvia columbariae* was considered inferior to the second, more valued type of *chia* that they described as having a red flower and larger seed and growing near Tecate (which is at elevations above the Sonoran Desert), where it was reported to be rare. *Salvia carduacea* grows in the vicinity of Tecate (*Moran 28681*, DES), where it is called *cardo.* It has larger seeds than *S. columbariae,* but its flower corollas are lavender, rather than red. *Salvia henryi* A. Gray (crimson sage) has a large, red corolla and seeds that become mucilaginous when wet (pers. obs.). However, it is not known to grow in Baja California. The identity of the favored *chia* remains a mystery.

Salvia columbariae was so important that it was responsible for a great massacre in a canyon so named for this clash. The story of the massacre was first published in *The High Country Quarterly,* Temecula, California, and later published by J. Knight (1964) and Harrison Doyle (1973). Massacre Canyon cuts into the San Jacinto Mountains in Riverside County. To those who lived in San Jacinto Valley in pre-Columbian days "life was represented by *chia;* death by the aboriginal spear" (Doyle 1973). The Soboba group is the only one still remaining of the six that once peacefully inhabited the fertile San Jacinto Valley below the mountains (Knight 1964:14–15). According to "Old Victoriana," their last chieftain who died in 1890, the battle took place long ago. Legend has it that drought destroyed the *chia* crop of the Temecula, a "tribe of strangers to the southwest of the Valley and war-like by nature." They moved northward to exploit the *chia* crop of one of the six groups, the Ivah. The Ivah's chief protested, but was met with an arrow that clipped his headdress. He and his group prepared for battle, meeting the Temecula the next day, who by then had gained reinforcements. The Ivahs were forced into a canyon where the Temeculas trapped them at a rock wall. Here they fought, "stopping only to die." Early white settlers who heard this story from Chief Victoriana named the canyon after this battle. This fight was said to be the last battle between Indian groups over food (Doyle 1973).

The Spanish Californians were quick to learn of *chia's* virtues as a food source and medicine, and the Anglos' interest in the plants did not wane for some time. Seeds found their way to purchasers in the markets and drug stores of southern California, southern Arizona, Sonora, Sinaloa, and Baja California near the turn of the century. Charles Saunders and Dr. Cephus Bard of Ventura, California, said that one pound of *chia* seed sold for as high as eight dollars in the 1890s (Doyle 1973). In the mid 1950s, Harrison Doyle cultivated *S. columbariae* seed. In an attempt to market his golden-colored seeds, he named it "golden *chia,*" to differentiate it from the grayish black seeds of *S. hispanica,* which was widely marketed in Mexico. (However, seeds of *S. columbariae* are also brownish gray when mature.) Those who became acquainted with his "golden *chia*" were quick to praise the plants and hoped to grow substantial quantities. One such interested person was a "tycoon in China who wanted seeds to start a lifesaving program for undernourished Asians" (Doyle 1973:2). Doyle realized the difficulty in trying to produce enough *chia* seed to market and compete successfully against the commonly sold and, in his mind, inferior Mexican *chia, S. hispanica* L. According to him, some firms started to push the Mexican *chia* as *S. columbariae,* and those that purchased and grew these seeds realized that they were fooled.

Another Anglo who enjoyed *chia* seed meal was Adolph Bulla, who, in 1958, was a 71-year-old hard rock miner and prospector of Red Mountain, California. He related to Eugene Conrotto (1958:19) how the desert environment, "especially the *Salvia columbariae,*" helped him retain his good health and happiness. He mixed a teaspoon of *chia* meal into his hotcake batter each morning and "sometimes a little more when there is an especially hard day's work ahead." He could "labor all day without eating again," and found the meal to be a "handy grub to take along on a prospecting trip for it eliminates the weight of more bulky foods, and at the same time gives more energy." He was the first white man Conrotto met that still regularly harvested and ate *chia* seed. Bulla explained that he could gather a "two-pound year's supply" in only a day during good years. He simply processed the seed by threshing it on a piece of canvas and blowing away the chaff. As far as Bulla was concerned, it was "a shame to see man lose *chia,*" because it was "really a wonderful food." Harrison Doyle was very impressed with Adolph Bulla upon reading Conrotto's story. Wanting to share *chia* stories with another *chia* admirer, Doyle went to Bulla for his own interview and found a man who looked and acted 20 years younger (Doyle 1963).

So how do the seeds of *S. columbariae* compare with those of *S. hispanica?* Although far from conclusive, Doyle offered some interesting insights. He took some of Bulla's seeds home and proceeded with an experiment. Doyle poured Bulla's golden *chia* and *S. hispanica* seeds into six separate labeled envelopes, which he then shuffled. He recorded his "state of energy and well-being" on the envelope (Doyle 1963:33). During the three mornings he used Bulla's seeds, he had the "unmistakable feeling of energy and well-being" and felt "30 years younger." The other three days when he used *S. hispanica* seeds were "more or less just ordinary."

However, he would probably be disappointed to know that seeds of *S. hispanica* were found to have similar amounts of protein, oil, and total dietary fiber (Weber et al. 1991).

Not everyone was impressed with *chia's* attributes. Edward Palmer (1891:140) believed that *chias* did not get the respect they deserved from the Anglo population: "As a food both nutritious and palatable it deserves to be better known. The white races are, perhaps, too apt to look with contempt upon the contents of the Indian granary, and though chia is never likely to rank as one of the greatest staples, it may come to be as universally esteemed among civilized as it is among the aborigines of the region where it grows."

Regardless, *S. columbariae* seed was a favored food by many. So important was *chia* that it was probably both encouraged and cultivated by early inhabitants. *Salvia columbariae* thrives on decomposed granite on disturbed slopes, such as roadcuts, and appears to respond favorably to fires to some degree. Amadeo Rea (1997) noted that *chia* and *Plantago* spp. grew more thickly in an area recently burned than in adjacent, nonburned areas. I have seen thick stands of exceptionally robust *chia* plants growing among numerous potsherds adjacent to the Verde River, Yavapai County, in an area possibly manipulated by pre-Columbian or historic cultures (*Hodgson et al. 6248,* DES). Evidence suggests that the Hohokam burned large tracts of desert to promote grasses and cool-season annuals that were important to them (Bohrer 1987, 1991). The Cahuilla periodically burned *chia* stands to facilitate next season's growth (Bean and Saubel 1972). That people intentionally set fires to obtain food resources is a well-known fact. Representatives from no less than 35 groups in central and northern California said that they burned an area after harvesting seeds to increase the next year's yield of grass seeds and edible tubers in late summer or fall (Lewis 1973; see Aschmann 1997:306–313). Undoubtedly this number is low, given that this knowledge may have been lost by the time serious ethnobotanical inquiry was being undertaken (see Timbrook 1990).

Harrison Doyle knew of *S. columbariae's* potential as an important healthfood. He enjoyed adding soaked seeds to hotcakes, bread, cookies, salads, ice cream, honey, or peanut butter. He especially enjoyed eating the seeds raw, with other fruits or nuts, or brewed as a tea. Doyle (1973:15) also realized that "to establish it nationally and internationally it would require a long period of education and financing."

FIGURE 124. ***Salvia carduacea*** Benth. habit and inflorescences. Near Anza, California, June 1982. Photograph courtesy of H. S. Gentry.

Salvia carduacea (fig. 124) was less often encountered than the more widespread *S. columbariae,* but its seeds were used in a similar fashion. Cahuillas gathered the seeds from June to November from populations covering many acres near Anza, California (Bean and Saubel 1972). They parched, ground, and mixed the seed meal with other seeds into a gruel. Santa Ysabel Diegueños added the seeds of this and *S. columbariae* to wheat to improve its flavor (Hedges and Beresford 1986).

Cahuillas gathered the seeds of *S. apiana* from July through September, then parched and ground them into flour (Bean and Saubel 1972). Southern Diegueños ground and ate the uncooked seeds of "white sage" (Spier 1923). Mention is made of how the Chumash, a group from southern California northwest of the Sonoran Desert, used *S. apiana.* They peeled and ate its young shoots, but drank water mixed with pulverized leaves to induce vomiting (Timbrook 1990).

Perhaps this is a good time to rekindle interest in the *chias,* particularly *S. columbariae.* Weber et al. (1991:125) suggested that *chia* seeds have the potential to be incorporated in human diets by being blended with other protein sources to produce a balanced protein. *Chia* seeds are competitive with other grain sources in that "The *chia* seed has more than one and one-half to twice the protein concentration of other grains and approximately three to ten times the oil concentration of most grains. Its high protein and oil concentration makes it a very attractive grain source for developing countries which have a shortage of protein and energy." However, they caution that because of *chia* seeds' high fiber concentration, only adults should include the seeds in their diets.

Lennoaceae | Lennoa Family

Pholisma | desert Christmas-tree, sandfood

P. arenarium **Nuttall**
scaly-stemmed sand plant, desert Christmas-tree

P. sonorae **(Torrey ex A. Gray) Yatskievych**
sandfood, camote de los medanos

Pholisma sonorae is a wonderfully strange, parasitic plant (figs. 125–127) that was known to the aboriginal populations of northwestern Mexico and adjacent United States, including the Hiá ceḍ O'odham. Its rhizomes (figs. 127, 128) provided a food source (Palmer 1871; Vasey and Rose 1890b; Havard 1895, 1896; Thackery and Gilman 1931; Saunders 1948; Castetter and Bell 1951; Thackery 1953; Childs 1954; Hedrick 1972; Bell et al. 1980; Nabhan 1980; Yatskievych 1985; Alvarez de Williams 1987; Nabhan et al. 1989a). Recorded use of this plant dates back to 1694, near the Sea of Cortez, where nomads, who later became known as the Hiá ceḍ O'odham, "lived by eating roots of wild sweet-potatoes" and other gathered plant foods (Nabhan 1980).

Col. Andrew B. Gray introduced *P. sonorae* to the scientific world, finding the plants near Pinacate Mountain, Sonora, in May 1854. With his Hiá ceḍ O'odham friends, he gathered and roasted the rhizomes on their campfire coals, as described by Col. Gray in a letter to Dr. John Torrey (Thackery 1953:22):

> Immediately upon entering these sand hills, our course being across them in a westerly direction, I observed the Indian dismount from his horse and commence digging with his hands. At first I could not perceive his object, but shortly discovered that he had pulled out of the sand a vegetable-looking substance, which was shaped somewhat like a mushroom. He showed great eagerness to obtain more, and made a sign that it was good to eat ... and the chief [sic], instead of supping with us, as usual, made a fire, and roasted his roots or plants on the hot coals (which took about 20 minutes), and commenced eating them ... out of courtesy, I moved over to the chief's [sic] fire, and he handed me one. At first I ate but little, and slowly, but in a few minutes, so luscious was it that I forgot my own mess, and ate heartily of it .... The taste, though peculiar, was not unlike the sweet potato, but more delicate.

Carl Lumholtz (1912:318–319) also found sandfood to be of great interest and regarded it highly:

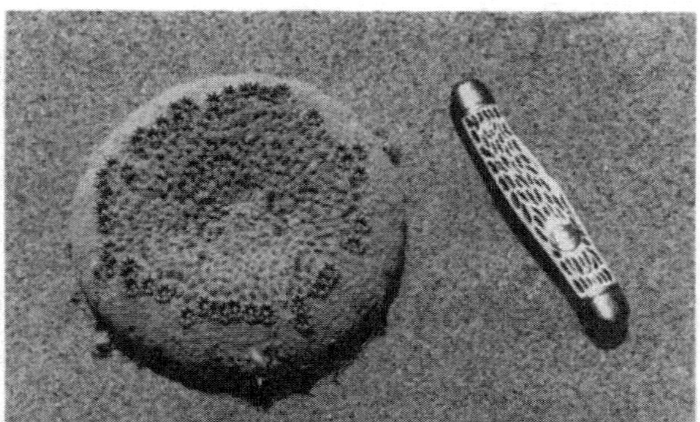

FIGURE 125. (left) ***Pholisma sonorae*** (Torr. ex A. Gray) Yatsk. Inflorescence a flattened disk with lilac-purple flowers. Ten miles east of San Luis, Sonora, along international border, April 1984. Photograph by Gary P. Nabhan, courtesy of Desert Botanical Garden, Phoenix, Arizona.

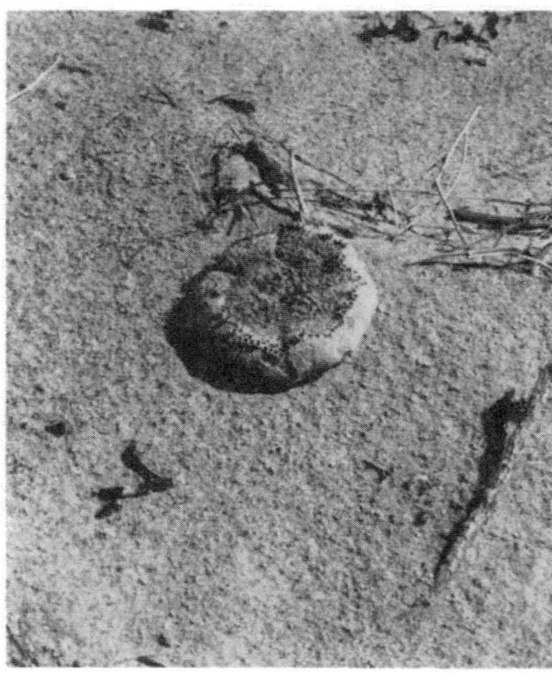

FIGURE 126. (right) ***Pholisma sonorae*** growing in a cotton field. Near Somerton, Yuma County, Arizona, June 1988. Photograph by Doug Mings, courtesy of Desert Botanical Garden, Phoenix, Arizona.

> I sampled one of them and found it to be succulent and excellent food. It is more tender than a radish, as well as more juicy, and the whole root can be eaten. It has a sweetish and agreeable flavor all its own. The Indians usually toast these plants on the coals, when they resemble sweet potatoes in taste, but I prefer to eat them raw. They are an especially delicious relish to a thirsty man, and they also quickly appease hunger; in fact, of all the many kinds of edible roots that I have tried in their uncooked state, used among natives in different parts of the earth, I know of none which can compare with this one in refreshing and palatable qualities.

Lumholtz went on to describe how important the stems, or *camotes,* were to Caravajales, the "Indian hermit of Los Papagos," who could find them out of season (Lumholtz 1912:333):

> He catches fish on the coast, also, but camotes, "the roots of the sands," form his principal means of subsistence. In fact he lives almost entirely on these camotes, and is able to find them out of season .... When his wife left him a few years before, he decided to go back again to live in the medanos where he was born.... Recently he had been in Quitovaquita for two days and had remained without eating during that time; then he had ridden to get the camotes for three days more without food.

The significance of sandfood to the Hiá ceḍ O'odham's traditional food-gathering patterns was made evident by Miguel Velasco, who said that his people were "the same the Mexican Papagos call *Hia Tuatk Ku:mda,*" or Sand Root Crushers (Bell et al. 1980:65).

People ate the underground stems raw or roasted or dried them in the sun, then ground them with mesquite pods (Nabhan 1980; Yatskievych 1985). Miguel Velasco related to Ofelia Zepeda (1985:24) how they gathered and ate sandfood: "Gathering the *hia tatk* 'sand roots' was not an easy thing because the sand was so deep and so soft that one would sink down to his knees and walking was difficult. He [Velasco] said that the meat of the roots was prepared much in the same way as the meat of the squash, that it was cut in long curling strips for easy carrying."

One elderly man recalled that he cut the plant stem into strips, dried them, and then rehydrated them when they were needed for a meal (Nabhan 1980). Beatrice Melvin related that they used to gather the stems and dry them "in the same way that you store squash, by cutting it in long strips and curling them in bunches to dry and to carry when traveling" (Zepeda 1985:29).

It has been alluded that sandfood was an important food source to the Cocopa (Havard 1895; Castetter and Bell 1951). It is not known for certain if it was this plant or *Orobanche cooperi* (which the Hiá ceḍ O'odham sometimes referred to as sandfood) that the Cocopa gathered. *Pholisma sonorae* was not mentioned by any of William Kelly's (1977) Cocopa friends.

Sandfood's underground stems usually die back to a small, relatively undifferentiated mass of tissue in and at the infection site of the host plant each year, soon after the plant sets fruit (Yatskievych 1985), although *P. sonorae* occasionally is able to overwinter some years (Cothrun 1969). It was therefore assumed that the underground stems usually could not be located and harvested prior to early March, when plants begin to develop an inflorescence, and after fruit set in July and August. However, Carl Lumholtz (1912) noted that the Hiá ceḍ O'odham knew how to gather the stems, or *camotes,* year-round. He described how Caravajales relied heavily on the *camotes* that he located and gathered out of season. Candelaria Orosco explained that one could find sandfood early in the season by

FIGURE 127. Gary Nabhan exposing succulent underground stems of ***Pholisma sonorae.*** Ten miles east of San Luis, Sonora, along international border, April 1984. Photograph courtesy of Desert Botanical Garden, Phoenix, Arizona.

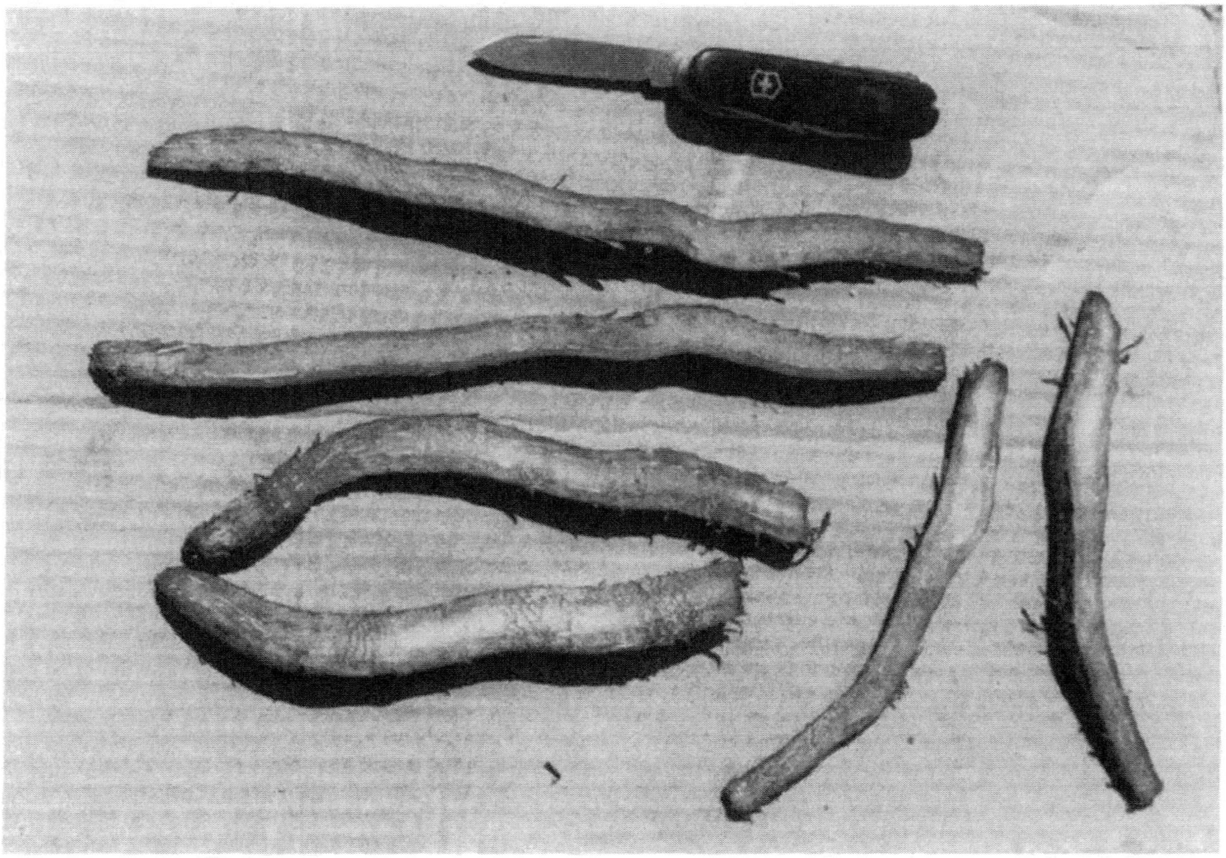

FIGURE 128. ***Pholisma sonorae*** succulent underground stems. All plants found in the area had been dug up and eaten by rabbits. Yusmex, Yuma County, Arizona, April 1987.

looking for the blackened, withered flower heads from the previous year (if they have not blown away) before digging into the sand to gather the stems (Nabhan et al. 1989a). The tell-tale tracks of jackrabbits leading up to the plants also aids in locating the underground stems. However, because the rabbits are seeking the moisture-laden stems, its location by humans is usually too late.

Sandfood stems have a very large amount of starch, with varying amounts of sugar (Yatskievych 1985). The taste has been described as similar to that of a delicate sweet potato, a cross between a celery and a pear, and ranging from bland to moderately sweet. When eaten raw, I find them pleasantly juicy and somewhat sweet, albeit, gritty. One O'odham woman related that the same plants they used to dig up and eat raw now have a more bitter taste (Bell et al. 1980). As with other starchy foods, roasting breaks down some of the starch and softens the stem (Yatskievych 1985). Fresh stems are encrusted with sand particles and are thus gritty. When Peter Brady and Col. Gray visited the Hiá cẹd O'odham, Brady noticed how the front teeth of these people were all worn. Their extremely poor dental health was thought by some to have been partially a result of eating so many sandfood stems. However, according to Tom Childs (1954), their worn teeth were due to eating Missmire clams raw, which they opened with their teeth.

Sandfood was also a very important source of water for both Anglos and natives alike (Vasey and Rose 1890b; Lumholtz 1912). Edward Palmer collected sandfood in "large quantities" at Lerdo, Mexico, and noted that the deeper the sand, the larger and juicier the plant stems (Vasey and Rose 1890b). Fresh stems have a moisture content of 83.5–89.7 percent (Yanovsky and Kingsbury 1938; Yatskievych 1985) and provide moisture to wildlife such as jackrabbits, who dig up and consume the stems.

Sandfood was harvested until the 1930s, but its use has declined since the Hiá cẹd O'odham and Quechan people were relocated away from where the plants grew (Nabhan 1980). As noted by Gary Nabhan et al.

(1989a), it is ironic and sad that sandfood, once harvested by Hiá ced O'odham and Quechan people for hundreds of years, was not threatened until after these people left the area. There is no evidence that they overexploited sandfood, perhaps because of the peoples' low population densities. Native peoples claim that plant populations declined once they stopped using it regularly. Gathering the underground stems may have encouraged seed dispersal to safe sites or encouraged production of more stems, which would provide more surface area for the production of flowers and fruit.

However, extensive agricultural clearing and off-road vehicles have quickly destroyed sandfood habitat, flowering and fruiting inflorescences, and the host plants on both sides of the U.S.-Mexico border. Although sandfood grows in agricultural settings (fig. 126), its long-term existence in these disturbed areas is not ensured. Although considered rare, sandfood was not even protected by the Arizona Native Plant Law until recent revisions in 1994 gave it minimal protection. The BLM has set aside a small area of sandfood habitat for protection in California, an area that still does not make populations safe (Nabhan et al. 1988). It is unfortunate, too, that the political climate is such that the only "good plant" is one that might harbor a miracle cure or possess some other economic self worth. Carl Lumholtz (1912:319) commented that "apparently this highly useful plant might be transplanted to advantage to other desert regions of the earth." Franklin Thackery (1953:24), a well-respected scientist, also thought of sandfood as a plant with promising economic potential: "If Ammobroma has anything like the food values claimed for it by the Indians it might indicate that some sort of a sprinkling system could be devised for use in the sand dunes thus finding a way to produce revenue from this large area now worthless."

Sandfood population and reproductive biological information is sorely needed. Nothing is known about its seed germination requirements. Ethnographic information on sandfood needs to be obtained from the Cocopa, Quechan, and other Colorado delta groups (Nabhan et al. 1989a), which will in return provide biological information. *Pholisma sonorae* is rare and deserves greater protection than what it receives. In 1990, Peter Warren, Karen Reichardt, Patrick Quirk, and I tried to locate individuals of sandfood in the sand dunes near Yusmex, Arizona, outside of Yuma. We did not find the plants, but discovered a great deal of sandfood habitat converted to asparagus fields. At that moment I decided that asparagus will never again be a part of my diet (and Thackery's idea might not be so strange).

The underground stems of *P. arenarium* has also been used for food by southern Californians and other groups inhabiting areas within the species' distribution in a manner similar to that of *P. sonorae,* although to a much lesser extent (Yanovsky 1936; Yatskievych 1985). Its stems accumulate smaller amounts of sugars than those of *P. sonorae* (Yatskievych 1985).

Loasaceae | Stickleaf or Blazing-star Family

Mentzelia | blazing-star, pegarropa

M. albicaulis Hooker

small-flowered blazing-star, white-stemmed blazing-star, selé

Mentzelia was a major plant food for many native peoples in the western United States, although references to those inhabiting the Sonoran Desert are few or concealed by misidentification. Its use dates back to pre-Columbian times, with the seeds recovered from a Hohokam site south of Tucson representing the first documentation of use in the southern Arizona desert (Bohrer et al. 1969). Seeds of the family are a valuable source of lipids and carbohydrates (Hill n.d.), with those of *M. albicaulis* having 6.4 percent fat, 3.9 percent protein, and 85.1 percent carbohydrates (Smith 1973).

Mentzelia albicaulis is a wide-ranging annual species that grows throughout much of western United States south into Baja California and northern Sonora (Christy 1998). Dr. John Torrey (1859:67) provided the earliest historical evidence for the use of *Mentzelia* (specifically *M. albicaulis*) when he described its "oily" seeds pounded and used to make a pinole. John Rothrock (1878:44) also noted how "southeastern California Indians pound up the seeds making one of their forms of pinole" and a kind of cake. Other groups who used the seeds of what was believed to be *M. albicaulis* for food include the Southern Paiute (Kelly 1932; Stewart 1941; Bye 1972); Hopi (Fewkes 1896; Hough 1898; Stephen 1936; Whiting 1939; Vestal 1940);

Navajo (Elmore 1943); and Yuman-speaking groups, including the Havasupai, Hualapai, and Yavapai (Hrdlička 1908; Spier 1928; Kroeber 1935; Mekeel 1935; Gifford 1936; Weber and Seaman 1985). River Pimas' knowledge of the plant has apparently been all but lost, perhaps because it has not been used for so long a time (Rea 1997).

Some groups, including the Yavapai, collected and threshed the seeds of *Mentzelia* by knocking them in conical or small baskets using seed beaters (Spier 1928; Kroeber 1935; Gifford 1936; Weber and Seaman 1985; Hill n.d.). Hopi girls usually gathered the seeds in the afternoon, believing that they would not fall out of the fruits until the sun passed halfway over the sky (Fewkes 1896). Others simply broke off the inflorescences or pulled up the entire plant (Smith 1973). People generally stored the dried threshed seeds or parched the seeds with coals in a winnowing tray before grinding them. The resulting oily meal was eaten alone or with bread or stored for future use. One Hualapai individual recalled that they roasted and ground the seeds, then baked the meal in solid chunks, which they ate dry (Mekeel 1935). Immature fruits were stored over a container, which allowed the collection of seeds as the fruits dried. Others sometimes stirred immature seeds into boiling water to make a gruel or parched, ground, and ate the unripe seeds with bread (Spier 1928). This may be the plant to which Leslie Spier (1923:336) was referring when describing how the Southern Diegueño ground the "oily seed for flour."

Of interest is the quantity of seeds once collected and harvested. *Mentzelia albicaulis* flowers from February to June (Christy 1998) and the tiny seeds mature from late February to July. One robust plant produces no more than a few tablespoons of seeds, yet large quantities were nevertheless collected. Three pounds of seeds were found in a storage jar unearthed at Cordova Cave, New Mexico (Kaplan 1963). The hundreds of pounds of "grass seeds" stored in willow baskets and other caches destroyed by the U.S. Cavalry in the 1860s (U.S. Senate 1936) is referable not to grass, but to *M. albicaulis* (Smith 1973; Hill n.d.). Such collecting efforts required the investment of a considerable amount of time and dense populations of plants.

Mentzelia albicaulis may be another important food plant whose distribution has been greatly reduced in relatively recent times, being far less abundant now than it probably was more than 150 years ago (Bohrer 1978). Extensive stands had to have been present to allow collection of such a large amount of seed to sustain a family through the winter (Smith 1973; Bohrer 1978). Several factors encouraged the reduction of *M. albicaulis* populations and subsequent loss of knowledge of its use among native peoples. With the appearance of, and increased contact with, Anglo settlers, the indigenous peoples' interaction with their resources was greatly altered. The introduction of nonnative plant species and new cultivates played an increasing role in the diets of indigenous groups (Hill n.d.) at the expense of the native plant species. Additionally, a change in traditional practices altered their diets and decreased the number of plants. For example, if *M. albicaulis* seeds were no longer sown in areas that were cleared and burned, the number of plants and seed bank would be affected.

Livestock grazing is also implicated as a major cause of the reduction of *M. albicaulis* populations (Bohrer 1978). In 1886, Capt. John Bourke of the 3rd Cavalry noted that livestock was impacting the resources, including *selé* populations (U.S. Senate 1936:151): "Since the coming of cattlemen in northern Arizona, cattle have eaten up much of the Zule *[selé]* and mesquite, and also scared away the wild animals, thus raising the problem of how the Hualapais are to live." It is suggested that cattle grazing further impacted its populations when *M. albicaulis* did not set abundant fruit during successive dry years, but was harvested by the local inhabitants (Bohrer 1978).

Malpighiaceae | Malpighia or Barbados-cherry Family

Malpighia | Singapore-holly, stingingbush

M. diversifolia **Brandegee**
manzana, manzanita, margarita

M. emarginata **Sessé & Moçiño de Candolle (syn.,** *M. umbellata* **Rose)**
granadilla, mora de campo

Malpighia diversifolia grows only in southern Baja California and flowers from August to October, whereas *M. emarginata* is found in southern Sonora and southward into Sinaloa, possibly just outside the limits of the Sonoran Desert (Wiggins 1964, cited as *M. umbellata*). The fleshy bright red drupes of *M. diversifolia* and orange drupes of *M. emarginata* provided an edible food to local inhabitants. It is probable that the bright red drupes of *M. ovata* Rose, a species that grows from western Sonora south to Oaxaca, were also eaten, although I know of no documentation of this.

Townsend Brandegee (1891a) noted that the inhabitants of Baja California's cape region used the fruits of an unknown *Malpighia* for food. He later described this plant as a new species, naming it *M. diversifolia,* and again commented on its edibility (Brandegee 1900–1901:104). He noted that people ate the small, red drupes, which were called *manzanita,* "without any special reason."

Malpighia emarginata supplied an important fruit source to the Pima Bajo at Ónavas, who consumed so many of the fruits that "in July there is much diarrhea" (Pennington 1980, cited as *M. umbellata*). They prepared sweet syrup by crushing and pressing the fruits through a metal strainer (or loosely woven basket) then boiling the liquid until it thickened. At Agiabampo, Sonora, the fruits were called *mora de campo* and eaten by the local inhabitants (Rose 1895, cited as *M. umbellata*). Howard Gentry noted that the Río Mayo people ate the ripe fruits. Certain beetles also feast on the fallen fruits (Martin et al. 1998).

Malvaceae | Mallow Family

Eremalche | white-mallow

E. exilis **(A. Gray) Greene**
white-mallow

Eremalche exilis is the only malvaceous plant that provided an edible food to Sonoran Desert peoples. The Pima once harvested young plants in late winter and spring as a famine food (Rea 1997). After cooking the leaves, they mixed them with white flour and then cooked this mixture. *Eremalche exilis* has not been recently documented on the reservation (Rea 1997), although it grows in nearby Sierra Estrella Regional Park, where it is rare (Sundell 1974).

Martyniaceae | Unicorn Family

Proboscidea | devil's-claw, unicorn-plant, gatitio

P. althaeifolia **(Bentham) Decaisne**
desert unicorn-plant, elephant's-tusk, devil's-claw, devil's-horn, espuela del diablo, cuernitos

P. parviflora **(Wooton) Wooton & Standley**
doubleclaw, devil's-claw, uña de gato, torito, gatuna, cuernitos

Proboscidea has been placed by some botanists within the family Pedaliaceae. *Proboscidea* seeds are edible and have high oil and protein contents

FIGURE 129. (left) ***Proboscidea parviflora*** (Wooton) Wooton & Standley. Note immature fruits in center. El Coyote, Sonora, July 1988 (*Hodgson et al. 5113,* DES).

FIGURE 130. (right) ***Proboscidea parviflora.*** **a.** Habit with immature fruits and flower; **b.** mature fruits and seeds, 5.2 miles southeast of Burro Creek bridge, Highway 93, September 1969 (*Pinkava 6338 et al.,* ASU). Courtesy of the Mesa Southwest Museum.

(Nabhan et al. 1981). Seed of southwestern annual proboscideas, such as *P. parviflora* (figs. 129, 130), were found to have 35–45 percent oil and 20–35 percent protein (Earle and Jones 1962; Ghosh and Beal 1979; Berry et al. 1981). The seeds and green, immature fruits (figs. 129–132) of wild and cultivated devil's claw provided food to various southwestern groups.

Western Apaches cracked and chewed the seeds of *P. parviflora* for the juice, which they described as being like milk (Buskirk 1986, cited as *Martynia* sp.). Seeds collected by children were taken to Apache prisoners-of-war in Oklahoma (Castetter and Opler 1936). Edward Palmer (1871, cited as *Martynia violacea*) noted that they also cooked and ate immature pods.

River Pimas and Tohono O'odham regularly ate the seeds, either boiled or raw, as a snack food (Castetter and Underhill 1935; Curtin 1949; Nabhan et al. 1981). A few River Pima and Tohono O'odham joke about girls who eat too many seeds of devil's claw. Girls do not eat the seeds for fear that they will bear only male children when they become mothers (Nabhan and Rea 1987) or that they will not be able to make love because their pubic hair will become stiff like the crest, or rostrum (G. P. Nabhan, pers. comm.). Pima George Kyyitan had heard that girls should not overindulge, but he never learned why (Rea 1997).

Proboscidea althaeifolia (fig. 131) provided edible seeds to the Cahuilla (Bean and Saubel 1972) and green fruits and seeds to the Yaqui (Watson 1889, cited as *Martynia palmeri*). Inhabitants of the Río San Miguel area probably used *P. parviflora* in the past, but have not in relatively recent times (Felger et al. 1976). Tarahumaras ate the seeds of mature fruits raw (Pennington 1963).

Little is written on the use of the large, fleshy root of *P. althaeifolia* for food (fig. 132). It was an important staple food of a Seri band living on Tiburón and San Esteban Islands (Felger and Moser 1976, 1985). They peeled the root and ate the outer portion (cortex) fresh. The inner part (pith) was bitter and not eaten. Edward Palmer noted that the large, yellow, carrotlike root weighed three to four pounds, but made no reference to its use as food by Yaquis (Watson 1889).

Although known as a food source, the fruit fibers are most important to basketmakers, particularly the River Pima and Tohono O'odham. Basketmakers integrate the fiber (or sprints) peeled from the "claws" (or rostrum) of mature fruit into their coiled basketry as binding and for making black designs (Nabhan et al. 1981; Bretting 1982; see Rea 1997; fig. 133). Baskets with solid coils of devil's claw fiber woven into their bottoms are leakproof. Such baskets were even used by dairies as milk containers before they became very expensive (G. P. Nabhan, pers. comm.).

Proboscidea parviflora ssp. *parviflora* var. *hohokamiana* Bretting may have been cultivated by Native Americans north of Mexico. The varietal name suggests that it was "of the Hohokam," although there is no evidence that it was cultivated by these people (Rea 1997). Excavations from Ak Chiñ, near Maricopa, showed that the white-seeded domesticated devil's claws were grown in the 1600s (Gasser 1987). The earliest published references concerning intentional planting appeared just after the turn of this century (see Hrdlička 1906). However, the most probable place of origin for the domesticated form of devil's claw is in southern Arizona among the River Pima and Tohono O'Odham between 1840 and 1870, when the demand for baskets increased (Bretting 1982; Nabhan and Rea 1987; G. P. Nabhan, pers. comm.). Recently, more Tohono O'odham families cultivated the domesticated devil's claw than any other single plant (Nabhan and Fritz 1977).

All three types of devil's claw *(P. althaeifolia, P. parviflora,* and the domesticate form of *P. parviflora)* have been used at some time for their fibers. However, the two readily grown annual forms of *P. parviflora* were used exclusively in the 19th century, although the white-seeded, long-clawed variety is preferred, even to this day (Rea 1997). Following the influx of cattle after the Civil War, more devil's claw was cultivated because wild plants decreased as a result of overgrazing (Nabhan and Rea 1987). Furthermore, sales and trade of baskets increased at this time (Nabhan and Rea 1987).

The cultivated form, *P. parviflora* ssp. *parviflora* var. *hohokamiana,* differs from the typical species in having white seeds, rather than black, and longer claws on the fruits (Bretting 1982). O'odham women say that the domesticate produces longer, smoother, wider, and more pliant fibers, which make their work easier (Nabhan and Rea 1987; Rea 1997). Four-clawed fruit appear

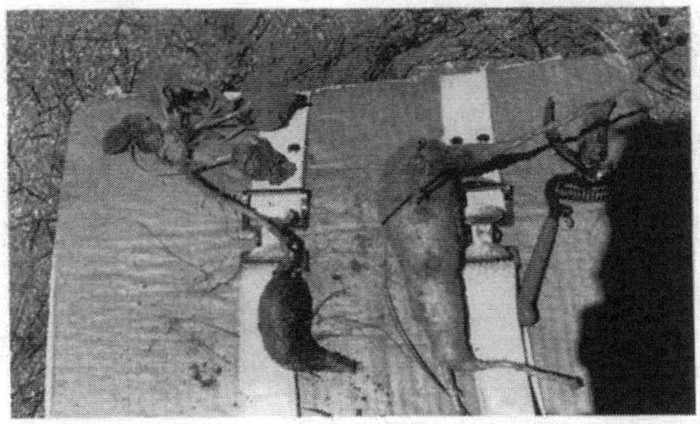

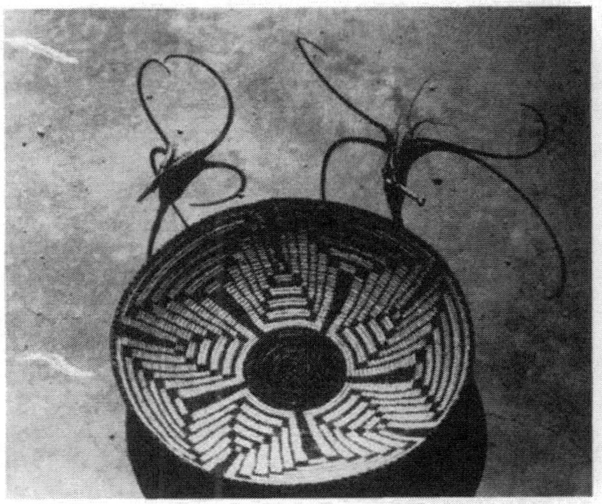

FIGURE 131. ***Proboscidea althaeifolia*** (Benth.) Decne. Note immature fruits in center and shiny, dark green leaves. Foothills of Patagonia Mountains, Santa Cruz County, Arizona, August 1988.

FIGURE 132. Tuberlike roots of ***Proboscidea althaeifolia.*** Foothills of Patagonia Mountains, Santa Cruz County, Arizona, September 1987 (*Hodgson 4652, 4653,* DES).

FIGURE 133. Tohono O'odham basket with fruit of ***Proboscidea parviflora*** (Woot.) Woot. & Standl. var. *hohokamiana* Bretting on right. Photograph by Gary P. Nabhan, courtesy of Desert Botanical Garden, Phoenix, Arizona.

occasionally in O'odham fields, but are selected against because two sets of claws are associated with the likelihood of having twin children, which is considered by some women to be a burden (Nabhan and Rea 1987).

It has been suggested that devil's claw was cultivated for food (Yarnell 1977). However, seed size, number of seed per fruit, and protein content of *P. parviflora* ssp. *parviflora* var. *hohokamiana* did not increase as compared to the wild typical species, *P. parviflora* ssp. *parviflora* var. *parviflora* (Nabhan et al. 1981; Bretting 1986). Significantly, the claws were found to be disproportionately larger relative to other parts of the fruit and provided more pliable, longer fibers, thus suggesting selection for uses other than food.

Moraceae | Mulberry Family

Ficus | fig

F. brandegeei **Standley**
zalate, anabá, tezcalama, higuera cimarróna

F. palmeri **S. Watson**
anabá, igerá, higuera cimarróna, salate, tezcalama, zalate

F. pertusa **Linnaeus f. (syn.,** *F. padifolia* **Kunth)**
amezquite, chuná, chinito, comuchín, nacapuli, matapalo

F. petiolaris **Kunth**
tescalama, amacostic, amate, amate amarillo, higuera, higueron, higuerote, palo maría, tezcalama, texcalamate, texcalamatl

Ficus palmeri is found from Yubay (approximately 29°N) south to the cape region of Baja California and on Tiburón, San Pedro Mártir, and Seal Islands (Wiggins 1964). It produces fruit twice a year, in late spring and midsummer (Aschmann 1959; del Barco 1980). Each of the larger trees was said to have yielded several bushels of fruits. The amount of precipitation appears to affect the quality of the figs. Fr. Ducrue noted that "if some rain falls, the figs are passably tasty, but if there has been no rain the fruit is without juice and practically tasteless" (Aschmann 1966:51). Although the fig of *F. palmeri* "very closely resembles the European fig in its shape, but smaller," there was "no comparison with its sweetness and lusciousness [of the latter]" (del Barco 1980:125). Wild figs had "very little juice and sweetness," which made them scarcely edible. Additionally, the small receptacles are leathery and contain gritty, hard achenes. Like the early missionaries, Townsend Brandegee (1891a:149–150) was not impressed with the wild figs, which seemed to be appreciated more by the animals: "The small figs are edible, but I think no one eats many of them, and certainly would not eat any without a good appetite.... When the small figs are ripe the tree is full of animal life; numerous insects are buzzing around, attracted by the sweet exudations of the fruit, and hummingbirds are continually flying through the branches." However, despite the questionable palatability of wild figs, people ate them.

The first production of fruits in late spring may have been of considerable importance to the inhabitants of the southern part of the central desert region of Baja California, where these plants are most abundant (Aschmann 1959). At this time these people experienced an acute shortage of other edible plants. Still, the missionaries expressed surprise that the natives, who called the fruits and plants *anaba,* would travel so far and suffer so much to acquire the fruits, as described by Fr. del Barco (1980:125–126): "Even though these would-be figs are not very good tasting, the Indians like them very much. Whenever it is known that one of these fig trees has ripe fruit, though it may be removed a distance of four or more leagues, the Indians go out in the morning to enjoy this fruit. They eat their fill, and what remains in the afternoon they bring home to their family in a net." The fig harvesters would climb the branches to procure as many fruits as possible (Aschmann 1959), which is a dangerous practice because the wood of fig trees is very "vitreous and breaks easily" (del Barco 1980:126). The ability of the women to harvest figs and other plant foods impressed del Barco (1980:126): "in this and similar projects the women are not less diligent nor more careless than the men. On the contrary, except for hunting and fishing, they do a better job." Once they had collected the fruits, the Cochimí cooked (probably roasted) and ate them.

Ficus brandegeei is endemic to Baja California, growing from the eastern escarpment of the Sierra de la Giganta, near Loreto, and in the cape region (Wiggins

1964). I expect that its fruits were used for food to some extent by the inhabitants of southern Baja California, including the Huichiti, Pericú, Guaicura, and southern Cochimí. However, I am unaware of its use being specifically documented. Ira Wiggins (1964) noted that nearly ripe fruits were collected in November.

Ethnobotanist Edward Palmer noted that *F. palmeri* fruits were eaten by the inhabitants of San Pedro Mártir Island, where he reported the plants to be rare (Watson 1889). This area in the Gulf of California overlaps portions of the areas originally occupied by the Seri. Here, this fig is the largest tree that produces fruits in the early spring and late fall, at which time they were collected by the Seri (Felger and Moser 1985, cited as *F. petiolaris* ssp. *palmeri* Felger and Lowe). They cooked the fruits in water with sea turtle oil until soft or ate the fruits fresh, being careful not to eat too many lest a headache develop.

Ficus pertusa grows from central Sonora south to Panama, whereas *F. petiolaris* grows from northern Sonora south to Guerrero and Morelos (Wiggins 1964). Edward Palmer noted that *F. pertusa,* which was found growing wild in the nearby mountainous canyons, was cultivated near Guaymas, Sonora (Watson 1889, cited as *F. fasciculatus* and *F. sonorae*). He thought the black fruits to be edible. Fr. Nentvig (1980:40) noted that in the "crags of mountains, canyons, and ravines" grew a "good-sized tree" that "thrust its roots into the rocky fissures." The local inhabitants called both the tree and fruit, which tasted like the common fig, *sassata.* Nentvig was undoubtedly referring to a wild fig, presumably *F. pertusa* or *F. petiolaris.* The Eudeve ate the fruits of a fig, which they called *chuna* or *sapoc* (Pennington 1982).

Tarahumaras collected and ate the fruits of *F. pertusa* and *F. petiolaris* (Bennett and Zingg 1935; Pennington 1963; cited in both as *F. padifolia*), the latter since the 18th century at Batopilas (Pennington 1963). People collected the bitter fruits in April and May by using a long pole to which they attached a wire hook or by shaking the branches until the fruits fell to the ground. They ate the mashed fruits with tortillas or added the pulp to atole. According to Tarahumara Ramon Valenzuela, who lives just upstream from Urique, the fruits are more important as a food for wildlife than for human consumption.

Morus | mulberry

M. microphylla Buckley

Texas mulberry, mora, moral, salsa mora

Morus microphylla is occasionally found along drainages in the Southwest and northern Mexico; it flowers from April to May (Wiggins 1964). The edible fruits consist of many small, juicy drupelets aggregated into a cluster. The use of these fruits for food is not well documented. This may be due to the brief period of time when the fruits are available and the fact that they are quickly consumed by birds and other animals. I have observed only a few small populations whose plants were with fruit. With regard to the palatability of the fruits, I agree with Standley (1912) and Medsger (1966), who described them as being too small and not very juicy, but having a pleasant, acidic flavor.

Southeastern Yavapais occasionally climbed the trees to collect the fruits, but usually collected them from the ground, in July, then ate them without further preparation (Gifford 1932). Northeastern and Western Yavapais obtained mulberry fruits in the Bradshaw and Kofa Mountains (Gifford 1936). Here they collected and ate them from the ground. The Tohono O'odham filled their baskets with whole branches if the mulberries were found around their village (Castetter and Underhill 1935). Sonorans in the Río San Miguel region consumed its fruits (Felger et al. 1976), but at Quitovac fruits of the commonly grown mulberry, *M. alba* L., were eaten fresh or in jellies (Nabhan et al. 1982). For both the Tohono O'odham and River Pima, mulberry was more important for the making of bows (see Russell 1908; Rea 1997).

Groups inhabiting areas outside the Sonoran Desert also ate mulberry fruits. These include the Hualapai (Watahomigie et al. 1982; the photograph depicts *M. alba*), Tarahumara, Ópata, and possibly Havasupai. The Tarahumara and Tepehuan ate the fruits raw or mashed and added to atole (Pennington 1963, 1969). Fr. Nentvig thought the small berries to be very tasty (Nentvig 1980, cited as *M. nigra*).

People used other parts of the plant for food and weapons. The Tarahumara (Bennett and Zingg 1935; Pennington 1963; Bye 1976, *Bye 6078,* ASU) and Tepehuan (Pennington 1969) cooked and ate the young leaves as a *quelite.* Fr. Nentvig noted that the Ópata did not use the leaves "which are utilized in other provinces" (Nentvig 1980:43). The Tarahumara also used a white sap for curdling milk to make cheese after collecting it off the branches (*Bye 6078*, ASU). Tarahumaras also valued *M. microphylla* for making bows, and it is suggested that they propagated the plants around their settlements (Pennington 1963).

Morus microphylla may have been introduced in Havasu Canyon (Kearney et al. 1960) and Cataract Canyon (Weber and Seaman 1985), both of which are within Havasupai country. It is not known whether the Havasupai ate the fruits, although they probably used the branches for making bows (Weber and Seaman 1985).

One additional nonfood use is worth mentioning. Fr. Andrés Pérez de Ribas (1968:102) noted that the "Yaquis, both men and women, stain their faces and arms with the juice of wild mulberry tree, which makes a dye of orange color." Its use as a dye plant did not diminish with time. Tomas Antonio Robertson (*in* Pérez de Ribas 1968:102) added that, "in the earlier years of the 20th century the dye of the wild mulberry was so esteemed that hundreds of carloads of mora wood were shipped into the U.S. to be transformed into dyes."

Nyctaginaceae | Four-o'clock Family

Boerhavia | spiderling

B. coulteri **(Hooker f.) S. Watson**
Coulter's spiderling

There is little documentation on the use of spiderlings for food. Coulter spiderling was one of the few greens used by the Seri, who cooked, mashed, and ate the green herbage (Felger and Moser 1985).

Boerhavia was recovered at archaeological sites at La Ciudad and at North Daisy Mountain in the New River Mountains north of Phoenix (Bohrer 1986). The Hohokam may have used the plants to provide steam when pit-baking other plants (Bohrer 1984), such as agaves or chollas. The Hohokam may have tolerated or encouraged *Boerhavia* at La Ciudad in areas that were intentionally burned, thus reducing soil moisture loss (and possibly slowing water runoff) in their fields.

Pisonia | catchbirdtree, devil's-claw

P. capitata **(S. Watson) Standley**
Mexican devil's-claw, gumbro, garambullo, bainora preito, bynora, caloca, cacoca, garabato

Little is known about the use of *P. capitata* for food. Howard S. Gentry described *garambullo* in characteristic fashion: "man and animal eat the orange berries [technically they are leathery achenes], very thorny, one of the wicked detainers to the brush traveler" (*Gentry 1273*, ARIZ). The Tarahumara used the plants (probably the fruits) for food (Bye 1976).

Salpianthus

S. macrodontus **Standley**
guayavilla

Salpianthus macrodontus produces large, fleshy roots that are up to seven centimeters in diameter and one meter in length. These roots were once one of the primary sources of food for the Guarijío (Gentry 1942, with an excellent photograph [plate 3, fig. 2] of exposed roots). They pounded, dried, and ground the roots into a fine powder, which they mixed with a small amount of water to make tortillas. By the late 1930s, Guarijios no longer ate the roots of *guayavilla*, because they had maize (Gentry 1942). By 1997, "most Guarijios had no name for the plant" (Martin et al. 1998:402).

Orobanchaceae | Broom-rape Family

Orobanche | broom-rape, cancer-root

***O. cooperi* (A. Gray) Heller (syn., *O. ludoviciana* Nuttall var. *cooperi* [A. Gray] Beck)**
broom-rape

***O. fasciculata* Nuttall**
clustered broom-rape

The fleshy, succulent, parasitic stems (both above and below ground) of broom-rapes, particularly the very thick stems of *O. cooperi,* provided food and moisture to various desert people, including the Cocopa, O'odham, and Cahuilla (Palmer 1878; Vasey and Rose 1891b, cited as *Aphyllon californicum;* Rusby 1907; Sparkman 1908; Chamberlain 1911; Curtin 1949; Vestal 1952; Bell et al. 1980; Nabhan et al. 1989a; Rea 1997).

I personally have learned that its stems are edible only at a particular stage of development. After finding *O. cooperi* with its beautiful, purple flowers in the sands of Cactus Plain, La Paz County, Yvonne Fortier and I eagerly bit into its very tempting, large, succulent, albeit gritty stems. They tasted terribly bitter. Upon relating this to our friend Culver Cassa, he patiently informed us that only the very young stems, which had just broken the ground's surface, were eaten. Indeed, one Tohono O'odham explained to Amadeo Rea (1997) that some of the broom-rapes were good to eat, but only if picked young and small, when they first began to emerge. The soft, underground stem is eaten raw and is sweet or somewhat bitter (opinions varied). Upon collection, the stems soon turn black. Older stems, particularly where they become hard, are very bitter and not used for food.

Broom-rapes were probably a more significant food for the River Pima at the turn of the century (Rea 1997). The stems resemble asparagus, and the Pima ate them raw or boiled or roasted the stems in ashes (Russell 1908). Whole plants of *O. cooperi* were cooked "without the addition of salt or sugar or other substance" (Hrdlička 1908:264). Leonora Curtin (1949:49, cited as *O. ludoviciana*) noted that "the tender young sprouts resemble asparagus and, although bitter, are used in the same manner." George Webb told Curtin the River Pima cooked the stems by covering them with hot ashes and baking them in the fireplace, a practice still done by "a few of the old people" in the early 1940s. They ate the lower part of the stem, but discarded the upper part. It is possible that *O. cooperi* was a starvation food source for the Gila River Pima. Amadeo Rea (1997) suggested that perhaps it was a significant food because it was available in the late winter and spring, when food supplies were often more limited. Older River Pimas knew of the plant and how it was once used for food, although they no longer eat it.

Orobanche cooperi stems were a significant food source to the Hiá ceḍ O'odham (Bell et al. 1980; Nabhan et al. 1989a). Miguel Velasco related to Ofelia Zepeda (1985) that they once gathered and ate broom-rape stems and sandfood *(Pholisma sonorae).* The Cahuilla harvested the young and tender underground stems of *O. cooperi* before it flowered, then roasted the stems in hot coals (Barrows 1900, cited as *O. ludoviciana*). They used the plant rarely in the 1960s, although older Cahuillas, like the River Pima, recalled using the stems for food (Bean and Saubel 1972, cited as *O. ludoviciana* var. *cooperi*). The stems were gathered from April to June.

Cocopas ate the stems of *O. cooperi,* but first boiled the stems to rid them of the bitter taste (Vasey and Rose 1891b). One Seri band cooked the stems in ashes for several hours (Felger and Moser 1976, 1985).

Little is known on the use of *O. fasciculata* by any group. Ramah Navajos were said to have baked the stems in ashes before eating them. However, Ramah Navajos either said they never heard of its use as food or knew of it but did not know how to prepare the stems (Vestal 1952). According to Chamberlain (1911, cited as *Aphyllon fasciculatum*), Gosiutes sometimes ate the stems.

Oxalidaceae | Woodsorrel Family

Oxalis | woodsorrel

O. albicans **Humboldt, Bonpland, and Kunth**
radish-root woodsorrel, hierba aigre, socoyole

O. stricta **Linnaeus**
upright yellow woodsorrel

Tepehuans boiled, drained and salted the "piquant" leaves of *O. stricta* and *O. stricta* (Pennington 1969), and Mountain Pima children ate the acidic young stems of *O. albicans* (Laferrière et al. 1991).

Passifloraceae | Passion-flower Family

Passiflora | passion-flower

P. arida **(Masters & Rose) Killip**
granadilla, rosal de la pasion, flor de la pasion, bolsita de la vibora

P. bryonioides **Kunth**
cupped passion-flower

P. foetida **Linnaeus**
scarlet-fruit passion-flower, corona de Cristo

P. palmeri **Rose**
granadilla, sandía de la pasion, bolsita de la vibora

The native passion-flowers in northern Mexico and the United States are not as conspicuous as those of the tropical areas, where some species are highly prized as ornamentals that bear large, showy flowers or edible fruit. Of the approximately 400 known species of *Passiflora,* about 50 or 60 species bear edible fruit (Martin and Nakasone 1970). Those cultivated for their fruit are often called *granadillas* (Lawrence 1951).

The fruits of Sonoran Desert passion-flowers did not constitute an important food source because they generally are dry within. However, fruits of *P. foetida* (fig. 134), *P. arida, P. palmeri,* and *P. bryonioides* are edible. *Passiflora foetida* is widely distributed in the Southwest and throughout Mexico, and this species grows near Mulegé, Baja California. Its fruit pulp has a pleasant, agreeable, sweet, slightly acidic, although "over-concentrated" taste (Martin and Nakasone 1970). Because of their excellent aroma, its fruits continue to be used to flavor drinks and juices. Fresh fruits are eaten without preparation or used for flavoring and can be stored for short periods.

Passiflora arida and *P. palmeri* grow throughout much of the southern three-fourths of Baja California, the latter growing mainly along the east coast of the Gulf

FIGURE 134. ***Passiflora foetida*** L. var. ***arizonica*** Killip. with juicy, pleasant-tasting, light green fruit. Gentry Agroecology Project, Desert Botanical Garden, Phoenix, Arizona, August 1988.

of California (Wiggins 1964). Fr. del Barco (1980:192–193) provided valuable information regarding both introduced and native species of *Passiflora* in Baja California and their use or lack of use by the inhabitants. He described a type of passion-flower called *rosal de la pasion* in Spain, so named because "its roses or flowers contain the signs of the Passion of our Lord Jesus Christ." Although it produced no fruit in Spain, plants fruited prolifically in New Spain, where it was extensively cultivated. People in Mexico liked the juicy, refreshing fruits of this introduced passion-flower very much. del Barco did not know why it was called *granadilla* as "it has absolutely no resemblance to pomegranates." This introduced passion-flower was not known, "nor was it found in New Spain until the Philippines were conquered and it was brought from there [or possibly from Peru]." The people also called it *granadilla de China* because "the people there [in Mexico] equated the Philippines with China, as well as the adjacent islands" (those people living in the Philippines who came to New Spain were called *chinos*, or Chinese).

Fr. del Barco (1980:192–193) recognized another kind of passion-flower, probably representing one of the native species: "When, a long time afterward [after the Philippines were conquered], the province of Texas was conquered, the Spaniards found it [passion-flower] there, because that country produces it on its own. Lately it has been found also in [Lower] California, where it grows in the courses of some arroyos without benefit of any cultivation." It is assumed that the passion-flower found in Texas was *P. foetida* and that the passion-flowers found growing along the arroyos of Baja California were *P. arida, P. fruticosa* Killip, or *P. palmeri*. These passion-flowers left much to be desired as an edible food, as noted by Fr. del Barco (1980:193): "But the plant is much smaller than that of New Spain [the cultivated species], originally from the Philippines, the bush as well as the flower and the fruit, which is about the size of a walnut in the large plants. The Californios do not eat this fruit, nor do they pay any attention to it, perhaps because their ancestors did not judge it fit for eating, as they found it contained nothing solid, and only that thick sort of humor." I found the fruits of *P. palmeri*, collected in March, to be edible, but not very juicy (*Hodgson 8836 et al.*, DES, ASU, SD, BCMEX).

However, not all people found the palatability of native passion-flowers to be questionable. Edward Palmer noted that the children on Carmen Island (in the Gulf of California, approximately 195 kilometers south of Guaymas, Sonora) relished the ripe, sweetish tasting fruit of *P. palmeri* (Rose 1892). Seris ate the fruits of *P. palmeri*, which they described as being sweet and having a smell like cantaloupe (Felger and Moser 1985). They ate the fruits fresh or sometimes cooked with meat. The Seri referred to *P. arida* as "coyote's passion vine" because of the inferior quality of its fruit as compared to those of *P. palmeri*. People compared the fragrance of *P. arida* fruits to guava, but had varying opinions as to the fruits' edibility and taste.

Passiflora bryonioides is occasionally found from southern Arizona in Pima County south to southern Mexico; it flowers from August through October. Its fruits mature in the fall and early winter. According to Joe Laferrière et al. (1991), Mountain Pima children occasionally eat the whitish fruits. I have found the fruits to be juicy, sweet, and pleasant tasting, but the plant's rarity precludes it as a significant food. It is not known if the fruits of *P. fruticosa* Killip or *P. mexicana* Jussieu (Mexican passion-flower), which are relatively dry and tasteless, were ever eaten.

Phytolaccaceae | Pokeberry or Pokeweed Family

Rivina | rouge plant, pigeon-berry

R. humilis Linnaeus
rouge plant, pigeon-berry, uruquiro, teihuist

The small, rose-colored, sweet, juicy fruits of *R. humilis* have a pleasant taste, but little is known on their use for food. People inhabiting western Chihuahua ate these fruits at least since the 18th century (Pennington 1963), and they were used for food and dye in Sonora (Gordon et al. 1972). In the 1950s, the Western Tarahumara collected the fruits along the lower slopes of Urique and Fuerte Canyons in October for food (Pennington 1963).

Plantaginaceae | Plantain Family

Plantago | plantain, Indian-wheat, rib-grass, way-bred

P. australis Lamarck ssp. *hirtella* (Kunth) Rahn (syn., *P. hirtella* Kunth)
Mexican plantain

P. heterophylla Nuttall
many-seeded plantain, pastora

P. lanceolata Linnaeus
buckhorn plantain, English plantain

P. major Linnaeus
common plantain, great plantain, lante, llanten

P. ovata Forsskal (syn., *P insularis* Eastwood)
woolly plantain

P. patagonica Jacquin
pursh plantain, pastora

P. rhodosperma Decaisne
red-seed plantain

P. virginica Linnaeus
pale-seed plantain

Dense populations of *Plantago* are found as winter/spring annuals following adequate winter rains in the Sonoran Desert. There seems to be relatively little written on the more xerophytic species, such as *P. ovata* and *P. patagonica,* despite their usually common occurrence.

River Pimas threshed, winnowed, and placed the seeds in water. The seeds swelled, making a mucilaginous drink, similar to that obtained from soaking the seeds of *Salvia columbariae* and *Descurainia* spp. They sometimes boiled the unground seeds in water. Ironically, the abandoned use of these three species may have been due to people's dislike of the mucilaginous texture (Rea 1997). Carl Lumholtz (1912) noted that the O'odham either ate the seeds uncooked or toasted and ground the seeds into a pinole.

Seris considered the seeds of *P. ovata* as an important food and stored the seeds in ollas (Felger and Moser 1976, 1985, cited as *P. insularis*). They mixed the seeds with sugar and sometimes water and used the glutinous mass as is or soaked it in water to make a cooling drink. The use of *Plantago* by Baja California inhabitants is not well documented. Some Baja Californians mixed the seeds of *P. ovata* with water and sugar (Hake 1980, 1983).

Plantago ovata seeds were also used for medicine, as a substitute for the true psyllium, *P. psyllium* L. (Kearney et al. 1960, cited as *P. insularis*). Its mucilaginous seeds are used for intestinal (controlling diarrhea and stimulating bowel activity), bronchial, and pulmonary problems (Millspaugh 1974; Sharma and Koul 1986). All species of *Plantago* have seed coats that are mucilaginous. Those of *P. ovata* have the highest mucilage content, nearly 20 percent (Sharma and Koul 1986). Other species, such as *P. lanceolata* and *P. major,* have only 8.9 and 5.5 percent mucilage content, respectively. *Plantago ovata* is grown in India on a large commercial scale (20,000 tons per year) for use as a laxative (Levington 1990). The mucilage attracts and absorbs water within the digestive tract, which is thus lubricated. The degree of swelling may be a measure of the swelling properties of the mucilage rather than the amount of mucilage (Sharma and Koul 1986). Like *chia,* this hygroscopic mucilage may be viscous enough to slow digestion and absorption in people's diets, thereby protecting those who are genetically predisposed to developing diabetes (Brand et al. 1990).

Much of the literature on wild food plants, both popular and ethnographic, includes a discussion of the use of the introduced plantain, *P. major,* whose leaves were eaten either raw, if young, or boiled in water, if older (Bennett and Zingg 1935; Castetter 1935; Medsger 1966; Weber and Seaman 1985).

Polygonaceae | Buckwheat Family

Antigonon | lovechain

A. leptopus Hooker & Arnott
queen's-jewels, San Miguel, San Miguelito, flor de San Miguel, vaiburin

Antigonon leptopus (fig. 135) is a perennial vine found along washes and canyons from central Sonora to Chihuahua and Oaxaca and from central Baja California to the cape region (Wiggins 1964). Its attractive, pink flowers are produced from

FIGURE 135. ***Antigonon leptopus*** Hook. & Arn. Dense, sprawling vines in flower; the area near here was visited two months later and the plants were still in full flower. Approximately seven to eight miles west of Guasabas, Sonora, July 1988.

April through November. Its roots provided food to Sonoran inhabitants.

According to an elder Pima at Ónavas, Sonora, the roots were baked for a short time and eaten during times of food shortage (Pennington 1980). The Yaqui, who called the plant *vaiburin,* ate the roots raw like jicama (or *Pachyrhizus* spp.; Watson 1889; Alvarez de Williams n.d.). Edward Palmer noted that the roots, which produced "long, black, and wiry large tubers," had a nutty flavor (Watson 1889).

Homer Aschmann (1952, 1959) believed that the Cochimí's *teddá,* whose seeds were an important food, was *A. leptopus.* Rather, *teddá* may have referred to the small annual *Oligomeris linifolia* (Vahl) J. F. Macbride (see *Oligomeris*) or, less likely, an amaranth, possibly *A. hybridus* (see *Amaranthus*).

Eriogonum | wild buckwheat

E. inflatum Torrey & Frémont
desert trumpet, Indian pipeweed, tivinagua

Little is known on the use of desert trumpet for food by Sonoran Desert people, although the young stems and leaves, which were collected in the spring, were eaten raw, boiled, or pickled (Saunders 1948; Weber and Seaman 1985). The Cahuilla gathered and ate the young stems and achenes of various species of *Eriogonum* during the spring and summer, respectively (Bean and Saubel 1972).

Rumex | dock, sorrel

R. crispus Linnaeus
curly dock, lengua de vaca

R. hymenosepalus Torrey
sand dock, cañaigre, caña agria, hierba colorada

R. violascens Rechinger f.
violet dock

Wild docks of the genus *Rumex* were a relatively versatile food source that supplied edible greens and fruits. All species have malic acid in the petioles and oxalic and citric acids in the leaf blades, which requires one to boil the leaves in more than one change of water to rid them of their sour taste.

Both the native species of dock and the introduced species, *R. crispus,* played a role in the River Pima's lives when plants were more abundant along the Salt and

FIGURE 136. ***Rumex hymenosepalus*** Torr. habit, with mature fruits and tuberlike root. Courtesy of the Mesa Southwest Museum.

Gila Rivers. Today, the native docks are absent on the reservation below the rivers' dams. At the turn of the century, Aleš Hrdlička (1908:264) noted that Pimas ate the stalks of *R. hymenosepalus* (fig. 136), which was considered a "common plant in the Gila valley." They cooked the stalks in pots or roasted them in the ashes and then ate the inside of the peeled stalks. Amadeo Rea's Pima friends had never heard of using this plant for food, although they knew that the herbage of other species were used as a *quelite* (Rea 1997). Maricopa May Makil explained to Leonora Curtin (1949) how to make a pie from the tender petioles of *R. hymenosepalus*. Although this is a relatively recent, nontraditional use, it was later substantiated by a Pima (Rea 1997). They washed and boiled the tender petioles, strained the juice, then added flour and cooked the mixture until it thickened. Sugar was combined in the sauce, which was poured into a pie crust and baked. The taste was said to be like rhubarb or lemon pie.

Rumex hymenosepalus was not so much an important food plant to the River Pima as it was an important medicinal plant, with the roots being used to treat various sores of the throat, mouth, and stomach (Rea 1997). These plants were important enough that they were transplanted and tended in a few people's yards. Its roots are rich in tannins, compounds that are known to be effective treatments for reducing infections and drying sores (Camazine and Bye 1980). One would not think of the bitter-tasting roots as a food source, but Frank Russell (1908) noted that the children "greedily devoured them." Perhaps they chewed the roots out of curiosity, as something to do, or for medicinal reasons.

In the early 1940s, the leaves of *R. crispus* and the native *R. violascens* were also used for greens throughout the Salt and Gila River reservations (Curtin 1949). Ruth Giff told Amadeo Rea (1997:206) that some people cooked these plants, but "old-time people" did not, and the plants were not "an old food." The leaves were boiled as one would prepare spinach or mixed with other greens. There has been no recorded use of dock for food by Pimas in the past 25 years. Of significance is the fact that the native docks, *R. hymenosepalus* and *R. violascens,* are not known to grow on their reservation (Rea 1997). *Rumex crispus* and *R. violascens* have been completely replaced by the more recently introduced *R. dentatus* L., a dock that River Pimas do not use.

Rumex crispus has been a significant food item to the Mohave and Quechan since its establishment and introduction. During the time of high floodwater in June, Mohave women sometimes gathered the greens while wading in water up to their waists (Stewart 1965). They broadcasted the achenes of curly dock on the Lower Colorado River banks and bottomlands in November and in the spring (Castetter and Bell 1951). No further care was given. They later gathered and cooked the emerging leaves as greens.

The achenes of docks also supplied a food item. Leonora Curtin (1949) noted that the River Pima roasted and ground the fruits of *R. crispus* in the 1940s. Quechans harvested the mature achenes later in the season, after collecting the emerging leaves (Castetter and Bell 1951). They broke off the inflorescence, which they then dried and threshed. After pounding and winnowing, they placed the fruits in a bowl with water to remove any remaining chaff (inner sepals). They never parched these fruits. The winnowed fruits were washed in several changes of water (water would not be so limiting here), ground into a flour, shaped into flat cakes, and dried before being toasted over hot coals. The Quechan occasionally mixed the meal with boiled fish or packed the hollow stems with cattail pollen before baking the stems on hot coals. The flour was also eaten as is or mixed with tepary beans or wheat flour. The meal was described as being bland, despite its tedious and time-consuming preparation.

Rumex violascens was plentiful in early spring in the Colorado River delta, thus providing the Cocopa an important food plant (Kelly 1977; Alvarez de Williams 1987). Although the leaves provided an edible green, it was the fruit that was most significant. Upon fruit maturation in early May, the Cocopa collected them, pounded the fruits in a mortar to remove the "skin" (probably inner sepals), and then placed the fruits in a bag (Kelly 1977). They leached the fruits by pouring water through the bag three or four times to remove the bitter taste, then ground the mass on a metate. This mixture was made into tortillas or boiled into gruel.

Portulacaceae | Purslane Family

Calandrinia | rock-purslane, red-maids

C. ciliata **(Ruiz & Pavón) de Candolle var.** ***menziesii*** **(Hooker) J. F. Macbride**
fringed red-maids

Little is known about the use of *C. ciliata* for food. California groups ate the tiny black seeds as pinole and the fleshy stems as a *quelite* (Chestnut 1902; Saunders 1948).

Claytonia | spring-beauty

C. perfoliata **Donn ex Willdenow**
miner's-lettuce, petota, Indian-lettuce

Documentation of *petota* for use as food by Sonoran Desert inhabitants is not known. María Beltran of Granados, Sonora, probably was referring to *petota* when she told Gary Nabhan and me that *petus,* described as having round leaves, was used as a *quelite* by a few people in the 1980s (Nabhan and Hodgson 1988). Miner's-lettuce has long been recognized as an edible food by Anglos and non-Sonoran groups, the plant being eaten raw or cooked (Yanovsky 1936). It is well known that *petota* was particularly important to early California miners' diets for the treatment of scurvy and other diseases.

Portulaca | purslane

P. oleracea **Linnaeus (including** ***P. retusa*** **Engelmann)**
common purslane, little-hogweed, verdolaga

P. pilosa **Linnaeus**
kiss-me-quick

The fleshy leaves and young stems of the weedy *P. oleracea* provided a relatively important food source that was high in vitamin C. This continues to be recognized as one of the most well-known edible greens. *Verdolaga* primarily germinates with the summer rains, soon after the germination of *Amaranthus palmeri,* but where there is irrigation, it will germinate any time from May to October (Meals for Millions Foundation 1980). *Verdolaga* is one of ten *quelites* consumed by the Tarahumara. The young seedlings are collected from the second week to the sixth week after germination in the summer and fall (Bye 1981). Fresh greens are sometimes available in grocery stores in Tucson or in the markets of Sonoran border towns. Young herbage is collected and eaten raw or, more often, cooked, sometimes with cheese, tomatoes, chiles, or onions (Rea 1997). Tipais still collect its young leaves and stems and cook them in small amounts of water with tomatoes, onions, and *chicharrones* (fried pork fat) or fried with onions and chiles (Weiss 1994).

Seeds of *Portulaca,* including *P. oleracea* and *P. pilosa,* were formerly used for food (Palmer 1878; Robbins et al. 1916; Elmore 1943; Hake 1980, 1983; Weiss 1994). However, their use was not known among the River

Pima (Rea 1997), even at the turn of this century (Russell 1908). Those who did gather the seeds were able to collect, winnow, sift, and grind large amounts of seeds into flour. Immature fruits could be gathered and saved for harvesting later because they will mature and dehisce, releasing hundreds of tiny black seeds (as I found, in a plant press). Zunis took advantage of this by gathering plants that were still in flower and placing them in large piles on mats to dry (Cushing 1920). They later beat the pile of plants to release the mature seeds.

The native, nonweedy species of purslane, *P. suffrutescens* Engelm. (shrubby purslane) and *P. halimoides* L. (syn., *P. parvula* A. Gray; silk-cotton purslane), may have been more abundant prior to the introduction of livestock (Bohrer 1978). If these plants were once used for food, their use was abandoned following *P. oleracea's* subsequent dominance as a result of habitat degradation with grazing pressures. María Estrella of Ónavas told Amadeo Rea and me that *P. suffrutescens* was not used as a *quelite*.

Resedaceae | Mignonette Family

Oligomeris | whitepuff

O. linifolia **(Vahl) J. F. Macbride**
line-leaf whitepuff, teddá

Little is known about this unassuming plant for use as a food. However, Richard Felger and Mary Moser (1976, 1985) noted that the Seris toasted and ground the seeds, then mixed the resulting meal with water to make a gruel. This and other clues may have helped to determine the identification of a plant that had been described as significant to Baja California *indigenes* in the central desert region (Clavigero 1937; Aschmann 1952, 1959, 1966; del Barco 1980).

Edward Cooke (1712:321; Andrews 1979:42; Mathes 1992:296) described a few plants he saw used by the Pericú, while exploring the cape region of Baja California: "A very small black seed they grind upon stones they have for that purpose, and then eat it by handfuls; my Men us'd to thicken their broth with it, and said it serv'd as well as flower [sic]. When ground and boil'd in water, it tastes somewhat like coffee."

The English pirate George Shelvocke (1726:411; Andrews 1979:99; Mathes 1992:329) also described the use of a black seed by the *indigenes* in the cape region in 1721: "What they use instead of bread is very remarkable, being a small black seed of an oily substance, which they grind in some such manner as we do our chocolate, and afterwards make it up in rolls, though the looks of it is not very inviting (being very black) yet the taste is not very disagreeable." Shelvocke apparently leaned heavily on the writings of Edward Cooke (1712) and Woodes Rogers (1712), privateers who did not go into as much detail in this case. Fr. del Barco (1980:196–198) provided a careful and lengthy description of a plant the Cochimí called *teddá*, whose seeds they highly valued for food. They developed an interesting and rather ingenious method of collecting the seeds, which were otherwise easily lost. Not only did they reduce this loss, but they established family boundaries as well:

> In years of good rains there grows in some places a plant that the Cochimies call *teddá*. It grows about one and a half handbreadths in small bunches growing out of one stalk and separated from one another. Its seeds are some grains about the size of anise. The plant sprouts, grows, and its seeds mature in a month and a half. No matter how quick they are in collecting it, when it gets ripe it falls to the ground and they lose it. In order to avoid this inconvenience, when the seed has developed but is still green the people go secure it in the following way: they take all the little branches which grow together out of each stalk, they twist them and, without breaking them, they make a knot with themselves in their highest part, which is where each little branch has a sort of spike with the seeds. Almost all of them remain thus collected into the knot, which is left loose in order that the seeds can finish ripening, but in such a way that, although they get very dry, they cannot fall on the ground. They continue in this fashion binding whatever stretch each family can manage, and with this act they take possession of it for the harvest of that year only, because each family has the right to collect that which it bound up.

Fr. del Barco continued to describe how they returned to and harvested the plants:

> When the teddá is dry they return there in order to harvest. To do this they place the tray at the foot of the stem, they bend the knot downward and undo it, and then they shake the spikes above the tray, making all the seeds fall into it. They continue realizing in this manner this harvest, which is, as far as seeds are concerned, after the medesá *[Cercidium microphyllum]* the most esteemed one for the Californios, both for its goodness as well as for its abundance with respect to the rest. This must be understood with the exception of some territories where cardón is abundant and teddá is scarce, because there the harvest of the former is probably esteemed more than that of the latter, since both seeds are very much appreciated by the Indians. I have said that the harvest of teddá is abundant with respect to that of other seeds, because really by itself it is not abundant. A family of three or four persons who work in the most copious harvest will collect only about two fanegas [approximately 3.2 bushels], apart from what they have eaten in the process of this work.

Fr. del Barco carefully described how the Cochimí toasted and stored the seeds of *teddá* (Aschmann 1966: 80–81):

> They eat the seeds toasted, and these, like any other seeds, are toasted in the following manner: they place a portion of the seeds in a flat basket, which is about the size of a *zaranda* [winnowing screen] but solid.... On top of the seeds they throw live coals, and, moving the basket with both hands, they circulate the embers through the seeds, in such a manner that while toasting the seeds they do not burn the basket. After the toasting has been completed they separate the embers, which by then are reduced to charcoal, and a large part of the seeds have popped as the result of heat, exposing within a white flour. Afterwards they clean out the husks [probably bracts and capsule walls] from which the seeds have come, winnowing in their flat baskets with the same dexterity that is used in Spain when winnowing wheat in *zarandas.* Thus cleaned, they grind the kernels and eat the flour which has been produced; or they cook it and make mush or cakes of it. The latter type of cooking occurs at the present time since the Indians now possess some pottery cooking vessels, and some women who know how to cook.

The *teddá* seeds swelled up when cooked, "and it nourishes and warms up the Indians" (del Barco 1980:198). They collected "as much of this as they can because it is one of the better foods which they possess" (Aschmann 1966:80). Also, as further explained by Fr. del Barco, they "store these seeds in order to eat them from October, the month in which they are collected, on into the following months." That *teddá* was one of the few foods stored attests to its importance. The Cochimí probably parched fresh seeds before storing them, because older seeds do not expand and expose a white "flour," or endosperm, upon being parched.

Homer Aschmann (1952, 1959) believed that *teddá* was *Antigonon leptopus,* but Fr. del Barco's usual excellent description makes possible its identification as being either *Amaranthus hybridus* or, more likely, *O. linifolia. Amaranthus hybridus* flowers from June to November, producing simple or, more often, branched stems with terminal or axillary spikes. Its seeds pop like popcorn when parched, as described by Frank Russell (1908:74): "the seeds are moistened, parched, which makes it resemble popcorn, ground on the metate, and eaten by taking alternately pinches of meal and sips of water." However, although the seeds of *A. hybridis* are nearer the size of anise, they generally are paler in color. In addition, Fr. del Barco knew amaranth and was well aware of another plant providing edible seeds that the Cochimí called *bledo* (see *Amaranthus*).

Oligomeris linifolia is an erect, single-stemmed or many-branched annual, with the branches produced from the base. It flowers from March to June, its inflorescence being a densely flowered spike terminating each branch. The seeds are numerous, very small (only 0.5 millimeter long), black, smooth, and shiny. Plants often form dense stands on desert flats and along washes, chiefly in somewhat saline soils, during favorable years of winter and spring precipitation, thus providing an adequate amount of seeds to harvest. It is not known if its seeds pop, swell, and show the whiteness of the endosperm. Plants whose black seeds were used by the Pericú, as described by Cooke (1712; Andrews 1979; Mathes 1992), Rogers (1712; Andrews 1979), and Shelvocke (1726; Andrews 1979; Mathes 1992), may actually have been those of a *Mentzelia, Amaranthus,* or *O. linifolia,* but which is not certain.

However, it is certain that *A. leptopus* was not *teddá.* The inflorescence of *A. leptopus* is a raceme and not a spike. More importantly, its "seeds" are achenes and are not at all like the fruits of anise, do not fall when shaken, do not "pop" or expose a white flour when parched, and taste terribly bitter.

Rhamnaceae | Buckthorn Family

Condalia | snakewood, gray-thorn

C. brandegeei **I. M. Johnston**

C. warnockii **M. C. Johnston var.** *kearneyana* **M. C. Johnston**

Warnock's snakewood, squawbush, crucillo

Condalia warnockii var. *kearneyana* is found from south-central Arizona south into central Sonora; it flowers from March through November in response to rain (Turner et al. 1995). The ethnographic literature often erroneously refers to *C. spathulata* as producing edible fruits occasionally eaten by the Tohono O'odham (Standley 1912; Castetter and Underhill 1935; Curtin 1949; Hedrick 1972). In all probability, the plant referred to was *C. warnockii* var. *kearneyana.* Plants can be easily confused with *C. globosa* I. M. Johnst. var. *pubescens* I. M. Johnst., which has extremely bitter-tasting fruits. Those of *crucillo* are not bitter, although they do have a somewhat soapy taste. Every bitter condalia may not have bitter fruit because the bitter principle is not found in some populations (Johnston 1962b). One can avoid an unpalatable experience by distinguishing the two condalias based on characteristics other than fruit taste. The pedicels of *C. warnockii* are much shorter than those of *C. globosa,* being only 0.5–3.0 millimeters long as compared to pedicels 2.5–6.5 millimeters long in the latter. *Condalia warnockii* has sepals that are usually persistent in fruit and a stone that is much longer than wide (fig. 137a). *Condalia globosa* has sepals usually deciduous in fruit and a stone that is nearly as wide as long (fig. 137b). Additionally, the two species occupy climatically distinct regions (Turner et al. 1995). *Condalia warnockii* var. *kearneyana* grows at elevations between 500 and 1,700 meters in areas that experience biseasonal rainfall, within the Arizona Upland in Arizona. *Condalia globosa* grows below 1,200 meters. Its range is west of that of *C. warnockii* var. *kearneyana,* in areas whose rainfall is almost entirely in the summer in the south to almost entirely in the winter in north-central Baja California, within the Lower Colorado River valley in Arizona.

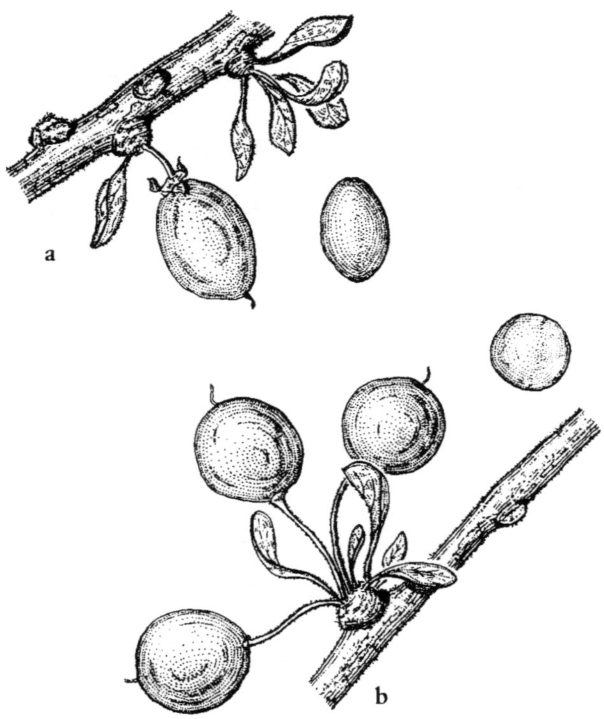

FIGURE 137. ***Condalia*** spp. **a. *Condalia warnockii*** M. C. Johnston var. ***kearneyana*** M. C. Johnston mature fruits and seed, Douglas, Cochise County, Arizona, September 1975 (*Earle s.n.,* DES); **b. *C. globosa*** Johnston var. ***pubescens*** Johnston mature fruits and seed, Kofa Mountains, La Paz County, Arizona, June 1975 (*Engard 547,* DES).

Little pulp is available in proportion to the relatively large seed. The Tohono O'odham often ate the fruits of *C. warnockii* var. *kearneyana* without preparation in the summer (Castetter and Underhill 1935, cited as *C. spathulata*).

Crucillo may have been encouraged or cultivated by the Hohokam at La Ciudad, the present location of Phoenix, Arizona (Bohrer 1991). Many of its stones were found in the trash pits and house floors through all periods of occupation, from A.D. 800 to 1100. The stones were relatively large, ranging in size from four to seven millimeters in length. Modern *crucillo* fruits are from three to six millimeters in length, with smaller stones. *Crucillo* is not known to grow in and around the Salt River valley nor has it been recovered from other Hohokam sites within the present range of *crucillo.* It has been suggested that sprouts may have developed from discarded or planted stones in the village and encouraged to grow (V. Bohrer, pers. comm.). Another plant producing edible fruits with stones similar in size and shape to *crucillo* is gray-thorn, *Ziziphus obtusifolius* var. *canescens,* a shrub commonly found along the floodplains of the Salt and Gila Rivers (see *Ziziphus*).

Condalia brandegeei is endemic to central Baja California, where it grows in canyons and on slopes (Wiggins 1964). Little is known about the edibility of its fruits, despite it having a more copious amount of pericarp relative to fruits of *C. warnockii*. These relatively large, pulpy fruits with large stones taste good (*Hodgson 9525 & Rebman,* DES, SD) and were probably eaten by Baja California inhabitants.

Karwinskia | coyotillo

K. humboldtiana **(J. A. Schultes) Zuccarini**
coyotillo, cachila, cacachila, china, tullidor, arbor que tulle, palo aspestoso

K. parvifolia **Rose**
buckthorn, cacachila, tuyidor, tullidor, capulincillo, capulincillo cimarrón, capulin, palo negrito, margarita, frutillo negrito, margarita del cerro

Karwinskia humboldtiana is found in central to southern Baja California and southern Texas south to Tamaulipas, Yucatan, and Oaxaca, whereas *K. parvifolia* (fig. 138) grows from central Sonora south into northern Sinaloa (Wiggins 1964). The two species may not be specifically distinct (see Turner et al. 1995).

The bluish purple fruits of both species are considered edible and sweet. However, there are numerous accounts of how the fruits, if eaten in excess, can cause paralysis and trembling in the legs, particularly in children. Indeed, the common name "arbor que tulle" means "the tree that cripples" (Carter *in* del Barco 1980:138). At San Bernardo, Sonora, the fruits were eaten, but they caused boys to become weak and tremble (*Gentry 1161,* ARIZ). Yaquis refer to the plant as *tuyidor* and consider the fruits to be very sweet (Alvarez de Williams n.d.). However, children who eat the stones generally get sick, as evidenced by one Yaqui father who noted that his child ate a large number of fruits and fell ill. A doctor could do nothing to help the child, but after administering domestic remedies, the youngster recovered. Edward Palmer noted that Tamaulipas children, so paralyzed, "are taken to a slaughter pen, and stomachs of freshly killed cattle are wrapped about the parts affected, an outer covering being employed to retain the warmth" (Standley 1923:717).

Baja California inhabitants looked upon *K. humboldtiana* differently. Fr. del Barco described the fruits as being "black and the size of a small garbanzo when ripe" (del Barco 1980:138). He further noted that, among the Cochimí, "grown up people do not eat it because they know it is patently injurious," although some children could not resist the juicy fruit: "Some children, either because they did not know this, or because they tasted it as a prank, and because it seemed all right to them, they were encouraged to eat a great quantity of it. I was witness to their becoming, in a few days, crippled. They remained like that for some months, then they experienced other accidents and they finally died."

FIGURE 138. ***Karwinskia parvifolia*** Rose var. ***pubescens*** (Standl.) Wiggins. Flowering shrub; note black glands on leaf margins. Located 6.3 miles west of Guasabas, Sonora, July 1988 (*Hodgson 5093 & DeLamater,* DES).

Even missionaries were said to have "tried to exterminate the plant everywhere" because of its potentially dangerous fruits (Clavigero 1937:56). While traveling into what was believed Cora and Pericú territory (these may have been Guaicura; see Mathes 1975b), Fr. del Barco noticed that some women at Mission Santiago carried a large quantity of this fruit in their baskets and intended to eat them. Upon recognizing the fruits and the women's intent, Fr. del Barco (1980:138) tried to dissuade them from eating the fruits: "But they would not be persuaded and they replied to me that the seeds

FIGURE 139. ***Ziziphus obtusifolius*** (Hook. ex Torr. & A. Gray) A. Gray var. *canescens* (A. Gray) M. C. Johnston. Branch with mature fruits and large seeds. Salt River Project right-of-way, South Mountain, Maricopa County, Arizona, May 1988.

[stones] were the ones that were bad and for that reason they did not eat them, but threw them out instead." He had no doubt that they were "speaking from long experience," and also recognized differences in the use of this plant by two neighboring cultures: "At the same time I became aware that the Pericúe were ahead of the Cochimies in their knowledge of this small fruit as these last ones [Cochimí] did not know how to make this distinction." Of interest too is the fact that Fr. del Barco "generally insisted on the superior ability of the Cochimí but admitted in this instance that the Pericú had a better understanding of the properties of plants such as this one" (Carter *in* del Barco 1980:138–139).

The toxic principles are anthracenones (Lampe and McCann 1985). When eaten, progressive paralytic neuropathy occurs, possibly ending in respiratory paralysis. Weakness arises only after a latent period of several weeks and paralysis may progress for a month or more. In severe cases in which the patient survives, recovery is slow and almost always incomplete.

Ziziphus | gray-thorn, jujube

Z. *amole* (Sessé & Moçiño) M. C. Johnston
amole, amole dulce, nanche de la costa, frutillo, manzanita, brasilillo

Z. *obtusifolius* (Hooker ex Torrey & A. Gray) A. Gray var. *canescens* (A. Gray) M. C. Johnston
gray-thorn, gray-leaved abrojo, lotebush, abrojo, papache, bachata, barbachatas, palo blanco, white crucillo, garrapata, garambullo

Z. *parryi* Torrey
Parry's jujube

Little is known about the use of *Z. amole* and *Z. parryi* fruits for food. *Ziziphus amole* reaches its northern limit in the Sonoran Desert in south-central Sonora (Turner et al. 1995). Although cited by Wiggins (1964) as growing in the cape region of Baja California, plants have yet to be found (Turner et al. 1995). Fruits of *Z. amole* are considered edible (Altschul 1973; *Hinton 3795, 5520*, DES), although they were also used as a substitute for soap (Standley 1923; Johnston 1963).

Ziziphus parryi grows on dry slopes from southeastern California south into northeastern Baja California; it flowers from February to April (Wiggins 1964, 1980). The Cahuilla gathered, dried, and ground its fruits into meal for atole (Barrows 1900, cited as *Condaliopsis parryi*) or ate them fresh (Bean and Saubel 1972, cited as *Condalia parryi*). They also made flour by grinding and leaching the seeds. In June, Mohaves and Maricopas gathered the "blue-black berries," which they ate after mashing the fruits in a basket to form a "foamy concoction" (Spier 1933, cited only as "crucifixion-thorn"; Castetter and Bell 1951).

Of the three species, *Z. obtusifolius* var. *canescens* (fig. 139) played the most significant role as a gathered food plant. The plant is widely distributed throughout the Sonoran Desert, but is absent on the Lower Colorado River (Johnston 1963; Turner et al. 1995). River Pimas gathered the fruits in basket bowls after they beat the plant down with sticks (Russell 1908, cited as *Z. lycioides*), a necessary procedure due to the plant's exceedingly thorny nature. Salt River Pimas considered the black fruits to be very sweet when fully ripe; they ate the fruits raw and discarded the seeds (Curtin 1949, *Curtin 38*, DES). They made a syrup by boiling the fruits in water, squeezing the water out by hand (seeds were thrown to the chickens), and allowing the sweet juice to cool and thicken. George Kyyitan told how he used to harvest the small fruits amid the numerous, very thorny branches (Rea 1997). He and his family would go across the Gila River early in the morning with a piece of canvas, which they put under the plant. They beat on the plant with a stick, then shook its branches to cause the fruits to fall on the canvas. Like the Salt River Pima, the Gila River Pima also ate the fruits raw. Sylvester Matthias knew that sometime before his generation, they made syrup from the fruits.

At Quitovac, Sonora, the Tohono O'odham ate the fruit and spit out the seeds (Nabhan et al. 1982; Felger et al. 1992). Maricopas ate the fruits of a *condalia* fresh, roasted in a frying pan, or cooked, strained, and boiled into a syrup (Hrdlička 1908, cited as *C. obovata*). This syrup was used on bread "or otherwise." The Seri often collected the fruits from packrat nests and ate the fruits without further preparation (Felger and Moser 1976, 1985).

Rhizophoraceae | Mangrove Family

Rhizophora | red mangrove

R. mangle Linnaeus
mangle, red mangrove, candelón, mangle dulce, mangle colorado, mangle rojo, mangle salado, mangle zapatero, mangle gateador

Use of *R. mangle* for food represents an interestingly efficient, creative way of using an available resource. The zygote develops into a seedling without an intervening seed stage (Turner et al. 1995). The reproductive unit, or propagule, is the hypocotyl (part of the embryo below the cotyledons that develops into the radical, or first root), which develops within and emerges from the fruit. It can grow 20 to 30 centimeters before the fruit falls off the parent plant (Wiggins 1964; Gill and Tomlinson 1969). The hypocotyls are hardy, long lived, and may last a year or more while floating in fresh or saltwater (Turner et al. 1995). These green hypocotyls supplied an edible food. After cooking the hypocotyls in ashes, Seris broke the outside with a stone and consumed the inner portion with sea turtle fat (Felger and Moser 1985). The hypocotyls were available to the Seri throughout the warmer months of the year. Those that washed up on shore were considered the best to eat. Plants also provide habitat for oysters, clams, and crabs, which are food sources used by the Seri.

Rosaceae | Rose Family

Prunus | wild plum, almond, cherry, plum, peach

P. fasciculata (Torrey) A. Gray
desert almond

P. fremontii S. Watson
desert apricot

P. ilicifolia (Nuttall ex Hooker & Arnott) D. D. Dietrich
hollyleaf cherry, islay

The fruit of wild *Prunus* species is characterized by a large stone and relatively little edible pulp. Fruit pulp was generally eaten fresh, but was sometimes dried and stored for later use. Only in southern California did indigenous peoples use the pits of *Prunus* to make "wild plum seed meal" (Timbrook 1982).

Prunus ilicifolia, or *islay*, was the most important wild plum, with its pits being used extensively. Plants grow from southern California southward to the cape region of Baja California, at and above the upper elevational limits of the Sonoran Desert. The name *islay* is a Hispanicized version of *slay'*, the Salinan word for the plant (Salinan refers to a group on the California coast north of the Chumash). All peoples within the range of *islay* sought out the plants for its sweet, juicy pulp and pits. Not only are the pits edible, they are probably high in protein and oil and were an important trade item. Jan Timbrook (1982) provides an excellent review of the importance of *islay* to native peoples in California, including the methods of preparation, effects of such preparation on the probable toxicity of the pits, and role of *islay* in the social framework of the cultures who depended on its fruits.

Pits were generally piled up until the pulp rotted and could be discarded, then shelled and further dried (Timbrook 1982). The pits were pounded or ground into a meal, this sometimes leached to remove more of the bitter taste. Leaching was done by steeping the pits in several changes of water or by pouring water through the ground meal. The meal was often roasted or cooked in water as mush and formed into cakes.

The Cahuilla were especially fond of the fruits. Ken Hedges (1985) suggested that the presence of *islay* may have played an important role in locating Cahuilla and possibly Southern Diegueño village sites. However, Frederick Hicks (1963:140) noted that *islay* does not "ordinarily occur in groves of sufficient extent to warrant semi-permanent camps for its exploitation." *Islay* and other wild plums "were usually within a short distance of acorn gathering sites, probably sought out during the acorn harvest," and "were also found within a mile or so of village sites" (Bean and Saubel 1972:120–121).

In his dissertation on the ethnobotany of the Cahuilla, David Barrows (1900:61) described the fruits and their use: "Its fruit is of a reddish-yellow color, and resembles very small gage plums. The pulp is, however, very thin and puckery and the pit preposterously large. It is the kernel of the latter and not the pulp that is mostly utilized. These plums are gathered in very large quantities in August and are spread in the sun until the pulp is thoroughly shrunk and dried. The thin shells of the pits are then easily broken open and the kernels extracted. These are crushed in the mortar, leached in the sand basket, and boiled into the usual atole."

That the pits of *P. ilicifolia* were an important food among all groups within its range is curious considering that they (and the pits of several other species of *Prunus*) probably contain the cyanogenic glycoside amygdalin, which reacts with the hydrolyzing enzymes in plant tissue to form hydrocyanic acid (Kingsbury 1964). Those who used the pits realized that the bitter fruits could make one sick if not prepared in a special way. The cyanide content of plants varies widely, depending on environmental factors and on the plant part used. Additionally, the hydrocyanic acid content may be lower in dried plant parts than in fresh parts, as was found for the leaves of *Prunus*. Drying the pits before and after shelling may lower their hydrocyanic acid content (Timbrook 1982). The Luiseño let chokecherries (*Prunus* sp.) sit for a few days to improve the taste (Sparkman 1908), suggesting that the fruits may also lose some of their hydrocyanic acid content upon drying. Also, the preparation of pits involved pounding, leaching, steeping, and boiling, processes that may have rapidly removed more of the free cyanide (Timbrook 1982). Drying, boiling, and steeping the roots of *cassava*, or *manioc (Manihot esculenta)*, removes the free cyanide rapidly (Lancaster et al. 1982).

The use of *islay* by California groups continued after 1900, despite population decline and acculturation (Timbrook 1982). The Cahuilla no longer prepared *islay* pits in the 1960s (Bean and Saubel 1972). They were considered a harsh food that did not taste very good and, if eaten regularly, caused a stomachache. However, when families did not have enough money to buy food, *islay* often became a dietary staple (Timbrook 1982). Delfina Cuero, a Northern Diegueño woman, recalled eating the fruits and pits while growing up. She and her family all worked for food as "they [ranchers for whom they often worked] never gave the Indians money. We didn't know what money was in those days" (Shipek 1968:25). She remembered spending much time hunting for food, greens, and honey, as well as doing hard, demanding jobs. Between clearing land, cutting and erecting fence posts, and cutting firewood, she, her mother, and grandmother "used to go all over looking for wild cherries at the right time of year." They ground the seeds into flour, which was winnowed and sifted before being eaten.

The only people who may still eat *Prunus* seeds are the Tipai (Hinton 1975), who enjoy the mature fruits that they gather in August (Weiss 1994). Their method of preparation is little different than that described by Leslie Spier (1923) in the summer of 1920. After eating the pulp, they remove and set aside the stone to dry in the sun for a day. They crack the stone, then remove and grind the embryo on a metate. They pour water through the meal several times, then boil the meal in water.

People living in the Sierra de San Francisco region of south-central Baja California still eat and are fond of the fruits of *islay* (*Hodgson 9551 & Rebman,* DES, BCMEX, ASU). It is not known if they use the pits for food.

Prunus fremontii inhabits the Lower Colorado Desert from southern California near Palm Springs southward to Ensenada and near Cataviña, Baja California. Its fruit is smaller than that of *P. ilicifolia,* and its pulp is thin and relatively tasteless. These fruits are no longer gathered for food, but Cahuillas still remembered the plant as a highly prized food source in the 1960s (Bean and Saubel 1972). They gathered the fruit in June, boiled and sweetened the fruits with sugar, then stored the mixture in jars as jelly. The Cahuilla ground and leached the large pits to make mush (Hedges 1985).

Prunus fasciculata was probably less important than other *Prunus* species, but its fruits were "undoubtedly used by the Cahuilla" (Bean and Saubel 1972:119).

Rubiaceae | Madder Family

Randia | indigo-berry

R. armata (Swartz) de Candolle

R. echinocarpa Sessé & Moçiño
papache, papache picudo, papache papachon, cirián chino, chacua, grangel, tecolochapo, tecolosapo

R. laevigata Standley
sapuche, crucecilla, crucecilla de la sierra, cascalojuche

R. megacarpa Brandegee
papache grande

R. obcordata S. Watson
papache, papachillo, papache borracho

R. sonorensis Wiggins
vachata negra

R. thurberi S. Watson
papache

Randia is well represented in the flora of Mexico. Many species provided edible fruits, with the seed placentae being pulpy and edible and often constituting a significant food source to both wildlife and people.

The inhabitants of the central desert region of Baja California ate the pulpy, globose fruits of *R. megacarpa*, which were apparently not an important item in their diet (Aschmann 1959, cited as *R. watsoni*). Fr. del Barco (1980:110) compared the fruits of a plant called *sapote prieto* (possibly *R. echinocarpa*) with the *sapote* found on the peninsula (possibly *R. megacarpa*):

> This fruit [of a mainland species] is about the size of an ordinary orange, of good flavor, soft and fresh. Its seeds are thick, and its skin is green even when the fruit is ripe. This skin is also thick and unusually tender. Because of this, and because its fleshy part is a very soft and black mass, and because it would be very inconvenient to peel it with a knife, this being in addition held to show little cleanliness, a spoon is therefore used to eat it, scooping out the marrow with it and leaving the skin. The sapote that is found in the above-mentioned place in California [Sierra de la Laguna] is notably smaller than the one already mentioned, and because it is wild it is not so smooth to the palate.

The German Jesuit Fr. Nentvig (1980:42) described a type of edible fruit that "comes from a small tree about a yard in height ... and the leaves as well as the fruit resemble those of the pear tree." The plant, called *sapuche* by the Spaniards and *tesavo* by the Ópata, was not a species of *Diospyros* (as suggested by Pradeau and Rasmussen, Nentvig's translators), but more likely *R. laevigata,* a small shrub bearing obovate leaves and pear-shaped fruits. Its fruits are green when immature, but upon ripening in November they are red (Martin et al. 1998). Guarijios and Tarahumaras ate mature fruits (Gentry 1942, 1963; Pennington 1963, 1969; Altschul 1973; von Reis and Lipp 1982). Ónavas Pimas (Pennington 1980) and Tepehuans (Pennington 1969) highly valued these fruits for food. María Beltran of Granados, Sonora, related that the fruits of "a smaller *sapuche*," possibly those of *R. laevigata* or the globose fruits of *R. sonorensis,* which ripen from September to November, were still eaten in the vicinity during the late 1980s (Nabhan and Hodgson 1988). Yaquis also consumed the mature fruits of *R. laevigata* and *R. sonorensis* (Alvarez de Williams n.d.). The only known reference to the use of *R. armata* is that of Paul Standley who noted that its fruits were eaten in El Salvador (Altschul 1973).

The rather odd-looking fruits of *R. echinocarpa* (figs. 140, 141b) also supplied food. The Guarijío, Tarahumara, Ónavas Pima, and Tepehuan gathered the green fruits as they began to ripen in the fall (Gentry 1942; Pennington 1963, 1969, 1980; Altschul 1973; pers. obs.). If the fruits were left on the plants to ripen, "strong-billed birds" and mammals were sure to consume them (Gentry 1942; Martin et al. 1998:431). The black, puddinglike mass has a bittersweet flavor and is full of seeds. Babies were especially fond of the pulp. These groups ate the pulp in large amounts with the seeds, which often caused constipation (H. S. Gentry, pers. comm.). Howard Gentry once ate the fruits for lunch, while in the wilds of Río Mayo country, having nothing else to eat (Martin et al. 1998). He enjoyed the first fruit, but could not finish the second because the fruits were very filling. *Randia echinocarpa* (and other members of the genus) fruits are important medicinally, being used to aid digestion and diabetes.

Birds and people alike eagerly sought the fruits of *R. thurberi* and "one seldom saw a fruit from which birds hadn't extracted the pulpy blackberry jam–like interior"

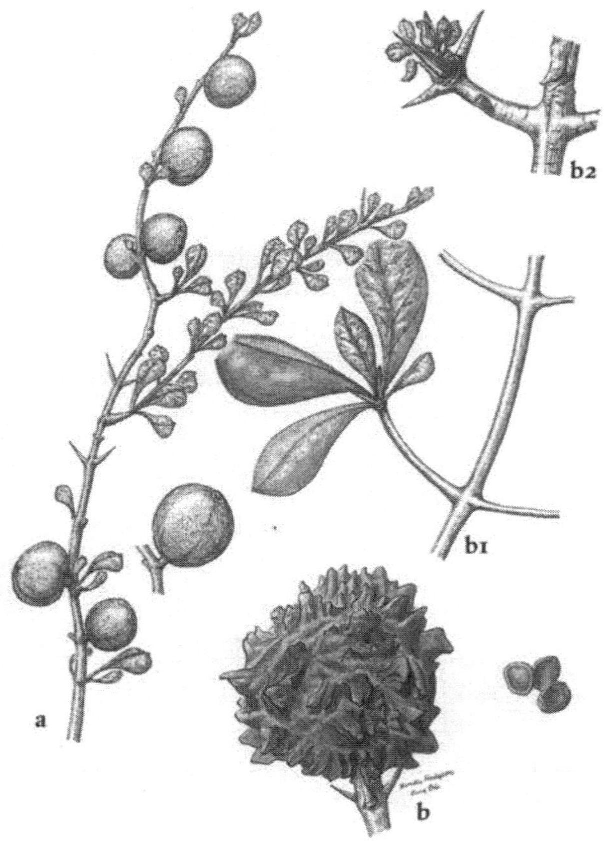

FIGURE 140. ***Randia echinocarpa*** Sessé & Moçiño branch with immature fruits. Approximately seven miles west of Alamos, Sonora, November 1987.

FIGURE 141. ***Randia*** spp. **a. *Randia obcordata*** S. Wats. branch and mature fruits, Desert Botanical Garden, Phoenix, Arizona; **b. *R. echinocarpa*** fruit and seeds, Alamos, Sonora, February 1953 (*Blakely 1698,* DES); **b1.** branch and leaves, Alamos, Sonora, February 1953 (*Blakely 1698,* DES); **b2.** branch with spines, Temascaltepec, Mexico, May 1935 (*Hinton 7817,* DES).

(Standley 1926; Altschul 1973). The mature yellowish green, globose fruits can be found from August to April (Turner et al. 1995). Seris, especially children, ate the sweet black pulp fresh, but the fruits were not considered a "regular food" (Felger and Moser 1985). The inhabitants around Guaymas, Sonora, also ate the fruits (Watson 1889).

According to Campbell Pennington (1980), Ónavas Pimas considered the fruits of *R. obcordata* (fig. 141a) as a delicacy. When eaten in quantity, however, the black, wrinkly fruits caused one to become drunk. Howard Gentry (1942) noted that the fruits were "sickening to humans," thus the common name, *papache borracho,* or "drunk."

Sapotaceae | Sapote or Sapodilla Family

Sideroxylon | bully

S. occidentale (Hemsley) Pennington
bebelama

Sideroxylon occidentale (fig. 142) grows as scattered populations from Comondú south to the cape region of Baja California and throughout much of Sonora (Wiggins 1964; Turner et al. 1995). Mature fruits are relatively large (1.5 centimeters long), blue-black, and usually have one seed embedded in a juicy

FIGURE 142. ***Sideroxylon occidentale*** (Hemsl.) Pennington. Branch with flower buds (left); note close-up of leaves and immature, green fruits (right). South of Hermosillo, Sonora, June 1975 (*Engard 551B & Gentry*, DES).

pericarp. Fresh fruits were considered sweet (*Gentry 17740*, ARIZ), and fruits were also edible dried (Altschul 1973). Seris harvested the fruits two or three times per year and ate the fruits fresh (Felger and Moser 1985, cited as *Bumelia occidentalis*). However, if one ate too much of the fresh fruit, one's mouth became sore (Bennett and Zingg 1935, cited as *B. occidentalis*). Women collected, spread out, and dried large quantities of fruits. The fruit, with the seeds removed, was safe to eat in unlimited quantities by that evening. The taste was described as being similar to that of raisins. Seris did not store the fruits, but extended the harvest period by collecting them from packrat nests.

Yaquis knew the plant as *bebelama de las aguas* and ate the fruits directly off the plant (Alvarez de Williams n.d., cited as *Bumelia occidentalis*). In Ópata territory in central Sonora, Fr. Nentvig (1980:42) described the fruits, which were called *bebelama* by the Spaniards and *juco* by the Ópata, as being quite sweet. However, he added "although they are terribly hot, there seem to be no ill effects upon the stomachs of the natives who ate them in large quantities in May, the time when this fruit ripens." He further described the tree from which the fruit came as being "of medium size" and with "small, tongue-shaped leaves." It is apparent that he is referring to the fruits of *S. occidentalis* (not *Bumelia laetivirens*, as determined by Pradeau and Rasmussen, Nentvig's translators).

There appears to be no reference to the use of *S. leucophyllum* S. Watson fruits for food by southern Baja California inhabitants. Townsend Brandegee (1900–1901:107) described the tomentose drupes as being white, with a fleshy pericarp. *Sideroxylon persimile* (Hemsley) Pennington ssp. *subsessiliflora* (Hemsley) Pennington, called *bebelama*, grows near the limits of the Sonoran Desert. Its blackish green fruits are very good to eat when ripe, during May and June east of Ónavas, Sonora (*E. Joyal 1970*, DES, ASU). Natives in the Río Mayo area usually cooked the fruits first to avoid burning their lips (Martin et al. 1998).

Simmondsiaceae | Jojoba Family

Simmondsia | jojoba, deernut

S. chinensis **(Link) Schneider**
jojoba, goatnut, deernut

Simmondsia chinensis (fig. 143) is commonly found in the arid zones of southern Arizona and California south into central Baja California and Sonora (Wiggins 1964; Rebman 1995b). These dioecious shrubs flower from December through July. The large seed of jojoba has been used for food and medicine. Although some consider jojoba seeds to be too bitter for consumption, I find them a welcomed, good-tasting snack that are potentially available throughout much of the year.

The Tohono O'odham ate the fruit fresh or parched (Castetter and Underhill 1935). Lower Colorado River groups used jojoba to some extent, supposedly gathering the fruits as they traveled (Castetter and Bell 1951). They molded the shelled seeds into an oily cake from which portions were broken off as needed and boiled slightly. The Hiá ceḍ O'odham were said to have used the seeds for medicine (Bolton 1948). Fr. Kino noted the presence of "much medicinal jojoba," while traveling in the gulf region in Hiá ceḍ O'odham territory. He described the fruits as being "like the almond, and with a very salutary and effective remedy for different kinds of sickness" (Bolton 1948 II:162). The Cahuilla only used the fruit in the preparation of a coffeelike beverage, which was made by roasting and grinding the seeds (Barrows 1900).

FIGURE 143. ***Simmondsia chinensis*** (Link) Schneid. habit with mature fruit.

Kiliwas ate the seeds in the form of pinole (Meigs 1939). The Cochimí did not use jojoba until after their contact with the Jesuits. Fr. del Barco (1980) noted that the plants in this region produced prolific amounts of fruit following winter rains of several days. According to del Barco, the Cochimí called the fruits "jojoba." He discussed the virtues of jojoba, copied "word for word" from a prescription printed in Mexico in 1749, with permission from the Royal Tribunal of Physicians (del Barco 1980:180–181). Jojoba was "extraordinarily effective" against urinary disorders, flatulence, indigestion, and "obstructions." It was also effective for facilitating childbirth and treating wounds, cancer, fever, abdominal cramps, and "to end fiery hangovers, which they call heartburn." In addition to these uses, Fr. del Barco included numerous others that were "widely experienced."

Of interest is that, according to Fr. del Barco (1980:183), *indigenes* in central and southern Baja California did not use jojoba "for anything before their conversion." He provides insight into how a group, might abandon the use of a particular plant, in this case the Cochimí, who were in fear of losing their soul should they eat jojoba:

> They did not use it for medicine because they were not acquainted with its virtues, nor for food, because they had a tradition among themselves that it caused vomiting, and therefore they do not eat it. It is plausible that their ancestors, when they began to eat it, must have eaten it in great quantity, and because it is by nature very fiery, it is natural that it should cause a great revolution in the body, and from this the severe vomiting ensued. And because they had the fear and believed that any vomiting is a mortal illness, while this torment lasted the victims and even all the rest around them must have been scared and thinking that death was near. Although they may have escaped from this experience, this memory of the danger in which they

> found themselves was left vividly marked in their memories. And so they transmitted to their descendants the customs to abstain from eating and to hate the jojoba which, instead of filling the stomach (their main occupation!) like other foods, with its terrible vomiting, makes one expel whatever he had previously eaten, with the danger of expelling the soul at the same time.

For nonnative peoples jojoba oil filled "a void left by olive oil when this latter is not available to make salads" (del Barco 1980:182). Jojoba oil is an indigestible liquid wax that acts as a purgative if taken in quantity (Mirov 1952). Fr. del Barco (1980:183) knew this because he commented that the oil causes "the bowels [to] expel it just as they received it, without its being digested by the stomach." He described how the soldiers who accompanied Fr. Consag on his trip by sea to the Colorado River experienced this rather unpleasant effect. Among their provisions they had jojoba oil, which they frequently used to cook their fish: "After using it for some time, they were made aware of the above-mentioned effect when they saw their clothes stained by the oil, without their having been aware when they had expelled it. Perhaps they used the oil to excess, because others who have used it in moderation have not experienced any novelty whatsoever."

Seris regarded the seeds as a survival food only (Felger and Moser 1976, 1985). As one elderly woman said, "it's not food, you just eat it." Some Seri value the seeds primarily for its use as a shampoo and for medicinal purposes.

Solanaceae | Nightshade or Potato Family

Capsicum | red pepper, cayenne pepper, Tabasco pepper

C. *annuum* Linnaeus var. *glabriusculum* (Dunal) Heiser & Pickersgill
wild chile, bird pepper, cayenne pepper, chiltepín, chile del monte, chillipiquin

Capsicum annuum var. *glabriusculum* is the most northern variety of the *C. annuum* complex, the typical variety being the most common and wide-ranging chile pepper in the Americas (Andrews 1984). *Capsicum annuum* also includes most domesticated chile peppers in international commerce today (Loaiza-Figueroa 1985). The term *chiltepín* refers to its oblong fruit and is the only nondomesticated chile that extends north of the Tropic of Cancer into arid subtropical and desert zones (Nabhan et al. 1989b). Its northern limits are in the Sonoran and Chihuahuan Deserts and in adjacent oak woodlands 50 kilometers north of the U.S.-Mexico border in southern Arizona, New Mexico, and Texas.

Wild *chiltepines* (figs. 144, 145) have been used for at least 8,000 years, as evidenced by the predominance of their seeds in coprolites (Callen 1965). *Chiltepines* are most popular in the desert regions of northwestern Mexico and the southwestern United States, where their presence is less common than further south (Nabhan et al. 1989b). In this region the red fruits mature in late September and October, when they are quickly eaten by birds or harvested by local inhabitants. The pungent fruits add flavor to monotonous diets and are rich sources of vitamins A, C, B_2, niacin, and potassium (Bye 1976; Cotter 1982; Andrews 1984). *Chiltepines* are also used to treat acid indigestion (Nabhan 1978b) and as a preservative for *carne seca* or *carne machaca,* due to its antioxidant properties (Cotter 1982).

River Pimas and Apaches relished *chiltepines,* although some may have lived 150 kilometers north of the plant's range and had to obtain the fruits through trade (Nabhan 1978b). The Tohono O'odham brought wild gathered *chiltepines* to the Gila River Pima for exchange (Russell 1908; Rea 1997) after having made their traditional annual pilgrimage into the desert mountains of southern Arizona and northern Mexico to gather the fruits (Nabhan et al. 1989b). Additionally, inhabitants of the Río San Miguel watershed, Sonora, collected green fruits in August or September, following the harvest of acorns, for bottling in vinegar and use as spices (Felger et al. 1976). The red fruits were collected and dried for use as a seasoning.

Yaquis used the *chiltepines* like chiles (Alvarez de Williams n.d.). Rosalio Moisés (Moisés et al. 1971:199) remembered that in the late 1940s he gathered large quantities of *chiltepines* and sold them: "We walked out in the brush looking for wild food... . Chiltipiquin grew wild all through the brush, and we could pick a sackful and sell it to the Mexican storekeeper in Vicam;

he paid 5 pesos a kilo [1946–1950]. We could pick two or three kilos of chiltipiquins a week."

Groups outside the Sonoran Desert, including the Tarahumara and Guarijío, also relished the fruits. Tarahumaras constructed stone walls around *chiltepín* plants to protect them from goats and other grazers (Nabhan 1978b). They added *chiltepines* to most bean, maize, and meat dishes (Bye 1976) and fried them with ground-cherry *(Physalis)* fruits (Pennington 1963). Some Tarahumara occasionally grew the plants from seed or transplants (Bye 1976). Plants found along the trails and near the base of boulders may have germinated from seeds contained in human feces or bird droppings. So highly valued were *chiltepines* that the sierran Tarahumara made a special two-week trip into the barrancas during October to collect and dry the fruits. A relish made from *chiltepines* soaked in water was an important product in interregional commerce between the barrancas and sierran cultures (Bennett and Zingg 1935). The Guarijío widely used the berries as a red-pepper seasoning, which was considered very hot but as having an excellent flavor (Gentry 1963).

It is doubtful that the popularity of *chiltepín* as a food and spice will decrease and be replaced by other domesticated peppers because *chiltepines* remain important in the folklore and cuisine of Sonorans, Indians, and Anglos (Nabhan et al. 1989b). *Chiltepines* continue to be the favorite food of the Gila River Pima; indeed, "if a Pima youngster knows but a few dozen words in his or her native language, one of these is likely to be *o'olas ko'okol*," the Piman name for *chiltepín* (Rea 1997: 54). Inhabitants of northern Mexico and recent immigrants from Mexico to the United States prize *chiltepines*. Although not as readily available in the United States as in northern Mexico, the wild *chiltepines* may help reinforce the Sonoran identity of Latinos living north of the border (Nabhan et al. 1989b). So highly valued are the wild *chiltepines* that "semicultivated" chiles deceptively marketed as wild *chiltepines* are recognized as different by those well accustomed to the wild chiles and are not accepted.

Chiltepines are harvested almost completely from wild populations (Nabhan et al. 1989b). Ethnobotanist Edward Palmer noted that in favorable years *chiltepines* were gathered in great quantities near Guaymas and throughout Sonora during the late 1880s and shipped

FIGURE 144. ***Capsicum annuum*** L. var. ***glabriusculum*** (Dunal) Heiser & Pickersgill. Close-up of the very hot, mature fruits given to us by María Beltran, Granados, Sonora, August 1988.

to San Francisco (Watson 1889, cited as *C. baccatum*). In the 1970s, local residents of *ejidos* and ranches who sought extra cash traveled to the sierras of Sonora, Chihuahua, and Sinaloa to collect the fruit (Nabhan 1978b, 1985; J. Duran, pers. comm.). The process of collecting the fruits was not a small operation. Near Meresichíc, Sonora, *chiltepín* gatherers fill pickup trucks with wild *chiltepines* that they sell in Hermosillo packaging houses. As many as 100 individuals participate in the harvest in the Ures *municipio* alone; at least another ten *municipios* are located in habitats where wild chiles are as prolific (Nabhan et al. 1989b). This suggests that 500 to 1,000 Sonorans my be involved in the wild harvest for the export market. U.S. buyers in Mexico purchase the *chiltepines* from the harvesters and load them into trucks to take back to urban centers, where they are sold fresh or as pickles, dried, or processed into hot sauce.

The quantity of *chiltepines* harvested from wild populations is staggering. In a good year, as many as 12 tons of the fruits may be harvested from a single Sonoran *municipio*, but the total harvest from Sonora may vary from 8 to 50 tons (Nabhan et al. 1989b). The amount of *chiltepines* harvested from Chihuahua and Sinaloa may be similar (Nabhan 1985). The popularity and demand for wild *chiltepines* continue to rise sharply. Additionally, fruit production and thus availability can fluctuate greatly from one year to the next (J. Duran, pers. comm.) and is dependent on many uncontrollable factors (Nabhan et al. 1989b). Weather (particularly drought and freezing temperatures for the northwestern *chiltepín* populations), grazing, and harvesting methods are the variables that affect the *chiltepines'* availability (Nabhan 1985; J. Duran, pers. comm.). As a result of the fluctuating availability and increased demand, *chiltepín* harvesting has become a highly competitive business. In the 1980s, harvesters were said to trample the plants or try to pull the plants up by the roots (J. Duran, pers. comm.). At El Coyote, northeastern Sonora, harvesters often cut the plants so low as to severely damage them, a practice unnecessary for obtaining the fruits. Howard S. Gentry recognized the plight of the *chiltepín* populations as a result of harvesting pressures in the late 1930s and early 1940s (Gentry 1942:234): "Recently, the natives of southern Sonora have started collecting the fruit for export to the United States ... if commercial exploitation of the [wild] plant is successful, it is probable that the great majority of plants will die under persisting breaking, and what has been a common plant will become rare. Or perhaps it will be cultivated."

FIGURE 145. ***Capsicum annuum*** var. ***glabriusculum***. **a.** Habit and mature fruits; **b.** fruit and seed, Tumacocori Mountains, Santa Cruz County, Arizona, October 1986 (*Hodgson 4456*, DES).

In northeastern Sonora, anyone caught damaging *chiltepín* plants during harvest time can be fined, theoretically, because *chiltepines* are now protected by the SARH Subsecretaria Forestal de México as well as by regulations established by certain *ejidos* (Nabhan 1985). Stricter controls on harvesting *chiltepines* should help to lessen pressure on wild stands of chiles. Cultivation of *chiltepín* plants should further reduce harvesting pressures and meet the demands for the fruits. Several *chiltepín* plantations of one hectare or more were planted near Hermosillo and in the Río Moctezuma and Río San Miguel watersheds with varying success (Nabhan et al. 1989b). Monocultural plantings have failed, due largely to the lack of understanding or consideration of the ecology of wild *chiltepín* populations. For example, northern populations of *chiltepines* are almost exclusively found growing beneath trees and shrubs. Vegetation analyses indicate that *chiltepines* grow beneath red-fruited nurse shrubs such as *Celtis pallida* Torr., *C. laevigata* Willd. var. *reticulata* L. Benson, and *Lycium* spp. (Nabhan 1987, cited as *Celtis reticulata*). At Rancho Argentina near Navajoa, Sonora, thousands of *chiltepines* were being successfully cultivated in association with known nurse plants such as *Leucaena* spp. during the late 1980s.

Chamaesaracha | false-nightshade, five-eyes

C. coronopus **(Dunal) A. Gray**
small ground-cherry, green-leaf five-eyes

C. sordida **(Dunal) A. Gray**
hairy five-eyes

Chamaesaracha sordida grows in the Sonoran Desert in Pima County, Arizona, whereas *C. coronopus* grows throughout Arizona into southern Utah and east to Kansas (Wiggins 1964). The use of their fruits by Sonoran people is unknown. However, Edward Castetter and Willis Bell (1951) may have referred to *C. coronopus* when describing an unknown plant similar to *Physalis,* but having smaller fruits that were eaten by the Mohave. Additionally, Tepehuans collected the fruits of an unidentified species (possibly *C. sordida*) in October (Pennington 1969).

Lycium | desert-thorn, matrimony-vine, wolfberry, tomatillo

L. andersonii **A. Gray**
Anderson thornbush, red-berry desert-thorn, manzanita, saliciesa

L. berlandieri **Dunal var.** *parviflorum* **(A. Gray) Terracciano**
silver desert-thorn, tomatillo, barehata, hoso, joso

L. exsertum **A. Gray**
Arizona desert-thorn, tomatillo

L. fremontii **A. Gray**
Fremont thornbush, Fremont desert-thorn, tomatillo

L. pallidum **Miers**
pale desert-thorn, rabbit-thorn, tomatillo

L. parishii **A. Gray**
Parish's thornbush, Parish's desert-thorn, tomatillo

L. richii **A. Gray (syn.,** *L. brevipes* **Bentham)**
tomatillo, frutilla

L. torreyi **A. Gray**
squawthorn, tomatillo

Wolfberries are commonly found throughout the Southwest and northern Mexico. Most of the edible species flower in the spring, from March to May, although *L. exsertum* (fig. 146) flowers as early as January. *Lycium fremontii* flowers a second time from August to December, whereas *L. berlandieri* flowers later, from March to September (Wiggins 1964). The red or orange, juicy fruits of the above-listed *Lycium* species are edible and played an important role in the diets of southwestern people. People generally ate the fully ripe fruits raw, sun-dried, or cooked in water to make soups, stews, syrup, sauces, or beverages (Coville 1892; Hough 1897; Russell 1908; Stevenson 1915; Castetter 1935; Elmore 1943; Saunders 1948; Curtin 1949; Wyman and Harris 1951; Weber and Seaman 1985; Felger and Moser 1985; Rea 1997). Eating the berries causes a temporary blackening of one's teeth (Russell 1908; Rea 1997). Wolfberries have been found to contain low percentages of phosphorous, calcium, magnesium, and sodium (Greenhouse 1979; Everitt and Alaniz 1981). However, fruits of *L. berlandieri,* which are collected from June through August, have relatively high percentages of protein and potassium (Everitt and Alaniz 1981).

River Pimas recognize four folk species of wolfberry (Rea 1997). A form that translates to "regular" wolfberry undoubtedly refers to the relatively large-fruited *L. fremontii,* and possibly embraces *L. torreyi* and *L. exsertum* as well. River Pimas used to pick large quantities of "regular" wolfberry fruits in the spring. They ate the fruits raw, cooked the berries in water with sugar to make a drink, or cooked the berries with water and a spoonful of flour to make a sauce (Curtin 1949, *Curtin 49,* DES; Rea 1997). To preserve the fruits, they dried whole berries or the cooked flour-berry mass in the sun and rehydrated the berries or mass when needed. Berries or pulp stored this way tasted sweeter than when eaten fresh. The berries of *L. fremontii* were still a popular food among the River Pima during the 1970s (Greenhouse 1979). However, they recognized a fourth folk taxon whose very small fruits were generally not collected (Rea 1997). This type of wolfberry corresponds to *L. californica,* which produces relatively dry, small fruits.

The Tohono O'odham collected and sold ten-pound bags of wolfberry fruits into the 1980s (G. P. Nabhan, pers. comm.). Hiá ceḍ O'odhams ate the fruits of *L. andersonii* and *L. fremontii* (Felger et al. 1992). The Seri also used the fruits of *L. fremontii,* which they gathered in March and May (Felger and Moser 1985). The Mohave, Quechan, Maricopa, and Cocopa ate various wolfberries, including *L. fremontii, L. exsertum,* and *L. andersonii* (Castetter and Bell 1951). People generally washed, boiled, and coarsely ground the berries after gathering them in a basket. They mixed the meal with water to make a beverage or stored the fruits in gourds or ollas. The mass was later eaten as is or pulverized, mixed with water, and drunk. The Maricopa prepared a beverage by boiling the berries briefly in hot water, then straining and mashing the berries (Spier 1933). Like other groups, they spread out the pulp in the sun to dry and stored the mass for later use.

Wolfberry fruits were undoubtedly eaten by Baja Californians. Edward Palmer collected *L. andersonii* in alkaline soil near La Paz in 1890 and mentioned that its fruits were edible (Vasey and Rose 1890c). "Modern inhabitants" ate the small, red fruits of *L. richii,* called *frutilla,* in the central desert region (Aschmann 1959:91). Meigs (1939) also noted that the Kiliwa ground and ate the seeds as pinole. Fr. del Barco (1980:185; see also Clavigero 1937) noted that the natives ate the fruits of a plant whose fruits they called *guigil,* which may have been the berries of *Lycium:*

> There is another plant that has a little red fruit like cherries, although not so big; perhaps two of them would make one good cherry. The Cochimies call this little fruit *guigil.* It does not have much flavor, but they eat it willingly, because from this and other things which are flavorless to us they are able to extract a flavor and a delight that we cannot attain. Before their conversion they always ate this fruit raw; now that they have clay pots they often eat it cooked. The missionary priests have observed that when women who have young children eat too much of this little fruit, many children become sick and many die, from which it is inferred that *guigil* generates bad milk. They are not always able to get this food, except when it has rained in more or less good showers during the winter. And because this happens only in occasional years, so likewise the *guigil* grows only very seldom. It has the fortunate property of growing swiftly and ripening around March or April, a particularly lean time for the Indians, since they have none of their foods except mezcal.

Annetta Carter (*in* del Barco 1980) noted that *guigil* was tentatively identified in Fr. del Barco's Spanish edition as *Castela tortuosa,* a plant that grows in south-central Mexico. *Castela peninsularis* Rose is endemic to the cape region of Baja California, which is some distance from the Cochimí. In addition, its fruits were probably not eaten by anyone. Townsend Brandegee (1891a, cited as *C. tortulosa*) noted that children easily

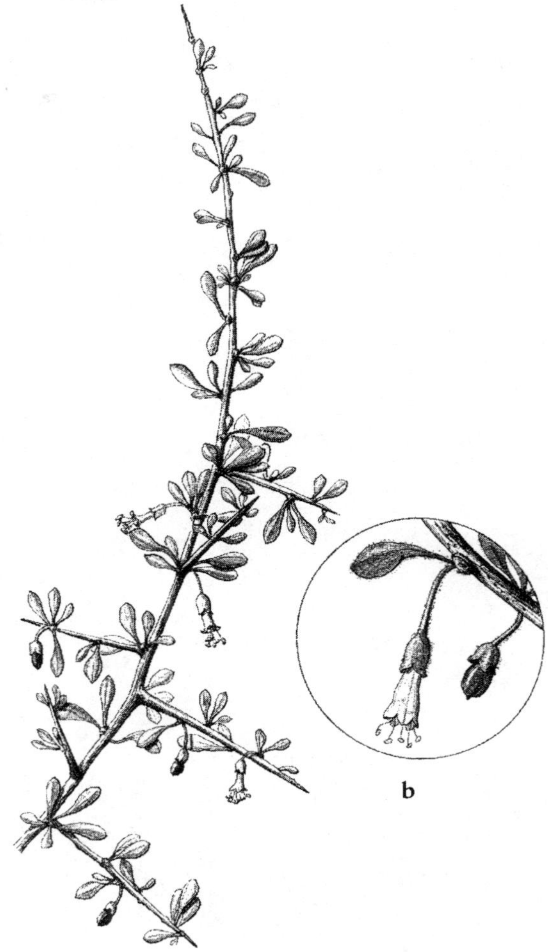

FIGURE 146. ***Lycium exsertum*** A. Gray. **a.** Branch with flowers and fruits, Big Horn Mountains, Maricopa County, Arizona, April 1980 (*Ducote 769,* DES); **b.** flower and mature fruit, Superstition Mountains, Pinal County, Arizona, March 1981 (*Hodgson 1186,* DES).

distinguished this shrub from *Lycium* when collecting fruits to eat. *Castela peninsularis* resembles wolfberry in its thorny nature and bright red fruits. These fruits have a bitter taste, however, unlike those of wolfberry. I have observed *L. fremontii* to produce abundant flowers and fruits during and following favorable winter rains. *Lycium berlandieri* var. *peninsulare* (Brandeg.) Hitchc., *L. fremontii* var. *fremontii, L. fremontii* var. *congestum* Hitchc., *L. megacarpum* Wiggins, and *L. richii* are fleshy-fruited tomatillos that also grow in the Sonoran Desert of the cape region of Baja California.

Not everyone looked upon wolfberry fruits favorably. Thomas Childs (1954:35) described two foods he could not accept while living with his Hiá ceḍ O'odham friends and in-laws: "Two kinds of grub I could not go: one is those large army worms with a large horn on their hind end. The other is what is called the squawberry. It is a reddish berry and when cooked is somewhat bitter. May the Lord forgive me from having to try to eat any again. Sick! I never got so sick in my life as I did when I tried to eat that berry!" Perhaps Childs ate the small, sometimes bitter-tasting fruits of *L. californicum*. Despite Childs's lack of enthusiasm for wolfberries, *L. fremontii* is a potentially important crop for arid regions, according to Gary Nabhan and Richard Felger (1984). Plants can tolerate poor-quality water and moderate freezing, yet produce numerous, large, and good-tasting fruits.

Physalis | ground-cherry, husk-tomato, Chinese-lantern, tomatillo

P. acutifolia **(Miers) Sandwith**
sharp-leaf ground-cherry, Wright ground-cherry, tomatillo, tomatillo cimarrón

P. angulata **Linnaeus**
cut-leaf ground-cherry, tomate de cascara, tomate

P. crassifolia **Bentham**
yellow nightshade ground-cherry, thick-leaved ground-cherry, tomate del culabra

P. hederifolia **A. Gray**
ivy-leaf ground-cherry

P. ixocarpa **Brotero ex Hornemann**
tomatillo

P. longifolia **Nuttall var.** ***longifolia*** **(syn., *P. virginiana* P. Miller var. *sonorae* [Torrey] Waterfall)**
long-leaf ground-cherry, tomatillo

P. philadelphica **Lamarck var.** ***immaculata*** **Waterfall**
Mexican ground-cherry, tomatillo

P. pubescens **Linnaeus**
husk-tomato, hairy ground-cherry, tomatillo, tomate fresadilla

People living in the Southwest and northern Mexico ate the mature berries of various ground-cherries in a variety of ways. They consumed them raw; cooked them into sauces, preserves, and jams; or dried, stored, and ground the berries into meal for bread (Stevenson 1915; Robbins et al. 1916; Bennett and Zingg 1935; Castetter 1935; Castetter and Bell 1951; Pennington 1963). Ground-cherry fruits fall to the ground one to two weeks before they are fully ripe. Fully ripe fruits are sweet and slightly acidic in taste and are high in vitamin C.

River Pimas knew *P. acutifolia* and *P. crassifolia* (fig. 147), whose name translated to "old man's testicles" (Curtin 1949; Rea 1997). Like most groups, they ate the sweet-tasting, black, fully ripe fruits without preparation. Edward Palmer found the fruits of *P. crassifolia*, collected near La Paz (Vasey and Rose 1890c), and fruits of *P. angulata*, collected near Guaymas (Watson 1889), to be edible. Tarahumaras, who often thought the plants to be a troublesome weed, nevertheless collected and fried the fruits with *chiltepines* (Pennington 1963).

Ground-cherries continue to be cultivated or semicultivated among different groups. *Physalis ixocarpa* occasionally escapes cultivation along ditch banks and hedge rows (Wiggins 1964). Robust plants of this ground-cherry were found in small gardens near Boquillas, Coahuila (*Hodgson 5292 & Nabhan*, DES).

FIGURE 147. ***Physalis crassifolia*** Benth. with immature fruits. Located 10.6 miles east of Carbo, Sonora, September 1988 (*Hodgson 5185*, DES).

Bohrer (1991) alluded to possible domestication of a *Physalis* by the Hohokam in the Salt River valley, but its identity is far from being resolved. Various ground-cherries are found in the markets of Mexico for use as a meat dressing or combination with red peppers (*Capsicum annuum;* Rose 1900; Bye 1979b). Ground-cherry fruits, which are marketed as tomatillos, are also commonly sold fresh in Southwest markets.

Solanum | nightshade, horse-nettle

S. *americanum* P. Miller (syn., *S. nodiflorum* Jacquin; *S. nigrum* Linnaeus var. *americanum* [P. Miller] O. Schultz; *S. nigrum* Linnaeus var. *virginicum* Linnaeus; and *S. nigrum* of various authors, not Linnaeus)
American black nightshade, marsh nightshade, chichiquelite, quelite, chuchilitas, manioche, pitoxe, mambia, hierba mora

***S. douglasii* Dunal**
green-spot nightshade

Solanum americanum grows in mesic sites or where moisture accumulates, such as along field margins and stream banks, in the southern and western United States and Mexico (Wiggins 1964). *Solanum douglasii* is found in similar habitats from central California south throughout Baja California east into Arizona and northeastern Mexico. With favorable moisture, both species flower most of the year.

Native nightshades providing edible fruits are few and infrequent in the Southwest and northern Mexico, due in part to the loss of mesic habitat. The few groups known to have eaten the mature purple or black berries of *S. americanum* include the inhabitants of the cape region, Baja California (Brandegee 1891a); Yaqui (Alvarez de Williams n.d.); Guarijío (*Gentry 1185, 1269,* ARIZ); and Tepehuan (Pennington 1969). Annetta Carter (Carter *in* del Barco 1980) determined that Fr. del Barco's *yerba mora,* whose fruit was edible when ripe, was *S. douglasii.* However, others considered the fruit to be too bitter to eat (Weber and Seaman 1985).

The leaves of *chichiquelites,* or *S. americanum* and *S. douglasii,* also provided edible greens to the Luiseño (Sparkman 1908), Eudeve (Pennington 1982), Yaqui (Alvarez de Williams n.d.), Tarahumara (Bennett and Zingg 1935; Pennington 1963; Bye 1976), Guarijío (*Gentry 1185,* ARIZ), and Tepehuans (Pennington 1969). Local inhabitants near Mulegé, Baja California, and Guaymas, Sonora (Watson 1889), ate these plants as a *quelite.* As with most *quelites,* only the youngest leaves were probably eaten.

Solanum eleagnifolium Cavanilles is a common summer annual that produces dry, yellow fruits, which are potentially toxic due to the presence of many glycoalkaloids, including solanine (Kingsbury 1964). Nevertheless, River Pimas used these ripe fruits for making cheese, a post-Hispanic activity. Leonora Curtin (1949, *Curtin 32,* DES) noted how they put powdered berries, tied in a small bag or cloth, in a can of warm milk with a piece of dried rabbit or cow stomach. They squeezed out the liquid and added salt to the resulting cheese. Ruth Giff also remembered making cottage cheese from the berries of this nightshade by putting the tasteless berries in a cloth before placing them in the milk, without the cow stomach (Rea 1997).

Sterculiaceae | Chocolate or Cacao Family

Guazuma | bastard-cedar

***G. ulmifolia* Lamarck**
pricklenut, guásima, aquiche, cuahuilote, palote negro, tapaculo, vacima, ajiyá, agiá, jijá, majagua de toro, tablote

The fruits and seeds of *guásima* supplied a food source to both humans and wildlife. Plants bloom from June to July, and fruit mature by the following spring, from March to May in south-central Sonora (Turner et al. 1995). The green, immature fruit of *guásima* is fleshy, mucilaginous, sweet, and pleasant tasting when eaten raw or cooked. Oviedo said of *guásima* (*in* Standley 1923:809): "The guácuma is a large tree that bears fruit like mulberries and the leaves are like those of mulberry but are smaller. From the fruit the Indians make a beverage on which they fatten ... for this they mash the fruit and put it in water." The Guarijío and Mexicans shared their fondness for these immature fruits with coatimundis (*Gentry 1923, 1176,* ARIZ). Tarahumaras used the inner portion of the presumably immature fruit for making a small cake (Pennington 1963). However, eating too many immature fruits caused diarrhea.

People also ground the mature seeds and hard, woody fruit into a meal. Around Ónavas, Sonora, Pimas differentiated between two types of *guásima* (Pennington 1980). The first type, possibly representing those plants whose leaves are tomentose on both surfaces (Pennington 1980, cited as *G. tomentosa* H.B.K.), produced fruits that were still often eaten in the 1970s. The second type may represent those plants whose leaves become dark green and glabrate on their upper surfaces, whose fruits were consumed infrequently in the past. The Pima dried and ground the seeds of both types into a meal used for making tortillas, atole, and pinole. Guarijios ground the mature seeds and fruit for making tortillas, atole, and pinole, and roasted and ground the seeds for coffee when coffee beans were unavailable (Gentry 1942, 1963; Martin et al. 1998).

The wide distribution of *guásima* may be due at least in part to human activities (Turner et al. 1995). Besides the fruits' usefulness as a food item for humans and livestock, other parts of the tree are used for various purposes. Its strong wood has been used for making ribs for small boats, house furniture (including beautiful chairs that one may still purchase), and paneling; for firewood; and as a source of charcoal for gunpowder (Standley 1923). Young stems provide a strong fiber for rope; silkworms are fed its leaves; livestock eat its leaves and young shoots; and the bark is used to treat malaria, leprosy, elephantiasis, and other problems. These uses have probably led to its accidental or deliberate introduction in suitable areas. Plants were successfully cultivated at the Desert Botanical Garden in Phoenix.

Theophrastaceae | Theophrasta Family

Jacquinia | braceletwood

J. macrocarpa **Cavanilles ssp.** *pungens* **(A. Gray) Stahl (syn.,** *J. pungens* **A. Gray)**
San Juanico, palo San Juan, pinicua, San Juan, flor de niño, palo de las animas, rosadilla, mata-peje, sacaté

The fruits of San Juanico are globose with a greenish red, hard "shell" on the outside when mature from late summer through the following spring. Inside this shell are a few thin seeds embedded in yellow pulp that is sweet, but with a somewhat bitter aftertaste. Birds, rodents (Janzen 1970), and possibly beetle larvae (Gentry 1942) consume the ripened fruits. Despite the fruits' sweet taste, their use by people for food is minimal. The Seri cracked the fruit on a metate and ate the soft pulp within (Felger and Moser 1985). Eating too many of the fruits caused dizziness and possible intestinal disorders. Yet, to cure the dizziness, one washed the face using an infusion of the flowers. Ónavas Pimas made a tea from the flowers to treat stomach disorders (Pennington 1980), although there is no indication that they ate the fruits. The leaves and fruits were extensively used as a fish poison along the west coast of Mexico (Standley 1924) and in lowland Veracruz (Janzen 1970).

Ulmaceae | Elm Family

Celtis | hackberry

C. iguanaea **(Jacquin) Sargent**
garabato, cumaro, granjeno, palo de arco, chaparro blanco, bainoro, vainoro

C. laevigata **Willdenow var.** *brevipes* **(S. Watson) Sargent (syn.,** *C. brevipes* **S. Watson); var.** *reticulata* **(Torrey) L. Benson (syn.,** *C. reticulata* **Torrey)**
netleaf hackberry, sugar-berry, cumaro, combro, uchica, garabato blanco, palo blanco

C. pallida **Torrey**
desert hackberry, spiny hackberry, shiny hackberry, granjeno, huasteco, capul, capui, garabato, garumbullo, gumbro, granjeno, bainoro, palo de águila, acebuche, rompecapa, vainoro

The fruits of hackberries are small, somewhat fleshy drupes with relatively large stones. When compared to other fruits of woody plants, those of *C. pallida* have relatively high percentages of crude protein, phosphorous, and calcium (Everitt and Alaniz 1981). *Celtis iguanaea* fruits, which mature in the summer and fall, are the largest of the three species and, in my opinion, are juicy, sweet, and the best tasting. Yaquis ate the fruits raw (Alvarez de Williams n.d.) and Ónavas Pimas considered the drupes to be a great delicacy (Pennington 1980). Tarahumaras also were fond of its fruits (Standley 1923; Pennington 1963). The Guarijío, however, did not eat the fruits "with great relish" (Gentry 1963).

Northeastern and Western Yavapais gathered red fruits of *C. laevigata* var. *brevipes* in June, then pot-boiled and ground them on a metate into a meal (Gifford 1936). Southeastern Yavapais collected the fruits of a "hackberry" (possibly *C. laevigata*) by running their hands along the stem; they then winnowed and ground the berries as a meal without cooking (Gifford 1932). They did not store hackberry fruits. The Tohono O'odham also ate the fruits of *C. laevigata,* with the women filling their carrying baskets with whole branches from trees found near a village (Castetter 1935). Lower Colorado River peoples occasionally gathered its fruits along their journeys to other areas (Castetter and Bell 1951). Others who ate the fruits of netleaf hackberry include the Eudeve (Pennington 1982, cited as *C. reticulata*) and Ónavas Pima (Pennington 1980, cited as *C. reticulata*), although plants were not found in the immediate area of the latter. Fr. Nentvig (1980) made note of the very sweet fruits of *cumaro,* erroneously determined by Pradeau and Rasmussen (Nentvig's translators) as a Cohune palm. María Beltran related to Gary Nabhan and me that both *cumaro* and *garumbullo* fruits were still eaten fresh around Granados, Sonora (Nabhan and Hodgson 1988).

Little has been written on the use of *C. pallida* fruits, despite Niethammer's (1974) opinion that they are more palatable, sweet, juicy, and easily obtainable (despite the plants' fierce spines) than those of the netleaf hackberry. Its fruits ripen throughout the summer and fall and are consumed by wildlife (Turner et al. 1995). Ónavas Pima (Pennington 1980) and Seri (Felger and Moser 1985) ate the fruits of *C. pallida* fresh.

Verbenaceae | Vervain or Verbena Family

Lantana | shrub-verbena

L. horrida **Kunth**
calico bush, confiturilla, sarza mora

L. velutina **Martius & Galeotti**
velvet shrub-verbena, sarza mora, confite, confiturilla, confiturilla blanca, tarepe

Lantana horrida grows from Mississippi west to New Mexico and south to Sonora and San Luis Potosi (Wiggins 1964). Its ripe, black, juicy fruits (fig. 148) are not only edible, but are sweet and good tasting. However, despite its availability and good taste, its use is not well documented. Ónavas Pimas (Pennington 1980) and Seris (Felger and Moser 1985) ate the fruits fresh. Likewise, little is known about the use of *L. velutina* fruits, which are found from central Sonora southward to Panama and in central Baja California (Wiggins 1964) from El Arco (near 28°N) south to the cape region (Wiggins 1980). Tarahumaras ate the mature, pink, juicy fruits, which they described as being "many balls growing around a center" (Bennett and Zingg 1935, cited as *L. involucrata*).

FIGURE 148. ***Lantana horrida*** Kunth. Close-up of leaves, orangish flowers, and blackish mature fruits. Located 13 miles west of Guasabas, Sonora, July 1988 (*Hodgson 5090 & DeLamater,* DES).

Lippia | lippia, mat-grass

L. palmeri **S. Watson**
orégano

Lippia palmeri (figs. 149, 150a) grows on islands in the Gulf of California and in Baja California and Sonora southward into Sinaloa (Wiggins 1964, 1980). Its herbage was important to inhabitants of northern Mexico for flavoring meats and fish (Bennett and Zingg 1935; Gentry 1942, 1963; Pennington 1963; Felger and Moser 1985). Cattle or deer that ate the leaves of *L. palmeri* were reported to have an especially flavorful meat (Gentry 1959; del Barco 1980). Seris collected, dried, and crushed the leaves as recently as the 1980s (Felger and Moser 1985). Ideally, they collected the plants after a heavy rain and before the plants flowered. If *orégano* was harvested when in flower, the inflorescences were removed because of their bitter taste; sometimes leaves from flowering plants were not collected. The Seri often stored large bundles of the leafy branches on the roof. Hunters carried small bags or bundles of the dried leaves mixed with salt for use as a meat flavoring. When Seris dried meat, they used the crushed leaves of *orégano* as a substitute for salt.

Near Guaymas, Sonora, *orégano* was used as a potherb near the turn of the century (Watson 1889). Here is found *L. palmeri* var. *spicata* Rose, which was called *origaro*. Edward Palmer noted that *origaro* was used in much the same way as thyme and sage was used in the United States, sometimes replacing commercial tea (Vasey and Rose 1890c).

Tarahumaras used *orégano* for flavorings or as an important *quelite*. They dried and crushed the leaves of *L. palmeri* between their hands to make a powder before using them as a flavoring (Bennett and Zingg 1935). Those inhabiting the western canyon country used *L. palmeri* and *L. berlandieri* Schauer (fig. 150b) as a *quelite* by boiling and draining the leaves, then eating them with beans (Pennington 1963) or as a relish with pinole (Bennett and Zingg 1935). The taste of *L. berlandieri* is more pungent than that of *L. palmeri*. Plastic bags filled with crushed leaves of *orégano* are sold in markets throughout much of Sonora.

FIGURE 149. ***Lippia palmeri*** S. Wats. Close-up of branches and subsessile inflorescence. Gentry Agroecology Project.

FIGURE 150. **a. *Lippia palmeri*** flowering branch; **a1.** inflorescence; grown at Gentry Agroecology Project, Desert Botanical Garden, Phoenix, Arizona, July 1986, from seed collected by H. S. Gentry in Cerro Prieto, Sonora (*Hodgson 4331*, DES); **b. *L. berlandieri*** Schauer long peduncle of inflorescence growing at Gentry Agroecology Project, July 1986.

Howard S. Gentry (1959) was especially fond of *L. palmeri,* noting its attributes and potential as an important crop: "Leaves and small twigs are plucked and dried for seasoning, frequently including the small spikes of white flowers. Leaf buds start with first of the summer rains about 1 July, flowers in September from October. Oregano is regularly found in local Mexican markets. Also exported to U.S. through Nogales and sold in Arizona markets. One ounce packets priced at 30 cents to 40 cents each [in 1950s]. Leaf response might be induced in spring in cultivation." When harvesting the aromatic herbage, one should collect the leaves in June, wash them thoroughly, tie the leaves in bundles, and hang the bundles to dry for seven to ten days (H. S. Gentry, pers. comm.). All stems and inflorescence pieces are removed from the leaves.

Other *orégano*-like plants that deserve notice include members of the genus *Aloysia* and *Burroughsia. Aloysia barbata* (Brandegee) Moldenke was described by Townsend Brandegee from fragments brought to him from "La Giganta," in southern Baja California. A man living in nearby Comondú used this plant for culinary purposes (Brandegee 1889, cited as *Lippia barbata* Brandeg.). At San Benito, Baja California, another person gave Brandegee material collected from "some point nearer the Pacific," which represented *Burroughsia fastigiata* (Brandegee) Moldenke (Brandegee 1889, cited as *Lippia fastigiata* Brandegee). The local inhabitants, who called the plant *damiana,* made tea from it. *Damiana* is a common name for various plants used for herbal teas, such as *Turnera diffusa* Willdenow. In addition, Havasupais preferred a tea made from boiled leaves of the common shrub *Aloysia wrightii* (A. Gray) Heller, or *oreganillo,* to that of Mormon-tea (*Ephedra* spp.) or commercial tea and coffee (Weber and Seaman 1985).

Vitex | chastetree

V. mollis **Kunth**
igualama, uvalama, torete, jari, atuto, jujuhuali

V. pyramidata **Robinson**
uvalama, toscalama

Vitex mollis grows at the upper elevational limits of the Sonoran Desert in central Baja California and Sonora (Wiggins 1964). People who ate its black fruits found them to be refreshing, although rather bitter (Watson 1889; Standley 1924; Pennington 1963, 1980, 1982; Altschul 1973). Fr. Nentvig (1980:41) thought the fruits, which ripened in September, to be "somewhat disagreeable" in taste. Guarijios ate the fruits raw or cooked and mashed with sugar. The fruits were occasionally sold in the markets of Mexico during the mid 1930s (Gentry 1942, 1963). Yaquis called the plant *ugualama* and ate the fruits without preparation or stored the fruits in bottles (Alvarez de Williams n.d.). Fruits were used to make wine in Meresichic, Sonora, in the Río Miguel watershed (Felger et al. 1976). Tarahumaras living in the vicinity of Urique, Chihuahua, still eat the fruits of this tree raw or with milk and sugar (pers. obs.).

Vitex pyramidata grows from Sonora to Yucatan (Wiggins 1964). Mature fruits are also black and were eaten raw or cooked (Altschul 1973; von Reis and Lipp 1982; *Gentry 2952,* ARIZ) like those of *V. mollis* (Martin et al. 1998). Guarijios collected the fruits in the summer (Gentry 1942, 1963). Fruits sold for 13 dollars per *fanega* (1.6 bushels) at Quiocoba, Sonora, in the mid 1930s (*Gentry 2952,* ARIZ).

Viscaceae | Mistletoe or Christmas Mistletoe Family

Phoradendron | mistletoe

P. californicum **Nuttall**
mistletoe, mesquite mistletoe, tojí, chile de espino

P. diguetianum **Van Tieghem**
mistletoe

Although the fruits of various species of this family are often considered potentially toxic, the pinkish red or white fruits of *P. californicum* and its varieties are edible. The white fruits of *P. tomentosum* (de Candolle) Engelm. ex A. Gray have a very bitter taste and should not be confused with the edible species, as discovered by Amadeo Rea (1997). Fruits of *P. californicum* were eaten by the River Pima, the Tohono O'odham, and Maricopa (Russell 1908; Castetter and Underhill 1935; Curtin 1949; Castetter and Bell 1951). River Pimas gathered and boiled the fruits without stripping them from the stem (Russell 1908). They simply took the branches in their fingers and ate off the berries. Forty years later, Leonora Curtin (1949) was told how the River Pima mashed, boiled, and ate the berries, which to them tasted like pudding.

It is interesting to note that the Gila River Pima classify mistletoe as a tree, "because it belongs to trees" (Rea 1997:255). In contrast, the Maricopa gathered the branches of its host plant and stripped them of the mistletoe fruits, which they boiled into a sticky, tasteless liquid that was combined with wheat gruel (Castetter and Bell 1951). The Tohono O'odham still gathered the fruit in the early 1900s. In the 1970s and early 1980s, those living at Quitovac, Sonora, did not use the fruits, although they recognized the plant (Nabhan et al. 1982).

The Cahuilla gathered the fruit of *P. californicum* from November through April, ground and mixed them with small amounts of ash (perhaps to remove any bitterness), and boiled the meal (Bean and Saubel 1972). Seris did not differentiate between *P. californicum,* which is common in their area, and the less frequent *P. diguetianum* (Felger and Moser 1985), even though the leaves of the latter are not scalelike, but more leaflike. Similar to the Gila River Pima, the Seri classified *P. californicum* according to which host plant it parasitized. The fruits were eaten only if the plants grew on certain legumes, such as *Prosopis, Olneya,* or *Acacia.* When growing on other plants, such as *Cercidium* and *Condalia,* the fruits were considered bitter. After knocking the mature fruits off the branches onto a blanket, the Seri often fed the berries to children.

Botanists once recognized different varieties of *P. californicum* based, in part, on fruit. *Phoradendron californicum* var. *californicum* and *P. californicum* var. *distans* Trel. were the most common of the desert mistletoes; these varieties parasitize *Prosopis, Olneya, Acacia,* and *Condalia* (Wiggins 1964). Both produce red fruits. The lesser-known, white-fruited variety, *P. californicum* var. *leucocarpum* Jeps., grew within the range of the species parasitizing *Prosopis.* Apparently, fruit color was not important to Seris when selecting the best-tasting berries, although they considered the white fruits (which could be the white-fruited form of *P. californicum* or *P. diguetianum*) as being sweet (Whiting 1957; Felger and Moser 1985). Likewise, modern taxonomists do not consider fruit color as an important character, and these varieties are not currently recognized. It is not known if there is any correlation between the amount of bitterness or sweetness of the different colored fruits of *P. californicum* or if these qualities are influenced by the type of host plant the mistletoe parasitizes, as suggested by Seri folklore. It is also not known if the white-fruited form of *P. californicum* parasitizes plants other than *Prosopis* or whether *P. diguetianum* parasitizes genera other than *Jacquinia, Castela, Jatropha, Maytenus,* and *Larrea.* Of these last genera, only *Larrea* appears in Seri classification of mistletoe.

Vitaceae | Grape Family

Vitis | grape

V. arizonica **Engelmann**
Arizona grape, canyon grape, parra, uva, uva cimarróna, vid

V. girdiana **Munson**
valley grape

V. peninsularis **M. E. Jones**
parras cimarrónas, narras

Vitis arizonica enters the Sonoran Desert in canyons and along streams in Pinal, Gila, and Pima Counties, Arizona and marginally in Sonora. *Vitis girdiana* grows in San Bernardino and Inyo Counties, California, extending into northern Baja California along desert mountain slopes (Wiggins 1964). *Vitis peninsularis* grows along streams and in canyons in the mountains of the cape region of Baja California.

Like the cultivated grape (*Vitis vinifera* L.), the small berries of *V. arizonica, V. peninsularis,* and *V. girdiana* are edible, although opinions varied as to their palatability. The berries of *V. arizonica* were often used as food, but were considered by some to be not very tasty (Palmer 1878; Castetter 1935). Edward Palmer (1871: 416, cited as *V. californica* Benth.) stated "the quantity of this fruit that an Indian will consume at one time is scarcely credible." Berries are small and somewhat sour, particularly if not fully ripe.

Palmer confused *V. californica* Bentham with its more eastern relative *V. arizonica.* He provided a lengthy discussion on *V. arizonica* distribution and possible cultivation, prior to Engelmann's recognizing it as an undescribed species (Palmer 1871:415–416):

> The ancient Pueblo Indians were in the habit of cultivating [wild grape, cited as *V. californica*], as is evident from the peculiar distribution of the plants near ruined settlements. In Arizona, near Fort Whipple, they are arranged in rows and are very old. At Camp Lincoln, on the Verde River, near which were a number of ancient Indian ruins, a small stream called Clear Creek passed close by, on each side of which was a narrow strip of rich land, covered with under-brush, among which were found several grape vines, planted at short intervals, that differed in many particulars from those native to the locality. The small kinds, found so universally in the woods, were growing abundantly all around, but no other spot could the cultivated kinds found on Clear Creek be discovered. The latter were near dilapidated habitations, the owners of which were evidently domestic in their habits. The vines were quite old, and had been repeatedly burnt off, as the stumps testified.

Palmer continued by describing the fruit as being superior in flavor to the wild grapes, some "foxy" in their nature, or resembling the "Isabella" and "Frontignac" grape. Specimens of each were sent to Engelmann in St. Louis, who had the seeds planted. Although it appeared to Palmer that five or six varieties were represented in the seed lot sent, it was Engelmann's opinion that they were one species distinct from an "eastern [U.S.] plant," but closely related to *V. californica.* Engelmann gave it the provisional name of *V. arizonensis.* Those grapes Palmer observed as "native to the locality" were in all probability "pure" *V. arizonica* (a taxon Engelmann described as distinct in 1868). Those grapes found in association with habitations, at least at Clear Creek, were probably domesticated selections from these native populations.

Western Apaches ate the ripe berries of *V. arizonica* raw or pounded, dried, and stored the meal in sacks, never in a vessel (Buskirk 1986). They also boiled the juice to make a wine. Southeastern Yavapais collected the grapes in the Pinal and Mazatzal Mountains (Gifford 1932). Gila River Pimas were familiar with the plants, which they knew from higher elevations, and its fruits, although edible, were considered quite sour (Rea 1997).

Cahuillas gathered the grapes of *V. girdiana* from June through August and ate them fresh or cooked them in stews (Bean and Saubel 1972). They also dried the fruits as raisins and boiled them in water before eating. The Cahuilla at Anza, California, made a wine in the late 1880s from this wild grape.

A type of wild grape grows in some of the deeper canyons of Baja California (Aschmann 1959:60) around Mission Guadalupe (near 24°N), south of the Sierra San Francisco, but north of the cape region. Local inhabitants consumed its fruit during the fall, but their diet did not seem to have benefited greatly from this food. Fr. Píccolo was quite impressed with the wild grapes he, a captain, and nine soldiers found. The group set out west from Loreto into the northern end of the Sierra de la Giganta to search for rancherias in May 1699, at the encouragement of the friendly natives (Burrus 1971). After trudging on for "many leagues," the exhausted group fell upon a "patch of wild grapes which extended for a full league" (Burrus 1971:161). The vines had very thick trunks and "if they were cultivated and pruned, they would abandon their wild nature; and even as they are, they produce an abundant crop of unripe grapes, and ripe ones in season." The Cochimí called the wild grapevine, its grapes, and those of European origin *kadeibi.*

The wild grapes were described by Fr. del Barco (1980:178, cited as *V. arizonica* by Carter) as being "small and they never ripen to sweetness but, rather, remain always sour, and they could be used only to make vinegar if they were collected in quantity." The cultivation of grapes was a high priority for the Jesuit missionaries upon arriving in Baja California. Fr. Juan de Ugarte, who, having been inspired by these wild grapes, requested that *V. vinifera* (European grape) be brought over from the mainland to the peninsula to be planted, this being the "first foreign tree" intentionally grown in either Alta or Baja California (del Barco 1980:179): "[Fr. Ugarte] first conceived the thought of bringing grapevines to California [from the Yaqui missions] for planting when he saw there these wild ones of which we speak, inferring that, since the soil of itself produced this kind, it would be suitable to plant in it a vine similar, although nobler without comparison."

Townsend Brandegee (1889:139) mentioned a type of grape that seemed "to belong to *V. californica,* rather than to *V. arizonica,* growing in the damp canyons near Comondú and Purísima (near Loreto at 26°N). In the canyons of the Sierra San Francisco, Baja California Sur (27'30°N), are found extensive populations of a type that produces large, very tasty grapes (*Hodgson 9568 & Rebman,* DES, SD, ASU, BCMEX; fig. 151). It

appears to be distinct from *V. girdiana,* which grows well north of these mountains, *V. peninsularis,* which grows to the south, and *V. vinifera,* which grows nearby at a small rancheria. Could the now extinct native people of the area have once used these grapes? Is it of hybrid origin between *V. vinifera* and another, as yet unknown grape, as suggested by Michael Moore (pers. comm.)? The identity of the large-fruited wild grape in the canyons of the Sierra San Francisco remains a puzzle.

Further south, the Guaicura and Pericú probably used fruits of *V. peninsularis.* Townsend Brandegee (1891a) noted that the local inhabitants of the cape region used the fruit of an unidentified wild grape for making a native wine. Fr. Nentvig (1980) also remarked that inhabitants of north-central Sonora made vinegar and wine from the grapes of a wild grapevine, or *V. arizonica.*

FIGURE 151. ***Vitis*** sp. Cañón Solidad, Sierra de San Francisco, Baja California, September 1995 (*Hodgson 9568 & Rebman,* DES, ASU, SD, BCMEX).

Appendixes

APPENDIX I

Plant Species and Parts Used

Species with references cited are not included in the text. FR: fruit (mature and immature, does not include achenes); SE: seeds (mature and immature, includes arils and achenes); LS: leaves, stems, herbage, flowering stalks in Agavaceae, Nolinaceae, and Crassulaceae, caudices in Agavaceae; RO: underground parts (rhizomes, bulbs, corms, roots); FL: flowers (includes pollen and flower buds); O: other; REF: references, given at end of appendix.

	FR	SE	LS	RO	FL	O	REF
Gymnospermae							
Ephedraceae							
Ephedra aspera		?	x				
E. californica		x	x				
E. fasciculata		?	x				
E. nevadensis		x	x				
E. trifurca		x	x				
E. viridis		x	x				
Angiospermae							
Monocotyledoneae							
Agavaceae							
Agave capensis			x?		?		
A. cerulata			x		?		
A. chrysoglossa			x				
A. colorata			x				
A. datylio			x?				
A. delamateri			x		?		
A. deserti			x		x		
A. felgeri			x				
A. fortiflora			x		?		
A. giganteus			x		?		
A. mckelveyana			x		?		
A. moranii			x		x		
A. murpheyi			x		?		
A. palmeri			x		?		
A. pelona			x		?		
A. shawii			x		x		
A. shrevei			x		?		
A. sobria			x		?		
A. subsimplex			x		?		
A. utahensis			x		?		
A. vivipara			x		x		
A. zebra			x		?		
Hesperoyucca whipplei		x	x		x		
Yucca arizonica	x	x	x		x		
Y. baccata	x	x	x		x		
Y. brevifolia		x	x		x		
Y. elata		?	x		x		

	FR	SE	LS	RO	FL	O	REF
Yucca schidigera	x	?			x		
Y. schottii	x	?					
Y. thornberi	x	?					
Y. valida	x	x					
Alismataceae							
Sagittaria cuneata				?			
S. latifolia				x			
Arecaceae							
Erythea armata	x	x	x				
E. brandegeei	x	?	x				
E. elegans	x	?	x				
Sabal uresana	x	?	x				
Washingtonia filifera	x	x	x				
W. robusta	x	x	x				
Commelinaceae							
Tradescantia occidentalis			x				
Cyperaceae							
Cyperus aristatus				x			42
C. erythrorhizos			x	x			
C. esculentus			x	x			
C. oderatus		x	x	x			
C. rotundus			x	x			
Schoenoplectus acutus		x		x			
S. americanus		x		x			
S. maritimus		x		x			
S. tabernaemontani		x		x	x		
Dioscoreaceae							
Dioscorea remotiflora				x			
Liliaceae							
Allium acuminatum				x			
A. bisceptrum var. *palmeri*				x			
A. fimbriatum				x			
A. haematochiton				x			
A. macropetalum				x			
A. parishii				x			
Calochortus ambiguus				x			
C. concolor				x			
C. dunnii				?			
C. flexuosus				x			
C. kennedyi				x			
C. plummerae				?			
C. weedii				?			
Dichelostemma capitatum ssp. *pauciflorum*				x	x		

	FR	SE	LS	RO	FL	O	REF
Hesperocallis undulata				x			
Tritelieopsis palmeri				x			
Nolinaceae							
Dasylirion wheeleri			x	x			
Dasylirion sp.			x				
Nolina beldingii			x				
N. bigelovii			x				
N. compacta			?				
N. matapensis			?				
N. microcarpa	x	x	x		x		
N. palmeri			?				
N. parryi			?				
Poaceae							
Bromus rigidus		x					38,48
Dactyloctenium aegyptium		x					10,47
Distichlis palmeri		x					
D. stricta		?					
Echinochloa colona		x					10,47
E. crus-galli		x					2,10,41,47
Elymus elymoides ssp. *elymoides* (syn., *Sitanion hystrix*)		x					29,41
Eragrostis mexicana		x					10
E. pectinacea		x					6
Eriochloa aristata		x					10
Hordeum pusillum		x					
Leptochloa viscida (syn., *Diplachne viscida*)		x					10
Leymus triticoides (syn., *Elymus triticoides*)		x					31,37
Muhlenbergia microsperma		x					18
M. rigens		x					34
Panicum hirticaule var. *miliaceum*		x					
P. obtusum		x					7,26
P. urvilleanum		x					37
Phalaris caroliniana		x					31
Phragmites australis		x				x	
Setaria vulpiseta (syn., *S. macrostachya*)		x					17,31
Sporobolus airoides		x					
S. contractus		x					
S. cryptandrus		x					
Urochloa fasciculata (syn., *Panicum fasciculatum*)		?					
Vulpia octoflora		x					11
Typhaceae							
Typha domingensis	x	x	x	x	x		
T. latifolia	x	x	x	x	x		
Zosteraceae							
Zostera marina		x					

	FR	SE	LS	RO	FL	O	REF
Dicotyledoneae							
Acanthaceae							
Justicia californica					x		
Aizoaceae							
Carpobrotus chilensis	x						
Mesembryanthemum crystallinum	x		x				
Mollugo verticillata				x			19,31
Trianthema portulacastrum		x?					
Amaranthaceae							
Amaranthus albus		x	x				
A. caudatus		x	x				
A. fimbriatus		x	x				
A. hybridus		x	x				
A. lepturus		x	x				
A. obcordatus		x	x				
A. palmeri		x	x				
A. retroflexus		x	x				
A. venulosus		x	x				
A. watsonii		x	x				
Anacardiaceae							
Cyrtocarpa edulis	x	x					
Malosma laurina	x?						
Rhus integrifolia	x	x					
R. kearneyi	x	x					
R. lentii	?	?					
R. ovata	x	x					
R. tepatate	?	?					
R. trilobata	x	x					
Apiaceae							
Coriandrum sativum		x		x			20,40
Daucus carota				x			7
D. pusillus				x			7
Apocynaceae							
Vallesia baileyana	?						
V. glabra	x						
V. laciniata	?						
Asclepiadaceae							
Asclepias erosa	x		x		x	x	19,24,31,43
A. speciosa	x		x		x	x	19,24,31,43
Marsdenia edulis	x						
Matelea arizonica	?						
M. balbisii	?						
M. caudata	x						
M. cordifolia	x						

	FR	SE	LS	RO	FL	O	REF
Matelea parvifolia	x						
M. petiolaris	x						
M. pringlei	x						
Sarcostemma arenarium	?				?		
S. clausum	?				?		
S. crispum	?				?		
S. cynanchoides	x		x		x	x	
S. hirtellum	?				?		
S. pannosum	x				?		

Asteraceae

	FR	SE	LS	RO	FL	O	REF
Almutaster pauciflorus (syn., *Aster pauciflorus*)			x				31
Ambrosia confertiflora			x	x			
Anisocoma acaulis			x				41
Artemisia dranunculus		x	x				6,30,33
A. ludoviciana		x					6,33
Bidens pilosa			x				
Cirsium arizonicum			x	x			45
C. mohavense			?				
C. neomexicanum			x				19,24,45
Dicoria canescens		x					
Eclipta prostrata (syn., *E. alba*)			x				31
Gaillardia pinnatifida		x?					45
Helianthus annuus		x			x		
H. niveus		?					
H. petiolaris		x					
Lactuca serriola			x				24
Lasthenia californica		x					
Layia glandulosa		x					38
Machaeranthera canescens		x					41
M. gracilis		x					10
Malacothrix glabrata (syn., *M. californica* var. *glabrata*)		x					38
Pectis angustifolia			x				
P. papposa			x		x		
Pluchea sericea				x			4
Sonchus asper			x				
S. oleraceus			x				
S. tenerrimus			x				
Tagetes filifolia			x				21

Bataceae

	FR	SE	LS	RO	FL	O	REF
Batis maritima			x	x			

Begoniaceae

	FR	SE	LS	RO	FL	O	REF
Begonia gracilis var. *nervipilosa*			x				

Berberidaceae

	FR	SE	LS	RO	FL	O	REF
Berberis haematocarpa	x						
B. harrisoniana	x						

	FR	SE	LS	RO	FL	O	REF
Bixaceae							
Amoreuxia gonzalezii	x	x	x	x	x		
A. palmatifida	x	x	x	x	x		
Bombacaceae							
Ceiba acuminata		x	x	x	x		
Boraginaceae							
Amsinckia intermedia		?	?				
A. tessellata		x	x				11,27
Bourreria sonorae	x	?					
Brassicaceae							
Brassica juncea		x	x				
B. nigra		x	x				
B. rapa		x	x				
B. tournefortii		?	x				
Capsella bursa-pastoris	x	x	x				12,19
Descurainia obtusa		x	x				
D. pinnata		x	x				
Lepidium flavum		x	x				
L. fremontii		x	x				
L. lasiocarpum		x	x				
L. nitidum		x	x				
L. oblongum		x	x				
L. thurberi		x	x				
L. virginicum		x	x				
Rorippa nasturtium-aquaticum			x				
R. palustris var. *hispida*			x				
Sisymbrium altissimum		x	x				16,24
S. irio		x	x				4,10,45
S. officinale			x				16,31
Stanleya pinnata		x	x				13,33,37,45
Thlaspi arvense		x					45
T. montanum		x					45
Thysanocarpus curvipes		x					12
T. erectens		?					
T. laciniatus		?					
Burseraceae							
Bursera fagaroides var. *elongata*		x					
B. microphylla		x					
Cactaceae							
Carnegiea gigantea	x	x					
Cylindropuntia acanthocarpa			x		x		
C. alcahes	?				?		
C. arbuscula	?				?		
C. bigelovii	x	x	x		x		
C. californica					?		
C. calmalliana	?				?		

	FR	SE	LS	RO	FL	O	REF
Cylindropuntia cholla	x	x			?		
C. ciribe	?				?		
C. echinocarpa					x		
C. fulgida	x	x	x		x		
C. × *kelvinensis*	x				x		
C. leptocaulis	x						
C. molesta	?				?		
C. munzii					?		
C. prolifera	?				?		
C. ramosissima	x		x				
C. spinosior	x		x		x		
C. tesajo	?				?		
C. × *tetracantha*	?						
C. thurberi	?						
C. versicolor	x		x		x		
C. whipplei		x					
Echinocactus polycephalus	x	x					
Echinocereus brandegeei	x	x					
E. engelmannii	x	x					
E. fasciculatus	x	x					
E. nicholii	x	x					
Echinocereus spp.	x	x					
Ferocactus cylindraceus	x	x	x		x		
F. emoryi	x	x	x		x		
F. fordii	x	x	?		x		
F. gracilis	x	x	?		?		
F. herrerae	x	x	x		x		
F. peninsulae	x	x?	?		x		
F. townsendianus	x	x	?		x		
F. viridescens	x	x	?		x		
F. wislizeni	x	x	x		x		
Ferocactus spp.	x	x					
Lophocereus schottii	x	x					
Mammillaria dioica	x	x					
M. goodridgei	x	x					
M. grahamii	x	x					
M. heyderi	x	x					
M. mainiae	x	x					
M. roseana	x	x					
M. sheldonii	x	x					
M. tetrancistra	x	x					
M. thornberi	x	x					
Mammillaria spp.	x	x					
Myrtillocactus cochal	x	x					
Opuntia basilaris	x		x		x		
O. bravoana	x				?		
O. chlorotica	?		?				?
O. × *curvospina*	?		?				
O. engelmannii	x	?	x				
O. ficus-indica	x		x				
O. gosseliniana	?						
O. littoralis	x		?				
O. oricola	?		?				
O. phaeacantha var. *major*	x		x				

	FR	SE	LS	RO	FL	O	REF
Opuntia pycnantha	?						
O. santa-rita	x		x		x		
O. tapona	x		x				
Pachycereus pecten-aboriginum	x	x					
P. pringlei	x	x					
Peniocereus greggii var. *transmontanus*	x	x		x	x		
P. striatus	x	x		x			
Pereskiopsis porteri	x						22
Stenocereus alamosensis	x	x					
S. eruca	x	x					
S. gummosus	x	x					
S. thurberi	x	x					
Capparaceae							
Cleome isomeris	x		x		x		
C. lutea		x	x		?		
C. serrulata	x	x	x				
C. tenuis		?	?				
Forchammeria watsoni	x						
Polanisia dodecandra			x				7
Wislizenia refracta			x				46
Caprifoliaceae							
Sambucus nigra ssp. *canadensis*	x						
Caryophyllaceae							
Stellaria media			x				1,24
Celastraceae							
Maytenus phyllanthroides		x					
Schaefferia cuneifolia	?						
S. shrevei	x						
Chenopodiaceae							
Allenrolfea occidentalis		x					
Arthrocnemum subterminale		x					3
Atriplex californica		x					
A. elegans		x	x				
A. lentiformis		x	?				
A. polycarpa		x	?				
A. rosea		x					44
A. wrightii		x	x				
Atriplex spp.		x?					
Chenopodium album		?	x				
C. ambrosioides		x	x				
C. berlandieri		x	x				
C. californicum		x	x				
C. fremontii		x	x				
C. leptophyllum		x	x				
C. murale		x	x				

	FR	SE	LS	RO	FL	O	REF
Chenopodium neomexicanum var. *palmeri*		x	x				
Cycloloma atriplicifolium		x					
Monolepis nuttalliana		x	x				
Salicornia europea		x					
S. pacifica		x					
Salsola tragus (syn., *S. iberica*)		x	x				16,24
Sarcobatus vermiculatus		x					15
Suaeda moquinii (syn., *S. torreyana*)		x	x				16

Convolvulaceae

	FR	SE	LS	RO	FL	O	REF
Ipomoea arborescens	x			x			
I. bracteata				x			
I. jicama				x			
I. purpurea			x		x		
Merremia aurea				x			

Crassulaceae

	FR	SE	LS	RO	FL	O	REF
Dudleya arizonica			x				
D. attenuata			x				
D. pulverulenta			x				
D. saxosa			?				
Dudleya spp.			x				

Cucurbitaceae

	FR	SE	LS	RO	FL	O	REF
Apodanthera palmeri	x?	x?					
A. undulata	x?	x?					
Cucurbita digitata		x					
C. foetidissima	x?	x		x?			
C. palmata		x					
Tumamoca mcdougalii	x						

Ebenaceae

	FR	SE	LS	RO	FL	O	REF
Diospyros californica	x						
D. sonorae	x	x					

Euphorbiaceae

	FR	SE	LS	RO	FL	O	REF
Cnidoscolus maculatus		x					
C. palmeri				x			
Manihot chlorosticta				x			

Fabaceae

	FR	SE	LS	RO	FL	O	REF
Acacia brandegeana		x					
A. cochliacantha	x	x					
A. greggii	x	x					
A. pennatula		x					
Astragalus nuttallianus		x					4,5
Caesalpinia platyloba		x					
C. pulcherrima		x					
Cercidium floridum	x	x			x		

	FR	SE	LS	RO	FL	O	REF
Cercidium microphyllum	x	x			x		
Crotalaria incana		x					
C. pumila		x					
Havardia mexicana (syn., *Pithecellobium mexicanum*)		?					
Hoffmanseggia glauca				x			
Leucaena brandegeei	x	x					23
L. microcarpa	x	x					23
Lysiloma candida		x					
L. microphyllum		x					
L. watsonii		x					
Medicago sativa		x	x				33
Olneya tesota		x					
Parkinsonia aculeata		x					
Phaseolus acutifolius		x					
P. filiformis		x					
P. ritensis	x	x					
Pithecellobium confine		x					
P. dulce	x	x					
P. leucospermum	x?	x					
P. sonorae		?					
Prosopis glandulosa var. *torreyana*	x	x			x		
P. pubescens	x	x			x		
P. velutina	x	x			x		
Trifolium mucronatum ssp. *lacerum* (syn., *T. lacerum*)			x				2,12,19,25
T. repens			x				12,19,25

Fagaceae

	FR	SE	LS	RO	FL	O	REF
Quercus agrifolia	x						
Q. chrysolepis	x						
Q. dumosa	x						
Q. emoryi	x						
Q. engelmannii	x						
Q. grisea	x						
Q. kelloggii	x						
Q. oblongifolia	x						
Q. palmeri	x						
Q. peninsularis	x						
Q. turbinella	x						

Fouquieriaceae

	FR	SE	LS	RO	FL	O	REF
Fouquieria burragei		?					
F. diguetii		?					
F. macdougalii		?			x		
F. splendens		x			x		

Geraniaceae

	FR	SE	LS	RO	FL	O	REF
Erodium cicutarium			x				
E. texanum			?				

Grossulariaceae

	FR	SE	LS	RO	FL	O	REF
Ribes quercetorum	x						48

	FR	SE	LS	RO	FL	O	REF
Juglandaceae							
Juglans major		x					
Koeberliniaceae							
Koeberlinia spinosa	x						
Lamiaceae							
Hedeoma nana		x					9
Hyptis emoryi		?					
H. suaveolens		x					
Salvia apiana		x					
S. carduacea		x					
S. columbariae		x					
Lennoaceae							
Pholisma arenarium				x			
P. sonorae				x			
Linaceae							
Linum lewisii		x					43
Loasaceae							
Mentzelia adhaerans		?					
M. albicaulis		x					
M. multiflora		?					
Mentzelia spp.		?					
Lythraceae							
Ammannia coccinea		x					10
Malpighiaceae							
Bunchosia sonorensis	?						
Malpighia diversifolia	x						
M. emarginata	x						
M. ovata	?						
Malvaceae							
Eremalche exilis			x				
Martyniaceae							
Proboscidea althaeifolia	x	x		x			
P. parviflora	x	x					
Moraceae							
Ficus brandegeei	x						
F. palmeri	x						
F. pertusa	x						
F. petiolaris	x						
Morus microphylla	x		x			x	

	FR	SE	LS	RO	FL	O	REF
Nyctaginaceae							
Boerhavia coulteri			x				
B. spicata (syn., *B. torreyana*)			?				
Pisonia capitata	x						
Salpianthus macrodontus				x			
Onagraceae							
Camissonia brevipes		x					10
C. claviformis		x	x				4,10
Orobanchaceae							
Orobanche bulbosa				?			
O. cooperi				x			
O. fasciculata				x			
Oxalidaceae							
Oxalis albicans			x				
O. stricta			x				
Passifloraceae							
Passiflora arida	x						
P. bryonioides	x						
P. foetida	x						
P. fruticosa	?						
P. mexicana	?						
P. palmeri	x						
Phytolaccaceae							
Rivina humilis	x						
Plantaginaceae							
Plantago australis ssp. *hirtella*		x					
P. heterophylla		x					
P. lanceolata		x					
P. major		x	x				
P. ovata		x					
P. patagonica		x					
P. rhodosperma		x					
P. virginica		x					
Polygonaceae							
Antigonon leptopus				x			
Eriogonum inflatum			x				
Polygonum argyrocoleon		x					10
P. aviculare		x					31
Rumex crispus		x	x				
R. hymenosepalus		x	x				
R. salicifolius var. *mexicanus* (syn., *R. mexicanus*)		?	?				
R. violascens		x	x				

	FR	SE	LS	RO	FL	O	REF
Portulacaceae							
Calandrinia ciliata		x	x				
Cistanthe ambigua (syn., *Calandrinia ambigua*)		?	?				
Claytonia perfoliata			x				
Portulaca oleracea		x	x				
P. pilosa		x	x				
Ranunculaceae							
Delphinium scaposum					x		28
Resedaceae							
Oligomeris linifolia		x					
Rhamnaceae							
Condalia brandegeei	x						
C. correllii	?						
C. warnockii var. *kearneyana*	x						
Karwinskia humboldtiana	x						
K. parvifolia	x						
Ziziphus amole	x						
Z. obtusifolius var. *canescens*	x						
Z. parryi	x						
Rhizophoraceae							
Rhizophora mangle	x						
Rosaceae							
Prunus fasciculata	x						
P. fremontii	x						
P. ilicifolia	x	x					
Rubiaceae							
Randia armata	x						
R. echinocarpa	x						
R. laevigata	x						
R. megacarpa	x						
R. obcordata	x						
R. sonorensis	x						
R. thurberi	x						
Salicaceae							
Populus fremontii					x		7,36,45
Sapotaceae							
Sideroxylon leucophyllum	?						
S. occidentale	x						
S. peninsularis	?						
Scrophulariaceae							
Mimulus guttatus			x				12,31

	FR	SE	LS	RO	FL	O	REF
Simmondsiaceae							
Simmondsia chinensis		x					
Solanaceae							
Capsicum annuum var. *glabriusculum*	x	x					
Chamaesaracha coronopus	?						
C. sordida	?						
Lycium andersonii	x						
L. berlandieri	x						
L. exsertum	x						
L. fremontii	x						
L. pallidum	x						
L. parishii	x						
L. richii	x						
L. torreyi	x						
Physalis acutifolia	x						
P. angulata	x						
P. crassifolia	x						
P. hederifolia	x						
P. ixocarpa	x						
P. longifolia var. *longifolia*	x						
P. philadelphica var. *immaculata*	x						
P. pubescens	x						
Solanum americanum	x		x				
S. douglasii	x		x				
Sterculiaceae							
Guazuma ulmifolia	x	x					
Theophrastaceae							
Jacquinia macrocarpa ssp. *pungens*	x						
Ulmaceae							
Celtis iguanaea	x						
C. laevigata var. *brevipes*, var. *reticulata*	x						
C. pallida	x						
Verbenaceae							
Aloysia barbata			x				
A. wrightii			x				
Burroughsia fastigiata			x				
Glandularia delticola (syn., *Verbena delticola*)			x				34
Lantana achyranthifolia (syn., *L. macropoda*)	?						
L. horrida	x						
L. velutina	x						
Lippia palmeri			x				
Vitex mollis	x						
V. pyramidata	x						

	FR	SE	LS	RO	FL	O	REF
Viscaceae							
Phoradendron californicum	x						
P. diguetianum	x						
Vitaceae							
Vitis arizonica	x						
V. girdiana	x						
V. peninsularis	x						
Vitis sp.	x						
Total taxa: 534	**199**	**234**	**173**	**55**	**52**	**5**	

References:

1. Altschul 1973; 2. Aschmann 1952; 3. Barrows 1900; 4. Bean and Saubel 1972; 5. Bohrer 1986; 6. Bye 1972; 7. Castetter 1935; 8. Castetter and Underhill 1935; 9. Castetter and Opler 1936; 10. Castetter and Bell 1951; 11. Chamberlain 1911; 12. Chestnut 1902; 13. Coville 1892; 14. Curtin 1949; 15. *Curtin 33b*, DES; 16. Elmore 1943; 17. Felger and Moser 1976; 18. Felger and Moser 1985; 19. Fernald and Kinsey 1958; 20. Fewkes 1896; 21. Gentry 1963; 22. Goldman 1916; 23. Hake 1983; 24. Harrington 1967; 25. Hedrick 1972; 26. Hough 1897; 27. Hrdlička 1908; 28. Kearney et al. 1960; 29. Kelly 1932; 30. Kelly 1964; 31. Kirk 1975; 32. Palmer 1871; 33. Palmer 1878; 34. Pennington 1980; 35. Reagan 1929; 36. Saunders 1948; 37. Sparkman 1908; 38. Standley 1912; 39. Stevenson 1915; 40. Steward 1938; 41. Swank 1932; 42. Sweet 1976; 43. Vestal 1952; 44. Weber and Seaman 1985; 45. Whiting 1939, 1966; 46. Alvarez de Williams 1987; 47. Yanovsky 1936; 48. Zigmond 1981.

APPENDIX II

Fruiting Periods of Selected Species Providing Edible Fruit

These diagrams show the beginning and end of the fruiting periods or, in some cases, the probable but undocumented fruiting times. For example, *Berberis haematocarpa* mature fruits are available from early May through mid-July and taper off from late July through late August. IFR, immature fruit; MFR, mature fruit.

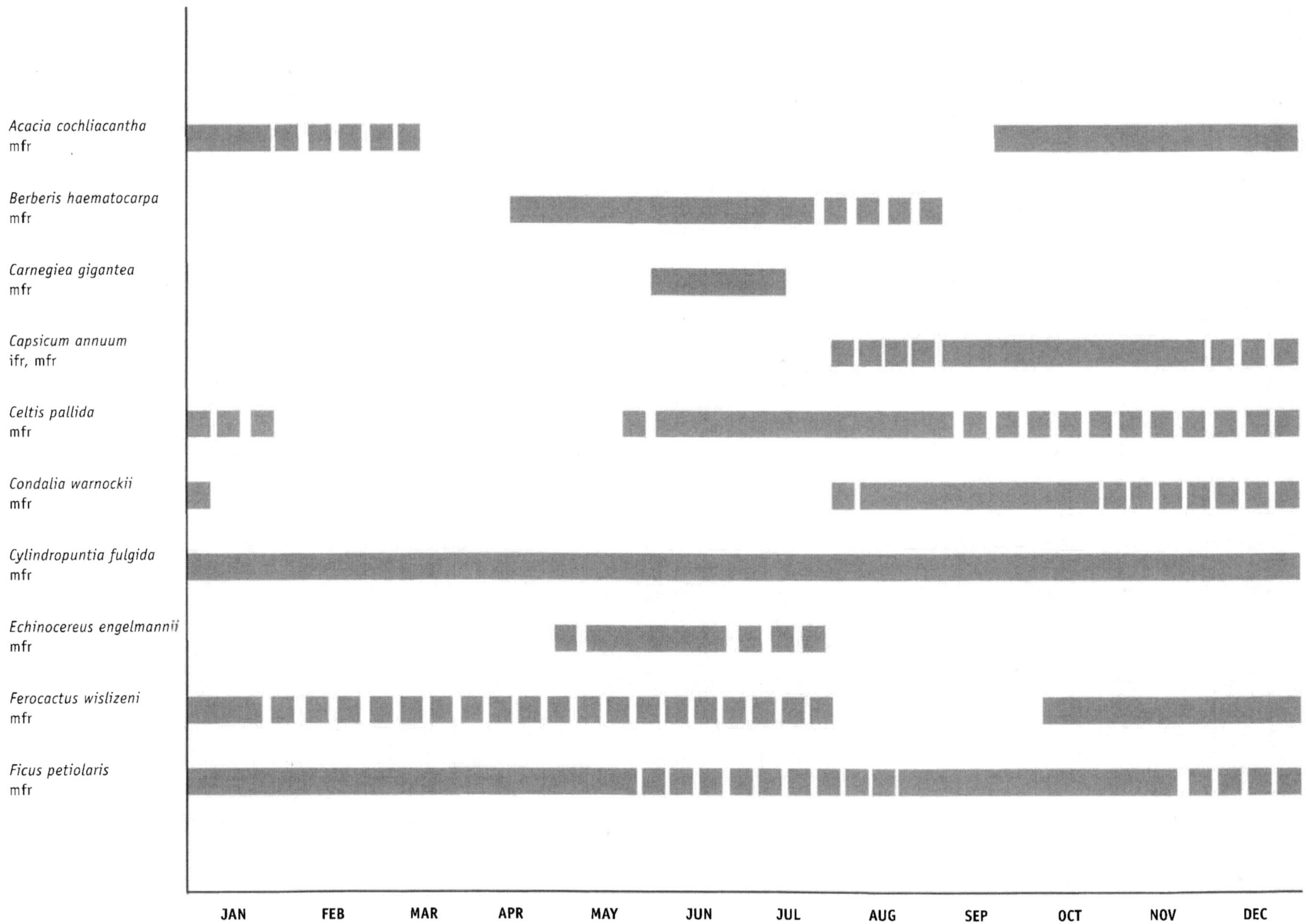

Acacia cochliacantha
mfr
Berberis haematocarpa
mfr
Carnegiea gigantea
mfr
Capsicum annuum
ifr, mfr
Celtis pallida
mfr
Condalia warnockii
mfr
Cylindropuntia fulgida
mfr
Echinocereus engelmannii
mfr
Ferocactus wislizeni
mfr
Ficus petiolaris
mfr
JAN
FEB
MAR
APR
MAY
JUN
JUL
AUG
SEP
OCT
NOV
DEC

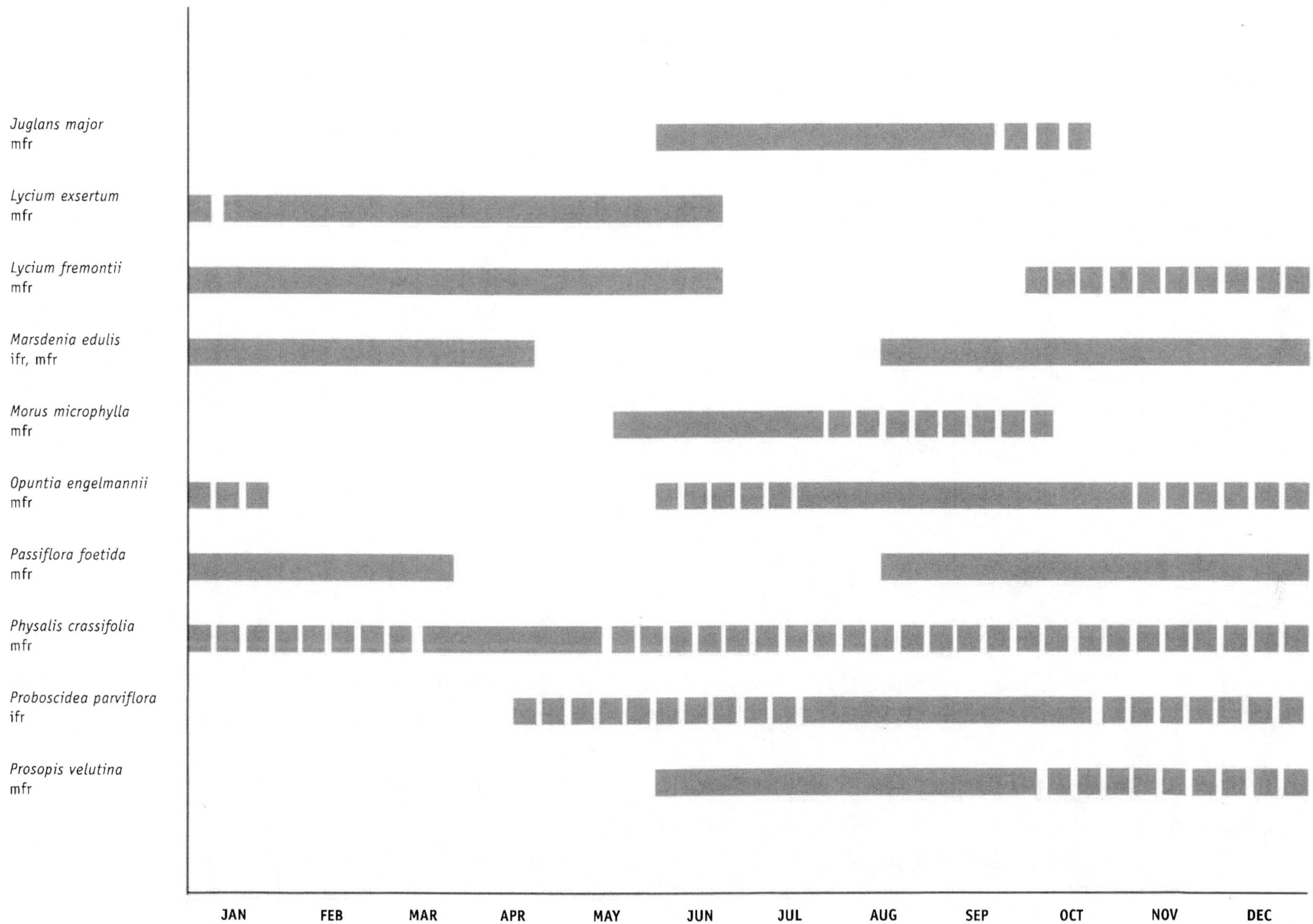
Juglans major
mfr
Lycium exsertum
mfr
Lycium fremontii
mfr
Marsdenia edulis
ifr, mfr
Morus microphylla
mfr
Opuntia engelmannii
mfr
Passiflora foetida
mfr
Physalis crassifolia
mfr
Proboscidea parviflora
ifr
Prosopis velutina
mfr
JAN
FEB
MAR
APR
MAY
JUN
JUL
AUG
SEP
OCT
NOV
DEC

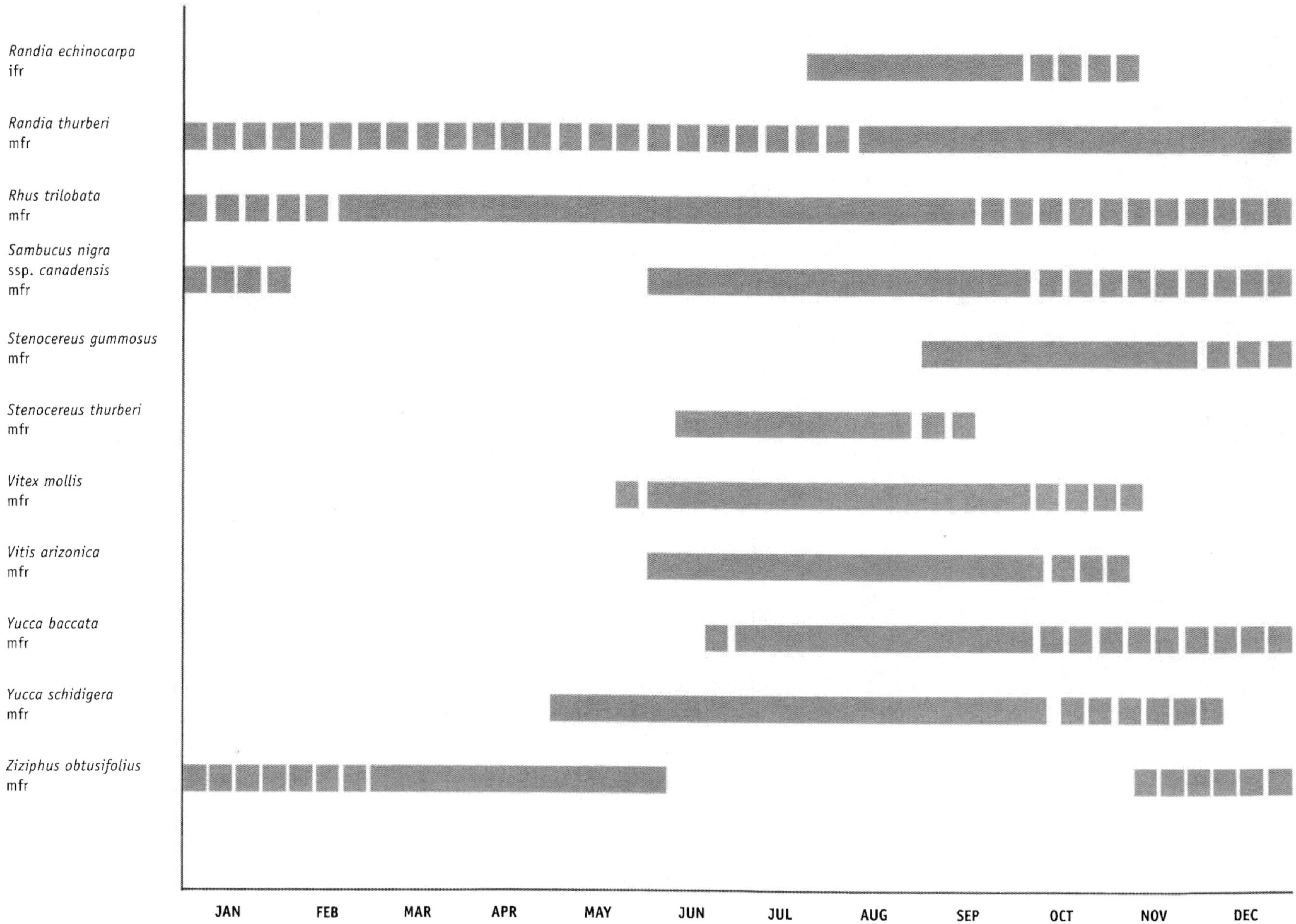
Randia echinocarpa
ifr
Randia thurberi
mfr
Rhus trilobata
mfr
Sambucus nigra
ssp. canadensis
mfr
Stenocereus gummosus
mfr
Stenocereus thurberi
mfr
Vitex mollis
mfr
Vitis arizonica
mfr
Yucca baccata
mfr
Yucca schidigera
mfr
Ziziphus obtusifolius
mfr
JAN
FEB
MAR
APR
MAY
JUN
JUL
AUG
SEP
OCT
NOV
DEC

APPENDIX III

Fruiting Periods of Selected Species Providing Edible Seeds

These diagrams show the beginning and end of the fruiting periods or, in some cases, the probable but undocumented fruiting times. See appendix II for an explanation of how to read the diagrams. ISE, immature seeds; MSE, mature seeds.

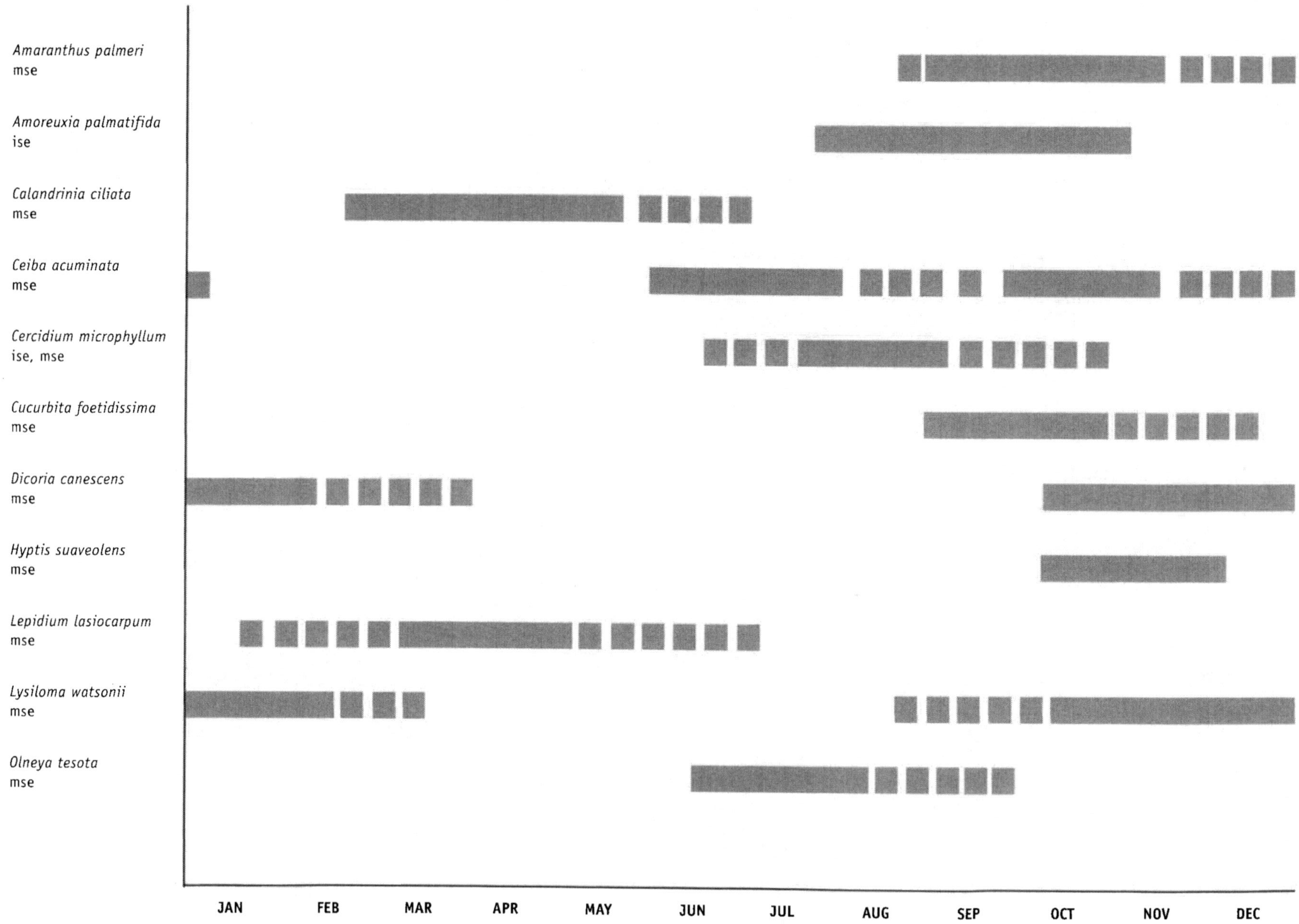

Amaranthus palmeri
mse
Amoreuxia palmatifida
ise
Calandrinia ciliata
mse
Ceiba acuminata
mse
Cercidium microphyllum
ise, mse
Cucurbita foetidissima
mse
Dicoria canescens
mse
Hyptis suaveolens
mse
Lepidium lasiocarpum
mse
Lysiloma watsonii
mse
Olneya tesota
mse
JAN
FEB
MAR
APR
MAY
JUN
JUL
AUG
SEP
OCT
NOV
DEC

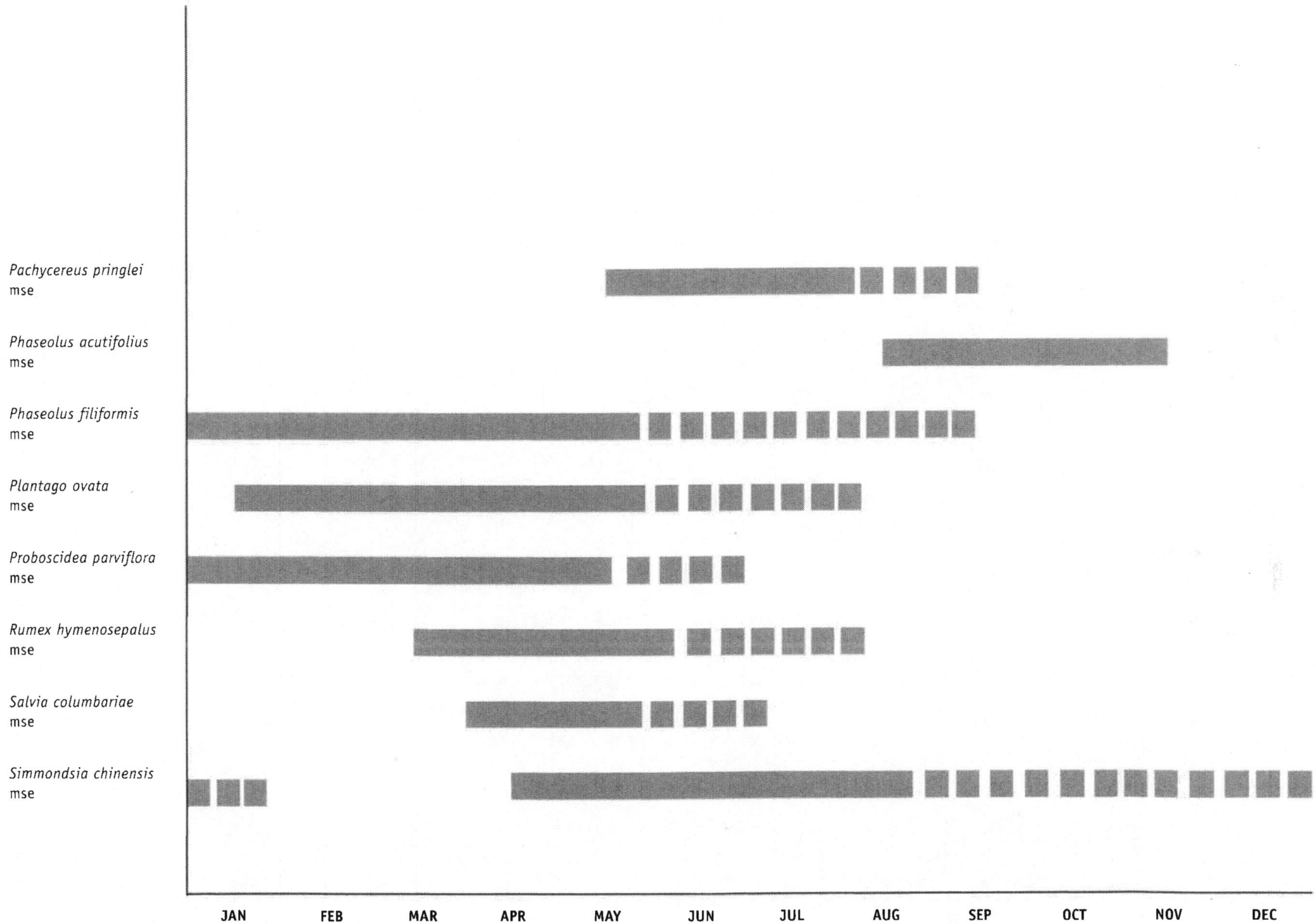
Pachycereus pringlei
mse
Phaseolus acutifolius
mse
Phaseolus filiformis
mse
Plantago ovata
mse
Proboscidea parviflora
mse
Rumex hymenosepalus
mse
Salvia columbariae
mse
Simmondsia chinensis
mse
JAN
FEB
MAR
APR
MAY
JUN
JUL
AUG
SEP
OCT
NOV
DEC

APPENDIX IV

Common Names (Non-English)

Scientific names in bold type refer to the common names that are used solely in Sonora and/or Baja California. For example, *ajo* is used for *Allium* spp. throughout much of Mexico, but only in Sonora or Baja California does the name refer to *Hesperocallis undulata*.

acebuche	*Celtis pallida*
agiá	***Guazuma ulmifolia***
agigandú	***Acacia brandegeana***
abrojo	***Ziziphus obtusifolius*** var. ***canescens***
agrillo	*Rhus trilobata*
aguabola	*Maytenus phyllanthoides*
aguiche	*Guazuma ulmifolia*
aguilla	***Cylindropuntia molesta***
aguja del pastor	*Erodium cicutarium*
agujitas	*Erodium cicutarium*
ahiyá, ajiyá	***Guazuma ulmifolia***
ajo	*Allium* spp., ***Hesperocallis undulata***
ajonjoli	*Crotalaria incana*
alchicoria dulce	*Sonchus asper, S. oleraceus*
alfilaria	*Erodium cicutarium*
algarroba	***Acacia greggii, A. pennatula***
algerita	*Berberis haematocarpa*
amacostic	*Ficus petiolaris*
amal	***Agave shawii***
amate	*Ficus petiolaris*
amate amarillo	*Ficus petiolaris*
amezquite	*Ficus pertusa*
amole	*Ziziphus amole*
amole dulce	*Ziziphus amole*
amul	***Agave deserti***
anabá	***Ficus brandegeei, F. palmeri***
arbor de hierro	***Olneya tesota***
arbor que tulle	*Karwinskia humboldtiana*
aschecani	*Chenopodium berlandieri*
atuto	*Vitex mollis*
babiso	***Erythea elegans***
bacanora	***Agave vivipara***
bacapore	*Parkinsonia aculeata*
bachata	***Ziziphus obtusifolius*** var. ***canescens***
bagota	***Parkinsonia aculeata***
bainora	*Celtis iguanaea, C. pallida*
bainora preito	*Pisonia capitata*
barbachatas	***Ziziphus obtusifolius*** var. ***canescens***
barba del sol	*Caesalpinia pulcherrima*
barbon	***Lophocereus schottii***
barehata	***Lycium berlandieri*** var. ***parviflorum***
batanene blanco	*Marsdenia edulis*
bebelama	*Sideroxylon occidentale*
bejuco de la candlai	*Ipomoea bracteata*
bellota	***Quercus emoryi, Q. oblongifolia***
berro	*Rorippa nasturtium-aquaticum*
bixhumi	*Sambucus nigra* ssp. *canadensis*
bis(z)naga	*Echinocactus* spp., ***Ferocactus cylindraceus, F. emoryi,*** *F. herrarae,* ***F. viridescens***
bis(z)naga de agua	***Ferocactus wislizeni***
bis(z)naga de dulce	*Echinocactus* spp.
bis(z)naga meloncillo	*Echinocactus* spp.
bledo	*Amaranthus* spp.
bolsita de la vibora	***Passiflora arida, P. palmeri***
brasilillo	*Ziziphus amole*
bynora	*Pisonia capitata*
cabecita	*Mammillaria* spp.
cabeza del viejo	***Lophocereus schottii***, *Mammillaria* spp.
cacachila	*Karwinskia humboldtiana, K. parvifolia*
cachila	*Karwinskia humboldtiana*
cacoca, caloca	*Pisonia capitata*
calabaza	*Cucurbita* spp.
calabaza amargosa	*Cucurbita foetidissima*
calabaza de coyote	***Cucurbita foetidissima***
calabaz(c)illa	*Cucurbita digitata, C. foetidissima*
calabazilla loco	*Cucurbita foetidissima*
camote de los medanos	***Pholisma sonorae***
camote de ratón	*Hoffmanseggia glauca*
caña agria	***Rumex hymenosepalus***
caña aigre	*Begonia gracilis*
cañaigre	***Rumex hymenosepalus***
cañatilla	*Ephedra trifurca*
candelón	*Rhizophora mangle*
cañutillo	***Ephedra californica***, *E. trifurca*
capui	*Celtis pallida*
capul	*Celtis pallida*

capulin	*Karwinskia parvifolia*
capulincillo	*Karwinskia parvifolia*
capulincillo cimarrón	*Karwinskia parvifolia*
cardo	***Salvia carduacea***
cardón	*Pachycereus pecten-aboriginum*, ***P. pringlei***
cardón barbón	*Pachycereus pecten-aboriginum*
cardón espinoso	*Pachycereus pecten-aboriginum*
cardón hecho	*Pachycereus pecten-aboriginum*
cardón pelón	***Pachycereus pringlei***
caribe	***Cnidoscolus maculatus***
carrizo	*Phragmites australis*
casahuate	*Ipomoea arborescens*
casahuate blanco	*Ipomoea arborescens*
cascalojuche	*Randia laevigata*
cebolla	***Allium*** spp.
ceiba	*Ceiba acuminata*
ceniza	*Agave shrevei*
chacmol	*Caesalpinia pulcherrima*
chacua	*Randia echinocarpa*
cham	***Hyptis suaveolens***
chamizo	*Atriplex spp.*, ***Atriplex lentiformis***
chamizo cenizo	***Atriplex elegans, A. polycarpa***
chaparro blanco	*Celtis iguanaea*
chia	***Salvia carduacea, S. columbariae***
chia gorde	*Hyptis suaveolens*
chia grande	*Hyptis suaveolens*
chichicoyote	*Cucurbita digitata*
chichiquelite	*Solanum americanum*
chichiwo	*Dioscorea remotiflora*
chico	***Allenrolfea occidentalis***
chile de espino	***Phoradendron californicum***
chile del monte	***Capsicum annuum* var. *glabriusculum***
chilenola	***Stenocereus eruca***
chillipiquin	*Capsicum annuum* var. *glabriusculum*
chiltepín	***Capsicum annuum* var. *glabriusculum***
chimulí	***Fouquieria macdougalii***
china	*Karwinskia humboldtiana*
chinita	***Sonchus asper, S. oleraceus***
chinito	***Ficus pertusa***
chipil	*Crotalaria pumila*
chirahui	***Acacia pennatula***
chirinola	***Stenocereus eruca***
chiroui	***Acacia cochliacantha***
cholla	*Cylindropuntia* spp.
cholla de coyote	***Cylindropuntia fulgida***
cholla del oso	***Cylindropuntia bigelovii***
cholla dorado	***Cylindropuntia echinocarpa***
cholla güerra	***Cylindropuntia bigelovii, C. echinocarpa***
chollita	*Mammillaria* spp.
chual	***Chenopodium berlandieri, C. leptophyllum***
chucharillo	*Acacia cochliacantha*
chuchilatas	***Solanum americanum***
chucum blanco	*Pithecellobium dulce*
chufa	*Cyperus esculentus*
chuná	***Ficus pertusa***
chuparosa	***Justicia californica***
cirián chino	*Randia echinocarpa*
ciribe	***Cylindropuntia bigelovii***
ciruelo	***Cyrtocarpa edulis***
clavellina	***Cylindropuntia alcahes***
cocanatain	*Ipomoea bracteata*
cochal	***Myrtillocactus cochal***
cochino	*Amaranthus albus*
cola de gato	*Typha domingensis, T. latifolia*
combro	***Celtis laevigata***
comuchín	*Ficus pertusa*
condumo	*Sambucus nigra* ssp. *canadensis*
confite	***Lantana velutina***
confitura	***Hyptis suaveolens***
confiturilla	*Hyptis suaveolens*, ***Lantana horrida, L. velutina***
confiturilla blanca	***Lantana velutina***
conivari	***Hyptis suaveolens***
coomeme	***Justicia californica***
copal	*Bursera* ssp., *B. fagaroides* var. *elongata*, ***B. microphylla***
coquito	*Cyperus rotundus, Hoffmanseggia glauca*
coquito de tierra	***Dichelostemma capitatum* ssp. *pauciflorum***
corona de Cristo	***Koeberlinia spinosa***, *Passiflora foetida*
cortadillo	***Yucca elata***
covena	*Dichelostemma capitatum* ssp. *pauciflorum*
coveria	*Dichelostemma capitatum* ssp. *pauciflorum*
coyotillo	*Karwinskia humboldtiana*
cresta de gallo	*Sporobolus airoides*
crucecilla	***Randia laevigata***
crucecilla de la sierra	***Randia laevigata***
crucillo	***Condalia warnockii* var. *kearneyana***
cuadrado	*Manihot chlorosticta*
cuaguayote	*Marsdenia edulis*
cuahuilote	*Guazuma ulmifolia*
cual	***Chenopodium berlandieri, C. leptophyllum***
cubata	*Acacia cochliacantha*
cucharo	***Pithecellobium leucospermum***

cuentas de Santa Elena	*Cyperus odoratus*
cuernitos	*Proboscidea althaeifolia, P. parviflora*
cumaro	*Celtis iguanaea,* ***C. laevigata***
dátil	***Yucca arizonica, Y. elata***
dátil cimarrón	***Yucca valida***
datilillo	***Agave datylio, Yucca valida***
datiliyo	***Agave datylio***
dipúa	***Cercidium microphyllum***
dipúgo	***Cercidium microphyllum***
ejotón	***Pithecellobium confine***
else	***Agave shawii***
encino	***Quercus oblongifolia***
encino negro	***Quercus emoryi***
encino prieto	***Quercus emoryi***
encino roble	***Quercus palmeri***
epazote	*Chenopodium ambrosioides, Lepidium lasiocarpum*
epazote de comer	*Chenopodium ambrosioides*
escomite	*Phaseolus acutifolius*
espadana	*Typha domingensis, T. latifolia*
espadilla	*Typha domingensis, T. latifolia*
espino	***Acacia cochliacantha***
espuela del diablo	***Proboscidea althaeifolia***
flora de camarón	*Caesalpinia pulcherrima*
flor de guacamaya	*Caesalpinia pulcherrima*
flor de la pasion	*Passiflora arida*
flor de nabo	*Brassica rapa*
flor de niño	*Jacquinia macrocarpa* var. *pungens*
flor de San Francisco	*Caesalpinia pulcherrima*
flor de San Miguel	*Antigonon leptopus*
flor de sol	*Carpobrotus chilensis, Helianthus annuus*
frijillo	***Phaseolus filiformis***
frijol	***Phaseolus filiformis***
frijolillo	*Phaseolus acutifolius*
frutillo (-a)	***Lycium richii,*** *Vallesia glabra, Ziziphus amole*
frutillo negrito	*Karwinskia parvifolia*
garabato	***Celtis iguanaea, C. pallida,*** *Pisonia capitata*
garabato blanco	***Celtis laevigata***
garambullo	***Celtis pallida, Lophocereus schottii,*** *Pisonia capitata, Ziziphus obtusifolius* var. *canescens*
garboncillo bolando	*Phaseolus acutifolius*
garrapata	*Ziziphus obtusifolius* var. *canescens*
gatitio	*Proboscidea* spp.
gatuna	*Proboscidea parviflora*
gatuno	***Acacia greggii***
giganton	*Helianthus annuus*
girasol	*Helianthus annuus*

granadilla	***Malpighia emarginata, Passiflora arida, P. palmeri,*** *Maytenus phyllanthroides*
grangel	*Randia echinocarpa*
granjeno	*Celtis iguanaea, C. pallida*
guachigelle	*Parkinsonia aculeata*
guaco	*Cleome serrulata*
guacóporo	***Parkinsonia aculeata***
guamúchil	*Pithecellobium dulce*
guásima	*Guazuma ulmifolia*
guayavilla	*Salpianthus macrodontus*
guayparin	***Diospyros californica, D. sonorae***
guinolo	*Acacia cochliacantha*
guinora	***Acacia cochliacantha***
gumbo-limbo	*Bursera* spp.
gumbro	*Celtis pallida, Pisonia capitata*
hadmunig	*Ceiba acuminata*
hecho	*Pachycereus pecten-aboriginum*
hierba aigre	*Oxalis albicans*
hierba colorada	***Rumex hymenosepalus***
hierba del burro	***Allenrolfea occidentalis***
hierba mora	*Solanum americanum*
higuera	*Ficus petiolaris*
higuera cimarróna	***Ficus brandegeei, F. palmeri***
higueron	*Ficus petiolaris*
higuerote	***Ficus petiolaris***
hintimorreal	*Ephedra aspera*
hombre viejo	***Lophocereus schottii***
hoso	***Lycium berlandieri***
huasteco	*Celtis pallida*
huauzontle	*Chenopodium berlandieri*
hueilaqui	***Caesalpinia platyloba***
hueizacat	*Typha domingensis, T. latifolia*
huelatave	*Vallesia glabra*
huevos de venado	***Peniocereus greggii* var. *transmontanus***
huinole	***Acacia cochliacantha***
huirote	***Sarcostemma cynanchoides***
huitatove	***Vallesia glabra***
huizache	*Acacia pennatula*
igerá	***Ficus palmeri***
igualama	*Vitex mollis*
islay	*Prunus ilicifolia*
itamo real	*Ephedra aspera*
jacamatraca, jarrmatraca	***Peniocereus striatus***
jari	*Vitex mollis*
jicama	***Ipomoea bracteata, I. jicama***
jito	*Forchammeria watsoni*
jobebi	***Erythrea aculeata***
jojoba	***Simmondsia chinensis***

jojolino	*Crotalaria pumila*
joso	***Lycium berlandieri***
jujuhuali	***Vitex mollis***
junco	*Koeberlinia spinosa, Parkinsonia aculeata*
junco marino	***Parkinsonia aculeata***
kapo	***Pectis papposa***
kapok	*Ceiba acuminata*
lambrisco	*Rhus trilobata*
lampote	*Helianthus annuus*
lante, llanten	*Plantago major*
lantisco	*Malosma laurina*
lechuguilla	***Agave palmeri, A. shrevei, A. vivipara,*** *Hesperoyucca whipplei*
lechuguilla ceniza	*Agave shrevei*
lemita	*Rhus trilobata*
lengua de vaca	*Rumex crispus*
limoncillo	***Pectis papposa***
lipasote	*Lepidium lasiocarpum*
machauhui	***Lysiloma watsonii***
maguey	*Agave* spp.
maiz de Texas	*Helianthus annuus*
majagua de toro	*Guazuma ulmifolia*
mala mujer	***Cnidoscolus palmeri***
mambia	*Solanum americanum*
mangle	*Maytenus phyllanthroides, Rhizophora mangle*
mangle aguabola	*Maytenus phyllanthroides*
mangle colorado	*Rhizophora mangle*
mangle dulce	***Maytenus phyllanthroides,*** *Rhizophora mangle*
mangle gateador	*Rhizophora mangle*
mangle rojo	*Rhizophora mangle*
mangle salado	*Rhizophora mangle*
mangle zapatero	*Rhizophora mangle*
manioche	***Solanum americanum***
manzana	***Malpighia diversifolia***
manzanita	***Lycium andersonii, Malpighia diversifolia,*** *Ziziphus amole*
margarita	*Karwinskia parvifolia,* ***Malpighia diversifolia***
margarita del cerro	*Karwinskia parvifolia*
mariposa	*Calochortus* spp.
marrube	*Marsdenia edulis*
matachín	*Caesalpinia pulcherrima*
matapalo	*Ficus pertusa*
mata-peje	*Jacquinia macrocarpa* var. *pungens*
mauto	***Lysiloma microphyllum***
medesá, medezá	***Cercidium microphyllum***
mehuelé, mevuelé	***Stenocereus thurberi***
melon de coyote	***Apodanthera undulata***
melon loco	***Apondanthera palmeri, A. undulata***
mescal ceniza	***Agave chrysoglossa***
mescalillo	***Agave datylio***
mescaliyo	***Agave datylio***
mescal lechuguilla	***Agave zebra***
mescal pardo	***Agave sobria***
mescal pelón	***Agave pelona***
mesquilito	***Agave capensis***
mesquite, mezquite	*Prosopis* spp.
mezcal, mescal	***Agave cerulata, A. subsimplex***
mezquite amarillo	*Prosopis glandulosa* var. *torreyana*
mezquite blanco	*Prosopis glandulosa* var. *torreyana*
mezquite chino	*Prosopis glandulosa* var. *torreyana*
mezquite colorado	*Prosopis glandulosa* var. *torreyana*
mirasol	*Helianthus annuus*
mora	*Morus microphylla*
morada cholla	***Cylindropuntia versicolor***
mora de campo	*Malpighia emarginata*
moral	*Morus microphylla*
mostaz(s)a	*Brassica nigra, B. rapa*
mostaza negra	*Brassica nigra*
musaro	***Lophocereus schottii***
nabo de canario	*Brassica rapa*
nacapuli	*Ficus pertusa*
nanche de la costa	*Ziziphus amole*
narras	***Vitis peninsularis***
nogal	*Juglans major*
nogal sylvestre	*Juglans major*
nopal	*Opuntia chlorotica, O. engelmannii, O. macrocentra,* ***O. oricola,*** *O. phaeacantha*
nopal grueso	***Opuntia* sp.**
nopal morado	***Opuntia santa-rita***
ocotillo	*Fouquieria spp.,* ***F diguetii,*** *F. splendens*
ocotillo blanco	***Fouquieria burragei***
ocotillo macho	*Fouquieria macdougalii*
ojotón	***Pithecellobium confine***
orache	*Artiplex* spp.
orégano	*Lippia palmeri*
organo	***Pachycereus pringlei***
ortiguilla	***Cnidoscolus palmeri***
otatave	*Vallesia glabra*
ortiga	***Cnidoscolus maculatus***
ozote	*Ipomoea arborescens*
palma	***Sabal uresana, Washingtonia robusta***
palma blanca	***Erythea armata, Washingtonia robusta***
palma ceniza	***Erythea armata***
palma colorado (-a)	***Erythea brandegeei, Washingtonia robusta***
palma criolla	***Yucca arizonica***

palma de castilla	***Washingtonia robusta***
palma del suelo	***Sabal uresana***
palma negra	***Erythea brandegeei***
palma rubra	***Washingtonia robusta***
palmetto	***Sabal uresana***
palmilla	***Erythea brandegeei,*** *Nolina microcarpa,* ***Washingtonia filifera,*** *Yucca elata*
palmilla de taco	***Erythea brandegeei***
palmita	***Nolina beldingii***
palmito	*Yucca elata*
palo adán	***Fouquieria burragei, F. diguetii***
palo amarillo	*Berberis haematocarpa*
palo aspestoso	*Karwinskia humboldtiana*
palo blanco	*Celtis laevigata,* ***Ipomoea arborescens, Lysiloma candida,*** *Maytenus phyllanthroides,* ***Ziziphus obtusifolius* var. *canescens***
palo bobo	***Ipomoea arborescens***
palo cabra	*Ipomoea arborescens*
palo colorado	***Caesalpinia platyloba***
palo de águila	*Celtis pallida*
palo de arco	*Celtis iguanaea*
palo de las animas	*Jacquinia macrocarpa* var. *pungens*
palo del muerto	*Ipomoea arborescens*
palo eba	***Pithecellobium leucospermum***
palo ebano	***Pithecellobium leucospermum***
palo fierro	***Olneya tesota, Pithecellobium confine, P. leucospermum***
palo garobo	*Acacia pennatula*
palo hierro	***Olneya tesota***
palo jito	*Forchammeria watsoni*
palo maría	*Ficus petiolaris*
palo negrito	*Karwinskia parvifolia*
palo San Juan	*Forchammeria watsoni, Jacquinia macrocarpa* var. *pungens*
palo santo	*Ipomoea arborescens*
palo santo armillo	***Ipomoea arborescens***
palote negro	*Guazuma ulmifolia*
palo verde	***Cercidium floridum, C. microphyllum,*** *Fouquiera macdougalii*
pamita	*Descurainia* spp., ***D. pinnata***
papache	*Randia echinocarpa, R. obcordata, R. thurberi,* ***Ziziphus obtusifolius* var. *canescens***
papache borracho	*Randia obcordata*
papache grande	*Randia megacarpa*
papache papachon	*Randia echinocarpa*
papache picudo	*Randia echinocarpa*
papachillo	*Randia obcordata*
pardo	***Agave sobria***
parra	*Vitis arizonica*
parras cimarrónas	***Vitis peninsularis***
pastora	*Plantago heterophylla, P. patagonica*
patata, patota	*Monolepis nuttalliana*
pato de arco	*Celtis iguanaea*
pavi	***Phaseolus acutifolius***
pazote	*Chenopodium ambrosioides,* ***Lepidium lasiocarpum***
péchita	***Prosopis glandulosa* var. *torreyana, P. velutina***
pegarropa	***Mentzelia* spp.**
peine de bruja	*Erodium cicutarium*
peonia	*Cyperus esculentus*
persimonio	***Diospyros sonorae***
petota	*Claytonia perfoliata*
pichilinge	***Fouquieria burragei***
pinicua	***Jacquinia macrocarpa* var. *pungens***
pitahaya	***Stenocereus gummosus,*** *S. thurberi*
pitahaya agria	***Stenocereus gummosus***
pitahaya agridulce	***Stenocereus gummosus***
pitahaya barbóna	***Lophocereus schottii***
pitahaya dulce	*Stenocereus thurberi*
pitahayita	***Echinocereus brandegeei,*** *Peniocereus striatus*
pitahita, pitayita	*Lophocereus schottii, Peniocereus striatus*
pitamo real	*Ephedra aspera*
pitayo agrio	***Stenocereus gummosus***
pitoxe	*Solanum americanum*
pochote	*Ceiba acuminata*
poinciana enana	*Caesalpinia pulcherrima*
popotilla(o)	*Ephedra aspera, E. nevadensis, E. trifurca*
quelite	*Amaranthus* spp., *A. caudatus, A. palmeri, Chenopodium* spp., *Solanum americanum*
quelite cenizo	*Chenopodium berlandieri*
quelite de las aguas	***Amaranthus palmeri***
quelite de perro	*Chenopodium murale*
quelite de puerco	***Chenopodium murale***
quelite manchado	*Amaranthus albus*
quelite morado	*Amaranthus hybridus*
quelite salado	*Chenopodium berlandieri*
quenopodia	*Chenopodium leptophyllum*
quiebra hacha	*Lysiloma microphyllum*
quisache costeño	*Acacia cochliacantha*
reina de la noche	*Peniocereus greggii* var. *transmontanus*
retama	*Parkinsonia aculeata*
rocio	*Carpobrotus chilensis*
rompecapa	*Celtis pallida*
rosadilla	*Jacquinia macrocarpa* var. *pungens*
rosal de la pasion	*Passiflora arida*
sabal	***Sabal uresana***
sacahuista	*Nolina microcarpa*

sacamatraca	***Peniocereus striatus***
sacaté	*Jacquinia macrocarpa* var. *pungens*
sacoton	*Sporobolus* spp.
sactilla	*Bidens pilosa*
saguaro	***Carnegiea gigantea***
saguera	***Pachycereus pringlei***
saguesa, sahueso	***Pachycereus pringlei***
sagui	***Panicum hirticaule* var. *miliaceum***
sairya	***Amoreuxia palmatifida***
saiya	***Amoreuxia gonzalezii, A. palmatifida***
saji	*Lysiloma microphyllum*
saladillo	***Atriplex lentiformis, A. polycarpa***
saladito	*Rhus trilobata*
saliciesa	***Lycium andersonii***
salsa mora	*Morus microphylla*
sandía de la pasion	***Passiflora palmeri,*** *Sarcostemma cynanchoides*
sanguinaria	*Ephedra aspera*
San Juan	*Forchammeria watsoni, Jacquinia macrocarpa* var. *pungens*
San Juanico	*Forchammeria watsoni, Jacquinia macrocarpa* var. *pungens*
San Miguel	*Antigonon leptopus*
San Miguelito	*Antigonon leptopus*
sapuche	***Randia laevigata***
saramatraca	***Peniocereus greggii* var. *transmontanus***
sarza mora	*Lantana horrida, L. velutina*
sauco	*Sambucus nigra* ssp. *canadensis*
sauwi	***Panicum hirticaule* var. *miliaceum***
sawo	*Dasylirion wheeleri*
saya	***Amoreuxia gonzalezii (?), A. palmatifida***
selé	*Mentzelia albicaulis*
senita	***Lophocereus schottii***
shiksh	***Sambucus nigra* ssp. *canadensis***
sidra	*Rhus trilobata*
sina	***Lophocereus schottii, Stenocereus alamosensis***
sinita	***Lophocereus schottii, Stenocereus alamosensis***
sinita barbona	***Echinocereus engelmannii***
sitavaro	*Vallesia glabra*
sitevase	***Vallesia glabra***
socoyole	*Oxalis albicans*
solate	*Yucca elata*
sota	***Yucca arizonica,*** *Y. elata*
sotol, soto	*Dasylirion wheeleri*
tabaquín	***Caesalpinia pulcherrima***
tablote	*Guazuma ulmifolia*
talayote	*Marsdenia edulis,* ***Matelea cordifolia, M. parvifolia,*** *Sarcostemma pannosum*
talcapache	***Caesalpinia pulcherrima***
tapaculo	*Guazuma ulmifolia*
tapiro	***Sambucus nigra* ssp. *canadensis***
tarepe	*Lantana velutina*
tavachín	*Caesalpinia pulcherrima*
tecolochapo	*Randia echinocarpa*
tecolosapo	*Randia echinocarpa*
teddá	***Oligomeris linifolia (?)***
teihuist	***Rivina humilis***
temaquí	***Amoreuxia palmatifida***
tepamo, tepame	*Acacia greggii, A. pennatula*
tépari	*Phaseolus acutifolius*
tépari del monte	***Phaseolus acutifolius***
tepeguaje	*Lysiloma watsonii*
tepemezquite	*Lysiloma microphyllum*
tepopote	*Ephedra nevadensis, E. trifurca*
tesajillo	***Cylindropuntia leptocaulis***
tesajo	***Cylindropuntia acanthocarpa, C. arbuscula, C. tesajo, C. versicolor***
tésota	***Acacia greggii, Olneya tesota***
tetezo	*Caesalpinia pulcherrima*
texcalamate	*Ficus petiolaris*
texcalamatl	*Ficus petiolaris*
tezcalama	***Ficus brandegeei, F. palmeri, F. petiolaris***
tivinagua	***Eriogonum inflatum***
tlamatsalin	*Sonchus oleraceus*
tojí	***Phoradendron californicum***
tomate	*Physalis angulata*
tomate de cascara	*Physalis angulata*
tomate del culabra	***Physalis crassifolia***
tomate fresadilla	*Physalis pubescens*
tomatillo	***Lycium berlandieri, L. exsertum, L. fremontii,*** *L. pallidum, L. parishii,* ***L. richii, L. torreyi,*** *Physalis* spp., ***P. acutifolia,*** *P. ixocarpa, P. longifolia,* var. *longifolia, P. philadelphica* var. *immaculata,* ***P. pubescens***
tomatillo cimarrón	*Physalis acutifolia*
tonchi	***Marsdenia edulis***
torete	*Vitex mollis*
torito	*Proboscidea parviflora*
tornillo	***Prosopis pubescens***
torote	*Bursera fagaroides* var. *elongata,* ***B. microphylla***
torote blanco	*Bursera fagaroides* var. *elongata*
torote colorado	***Bursera microphylla***
torote espinosa	***Fouquieria macdougalii***
torote jabonsillo	*Fouquieria macdougalii*
torote prieto	*Fouquieria macdougalii*

torote verde	***Fouquieria macdougalii***
toscalama	*Vitex pyramidata*
totosali	***Agave shrevei***
tracamatraca	***Peniocereus striatus***
trigo del mar	*Zostera marina*
trigo gentil	***Distichlis palmeri***
tule	*Cyperus* spp., *Phragmites australis, Schoenoplectus maritimus, S. tabernaemontani, Typha* spp.
tulillo	*Cyperus esculentus*
tullidor, tuyidor	*Karwinskia humboldtiana, K. parvifolia*
tulumisi	***Physalis angulata***
tuna	*Opuntia engelmannii,* ***O. santa-rita***
tuna agria	***Opuntia cholla,*** *O. imbricata,*
tuna barbona	***Lophocereus schottii***
tutus	*Pachycereus pecten-aboriginum*
uclatave	***Vallesia glabra***
uchica	***Celtis laevigata***
uña de gato	***Acacia greggii, Olneya tesota,*** *Proboscidea parviflora*
uruquiro	*Rivina humilis*
uva	*Vitis arizonica*
uva cimarróna	***Vitis arizonica***
uvalama	*Vitex mollis, V. pyramidata*
vachata negra	*Randia sonorensis*
vacima	*Guazuma ulmifolia*
vaiburin	***Antigonon leptopus***
vainoro	*Celtis iguanaea, C. pallida*
velas de coyote	***Cylindropuntia fulgida***
verdolaga	*Portulaca oleracea, Trianthema portulacastrum*
verdolaga blanca	*Trianthema portulacastrum*
verdolaga de cochi	*Trianthema portulacastrum*
verdolaga del sapo	***Trianthema portulacastrum***
vid	*Vitis arizonica*
vidrillo	*Batis maritima*
vinol	*Acacia cochliacantha*
vinorama	***Acacia brandegeana***
wapato	*Sagittaria latifolia*
yamp	*Agave utahensis*
yepouchecha	***Acacia pennatula***
yori muni	*Phaseolus acutifolius*
yuca	*Manihot chlorosticta,* ***Merremia aurea, Yucca arizonica, Y. elata***
zacate alcalino	*Sporobolus airoides*
zacate alcalino espigado	*Sporobolus contractus*
zacate del mar	*Zostera marina*
zacate encubierto	*Sporobolus cryptandrus*
zacate espigado	*Sporobolus contractus*
zacate gramilla	*Panicum obtusum*
zacate salado	***Distichlis palmeri***
zacaton de arena	*Sporobolus contractus, S. cryptandrus*
zacaton des granador	*Sporobolus cryptandrus*
zalate	***Ficus brandegeei, F. palmeri***
zicana	*Ipomoea bracteata*

LITERATURE CITED

Alcorn, J. 1995. The scope and aims of ethnobotany in a developing world. Pp. 23–39 *in* Ethnobotany: Evolution of a discipline. R. Schultes and S. von Reis, eds. Dioscorides Press, Portland, Ore.

Altschul, S. 1973. Drugs and foods from little-known plants. Harvard University Press, Cambridge, Mass.

Alvarez de Williams, A. 1975. Travelers among the Cucapá. Dawson's Book Shop, Los Angeles, Calif.

Alvarez de Williams, A. 1987. Environment and edible flora of the Cocopa. Environment Southwest 519:22–27.

Alvarez de Williams, A. 1989. The Cucapá Indians of the Colorado River delta. CEDO News 2(2):17,19.

Alvarez de Williams, A. n.d. Unpublished notes, copy deposited at Desert Botanical Garden, Phoenix, Ariz.

Anderson, E. 1999. Some nomenclatural changes in the Cactaceae, subfamily Opuntioideae. Cactus and Succulent Journal (U.S.) 71(6):324–325.

Anderson, E. 2001. The cactus family. Dioscorides Press/ Timber Press, Portland, Ore.

Andrews, J. 1984. Peppers: The domesticated capsicums. University of Texas Press, Austin.

Andrews, T. 1979. English privateers at Cabo San Lucas: The descriptive accounts of Puerto Seguro by Edward Cooke (1712) and Woodes Rogers (1712). Dawson's Book Shop, Los Angeles, Calif.

Ariffin, R. 1984. Proximate analysis of Sonoran Desert food plants. M.S. thesis, University of Arizona, Tucson.

Arizona-Sonora Desert Museum. 2000. Desert Ironwood Primer. Biodiversity and uses associated with ancient legume and cactus forests in the Sonoran Desert. Arizona-Sonora Desert Museum, in collaboration with the Department of the Interior and Pima County. Tucson, Arizona.

Aschmann, H. 1952. A primitive food preparation technique in Baja California. Southwestern Journal of Anthropology 8(1):36–39.

Aschmann, H. 1959. The central desert of California: Demography and ecology. University of California Press, Berkeley.

Aschmann, H., trans. and ed. 1966. The natural and human history of Baja California. Dawson's Book Shop, Los Angeles, Calif.

Aschmann, H. 1986. Learning about Baja California Indians: Sources and problems. Journal of California and Great Basin Anthropology 8(2):238–245.

Aschmann, H. 1997. The evolving landscape: Homer Aschmann's geography. Johns Hopkins University Press, Baltimore, Md.

Austin, M. 1988. Cactus thorn. University of Nevada Press, Reno.

Axelrod, D. 1950. Evolution of desert vegetation in western North America. Pp. 215–306 *in* Carnegie Institute of Washington Publication no. 590, Washington, D.C.

Baegert, J. 1952. Observations in Lower California. M. M. Brandenburg and C. L. Baumann, trans. University of California Press, Berkeley.

Baegert, J. 1982. The letters of Jacob Baegert 1749–1761. E. Schulz-Bischof, trans. Dawson's Book Shop, Los Angeles, Calif.

Bailey, F. 1940. Navajo food and cooking methods. American Anthropologist 42:270–290.

Bailey, L. H. 1937. *Erythea.* Gentes Herbarium 4:83–118.

Bainbridge, D. 1985. Acorns as food: Oak bibliography no. 1, with an introduction, country use list, and nutrient analysis. Sierra Nature Prints, Twain Harte, Calif.

Balls, E. 1970. Early uses of California plants. University of California Press, Berkeley.

Barrows, D. 1900. The ethnobotany of the Cahuilla Indians of southern California. University of Chicago Press, Chicago, Ill.

Beals, R. 1945. The contemporary culture of the Cáhita Indians. Smithsonian Institution Bureau of American Ethnology Bulletin no. 142. U.S. Government Printing Office, Washington, D.C.

Bean, L., and K. Saubel. 1961. Cahuilla ethnobotanical notes: The aboriginal use of oak. Pp. 237–345 *in* Archaeological Survey annual report. University of California, Los Angeles.

Bean, L., and K. Saubel. 1972. Temalpakh: Cahuilla Indian knowledge and usage of plants. Malki Museum, Banning, Calif.

Beatley, J. 1976. Vascular plants of Nevada Test Site and central-southern Nevada: Ecologic and geographic distributions. National Technical Information Service, Springfield, Mass.

Becker, R. 1982. The nutritive value of *Prosopis* pods. Pp. M-1–M-9 *in* Mesquite utilization: Proceedings of the symposium. H. Parker, ed. College of Agricultural Sciences, Texas Tech University, Lubbock.

Bee, R. 1989. Indians of North America: The Yuma. Chelsea House Publishers, New York, N.Y.

Beetle, A. 1981. Noteworthy grasses from Mexico. VII. Phytologia 47(5):379–383.

Bell, F. 1980. Interview with Fernando Flores, Arlington, Arizona, March. Unpublished notes, copy deposited at Desert Botanical Garden, Phoenix, Ariz.

Bell, F., K. Anderson, and Y. Stewart. 1980. The Quitobaquito cemetery and its history. Western Archaeological Center, U.S. Department of the Interior, National Park Service, Tucson, Ariz.

Bell, W., and E. Castetter. 1937. Ethnobiological studies in the American Southwest. Vol. V. The utilization of mesquite and screwbean by the aborigines in the American Southwest. University of New Mexico Bulletin, Biological Series 5(2).

Bell, W., and E. Castetter. 1941. Ethnobiological studies in the American Southwest. Vol. VII. The utilization of yucca, sotol, and beargrass by the aborigines in the American Southwest. University of New Mexico Bulletin, Biological Series 5(5).

Bemis, W., J. Berry, M. Kennedy, D. Woods, M. Moran, and A. Deutschman Jr. 1967. Oil composition of *Cucurbita.* Journal of the American Oil Chemists' Society 44:429–430.

Bennett, W., and R. Zingg. 1935. The Tarahumara. University of Chicago Press, Chicago, Ill.

Benson, L. 1969. Cacti of Arizona. 3rd ed. University of Arizona Press, Tucson.

Benson, L., and R. Darrow. 1981. Trees and shrubs of the southwestern deserts. 3rd ed. University of Arizona Press, Tucson.

Berry, J., W. Bemis, C. Weber, and T. Philip. 1975. Cucurbit root starches: Isolation and some properties of starches from *C. foetidissima* H.B.K. and *C. digitata* Gray. Journal of Agricultural Food Chemistry 23:825–826.

Berry, J., C. Weber, M. Dreher, and W. Bemis. 1976. Chemical composition of buffalo gourd, a potential food source. Journal of Food Science 41:465–466.

Berry, J., P. K. Bretting, G. P. Nabhan, and C. Weber. 1981. Domesticated *Proboscidea parviflora:* A potential oilseed crop for arid lands. Journal of Arid Environments 4:147–160.

Bogler, D. In press. A Monograph of *Dasylirion* (Nolinaceae). Systematic Botany Monographs. The American Society of Plant Taxonomists, Ann Arbor, Mich.

Bogler, D., and B. Simpson. 1995. A chloroplast DNA study of the Agavaceae. Systematic Botany 20(2):191–205.

Bohrer, V. 1957. Chinchweed *(Pectis papposa),* a Zuni herb. El Palacio 64(11/12):365.

Bohrer, V. 1970. Ethnobotanical aspects of Snaketown, a Hohokam village in southern Arizona. American Antiquity 35:413–430.

Bohrer, V. 1975. The prehistoric and historic role of the cool-season grasses in the Southwest. Economic Botany 29(3):199–207.

Bohrer, V. 1978. Plants that have become locally extinct in the Southwest. New Mexico Journal of Science 18(2):10–18.

Bohrer, V. 1984. Domesticated and wild crops in the CAEP study area. Pp. 183–259 *in* Prehistoric cultural development in central Arizona: Archaeology of the Upper New River region. P. Spoerland and G. Gumerman, eds. Occasional Paper no. 5. Southern Illinois University, Carbondale Center for Archaeological Investigations, Carbondale, Ill.

Bohrer, V. 1985. Chenopodiaceae and Amaranthaceae, La Ciudad, Arizona: Ethnobotanical report for January. Unpublished manuscript, copy deposited at Desert Botanical Garden, Phoenix, Ariz.

Bohrer, V. 1986. An overview of the plant remains from La Ciudad, Arizona: Ethnobotanical report for November. Unpublished manuscript, copy deposited at Desert Botanical Garden, Phoenix, Ariz.

Bohrer, V. 1987. The plant remains from La Ciudad, a Hohokam site in Phoenix. Pp. 67–237 *in* Specialized studies in the economy, environment, and culture of La Ciudad. J. Kisselburg, G. Rice, and B. Shears, eds. ASU Anthropological Field Studies no. 20. Department of Anthropology, Arizona State University, Tempe.

Bohrer, V. 1991. Recently recognized cultivated and encouraged plants among the Hohokam. Kiva 56(3):227–235.

Bohrer, V. 1992. New life from ashes. II. A tale of the burnt brush. Desert Plants 10(3):122–125.

Bohrer, V., H. Cutler, and J. Sauer. 1969. Carbonized plant remains from two Hohokam sites, Arizona BB:13:41 and Arizona BB:13:50. The Kiva 35(1):1–10.

Bolley, D., R. McCormack, and L. Curtis. 1950. The utilization of the wild perennial gourds. Journal of American Oil Chemical Society 27:571–574.

Bolton, H. 1936. Rim of Christendom: A biography of Eusebio Francisco Kino, Pacific Coast pioneer. MacMillan, New York, N.Y.

Bolton, H. 1948. Kino's Historical Memoir of Pimería Alta. 2 vols. University of California Press, Berkeley.

Bourke, J. 1888. The medicine-men of the Apache. Pp. 443–603 *in* Smithsonian Institution Bureau of American Ethnology 9th annual report. U.S. Government Printing Office, Washington, D.C.

Bourke, J. 1891. On the border with Crook. Charles Scribner's Sons, New York, N.Y. 1980. Reprinted as Classics of the old West, Time-Life Books, Inc., Alexandria, Va.

Bourke, J. 1895. The folk-foods of the Rio Grande Valley and of northern Mexico. Journal of American Folk Lore 8:41–71.

Bouscaren, S., J. Waines, L. Boykin-Bouscaren. 1983. Cultivation and use of teparies in Sonora, Mexico. Desert Plants 5(1):38–42.

Bowen, R. 1939. Saguaro harvest in Papagoland. Desert Magazine 2(8):3–5.

Bowers, J. 1980. Flora of Organ Pipe Cactus National Monument. Journal of the Arizona-Nevada Academy of Science 15(1):1–47.

Brand, J., B. Snow, G. Nabhan, and A. Truswell. 1990. Plasma glucose and insulin responses to traditional Pima Indian meals. American Journal for Clinical Nutrition 51:416–420.

Brandegee, T. S. 1889. Plants from Baja California. Proceedings of the California Academy of Sciences Ser. II, 2:117–217.

Brandegee, T. S. 1891a. Flora of the cape region of Baja California. Proceedings of the California Academy of Sciences Ser. II, 3(1):108–182.

Brandegee, T. S. 1891b. Field notes on the plants of Baja California. Zoe II:145–152.

Brandegee, T. S. 1891c. Cactaceae of the cape region of Baja California. Zoe II:18–22.

Brandegee, T. S. 1894. Additions to the flora of the cape region of Baja California. II. Zoe IV(4):398–408.

Brandegee, T. S. 1900a. Voyage of the Wahlberg. Zoe V(2):19–28.

Brandegee, T. S. 1900b. A new *Tapira edulis* from Baja California. Zoe V:78–79.

Brandegee, T. S. 1900–1901. New species of plants, mainly from Baja California. Zoe V:104–109.

Brandegee, T. S. 1904. Palms of Baja California. Zoe V:187–189.

Brazdovicova, B., D. Kostalova, J. Tomko, and H. Yang Jin. 1980. Isolation and identification of alkaloids from fruits of *Berberis thunbergii* DC. Chemicke Zvesti 34:259–262.

Bretting, P. K. 1982. Morphological differentiation of *Proboscidea parviflora* ssp. *parviflora* (Martyniaceae) under domestication. American Journal of Botany 69(10): 1531–1537.

Bretting, P. K. 1986. Changes in fruit shape in *Proboscidea parviflora* ssp. *parviflora* (Martyniaceae) with domestication. Economic Botany 40:170–176.

Brian, N., W. Hodgson, and A. Phillips III. 2000. Additions to the flora of the Grand Canyon National Park (and Grand Canyon region). II. Journal of the Arizona-Nevada Academy of Science 32(2):117–127.

Bright, W. 1935. Your garden and mine. Desert Plant Life VII(2):20–21.

Browne, J. 1869. Adventures in the Apache country: A tour through Arizona and Sonora, with notes on the Silver Regions of Nevada. Harper and Bros., New York, N.Y. 1974. Reprint, University of Arizona Press, Tucson.

Brum, G. 1973. Ecology of the saguaro *(Carnegiea gigantea):* Phenology and establishment in marginal populations. Madroño 22:195–204.

Brummitt, R., and C. Powell, eds. 1992. Authors of plant names. Royal Botanic Gardens, Kew, England.

Burkart, A., and B. Simpson. 1977. The genus *Prosopis* and annotated key to the species of the world. Pp. 201–215 *in* Mesquite: Its biology in two desert scrub ecosystems. B. Simpson, ed. Dowden, Hutchinson, and Ross, Inc., Stroudsburg, Pa.

Burrus, E., trans. and ed. 1966. Wenceslaus Linck's diary of his 1766 expedition to northern Baja California. Dawson's Book Shop, Los Angeles, Calif.

Burrus, E., trans. and ed. 1967. Wenceslaus Linck's reports and letters, 1762–1778. Dawson's Book Shop, Los Angeles, Calif.

Burrus, E., trans. and ed. 1971. Juan Maria de Salvatierra, S.J.: Selected letters about Lower California. Dawson's Book Shop, Los Angeles, Calif.

Burrus, E. 1984. Jesuit relations, Baja California. Dawson's Book Shop, Los Angeles, Calif.

Buskirk, W. 1986. The Western Apache: Living with the land before 1950. University of Oklahoma Press, Norman.

Bye, R., Jr. 1972. Ethnobotany of the Southern Paiute Indians in the 1870s; with a note on the early ethnobotanical contributions of Dr. Edward Palmer. Pp. 87–104 *in* Great Basin cultural ecology: A symposium. Don D. Fowler, ed. Desert Research Institute Publications in the Social Sciences no. 8, Reno, Nev.

Bye, R., Jr. 1976. Ethnoecology of the Tarahumara of Chihuahua, Mexico. Ph.D. dissertation, Harvard University, Cambridge, Mass.

Bye, R., Jr. 1979a. Incipient domestication of mustards in northwestern Mexico. Kiva 44:237–256.

Bye, R., Jr. 1979b. An 1878 ethnobotanical collection from San Luis Potosi: Dr. Edward Palmer's first major Mexican collection. Economic Botany 33:135–162.

Bye, R., Jr. 1981. Quelites: Ethnoecology of edible greens—past, present, and future. Journal of Ethnobiology 1(1):109–123.

Bye, R., Jr. 1986. Voucher specimens in ethnobiological studies and publications. Journal of Ethnobiology 6(1):1–8.

Bye, R., Jr., D. Burgess, and A. Trias. 1975. Ethnobotany of the Western Tarahumara of Chihuahua, Mexico. Botanical Museum Leaflets, Harvard University 24:85–112.

Callen, E. 1965. Food habits of some pre-Columbian Indians. Economic Botany 19:335–343.

Calloway, D., R. Giaugue, and F. Costa. 1974. The superior mineral content of some American Indian foods in comparison to federally donated counterpart commodities. Ecology of Food and Nutrition 3:203–211.

Camazine, S., and R. Bye Jr. 1980. A study of the medical ethnobotany of the Zuni Indians of New Mexico. Journal of Ethnopharmacology 2:365–388.

Carothers, S., and B. Brown. 1991. The Colorado River through Grand Canyon. University of Arizona Press, Tucson.

Carter, A. 1970. Some ethnobotanical notes on the plants of the Sierra de la Giganta, Baja California Sur. Pacific Coast Archaeological Society Quarterly 6(1):29–34.

Carter, A. 1974. The genus *Cercidium* in the Sonoran Desert of Mexico and the U.S. Proceedings of the California Academy of Sciences Ser. IV, 40:15–57.

Castetter, E. 1935. Uncultivated native plants used as sources of food. Ethnobiological Studies in the American Southwest. Vol. I. University of New Mexico Bulletin, Biological Series 4(1).

Castetter, E., and W. Bell. 1937. The aboriginal utilization of the tall cacti in the American Southwest. Ethnobiological Studies in the American Southwest. Vol. IV. University of New Mexico Bulletin, Biological Series 5(1).

Castetter, E., and W. Bell. 1942. Pima and Papago Indian agriculture. Inter-Americana Studies. Vol. I. University of New Mexico Press, Albuquerque.

Castetter, E., and W. Bell. 1951. Yuman Indian agriculture. University of New Mexico Press, Albuquerque.

Castetter, E., and M. Opler. 1936. The ethnobiology of the Chiricahua and Mescalero Apache. A. The use of plants for food, beverages, and narcotics. University of New Mexico Bulletin, Biological Series 4(5).

Castetter, E., and R. Underhill. 1935. The ethnobiology of the Papago Indians. Ethnobiological Studies in the American Southwest. Vol. II. University of New Mexico Bulletin, Biological Series 4(3).

Castetter, E., W. Bell, and A. Grove. 1938. The early utilization and the distribution of *Agave* in the American Southwest. Ethnobiological Studies in the American Southwest. Vol. VI. University of New Mexico Bulletin, Biological Series 5(4).

Chamberlain, R. 1911. The ethnobotany of the Gosiute Indians of Utah. American Anthropological Association Memoir 11:329–405.

Chamberland, M. 1991. Biosystematics of the *Echinocactus polycephalus* complex (Cactaceae). M. S. thesis, Arizona State University, Tempe.

Chamberland, M. 1995. Vascular plants of Arizona: Cactaceae. Part 2. Cactus family: *Echinocactus* Link & Otto. Journal of the Arizona-Nevada Academy of Science 29(1):13–14.

Cheatham, S., M. C. Johnston, with L. Marshall. 1995. Useful wild plants of Texas, the southeastern and southwestern United States, the southern Plains, and northern Mexico. Vol. 1. Useful Wild Plants, Inc., Austin, Tex.

Chestnut, V. 1902. Plants used by the Indians of Mendocino County. Contributions U.S. National Herbarium 7(3):295–408.

Childs, T. 1954. Sketch of the Sand Indians. Kiva 19(2/4) 27–39.

Christy, C. 1998. Vascular plants of Arizona: Loasaceae—stickleaf or blazing-star family. Journal of the Arizona-Nevada Academy of Science 30(2):96–111.

Clary, K. 1997. Phylogeny, character evolution, and biogeography of *Yucca* L. (Agavaceae) as inferred from plant morphology and sequences of the internal transcribed spacer (ITS) region of the nuclear ribosomal DNA. Ph.D. dissertation, University of Texas, Austin.

Clavigero, F. 1937. The history of (Lower) California. Sara Lake and A. A. Gray, trans. Stanford University Press, Stanford, Calif.

Cochrum, E., and Y. Petryszyn. 1991. The long nose bat, *Leptonycteris:* An endangered species in the Southwest? Occasional Papers of the Museum of Texas Tech University 142:1–32.

Conrad, B. 1981. Community dynamics of old fields in the Sonoran Desert. M.S. thesis, Arizona State University, Tempe.

Conrotto, E. 1958. He works all day on hotcakes'n chia. Desert Magazine 21(4):19.

Cooke, E. 1712. Cabo San Lucas: November–December 1709. Pp. 315–327 *in* A voyage to the South Sea and around the world, perform'd in the years 1708–1711, by the ships Duke and Duchess of Bristol, London. 2 vols. B. Lintot and R. Gosling, London.

Cornett, J. W. 1984. Coachella Valley's thousand palms. The Nature Conservancy News 34(5):18–21.

Cornett, J. W., and J. H. Stewart. 1986. Palm burning and increased spadix production. Southwestern Naturalist 31(4):552.

Cothrun, J. D. 1969. Some aspects of the germination and attachment of *Ammobroma sonorae,* a root parasite of desert shrubs. Ed.D. dissertation, Oklahoma State University, Stillwater.

Cotter, D. 1982. The scientific contribution of New Mexico to the chile pepper. Pp. 16–27 *in* Southwestern agriculture: Pre-Columbian to modern. H. Dethloff and I. May Jr., eds. Texas A&M University Press, College Station.

Coville, F. 1892. The Panamint Indians of California. American Anthropologist 5:351–361.

Coville, F. 1903. Desert plants as a source of drinking water. Pp. 499–506 *in* Smithsonian Institution annual report. U.S. Government Printing Office, Washington, D.C.

Coyle, J., and N. Roberts. 1975. A field guide to the common and interesting plants of Baja California. Natural History Publishing Co., La Jolla, Calif.

Crosswhite, F. 1980. The annual saguaro harvest and crop cycle of the Papago, with reference to ecology and symbolism. Desert Plants 2:2–61.

Curtin, L. M. 1947. Healing herbs of the Upper Rio Grande. New Mexico Laboratory of Anthropology, Santa Fe, N.M.

Curtin, L. M. 1949. By the prophet of the Earth: Ethnobotany of the Pima. 1984. Reprint, University of Arizona Press, Tucson.

Curtis, L. 1946. The possibilities of using species of perennial cucurbits as a source of vegetable fats and protein. Chemurgic Digest 13:221–224.

Curtis, L. 1979. New crops for desert farming. New Farm 1(3):52–60.

Cushing, F. 1882. The nation of the willows. Atlantic Monthly 50:362–374, 541–559.

Cushing, F. 1920. Zuni breadstuff. Indian Notes and Monographs. Vol. 8. Museum of the American Indians, Heye Foundation, New York, N.Y.

Cushing, F. 1965. The nation of the willows. Northland Press, Flagstaff, Ariz.

Cutler, H., and T. Whitaker. 1961. History and distribution of the cultivated cucurbits in the Americas. American Antiquity 26:469–485.

Davis, E. W. 1995. Ethnobotany: An old practice, a new discipline. Pp. 40–51 *in* Ethnobotany: Evolution of a discipline. R. Schultes and S. von Reis, eds. Dioscorides Press, Portland, Ore.

del Barco, M. 1980. The natural history of Baja California. F. Tiscareno, trans. Dawson's Book Shop, Los Angeles, Calif.

del Barco, M. 1981. Ethnology and linguistics of Baja California. F. Tiscareno, trans. Dawson's Book Shop, Los Angeles, Calif.

Densmore, F. 1928. Uses of plants by the Chippewa Indians. Pp. 295–397 *in* Smithsonian Institution Bureau of American Ethnology 44th annual report. U.S. Government Printing Office, Washington, D.C.

Dobbs, J. 1933. Delicatessen of the desert. Desert Plant Life 5(3):42.

Dobyns, H. 1949. Reports on investigations on the Papago Reservation. Cornell University Department of Sociology-Anthropology. Unpublished manuscript, copy deposited at Desert Botanical Garden, Phoenix, Ariz.

Dobyns, H. 1978. Who killed the Gila? The Journal of Arizona History 19(1):17–30.

Dobyns, H. 1981. From fire to flood: Historic human destruction of Sonoran Desert riverine oases. Anthropological Papers no. 20. Ballena Press, Socorro, N.M.

Doebley, J. 1984. "Seeds" of wild grasses: A major food of southwestern Indians. Economic Botany 38(1):52–63.

Doelle, W. H. 1976. Desert resources and Hohokam subsistence: The Conoco-Florence project. Arizona State Museum Archaeological Series no. 103, Tucson, Ariz.

Doelle, W. H. 1980. Nonriverine resource use: An archaeological study in western Papagueria. Unpublished manuscript, copy deposited at Desert Botanical Garden, Phoenix, Ariz.

Doyle, H. 1963. Chia. Desert Magazine 26(10)18–19.

Doyle, H. 1973. Golden chia, ancient Indian food. Hillside Press, Vista, Calif.

Dreher, M., and J. Berry. 1983. Buffalo gourd root starch. Part 1. Properties and structure. Starch/Starke 35:76–81.

Driver, H. E., and W. Massey. 1957. Comparative studies of North American Indians. Transactions of the American Philosophical Society 47(2):165–456.

Duke, J., and E. Terrell. 1974. Crop diversification matrix: An introduction. Taxon 23(6):759–800.

Earle, F., and Q. Jones. 1962. Analyses of seed samples from 113 plant families. Economic Botany 16:221–250.

Ebeling, W. 1986. Handbook of Indian foods and fibers of arid America. University of California Press, Berkeley.

Ecker, L. 1990. Population enhancement of a rare cactus, *Mammillaria thornberi* Orcutt (Cactaceae) M.S. thesis, Arizona State University, Tempe.

Ehleringer, J. 1983. Ecophysiology of *Amaranthus palmeri,* a Sonoran Desert summer ephemeral. Oecologia 57:107–112.

Elmore, F. 1943. Ethnobotany of the Navajo. University of New Mexico Bulletin 1(7):16–128.

Elsasser, A. 1980. Explorations of Hernando Alarcón in the Lower Colorado River region, 1540. Journal of California and Great Basin Anthropology 2(2):8–37.

Emory, W. 1848. Notes of a military reconnaissance, from Fort Leavenworth, in Missouri, to San Diego, in California, including part of the Arkansas, del Norte, and Gila Rivers. 30th Congress, 1st session, Ex. Doc. no. 41. Wendell and Van Bentthuysen, Washington, D.C. 1951. Reprinted as Lieutenant Emory reports: A reprint of Lieutenant W. H. Emory's notes on a military reconnaissance, University of New Mexico Press, Albuquerque.

Engelhardt, Z. 1908. The missions and missionaries of California. Vol. I. Lower California. The James H. Barry Co., San Francisco, Calif.

Enos, D. 1988. Pesticides continue to plague Indians. Scottsdale Progress, August 8.

Enos, S. 1945. Papago legend of the sahuaro. Arizona Quarterly 1(1):64–69.

Euler, R., and V. Jones. 1956. Hermetic sealing as a technique of food preservation among the Indians of the American Southwest. Proceedings of the American Philosophical Society 100(1):87–99.

Everitt, J., and M. Alaniz. 1981. Nutrient content of cactus and woody plant fruits eaten by birds and mammals in south Texas. Southwestern Naturalist 26:301–305.

EWILHEL. 1998. Agave alert: Potential toxicity and labeling concerns. Available via E-mail: ewilhel@klarify.com [May 4, 1998].

Felger, R. 1977. Mesquite in southwestern Indian cultures. Pp. 150–176 *in* A tree in perspective: *Prosopis* in desert scrub ecosystems. B. Simpson, ed. Dowden, Hutchinson, and Ross, Inc., Stroudsburg, Pa.

Felger, R. 1980. Vegetation and flora of the Gran Desierto, Sonora, Mexico. Desert Plants 2(2):87–114.

Felger, R., and M. Moser. 1970. Seri use of *Agave* (century plant). Kiva 35(4):159–167.

Felger, R., and M. Moser. 1971. Seri use of mesquite *(Prosopis glandulosa* var. *torreyana)*. Kiva 37(3/4):53–60.

Felger, R., and M. Moser. 1973. Eelgrass (*Zostera marina* L.) in the Gulf of California: Discovery of its nutritional value by the Seri Indians. Science 181:355–356.

Felger, R., and M. Moser. 1974. Columnar cacti in Seri Indian culture. Kiva 39(3/4):257–275.

Felger, R., and M. Moser. 1976. Seri Indian food plants: Desert subsistence without agriculture. Ecology of Food and Nutrition 5:13–27.

Felger, R., and M. Moser. 1985. People of the desert and sea: Ethnobotany of the Seri. University of Arizona Press, Tucson.

Felger, R., and G. P. Nabhan. 1976. Deceptive barrenness. Ceres, FAO Review on Development 9(2):34–39.

Felger, R., and G. P Nabhan. 1978. Agroecosystem diversity: A model from the Sonoran Desert. Pp. 129–149 *in* Social and technological management in dry lands: Past and present, indigenous and imposed. N. Gonzalez, ed. AAAS Selected Symposium no. 10. Westview Press, Boulder, Colo.

Felger, R., G. P. Nabhan, and T. Sheridan. 1976. Ethnobotany of the Rio San Miguel, Sonora, Mexico. Unpublished manuscript, copy deposited at the Desert Botanical Garden, Phoenix, Ariz.

Felger, R., M. Moser, and E. Moser. 1980a. Seagrasses in Seri Indian culture. Pp. 260–276 *in* Handbook of seagrasses biology: An ecosystem perspective. R. C. Phillips and C. P. McRoy, eds. Garland STPM Press, New York, N.Y.

Felger, R., D. Cornejo, L. Leigh, and C. Stigers. 1980b. Semillas magicas del desierto. Un modelo de agricultura apropiada del Desierto Sonorensis. Pp. 70–80 *in* IV Simposio sobre el Medio Ambiente del Golfo de California—la Produccion Sostenida de Alimentos, Materias Primas y Empleos. Instituto Nacional de Investigaciones Forestales, México, D.F.

Felger, R., P. Warren, S. Anderson, and G. Nabhan. 1992. Vascular plants of a desert oasis: Flora and ethnobotany of Quitobaquito, Organ Pipe Cactus National Monument, Arizona. Proceedings of the San Diego Society of Natural History 8:1–39.

Fernald, M., and A. Kinsey. 1958. Edible wild plants of eastern North America. Idlewild Press, Cornwall-on-Hudson, N.Y.

Fewkes, J. W. 1896. A contribution to ethnobotany. American Anthropology 9:14–21.

Fish, S. 1984. Agriculture and subsistence implications of the Salt-Gila aqueduct project pollen analysis. Pp. 111–138 *in* Hohokam archaeology along the Salt-Gila aqueduct, Central Arizona Project. Vol. VII. Environment and subsistence. L. Teague and P. Crown, eds. Cultural Resource Management Section, Arizona State Museum, Archaeological Series no. 150, Tucson, Ariz.

Fish, S., P. R. Fish, C. Mikisicek, and J. Madsen. 1985. Prehistoric agave cultivation in southern Arizona. Desert Plants 7(2):107–112.

Fish, S., P. R. Fish, and J. Madsen. 1990. Analyzing regional agriculture: A Hohokam example. Pp. 189–218 *in* The archaeology of regions: The case for full-coverage survey. S. Fish and S. Kowalewski, eds. Smithsonian Institution Press, Washington, D.C.

Fish, S., P. R. Fish, and J. Madsen. 1992. Evidence for large-scale agave cultivation in the Marana community. Pp. 73–87 *in* The Marana community in the Hohokam world. S. Fish, P. Fish, and J. Madsen, eds. University of Arizona Press, Tucson.

Fleming, T., R. Nunez, and L. Sternberg. 1993. Seasonal changes in the diets of migrant and non-migrant nectarivorous bats as revealed by carbon stable isotype analyses. Oecologia 94:72–75.

Fontana, B. 1974. Man in arid lands: The Piman Indians of the Sonoran Desert. Pp. 489–528 *in* Desert biology. Vol. II. G. Brown Jr., ed. Academic Press, New York, N.Y.

Fontana, B. 1980. Ethnobotany of the saguaro, an annotated bibliography. Desert Plants 2:62–78.

Ford, R. 1978. Ethnobotany: Historical diversity and synthesis. Pp. 33–49 *in* The nature and status of ethnobotany. R. Ford, ed. Anthropological Papers no. 67. Museum of Anthropology, University of Michigan, Ann Arbor.

Forde, D. 1931. Ethnography of the Yuma Indians. University of California Publications in American Archaeology and Ethnology 28:4.

Fowler, C. 1995. Some notes on ethnographic subsistence systems in Mojavean environments in the Great Basin. Journal of Ethnobiology 15(1):99–117.

Fowler, C. 1999. Plant "wifery" in the Great Basin: Indigenous and diffused. Paper presented at the XVI International Botanical Congress, August 1–7, St. Louis, Missouri.

Frati-Munari, A., J. Fernandez-Harp, H. de la Riva, R. Ariza-Andraca, and M. del Carmen Torres. 1983. Efecto del nopal (*Opuntia* sp.) sobre los lipidos sericos, la glucemia y el peso corporal. Archivos de Investigacíon Médico (México) 14:117–125.

Frati-Munari, A., B. Gordillo, P. Atamiro, and C. Ariza. 1988. Hypoglycemic effect of *Opuntia streptacantha* Lemaire in NIDDM. Diabetes Care 11:63–66.

Freeman, G. 1912. Southwestern beans and teparies. University of Arizona Agricultural Experiment Station Bulletin 68:1–55.

Gallagher, M. 1976. Contemporary ethnobotany among the Apache of the Clarkdale, Arizona, area. Coconino and Prescott National Forests. Report no. 14. U.S. Department of Agriculture, Forest Service, Southwestern Region.

Gasser, R. 1982. Hohokam use of desert foods. Desert Plants 3(4):216–234.

Gasser, R. 1987. Subsistence in a bag of soil. Environment Southwest 519:6–9.

Gasser, R., and S. Kwiatkowski. 1991a. Food for thought: Recognizing patterns in Hohokam subsistence. Pp. 417–459 *in* Exploring the Hohokam: Prehistoric desert peoples of the American Southwest. G. Gumerman, ed. Amerind Foundation, Dragoon, University of New Mexico Press, Albuquerque.

Gasser, R., and S. Kwiatkowski. 1991b. Regional signatures of Hohokam plant use. Kiva 56(3):207–226.

Gathman, A., and W. Bemis. 1983. Heritability of fatty acid composition of buffalo gourd seed oil. Journal of Heredity 74:199–200.

Gentry, H. S. 1942. Rio Mayo plants. Carnegie Institution of Washington Publication no. 527, Washington, D.C.

Gentry, H. S. 1959. Economic crops for arid lands. Unpublished manuscript, copy deposited at Desert Botanical Garden, Phoenix, Ariz.

Gentry, H. S. 1963. The Warihio Indians of Sonora-Chihuahua: An ethnographic survey. Smithsonian Institution Bureau of American Ethnological Bulletin no. 186, Anthropology Papers no. 65. U.S. Government Printing Office, Washington, D.C.

Gentry, H. S. 1972. The agave family in Sonora. Agricultural Handbook no. 399. U.S. Department of Agriculture, Washington, D.C.

Gentry, H. S. 1978. The agaves of Baja California. Occasional Papers of the California Academy of Sciences no. 130, San Francisco, Calif.

Gentry, H. S. 1982. The agaves of continental North America. University of Arizona Press, Tucson.

Genung, W. 1959. Ecological and cultural factors affecting chemical control of subterranean cutworms in the Everglades. Proceedings of the Florida State Horticultural Society 72:163–167.

Ghosh, A., and J. Beal. 1979. Seed lipid constituents of three species of *Proboscidea*. Journal of Natural Products 42:287–292.

Gibson, F. 1935. *Agave murpheyi,* a new species. Contributions from the Boyce Thompson Institute 1:83–85.

Gifford, E. W. 1931. The Kamia of Imperial Valley. U.S. Bureau of Ethnology Bulletin no. 97, Washington, D.C.

Gifford, E. W. 1932. The Southeastern Yavapai. University of California Publications in American Archaeology and Ethnography 29(3):177–252.

Gifford, E. W. 1933. The Cocopah. University of California Publications in American Archaeology and Ethnography 31:257–334.

Gifford, E. W. 1936. Northeastern and Western Yavapai. University of California Publications in American Archaeology and Ethnography 34:247–354.

Gifford, E. W. 1940. Culture element distributions. XII. Apache-Pueblo. Anthropological Records 4(1):1–207.

Gifford, E. W., and R. H. Lowie. 1928. Notes on the Akwa'ala Indians of Lower California. University of California Publications in American Archaeology and Ethnology 23:339–352.

Gill, A., and P. Tomlinson 1969. Studies on the growth of red mangrove (*Rhizophora mangle* L.). Biotropica 1:1–9.

Gish, J. 1987. Structured diversity in the resource base of a Hohokam village: The pollen evidence from La Ciudad. Pp. 1–66 *in* Specialized studies in the economy, environment, and culture of La Ciudad. J. Kisselburg, G. Rice, and B. Shears, ed. ASU Anthropological Field Studies no. 20. Department of Anthropology, Arizona State University, Tempe.

Glendening, G. E., and H. A. Paulsen Jr. 1975. Reproduction and establishment of velvet mesquite as related to invasion of semi-desert grasslands. U.S. Department of Agriculture, Forest Service Technical Bulletin no. 1127. U.S. Government Printing Office, Washington, D.C.

Goldman, E. 1916. Plant records of an expedition to Lower California. Contributions U.S. National Herbarium 16(14):309–389.

Gontzea, I., and P. Sutzescu. 1968. Natural antinutritive substances in foodstuffs and forages. S. Karger, New York, N.Y.

Goodwin, G. 1942. The social organization of the Western Apache. University of Chicago Press, Chicago, Ill.

Gordon, D., R. Murrieta, L. Michel, and F. Velazquez. 1972. Vegetacion del estado de Sonora. Comision technico consultiva para la determinacion regional de los coeficientes de agostadero, S.A.G. Brigada, Sonora. Subagencia de agriculture y ganaderia, Hermosillo, Sonora.

Green, M. 1986. Settlement, subsistence, and specialization in the Northern Periphery: Research design for mitigative recovery at sites in the new Waddell Dam borrow areas. Archaeological Consulting Services Report 40:1–54.

Greenhouse, R. 1979. The iron and calcium content of some traditional Pima foods and the effects of preparation methods. M.S. thesis, Arizona State University, Tempe.

Greenhouse, R. 1986. Plants and people of the Sonoran Desert. Agave 1(4):4.

Greenhouse, R., R. Gasser, and J. Gish. 1981. Cholla bud roasting pits: An ethnoarchaeological example. Kiva 46(4):227–242.

Gumerman, G., J. Hanson, D. Brew, K. Tomoff, and C. Weed. 1975. The hydrology of prehistoric farming systems in a central Arizona ecotone. Lyndon B. Johnson Space Center, Houston, Tex.

Haiman, R. 1974. Human modification of the coastal vegetation of northwestern Baja California. Journal of the Arizona-Nevada Academy of Science 9 (Supplement):26.

Hake, H. 1980. Introducción al estudio y al uso práctico de las plantas alimenticias del estado de Baja California. Pp. 85–115, *in* V Simposio Sobre el Medio Ambiente del Golfo de California. Mexicali y Puerto de San Felipe, Baja California. Memoria, Instituto Nacional de Investigaciones Forestales, México, D.F.

Hake, H. 1983. Especies nativas de utilidad alimenticia de Baja California Sur. Pp. 53–68, *in* Segunda Reunión Nacional Sobre Ecología, Manejo y Domesticación de las Plantas Útiles del Desierto. Publicación Especial No. 43, Subsecretaria Forestal Instituto Nacional de Investigaciones Forestales. México, D.F.

Hakluyt, R. 1904. Relation of Fernando de Alarcón: May–September 1540. Pp. 279–318 *in* The principal navigations, voyages traffiques & discoveries of the English nation. Vol. IX. James MacLehose and Sons, Glasgow.

Harden, M. L., and R. Zolfaghari. 1988. Nutritive composition of green and ripe pods of honey mesquite (*Prosopis glandulosa,* Fabaceae). Economic Botany 42(4):522–532.

Harlan, J. 1968. On the origin of barley. Pp. 9–31 *in* Barley: Origin, botany, culture, winter hardiness, genetics, utilization. U.S. Department of Agriculture Handbook no. 338, Washington, D.C.

Harrington, H. 1967. Edible native plants of the Rocky Mountains. University of New Mexico Press, Albuquerque.

Havard, V. 1895. Food plants of the North American Indians. Bulletin of the Torrey Botanical Club 22:98–123.

Havard, V. 1896. Drink plants of the North American Indians. Bulletin of the Torrey Botanical Club 23:33–46.

Hayden, J. D. 1967. A summary prehistory and history of the Sierra Pinacate, Sonora. American Antiquity 32:335–344.

Hayden, J. D. 1969. Gyratory crushers of the Sierra Pinacate, Sonora. American Antiquity 34(2):154–161.

Hedges, M. 1985. Indians of the Anza-Borrego: Land use and settlement patterns. Environment Southwest Autumn:6–11.

Hedges, M., and C. Beresford. 1986. Santa Ysabel ethnobotany. San Diego Museum of Man Ethnic Technology Notes no. 20, San Diego, Calif.

Hedrick, U., ed. 1972. Sturtevant's edible plants of the world. Dover Publications, Inc., New York, N.Y.

Heiser, C. 1976. The Sunflower. University of Oklahoma Press, Norman.

Heizer, R. 1949. Honey-dew sugar in western North America. Antiquity 19(5):140–145.

Henderson, R. 1951. Mescal roast. Desert Magazine 14(10):8.

Herbert, C. 1955. Saguaro harvest in the land of the Papagos. Desert Magazine 18(11):14–17.

Herbert, C. 1969. Papago saguaro harvest. Arizona Highways 45(1):2–7.

Hesse, F. 1959. A dietary study of the Pima Indian. American Journal for Clinical Nutrition 7:532–537.

Hickman, J. 1993. The Jepson manual. University of California Press, Berkeley.

Hicks, F. 1963. Ecological aspects of aboriginal culture in the western Yuman area. Ph.D. dissertation, University of California, Los Angeles.

Hill, R. J. n.d. Observations on the ethnobotany of the genus *Mentzelia* (Loasaceae). Unpublished manuscript, copy deposited at Desert Botanical Garden Herbarium, Phoenix, Ariz.

Hinton, L. 1975. La Muerta Diegueño ethnobotany. Journal of California Anthropology 2(2):214–222.

Hinton, T. 1956. A description of the contemporary use of an aboriginal Sonoran food. Kiva 21(3/4):27–28.

Hodgson, W. 1982. Edible native and naturalized plants of the Sonoran Desert north of Mexico. M.S. thesis, Arizona State University, Tempe.

Hodgson, W. 1989. A tale of two saiyas: Conserving plant lore and gene pools. Agave 3(3):12–14.

Hodgson, W. 1993. Bixaceae: Lipsticktree family. Journal of the Arizona-Nevada Academy of Science 27(2):188–189.

Hodgson, W. 1994a. Status report on *Agave murpheyi* Gibson. Report to U.S. Fish and Wildlife Service, Arizona Ecological Services State Office, Phoenix, Ariz.

Hodgson, W. 1994b. Status report on *Agave delamateri,* sp. nov. Report to U.S. Fish and Wildlife Service, Arizona Ecological Services State Office, Phoenix, Ariz.

Hodgson, W. 1999a. Agavaceae (agave family). Part 1. *Agave* L. Vascular plants of Arizona. Journal of the Arizona-Nevada Academy of Science 32(1):1–21.

Hodgson, W. 1999b. Agaves and humans: The continuing story of a continuing connection. Sonoran Quarterly 53(4):6–8.

Hodgson, W., and L. Slauson. 1995. *Agave delamateri* (Agavaceae) and its role in the subsistence patterns of pre-Columbian cultures in Arizona. Haseltonia 3:130–140.

Hodgson, W., G. Nabhan, and L. Ecker. 1989. Conserving rediscovered agave cultivars. Agave 3(3):9–11.

Holmgren, P., N. Holmgren, and L. Barnett, eds. 1990. Index Herbariorum. Part I. The herbaria of the world. 8th ed. New York Botanical Garden, Bronx, N.Y.

Honma, S. 1956. Bean interspecific hybrid. Journal of Heredity 41:217–220.

Hough, W. 1897. The Hopi in relation to their plant environment. American Anthropologist 10:33–44.

Hough, W. 1898. Environmental interrelations in Arizona. American Anthropologist 11:133–155.

Housely, L. K. 1975. *Opuntia imbricata:* Distribution on old Jemez Indian habitation sites. M.S. thesis, Claremount Graduate School, Claremount, Calif.

Howard, E. 1887. Reports of agents in Arizona: Pima agency, 1887. Annual Reports of Commissioner for Indian Affairs to the Secretary of Interior. U.S. Government Printing Office, Washington, D.C.

Howell, D. 1985. The bat, the blossom, and the biologist. Summary of British Broadcasting Company film. Desert Plants 7(2):34.

Howell, D., and D. Roth. 1981. Sexual reproduction in agaves: The benefits of bats, the cost of semelparous advertising. Ecology 62:1–7.

Hrdlička, A. 1905. Notes on the San Carlos Apache. American Anthropologist 7:480–495.

Hrdlička, A. 1906. Notes on the Pima of Arizona. American Anthropologist 7:39–46.

Hrdlička, A. 1908. Physiological and medical observations among the Indians of southwestern U.S. and northern Mexico. Smithsonian Institution Bureau of American Ethnology Bulletin no. 34. U.S. Government Printing Office, Washington, D.C.

Huerta, G. 1988. Los aspectos biologicos de la exploracion en el territorio de Baja California. Boletin de la Sociedad Mexicana de Geografia y Estadistica 88(1/2):242.

Humphrey, R. 1975. Phenology of selected Sonoran Desert plants at Punta Cirio, Sonora, Mexico. Journal of the Arizona-Nevada Academy of Science 10:50–67.

Index Kewensis. 1997. CD rom, version 2.0. Royal Botanic Gardens, Kew, Oxford University Press, Oxford, England.

Jacks, T., T. Hensarling, and L. Tatsu. 1971. Cucurbit seeds. I. Characterizations and uses of oils and proteins: A review. Economic Botany 26:135–141.

Janzen, D. 1969. Seed dispersal versus seed size, number, toxicity, and dispersal. Evolution 23:1–27.

Janzen, D. 1970. *Jacquinia pungens,* a heliophile from the understory of tropical deciduous forest. Biotropica 2:112–119.

Jöel, J. 1976. Some Paipai accounts of food gathering. Journal of California Anthropology 3(1):58–71.

Johns, T. 1990. With bitter herbs they shall eat it: Chemical ecology and the origins of human diet and medicine. University of Arizona Press, Tucson.

Johnston, M. 1962a. The North American mesquites: *Prosopis* sect. *Algarobia* (Leguminosae). Brittonia 14(1):72–89.

Johnston, M. 1962b. Revision of *Condalia* including *Microrhamnus* (Rhamnaceae). Brittonia 14(4):332–368.

Johnston, M. 1963. The species of *Ziziphus* indigenous to the United States and Mexico. American Journal of Botany 50:1020–1027.

Jones, Q., and F. Earle. 1966. Chemical analysis of seeds. II. Oil and protein content of 759 species. Economic Botany 20:127–155.

Jones, V. 1945. Use of honey-dew as food. Masterkey 19(5):145–149.

Jordan, P., and P. Nobel. 1979. Infrequent establishment of seedlings of *Agave deserti* (Agavaceae) in the northwestern Sonoran Desert. American Journal of Botany 66:1079–1084.

Joyal, E. 1995. An ethnoecology of *Sabal uresana* Trelease (Arecaceae) in Sonora, Mexico. Ph.D. dissertation, Arizona State University, Tempe.

Joyal, E. 1996. The use of *Sabal uresana* (Arecaceae) and other palms in Sonora, Mexico. Economic Botany 50(4):429–445.

Kaplan, L. 1963. Archaeoethnobotany of Cordova Cave, New Mexico. Economic Botany 17(4):350–359.

Kartesz, J., and C. Meacham. 1999. Synthesis of the North American flora. CD rom, version 1.0. North Carolina Botanical Garden, Chapel Hill.

Kearney, T., R. Peebles, J. T. Howell, and E. McClintock. 1960. Arizona flora. University of California Press, Berkeley.

Keasey, M. 1975. Harvesting time in the saguaro forest. Pacific Discovery 28(2):25–29.

Keil, D. 1970. Vegetation and flora of White Tanks Mountains Regional Park. M.S. thesis, Arizona State University, Tempe.

Kelly, I. 1932. Ethnography of the Surprise Valley Paiute. University of California Publications in Archaeology and Ethnology 31(3):67–210.

Kelly, I. 1932–1934. Southern Paiute field notes: Las Vegas, Vol. 1; Chemehuevi, Vol. 1; Moapa; St. George; Shivwits. Unpublished manuscript, copy on file at the Department of Anthropology, University of Nevada, Reno; also University Archives, University of California at Berkeley, microfilm copies (except Las Vegas, Vol. 1, and Chemehuevi).

Kelly, I. 1964. Southern Paiute ethnography. University of Utah Anthropological Papers no. 69, Salt Lake City.

Kelly, W. 1977. Cocopah Ethnography. Anthropological Papers of the University of Arizona no. 29, Tucson.

Kephart, H. 1921. Camping and woodcraft: A handbook for vacation campers and travelers in the wilderness. McMillan, New York, N.Y.

King, F. 1984. Plants, people, and paleoecology. Illinois State Museum Scientific Paper no. 20, Springfield.

Kingsbury, J. 1964. Poisonous plants of the United States and Canada. Prentice-Hall, Inc., Englewood Cliffs, N.J.

Kingsolver, J., C. Johnson, S. Swier, and A. Teran. 1977. *Prosopis* fruits as a resource for invertebrates. Pp. 108–122 *in* Mesquite: Its biology in two desert scrub ecosystems. B. Simpson, ed. Dowden, Hutchinson, and Ross, Inc., Stroudsburg, Pa.

Kirk, D. 1975. Wild edible plants of the United States. Naturegraph Publishers, Inc., Healdsburg, Calif.

Kissell, M. 1916. Basketry of the Papago and Pima. Anthropological Papers of the American Museum of Natural History 17:115–264. 1972. Reprint, Rio Grande Press, Glorieta, N.M.

Knight, J. 1964. Chia fostered the battle of Massacre Canyon. Desert Magazine 27(9):14–15.

Knowler, W., P. Bennett, R. Hamman, and M. Miller. 1978. Diabetes incidence and prevalence in Pima Indians: A 19-fold greater incidence than in Rochester, Minnesota. American Journal for Epidemiology 108:497–504.

Krizman, R. 1972. Environment and season in a tropical deciduous forest in northwestern Mexico. Ph.D. dissertation, University of Arizona, Tucson.

Krmpotic, M. 1923. Life and works of the Rev. Ferdinand Konscak, S.J. The Stratford Co., Boston, Mass.

Kroeber, A. 1931. The Seri. Southwest Museum Papers no. 6, Los Angeles, Calif.

Kroeber, A. 1935. Walapai ethnography. Memoirs of the American Anthropological Association no. 42, Menasha, Wis.

Kroeber, C. 1980. Lower Colorado River people: Host and hunger. Journal of California and Great Basin Anthropology 2(2):187–198.

Kuhnlein, H. 1985. Wild foods for modern diets. Nutrition Update 2:153–169.

Laferrière, J. E., C. W. Weber, and E. A. Kohlhepp. 1991. Use and nutritional composition of some traditional Mountain Pima plant foods. Journal of Ethnobiology 11(1):93–114.

Lampe, K., and M. A. McCann. 1985. AMA handbook of poisonous and injurious plants. American Medical Association, Chicago, Ill.

Lancaster, P., J. Ingram, M. Lim, and D. Coursay. 1982. Traditional cassava-based foods: Survey of processing techniques. Economic Botany 36(1):12–45.

Landrum, L. 1993. Fagaceae: Oak family. Journal of the Arizona-Nevada Academy of Science 27(2):203–214.

Lawrence, G. 1951. Taxonomy of vascular plants. The Macmillan Co., New York, N.Y.

Lehr, J. H. 1978. A catalogue of the flora of Arizona. Northland Press, Flagstaff, Ariz.

Lehr, J. H., and D. Pinkava. 1980. A catalogue of the flora of Arizona. Supplement I. Journal Arizona-Nevada Academy of Science 15:17–32.

Lehr, J. H., and D. Pinkava. 1982. A catalogue of the flora of Arizona. Supplement II. Journal Arizona-Nevada Academy of Science 17:19–26.

Lenz, L. 1998. *Yucca capensis* (Agavaceae, Yuccoideae), a new species from Baja California Sur, Mexico. Cactus and Succulent Journal (U.S.) 70(6):289–296.

Leung, W. 1961. Food composition table for use in Latin America. Institute of Nutrition of Central America and Panama (Guatemala) and Interdepartmental Committee on Nutrition for National Defense (U.S.A.), National Institutes of Health, Bethesda, Md.

Levington, A. 1990. Plants for people. Oxford University Press, New York, N.Y.

Lewis, H., ed. 1973. Patterns of Indian burning in California: Ecology and ethnohistory. Ballena Press, Socorro, N.M.

Lindsay, G., J. H. Cota, M. Lee, L. Mitich, and F. Thrombley. 1996. The taxonomy and ecology of the genus *Ferocactus*. Tireless Termites Press, San Diego, Calif.

Loaiza-Figueroa, F. 1985. Evolution of the genus *Capsicum* (Solanaceae) in Mexico. M.S. thesis, New Mexico State University, Las Cruces.

Luckingham, B. 1989. Phoenix: The history of a southwestern metropolis. University of Arizona Press, Tucson.

Lumholtz, C. S. 1902. Unknown Mexico: A record of five years' exploration among the tribes of the western Sierra Madre; in the Tierra Caliente of Tepic and Jalisco and among the Tarascos of Michoacan. 2 vols. Charles Scribner's Sons, New York, N.Y.

Lumholtz, C. S. 1912. New trails in Mexico. Charles Scribner's Sons, New York, N.Y. 1971. Reprint, Rio Grande Press, Glorieta, N.M.

Marsh, R. 1969. Two contemporary Papago recipes of indigenous plants and the American Southwest botanical implications. Kiva 34(4):242–246.

Marshall, W. T., and T. M. Bock. 1941. Cactaceae. Abbey Garden Press, Pasadena, Calif.

Martin, F., and H. Nakasone. 1970. The edible species of *Passiflora*. Economic Botany 24:333–343.

Martin, P., D. Yetman, M. Fishbein, P. Jenkins, T. Van Devender, and R. Wilson, eds. 1998. Gentry's Rio Mayo plants: The tropical deciduous forest and environs of northwest Mexico. The Southwest Center Series. University of Arizona Press, Tucson.

Martinez, M. 1936. Plantas Utiles de la Republica Mexicana. Ediciones Botas, México City, D.F.

Martinez, M. 1947. Baja California. Reseña Histórica del Territorio y de su Flora. Ediciones Botas, México City, D.F.

Martinez, M. 1979. Catalogo de Nombres Vulgares y Cientificos de Plantas Mexicanas. Fondo de Cultura Economica, México City, D.F.

Martinez-Morales, R., and S. Meyer. 1985. A demographic study of maguey verde *(Agave salmiana* ssp. *crassispina)* under conditions of intense utilization. Desert Plants (2):61–64;101–102.

Massey, W. 1949. Tribes and languages of Baja California. Southwestern Journal of Anthropology 5(3):272–307.

Massey, W. 1966. Archaeology and ethnohistory of Lower California. Pp. 38–58 *in* Handbook of middle American Indians. Vol. 4. R. Wauchope et al., eds. University of Texas Press, Austin.

Mathes, W. M. 1969. First from the Gulf to the Pacific: The diary of the Kino-Atondo peninsular expedition. Dawson's Book Shop, Los Angeles, Calif.

Mathes, W. M. 1973. The conquistador in California, 1535. Dawson's Book Shop, Los Angeles, Calif.

Mathes, W. M. 1974. A case of idolatry among the Cochimí. The Masterkey 48(3):98–107.

Mathes, W. M. 1975a. Opinion given by Licentiate Diego de la Nava: April–June 1632. Pp. 53–59 *in* Spanish approaches to the island of California, 1628–1632. W. Michael Mathes, ed. and trans. The Book Club of California, San Francisco, Calif.

Mathes, W. M. 1975b. Some new observations relative to the indigenous inhabitants of La Paz, Baja California Sur. The Journal of California Anthropology 2(2):180–182.

Mathes, W. M. 1979. Clemente Guillén, explorer of the south: Diaries of the overland expeditions to Bahia Magdalena and La Paz, 1719, 1720–1721. Dawson's Book Shop, Los Angeles, Calif.

Mathes, W. M. 1981. Problems of ethnohistorical research in Baja California. Journal of California and Great Basin Anthropology 3(1):44–48.

Mathes, W. M. 1989. Baja California: A special area of contact and colonization, 1535–1697. Pp. 407–422 *in* Columbian consequences: Archaeological and historical perspectives on the Spanish borderlands west. Vol. 1. Smithsonian Institution Press, Washington, D.C.

Mathes, W. M. 1990. Relations of Francisco de Ortega, 1633–1634. Pp. 347–352, 436–452 *in* California I: Documentos para la historia de la explotacion comercial de California 1611–1679. W. M. Mathes, ed. Ediciones José Porrua Turanzas, Madrid.

Mathes, W. M., ed. 1992. Ethnology of the Baja California Indians. Vol. 5. Garland Publishing Co., New York, N.Y.

McDowell, M. 1920. Report on the Papago Indians. Reports of the Department of Interior Fiscal Year 1919. U.S. Government Printing Office, Washington, D.C.

McKelvey, S. 1938. Yuccas of the Southwestern U.S. Part 1. Arnold Arboretum of Harvard University, Jamaica Plain, Mass.

McKelvey, S. 1947. Yuccas of the Southwestern U.S. Part 2. Arnold Arboretum of Harvard University, Jamaica Plain, Mass.

McLaughlin, S. 1989. Natural floristic areas of the western U.S. Journal of Biogeography 16:239–248.

McVaugh, R. 1956. Edward Palmer: Plant explorer of the American West. University of Oklahoma Press, Norman.

McVaugh, R. 1987. Flora Novo-Galiciana. Vol. 5. Leguminosae. W. Anderson, ed. University of Michigan Press, Ann Arbor.

Meals for Millions Foundation. 1980. O'odham *I: waki:* Wild greens of the desert people. Southwest Program, Tucson, Ariz.

Medsger, O. 1966. Edible wild plants. MacMillan Publishing Co., New York, N.Y.

Meigs, P. 1935. The Dominican mission: Frontier of Lower California. University of California Publications in Geography 7:1–192.

Meigs, P. 1939. The Kiliwa Indians of Lower California. University of California Publications Ibero-Americana no. 15, Berkeley, Calif.

Mekeel, S. 1935. Subsistence plant foods and preparation. Pp. 48–57 *in* Walapai ethnography. A. L. Kroeber, ed. American Anthropological Association Memoir no. 42, Menasha, Wis.

Mellink, E., G. Nabhan, and H. Suzan. 1991. Ironwood tree/ el palofierro *(Olneya tesota)*. CEDO News 4(2):27–30.

Merrick, L., and G. Nabhan. 1984. Natural hybridization of wild *Cucurbita sororia* group and domesticated *C. mixta* in southern Sonora, Mexico. Cucurbit Genetics Cooperative Newsletter 7:73–75.

Metcalf, R., A. Rhodes, R. Metcalf, J. Ferguson, E. Metcalf, and P. Lu. 1982. Cucurbitacin contents and diaboticite (Coleoptera: Chrysomelidae) feeding upon *Cucurbita* spp. Environment Entomology 11(4):931–938.

Miksicek, C. 1983. Archaeobotanical aspects of Las Fosas: A statistical approach to prehistoric plant remains. Pp. 671–700 *in* Hohokam archaeology along the Salt-Gila aqueduct, Central Arizona Project. Vol. VI. Habitat sites on the Gila River. L. Teague and P. Crown, eds. Arizona State Museum Archaeological Series no. 150, University of Arizona, Tucson.

Millspaugh, C. 1974. American medicinal plants. Dover Publications, Inc., New York, N.Y.

Minnis, P. 1991. Famine foods of the North American desert borderlands in historical context. Journal of Ethnobiology 11(2):231–257.

Minnis, P., and S. Plogg. 1976. A study of site-specific distribution of *Agave parryi* in east-central Arizona. Kiva 41(3/4):299–308.

Mirov, N. 1952. *Simmondsia* or jojoba: A problem in economic botany. Economic Botany 6:41–47.

Moerman, D. 1998. Native American ethnobotany. Timber Press, Portland, Ore.

Moisés, R., J. Holden Kelly, and W. Holden. 1971. A Yaqui life: The personal chronicle of a Yaqui Indian. University of Nebraska Press, Lincoln.

Mokady, S., and A. Dolev. 1970. Nutritional evaluation of tubers of *Cyperus esculentus* L. Journal of the Science of Food and Agriculture 21:211–214.

Molto, J., and H. Fujita. 1995. La Matancita: A Las Palmas mortuary site from the west cape region of Baja California Sur, Mexico. Pacific Coast Archaeological Society Quarterly 31(1/2)20–55.

Moran, R. 1968. Cardón. Pacific Discovery 21:2–9.

Moran, R. 1969. Twelve new dicots from Baja California, Mexico. San Diego Society of Natural History Transactions 15(17):265–295.

Moran, R. 1977. Palms in Baja California. Environment Southwest 478:10–14.

Moran, R. 1979. Palmas of Valle de las Palmas. Environment Southwest Spring:16–18.

Moriarty, J., and B. Smith, trans. and eds. 1970. The Cora Indians of Baja California: The relacion of Father Ignacio María Nápoli, S.J., September 20, 1721. Dawson's Book Shop, Los Angeles, Calif.

Morton, J. 1962. Spanish-needles (*Bidens pilosa* L.) as a wild food resource. Economic Botany 16:173–179.

Morton, J. 1963. Principal wild food plants of the United States. Economic Botany 17:319–330.

Morton, J. 1975. Cattails (*Typha* spp.): Weed problem or potential crop? Economic Botany 29:7–30.

Nabhan, G. P. 1975. Teparies and other native beans *(Phaseolus)* in southwestern North America. Journal Arizona-Nevada Academy of Science 11:18–19.

Nabhan, G. P. 1978a. Tepary bean domestication: Ecological and nutritional changes during *Phaseolus acutifolius* evolution. M.S. thesis, University of Arizona, Tucson.

Nabhan, G. P. 1978b. Chiltepines! Wild spice of the American Southwest. El Palacio 84:30.

Nabhan, G. P. 1979a. The ecology of floodwater farming in arid southwestern North America. Agro-Ecosystems 5:245–255.

Nabhan, G. P. 1979b. Southwestern Indian sunflowers. Desert Plants 1(1):23–26.

Nabhan, G. P. 1979c. Amaranth cultivation in the U.S. Southwest and northwest Mexico. Amaranth Proceedings 1979:129–133.

Nabhan, G. P. 1980. *Ammobroma sonorae,* an endangered parasitic plant in extremely arid North America. Desert Plants 2:188–196.

Nabhan, G. P. 1982. The desert smells like rain: A naturalist in Papago Indian country. North Point Press, San Francisco, Calif.

Nabhan, G. P. 1983. Seedkeepers in their own right: Binational team works to save saltgrass genes. Seedhead News no. 4. Native Seeds/SEARCH, Tucson, Ariz.

Nabhan, G. P. 1984a. Sonoran panicgrass: Does it merit U.S. endangered species status? Seedhead News no. 5. Native Seeds/SEARCH, Tucson, Ariz.

Nabhan, G. P. 1984b. Petition to place Sonoran panicgrass, *Panicum sonorum* Beale, on the U.S. list of endangered and threatened wildlife and plants. Office of Arid Land Studies, Tucson, Ariz.

Nabhan, G. P. 1985. Gathering the desert. University of Arizona Press, Tucson.

Nabhan, G. P. 1987. Nurse plant ecology of threatened desert plants. Pp. 377–383 *in* Conservation and management of rare and endangered plants. T. Elias, ed. Rare and Endangered Plant Conference and Symposium, 5–11 November 1986, Sacramento, Calif.

Nabhan, G. P. 1989a. Plants at risk in the Sonoran Desert: An international concern. Agave 3(3):14–15.

Nabhan, G. P. 1989b. Interview with Chico Shuni and other Hia Ced O'odham, Organ Pipe Cactus National Monument, December. Unpublished notes, copy deposited at Desert Botanical Garden, Phoenix, Ariz.

Nabhan, G. P. 1992. Field notes on agave use in Sonora. Unpublished manuscript, copy deposited at Desert Botanical Garden Herbarium, Phoenix, Ariz.

Nabhan, G. P., and J. M. DeWet. 1984. *Panicum sonorum* in Sonoran Desert agriculture. Economic Botany 38(1):65–82.

Nabhan, G. P., and R. Felger. 1978. Teparies in southwestern North America. Economic Botany 32(1):2–19.

Nabhan, G. P., and R. Felger. 1985. Wild desert relatives of crops: Their direct uses as food. Pp. 19–34 *in* Plants for arid lands: Proceedings of the Kew international conference on economic plants for arid lands. G. Wilkens, J. Goodin, and D. Field, eds. George Allen and Unwin, London.

Nabhan, G. P., and G. Fritz. 1977. Devil's claw *(Proboscidea):* Cash crop in the Papago basketry industry. Journal of the Arizona Academy of Science 12:4–5.

Nabhan, G. P., and W. Hodgson. 1988. Interview with María Beltran, Granados, Sonora, February. Unpublished notes, copy deposited at Desert Botanical Garden, Phoenix, Ariz.

Nabhan, G. P., and A. Rea. 1987. Plant domestication and folk-biological change: The Upper Piman/devil's claw example. American Anthropologist 89(1):57–73.

Nabhan, G. P., and H. Teiwes. 1983. Tepary beans, O'odham farmers, and desert fields. Desert Plants 5(1):15–39.

Nabhan, G. P., C. Weber, and J. Berry. 1979. Legumes in Papago-Pima Indian diet and ecological niche. Kiva 44:173–190.

Nabhan, G. P., J. Berry, and C. Weber. 1980. Wild beans of the greater Southwest: *Phaseolus metcalfei* and *P. ritensis.* Economic Botany 34(1):68–85.

Nabhan, G. P., A. Whiting, H. Dobyns, R. Hevly, and R. Euler. 1981. Devil's claw domestication: Evidence from southwestern Indian fields. Journal of Ethnobiology 1:135–164.

Nabhan, G. P., A. Rea, K. Reichardt, E. Mellinck, and C. Hutchinson. 1982. Papago influence on habitat and biotic diversity: Quitovac oasis ethnoecology. Journal of Ethnobiology 2(2):124–143.

Nabhan, G. P., P. L. Warren, and M. Parton. 1985. Mesquite resources of the Colorado River Indian Tribes Reservation. Office of Arid Lands Studies, Tucson, Ariz.

Nabhan, G. P., V. Gass, and P. Quirk. 1986. Thornber's fishhook cactus: Conserving a declining species. Agave 2(2):4–8.

Nabhan, G. P., W. Hodgson, and L. Hernandez. 1988. Plant genetic resources threatened in North American deserts: The FLORUTIL Conservation Project. Pp. 59–65 *in* Strategies for classification and management of native vegetation for food production in arid zones. General Technical Report no. RM-150. U.S. Forest Service and Secretaria Agricultura y Recursos Hidraulicos (SARH).

Nabhan, G. P., W. Hodgson, and F. Fellows. 1989a. A meager living on lava and sand? Hia ceḍ O'odham food resources and habitat diversity in oral and documentary histories. Journal of the Southwest 31(4):508–533.

Nabhan, G. P., M. Slater, and L. Yarger. 1989b. New crops for marginal peoples in marginal lands: Wild chiles as a case study. Pp. 17–23 *in* Agroecology and small farm development. M. Altieri and S. Hecht, eds. CRC Press, Boca Raton, Fla.

Nabhan, G. P., E. Saucedo Monarque, P. Olwell, P. Warren, W. Hodgson, C. Gallindo-Duarte, R. Bittman, and S. Anderson. 1989c. A preliminary list of plants at risk in the Sonoran Desert of the U.S. and Mexico. Agave 3(3):15.

Nabhan, G. P., D. House, H. Suzan, W. Hodgson, L. Hernandez, and G. Malda. 1991. Conservation and use of rare plants by traditional cultures of the U.S./Mexico borderlands. Pp. 127–146 *in* Biodiversity: Culture, conservation, and ecodevelopment. M. Oldfield and J. Alcorn, eds. Westview Press, Boulder, Colo.

Napton, L. K. 1969. The lacustrine subsistence pattern in the desert West. Pp. 28–97 *in* Archaeological and paleobiological investigations in Lovelock Cave, Nevada: Further analysis of human coprolites. L. K. Napton, ed. University of California, Kroeber Anthropological Social Papers, Special Publication no. 2, Berkeley, Calif.

Nelson, R., and S. Nelson. 1973. Fifty hikes in Arizona. Tecelote Press, Inc., Tombstone, Ariz.

Nentvig, L. 1980. Rudo Ensayo: A description of Sonora and Arizona in 1764. A. Pradeau and R. Rasmussen, trans. University of Arizona Press, Tucson.

Nequatewa, E. 1943. Some Hopi recipes for the preparation of wild plant foods. Plateau 16(1):18–20.

Neumann, A., R. Holloway, and C. Busby. 1989. Determination of prehistoric use of arrowhead (*Sagittaria,* Alismataceae) in the Great Basin of North America by scanning electron microscopy. Economic Botany 43(3):287–296.

Niethammer, C. 1974. American Indian food and lore. Collier/MacMillan, New York, N.Y.

Nobel, P. 1984. Productivity of *Agave deserti:* Measurement by dry weight and monthly prediction using physiological responses to environmental parameters. Oecologia 64:1–7.

Nobel, P. 1987. Water relations and plant size aspects of flowering for *Agave deserti.* Botanical Gazette 148:79–84.

O'Dea, K., R. Spargo, and P. Nestel. 1982. Impact of westernization on carbohydrate and lipid metabolism in Australian aborigines. Diabetologia 22:148–153.

O'Leary, J. 1988. Halophytic food crops for arid lands. Pp. 1–4 *in* Strategies for classification and management of native vegetation for food production in arid zones. General Technical Report no. RM-150. U.S. Forest Service and Secretaria Agricultura y Recursos Hidraulicos (SARH).

Olwell, P. 1986. Endangered and threatened wildlife and plants: Determination of *Tumamoca macdougalii* to be endangered. Federal Register 51:15906–15911.

Opler, M., ed. 1973. Grenville Goodwin among the Western Apache: Letters from the field. University of Arizona Press, Tucson.

Orcutt, C. 1885. Palms. Western American Scientist 1:5.

Orcutt, C. 1887. A lemonade and sugar tree. Western American Scientist 3:45–47.

Ortega, J., and J. Balthasar. 1944. Apostolicos afanes de la compañía de Jesús: escripto por un padre de la misma sagrada religión de su provincia de México. México City. First published in Barcelona, 1754.

Ortiz, A., ed. 1983. Handbook of North American Indians: Southwest. Vol. 10. Smithsonian Institution, Washington, D.C.

Palmer, E. 1871. Food plants of the North American Indians. U.S. Department of Agriculture Report to the Commissioner of Agriculture for 1870. U.S. Government Printing Office, Washington, D.C.

Palmer, E. 1878. Plants used by the Indians of the United States. American Naturalist 12:593–606, 646–655.

Palmer, E. 1890. Customs of the Coyotero Apache. Zoe I:161–172.

Palmer, E. 1891. Chia. Zoe II:140–142.

Parker, K. 1989. Height structure and reproductive characteristics of senita, *Lophocereus schottii* (Cactaceae) in southern Arizona. Southwestern Naturalist 34:392–401.

Pennington, C. 1963. The Tarahumara of Mexico: Their environment and material culture. University of Utah Press, Salt Lake City.

Pennington, C. 1969. The Tepehuan of Chihuahua: Their material culture. University of Utah Press, Salt Lake City.

Pennington, C. 1980. The Pima Bajo of Central Sonora, Mexico. Vol. I. University of Utah Press, Salt Lake City.

Pennington, C. 1982. La cultura de los Eudeve del noroeste de México. Pp. 9–34 *in* Noroeste de México no. 6. Centro Regional del Noroeste del Instituto Nacional de Antropologia e Historia. B. Braniff and R. Felger, eds. Hermosillo, Sonora.

Pérez de Ribas, A. 1968. My life among the savages of New Spain. T. A. Robertson, trans. Ward Ritchie Press, Los Angeles, Calif.

Phillips, A., B. Phillips, P. Hogan, and W. Hodgson. 1994. Hualapai ethnobotanical native species plant study, second reconnaissance river trip report. Unpublished report, copy deposited at Desert Botanical Garden Herbarium, Phoenix, Ariz.

Píccolo, F. 1967. Informe on the New Province of California 1702. G. Hammond, trans. and ed. Dawson's Book Shop, Los Angeles, Calif.

Piña Puente, F. 1983. Catalogo de especies de plantas utiles no maderables con importancia economica. Catalogo no. 9, Septiembre. Subsecretaria Forestal Instituto Nacional de Investigaciones Forestales.

Pinkava, D. 1995. Cactaceae. Part 1. Cactus family: The cereoid cacti. Journal of the Arizona-Nevada Academy of Science 29(1):6–12.

Pinkava, D. 1999. Cactaceae: Cactus family. Part 3. *Cylindropuntia* (Engelm.) Knuth. Vascular plants of Arizona: Cactaceae—*Cylindropuntia.* Journal of the Arizona-Nevada Academy of Science 32(1):32–47.

Potter-Basso, G. 1991. *Yucca baccata:* From the beginning. Arid Lands Newsletter 31(Fall/Winter):24–29.

Pratt, R., and G. Nabhan. 1988. Evolution and diversity of *Phaseolus acutifolius* genetic resources. Pp. 409–440 *in* Genetic resources of *Phaseolus* beans: Their maintenance, domestication, evolution, and utilization. P. Gepts, ed. Kluwer Academic Publishers, Boston, Mass.

Rankin, A., and K. Katzer. 1989. Agricultural systems in the ACS Waddell Project area. Pp. 981–1020 *in* Settlement, subsistence, and specialization in the Northern Periphery: The Waddell Project. M. Green, ed. Archaeological Consulting Services, Ltd., Cultural Resources Report no. 65, Tempe, Ariz.

Rea, A. 1983. Once a river: Bird life and habitat changes on the Middle Gila. University of Arizona Press, Tucson.

Rea, A. 1987. Introducing ethnobotany. Environment Southwest 519:3–4.

Rea, A. 1997. At the desert's green edge: An ethnobotany of the Gila River Pima. University of Arizona Press, Tucson.

Reagan, A. 1929. Plants used by the White Mountain Apache. Wisconsin Archaeologist 8:143–162.

Reagan, A. 1930. Notes on the Indians of the Fort Apache Region. American Museum of Natural History Anthropological Papers 31(5):281–345.

Rebman, J. 1995a. Biosystematics of *Opuntia* subgenus *Cylindropuntia* (Cactaceae), the chollas of Lower California, Mexico. Ph.D. dissertation, Arizona State University, Tempe.

Rebman, J. 1995b. Simmondiaceae: Jojoba family. Arizona-Nevada Academy of Science 29(1):63–64.

Reichenbacher, F. 1984. Rare plants of the Central Arizona Project Tucson aqueduct, phase B. Report to the U.S. Fish and Wildlife Service, Albuquerque, N.M.

Reiser, C. 1994. Rare plants of San Diego County. Aquafir Press, Imperial Beach, Calif.

Rice, K. 1994. Vegetation and flora of the Superstition Wilderness Area, central Arizona. M.S. thesis, Arizona State University, Tempe.

Robbins, W., J. Harrington, and B. Freire-Marreco. 1916. Ethnobotany of the Tewa Indians. Smithsonian Institution Bureau of American Ethnology Bulletin no. 55. U.S. Government Printing Office, Washington, D.C.

Rogers, D., and S. G. Appan. 1973. *Manihot* Manihotoides (Euphorbiaceae). Flora Neotropica Monograph no. 13. Hafner Press, New York, N.Y.

Rogers, W. 1712. A cruising voyage round the world. Andrew Bell, London.

Rose, J. N. 1892. List of plants collected by Dr. Edward Palmer in 1890 on Carmen Island. Contributions from the U.S. National Herbarium I(V):129–134.

Rose, J. N. 1895. Report on a collection of plants made in the states of Sonora and Colima, Mexico, by Dr. Edward Palmer, in the years 1890 and 1891. Contributions from the U.S. National Herbarium I(9):286–434.

Rose, J. N. 1900. Notes on the useful plants of Mexico. Contributions from the U.S. National Herbarium V(5):209–259.

Ross, W. 1944. The present-day dietary habits of the Papago Indians. M.S. thesis, University of Arizona, Tucson.

Rothrock, J. 1878. Reports on the botanical collections made in portions of Nevada, Utah, California, Colorado, New Mexico, and Arizona during the years 1871, 1872, 1873, 1874, and 1875. Vol. VI. Botany. Pp. 1–404 *in* Report upon United States geographical surveys west of the one hundredth meridian, in charge of First Lieut. Geo. M. Wheeler. U.S. Government Printing Office, Washington, D.C.

Rusby, H. 1906. The August wild foods of the United States. Pp. 436–452 *in* Country Life in America. Vol. 10. Double Day, Page, and Co., New York, N.Y.

Rusby, H. 1907. The wild foods of March. P. 546 *in* Country Life in America. Vol. 11. Double Day, Page, and Co., New York, N.Y.

Russell, F. 1908. The Pima Indians. Smithsonian Institution Bureau of American Ethnology 26th annual report, 1904–1905. U.S. Government Printing Office, Washington, D.C. 1980. Reprint, University of Arizona Press, Tucson.

Rzedowski, J., and H. Kruse. 1979. Algunas tendencias evolutivas en *Bursera* (Burseraceae). Taxon 28(1):103–116.

Sales, L. 1956. Observations on California 1772–1790. C. Rudkin, trans. and ed. Glen Dawson, Los Angeles, Calif.

Sauer, J. 1967. The grain amaranths and their relatives: A revised taxonomic and geographic survey. Annals of the Missouri Botanical Garden 54:103–137.

Saunders, C. 1948. Edible and useful wild plants of the United States and Canada. Dover Publications, Inc., New York, N.Y.

Saunders, R., R. Becker, D. Meyer, E. del Valle, and M. Torres. 1985. Identification of commercial milling techniques to produce high sugar, high fiber, high protein, and high galactomannan gum fractions from *Prosopis* pods. *In* Symposium on establishment and productivity of tree plantings in arid regions. P. Felker, ed. Texas A&I University, Kingsville, Tex.

Scheerens, J., A. Tinsley, F. Abbas, C. Weber, and J. Berry. 1983. The nutritional significance of tepary bean consumption. Desert Plants 5(1):11–14, 50–56.

Schmidt, R., Jr. 1989. The arid zones of Mexico: Climatic extremes and conceptualization of the Sonoran Desert. Journal of Arid Environments 16:241–256.

Shahani, H., F. Dollear, K. Markley, and J. Quimby. 1951. The buffalo gourd, a potential oilseed crop of the southwestern drylands. Journal of American Oil Chemical Society 28:90–95.

Sharma, P., and A. Koul. 1986. Mucilage in seeds of *Plantago ovata* and its wild allies. Journal of Ethnopharmacology 17:289–295.

Shelvocke, G. 1726. Cabo San Lucas: August 1721. Pp. 390–415 *in* A voyage round the world by the way of the great South Sea perform'd in the years 1719, 20, 21, 22, in the Speedwell of London. J. Senex, London.

Shipek, F. 1968. The autobiography of Delfina Cuero, a Diegueño Indian. Dawson's Book Shop, Los Angeles, Calif.

Shreve, F. 1964. Vegetation of the Sonoran Desert. Part I. Pp. 1–186 *in* Vegetation and flora of the Sonoran Desert. F. Shreve and I. Wiggins, eds. Stanford University Press, Stanford, Calif.

Siemens, D., C. Johnson, and K. Ribardo. 1992. Alternative seed defense mechanisms in congeneric plants. Ecology 73(6):2152–2166.

Sitgreaves, L. 1853. Report on an expedition down the Zuni and Colorado Rivers. U.S. Government Printing Office, Washington, D.C.

Slauson, L. 1996. A morphometric and pollination ecology study of *Agave chrysantha* Peebles and *Agave palmeri* Engelm. (Agavaceae). Ph.D. dissertation, Arizona State University, Tempe.

Smith, C. 1973. *Selé,* a major vegetal component of the aboriginal Hualapai diet. Plateau 45(3):102–110.

Solbrig, O. F., and P. D. Cantino. 1976. Reproductive adaptations in *Prosopis* (Leguminosae, Mimosoideae). Journal of Arnold Arboretum 56(2):185–210.

South, M. 1939. Mescal roast. Desert Magazine 3(12):12.

Sparkman, P. 1908. The culture of the Luiseño Indians. University of California Publications in American Archaeology and Ethnology 8:187–234.

Spier, L. 1923. Southern Diegueño customs. University of California Publications in American Archaeology and Ethnology 20:296–358.

Spier, L. 1928. Havasupai ethnography. American Museum of Natural History Anthropological Papers 29:83–392.

Spier, L. 1933. Yuman tribes of the Gila River. University of Chicago Press, Chicago, Ill.

Standley, P. 1912. Some useful native plants of New Mexico. Pp. 447–463 *in* Annual report of the Smithsonian Institution. U.S. Government Printing Office, Washington, D.C.

Standley, P. 1920–1926. Trees and shrubs of Mexico. Contributions from the U.S. National Herbarium. Vol. 23: Part 1 (1920), Part 2 (1922), Part 3 (1923), Part 4 (1924), Part 5 (1926). U.S. Government Printing Office, Washington, D.C.

Steenbergh, W., and C. Lowe. 1977. Ecology of the saguaro. Part 2. Reproduction, germination, establishment, growth, and survival of the young plant. National Park Service Scientific Monograph Series no. 8, Washington, D.C.

Steggerda, M., and R. Eckardt. 1941. Navajo foods and their preparation. American Dietetic Association Journal 17:217–225.

Stephen, A. 1936. The Hopi journal of Alexander H. Stephen. Columbia Contributions in Anthropology 23(2), New York, N.Y.

Stevenson, M. 1915. Ethnobotany of the Zuni Indians. Pp. 35–102 *in* Smithsonian Institution Bureau of American Ethnology 30th annual report. U.S. Government Printing Office, Washington, D.C.

Steward, J. 1938. Basin-Plateau aboriginal sociopolitical groups. Smithsonian Institution Bureau of Ethnology Bulletin no. 120. U.S. Government Printing Office, Washington, D.C. 1970. Reprint, University of Utah Press, Salt Lake City.

Stewart, K. 1965. Mohave Indian gathering of wild plants. Kiva 31(1):46–53.

Stewart, O. 1941. Culture element distribution. XIV. Northern Paiute. University of California Anthropological Records 4(3):361–445.

Stone, M. 1943. Bean people of the cactus forest. Desert Magazine 6(11):5–10.

Stratton, R. 1857. Captivity of the Oatman girls: Being an interesting narrative of life among the Apache and Mohave Indians. Carlton and Porter, New York, N.Y. 1982. Reprinted as Classics of the old West, Time-Life Books, Alexandria, Va.

Stuart, B. 1945. Pug-a-roo gathers mescal. Masterkey 19(3):79–81.

Sundell, E. 1974. Vegetation and flora of Sierra Estrella Regional Park. M.S. thesis, Arizona State University, Tempe.

Sutton, M. 1993. Midden- and coprolite-derived subsistence evidence: An analysis of data from the La Quinta site, Salton Basin, California. Journal of Ethnobiology 13(1):1–15.

Suzan, H., G. Nabhan, and D. Patten. 1994. Nurse plant and floral biology of a rare night-blooming cereus, *Peniocereus striatus* (Brandegee) F. Buxbaum. Conservation Biology 2:461–470.

Swank, G. 1932. The ethnobotany of the Acoma and Laguna Indians. M.A. thesis, University of New Mexico, Albuquerque.

Sweet, M. 1976. Common edible and useful plants of the West. Naturegraph Publishers, Inc., Healdsburg, Calif.

Swenson, W. 1969. Comparisons of insects on mesquite in burned and unburned areas. M.S. thesis, Texas Technological College, Lubbock.

Taravel, S. 1931. The Indian uprising in Lower California, 1734–1737. M. Wilbur, trans. The Quivira Society, Los Angeles, Calif.

Taylor, N. 1985. The genus *Echinocereus*. A Kew Magazine Monograph. The Royal Botanic Gardens, Kew, England, in association with Timber Press, Portland, Ore.

Thackery, F. 1953. Sand food of the Papagos. Desert Magazine 16(4):22–24.

Thackery, F., and M. Gilman. 1931. A rare parasitic food of the Southwest. Pp. 409–416 *in* Smithsonian Institution annual report for 1930. Publication no. 3094. U.S. Government Printing Office, Washington, D.C.

Thackery, F., and A. Leding. 1929. The giant cactus of Arizona. Journal of Heredity 20:401–414.

Thomas, R. 1963. Papago land use west of the Papago Indian Reservation south of the Gila River and the Problem of San Papago identity. Unpublished manuscript, copy deposited at the Desert Botanical Garden, Phoenix, Ariz.

Thompson, S., C. Weber, and J. Bemis. 1978. Protein quality of buffalo gourd seed and seed fractions. Nutrition Reports International 18:515–520.

Thorburn, A., J. Brand, and A. Truswell. 1987. Slowly digested and absorbed carbohydrate in traditional bushfoods: A protective factor against diabetes? American Journal of Clinical Nutrition 45:98–106.

Thornber, J., and F. Bonker. 1932. The fantastic clan: The cactus family. The MacMillan Co., New York, N.Y.

Timbrook, J. 1982. Use of wild cherry pits as food by the California Indians. Journal of Ethnobiology 2(2):162–176.

Timbrook, J. 1990. Ethnobotany of Chumash Indians, California, based on collections by John P. Harrington. Economic Botany 44(2):236–253.

Tiscareno, F., trans., and J. Robinson, ed. 1969. José Joaquin Arillaga: Diary of his surveys of the frontier, 1796. Dawson's Book Shop, Los Angeles, Calif.

Torrey, J. 1859. Botany of the United States and Mexican boundary. Pp. 29–270 *in* W. Emory, ed. Report on the United States and Mexico boundary survey, made under the direction of the Secretary of the Interior, by William H. Emory. A. O. P. Nicholson, Washington, D.C.

Treutlein, T., trans. 1949. Pfefferkorn, von I.: A description of Sonora. University of New Mexico Press, Albuquerque.

Truman, K. n.d. Chia: A pre-Columbian oilseed. Unpublished manuscript, copy deposited at Desert Botanical Garden Herbarium, Phoenix, Ariz.

Turner, N., and A. Bell. 1973. The ethnobotany of the Southern Kwatiutl Indians of British Columbia. Economic Botany 27(3):257–310.

Turner, R., J. Bowers, and T. Burgess. 1995. Sonoran Desert plants: An ecological atlas. University of Arizona Press, Tucson.

Underhill, R. 1936. The autobiography of a Papago Woman. Memoirs of the American Anthropological Association no. 46, Menasha, Wis.

Underhill, R. 1946. Papago Indian religion. Columbia University Press, New York, N.Y.

Underhill, R. 1951. People of the crimson evening. United States Indian Service, Riverside, Calif.

U.S. Department of Agriculture Soil Conservation Service. 1950. Sulphur Springs Valley area, Arizona. P. 14 *in* U.S. Department of Agriculture Soil Survey Series 1940. U.S. Government Printing Office, Washington, D.C.

U.S. Department of the Interior. 1985. Endangered and threatened wildlife and plants; review of plant taxa for listing as threatened or endangered species. Federal Register 50(172):25–32.

U.S. Senate. 1936. Walapai papers. Document no. 273, 74th Congress, 2nd Session. U.S. Government Printing Office, Washington, D.C.

Vasey, G., and J. Rose. 1890a. List of plants collected by Dr. Edward Palmer in 1888 in southern California. Contributions from the U.S. National Herbarium 1(1):1–8.

Vasey, G., and J. Rose. 1890b. List of plants collected by Dr. Edward Palmer in Lower California in 1889: Plants collected near the head of the Gulf of Lower California. Contributions from the U.S. National Herbarium 1(1): 27–28.

Vasey, G., and J. Rose. 1890c. List of plants collected by Dr. Edward Palmer in 1890 in Lower California and western Mexico. Contributions from the U.S. National Herbarium 1(1):63–92.

Vasey, G., and J. Rose. 1891a. List of plants collected by Dr. Edward Palmer in the region of Lower California, with notes and descriptions of new species. Contributions from the U.S. National Herbarium 1(1):9–27.

Vasey, G., and J. Rose. 1891b. List of plants collected by Dr. Edward Palmer in 1890 in western Mexico and Arizona. Contributions from the U.S. National Herbarium 1(4): 91–116.

Venegas, M., and A. Burriel. 1966. A natural and civil history of California. Vol. I and II. Readex Microprint Corporation, Great Americana Series.

Vestal, P. 1940. Notes on a collection of plants from the Hopi Indian region of Arizona made by J. G. Owens in 1891. Botanical Museum Leaflets, Harvard University 8:153–168.

Vestal, P. 1952. Ethnobotany of the Ramah Navaho. Reports of the Ramah Project no. 4. Papers of the Peabody Museum of American Archaeology and Ethnology 40(4), Cambridge, Mass.

von Reis, S., and F. Lipp Jr. 1982. New plant sources for drugs and foods from the New York Botanical Garden Herbarium. Harvard University Press, Cambridge, Mass.

Waddell, J. 1973. The place of the cactus wine ritual in the Papago Indian ecosystem. Sixth International Congress of Anthropological and Ethnological Sciences, Chicago, Ill.

Wagner, H., trans. 1929. Father Antonio de la Ascensión's account of the voyage of Sebastián Vizcaíno, 1602. Pp. 190–234 *in* Spanish voyages to the northwest coast of America in the sixteenth century. California Historical Society, San Francisco, Calif.

Wallen, D., and J. Ludwig. 1978. Energy dynamics of vegetative and reproductive growth in Spanish bayonet, *Yucca baccata* Torr. Southwestern Naturalist 23:409–422.

Warrick, G., and P. Krausman. 1989. Barrel cacti consumption by desert bighorn sheep. Southwestern Naturalist 34(4):483–486.

Watahomigie, L., M. Powskey, and J. Bender. 1982. Hualapai ethnobotany. Hualapai Bilingual Program, Peach Springs School District no. 8, Peach Springs, Ariz.

Watson, D., trans. and ed. 1934. The founding of the first California missions. Nueva California Press, San Francisco, Calif.

Watson, S. 1889. Contributions to American botany. I. Upon a collection of plants made by Dr. Edward Palmer in 1887 about Guaymas, Mexico, at Muleje and Los Angeles Bay in Lower California, and on the island of San Pedro Martir in the Gulf of California. Proceedings of the American Academy of Arts and Sciences 24:36–82.

Watson, S., W. Brewer, and A. Gray. 1880. Botany: Geological survey of California. 1(iii). 2 vols. John Wilson and Son University Press, Cambridge, Mass.

Watt, B., and A. Merrill. 1963. Composition of foods. Agricultural Handbook no. 8. U.S. Department of Agriculture, Washington, D.C.

Webber, J. 1953. Yuccas of the Southwest. Agricultural Monograph no. 17. U.S. Department of Agriculture, Washington, D.C.

Weber, C., H. Gentry, E. Kohlhepp, and P. McCrohan. 1991. The nutritional and chemical evaluation of chia seeds. Ecology of Food and Nutrition 20:119–125.

Weber, F. 1968. The missions and missionaries of Baja California. Dawson's Book Shop, Los Angeles, Calif.

Weber, S., and P. Seaman, eds. 1985. Havasupai habitat: A. F. Whiting's ethnography of a traditional Indian culture. University of Arizona Press, Tucson.

Weight, L. 1977. Squawbush—it's for eating and wearing. Desert Magazine 40(2):36–37.

Weiss, A. 1994. The impact of nutritional change on the emergence of diabetes in two Tipai Cochimí communities in Baja California. Ph.D. dissertation, University of California at Irvine. UMI Dissertation Services, Ann Arbor, Mich.

White, L. 1942. The Pueblo of Santa Ana. Memoirs of the American Anthropological Association no. 60, Menasha, Wis.

White, S. 1948. The vegetation and flora of the region of the Rio de Bavispe in northeastern Sonora, Mexico. Lloydia 11(4):229–302.

Whiting, A. 1939. Ethnobotany of the Hopi. Museum of Northern Arizona Bulletin no. 15, Flagstaff, Ariz. 1966. Reprint, Northland Press, Flagstaff, Ariz.

Whiting, A. 1957. Some preliminary notes on the ethnobotany of the Seri. Unpublished files, Arizona State Museum, University of Arizona, Tucson.

Whiting, A. 1966. Ethnobotany of the Hopi. Northland Press, Flagstaff, Ariz.

Whittemore, I. 1893. The Pima Indians, their manners and customs. Pp. 51–96 *in* Among the Pimas, or the missions to the Pima and Maricopa Indians. Ladies Union Mission School Association, Albany, N.Y.

Wiggins, I. 1964. Flora of the Sonoran Desert. Part II. Pp. 189–1740 *in* Vegetation and flora of the Sonoran Desert. F. Shreve and I. Wiggins, eds. Stanford University Press, Stanford, Calif.

Wiggins, I. 1980. Flora of Baja California. Stanford University Press, Stanford, Calif.

Wilke, P. 1978. Late prehistoric human ecology at Lake Cahuilla: Coachella Valley, California. Contributions of the University of California Archaeological Facility no. 38, Berkeley.

Wilke, P., M. DeDecker, and L. Dawson. 1979. *Dicoria canescens* Torr. & Gray: An aboriginal food plant in the arid west. Journal of California and Great Basin Anthropology 1:188–192.

Winklemann, M. 1992. Pharmacological properties of some Piman (O'odham) medicinal plants for the treatment of diabetes. Seedhead News no. 1. Native Seeds/SEARCH, Tucson, Ariz.

Wolf, C. 1935. California plant notes. Part 1. Occasional Papers of the Rancho Santa Ana Botanic Garden series 1(1):31–43.

Woodward, A. 1938. The "honey" of the early California Indians: A strange ethnological error. Masterkey 13:175–180.

Wyllys, R. 1931. Padre Luis Velarde's relacion of Pimeria Alta, 1716. New Mexico Historical Review 6:111–157.

Wyman, L., and S. Harris. 1951. The ethnobotany of the Kayenta Navajo. University of New Mexico Publications in Biology no. 5, Albuquerque.

Yanovsky, E. 1936. Food plants of the North American Indians. U.S. Department of Agriculture Miscellaneous Publications no. 237. U.S. Government Printing Office, Washington, D.C.

Yanovsky, E., and R. Kingsbury. 1938. Analyses of some Indian food plants. Association of Official Agricultural Chemists 21:648–665.

Yarnell, R. 1977. Native plant husbandry north of Mexico. Pp. 861–874 *in* The origins of agriculture. C. Reed, ed. Mouton, The Hague.

Yatskievych, G. 1985. Notes on the biology of the Lennoaceae. Cactus and Succulent Journal (U.S.) 57(2):73–79.

Yensen, N., E. Glenn, and M. Fontes. 1983. Biogeographical distribution of salt marsh halophytes on the coasts of the Sonoran Desert. Desert Plants 5(2):76–81.

Yensen, N., S. de Yensen, and C. Weber. 1988. A review of *Distichlis* for production and nutritional values. Pp. 809–822 *in* Arid lands today and tomorrow: Proceedings of an international research and development conference. E. Whitehead, C. Hutchinson, B. Timmermann, and R. Varady, eds. Westview Press, Boulder, Colo.

Yetman, D., and A. Burquez. 1996. A tale of two species: Speculation on the introduction of *Pachycereus pringlei* in the Sierra Libre, Sonora, Mexico by *Homo sapiens*. Desert Plants 12(1):23–32.

Young, D. 1975. Correction of the geographic distribution of *Rhus microphylla* (Anacardiaceae). Madroño 23(2):78.

Zepeda, O. 1985. Sand Papago Oral History Project. National Park Service, Western Archaeological Center, Tucson, Ariz.

Zigmond, M. 1981. Kawaiisu ethnobotany. University of Utah Press, Salt Lake City.

Zwinger, A. 1983. A desert country near the sea. Harper and Row, New York, N.Y.

INDEX

Note: Italicized pages indicate illustrations. See Appendix IV for correlation of non-English common names. Appendix pages are not included in index.

abrojo: gray-leafed (*Ziziphus obtusifolia*), 226

Acacia (acacia), 244; *brandegeana,* 162, 196; *cochliacantha* (boat-thorn, spoon-thorn), 162–63; *constricta, 84; cymbispina,* 162; *farnesiana,* 162; *greggii* (catclaw), 162, 163; *pennatula,* 162, 163

Acanthaceae (Acanthus Family), 75

achenes, 86, 87–88, 220–21

acorns, 5, 179, 189; collecting and processing, 190–95

Agavaceae (Agave Family), 13–51

Agave (agave), 64, 77, 83, 129, 131; *americana,* 39; *applanata,* 39; *aurea,* 23, 27, 28; *avellanidens,* 23, 27; *capensis,* 13, 23, *24,* 28, 41; *cerulata,* 13, 14, 23, *24,* 27, 30, 34; *chrysantha* (golden-flowered), 13, *16,* 18, 21, 40, 42, 43; *chrysoglossa,* 13, 30–31; *colorata,* 13, 30, 41; cultivation of, 34–35; *datylio,* 13, 23, 27, 28; *delamateri,* 13, 16, 18, *37–39*; *deserti,* 13, *15,* 19, *20,* 21, 22, 23, *24,* 25, 27, 31, 33, 40, 43; *felgeri* (Felger's), 13; *fortiflora,* 13, 30, 41; *gigantensis,* 13, 23, *24,* 27; *margaritae, 24*; *marmorata,* 34; *mckelveyana,* 13, 18, 19, 22, 31; *moranii,* 13, 23, 24, 33; *murpheyi* (Hohokam), 1, 13, 16, 18, 19, 21, 30, 34–37, 38, 39, 42; *palmeri* (Palmer's), 13, *16,* 18, 21, 31, 41, 42, 43; *parryi,* 16, 21; *parviflora,* 14; *pelona,* 13, 14, 30; *polianthiflora,* 14; *promontori,* 23, 24, 28; *schottii,* 21; *sebastiana,* 33, 41; *shawii,* 13, 22, 23, *24,* 27, 33, 42; *shrevei,* 13, 31, 33, 41, 42; *sobria,* 13, 23, *24,* 27, 28; *subsimplex,* 13, 30, 115; *tequilana,* 41; *toumeyana,* 16, 18, 19; *utahensis* (Utah), 13, 18, 20, 31, 32, 44, 182; *viscainoensis,* 23, *24*; *vivipara,* 13, *30,* 31, 41, 42; *zebra,* 13, *29,* 30

agriculture. *See* cultivation

Ahill, Juanita, *103, 105*

Aizoaceae (Aizoon Family), 75–76

ajo-lily (*Hesperocallis undulata*), 60–61

ajonjoli (*Crotalaria incana*), 167–68

Ak Chiñ, 47, 211

Alamos, 68, 98, 160, 178

Alarcón, Hernando de, 50, 179, 201

Alarobius prosopis, 188

alcohol, 63, 149, 243, 245; agave-based, 27, 28, 31, 41, 42

Alismataceae, 51

Allenrolfea occidentalis, 149–50

Allium: *acuminatum,* 58; *bisceptrum* var. *palmeri,* 58, 59; *fimbriatum,* 58; *haematochiton,* 58; *macropetalum,* 58, 59; *palmeri,* 58, 59; *parishii,* 58; *unifolium,* 59

all-thorn (*Koeberlinia spinosa*), 198

almond: desert (*Prunus fasciculata*), 227, 228

Aloysia: *barbata,* 243; *wrightii,* 243

Alvarez de Williams, Anita, 65, 68

amacostic (*Ficus petiolaris*), 212

Amaranthaceae (Amaranth Family), 77–80

Amaranthus (amaranth), 18, 97; *albus,* 77; *caudatus,* 77, 78, 79; *fimbriatus* (fringed), 77, 79, 80; *hybridus* (grain, smooth, spleen), 77, 80, 219, 223; *lepturus,* 77; *obcordatus* (trans-Pecos), 77; *palmeri* (Palmer's), *77–79,* 80, 221; *retroflexus* (rough, red-root), 77, 78; *venulosus* (baja), 77; *watsonii* (Watson's), 77, 80

Amargosan-Pinacateños, 186

Ambrosia confertiflora, 86

amole: *Yucca* spp., 44–51; *Ziziphus amole,* 226

Amoreuxia, 51, 157, 162; *gonzalezii,* 1, 3, 91, 92, *93,* 94; *palmatifida,* 3, *91, 92,* 93, 94; *wrightii,* 93

Anacardiaceae, 81–83

Anglos, 179, 202

Antigonon leptopus, 218–19, 223

Anza, 203, 245

Apaches, 16, 18, 39, 62, 233. *See also various bands; groups*

aphids, 69

Aphyllon fasciculatum, 215

Apocynaceae, 84

Apodanthera: *palmeri,* 157; *undulata, 157*

apple: cactus- (*Opuntia engelmannii*), 125

apricot: desert (*Prunus fremontii*), 227, 228

Aravaipa Apache, 101

archaeology, 72, 80, 143, 157, 159, 176, 186, 196, 203, 211, 214, 233, 245; agave in, 32, 37, 38, 39, 40; *Dicoria* use, 86–87; *Echinocereus* in, 117–18; *Mentzelia* seed, 207, 208

Arecaceae, 52–56

Arillaga, Lt. Gov., 25, 165

Aripes, 23, 137, 156

Arizona, 2, 55, 100, 123, 147, 159, 217, 244; pre-Columbian agave cultivation in, 34–35, 37–39. *See also various places by name*

arrowhead: arum-leaf (*Sagittaria cuneata*), 51; long-barb (*S. longiloba*), 51

arrow-weed (*Pluchea sericea*), 72, 79, 178, 179, 182, 183, 184

Arundinaria longifolia, 131, 146, 178

Arundo donax, 69, 70, 131

Aschmann, Homer, 76, 100, 132, 142, 157, 160, 219, 223; on agave, 15–16, 25, 26, 29, 40, 41; on *Amoreuxia,* 92, 94; on prickly-pear, 125, 129

Asclepiadaceae, 84–86

Asphondylia opuntiae, 130

Asteraceae (Aster Family), 86–89

atole, 96, 102, 107, 111, 162, 186–87, 200

Atondo, Isidro de, 27, 141

Atriplex, 113; *californica,* 150; *elegans,* 150; *lentiformis,* 150–51; *polycarpa,* 150, 151; *wrightii,* 110–11, 150, 151

Baboquivari Mountains, 21, 59, *127*

bacanora (*Agave vivipara*), 13, 42

bacanora (liquor), 31, 41

bachata (*Ziziphus obtusifolius*), 226

Baegert, Johann, 2, 129, 132, 155, 156, 161, 180; on agave use, 27–28, 29, 40; on pitahaya agria, 137, 139; on pitahaya dulce, 142, 143, 144

Baja California, 1–2, 76, 78, 82, 84, 92, 97, 100, 123, 129, 131, 136, 147, 152, 157, 160, 161, 165, 180, 195, 201, 218, 225, 229, 237, 239; agave use in, 14, 15–16, 23, 24–28, 33–34, 39, 40–41; barrel cactus use in, 120, 121; cholla use in, 112, 115;

cochal in, 124–25; *Echinocereus* in, 116, 117, 118; *Ephedra* use in, 11–12; figs in, 212–13; grapes in, 244, 245–46; *Ipomoea* in, 153–54; *Lysiloma* in, 168, 169; *Merremia aurea,* 155–57; ocotillo use, 195–96; *Oligomeris* use, 222–23; palms in, 52, 55, 56; passion-flower in, 216–17; pitahaya dulce use in, 141–42; *Pithecellobium* in, 177, 178; reeds in, 68–69, 70; *Stenocereus* spp. in, 137, 140; yucca use, 49–50; Yuman groups in, 28–29. *See also various groups; places by name*
Baja California Sur, 81, 83, 137, 181
baja-lily: Palmer's (*Triteleiopsis palmeri*), 61–62
Barbados-cherry Family (Malpighiaceae), 209
Barbados flower, pride of Barbados (*Caesalpinia pulcherrima*), 163
barberry: Harrison's (*Berberis harrisoniana*), 90
Barberry Family (Berberidaceae), 90
Barco, Miguel del, 2, 7, 15, 51, 76, 81, 82, 129, 132, 139, 144, 154, 160, 162, 180, 195, 196, 212, 229, 237, 239, 245; on agaves, 23, 25, 26, 27, 28, 29; on amaranth, 78, 79; on barrel cactus use, 120–22; on cholla, 112, 115; on exudate gathering, 69, 70; on jojoba, 232–33; on *Karwinskia* use, 225–26; on *Merremia aurea* use, 156–57; on *Oligomeris* use, 222–23; on palms, 52–53, 56; on paloverde, 165, 166, 167; on passion-flower, 216–17; on pitahaya dulce, 141, 142, 143
barley: little (*Hordeum pusillum*), 64, 66
barrel cactus: California (*Ferocactus cylindraceus*), 32, 118, *119,* 120, 121, 122; compass (*F. wislizeni*), 118, *119*; Emory's (*F. emoryi*), 118, *119*; many-headed (*Echinocactus polycephalus*) 116; as water source, 118–20
Barrows, David, 44, 64, 98, 115, 128, 153, 193, 228
basketry, 63, 71, 211
bastard-cedar (*Guazuma* spp.), 239
Bataceae, 90
Batis maritimus, 90
beachwort (*Batis maritima*), 90
Beals, Ralph, 145
Bean, Lowell, 22, 64, 193
beans: lima, 5; Santa Rita Mountain (*P. ritensis*), 172, 176–77; slimjim, coyote (*Phaseolus filiformis*), *172,* 176; tepary (*P. acutifolius*), 5, 77, *172–76*
bear-grass, 45; Bigelow's (*Nolina bigelovii* 64; *N. beldingii,* 64; *N. microcarpa,* 17, 18, 32, 192
Bear-grass Family (Nolinaceae), 62–64
Beech Family (Fagaceae), 189–95
beeplant: Rocky Mountain (*Cleome serrulata*), 147; yellow (*C. lutea*), 147
bees: carpenter (*Xylocarpa* spp.), 21
beetles, 56, 159, 189; bruchid, 167, 171, 181, 187–88
beggar-ticks: hairy (*Bidens pilosa*), 86
Begoniaceae (Begonia Family), 90
Begonia gracilis var. *nervipilosa* (begonia), 90
Bell, William, 68, 102, 112, 198, 236
Beloperone californica, 75
Beltran, María, *31,* 93, 97, 129, 146, 157, 198, 221, 229, 241
Berberidaceae, 90
Berberis: *haematocarpa,* 90; *harrisoniana,* 90
berries. *See* drupes
berry: pigeon- (*Rivina humilis*), 217; sugar- (*Celtis laevigata*), 240, 241
Bidens pilosa, 86
Bidwell, John, 69
bird-of-paradise bush (*Caesalpinia pulcherrima*), 163
bisnaga meloncillo, de dulce (*Echinocactus* spp.), 116
Bittersweet Family (Celastraceae), 149
Bixaceae, 91–94
biznaga (*Ferocactus* spp.), 122; pulp of, 120–21; as water source, 118–20
blackbead (*Pithecellobium* spp.), 177–78
blackjack (*Bidens pilosa*), 86
bladderpod (*Cleome isomeris*), 147
blazing-star: small-flowered, white-stemmed (*Mentzelia albicaulis*), 207–8
Blazing-star Family (Loasaceae), 207–8
bledo (*Amaranthus* spp., *Chenopodium* spp.), 77, 78
bluedicks (*Dichelostemma capitatum*), 59–60
Boerhavia coulteri, 214
Bohrer, Vorsila, 64, 66, 116
Bombacaceae, 95–96
Boraginaceae (Borage Family), 97
Borjeños, 23, 39
Bourke, John Gregory, 17, 130, 208
Bourreria sonorae, 97
braceletwood (*Jacquinia* spp.), 240
Bradshaw Mountains, 34, 83, 101, 197
Brahea brandegeei, 52, 56
Brandegee, Townsend, 2, 27, 51, 139, 155, 160, 169, 199, 209, 212, 237, 243, 245; on *Amoreuxia,* 92–93
Brassica: *juncea,* 97; *nigra,* 97; *rapa,* 97, 98; *tournefortii,* 4–5, 7, 62, 97
Brassicaceae, 97–99
Brodiaea capitata, 60
broom-rape (*Orobanche* spp.), 215
Broom-rape Family (Orobanchaceae), 215
broomrape's mother (*Ambrosia confertiflora*), 86
bruchids, 167, 171, 181, 187–88
buckbrush (*Ceanothus greggii*), 18
buckthorn (*Karwinskia parvifolia*), *225*
Buckthorn Family (Rhamnaceae), 224–27
buckwheat: wild (*Eriogonum* spp.), 219
Buckwheat Family (Polygonaceae), 218–21
buffelgrass (*Pennisetum ciliare*), *4,* 146, 171
bug: leaf-footed (*Mozena obtusa*), 188
bulbs: desert-lily, 60–61
Bulla, Adolph, 202
bull-nettle (*Cnidoscolus* spp.), 160–61
bully (*Sideroxylon occidentalis*), 230–*31*
Bumelia occidentalis, 231
bur-marigold (*Bidens pilosa*), 86
Burroughsia fasciculata, 243
bursage: slim-leaf (*Ambrosia confertiflora*), 86
Bursera (bursera): *fagaroides* var. *elongata,* 100; *microphylla,* 100
Burseraceae, 100
Buskirk, Winfred, 62, 147, 152
butterfly-tulip (*Calochortus* spp.), 59

cabeza de viejo: *Lophocereus schottii,* 122–23; *Mammillaria* spp., 123
Cabo San Lucas, 28, 50
Cacao Family (Sterculiaceae), 239–40
Cactaceae (Cactus Family), 100–146
cactus, 18; beavertail (*Opuntia basilaris* var. *basilaris*), 125, 126; cottontop, many-headed barrel (*Echinocactus polycephalus*), 116; deerhorn (*Peniocereus greggii*), 134; desert Christmas (*Cylindropuntia leptocaulis*), 106, 107, 111, 114, *115*; giant (*Carnegia gigantea*), 100; octopus (*Stenocereus alamosensis*), 136; pincushion (*Mammillaria* spp.), 123; strawberry, saint's (*Echinocereus engelmannii*), 116; Thornber's fishhook (*M. thornberi*), 123–24. *See also various types*
cactus-apple (*Opuntia engelmannii*), 125
Caesalpinia: *gillesii,* 163; *platyloba,* 163; *pulcherrima,* 163

Cáhita, 129, 145, 178
Cahuilla, 44, 59, 60, 64, 71, 83, 86, 88, 98, 147, 152, 153, 157, 163, 165, 193, 195, 210, 215, 219, 226, 228, 232, 244, 245; agave use, 17, 22, 33; amaranth use, 78, 79; *Atriplex* use, 150, 151; barrel cactus use, 120, 121; chia use, 201, 203; cholla use, 112, 115; elderberry use, 148, 149; mesquite use, 178, 179, 187; palm use, 55–56; prickly-pear use, 126, 128
Cahuilla, Lake, 58, 72
Calandrinia ciliata, 221
calendar year: and harvests, 102, 103, 142, 184
calico bush (*Lantana horrida*), 241
California, 50, 55, 75, 82, 147, 221, 244; agave in, 33, 42; club- and bulrush use in, 57–58. *See also various groups; places by name*
California, Gulf of, 72–73, 97, 122
Calochortus: ambiguus, 59; *concolor,* 59; *dunnii,* 59; *flexuosus,* 59; *kennedyi,* 59; *plummerae,* 59; *weedii,* 59
camote, 168. *See also Ipomoea*
camote de los medanos (*Pholisma sonorae*), *204–7*
cañaigre, caña agria (*Rumex hymenosepalus*), 90, 219, *220*
candlewood (*Fouquieria* spp.), 195–96
candy: cactus, 116, 121
cane: *Arundo donax,* 69, 70; *Phragmites* spp., 68–70
CAP. *See* Central Arizona Project
Capparaceae (Caper Family), 147–48
Caprifoliaceae, 148–49
Capsicum annum 233–35
capul: *Celtis pallida,* 240–41; *Schaefferia cuneifolia,* 149
cardo (*Salvia carduacea*), 199, 202, *203*
cardón (*Pachycereus* spp.), 73, 160; hecho, barbón, espinoso (*P. pecten-aboriginum*), 131; pelón (*P. pringlei*), 131; uses of, 131–34
carelessweed (*Amaranthus palmeri*), *77*
Carmen Island, 122, 139, 217
Carnegia gigantea, 47, *100,* 120, 123; fruit preparation, 101–2; Tohono O'odham and, 102–6
Carpobrotus chilensis, 75
carrizo: *Arundo donax,* 70; *Phragmites australis,* 68–70
Carrizo Apaches, 147
Carter, Annetta, 2, 29, 50, 76, 154, 157, 169, 237, 239
Casa Blanca, 114, 175
Cashew Family (Anacardiaceae), 81–83
Castela: emoryi, 198; *peninsularis,* 237; *tortuosa,* 237
Castetter, Edward, 18, 68, 102, 112, 198, 236
catclaw (*Acacia* spp.), 162
cattail (*Typha* spp.), 32, 58; broad-leaf (*T. latifolia*), 71; southern (*T. domingensis*), *71*
Cattail Family (Typhaceae), 71
cattle: impacts of, 3, 56, 59, 177, 211, 242
cattle-spinach (*Atriplex polycarpa*), 150
Ceanothus greggii, 18
cedar: bastard- (*Guazuma* spp.), 239
Cedros Island, 33, 40–41, 122
Ceiba acuminata (ceiba), *95–96*
Celastraceae, 149
Celtis, 7; *brevipes,* 240; *iguanaea,* 240, 241; *laevigata,* 235, 240, 241; *pallida,* 235, 240–41; *reticulata,* 240, 241
Central Arizona Project (CAP), 123, 159
Cercidium, 101, 244; *floridum, 164,* 165, 167; *microphyllum,* 141, *164,* 165, 166–67; *praecox,* 4, 165, 166; x *sonorae,* 165
cereus: night-blooming (*Peniocereus greggii*), 134
Chamaesaracha: coronopus, 236; *sordida,* 236
chamizo (*Atriplex* spp.), 150–51
chastetree (*Vitex* spp.), 243
Chemehuevi, 31, 50, 80, 200
Chenopodiaceae, 149–53
Chenopodium, 18, 66, 77, 78, 97; *album,* 151, 152; *ambrosioides,* 151, 152; *berlandieri,* 151–52; *californicum,* 151, 152; *fremontii,* 151, 152; *leptophyllum,* 151, 152; *murale,* 151, 152; *neomexicanum,* 151; *palmeri,* 151
cherry: Barbados- (*Malpighiaceae*), 209; ground-, 234, 239; hollyleaf (*Prunus ilicifolia*), 227–28
chia: grande, gorde (*Hyptis suaveolens*), 198–99; *Salvia* spp., 5, 199–203
Chihuahua, 34, 39, 100, 158, 177, 217
Childs, Tom, 112, 141, 186, 206, 237–38
chile: wild, del monte (*Capsicum annuum* var. *glabriusculum*), *233–35*
chiltepin, chillipiquin (*Capsicum annuum*), *233–35*
chinchweed (*Pectis papposa*), 88–*89*
Chinese-lantern (*Physalis* spp.), 238
Chiricahua Apaches, 101
Chocolate Family (Sterculiaceae), 239–40
chokecherries (*Prunus* sp.), 228
cholla: brincadora (*Cylindropuntia alcahes*), 112; buckhorn (*C. acanthocarpa*), 106, *107,* 108–11, 112, 113; cane (*C. spinosior*), 106, 108, 112–13, 114; chain-fruit, de coyote (*C. fulgida*), 106, 107, 111, 112, 113, *114*–15, 116; chain-link, pelona (*C. cholla*), 112, 115; coastal (*C. prolifera*), 112; cultivation of, 64, 115–16; diamond (*C. ramosissima*), 106, 107; fruit of, 112–13; Gila (*C.* x *kelvinensis*), 106, 111, 112, 113–14; Gila River Pima and, 108–11, 114; pencil (*C. arbuscula*), 106, 111, *113*; silver, golden (*C. echinocarpa*), 106, 108, 111, 113; staghorn, morada (*C. versicolor*), 106, 111, 112, *113*; teddy-bear, del oso, güerra (*C. bigelovii*), 106, 107, 108, 112, 114, 115; Thurber's (*C. thurberi*), 112; Whipple's (*C. whipplei*), 106, 113
Chona, María, 111
Christmas Mistletoe Family (Viscaceae), 243–44
Christmas-tree: desert (*Pholisma arenarium*), 204
Chumash, 43–44, 203
chuparosa (*Justicia californica*), 75
Cibecue Apaches, 107, 130, 147, 191, 199
cinchweed: many-bristle (*Pectis papposa*), 88–*89*
ciribe (*Cylindropuntia bigelovii*), 106, 107, 114
ciruelo (*Cyrtocarpa edulis*), 81, 167
Clarkdale Apaches, 82–83, 87, 163, 184, 191, 196
clavellina (*Cylindropuntia alcahes*), 112
Clavigero, Fr., 29, 139, 155, 160, 161, 162, 180
clay, 189
Claytonia perfoliata, 221
cleaning agents, 49, 158–59
Cleator, 101, 164, 199
Cleome: isomeris, 147; *lutea,* 147; *serrulata,* 147
clones: agave, 26, 34, 37, 39, 40
club-rush: chairmaker's (*Schoenoplectus americanus*), 57; hard-stem (*S. acutus*), 57; salt-marsh (*S. maritimus*), 57; soft-stem (*S. tabernaemontani*), 57
Cnidoscolus: angustidens, 160; *maculatus,* 160; *palmeri,* 160, *161*
coachwhip (*Fouquieria splendens*), 195–96
Cochimí, 7, 15, 29, 69, 76, 121, 132,

139, 145, 156, 169, 213, 219, 237, 245; agave and, 14, 17, 23, 25–27, 28, 33–34; amaranth and, 78, 79; cholla use, 112, 115; jojoba and, 39, 232–33; *Karwinskia* use, 225, 226; paloverde use, 165, 166; pitahaya dulce use, 141, 142, 144; prickly-pear use, 125, 126, 129; senita use, 122, 123; on teddá use, 222–23. *See also* Borjeños

cocklebur (*Xanthium* sp.), 182

Cocopa, 3, 51, 50, 57, 65, 69, 112, 121, 126, 150, 152, 165, 168, 194, 215, 221, 236; agave use, 17, 22, 23–24; amaranth use, 78, 79; cattail use, 71, 72; mesquite use, 178, 179–80, 182, 183, 186; palm use, 52, 55; panic grass use, 67, 68; sandfood, 205, 207

Colorado River, 51, 65, 67, 68, 72, 179

Colorado River delta, 64, 68, 221

Colorado River Indian Tribe, 68, 189

Commelinaceae, 56

Comondú, 27, 92, 94, 143, *169*

companion child, 62

Condalia, 7; *brandegeei*, 224, 225; *globosa*, 224; *parryi*, 226; *spathulata*, 224; *warnockii*, 64, *224*

Condaliopsis parryi, 226

confiturilla, confitura, confite: *Hyptis suaveolens*, 198–99; *Lantana* spp., 241

conivari (*Hyptis suaveolens*), 198–99

Consag, Fernando, 52, 121, 233; on agave use, 28–29

construction: palms used in, 52, 54, *55*; reeds used in, 69

Convention for the International Trade of Endangered Species, 134

Convolvulaceae, 153–57

Cooke, Edward, 50, 79, 81, 97, 154, 156, 157, 161, 222

copal (*Bursera* spp.), 100

coquito: *Cyperus rotundus*, 57; *Dichelostemma captitatum*, 59–60; *Hoffmanseggia glauca*, 168

Cora, 52, 81, 137, 141, 156, 161, 225; agave use, 23, 28; reed use, 69, 70

corms, cormlets, 64; Lily family, 59–60, 61–62

corona de Cristo: *Koeberlinia spinosa*, 198; *Passiflora foetida*, 216

cottontree (*Ceiba acuminata*), *95–96*

Cottontree Family (Bombacaceae), 95–96

cottonwood (*Populus* spp.), 150

Coursetia glandulosa, 106

covena, coveria (*Dichelostemma capitatum*), 59–*60*

Coville, Frederick, 118, 119, 120

Crassulaceae, 157

creeping-devil (*Stenocereus eruca*), 136, 137

creosote bush (*Larrea divaricata*), 134, 136, 140

Crotalaria: *incana*, 167–68; *pumila*, 167–*68*

crucifixion-thorn (*Koeberlinia spinosa*), 198

crucillo (*Condalia warnockii*), 64, *224*; white (*Ziziphus obtusifolius*), 226

Cucurbita: *digitata*, *158*, 159; *foetidissima*, 158–59; *palmata*, 158, 159

Cucurbitaceae, 157–59

Cuero, Delfina, 22, 157, 179, 194, 228

cultivation, 65, 94, 98, 118, 130, 152, 159, 162, 163, *164*, 198, 213, 224, 235, 240; agave, 34–35, 37, 39; amaranth, 77, 80; barley, 64, 66; cholla, 115–16; *Cnidoscolus* spp., 160–61; ground-cherries, 238–39; panic grass, 67, 68; passion-flower, 216, 217; *Proboscidea*, 211, 212; sunflower, 87, 88; tepary bean, 172, 173–74, 175

Curtin, Leonora, 72, 76, 89, 113, 114, 130, 152, 165, 215, 220, 244; on *Atriplex* use, 150, 151

Cycloloma atriplicifolium, 152

Cylindropuntia: *acanthocarpa*, 106, *107*, 108–11, 112, 113; *alcahes*, 112; *arbuscula*, 106, 111, 112, *113*; *bigelovii*, 106, 107, 108, 112, 114, 115; *californica*, 112; *calmalliana*, 112; *cholla*, 112, 115; cultivation of, 115–16; *echinocarpa*, 106, 108, 111, 112, 113; *fulgida*, 106, 107, 111, 112, 113, *114*–15, 116; Gila River Pima and, 108–11, 114; *imbricata*, 115, 116; x *kelvinensis*, 106, 111, 112, 113–14; *leptocaulis*, 106, 107, 111, 112, 114, *115*; *molesta*, 112; *munzii*, 112, 115; *prolifera*, 112; *ramosissima*, 106, 107, 115; *spinosior*, 106, 108, 112–13, 114; *tesajo*, 112, 115; x *tetracantha*, 112; *thurberi*, 106, 112; *versicolor*, 106, 111, 112, *113*; x *viridiflora*, 116; *whipplei*, 106, 113

Cyperaceae, 57–58

Cyperus: *erythrorhizos*, 57; *esculentus*, 57; *odoratus*, 57; *rotundus*, 57; *utriculata*, 57

Cyrtocarpa edulis, 81, 167

daisy, railway- (*Bidens pilosa*), 86

Dasylirion wheeleri, *62*–63, 105

dátil, dátilillo (*Yucca* spp.), 44–51, 156

Death Valley Shoshones, 50, 182

deernut (*Simmondsia chinensis*), 8, 39, 101, 232–33

DeLamater, Rick, 34, 37, *48*

Descurainia, 99; *obtusa*, 98; *pinnata*, 98

desert-lily (*Hesperocallis undulata*), 60–*61*

desert spoon (*Dasylirion wheeleri*), *62*–63, 105

desert-thorn: Arizona (*Lycium exsertum*), 236; Fremont (*L. fremontii*), 236; pale (*L. pallidum*), 236; Parish's (*L. parishii*), 236; red-berry (*L. andersonii*), 236, 237; silver (*L. berlandieri*), 236, 237

desert trumpet (*Eriogonum inflatum*), 219

desert-yaupon (*Schaefferia cuneifolia*), 149

devil's claw: *Acacia greggii*, 162; Mexican (*Pisononia capitata*), 214; *Proboscidea* spp., 3–4, 209

devil's head (*Echinocactus polycephalus*), 116

devil's horn (*Proboscidea althaeifolia*), 209

devil's pincushion (*Echinocactus* spp.), 116

diabetes, 5, 99, 125, 126, 135–36, 175–76, 190

Dichelostemma: *capitatum*, 3, 59–*60*; *pulchellum*, 59, 60

Dicoria canescens (desert dicoria), 86–87

Didiu, 23, 166–67

Diegueños, 52, 75, 178, 228; acorn use, 192, 193, 194; agave use, 16, 22, 23, 24, 25. *See also* Northern Diegueños; Southern Diegueños

Dinapate wrightii, 56

Dioscorea: *convolvulacea*, 58; *remotiflora*, *58*

Dioscoreaceae, 58

Diospyros: *californica*, 160; *sonorae*, 160

dipúgo, dipúa (*Cercidium microphyllum*), 164, 165, 166

Distichlis: *palmeri*, 3, 64, 65, 78; *spicata*, 65

Ditepalae, 42

division of labor. *See* gender roles

Dobbs, John, 117, 119

dock: curly (*Rumex crispus*), 219–20; sand (*R. hymenosepalus*), 90, 219, *220*; violet (*R. violascens*), 219, 220, 221

Doebley, John, 64

Dogbane Family (Apocynaceae), 84

doubleclaw (*Proboscidea parviflora*), 209

Doyle, Harrison, 200, 202–3
drinks, 98, 117, 149, 198, 218, 243, 245; chia seed, 199–200, 201; mesquite bean, 179, 183, 184, 186; *Rhus* drupe, 82–83. *See also* water
Dripping Springs, 192
dropseed: narrow-spike (*Sporobolus contractus*), 70; sand (*S. cryptandrus*), 70
drought, 68, 70, 131
drupes, 81, 82–83, 149, 160
duckpotato (*Sagittaria latifolia*), 51
Ducrue, Fr., 166, 169, 212
Dudleya: *arizonica,* 157; *attenuata,* 157; *pulverulenta,* 157; *saxosa,* 157
Durango, 39

Eastwood, Alice, 2
Ebenaceae (Ebony Family), 160
echeveria: rock- (*Dudleya saxosa*), 157
Echinocactus: *acanthodes,* 120, 121; *cylindraceus,* 120; *horizonthalonius,* 116; *polycephalus,* 116
Echinocereus: *brandegeei,* 117, 118; *engelmannii,* 116, *117,* 118, 123; *fasciculatus,* 116, *118*; *fendleri,* 116, 118; *nicholii,* 116, 118
eel-grass (*Zostera marina*), 65, 72–73, 134
Eel-grass Family (Zosteraceae), 72–73
elder, elderberry: black, Mexican (*Sambucus nigra*), 148–49
elephant-tree (*Bursera microphylla*), 100; fragrant (*B. fagaroides*), 100
Elm Family (Ulmaceae), 240–41
Elsasser, Albert, 50–51
epazote: *Chenopodium ambrosioides,* 151; *Lepidium lasiocarpum,* 99
Ephedra (ephedra), 243; *aspera* (boundary), 11; *californica,* 11, 12; *fasciculata,* 11; *nevadensis,* 11; *trifurca, 11*; *viridis,* 11
Ephedraceae (Ephedra Family), 11–12
Eremalche exilis, 209
Eriogonum inflatum, 219
Erodium: *cicutarium,* 196; *texanus,* 196
Erythea: *armata,* 52, *55*; *brandegeei,* 52, 56; *elegans,* 52; *roezlii,* 52
Estrella Estrella, María, 76, 222
Estrella Tánori, Pedro, 1, 41, 76, 93, 94
Eudeve, 131, 178, 213, 241
Euphorbiaceae, 160–62
Exogonium bracteatum, 153, 154
exotics, 1, 7, 147, 151, 177, 208; agaves as, 25–26; dock as, 219–20; ice plants as, 75–76; impacts of, 4–5, 62; mustards as, 97–98; passion-flower, 216, 217
exudate, 68–69, 70, 83, 85, 115, 169, 188, 189

Fabaceae, 162–89
Fagaceae, 189–95
famine foods, 51, 149, 150, 151, 157, 179, 215
feathertree (*Lysiloma* spp.), 168–69
Felger, Richard, 132–33, 159, 173, 222, 238
Ferocactus: *acanthodes,* 118, 120; candy from, 116, 121; *chrysacanthus,* 122; *covillei,* 120; *cylindraceus,* 32, 118, *119,* 120, 121, 122; *diguetti,* 122; *emoryi,* 118, *119,* 120, 121; *fordii,* 121, 122; *gracilis,* 121; *herrarae,* 118, 121, 122; *peninsulare,* 121; *townsendianus,* 121; *viridescens,* 118, 122; *wislizeni,* 118, *119,* 120, 121, 122; as water source, 118–20
Ficus (fig): *brandegeei,* 212–13; *padifolia,* 212; *palmeri,* 212, 213; *pertusa,* 212, 213; *petiolaris,* 212; *petiolaris* ssp. *palmeri,* 213
fig: Hottentot- (*Carpobrotus* spp.), 75; Indian- (*Opuntia ficus-indica*), 125, 128, 129; sea- (*Carpobrotus chilensis*), 75; *Mesembryanthum* spp., 75–76
Fig-marigold Family (Aizoaceae), 75–76
filaree (*Erodium* spp.), 196
fir, joint-: Arizona (*Ephedra fasciculata*), 11; California (*E. californica*), 11; long-leaf (*E. trifurca*), *11*; mountain (*E. viridis*), 11; Nevada (*E. nevadensis*), 11; rough (*E. aspera*), 11
fire, 3, 64, 203
five-eyes: green-leaf (*Chamaesaracha coronopus*), 236; hairy (*C. sordida*), 236
floods, 66–67, 68, 78
Flores, Fernando, 165, 186
Flores, Rosa, *161,* 173
flour, 65, 67, 70, 73, 87, 88, 89, 128, 149, 152, 226; amaranth, 79, 80; mesquite, 179, 185–86; ocotillo, 195–96; paloverde seed, 165, 166
flower buds: barrel cactus, 121, 122; cholla, 106–12
flowers, 33, 50, 64, 75, 83, 136, 176, 189; barrel cactus, 121, 122
flower stalks, flowering stalks, 24, 62, 64, 71
Forchammeria watsoni (forchammeria), 148
Fort Apache Indian Reservation, 17, 152
Fouquieria: *burragei,* 195; *diguetti,* 195; *macdougalii,* 195; *splendens,* 195–96
Fouquieriaceae, 195–96
Four-o'clock Family (Nyctaginaceae), 214
Fowler, Kay, 181–82, 191
Frankincense Family (Burseraceae), 100
Franseria tenuifolia, 86
fruits, 58, 64, 81, 87, 90, 91, 94, 97, 116, 148, 153, 164, 209, 213, 229, *231,* 232, 239; acacia, 162–63; barrel cactus, 121, 122; cardón, 131–34; *Celtis* spp., 240–41; cholla, 112–13, 114–15; cochal, 124–25; *Condalia,* 224, 225; dock, 219, 220–21; *Echinocerus, 117,* 118; gourd, 158–59; kapok, 95–*96*; *Matelea* spp., 84–85; mistletoe, 243–44; palm, 52, 53–54, 55–56; panic grass, 66–67; passion-flower, 216–17; pitahaya, 137–39, 140–46; *Pithecellobium dulce,* 177–78; prickly-pear, 126–30; *Peniocereus,* 134, 136; *Prunus,* 227–28; saguaro, *100*–106; wolfberry, 236–37; yucca, 45, 47, *48, 49*; *Ziziphus,* 226–27
frutilla: *Lycium richii,* 236; *Vallesia glabra,* 84
frutillo: *Karwinskia parvifolia,* 225; *Ziziphus amole,* 226
Funastrum: *cynanchoides,* 85; *heterophyllum,* 85

Gallagher, Marsha, 18, 45, 82, 184, 191
garabato: *Celtis* spp., 240; *Pisonia capitata,* 214
garambullo: *Lophocereus schottii,* 122–23; *Pisonia capitata,* 214; *Ziziphus obtusifolius* var. *canescens,* 226
garlic (*Allium* spp.), 58
garumbullo (*Celtis pallida*), 240–41
gender roles, 67, 68, 97, 192, 231; agaves and, 17, 18–19, 26, 32; cholla buds and, 108–10; mesquite beans and, 179–80; saguaro fruit and, 101, 104, 105
Gentry, Howard S., 95, 121, 146, 167, 168, 177, 196, 198, 214, 229, 243; on agave, 27, 29, 30, 41, 42; on *Amoreuxia,* 91, 94
Geraniaceae (Geranium Family), 196
Giff, Joe, 5, 187
Giff, Ruth, 57, 102, 110, 111, 117, 165, 168, 193, 220, 239; ironwood preparation, 170–71; on mesquite use, 185, 187, 189
Gifford, Edward, 2, 18, 60, 62, 64,

67, 108, 113, 128, 164, 170, 196
Gila Bend, 102
Gila River Indian Community, 123
Gila River Pima Reservation, 51, 61, 70, 114, 123, 130, 150, 175
Gila River Pimas, 2, 47, 55, 57, 59, 70, 80, 85, 86, 102, 117, 134, 141, 158, 163, 173, 187, 199, 215, 220, 227, 244, 245; agave use, 19–20, 21, 33, 40; chiltepin use, 233, 234; and cholla, 108–11, 113, 114; desert-lily and, 60–61; diabetes in, 5, 176; ironwood use, 170–71; panic grass at, 67, 68; prickly-pear use, 125, 128; senita use, 122–23
Gila River Valley, 58, 59, 70, 87, 102, 123, 136, 220; agave in, 39, 42; cholla in, 113–14; *Echinocereus* in, 117, 118
Gilmore, Dr. M., 69
girasol (*Helianthus annuus*), 87
glasswort (*Salicornia* spp.), 153
Globe, 37
globeberry: Tumamoc (*Tumamoca macdougalii*), 159
globemallow (*Sphaeralcea ambigua*), 19, 101
goatnut (*Simmondsia chinensis*), 8, 39, 101, 232–33
goldfields: California (*Lasthenia californica*), 88
goosefoot (*Chenopodium* spp.), 77; California (*C. californicum*), 151, 152; Fremont's (*C. fremontii*), 151, 152; nettle-leaf (*C. murale*), 151, 152; New Mexico (*C. neomexicanum*), 151; pit-seed (*C. berlandieri*), 151–52; slim-leaf (*C. leptophyllum*), 151, 152
Goosefoot Family (Chenopodiaceae), 149–53
Gosiutes, 215
gourd: buffalo, Missouri (*Cucurbita foetidissima*), 158–59; finger-leaved, coyote (*C. digitata*), *158*, 159
Gourd Family (Cucurbitaceae), 157–59
Graham Mountains, 16, 191
granadilla: *Malpighia emarginata*, 209; *Maytenus phyllanthoides*, 149; *Passiflora* spp., 216–17
Granados, 97, 146, 241
Grand Canyon, 32, 39, *43*, 72, 130
Gran Desierto, 62
Granite Peak, 18, 128, 192
grape: Arizona, canyon (*Vitis arizonica*), 244–45; holly- (*Berberis haematocarpa*), 90; valley (*V. girdiana*), 244, 245
Grape Family (Vitaceae), 244—46
grass: bear-, 17, 18, 32, 45, 64, 192; eel- (*Aostera Marina*), 65, 72—73, 134; mat- (*Lippia palmeri*), *242*—43; nut, 57; pepper- (*Lepidium* spp.), 5, 98–99
Grass Family (Poaceae), 64–70
Gray, Andrew B., 204, 206
gray-thorn: *Condalia* spp., 224; *Ziziphus obtusifolius* var. *canescens*, 226
Greenhouse, Ruth, 110, 188
greens: amaranth, 76, 77–78, 80, 86, 89, 94, 147, 153, 196, 219, 221, 239; goosefoot, 151–52; Mustard Family, 97–98, 99
ground-cherry, 234, 239: cut-leaf (*P. angulata*), 238; hairy (*P. pubescens*), 238; ivy-leaf (*P. hederifolia*), 238; long-leaf (*P. longifolia*), 238; Mexican (*P. philadelphica*), 238; sharp-leaf, Wright (*P. acutifolia*), 238; small (*Chamaesaracha coronopus*), 236; yellow nightshade, thick-leaved (*P. crassifolia*), 238
Guaicuras, 81, 132, 137, 145, 155, 165, 213, 246; agave use among, 23, 27–28, 29; pitahaya dulce use, 140, 142, 143
Guarijío, 54, 58, 84, 93, 95, 121, 129, 131, 146, 154, 163, 171, 198, 214, 229, 234, 239, 243; acacia use, 162, 163; amaranth use, 78, 80; *Crotalaria* use, 167, 168; panic grass use, 67–68; *Pithecellobium* use, 177, 178
Guasabas, 93, 97, 129
guásima (*guazuma ulmifolia*), 239–40
Guaymas, 80, 84, 97, 98, 134, 160, 213, 230, 234, 238, 239, 242; palms near, 52, 53
Guazuma ulmifolia, 239–40
Guillén, Clemente, 27, 28, 145, 156, 157
gumbro: *Celtis pallida*, 240–41; *Pisonia capitata*, 214

hackberry (*Celtis*), 7, 235; desert, spiny, shiny, (*Celtis pallida*), 240–41; netleaf (*Celtis laevigata*), 240, 241
halophytes, 65, 151, 153
Havard, Valery, 141, 193
Havasupais, 12, 47, 49, 59, 87–88, 89, 178, 208, 213, 214, 243
hecho (*Pachycereus pecten-aboriginum*), *131*
hedgehog cactus (*Echinocereus* spp.); Engelmann's (*E. engelmanni*), 116; Nichol's (*E. nicholii*), 116, 118
Helianthus: *annuus*, 87, 88; *lenticularis*, 87; *niveus*, 87, *88*; *niveus* ssp. *canescens*, 88; *petiolaris*, 87, 88
herbicides, 5, 79
Hermosillo, 53, 235
heron's-bill (*Erodium* spp.), 196
Hesperaloe, 43
Hesperocallis undulata, *60–61*
Hesperoyucca whipplei, *43*–44
Hiá ceḍ O'odham, 21, 59, 60, 61, 92, 112, 116, 118, 122, 123, 141, 148, 165, 176, 195, 200, 215, 232, 236; mesquite use, 178, 182, 186; *Peniocereus* use, 135, 136; saguaro use, 100, 102; sandfood, 204, 205–6, 207
hierba: aigre (*Oxalis albicans*), 216; del burro (*Allenrolfea occidentalis*), 149; colorado (*Rumex hymenosepalus*), 219, *220*–50; mora (*Solanum americanum*), 239
Hoffmannseggia: *densiflora*, 168; *glauca* (hog-potato), 168
hogweed: little- (*Portulaca oleracea*), 221–22
Hohokam, 64, 66, 80, 98, 151, 203, 207, 214, 224, 239; agave and, 34–35, 37, 39; cholla and, 115–16; *Echinocereus* use, 117–18
Holacantha emoryi, 198
holdback (*Caesalpinia* spp.), 163
holly: Singapore- (*Malpighia* spp.), 209
holly-grape: red- (*Berberis haematocarpa*), *90*
Honeysuckle Family (Caprifoliaceae), 148–49
Hopis, 16, 56, 86, 88, 151, 207, 208
Hordeum pusillum, 64, 66
horse-purslane: desert (*Trianthema portulacastrum*), *76*
Hottentot-fig (*Carpobrotus* spp.), 75
Hrdlička, Aleš, 60, 78, 113, 114, 134, 151, 152, 153, 170, 220
Hualapai, 12, 49, 59, 83, 122, 200, 208, 213; agave use, 20, 22, 32–33, 44
Huichiti, 23, 27, 28, 81, 141, 143, 213
hummingbird-bush (*Justicia californica*), 75
husk-tomato (*Physalis* spp.), 238–39
Hyalopterus arundinis, 69
hybridization, 65, 118, 159, 246; cholla, 113–14, 116
Hyptis: *collina*, 199; *suaveolens*, 198–99

ice plant: *Carpobrotus* spp., 75; common (*Mesembryanthemum crystallinum*), 75–76

Indian-fig (*Opuntia ficus-indica*), 125, 128, 129
Indian-lettuce (*Claytonia perfoliata*), 221
Indian-spinach (*Monolepis nuttalliana*), 152–53
iodinebush: *Allenrolfea occidentalis*, 149–50; *Suaeda moquinii*, 150
Ipomoea: *arborescens*, 4, 153, *154*; *bracteata*, 153–54; *jicama*, 153, 154, 155; *purpurea*, 153, 155
ironwood: desert (*Olneya tesota*), 134, 136, 170–71
irrigation water: diversion of, 3–4
islay (*Prunus ilicifolia*), 227–28
Isomeris arborea, 147

Jacquinia macrocarpa ssp. *pungens*, 148, 240
Jatropha macrorhiza, 92
Jerusalem thorn (*Parkinsonia* spp.), 171
Jesuits, 2, 179–80
jicama: *Ipomoea* spp., 153–54, 155; *Pachyrhizus erosus*, 154–55
joint-fir: Arizona (*Ephedra fasciculata*), 11; California (*E. californica*), 11; long-leaf (*E. trifurca*), *11*; mountain (*E. viridis*), 11; Nevada (*E. nevadensis*), 11; rough (*E. aspera*), 11
jojoba (*Simmondsia chinensis*), 8, 39, 101, 232–33
Jojoba Family (Simmondsiaceae), 232–33
Joshua tree (*Yucca brevifolia*), 44
Jovas, 162
Joyal, Elaine, 53–54
Juglandaceae, 196–98
Juglans major, 196–98
jujube (*Ziziphus parryi*), 226
junco: *Koeberlinia spinosa*, 198; *Parkinsonia aculeata*, 171
Junco Family (Koeberliniaceae), 198
Juniperus (juniper), 18
Justicia californica, 75

Kada kaaman, 69
Kamia, 22, 23, 71, 112, 126
kapok (*Ceiba acuminata*), *95–96*
Kapok-tree Family (Bombacaceae), 95–96
Karwinskia: *humboldtiana*, 225–26; *parvifolia*, *225*
Kelly, William, 24, 112, 180, 187
Kermen, Laura, 1, 21
Kiliwas, 12, 43, 50, 52, 69, 126, 137, 165, 171, 180, 194, 232, 237; agave use, 16, 23, 24–25, 33; barrel cactus use, 121–22; cardón use, 131–32; cholla use, 112, 115
Kino, Eusebio Francisco, 2, 69, 136, 137, 141, 155, 232
kiss-me-quick (*Portulaca pilosa*), 221–22
Koeberliniaceae, 198
Koeberlinia spinosa, 198
Kofa Mountains, 83, 102
Kumeyaay, 23, 24, 179
Kyyitan, George, 98, 113, 114, 184, 210, 226–27

lac insect, 32, 106
La Ciudad, 3, 34, 64, 115–16, 214, 224
lamb's quarter (*Chenopodium* spp.), 78, 151
Lamiaceae, 198–203
Lantana: *horrida*, *241*; *velutina*, 241
La Paz, 28, 39, 97, 143, 145, 156, 237, 238
Larrea divaricata, 134, 136, 140, 244
Las Maravillas, Rancho, 29–30
Las Palmas Bay, 53
Last Chance Mountain, 86–87
Lasthenia californica, 88
Las Vegas Southern Paiute, 47
laurel-sumac (*Malosma laurina*), 81–82
Laymon, 23, 27
lechuguilla: *Agave* spp., 13, 27, 30, 31; *Hesperoyucca whipplei*, 43–44
lechuguilla (liquor), 41
leek: wild (*Allium* spp.), 58
Legume Family (Fabaceae), 162–89
lemita, lemonade-berry (*Rhus trilobata*), *82*
Lennoaceae (Lennoa Family), 204–7
lens-scale (*Atriplex lentiformis*), 150–51
Lepidium, 5, 98; *flavum*, 99; *fremontii*, 99; *lasiocarpum*, 99; *nitidum*, 99; *oblongum*, 99; *thurberi*, 99; *virginicum*, 99
Leptonycteris spp., 42
lettuce: miner's-, Indian- (*Claytonia perfoliata*), 221
Leucaena spp., 235
Liliaceae (Lily Family), 58–62, 64
lily: ajo-, desert- (*Hesperocallis undulata*), 60–*61*; mariposa- (*Calochortus* spp.), 59; Palmer-, blue sand-, Palmer's baja- (*Triteleiopsis palmeri*), 61–62, 97; sego- (*Calochortus* spp.), 59; snake- (*Dichelostemma capitatum*), 59–*60*
limoncillo (*Pectis papposa*), 88, *89*
Linck, Fr., 23, 27, 39, 137, 141
Lippia palmeri: *barbata*, 243; *berlandieri*, 242; *fastigiata*, 243; *palmeri*, 140, *242*–43
Lipsticktree family (Bixaceae), 91—94
little-hogweed, (*Portulaca oleracea*), 221–22
live-forever: Arizona (*Dudleya arizonica*), 157; chalk (*D. pulverulenta*), 157; taper-tip (*D. attenuata*), 157
livestock, 42–43, 78, 122, 177, 208
Loasaceae, 207–8
Lophocereus schottii, 14, 122–23
Loreto, 70, 122, 126, 180, 212
Los Angeles County: barrel cactus and, 121, 122
Los Hornos, 117–18
lotebush (*Ziziphus obtusifolius*), 226
love chain (*Antigonon leptopus*), 218–*19*
love-lies-bleeding (*Amaranthus caudatus*), 77
Lower Colorado River Valley, 4–5, 48, 72, 201, 232, 241
Luiseño, 99, 152, 228, 239
Lumholtz, Carl, 131, 204–5, 207, 218
Lycium, 7, 235; *andersonii*, 236, 237; *berlandieri*, 236, 237; *brevipes*, 236; *californicum*, 238; *exsertum*, 236, *237*; *fremontii*, 236, 237; *megacarpum*, 237; *pallidum*, 236; *parishii*, 236; *richii*, 236, 237; *torreyi*, 236
Lysiloma: *candida*, 168–*69*; *divaricata*, 168; *microphyllum*, 168, 169; *thornberi*, 168; *watsonii*, 168, 169

MacDougal, Daniel T., 24, 118
Machaerocereus: *eruca*, 136; *gummosus*, 137
Madder Family (Rubiaceae), 229–30
Magdalena Plain, 27, 137
maguey (*Agave* spp.), 25–26, 64. *See also Agave*
mahonia (*Berberis haematocarpa*), 90
mala mujer (*Cnidoscolus palmeri*), 160
mallow: white- (*Eremalche exilis*), 209. *See also* globemallow
Mallow Family, 209
Malosma laurina, 81–82
Malpighia: *diversifolia*, 209; *emarginata*, 209; *ovata*, 209; *umbellata*, 209
Malpighiaceae (Malpighia Family), 209
Malvaceae (Mallow Family), 209
Mammillaria: *goodridgei*, 123; *grahamii*, 123; *grahamii* var. *oliveiae*, 123; *heyderi*, 123; *mainiae*, 123; *roseana*, 123; *sheldoni*, 123; *tetrancistra*, 123; *thornberi*, 123–24
mangle: *Maytenus phyllanthoides*, 149; *Rhizophora mangle*, 227
mangrove: red (*Rhizophora mangle*), 227
Mangrove Family (Rhizophoraceae), 227

Manihot (manihot): *chlorosticta,* 51, 92, 154, 156, 157, 161–62; *esculenta,* 228
manzana, manzanita: *Lycium andersonii,* 236, 237; *Malpighia diversifolia,* 209; *Ziziphus amole,* 226
margarita: *Karwinskia parviflora,* 225; *Malpighia diversifolia,* 209
Maricopa, 49, 98, 102, 112, 150, 182, 220, 227, 236, 243, 244; cattail use, 71, 72
marigold: bur- (*Bidens pilosa*), 86; fig- (*Aizoaceae*), 75–78; foetid- (*Pectis papposa*), 88
mariposa, mariposa-lily: desert, red (*Calochortus kennedyi*), 59; doubting (*C. ambiguus*), 59; golden-bowl (*C. concolor*), 59; winding, straggling (*C. flexuosus*), 59
Marsdenia edulis, 84
Martyniaceae, 209–11
Martynia palmeri, 210
Matelea: altatensis, 85; *arizonica, 85*; *caudata,* 84; *chrysantha,* 85; *cordifolia,* 84–85; *fruticosa,* 85; *parvifolia,* 84; *petiolaris,* 84; *pringlei,* 84, 85; *producta, 85*; *tristeflorum,* 84; *umbellata,* 85
mat-grass (*Lippia palmeri*), *242*–43
Mathes, W. Michael, 29, 39, 167
matrimony-vine (*Lycium* spp.), 236
Matthias, Sylvester, 89, 92, 102, 120, 121, 123, 149, 169, 171, 227; on mesquite use, 184, 187, 189
mauto (*Lysiloma microphyllum*), 168
Mayo, 41, 58, 72, 131, 141, 145, 160, 178, 198
Mayo, Río, 122, 137, 148, 154, 198–99, 231
Maytenus phyllanthoides (Florida mayten), 149
Mazatzal Mountains, 47, 192, 245
medesá, medesé, medezá (*Cercidium microphyllum*), 141, 164, 165, 166
medicinal plants, 12, 57, 139, 148, 169, 202, 218, 220, 240; *Hyptis suaveolens,* 198, 199; jojoba as, 232, 233; Mustard Family, 98–99; *Peniocereus* as, 134–36; yucca as, 45, 50; prickly-pear as, 125, 126
Meigs, Peveril, 16, 24, 25, 50, 121, 129, 180, 190
Melochia tomentosa, 136
melon: coyote (*Cucurbita palmata*), 158; de coyote (*Apodanthera undulata*), *157;* loco (*Apodanthera* spp.), *157*
Melvin, Beatrice, 116, 205
Mentzelia, 223; *albicaulis,* 3, 207–8
Meresichic, 235, 243
Merremia aurea, 28, 51, 154, 155–57, 162
mescal, *Agave* spp. 13, 14, 25, 83
mescal (liquor), 27, 28, 41
Mescal Mountains, 16, 192
Mesembryanthemum: acinaiciforme, 75; *aequilaterale,* 75; *chilense,* 75; *crystallinum,* 75–76
Mesem Family (Aizoaceae), 75–76
mesquite, 4, 145; honey, western honey (*Prosopis glandulosa*), 178, 179, 180, 181–82, 184, 188, 189; *juliflora,* 167; screwbean (*P. pubescens*), 178, 179–80, *182*–83; velvet (*P. velutina*), 5, 178, 179, 182, 183–87, 188, 189
mesquite girdler (*Oncideres rodostricta*), 189
Mexicans, 58, 68, 80, 146, 163, 239; chiltepin use, 234, 235; queen-of-the-night use, 135, 136
Mexican-tea (*Chenopodium ambrosioides*), 151
mezcal (*Agave* spp.), 13, 25, 26–27
mezquite (*Prosopis* spp.), 167, 178
Mignonette Family (Resedaceae), 222–23
milkvine: Arizona (*Matelea arizonica*), *85*; Sonoran (*M. cordifolia*), 84–85; Texas (*M. producta*), 85
milkweed: climbing (*Sarcostemma cynanchoides*), *85, 86*
Milkweed Family (Asclepiadaceae), 84–86
Milla capitata, 60
Mimosestes, 171; *protractus,* 188
miner's-lettuce (*Claytonia perfoliata*), 221
mint, 5; bush (*Hyptis suaveolens*), 198–99
Mint Family (Lamiaceae), 198–203
missions, missionaries, 2, 70, 81, 129, 142; agaves and, 24, 25–26, 29, 39, 40; mesquite and, 180–81; palms and, 52–53; *Phragmites* exudate and, 68–69. *See also by name*
mistletoe (*Phoradendron* spp.), 243–44
Mistletoe Family (Viscaceae), 243–44
Moapa Southern Paiute, 69, 182
Mogollon, 37, 39
Mohave, 49, 51, 71, 78, 87, 89, 98, 150, 152, 168, 200, 220, 236; agave use, 18, 21–22; mesquite, 178, 182, 183
Mohave Desert, 31, 47, 116, 122, 147, 181
Moisés, Rosalio, 31, 80, 130, 145–46, 148, 186, 233
monkeypod (*Pithecellobium dulce*), 177–78
Monolepis nuttalliana, 152–53
Monquí, 23, 144–45, 156
mora, moral: *Malpigia emarginata,* 209; *Morus microphylla,* 213–14
Moraceae, 212–14
Mormon-tea Family (Ephedraceae), 11–12
morning-glory: tree (*Ipomoea arborescens*), 153, *154*
Morning-glory Family (Convolvulaceae), 153–57
Morton, Julia, 86
Morus: microphylla, 213–14; *nigra,* 213
Moser, Mary, 132–33, 222
mostaza (*Brassica* spp.), 97
moths, 45, 136
Mountain Pima, 31, 57, 90, 216, 217
Mozena obtusa, 188
mulberry: Texas (*Morus microphylla*), 213–14
Mulberry Family (Moraceae), 212–14
Mulegé, 94, 216, 239
mustard, 5; Asian (*Brassica tournefortii*), 97; black (*B. nigra*), 97; Chinese (*B. juncea*), 97; tansy- (*Descurainia* spp.), 98–99
Mustard Family (Brassicaceae), 97–99
Myrtillocactus cochal, 124–25

Nabhan, Gary, 3, *35,* 39, 40, 76, 157, 173, 221, 238
nacapuli (*Ficus pertusa*), 212
Nápoli, Ignacio, 52, 53, 69, 70, 81, 156, 157
Natividad Island, 33, 41
Nava, Diego de la, 39, 181
Navajo, 18, 56, 151, 208
Navajoa, 91, 94, 98, 178, 235
Nentvig, Fr., 54, 85–86, 146, 149, 161, 162, 213, 229, 243, 246
Neoevansia striata, 134, 136
nettle, bull- (*Cnidoscolus* spp.), 160–61
netvine (*Marsdenia* spp.), 84
Névome, 146
New River Mountains, 34, 35, 37, 42, 196, 214
nicker (*Caesalpinia* spp.), 163
nightshade: American black, marsh (*Solanum americanum*), 239; false- (*Chamaesaracha* spp.), 236; green-spot (*S. douglasii*), 239
Nightshade Family (Solanaceae), 233–39
Noceo family, *104,* 105
nogal, nogal silvestre (*Juglans major*), 196–98
Nolina, 45; *beldingii,* 64; *beldingii* var. *deserticola,* 64; *bigelovii* (Bigelow's), 64; *microcarpa,* 17, 18, 32, 192

Nolinaceae, 62–64
nopal (*Opuntia* spp.), 125, 126
Norris, Juanita, 47, 50
Northeastern Yavapais, 46, 60, 77, 83, 87, 108, 128, 148, 152, 184, 192, 195, 197, 213, 241; paloverde use, 164–65; saguaro fruit, 101–2
Northern Tonto Apaches, 17, 62, 87, 192
nut-grass: purple (*Cyperus rotundus*), 57; yellow (*C. esculentus*), 57
Nyctaginaceae, 214
nypa (*Distichlis palmeri*), 65

oak: California black (*Quercus kelloggii*), 189, 190, 193; canyon live (*Q. chrysolepis*), 189, 190, 192, 193, 194, 195; coast live (*Q. agrifolia*), 189, 190, 193, 195; Emory's (*Q. emoryi*), 189, *190, 191*, 192, 193, 195; Engelmann's (*Q. engelmannii*), 189, 190, 194; gray, Arizona (*Q. grisea*), 189, 190, 192; Mexican blue (*Q. oblongifolia*), 189, 190, 193, 195; scrub (*Q. dumosa*), 189, 190, 194, 195; scrub live (*Q. turbinella*), 189, 190, 192, 194
oases: palm, 55, 56
Ochurte, Joséfina, 49, 129, 194
ocotillo (*Fouquieria* spp.), 195–96; tree (*F. macdougalii*), 195
Ocotillo Family (Fouquieriaceae), 195–96
Ojo Caliente (Coahuila), 147
Oligomeris linifolia, 80, 219, 222–23
Olneya tesota, 134, 136, 170–71, 244
Ónavas Pima, 42, 93, 95, 114, 129, 131, 145, 149, 154, 157, 163, 178, 186, 195, 219, 240, 241; greens used by, 76, 222; palms used by, 53, 54; *Randia* use, 229, 230
onion: aspen (*Allium bisceptrum* var. *palmeri*), 58, 59; fringed (*A. fimbriatum*), 58; large-petal (*A. macropetalum*), 58, 59; Parish's (*A. parishii*), 58; red-skin (*A. haematochiton*), 58; taper-tip (*A. acuminatum*), 58
O'odham, 153. *See also* Hiá ced O'odham; Gila River Pimas; Mountain Pimas; Pimas; River Pimas; Salt River Pimas; Tohono O'odham
Ópata, 93, 134, 141, 186–87, 213, 229, 231
Opuntia, 5; *basilaris*, 125, 126, 128, 129; *bravoana*, 125, 126, 129; *chlorotica*, 125, 126, 128; x *curvospina*, 128; *engelmannii*, 106, 113, 125, *126, 127*, 128, 129, 130; *erinacea*, 128; *ficus-indica*, 125, 126, 128, 129; *gosseliniana*, 125, 126; *littoralis*, 125, 126, 129; *macrocentra*, 125, 126; *megacantha*, 125, 126, 128; *oricola*, 125, 126, 128; *phaeacantha*, 125, 126, 128, 130; *polyacantha*, 125; *pycnantha*, 125, 126; *santa-rita*, 125, 126; *tapona*, 125, 126, 129; *violacea*, 125. *See also* Cylindropuntia
orache (*Atriplex* spp.), 150–51
Orcutt, Charles, 52, 55, 69, 83
orégano (*Lippia palmeri*), 140, *242–43*
organ pipe cactus (*Stenocereus thurberi*), 4, 102, 106, 122, 129, 132, 137, *140–46*
Organ Pipe Cactus National Monument, 59, 123–24, 136
Orobanchaceae, 215
Orobanche: *cooperi*, 86, 205, 215; *fasciculata*, 215; *ludoviciana*, 215
Orozco, Candalaria, 102, 205–6 [Orosco?]
Ortega, Francisco de, 25, 27, 39, 143, 161, 181
Our Lord's candle, 43–44
overgrazing, 3, 42–43, 56, 59, 171, 177, 211
Oxalidaceae, 216
Oxalis: *albicans*, 216; *stricta*, 216
ownership: of mesquites, 178–79; of oaks, 192; of teddá, 222

Pachycereus: *pecten-aboriginum*, 4, *131*; *pringlei*, 73, 106, 131–*32*, *133*; *schottii*, 122; uses of, 131–34
Pachycormus discolor, 83
Pachyrhizus erosus, 154
packrat middens, 40, 227
paint: from beeplant, 147
Paipais (Akwa'ala), 23, 24, 49, 71, 112, 126, 129, 194
Paiutes, 68, 69, 200
palma: *Erythea* spp., 52, 53; *Sabal uresana*, 53–*54*; *Washingtonia robusta*, 53, 55; *Yucca arizonica*, 44
Palmer, Edward, 2, 33, 45, 51, 69, 83, 84, 91, 97, 120, 141, 150, 152, 154, 157, 198, 207, 210, 213, 217, 219, 225, 237, 238, 242; on chia use, 199, 200, 203; on chiltepin harvesting, 234–35; on grass use, 65, 67; on *Vitis* spp., 244–45
Palmer-lily (*Triteleiopsis palmeri*), 61–62, 97
palmetto (*Sabal uresana*), 53–*54*
Palm Family (Arecaceae), 52–56
palmilla: *Erythea brandegeei*, 52; *Washingtonia filifera*, 55; *Yucca elata*, 44
palmito: *Erythea* hearts, 52–53; *Yucca elata*, 44
palms: blue fan (*Erythea armata*), 52; California fan (*Washingtonia filifera*), 55; red (*Erythea brandegeei*), 52; skyduster fan, Washington fan (*Washingtonia robusta*), 55
palo aspestoso (*Karwinskia humboldtiana*), 225–26
palo blanco: *Celtis laevigata*, 240, 241; *Ipomoea arborescens*, 153; *Lysiloma candida*, 168, 169; *Maytenus phyllanthoides*, 149; *Ziziphus obtusifolius* var. *canescens*, 226
palo bobo (*Ipomoea arborescens*), 153, *154*
palo brea (*Cercidium praecox*), 165, 166
palo cabra (*Ipomoea arborescens*), 153, *154*
palo de águila (*Celtis pallida*), 240–41
palo de arco (*Celtis iguanaea*), 240, 241
Palomar Cañon, 24
palo San Juan: *Forchammeria watsoni*, 148; *Jacquinia macrocarpa*, 240
palo santo (*Ipomoea arborescens*), 153, *154*
palote negro (*Guazuma ulmifolia*), 239–40
paloverde, 101; blue (*Cercidium floridum*), 164, 165, 166; *Fouquieria macdougalii*, 195; littleleaf, yellow, foothill (*C. microphyllum*), 164, 165, 166–67; Mexican (*Parkinsonia aculeata*), 171
Panamints, 50, 68, 116, 126, 128, 181
Panicum (panic grass): *capillare* (common), 66; *fasciculatum*, 66; *hirticaule* var. *miliaceum* (Sonoran), 3, 64; *obtusum* (blunt), 66; *sonorum* (Sonoran, Mexican), 66–68; *urvilleanum* (desert), 66
papache: *Randia* spp., 229–30; *Ziziphus obtusifolius* var. *canescens*, 226
parasites, 86, 130, 204, 215, 243–44
Parkinsonia: *aculeata*, 171; *florida*, 164; *microphylla*, 119, 164, 165
Passiflora (passion-flower): *arida*, 216–17; *bryonioides* (cupped), 216, 217; *foetida* (scarlet-fruit), 216, 217; *fruticosa*, 217; *mexicana*, 217; *palmeri*, 216, 217
Passifloraceae (Passion-flower Family), 216–17
patata, patota (*Monolepis nuttalliana*), 152–53
pazote: *Chenopodium ambrosioides*, 151; *Lepidium lasiocarpum*, 99
Peach Springs school, 32–33

Pea Family (Fabaceae), 162–89
pearlberry (*Vallesia glabra*), 84
péchita (*Prosopis* spp.), 178, 186–87
Pectis: *angustifolia* (lemon-scented pectis), 88; *papposa*, *88–89*
Pedaliaceae, 209
Peniocereus: *greggii*, 134–36; *striatus*, 134, 136
Pennington, Campbell, 129, 157, 230
Pennisetum ciliare, *4*, 146, 171
pepper: (*Capsicum annuum*), 233–*35*
pepper-grass (*Lepidium* spp.), 5, 98–99
pepperwort: bush (*Lepidium fremontii*), 99; hairy-pod (*L. lasiocarpum*), 99; poorman's (*L. virginicum*), 99; shining (*L. nitidum*), 99; Thurber's (*L. thurberi*), 99; veiny (*L. oblongum*), 99; yellow (*L. flavum*), 99
Pérez de Ribas, Andrés, 146, 214
Pericú, 81, 132, 154, 155, 161, 165, 213, 246; agave use, 23, 27, 28, 29; *Karwinskia* use, 225–26; *Oligomeris* use, 222, 223; pitahaya dulce use, 141, 142, 143
persimmon (*Diospyros* spp.), 160
Persimmon Family (Ebenaceae), 160
pest control, 5, 56, 136
Phaseolus: *acutifolius*, 77, 172–76; *filiformis*, *172*, 176; *maculatus*, 177; *metcalfei* group, 176–77; *ritensis*, 172, 176–77; *vulgaris*, 175
Phillips, Art, III, *43*
Pholisma: *arenarium*, 204, 207; *sonorae*, 51, *204–7*
Phoradendron: *californicum*, 243–44; *diguetianum*, 243, 244; *tomentosum*, 243
Phragmites: *australis*, 64, 68–69, 143; *communis*, 68, 69
Physalis, 234; *acutifolia*, 238; *angulata*, 238; *crassifolia*, 238; *hederifolia*, 238; *ixocarpa*, 238; *longifolia* var. *longifolia*, 238; *philadelphica*, 238; *pubescens*, 238; *virginiana*, 238
Phytolaccaceae, 217
Picacho Mountains, 40
Piccolo, Francisco María, 68–69, 142, 144, 145, 166, 245
pickleweed: *Allenrolfea occidentalis*, 149–50; *Salicornia* use, 153
pigeon-berry (*Rivina humilis*), 217
pignut (*Hyptis suaveolens*), 198–99
pig's face (*Mesembryanthemum crystallinum*), 75–76
pigweed: *Amaranthus* spp., 77; rough (*A. retroflexus*), 77; *Trianthema portulacastrum*, *76*; winged- (*Cycloloma atriplicifolium*), 152
Pima Bajo, 33, 100, 131, 141, 178, 186, 195, 209
Pimas, 2, 50, 57, 71, 76, 85, 93, 95, 102, 148, 209; agave use, 17, 20–21, 39, 40; amaranth use, 78, 79; *Atriplex* use, 150–51; medicinal plants of, 12, 135. *See also* Gila River Pimas; Mountain Pimas; Pima Bajo; River Pimas; Salt River Pimas
Pinacates, 122, 176, 186, 204
Pinal Apaches, 101
Pinal Mountains, 192, 245
pincushion: fishhook (*Mammillaria* spp.), 123
pine nuts, 24, 179
pinicua (*Jacquinia macrocarpa*), 240
Pinkava, Donald, 106
pinole, 12, 67, 80, 149, 168, 171, 186, 196, 218, 221; chia, 199–200
Pinus edulis (piñon), 3, 179
pipeweed: Indian (*Eriogonum inflatum*), 219
Pisonia capitata, 214
Pistacia mexicana, 81
pitahaya, 24, 120; barbona (*Lophocereus schottii*), 122–23; bittersweet, agria, agridulce (*Stenocereus gummosus*), 137–40, 144; dulce (*S. thurberi*), 102, 106, 122, 129, 132, 137, *140–46*
pitahita, pitahayita (*Peniocereus striatus*), 134, 136
pit-baking, 43, 47, 62, 64, 98; agave, 14, 15, 17, 22–23, 25, 29, 32, 41; cholla, 107, 108–9, 113; pre-Columbian, 34, 214
pit-"cooking": mesquite beans, 182–83
Pithecellobium: *confine*, 177; *dulce*, *177–78*; *leucospermum*, 177, 178; *undulatum*, 179
Plantaginaceae (Plantain Family), 218
Plantago (plantain), 5, 102, 203; *australis* (Mexican), 218; *heterophylla* (many-seeded), 218; *hirtella*, 218; *insularis*, 218; *lanceolata* (buckhorn, English), 218; *major* (common, great), 218; medicinal use of, 98, 99; *ovata* (woolly), 218; *patagonica* (pursh), 218; *rhodosperma* (red-seeded), 218; *virginica* (pale-seed), 218; water- (*Alismataceae*), 51
Pleasant Valley, 191
Pluchea sericea, 72, 79, 178, 179, 182, 183, 184
plum: wild (*Prunus* spp.), 227–28
plum-tree, plum (*Cyrtocarpa edulis*), 81
Poaceae, 64–70
pods, 164; mesquite, 178–80, 181–87, 188
Pokeberry, Pokeweed Family (Phytolaccaceae), 217
pollen: cattail, 58, 72
Polygonaceae, 218–21
Populus spp. 150
Portulaca, 3; *oleracea*, 76, 78, 221–22; *parvula*, 222
pilosa, 221–22; *retusa*, 221; *suffrutescens*, 222
Portulacaceae, 221—22
potato: rat- (*Hoffmanseggia glauca*), 168
Potato Family (Solanaceae), 233–39
potherbs, 78, 147, 242. *See also* greens; quelites
poverty-weed: Nuttall's (*Monolepis nuttalliana*), 152–53
pre-Columbian peoples, 157, 163, 173, 176, 196, 207, 214, 233, 245; agave use by, 30, 34–35, 37, 38, 39; chia and, 202, 203; mesquite use by, 183, 186
prickle-nut (*Guazuma ulmifolia*), 239–40
prickly-pear, 64, 106; chaparral (*Opuntia oricola*), 125; coastal (*O. littoralis*), 125, 129; Engelman (*O. engelmannii*), 106, 113, 125, *126*, *127*, 128, 129, 130; pancake, clockface (*O. chlorotica*), 125, 126, 128; plains (*Opuntia polyacantha*), 125; purple (*O. macrocentra*; *O. santa-rita*), 125; Santa Rita (*O. santa-rita*), 125; tulip (*O. phaeacantha*), 125, 128, 130; violet (*O. gosseliniana*), 125
Proboscidea: *althaeifolia*, 209, *211*; *parviflora*, 3–4, 209, *210–12*
Prosopis, 4, 145, 244; *articulata*, 180; *glandulosa* var. *torreyana*, 178, 179, 180, 181–82, 184, 188, 189; *juliflora*, 167, 178, 180; *palmeri*, 180; *pubescens*, 178, 179–80, *182–83*; *velutina*, 5, 178, 179, 182, 183–87, 188, 189
Prunus, 69; *fasciculata*, 227, 228; *fremontii*, 227, 228; *ilicifolia*, 227–28
Puerto Peñasco, 65, 90, 153
Pug-a-roo, 32
pulp: barrel cactus, 120–21; *Echinocereus*, 117; saguaro, 105, 106
Purisma, 169
purslane: common (*Portulaca oleracea*), 78, 221–22; horse- (*Trianthema portulacastrum*), *76*; rock- (*Calandrinia* spp.), 221; shrubby (*P. suffrutescens*), 222; silk-cotton (*P. parvula*), 222

Purslane Family (Portulacaceae), 221–22

quailbush (*Atriplex lentiformis*), 150
Quechan, 71, 78, 98, 150, 168, 200, 236; agave use, 18, 22; dock use, 220–21; mesquite use, 178–79, 182; and sandfood, 206, 207
Queen Creek, 34, 64
queen-of-the-night (*Peniocereus greggii*), 134
queen's jewels (*Antigonon leptopus*), 218–*19*
quelites, 5, 7, 86, 99, 213, 220, 221, 239, 242; *Amaranthus* spp., 77–78; *Chenopodium* as, 151–52; mustard as, 97–98
Quercus, 3, 179; *agrifolia*, 189, 190, 193, 195; *arizonica*, 192; *brandegeei*, 195; *chrysolepis*, 189, 190, 192, 193, 194, 195; *dumosa*, 189, 190, 193, 194, 195; *dunnii*, 194; *emoryi*, 5, 189, *190*, *191*, 192, 193, 195; *engelmanni*, 189, 190, 194; *gambelii*, 192; *grisea*, 189, 190, 192; *kelloggii*, 189, 190, 193; *oblongifolia*, 189, 190, 193, 195; *palmeri*, 189, 190, 192; *peninsularis*, 189, 194; *turbinella*, 189, 190, 192, 194
Quijotoa Mountains, 102
Quiocoba, 243
quisache costeño (*Acacia cochliacantha*), 162
Quitobaquito, 21
Quitovac, 21, 97, 118, 125, 141, 148, 171, 213, 227, 244; greens in, 76, 97; saguaro in, 102, 106

rabbit-thorn (*Lycium pallidum*), 236
ragweed: weak-leaf burr- (*Ambrosia confertiflora*), 86
railway-daisy (*Bidens pilosa*), 86
Ramah Navajo, 59, 215
Randia: *armata*, 229; *echinocarpa*, 229, *230*; *laevigata*, 229; *megacarpa*, 229; *obcordata*, 229, *230*; *sonorensis*, 229; *thurberi*, 229–30
rape (*Brassica rapa*), 97, 98; broom- (*Orobanche* spp.), 215
Raphael, Carmelita, 109
Rathbunia alamosensis, 136
rat-potato (*Hoffmanseggia glauca*), 168
rattlebox, 167–68; low (*Crotalaria pumila*), 167–68
Rea, Amadeo, 2, 41, 47, 50, 57, 58, 76, 89, 92, 98, 102, 109, 120, 123, 136, 158, 165, 168, 198, 203, 215, 220, 243; on mesquite, 183, 184
Rebman, Jon, 106
red-maids: fringed (*Calandrinia ciliata*), 221
redroot (*Amaranthus palmeri*), 77
reed: common (*Phragmites* spp.), 68–70
Reichenbacher, Frank, 159
reina de la noche (*Peniocereus greggii*), 134
Resedaceae, 222–23
Rhamnaceae, 224–27
rhizomes: club- and bulrush, 57–58
Rhizophoraceae, 227
Rhizophora mangle, 227
Rhus, 7; *integrifolia*, 82, 83; *kearneyi*, 82, 83; *lentii*, 83; *microphylla*, 83; *ovata*, 69, 82, 83, 198; *tepatate*, 83; *trilobata*, *82*–83
River Paipai, 24
River Pimas, 5, 19, 47, 71, 89, 92, 98, 99, 120, 122, 125, 136, 148, 149, 152, 153, 165, 168, 170, 173, 200, 208, 213, 215, 218, 226, 233, 236, 238, 239; acorns, 192–93; amaranth use, 77–78; *Atriplex* use, 150, 151; cholla use, 108, 113, 114; dock use, 219–20; mesquite use, 179, 182, 184–86, 187, 189; mistletoe use, 243–44; *Proboscidea* use, 210, 211; saguaro and, 100, 102, 103; walnut use, 197–98. *See also* Gila River Pimas; Salt River Pimas
Rivina humilis, 217
roasting pits: agave, 14, 17, 22–23, 25, 29, 32, 34, 41, 43, 47, 62, 64; cholla bud, 108–*9*
Robertson, Tomas Antonio, 214
Rogers, Woodes, 50, 79, 81, 222
roots, 71, 90, *95*, 160, 168, 214, 219; *Amoreuxia*, 91–92, 93; gourd, 158–59; *Ipomoea*, 153–54, 155; *Proboscidea althaeifolia* use, 210–11; queen-of-the-night, 134–35; yucca, 50–51
Rorippa: *nasturtium-aquaticum*, 99; *palustris* var. *hispida*, 99
Rosaceae (Rose Family), 227–28
rose, wood- (*Merremia aurea*), 28, 51, 154, 155–57
Rose, J. N., 2, 98
Rothrock, John, 34, 199, 201, 207
rouge plant (*Rivina humilis*), 217
Rubiaceae, 229–30
Rumex: *crispus*, 219–20; *dentatus*, 220; *hymenosepalus*, 90, 219, *220*; *violascens*, 219, 220, 221
rush, club-: chairmaker's (*Schoenoplectus americanus*), 57; hard-stem (*S. acutus*), 57; salt-marsh (*S. maritimus*), 57; soft-stem (*S. tabernaemontani*), 57
rush-pea: waxy (*Hoffmanseggia glauca*), 168
Russell, Frank, 78, 80, 89, 102, 113, 130, 149, 165, 182, 185, 220

Sabal uresana (sabal), 53–*54*, *55*
Sacaton, 123, 175
sacaton: alkali (*Sporobolus airoides*), 64, 70
sage: California (*Salvia columbariae*), 5, 98, 99, 199–203; California white (*S. apiana*), 199, 203; coastal (*Quercus dumosa*), 189; thistle (*S. carduacea*), 199, 202, *203*
Sagittaria, 51; *cuneata*, 51; *greggii*, 51; *longiloba*, 51
saguaro (*Carnegia gigantea*), 47, *100*, 123; fruit processing, 101–2; syrup processing, 63, 120; Tohono O'odham and, 102–6
Saguaro National Park, 123, 124
sagui (*Panicum sonorum*), 66–68
saiya (*Amoreuxia* spp.), 1, 91–93
Salado, 37, 39, 80
Sales, Luis, 23, 25, 29, 33, 141
Salicornia: *europea*, 153; *pacifica*, 153
Salix, 79, 184
Salpianthus macrodontus, 214
saltbush, 113; California (*Atriplex californica*), 150; wheel-scale (*A. elegans*), 150; Wright's (*A. wrightii*), 110–11
salt grass: *Distichlis spicata*, 65; Palmer (*D. palmeri*), 3, 64, 65, 78
Salton Basin, Sea, 55, 72. *See also* Cahuilla, Lake
Salt River Pima, 5, 12, 47, 76, 78, 87, 117, 148, 151, 220; agave use, 19–20, 40; *Ziziphus* use, 226–27
Salt River Reservation, 77–78
Salt River valley, 3, 34, 58, 116, 183; agave in, 39, 42; dock on, 219–20
saltwort: *Batis maritima*, 90; *Salicornia* spp., 153
Saltwort Family (Bataceae), 90
Salvatierra, Fr., 2, 51, 126, 142, 144–45, 155, 156, 161
salvia (*Hyptis* spp.), 198–99
Salvia (salvia): *apiana*, 199, 203; *carduacea*, 199–200, 202, *203*; *columbariae*, 5, 98, 99, 199–203; *henryi*, 202; *hispanica*, 202–3
Sambucus: *mexicana*, 148; *nigra* ssp. *canadensis*, 148–49
San Benito Island, 33, 41, 122
San Bernabe, 27, 93
San Bernardo, 98, 177, 225
San Borjas, 23, 41

San Carlos Apaches, 16, 62, 64, 87, 101, 113, 134, 152, 198, 199; barrel cactus use, 120, 121; *Dichelostemma* use, 59, 60
San Carlos Bay, 56, 137
sandfood (*Pholisma sonorae*), *204–7*
sandia de la pasion: *Passiflora palmeri,* 216; *Sarcostemma cynanchoides,* 85
San Diego Diegueño, 157
sand plant: scaly-stemmed (*Pholisma arenarium*), 204
San Esteban Island, 34, 167, 210
sand-lily: Palmer's blue- (*Triteleiopsis palmeri*), 3, 5, *61*–62, 97
San Felipe, 81, 137
San Felipe Desert, 131–32, 171
San Francisco Javier, 70, 112
San Ignacio, 33, 50, 69
San Javier, 70, 162
San José del Cabo, 84, 92
San Juanico: *Forchammeria watsoni,* 148; *Jacquinia macrocarpa,* 240
San Luisito, 21, 34
San Miguel, San Miguelito (*Antigonon leptopus*), 218–*19*
San Miguel, Río, 54, 163, 210, 233, 235, 243
San Pedro Mártir, 212, 213
Santa Catalina Mountains, 21, *48, 113,* 191
Santa Cruz River, 57, 70, 171
Santa Rosa, 92, 102
Santa Ysabel Diegueños, 12, 22, 44, 128, 179, 193–94, 201
Santiago, 225–26
sap: mulberry, 213–14
Sapotaceae (Sapote, Sapodilla Family), 230–31
Sarcostemma: *arenarium,* 86; *clausum,* 86; *crispum,* 86; *cyanchoides,* 85, *86*; *hirtellum,* 86; *pannosum,* 85–86
SARH Subsecretaria Forestal de México, 235
Saubel, Katherine, 22, 64, 193
Saunders, Charles, 202
scale, lens- (*Atriplex lentiformis*), 150–51
Schaefferia cuneifolia (desert-yaupon), 149
Schoenoplectus: *acutus,* 57, 58; *americanus,* 57; *maritimus,* 57; *tabernaemontani,* 57–58; *validus,* 57
Scirpus: *acutus,* 57, 58; *americanus,* 57; *lacustris,* 57; *maritimus,* 57; *validus,* 58
screwbean (*Prosopis pubescens*), 178, 179
sea-fig: *Carpobrotus chilensis,* 75; *Mesembryanthum* spp., 75–76
seasoning: *Lippia* as, 242–43; *Pectis* as, 88–89
seawrack (*Zostera mariana*), 72–73
second harvest, 102, 106, 131, 134, 139, 144
Sedge Family (Cyperaceae), 57–58
sedges: purple flat-, purple nut- (*Cyperus rotundus*), 57; red-root flat- (*C. erythrorhizos*), 57; rusty flat- (*C. odoratus*), 57; yellow nut- (*C. esculentus*), 57
seeds, 50, 52, 62, 64, 76, 81, 94, 96, 97, 100, 113, 128, 139, 144, 147, 152, 153, 158, 160, 163, 168, 218, 219, 226, 232; amaranth, 79–80; *Atriplex,* 150–51; barrel cactus, 121–22; bruchid beetles and, 187–88; cardón, 132, 134; chia, 199–200; eel-grass, 72–73; *Hyptis suaveolens,* 198, 199; ironwood, 170–71; *Mentzelia,* 207, 208; mesquite, 185, 188–89; muscilaginous, 98, 99; ocotillo, 195–96; *Oligomeris,* 222, 223; paloverde, 164–65, 166–67; pickleweed, 149, 150; *Proboscidea,* 209–10; *Prunus,* 227–28; purslane, 221–22; saguaro, 101, 102, 106; tansy-mustard, 98–99; teddá, 222, 223. *See also* fruits
seepweed: desert (*Suaeda moquinii*), 109
sego-lily (*Calochortus* spp.), 59
senita (*Lophocereus schottii*), 122–23
Seris, 47, 62, 65, 70, 80, 90, 93, 106, 122, 136, 137, 149, 159, 160, 171, 173, 195, 217, 218, 222, 227, 230, 231, 233, 236, 240, 241, 242, 244; agave use, 14, 30–31, 34; barrel cactus use, 118, 120, 121; cardón use, 131, 133–34; cholla use, 114–15; eel-grass use, 72–73; mesquite use, 178, 181, 189; Milkweed Family use, 84–85; palm use, 52, 54, 56; pepper-grass use, 98–99; pitahaya agria, 139–40; pitahaya dulce use, 141, 145; *Proboscidea althaeifolia* use, 210–11
Serra, Junipero, 23, 39
shakeshake (*Crotalaria incana*), 167–68
shampoos, 49, 233
Shoshone, 3, 32, 50, 181
Shuni, Chico, 118, 135
Sideroxylon: *occidentale,* 230–*31*; *persimile,* 231
Sierra de la Giganta, 51, 143, 162, 169, 195, 212, 245; agave in, 27, 28, 29
Sierra del Viejo, 29, 30, *63*
Sierra Estrella, 19–20, 40, 102
Sierra Estrella Regional Park, 59, 61, 209
Sierra Juarez, 24, 25, 194
Sierra San Francisco, 92, 245
Sierra San Pedro Martir, 25, 27, 28, 29, 194
Simmondsiaceae, 232–33
Simmondsia chinensis, 8, 39, 101, 232–33
sina: *Lophocereus schottii,* 122–23; *Stenocereus alamosensis,* 136
Sinaloa, 2, 30, 95, 131, 155, 160
sinita: *Stenocereus alamosensis,* 136; *Echinocereus engelmannii,* 116
Sistiaga, Fr., 141
Sisymbrium canescens, 98
skunkbush (*Rhus trilobata*), *82*–83
Slauson, Liz, 41
snake-lily (*Dichelostemma* spp.), 59–60
Snaketown, 66, 98
snakewood: Warnock's (*Condalia warnockii*), 224
soapweed (*Yucca* spp.), 44–51
Solanaceae, 233–39
Solanum: *americanum,* 239; *douglasii,* 239; *eleaganifolium,* 239; *nigrum,* 239; *nodiflorum,* 239
Sonchus: *asper,* 89; *oleraceus,* 89; *tenerrimus,* 89
Sonoita, 102
Sonora, 2, 41, 52, 64, 80, 84, 95, 100, 121, 137, 159, 160, 169, 174, 177, 195, 198; agave in, 29–31, 39
Sonoran Desert, 1, 3
sotol (*Dasylirion wheeleri*), 62–63
South, Marshall, 22–23, 26
Southeastern Yavapais, 46, 83, 101, 164, 170, 184, 192, 199, 213, 245; prickly-pear use, 126, 128; walnut use, 196–97
Southern Diegueños, 23, 24, 112, 126, 194, 203, 228
Southern Paiute: agave use, 31–32, 39, 47, 50, 68, 130, 181, 207
Southern Tonto Apache, 17, 62, 64, 191–92, 198
South Mountain (Salt River Mountains), 40, 102, 130
Southwest Boll Weevil Eradication Program, 5
sow-thistle: annual, common (*Sonchus oleraceus*), 89; slender (*S. tenerrinus*), 89; spiny-leaf (*S. asper*), 89
Spa, Sam, 24, 180, 187
Spanish bayonet (*Yucca elata*), 44
Spanish dagger (*Yucca schidigera*), 44
Spanish needles (*Bidens pilosa*), 86
Spanish-tea (*Chenopodium ambrosioides*), 151
spearleaf (*Matelea parvifolia*), 84
Sphaeralcea ambigua (globemallow), 19, 101
spiderflower (*Cleome* spp.), 147

spiderling: Coulter's (*Boerhavia coulteri*), 214
spiderwort: prairie (*Tradescantia occidentalis*), 56; yellow (*Cleome lutea*), 147
Spiderwort Family (Commelinaceae), 56
Spier, Leslie, 194
spinach: cattle- (*Atriplex polycarpa*), 150; Indian- (*Monolepis nuttalliana*), 152–53
Sporobolus: *airoides,* 64, 70; *contractus,* 70; *cryptandrus,* 70; *virginicus,* 70
Spring-beauty (*Claytonia perfoliata*), 221
Spurge Family (Euphorbiaceae), 160–62
squawbush, squawberry: *Condalia warnockii, 224*; *Rhus trilobata, 82*
Stafftree Family (Celastraceae), 149
Stenocereus: *alamosensis,* 136, 137; *eruca,* 136, 137; *gummosus,* 136, 137–40, 143, 144; *thurberi,* 4, 102, 106, 120, 122, 129, 132, 137, *140–46*
Sterculiaceae, 239–40
Stickleaf Family (Loasaceae), 207–8
sticktights (*Bidens pilosa*), 86
stingingbush (*Malpighia* spp.), 209
Stonecrop Family (Crassulaceae), 157
stork's-bill: large-flowered, Texas (*Erodium cicutarium*), 196; red-stem (*E. cicutarium*), 196
Suaeda moquinii, 18, 109, 150
sugar-berry (*Celtis laevigata*), 240, 241
sumac: ill-scented (*Rhus trilobata*), *82*; Kearney's (*R. kearneyi*), 82; laurel- (*Malosma laurina*), 81—82; lemonade (*R. integrifolia*), 82; sugar (*R. ovata*), 82
Sumac Family (Anacardiaceae), 81–83
sunflower: common (*Helianthus annuus*), 87; prairie (*H. petiolaris*), 87; showy (*H. niveus*), 87
Superstition Mountains, 18, 47, 59, 101, 192
syrup, 122, 141, 209, 226; saguaro, 102, 105, 106, 120

Table Mesa (New River Mtns.), 35, 37
Table Top Mountain, 40, 59
tablote (*Guazuma ulmifolia*), 239–40
Tachardiella larreae, 32
talayote: *Marsdenia edulis,* 84; *Matelea cordifolia,* 84; *Sarcostemma pannosum,* 85
tamarind: little-leaf false- (*Lysiloma watsonii*), 168, 169
Tamarix spp. (tamarisk), 65, 68
tansy-mustard: blunt (*Descurainia obtusa*), 98; western (*D. pinnata*), 98
tapaculo (*Guazuma ulmifolia*) 239–40
Tapirira edulis, 81
tapiro (*Sambucus mexicana*), 148–49
Tarahumaras, 62, 78, 85, 86, 89, 131, 141, 152, 168, 178, 195, 217, 229, 234, 238, 239–40, 241, 242, 243; agave use, 31, 33, 34, 41; greens, 99, 221; *Ipomoea* use, 153, 154; kapok use, 95–96; mulberry use, 213–14; mustard use, 97–98
Taravel, Fr., 33, 137
tea: Mexican-, Spanish- (*Chenopodium ambrosioides*), 151
tecolochapo, tecolosapo (*Randia echinocarpa*), 229
teddá (*Oligomeris linifolia*), 222–23
Tegeticula: *maculata,* 45; *yuccasella,* 45
temaqui (*Amoreuxia palmatifida*), 91, 93
Tempe, 117–18
teparies (*Phaseolus acutifolius*), *172–76*
Tepehuans, 62, 80, 95, 154, 157, 213, 216, 229, 236, 239
tesajillo (*Cylindropuntia leptocaulis*), 106, 111
tesajo (*Cylindropuntia* spp.), 106, 112, 115
Theophrastaceae (Theophrasta Family), 240
thistle, sow-, 89
thorn: all- (*Koeberlinia spinosa*), 198; crucifixion- (*Koeberlinia spinosa*), 198; rabbit- (*Lycium pallidum*), 236
thornbush: Anderson (*Lycium andersonii*), 236; Fremont (*L. fremontii*), 236; Parish's (*L. parishii*), 236
thornscrub: Sinaloan, 95, 131, 145
Tiburón Island, 93, 122, 139, 167, 210, 212; agave from, 30–31; tepary beans on, 172, 173
Timbisha Shoshones, 3, 181–82, 191
Tipais, 23, 49, 52, 97, 99, 112, 118, 121, 123, 147, 148, 152, 228; acorn use, 194–95; chia use, 201–2; *Hesperoyucca whipplei* use, 43, 44; prickly-pear use, 125, 126, 129
Tirado, Ricardo Flores, 29–30, 63
Tohono O'odham, 3–4, 7, 59, 60, 62, 64, 70, 75, 78, 85, 86, 92, 97, 98, 122, 123, 141, 151, 152, 153, 165, 171, 195, 213, 215, 224, 227, 232, 233, 236, 241; acorns, 192, 193; agave cultivation by, 34, 39; agave use, 17, 18, 21, 30; amaranth use, 77, 79, 80; barrel cactus use, 118, 120; cholla and, 111, 114; diet, 5, 175, 176; elderberry use, 148–49; mesquite use, 179, 186; mistletoe use, 243, 244; prickly pear use, 125, 128, 130; *Proboscidea* use, 210, 211; queen-of-the-night, 134–35, 136; saguaro and, 100, 102–6; and tepary beans, 173–74, 175; yucca use, 47, 50
Tohono O'odham Reservation, 92, 123; teparies on, 174–75
tomatillo: *Lycium* spp., 236; *Physalis* spp., 238
tomato, husk- (*Physalis* spp.), 238–39
Tonto Apaches, 18, 45–46, 62. *See also* Northern Tonto Apaches; Southern Tonto Apaches
Tonto Basin, 34, *36,* 37, 38
Torchwood Family (Burseraceae), 100
torote: *Bursera* spp., 100; *Fouquieria macdougalii,* 195
Torrey, John, 204, 207
Tortilla Flat, 126, 184
trade, 39, 47, 59, 113, 120, 122, 141, 200, 227; in acorns, 192–93, 194; in agave, 18, 20, 21, 22, 29; in chiltepines, 234–35; in mesquite beans, 179, 180, 186
Tradescantia occidentalis, 3, 56
tread softly (*Cnidoscolus* spp.), 160
tree: elephant- (*Bursera microphylla*), 100; Kapok- (Bombacaceae), 95–96; plum- (*Cyrtocarpa edulis*), 81
Trianthema portulacastrum, 76
Tricerma phyllanthoides, 149
trigo: del mar (*Zostera marina*), 72–73; gentil (*Distichlis palmeri*), 3, 64, 65
Triteleiopsis palmeri, 3, 5, *61–62,* 97
tule: *Phragmites australis,* 68–70, 143; *Schoenoplectus* spp., 57–58
tulip, butterfly- (*Calochortus* spp.), 59
Tumacacori, 66
Tumamoca macdougalii, 159
tumbleweed (*Amaranthus albus*), 77
tuna: *Lophocereus schottii,* 122–23; *Opuntia* spp., 125
Turnera diffusa, 243
turtleweed (*Batis maritima*), 90
twinbugs: desert (*Dicoria canescens*), 86–87
Typha, 32; *domingensis,* *71*; *latifolia,* 71
Typhaceae, 71

Ugarte, Juan de, 25–26, 142, 245
Ulmaceae, 240–41
Unicorn Family (Martyniaceae), 209–11
unicorn-plant: desert (*Proboscidea altheaifolia*), 209
Uniola palmeri, 65
uña de gato: *Acacia greggii,* 162; *Proboscidea parviflora,* 209

Ures, 52, 53, 235
Urochloa fasciculatum, 66

vacima (*Guazuma ulmifolia*), 239–40
vaiburin (*Antigonon leptopus*), 218–*19*
Valenzuela, Esteban C., 25, 27, 143, 161
Valenzuela, Ramon, 213
Valle de las Palmas, 55
Vallesia: *baileyana,* 84; *dicholoma,* 84; *glabra,* 84; *laciniata,* 84
Velarde, Luis, 173
Velasco, Miguel, 102, 205
Venegas, Fr., 69, 70, 155, 156, 161
verbena: velvet shrub- (*Lantana velutina*), 241
Verbenaceae (Verbena Family), 241–43
Verde River, Verde Valley, 34, 184, 203, 245
Verde Valley Yavapais, 192
verdolaga: *Portulaca oleracea,* 221–*22*; *Trianthema portulacastrum,* *76*
Vervain Family (Verbenaceae), 241–43
Victoriana, 202
Vincetoxicum caudatum, 84
vine: matrimony- (*Lycium* spp.), 236
Viscaceae, 243–44
Vitaceae, 244–46
Vitex: *mollis,* 243; *pyramidata,* 243
Vitis: *arizonica,* 244–45; *californica,* 244–45; *girdiana,* 244, 245; *peninsularis,* 244, 246; *vinifera,* 246
Vizcaíno, Sebastián, 39, 81, 137, 145, 201
Vizcaíno Desert, 117

walnut: Arizona (*Juglans major*), 196–98
Walnut Family (Juglandaceae), 196–98
wandering-jew (*Tradescantia* spp.), 56
Washingtonia: *filifera,* 52, 55–56; *robusta,* 52, 53, 55, 56
water: agaves as source of, 33–34; barrel cactus as source of, 118–20; and pitahaya dulce fruits, 142–43; from sandfood, 206
watercress (*Rorippa nasturtium-aquaticum*), 99
Water-plantain Family (Alismataceae), 51
water-willow (*Justicia* spp.), 75
weaving, 54, 63, 69, 70
Webb, George, 113, 120, 130, 165, 215
weed: arrow (*Pluchea sericea*), 72, 79, 178, 182, 183, 184; poverty (*Monolepis nuttalliana*), 152–53
Weiss, Audrey, 99, 118, 147, 148, 194–95
Western Apaches, 62, 64, 71, 77, 87, 101, 120, 147, 152, 177, 183, 196, 210, 245; acorn, 191–92; agave use, 16–17, 18, 33, 39; prickly-pear, 125, 126; yucca use, 45, 50
Western Yavapais, 60, 83, 102, 128, 152, 182, 213, 241; agave use, 22, 32; cholla use, 108, 113
White Mountain Apaches: agave, 16, 17, 64, 101, 199; cholla use, 107, 112–13
whitepuff: line-leaf (*Oligomeris linifolia*), 222–23
White Tank Mountains, 40, 59, 111
Wilcoxia striata, 134
willow (*Salix* spp.), 69, 79, 184; water- (*Justicia* spp.), 75
wine. *See* alcohol
wolfberry (*Lycium* spp.), 236
wood-rose (*Merremia aurea*), 28, 51, 154, 155–57
woodsorrel: radish-root (*Oxalis albicans*), 216; upright yellow (*O. stricta*), 216
Woodsorrel Family (Oxalidaceae), 216

Xanthium sp., 182
Xanthosoma phaseoli, 175
Xylocarpa spp., 21

yam (*Dioscorea* spp.), 58
Yam Family (Dioscoreaceae), 58
yamp (*Agave utahensis*), 13, 32
Yamparika, 32
Yaquis, 72, 78, 80, 93, 130, 136, 148, 153, 163, 210, 219, 225, 229, 231, 239, 241, 243; agave use, 31, 41; cardón use, 131, 134; chiltipiquin use, 233–34; kapok use, 95–96; mesquite use, 178, 180, 186; palm use, 54, 56; pitahaya dulce use, 141, 145–46
yaupon: desert- (*Schaefferia cuneifolia*), 149
Yavapais, 2, 46, 69, 83, 87, 120, 125, 192, 208; agave use, 17, 18–19, 32, 39. *See also* Northeastern Yavapais; Western Yavapais
yellowcress: bog (*Rorippa palustris* var. *hispida*), 99
yellowshow: Mexican (*Amoreuxia palmatifida*), *91*; Santa Rita Mountain (*A. gonzalezii*), 91
Yensen, Nicolas, 65, 90
yuca, 50; *Manihot chlorosticta,* 51, 92, 154, 156, 157, 161–62; *Merremia aurea,* 28, 51, 154, 155–57; *Yucca* spp., 44, 156. *See also Ipomoea*
Yucca (yucca), 17, 28, 64; *arizonica,* 44, 45, 47, *48,* 50; *baccata* (banana, blue, fleshy-fruited), 44, 45–*46,* 47, 49; *brevifolia,* 44, 45, 50; *capensis,* 156; *elata* (soaptree), 19, 44, 45, *47,* 50; *schidigera* (Mohave), 44, 45, *49,* 50, 51; *schottii* (hoary), 44, 45, 47, *48*; *thornberi* (Thornber's), 44, 45, 47; *valida,* 44, 50, 51, 156; *whipplei. See Hesperoyucca whipplei*
Yuma, Yuma Crossing, 97, 179
Yuman speakers, Yumans, 28–29, 67, 68. *See also by group*

zacate: alcalino espigado (*Sporobolus contractus*), 70; del mar (*Zostera marina*), 72–73; encubierto (*S. cryptandrus*), 70; salado (*Distichlis palmeri*), 3, 64, 65
zacaton: alkalino (*Sporobolus airoides*), 70; de arena (*S.* spp.), 70; des granador (*S. cyrptandrus*), 70
Ziziphus: *amole,* 226; *lycioides,* 226; *obtusifolius* var. *canescens,* 224, *226*–27; *parryi,* 226
Zosteraceae, 72–73
Zostera marina, 65, 72–73, 134
Zunis, 88–89, 151, 152, 158, 222

ABOUT THE AUTHOR

Wendy C. Hodgson has lived in the Sonoran Desert for thirty years, having moved to Arizona from upstate New York. In 1974 she began working as an illustrator and assistant to Howard S. Gentry at the Desert Botanical Garden in Phoenix. She began to study and document the flora of the Southwest and northern Mexico in the late 1970s. In 1982 she earned a master's degree from Arizona State University in botany, taxonomy, and systematics under Donald Pinkava. Today Ms. Hodgson is a research botanist and herbarium curator at the Desert Botanical Garden. Her fieldwork includes documenting plants in the Grand Canyon and on the Colorado Plateau, deciphering Agavaceae taxonomy and systematics, and studying how people of the Southwest and northern Mexico use plants.

Das Franco-Regime in Spanien

Walther L. Bernecker

Das Franco-Regime in Spanien

Der Streit um einen chamäleonhaften Systemtypus

PETER LANG
EDITION

Bibliografische Information der Deutschen Nationalbibliothek
Die Deutsche Nationalbibliothek verzeichnet diese Publikation in der Deutschen Nationalbibliografie; detaillierte bibliografische Daten sind im Internet über http://dnb.d-nb.de abrufbar.

ISBN 978-3-631-67938-8 (Print)
E-ISBN 978-3-653-07167-2 (E-PDF)
E-ISBN 978-3-631-70169-0 (EPUB)
E-ISBN 978-3-631-70170-6 (MOBI)
DOI 10.3726/978-3-653-07167-2

Peter Lang Edition ist ein Imprint der Peter Lang GmbH.

Peter Lang – Frankfurt am Main · Bern · Bruxelles · New York · Oxford · Warszawa · Wien

Diese Publikation wurde begutachtet.

www.peterlang.com

Zusammenfassung / Abstract

Seit Jahrzehnten sind sich Zeitgenossen und Wissenschaftler darüber uneinig, wie die Diktatur Francos (1936/39–1975) typologisch einzuordnen ist. Dabei wurde immer wieder auch auf die Eigenbezeichnungen des Regimes zurückgegriffen. Anfangs, vor allem bis zum Ende des Zweiten Weltkriegs, war daher vielfach die Rede von einer spanischen Variante des Faschismus. Als Franco selbst sich allmählich vom politischen System der Achsenmächte distanzierte, stellte er sein Regime (spätestens ab 1945) als ein nationalkatholisches System dar und betonte die konservativ-antikommunistischen Elemente. Kritiker des Franquismus sprachen zugleich von einer Militärdiktatur. In der Phase des Kalten Krieges (und zur Abgrenzung von totalitären Regimen) setzte sich die Charakterisierung als „autoritäres System" weitgehend durch, und in den letzten anderthalb Jahrzehnten der Diktatur sprachen sowohl Franquisten als auch Sozialwissenschaftler immer häufiger von einem Entwicklungsregime.
Der Band präsentiert und diskutiert die verschiedenen typologischen Ansätze, er weist deren Reichweite und Grenzen auf und eröffnet Perspektiven für die weitere Debatte.

Spanish contemporaries as well as historians have been discussing the question how to classify (in terms of typology) Franco's dictatorship (1936/39–1975) for several decades now. In doing so it has become general practice to revert to the regime's own nomenclature. Thus – especially from the beginning of Franco's regime until the end of World War II – a common term was "the Spanish variety of fascism". However, when Franco began to distance himself from the political system of the Axis Powers, he referred to his regime (at least from 1945 onwards) as a national-catholic system, hereby stressing conservative-anticommunist elements. Critics of Francoism added the label "military dictatorship". During the Cold War period, the characterization "authoritarian system" was used frequently, especially in contrast to the term "totalitarian regime". In the last 15 years of the dictatorship, Francoists as well as social scientists were talking about a "conservative developmental regime".

This book volume presents and discusses the different typological approaches, shows the range and limits of these approaches, and opens up perspectives for further discussion.

This book volume presents and discusses the different typological approaches, it shows the range and limits of these approaches, and opens up perspectives for further discussion.

Inhaltsverzeichnis

I. **Einleitung und Fragestellung** ... 9

II. **Franquismus als Faschismus** ... 13
1. Spanischer Faschismus in der Zweiten Republik (1931–1936) ... 13
2. „Alter" und „neuer" Faschismus zwischen Bürgerkrieg und Weltkrieg: die Falange ... 36
3. Niedergang des Faschismus als Staatsideologie ... 50

III. **Militärdiktatur, Nationalkatholizismus, Autoritarismus, Entwicklungsdiktatur: alternative Typologisierungen** ... 59
1. Der Franquismus: eine Militärdiktatur ... 59
2. Der Nationalkatholizismus als Wesen des Franco-Regimes ... 66
3. Franquismus als prototypische Form des Autoritarismus ... 85
4. Die Franco-Ära: ein konservatives Entwicklungsregime ... 92

IV. **Fazit: Der Franquismus – eine chamäleonhafte Diktatur?** ... 109

Bibliographie ... 117

I. Einleitung und Fragestellung

Die Debatte über den Charakter des Franco-Regimes ist so alt wie dieses selbst und hält bis heute an.[1] Die antifranquistischen Kämpfer im Bürgerkrieg (1936–1939) bezeichneten den im ‚nationalen Lager' entstehenden „Neuen Staat" von Anfang an als „faschistisch". Hierfür schienen mehrere Argumente zu sprechen: Zum einen war bekannt, dass Franco von den faschistischen Mächten Deutschland und Italien unterstützt wurde, zum anderen wurde die faschistische Falange-Partei, nach ihrer Vereinigung mit anderen Rechtsorganisationen, zur einzig zugelassenen politischen Organisation im Franco-Lager erklärt; schließlich wurden die Arbeiterbewegung und ihre Interessenvertretungen zerschlagen, eine Gleichschaltung auf vielen Gebieten versucht, der staatliche Terror massiv als Mittel zur Einschüchterung der Zivilbevölkerung eingesetzt. Die zeitgenössische Charakterisierung des Franquismus als „faschistisch" hat den Bürgerkrieg und die ersten Jahre des Regimes überstanden und ist (vor allem von dessen Gegnern) immer wieder – zumeist in politisch-polemischer Absicht – verwendet worden.

Demgegenüber haben sich schon früh weitere Interpretationsrichtungen herausgebildet, die darauf abhoben, dass das Regime spätestens ab 1943 nicht nur von faschistischen Symbolen und Gesten abrückte, sondern sich auch vom politischen System der Achsenmächte distanzierte. Sie verwies darauf, dass die Bezeichnung „totaler Staat" in Spanien nur selten verwendet wurde und die „Einheit von Staat und Gesellschaft" nie mehr als eine Rechtfertigungsfloskel für die „Nationale

1 Von den neueren Titeln zu diesem Thema vgl. Navarro, Vicenc: El subdesarrollo social de España. Barcelona 2006, bes. S. 127–145. Thomàs, Joan Maria: El gran golpe. (El ‚caso Hedilla' o cómo Franco se quedó con Falange.) Barcelona 2014.

Bewegung“ war. Im Vokabular und in der Mentalität eines traditional denkenden Diktators wie Franco kam totalitäres Gedankengut kaum vor. Nach 1945 drängte er, auch wegen der internationalen Ächtung des Regimes, den Einfluss der faschistischen Falange weiter zurück; zugleich verzichtete er darauf, die faschistische Ideologie der Einheitspartei weiter zu entwickeln. Franquismus und Faschismus könnten daher keineswegs gleichgesetzt werden. Die Entwicklung des Regimes, vor allem seit Ende der 1950er Jahre, schien dieser Interpretation recht zu geben. An die Stelle des Faschismus traten als analytische Kategorien zur Interpretation des Franquismus Bezeichnungen wie Nationalkatholizismus, Autoritarismus, Militärdiktatur oder konservatives Entwicklungsregime.

Zu diesen Interpretationsparadigmata gesellten sich im Laufe der Jahre zahlreiche weitere Deutungsansätze.[2] Da bei all diesen Typologisierungsversuchen die durchgehend zu beobachtenden Charakteristika, somit die konstanten Züge des Systems im Mittelpunkt der Analyse stehen, werden die prozesshaft-dynamischen Elemente eher zurückgedrängt. Die primär statische Anlage der Analysen ist allerdings wenig geeignet, Kräfteverschiebungen und Formveränderungen zu erfassen. Während etwa die „faschistische“ Interpretation einzelne Aspekte der Genese und der Frühphase des Regimes betont und die gewonnenen Ergebnisse auf den gesamten Zeitraum der franquistischen Herrschaft überträgt, verfährt die „autoritäre“ Deutung umgekehrt und neigt dazu,

2 Überblicke und verschiedene Konzeptualisierungsansätze enthalten die Sondernummer 8 von Papers. Revista de Sociología (El régimen franquista). Barcelona 1978 und Franz, Hans-Werner: Der Frankismus. Zur politischen Herrschaftssoziologie Spaniens während der Franco-Ära. Frankfurt a. M. 1981, S. 77–129. Vgl. als Überblick auch Prutsch, Ursula: Iberische Diktaturen. Portugal unter Salazar, Spanien unter Franco. Innsbruck 2012.

sämtliche faschistischen Einflüsse zu leugnen. Ein Vergleich der verschiedenen Konzeptualisierungsbemühungen lässt deutlich werden, dass der Entstehungs- und Frühphase des Regimes – somit den ideologischen Prämissen, der Genese im Bürgerkrieg, der prekären Stabilisierung in den 1940er Jahren – für dessen Charakterisierung eine besondere Bedeutung zukommt. Insbesondere gilt dies für die Frage nach den faschistischen Elementen im Franquismus.

Im Folgenden werden verschiedene Ansätze zur Konzeptualisierung des Franquismus vorgestellt und diskutiert. Der erste Versuch der Einordnung in ein System politischer Regime war der Faschismus, der auch in diesem Essay an erster Stelle und zugleich am ausführlichsten debattiert wird, da alle anderen Charakterisierungen in Abgrenzung und Kontrastierung zum Faschismus entstanden sind. Allein die Tatsache, dass die Debatte über den „Charakter" des Franco-Regimes bis heute – also noch Jahrzehnte nach seinem Ende – anhält, lässt die Schwierigkeit erkennen, geeignete Kriterien zu entwickeln, die eine analytisch präzise Verortung dieses aus einem Bürgerkrieg hervorgegangenen und Jahrzehnte währenden Regimes ermöglichen. Auch die folgenden Ausführungen zu anderen Systematisierungs- und Typologisierungsvorschlägen wie Militärdiktatur, Nationalkatholizismus, Autoritarismus und konservatives Entwicklungsregime können und wollen nicht den Anspruch erheben, eine endgültige Antwort auf die Frage nach der Typologie des Franquismus zu geben. Ganz im Gegenteil: Es wird darum gehen, die Reichweite, aber auch die Grenzen bisheriger Typologisierungs- und Verortungsversuche aufzuzeigen und damit zugleich auf die Veränderungen des Regimes, auf seine (relative) Anpassungsfähigkeit hinzuweisen, die es durchaus angebracht erscheinen lässt, den Franquismus mit einem Chamäleon zu vergleichen – ist doch gerade die Anpassungsfähigkeit eines Chamäleons an seine Umwelt eine entscheidende Voraussetzung für sein Überleben.

II. Franquismus als Faschismus

1. Spanischer Faschismus in der Zweiten Republik (1931–1936)

Im Folgenden werden die Vorbedingungen und Entfaltungsmöglichkeiten des spanischen Faschismus in den Jahren der Zweiten Republik dargestellt. Zu Recht ist nämlich darauf hingewiesen worden, dass phänomenologische Aspekte wie die Ideologie und bestimmte Erscheinungsformen oder die angestrebte Struktur des politischen Systems zur Erklärung des Faschismus weniger beitragen als die Analyse der sozialen Bedingungen seiner Entstehung, der Kräfteverhältnisse und der Klassenauseinandersetzungen vor der Institutionalisierung des Regimes.[3]

Lange Zeit ist in der Publizistik und in der Historiographie die Falange als die einzige genuin spanische Form des Faschismus in der Zweiten Republik dargestellt worden. Als der Ausgang des Bürgerkrieges feststand, begann im Lager der Sieger eine Politisierung der Rolle der Falange, die – gröblich verzerrt – als das einzige Bollwerk gegen die ‚roten' Kräfte der Republik idealisiert wurde. Die Niederlage der Achsenmächte im Zweiten Weltkrieg machte zwar eine Uminterpretation der Falange als Verteidigerin des Katholizismus (unter Vernachlässigung ihrer faschistischen Elemente) erforderlich, was Anlass zu nicht wenigen Irritationen unter den „alten Kämpfern" (*camisas viejas*) gab; das sodann offiziell dekretierte Schweigen über die Partei, insbesondere über ihre republikanischen Jahre, ließ aber ohnehin sehr schnell jegliche Diskussion über deren ‚faschistischen' oder ‚revolutionären'

3 Tezanos, José Félix: „Notas para una interpretación sociológica del franquismo". In: Sistema 23, 1978, S. 47–99.

Charakter verstummen. Überzeugte Altfalangisten zogen sich in die innere Emigration oder in erfolglose konspirative Zirkel zurück, und Neufalangisten sahen in der Einheitspartei sowieso nur ein Mittel, einen lukrativen Posten in der aufgeblähten Regierungs- und Verwaltungsbürokratie zu erhalten. Von einigen frühen Pionierstudien abgesehen[4], stagnierte die Forschung über die faschistische Basis des franquistischen Staates. Erst allmählich hat die Geschichtsschreibung eine doppelte Korrektur an dem lange Zeit vorherrschenden Bild anbringen können: Einerseits besteht heute kein Zweifel mehr an der eklatanten Schwäche der Falange, bevor sie zur ‚Staatspartei' des Franco-Regimes wurde; andererseits muss darauf hingewiesen werden, dass die spanische Form des Faschismus sich keineswegs auf die Falange beschränkte. Die Schwäche der später als einzige faschistische Partei dargestellten Falange hängt gerade mit der relativen Bedeutung anderer Frühformen des spanischen Faschismus zusammen.[5]

---

4 Southworth, Herbert: Antifalange. Paris 1967; Payne, Stanley G.: A history of Spanish fascism. Stanford 1961; ders.: El fascismo. Madrid 1982; Nellessen, Bernd: Die verbotene Revolution. Aufstieg und Niedergang der Falange. Hamburg 1963; vgl. auch die Bibliographie in Rees, Philip (Hg.): Fascism and Pre-Fascism in Europe, 1890–1945. A Bibliography of the Extreme Right. Brighton 1984, bes. S. 100–116.

5 Zur Deutung der republikanischen Rechtsgruppen, die im Bürgerkrieg die aufständischen Generäle unterstützten, als zumindest potenziell faschistische Reaktion auf eine Krise der spanischen Gesellschaft, vgl. Preston, Paul: „Spain". In: Woolf, S. J. (Hg.): Fascism in Europe. London 1981, S. 329–351; Preston, Paul: La destrucción de la democracia en España. Madrid 1978; ders.: „Alfonsist Monarchism and the Coming of the Spanish Civil War". In: Journal of Contemporary History 7, 1972, S. 89–114; ders.: „The 'Moderate' Right and the Undermining of the Second

Die erste spanische Rezeption des italienischen Faschismus erfolgte bereits in den 1920er Jahren. Die Diktatur Miguel Primo de Riveras (1923–1930) kann zwar nicht als faschistisches Regime bezeichnet, sondern muss in der aus dem 19. Jahrhundert überkommenen Tradition militärischer *pronunciamientos* gesehen werden; andererseits bewunderte und imitierte Primo de Rivera die faschistische Politik Italiens (und versuchte, seine Einheitspartei *Unión Patriótica* nach dem Vorbild des *Partito Nazionale Fascista* zu gestalten). Die spanische Krise von 1917–1923 konnte vorübergehend und oberflächlich durch die ‚paternalistische' Diktatur Primo de Riveras verdeckt werden, ohne dass faschistische Rezepturen angewandt werden mussten. Der Versuch des Diktators, einen ‚neuen Staat' zu gründen, schlug zwar fehl; er sollte aber in vielerlei Hinsicht für das spätere Franco-Regime richtungsweisend werden.[6]

Im Übergang von der Monarchie zur Republik artikulierte sich der bis dahin primär ‚intellektuelle' Faschismus – deutlich greifbar etwa in der von Ernesto Giménez Caballero 1927 gegründeten Zeitschrift *La Gaceta Literaria*[7] – in der

---

Republic in Spain 1931–1933". In: European Studies Review 3, 1973, S. 369–394; Ben-Ami, Shlomo: „The Forerunners of Spanish Fascism: Unión Patriótica and Unión Monárquica". In: European Studies Review 9, 1979, S. 49–78.

6 Ben-Ami, Shlomo: „The Dictatorship of Primo de Rivera: A Political Reassessment". In: Journal of Contemporary History 12, 1977, S. 65–84; ders.: Fascism from Above: The Dictatorship of Primo de Rivera in Spain, 1923–1930. Oxford 1983; Pastor, M.: Los orígenes del fascismo en España. Madrid 1975.

7 In seinem Buch „Genio de España" (1932) fasste Ernesto Giménez Caballero seine politische Doktrin zusammen; er verdammte den liberalen Staat, betonte die Notwendigkeit eines „Cäsar" für Spanien und forderte „faschistische Katholizität". Vgl. Foard,

Gründung mehrerer Splitterparteien, die jedoch weder über eine geschlossene Ideologie noch über eine erwähnenswerte Anhängerschaft verfügten. Allen faschistischen Splittergruppen jener Jahre war gemein, dass sie weit eher das Produkt einer radikalen ‚Intelligentsia' als die Folge einer nationalen Krise waren. Die kleine Gruppe um Ramiro Ledesma Ramos, die 1931 in Madrid einige Monate lang die Wochenzeitschrift *La Conquista del Estado* herausgab, kann als erste genuin faschistische Organisation – die den Begriff Faschismus zur Selbstidentifizierung allerdings noch vermied – bezeichnet werden.[8] In revolutionär-sozialistischen Formulierungen wandte sich die Gruppe gegen alle politischen Formationen, verurteilte die Monarchie ebenso wie die Republik und warb für eine nationale Revolution zum Aufbau eines „Neuen Staates". Ledesma beschwor zwar das ruhmreiche Spanien der Katholischen Könige – deren Emblem (Joch und Pfeile) er übernahm – und appellierte an die nationale Einheit, kehrte aber nicht zu traditionalistischen Formen und Prinzipien der katholischen Staatsidee zurück; sein Programm war vielmehr von einem dezidiert akatholischen Zug durchdrungen. Die sozioökonomischen Forderungen der Gruppe entsprachen in vielerlei Hinsicht sozialistischen Programmen: Neben die

---

D.W.: Ernesto Giménez Caballero o la revolución del poeta: estudio sobre el nacionalismo cultural hispánico en el siglo XX. Madrid 1975.

8 Zur Gruppe „La Conquista del Estado" um Ledesma Ramos vgl. Sánchez Diana, J. M.: Ramiro Ledesma Ramos: biografía política. Madrid 1975; Moreno Hernández, M.: El nacionalsindicalismo de Ramiro Ledesma Ramos. Madrid 1963; hagiographisch ist Borrás y Bermejo, T.: Ramiro Ledesma Ramos. Madrid 1971; Ledesmas Doktrin ist enthalten in Ledesma Ramos, Ramiro: Fascismo en España? Barcelona 1968 (Erstveröffentlichung 1935).

Enteignung der Grundbesitzer trat die Verstaatlichung der Schlüsselindustrien, der Banken, der Versicherungsgesellschaften und des Transportwesens, Staatskontrolle über den Außenhandel und Abwehr ausländischer Einflüsse. Ledesmas Positionen waren antibürgerlich und radikal, antichristlich und materialistisch; seine Vorbilder waren Hitler und Mussolini, seine Adressaten – neben der Mittelschichtintelligentsia – die städtischen Arbeiter.

Ganz anders verhielt es sich mit der zweiten Splittergruppe, die ein offen faschistisches Programm verfocht: dem Valladolider Kreis um Onésimo Redondo und die Wochenzeitung *Libertad*. Diese Gruppierung rief zwar ebenfalls zum Kampf um ein einiges, großes und freies Spanien auf – ihr später von der Falange übernommener Wahlspruch lautete: *España una, grande, libre* –, erstrebte auch die Wiederherstellung der imperialen Würde Spaniens; im Gegensatz zu der Ledesma-Gruppe ging Redondo jedoch von der Identität katholischen und nationalen Wollens aus. Die Verurteilung des liberalen Systems, die Forderung nach imperialer und sozialer Würde, der Protest gegen die Zerrissenheit des Vaterlandes, die unklaren sozioökonomischen Programmpunkte hatten lediglich einen gemeinsamen Nenner: den entschiedenen Katholizismus des kirchentreuen Juristen Redondo, dessen *Juntas Castellanas de Actuación Hispánica* nie über ein romantisch verbrämtes Kellerdasein hinauskamen.[9]

Angesichts der krisenhaft stagnierenden Entwicklung beider Gruppen kamen Ledesma und Redondo im Spätsommer 1931 überein, ihre beiden Organisationen zu den *Juntas*

---

9 Zur Redondo-Gruppe vgl. Nellessen: Verbotene Revolution, S. 54–57; Redondo y Ortega, Onésimo: Onésimo Redondo: textos políticos. Madrid 1975; ders.: Obras completas: edición cronológica. 2 Bde. Madrid 1955.

de Ofensiva Nacional Sindicalista (JONS) zusammenzuschließen. In der neuen Gruppierung war der urbane Materialismus Ledesmas mit dem kämpferischen Katholizismus Redondos vereinigt. Im Wesentlichen bestand die JONS-Programmatik aus fünf Punkten: Einheit Spaniens, Respekt vor der religiösen Tradition, Appell an die Jugend, Antimarxismus, sozioökonomische Revolution (mittels Zwangssyndikalisierung, öffentlicher Kontrolle des Reichtums und „Erhebung der Arbeiter in ihre Würde"). Nationales Emblem der JONS wurden Joch und Pfeile auf der (ursprünglich anarchosyndikalistischen) schwarz-roten Fahne. Der Verbalradikalismus des JONS-Programms verschaffte der Organisation einige wenige Anhänger unter kommunistischen und anarchosyndikalistischen Dissidenten, die in der Verwerfung des bestehenden Staates und dem Mittel der direkten Aktion übereinstimmten. Insgesamt blieb die JONS jedoch eine quantitativ unbedeutende Gruppe. Ende 1933 soll sie nicht mehr als 200 eingeschriebene Mitglieder gehabt haben, die sich primär aus Studenten, städtischen Angestellten im Dienstleistungssektor, einigen Tagelöhnern und Kleinbauern in agrarischen Gegenden rekrutierten. Formal bestand die JONS zwar landesweit, faktisch jedoch konzentrierten sich ihre Aktivitäten auf Madrid, Valladolid, Galicien und Valencia.[10] Ihr verschwommenes Programm ermöglichte die oberflächliche Integration zweier (sich eigentlich ausschließender) Flügel, eines proletarisch-achristlichen und eines ländlich-katholischen, unter dem gemeinsamen Zielbanner eines nationalen und imperialen Spanien.

---

10 Ellwood, Sheelagh: Prietas las filas. Historia de Falange Española, 1933–1983. Barcelona 1984, S. 33; vgl. auch die Anthologie von JONS-Artikeln: JONS, antología y prólogo de Juan Aparicio. Barcelona 1939.

Die dritte in jenen Jahren entstandene faschistische Splittergruppe war die von José Antonio Primo de Rivera, dem ältesten Sohn des früheren Diktators, Ende Oktober 1933 gegründete *Falange Española* (FE). Es ist oft darauf hingewiesen worden, dass die neue Partei mit dem Ausdruck poetischer Romantik junger Literaten sprach, die aus universitär-intellektueller Perspektive eine Lösung für die Probleme des zerrissenen Spanien zu präsentieren vorgaben. José Antonio selbst betonte immer wieder, die Falange sei ein *movimiento intelectual*, eine *obra de intelectuales*. Der „poetische" Charakter, den die FE in der Öffentlichkeit erweckte, trug nicht unerheblich zur Verharmlosung dieser Bewegung in den Medien bei; weitgehend unbeachtet blieb die bereits auf der Gründungsversammlung vorgetragene Forderung, die politischen Parteien als „unnatürliche" Elemente im Organismus des Staates abzuschaffen, den alten Nationalismus der 1920er Jahre durch einen neuen, aggressiv-revolutionären zu ersetzen, den Einsatz von Gewalt nicht zu scheuen.[11]

Die Falange war anfangs deutlich um die Vermeidung des Eindruckes bemüht, es gehe ihr nur um die Errichtung einer spanischen Variante des italienischen Faschismus. Sie war viel zu sehr an konservativen und ‚nationalen' Wählerschichten interessiert, als dass sie sich allzu deutlich mit einer

---

11 Primo de Rivera, José Antonio: "Discurso de la Fundación de Falange Española. Teatro de la Comedia, Madrid 29-X-1933". In: Ders.: Escritos y discursos. Obras completas. Bd. 1. Madrid 1976, S. 193–194. Hierzu Pérez-Ramos, Bárbara: Intelligenz und Politik im Spanischen Bürgerkrieg 1936–1939. Bonn 1982, S. 26–30. Zu José Antonio vgl. den umfangreichen bibliographischen Überblick von Alvarez Gutiérrez, Luis: „Ensayo bibliográfico sobre José Antonio Primo de Rivera". In: Palacio Atard, Vicente (Hg.): Estudios de Historia contemporánea. Bd. 1. Madrid 1976, S. 441–495.

ausländischen und revolutionären Bewegung identifizieren konnte. Die Selbstbezeichnung „Faschismus“ wurde daher vorerst vermieden, und die Einsetzung eines Triumvirats als Leitungsorgan der neuen Partei schien allen Führerkulttendenzen zu widersprechen. Zu den Charakteristika der frühen Falange zählten das nostalgische Bestreben, die ehemalige Größe Spaniens wiederzuerlangen, der gegen separatistische Tendenzen und ausländischen „Kolonialismus“ auf spanischem Boden (Gibraltar) orientierte Nationalismus, ein nicht klar definierter Imperialismus,[12] der Katholizismus als traditionelle spanische Religion und eine grenzenlose Bewunderung militärischer Werte.[13] Antisemitismus und eine Rassenideologie fehlten ebenso wie explizit formulierte außenpolitische Zielforderungen. Stattdessen beschwor die Falange den diffusen Gedanken der *hispanidad* und der Errichtung eines starken Staates nach dem Vorbild des Habsburgerreichs. Zu den ‚linken‘ Programmpunkten zählten die Forderung nach Einschränkung des ausländischen wirtschaftlichen

---

12 Imperialistische Expansion zur Ablenkung des revolutionären Elans der spanischen „Massen“ nach außen ist für Southworth das Distinktivum des spanischen Faschismus von anderen politischen Rechtsgruppierungen. Southworth, Herbert.R.: "The Falange: An Analysis of Spain’s Fascist Heritage". In: Preston, Paul (Hg.): Spain in Crisis. The Evolution and Decline of the Franco Régime. Hassocks 1976, S. 1–22.

13 Zum Falangeprogramm vgl. Nellessen, Payne, Ellwood; zusammengefasst bei Bernecker, Walther L.: „Spanien“. In: Wende, Frank (Hg.): Lexikon zur Geschichte der Parteien in Europa. Stuttgart 1981, S. 647–649; die deutsche Fassung des falangistischen Wirtschafts- und Sozialprogramms in Bernecker, Walther L. (Hg.): Gewerkschaftsbewegung und Staatssyndikalismus in Spanien. Quellen und Materialien zu den Arbeitsbeziehungen 1936–1980. Frankfurt a.M. 1985, S. 35–38.

Einflusses, die Errichtung von Wirtschaftssyndikaten nach dem Vorbild des italienisch-korporativen Systems, die Enteignung von Großbetrieben und des nicht genutzten Großgrundbesitzes. José Antonios Ziel bestand darin, den Versuch seines Vaters zu vollenden, Spanien zu „regenerieren“. Ein radikal-integrativer nationalistischer Autoritarismus sollte das parlamentarische System ersetzen und sozioökonomische Interessen koordinieren.

Die Falange appellierte anfangs an Studenten, die sich vom Radikalismus angezogen, vom gleichzeitigen Internationalismus der Linken aber abgestoßen fühlten; sie versuchte, die alfonsinischen Monarchisten zu integrieren; außerdem wandte sie sich an die konservativen Kräfte, die weder von den Karlisten noch von den übrigen Rechtsparteien erfasst worden waren; schließlich gehörten auch frühere Anhänger der *Unión Patriótica* der Diktaturepoche zu ihren Adressaten. Insgesamt setzte sich die falangistische Klientel aus Mittelschichtangehörigen zusammen, die die Oberschicht bewunderten und nachahmten. José Antonio selbst und einige weitere Falangisten entstammten der Oberschicht, zu der sich der Falangegründer auch ausdrücklich bekannte („Ja, wir tragen Krawatten, und man kann von uns ruhig sagen, wir seien *señoritos.*“). Vor allem bei den Studenten kam ein weiterer Motivationsfaktor hinzu: eine Art Rebellion gegen die konservativ-reaktionären Lösungsvorschläge ihrer Vätergeneration. Die Falange präsentierte sich diesen Jugendlichen als Möglichkeit zur Artikulation von Opposition gegenüber dem Status quo, ohne ‚links‘ sein zu müssen.

Ebenso wie die JONS blieb auch die Falange eine unbedeutende Splittergruppe. Vor 1936 konnte sie keine nennenswerte Gefolgschaft mobilisieren. Vergleicht man die Wahlergebnisse Spaniens mit denen anderer Länder, in denen das parlamentarische System noch einigermaßen intakt funktionierte, so wird deutlich, dass die faschistische Wählerbasis nicht nur in absoluten Zahlen minimal war, sondern im europäischen Vergleich auch das Schlusslicht bildete. In den letzten Wahlen vor dem Bürgerkrieg (Februar 1936) erhielt die Falange 44.000 Stimmen, d. h. verschwindende 0,7 % der Wähler entschieden sich für sie. In allen anderen bedeutenden europäischen Staaten, die eine Partei faschistischen Typs hatten, erhielt diese unter politischen Wettbewerbsbedingungen mehr Stimmen.[14]

Da sowohl die Entwicklung der Falange als auch die der JONS stagnierte, erfolgte am 13. Februar 1934 der Zusammenschluss beider Organisationen zur *Falange Española de las Juntas de Ofensiva Nacional Sindicalista* (FE de las JONS). Dieser bereits wenige Monate nach der Falangegründung erfolgte Zusammenschluss stellt das erste Beispiel der Unfähigkeit der Falange dar, sich als eigenständige und effiziente politische Kraft zu konstituieren, ohne taktische und strategische Allianzen mit anderen Kräften einzugehen.[15] Die gesamte Falangegeschichte war eine Aufeinanderfolge von Allianzen und Kompromissen mit dem Ziel, ein Überleben der Bewegung zu ermöglichen. Der Zusammenschluss mit den JONS schien der Falange nur Vorteile zu bringen: Sie verzichtete auf keines ihrer Grunddogmen, konnte sich aber andererseits die organisatorische Überlegenheit der JONS zunutze machen.[16]

---

14 Payne, Stanley G.: „Spanish Fascism in Comparative Perspective". In: Turner, Henry A. (Hg.): Reappraisals of Fascism. New York 1975, S. 147.

15 Hierauf weisen nachdrücklich Ellwood: Prietas las filas, S. 21 und Payne: Spanish Fascism hin.

16 Vorest wurden durch den Zusammenschluss von JONS und Falange viele zuvor weit radikalere JONS- Programmpunkte abgeschwächt. Ledesma Ramos etwa hatte die Enteignung des gesamten Großgrundbesitzes gefordert; als er mit seinem Postulat nicht durchdringen konnte, verließ er die Partei. Syndika-

Hatte die Falange im Oktober 1933, bei ihrer Gründung, die Affinitäten zum Faschismus noch verdeckt, so legte der Zusammenschluss mit den JONS, die aus ihrer Bewunderung für Hitler und Mussolini nie einen Hehl gemacht hatten, die faschistischen Tendenzen vollends offen. Auch Primo de Rivera bekannte nun öffentlich, den italienischen Faschismus zu imitieren; in der Falange sah er ein Instrument, ihn in Spanien zu verankern.

Die Fusion von Falange und JONS sollte allerdings auch die ersten Probleme aufwerfen, da FE de las JONS ein Amalgam darstellte, in dem verschiedene ideologische Richtungen zusammengefasst waren: die Ledesma-Gruppe *La Conquista del Estado* mit ihrer Position einer „Revolution gegen die Bourgeoisie"; die Redondo-Gruppe um die *Juntas Castellanas de Actuación Hispánica* mit ihrem Konzept der „Revolution ohne die Bourgeoisie"; schließlich *Falange Española* mit dem Ziel einer „Revolution der Bourgeoisie". Diese verschiedenen Faschismusvarianten sollten nie zu einer derartigen Homogenität verschmelzen, dass FE de las JONS eine eindeutige ideologische Position vertreten hätte.

Das Jahr 1934 erlebte nicht nur die Fusion von FE und JONS, sondern sechs Monate später auch das erste Bündnis der neuen Organisation. Primo de Rivera schloss mit den alfonsinischen Monarchisten der *Renovación Española* eine Allianz, in der die grundsätzliche politische Übereinstimmung der beiden Organisationen hervorgehoben wurde. Die Allianz lässt deutlich werden, dass Primo de Rivera bereit war, das materielle und politische Überleben seiner Partei auch auf Kosten ihrer ideologischen Unabhängigkeit und Reinheit zu sichern. Während nämlich der Zusammenschluss von Fa-

---

listische Forderungen wurden abgeschwächt, die ursprünglich antiklerikalen Programmpunkte der JONS gestrichen.

lange und JONS noch auf der Grundlage übereinstimmender ideologischer Charakteristika erfolgen konnte, war das Abkommen mit der *Renovación Española* völlig anders geartet. Beide Organisationen stimmten zwar in politischen Grundüberzeugungen wie Antimarxismus, Antirepublikanismus, Patriotismus und Religion überein. Die Restauration der Monarchie war aber unvereinbar mit dem nationalsyndikalistischen Staat, wie ihn etwa Ledesma Ramos erstrebt hatte. Gegen eine finanzielle Monatsunterstützung „verkaufte" José Antonio die Falange; sein Hauptziel blieb das Überleben der Partei, in allen anderen Fragen war er zu Kompromissen bereit.

Die Anpassungstendenzen durchziehen die weitere Geschichte der Falange: 1934 stellte sie sich ungebeten den Staatsorganen zur Verfügung, um den Oktober-Aufstand in Asturien und Katalonien zu unterdrücken; 1935/36 akzeptierte sie finanzielle Unterstützung des faschistischen Italien[17]; 1936 scheiterte die Bildung eines Wahlbündnisses von Falange und anderen Rechtsparteien nur knapp. Trotz aller Bemühungen blieben die vereinigten faschistischen Parteien bis 1936 politisch jedoch einflusslos. Um das Scheitern des Faschismus in der Zweiten Republik erklären zu können, müssen jene ‚Vorbedingungen' genauer betrachtet werden, die in anderen europäischen Ländern faschistische Massenbewegungen ermöglicht haben. Bei der Erforschung faschistischer Bewegungen haben sich die Fragen nach den Voraussetzungen und Vorbedingungen, der sozialen Basis,

---

17 Coverdale, John F.: Italian Intervention in the Spanish Civil War. Princeton 1975, S. 31–65; hierzu auch Viñas, Angel: La Alemania nazi y el 18 de julio. Madrid 1977. Neuerdings Rodrigo, Javier: La guerra fascista: Italia en la Guerra Civil Española, 1936–1939. Madrid 2016.

der sozialen Funktion und dem Telos der einzelnen faschistischen Bewegungen als relevant erwiesen.[18] Da jedoch alle faschistischen Organisationen Spaniens unter parlamentarischen Wettbewerbsbedingungen gewissermaßen im Anfangsstadium verblieben, sodass sie kaum als Bündnispartner oder gar ‚Agenten' einflussreicher Gruppierungen (konservative Kräfte, ‚Kapitalisten') betrachtet werden können, erübrigt sich weitgehend die Frage nach der sozialen Funktion des spanischen Faschismus.[19] Bei einer Untersuchung der fehlenden ‚Vorbedingungen' stößt man im Wesentlichen auf vier Gründe, die den mangelnden Erfolg des Faschismus in Spanien erklären.[20]

---

18 Thamer, Hans-Ulrich/Wippermann, Wolfgang: Faschistische und neofaschistische Bewegungen. Probleme empirischer Faschismusforschung. Darmstadt 1977, S. 1.

19 Über die soziale Zusammensetzung der Falange-Mitgliedschaft in jenen Jahren ist wenig bekannt. Von den 1.100 Mitgliedern der Madrider Organisation zu Beginn des Jahres 1936 waren rund 50 % Arbeiter; dieser auf den ersten Blick erstaunlich hohe Prozentsatz wird allerdings schnell durch den Hinweis auf die absolute Mitgliederzahl relativiert: Die etwas über 500 Madrider Arbeiter, die der Falange beigetreten waren, stellten unter den mehreren hunderttausend Arbeitern der Hauptstadt eine verschwindende Minorität dar. Hierzu Payne, Stanley G.: „Social Composition and Regional Strength of The Spanish Falange". In: Ugelvik Larsen, S. (Hg. u. a.): Who were the Fascists. Social Roots of European Fascism. Bergen 1980, S. 423–434.

20 Luis Araquistáin, einer der intellektuell führenden Marxisten in der Sozialistischen Partei (PSOE), hatte 1934 bereits die Aspekte hervorgehoben, weshalb eine faschistische Bewegung in Spanien wenige Entfaltungsmöglichkeiten vorfand. Seine zeitgenössische Beobachtung hat bis heute ihre Gültigkeit nicht verloren: „In Spain there can be no fascism of the Italian or German type. There are no demobilized men, as there were in Italy; there are

Zum Ersten ist auf das Fehlen einer nationalen Identitätskrise zu verweisen, was auf den unterschiedlichen Verlauf der spanischen (im Vergleich zur deutschen und italienischen) Nationalgeschichte zurückzuführen ist. Stanley Payne hat hervorgehoben[21], dass in Spanien kaum jene „präfaschistische Kultur“ anzutreffen war, die sich in Italien aus dem Radikalnationalismus der *Associazione Nazionalista Italiana*, aus irredentistischen und kolonialistischen Elementen, aus den unter Literaten, Philosophen und Politikern vorherrschenden neoidealistischen Doktrinen und Irrationalismen, schließlich aus der Verunglimpfung des Parlamentarismus durch herausragende Vertreter der Intelligentsia speiste. Demgegenüber gelang es in Spanien dem *regeneracionismo* zu Beginn des 20. Jahrhunderts nicht, eine moderne Form des Nationalismus zu schaffen, was offensichtlich damit zusammenhing, dass Spanien weder am Ersten Weltkrieg teilnahm noch ein Irredentaproblem hatte; außerdem wurde die Modernisierungsdiskussion von einem Klima des Kulturpessimismus beherrscht, der der Entwicklung eines aggressiven Nationalismus ebenfalls abträglich war. Da Spanien nicht am Ersten Weltkrieg teilnahm, gab es auch keine ehemaligen Frontsoldaten, die – wie in Deutschland und Italien – durch das Kriegsende in eine materielle und psychische Existenzkrise gestürzt wurden und als Folge sozialer Entwurzelung

---

no hundreds of thousands of young university men with no future, nor millions of unemployed, as in Germany. There is no Mussolini, nor even a Hitler; there are no imperialist ambitions nor sentiments of revenge, no problems of expansion, nor even a bad Jewish problem. Out of what could Spanish fascism be concocted? I cannot imagine the recipe.” Araquistáin, Luis: „The Struggle in Spain”. In: Foreign Affairs 3, 1934, S. 458–471, Zitat S. 470.

21 Zum folgenden Payne: Spanish Fascism.

bzw. nationaler Frustration den paramilitärischen Organisationen zuliefen. Schließlich waren in Spanien – im Gegensatz wieder zu Italien – die Gegenden, in denen sich eine nationale Identität entwickelte, die peripheren Regionen des Landes, insbesondere Katalonien, während das politische Zentrum Kastilien weder von der Sozial- noch von der Wirtschaftsstruktur her einen dynamisch-modernisierenden Nationalismus hervorbringen konnte. Die Reaktion auf den zentrifugalen Nationalismus der Peripherie nahm sodann weit eher die Form des politischen Antikatalanismus als die eines gesamtspanischen Nationalismus an. Trotz dieses Befundes muss andererseits darauf hingewiesen werden, dass der Schock der Niederlage von 1898 im Krieg gegen die USA und der Verlust der letzten überseeischen Kolonien weitreichende Folgen hatte: Nostalgie nach einem Imperium war allen spanischen Rechtsgruppen in den 1930er Jahren gemein.[22]

Zum Zweiten ist auf eine bedeutende Rechte hinzuweisen, die hinsichtlich des Autoritarismus, des Nationalismus und der Opposition gegen Liberalismus und Kommunismus eine politische Alternative zu den faschistischen Parteien darstellte. Wirtschaftspolitisch trat diese Zwischenkriegs-Rechte für ein korporatives System ein, das jedoch primär der Stärkung der bestehenden sozialen Kräfteverhältnisse dienen sollte; die sozialrevolutionären Programmpunkte der faschistischen Nationalsyndikalisten lehnte sie ab. Derartige Bewegungen der ‚neuen' Rechten gab es in der Zwischenkriegszeit in nahezu allen europäischen Staaten; sie waren aber in den sozial und ökonomisch relativ zurückgebliebenen Ländern Süd- und

22 Vgl. Harrison, John: „The Regenerationist Movement in Spain after the Disaster of 1898". In: European Studies Review 9, 1979, S. 1–27. Vgl. auch Preston: Spain.

Osteuropas besonders stark, in denen die überkommenen sozialen Sektoren und Eliten größeren Einfluss behalten hatten und die radikalen sozialen Kräfte weniger entwickelt waren. Das Paradoxe an der politischen ‚Alternative von rechts' bestand darin, dass sie in der Zweiten Republik keineswegs als Konkurrenz zu den faschistischen Parteien betrachtet wurde. Im Gegenteil: Was sich in historischer Perspektive als Alternative präsentiert, wurde von Zeitgenossen als spanischer Faschismus betrachtet. Primär ist hierunter eine Reihe autoritärer Rechtsparteien zu verstehen, die José María Gil Robles 1933 in der *Confederación Española de Derechas Autónomas* (CEDA) zusammenfasste. Diese betrieb sofort nach ihrer Gründung eine extrem antisozialistische Agitation und stellte das faschistische Regime Mussolinis in vielerlei Hinsicht als Vorbild für Spanien hin. In ihrem Programm, ihrer Wählerbasis und ihrer politischen Haltung ist die CEDA der Christlichsozialen Partei Österreichs vergleichbar.

Im Wahlkampf von 1933 gab Gil Robles Anlass genug, ihn mit faschistischen Bestrebungen zu identifizieren: er zeigte unverhohlen Sympathien für die ausländischen faschistischen Bewegungen,[23] setzte die Massenmedien – dem Hitlerschen Beispiel folgend – manipulativ ein, ließ auf die Landbevölkerung vielerlei wirtschaftliche und ideo-

---

23 Preston hat in seinen Arbeiten über die Zweite Republik deutlich hervorgehoben, wie Stil und Ziel der legalistischen Rechten mit der Existenz der Republik unvereinbar waren. Das historische Urteil über die CEDA ist widersprüchlich. Äußerst kritisch interpretieren ihre Rolle Preston: La destrucción de la democracia, und Montero, José R.: La CEDA: el catolicismo social y político en la II República. 2 Bde. Madrid 1977. Eine freundliche Deutung, unter Betonung der christlichsozialen Rhetorik der CEDA, enthält Robinson, Richard A. H.: The Origins of Franco's Spain. Newton Abbot 1970.

logische Aggressionen ausüben, agitierte offen gegen das demokratisch-republikanische System, bezeichnete die Demokratie als Mittel zur Eroberung eines neuen korporativen Staates. Zuerst koalierte er mit den Monarchisten, in der zweiten Wahlrunde mit den Radikalrepublikanern. Der Wahlsieg der Rechten – die CEDA wurde stärkste Partei – erschien vielen Sozialisten als erster Schritt auf dem Weg zur Errichtung eines autoritär-korporativen Staates.[24] Als die Radikalrepublikaner die Regierung bildeten und parlamentarisch von der CEDA abhängig waren, konnte Gil Robles ihnen politische Bedingungen diktieren und, für den Fall ihrer Nicht-Erfüllung, mit Verlagerung seiner Aktionen auf „ein anderes als das parlamentarische" Gebiet drohen.[25] Der Bezug zur gleichzeitigen Unterdrückung der sozialistischen Bewegung in Österreich war unüberhörbar; Italien und Deutschland wurden als Vorbilder zur Beendigung der ‚Unordnung' dargestellt. Gil Robles ließ sich in Massenveranstaltungen der *Juventud de Acción Popular* (JAP), der Jugendorganisation seiner Partei, als „oberster Führer" feiern und lauthals *Jefe! Jefe! Jefe!* – das Äquivalent zu *Duce* oder Führer – skandieren. Lokalpolitiker der CEDA verkündeten, die „Massen" von *Acción Popular*, der wichtigsten Einzel-

---

24 Eine besondere Rolle spielte in diesem Zusammenhang die 1934 von Luis Araquistáin gegründete Zeitschrift *Leviatán*, die sich schnell zum wichtigsten theoretischen Organ des linken PSOE-Flügels entwickelte und sich vorest nahezu ausschließlich mit der „faschistischen Bedrohung" befasste. Hierzu Preston, Paul: „La lucha contra el fascismo en España: ‚Leviatán' y las contradicciones de la izquierda socialista, 1934–1936". In: Sistema 34, 1980, S. 71–89.

25 Gil Robles, José María: Discursos parlamentarios. Madrid 1971, S. 297–300; vgl. auch ders.: No fue posible la paz. Barcelona 1968.

partei des Rechtsbündnisses, würden die Macht erobern, um die Errettung Spaniens vorzubereiten; der Eintritt von drei CEDA-Ministern in die Regierung schließlich (1934) wurde von der Linken als der letzte Vorbereitungsschritt zur Errichtung eines faschistischen Regimes gedeutet.[26] Der asturische Oktoberaufstand gegen die Rechtsregierung wurde von der defensiven Überzeugung der Arbeiter getragen, sie kämpften als einzige Proletarier in Europa gegen den Faschismus.

In den Jahren der Zweiten Republik akzeptierte die Rechte den parlamentarischen Legalismus primär als Mittel zur Machterringung; ihr Ziel war jedoch die Überwindung des republikanischen Parlamentarismus und die Ersetzung des demokratischen Systems durch ein korporatives. Ihr Auftreten (uniformierte Jugendorganisation, Aufmärsche, ‚halbfaschistischer' Armgruß), der Führerkult und die ständestaatliche Programmatik ließen die CEDA in den Augen der Linken als die ‚faschistische Gefahr' schlechthin erscheinen. Nicht die völlig unbedeutende Falange galt als spanische Form des Faschismus, sondern die Partei von Gil Robles.[27] Aus heutiger Sicht wird die CEDA kaum als faschistische Partei bezeichnet werden können, wenn sie auch phänomenologisch und strukturell viele Affinitäten zum Typus faschistischer Parteien aufwies. In der sich zusehends polarisierenden innenpoliti-

---

26 Die Beispiele des CEDA-Auftretens nach Preston, Paul: „La Revolución de Octubre en España: La lucha de las derechas por el poder". In: Sistema 14, 1976, S. 95–115.

27 Artikel in dem konservativ-katholischen Sprachrohr *El Debate* rechtfertigten die legalistische Taktik der Rechten unter Hinweis auf den Erfolg, den Hitler mit ihr hatte; Leitartikel priesen den Antikommunismus von Dollfuß, Hitler und Mussolini; vor allem aber plädierte die Zeitung für die Übernahme eines korporativen Staates, der nach dem portugiesischen und österreichischen Vorbild aufgebaut sein sollte.

schen Situation der Krisenjahre der Zweiten Republik galt das Etikett „faschistisch“ auch weniger zur analytischen Identifizierung einer Partei als vielmehr zur kämpferisch-plakativen Benennung des Gegners. Das Hauptproblem der Falange zwischen 1933 und 1935 bestand darin, sich selbst als effiziente und genuin spanische Form eines radikalintegralen Nationalismus zu präsentieren und zugleich eine Massenbasis zu erhalten; beide Versuche scheiterten, letzterer auch deshalb, weil die CEDA – in geringem Umfang auch die monarchistischen Gruppen der Karlisten und Alfonsiner – sozial den Raum des rechten Mittelschichtenradikalismus okkupierte, den eine faschistische Bewegung zur Rekrutierung einer größeren Anhängerschaft benötigt hätte. Die radikaleren antiklerikalen Mittelschichten wiederum lehnten die nationalistischen Punkte des Falangeprogramms ab und bekannten sich nachdrücklich zu einem säkularisierten Republikanismus. Die *latecomer*-Bewegungen JONS und Falange fanden daher ihr natürliches Reservoir weitgehend ausgeschöpft. Hinzu kam, dass aufgrund der Existenz einer radikalen Rechten zumindest bis Februar 1936 keine Notwendigkeit bestand, auf die von der Falange propagierten antiparlamentarischen Methoden zu rekurrieren. Außerdem wandten sich Kräfte der traditionellen Rechten in dem Maße wieder von der faschistischen FE de las JONS ab, in dem die Republik unter CEDA-Einfluss ohnehin nach rechts abdriftete. Die syndikalistischen Forderungen der Falange und die Anklänge in ihrem Parteiprogramm an das Prinzip sozialer Gerechtigkeit trugen sicherlich ebenfalls zur faschistischen „Ausblutung“ bei.[28]

28 Anfang 1935 erfolgte eine weitere Schwächung der Falange, als Ledesma Ramos wieder aus der gemeinsamen Partei austrat.

Auch eine dritte ‚Vorbedingung' für die Entstehung einer faschistischen Massenbewegung fehlte in Spanien: eine starke, organisierte Linke, gegen die sich der Faschismus hätte formieren können. Wiewohl in seiner ordnungspolitischen Theorie antikapitalistisch und antisozialistisch eingestellt, beschränkte sich der Faschismus in der praktischen Politik auf die antisozialistische Frontstellung. Faschistische Bewegungen erschienen dem beunruhigten (Klein-) Bürgertum als Rettung vor der „bolschewistischen Gefahr". Im spanischen Fall nun konnte die Massenbewegung des Anarchismus und Anarchosyndikalismus mit seiner antipolitischen und antiparlamentarischen Ausrichtung die Rolle des zu bekämpfenden innenpolitischen Feindes nicht spielen. Und die parlamentarische Linke, insbesondere die Sozialisten, waren untereinander so zersplittert, dass sie nicht als Gefahr für Staat und bürgerliche Gesellschaft erschienen. Die antimarxistische Motivation zur Herausbildung einer starken faschistischen Bewegung fehlte daher in Spanien.[29] Auf die Bedeutung einer mächtigen Linken für das Anwachsen einer faschistischen Partei zu einer Massenorganisation verweist ansatzweise die Entwicklung im ersten Halbjahr 1936: Nach dem Sieg der Volksfront, als die Gefahr revolutionärer Strukturveränderungen für die herrschenden Schichten greifbare Realität geworden war, stieg die Mitgliederzahl der jahrelang stagnierenden Falange steil (auf angeblich mindestens 10.000) an, konnte politisch jedoch nicht mehr zu Buche schlagen, da sie im März 1936 bereits verboten wurde. Die Falange wurde

29 Zur Stärke und Organisation der Linken in der Zweiten Republik vgl. Bernecker, Walther L.: Anarchismus und Bürgerkrieg. Zur Geschichte der Sozialen Revolution in Spanien 1936–1939. Hamburg 1978, S. 20–26 (2., mit einer neuen Einleitung versehene Auflage. Nettersheim 2006).

dadurch in terroristische Aktivitäten und konspirative Tätigkeiten abgedrängt, anstatt zu einer machtvollen politischen Massenbewegung zu werden. Bis zu den Volksfrontwahlen wurde für die Interessen und Befürchtungen der Mittel- und Oberschichten somit die „demokratische Lösung“ anvisiert; und als sich danach die Überzeugung breitmachte, dass besagte Interessen nur durch eine bewaffnete und antidemokratische Intervention verteidigt werden könnten, ergab sich wie selbstverständlich der Rekurs auf die Armee.

Schließlich müssen Stärke bzw. Schwäche des Faschismus mit dem Stand der kapitalistischen Industrieentwicklung und der Krise des kapitalistischen Systems in Beziehung gesetzt werden. Die ‚klassischen' Faschismusausprägungen in Italien und Deutschland stellten je spezifische Antworten auf ‚nationale' Krisen dar. Es herrscht Übereinstimmung darüber, dass jeder ‚nationale' Faschismus in seiner Beziehung zu dem entsprechenden Kapitalismus, aus dem er hervorging, analysiert werden muss, dass primär nationale Besonderheiten der sozialen und wirtschaftlichen Nachkriegs- und Weltwirtschaftskrise Berücksichtigung finden müssen. In den 1930er Jahren war der sozioökonomische Entwicklungsstand Spaniens bei weitem noch nicht dem mitteleuropäischer Staaten vergleichbar; der spanische Kapitalismus war überwiegend Agrarkapitalismus. Die politische Stärke der traditionellen Oligarchien hatte zur Folge, dass der Faschisierungsprozess der Mittelschichten im europäischen Vergleich später und weniger durchgreifend erfolgte.[30] Der regionale und wenig entwickelte Charakter der spanischen Industrialisierung hatte bereits früher bewirkt, dass die Industriebourgeoisie und das Kleinbürgertum zur Realisierung ihrer politischen Vor-

30 Die folgende Argumentation im Wesentlichen nach Tezanos: Notas.

stellungen auf wechselnde Allianzen zurückgreifen mussten. Teilweise verbündeten sie sich mit den traditionellen Führungseliten (charakteristisch etwa für die Restaurationsära), teilweise mit der regional konzentrierten, in Gewerkschaften organisierten und politisierten Arbeiterschaft (beispielsweise im Übergang zur Zweiten Republik). Im Unterschied zu Italien und Deutschland wurde Spanien sodann, aufgrund seiner geringeren Verflechtung mit der Weltwirtschaft und seiner wenig entwickelten Industrialisierung, erst spät von der allgemeinen Wirtschaftskrise erfasst. Diese Phasenverschiebung trägt auch zur Erklärung des zeitverschobenen Aufschwungs des Faschismus bei, wobei sich in der historischen Forschung immer mehr die Erkenntnis durchgesetzt hat, dass neben die endogenen Strukturprobleme als Bedingungsfaktoren des Bürgerkrieges auch die Folgeerscheinungen der Weltwirtschaftskrise zu setzen sind. „Als die Folgewirkungen der Depression auf die strukturellen Schwierigkeiten und Reformen stießen, mit denen sich das neue demokratische Regime von 1931 auseinanderzusetzen hatte, wurde die Situation so schwierig, dass man zu dem Schluss kommen muss, dass die Wirtschaftskrise indirekt den liberalen Versuch der Zweiten Republik in Spanien unrealisierbar werden ließ.“[31]

Da in Spanien keine eindeutige hegemoniale gesellschaftliche Gruppe vorhanden war, andererseits der Faschismus – aus den oben angeführten Gründen – ‚unterentwickelt‘ war, ergriff das Militär, auf Drängen der traditionellen Eliten hin, die Initiative zur Lösung *manu militari* einer sich zusehends polarisierenden Konfliktsituation. Das Frühjahr 1936 erlebte im Grunde genommen zwei zeitlich zusammenfallende Aufstandsbewegungen unterschiedlichen Typs: Während

31 Balcells, Albert: Crisis económica y agitación social en Cataluña (1930–1936). Barcelona 1971, S. 71.

die verunsicherten Mittelschichten eher eine faschistische Lösung der Krisensituation anvisierten, kamen die um ihre sozioökonomischen Interessen bangenden Oberschichten nach dem Sieg der Volksfront zu der Überzeugung, dass die Armee ihren Zwecken besser und unverzüglicher helfen konnte als eine faschistische Bewegung.[32] Sie erstrebten, unter Führung des Militärs und mit Unterstützung der Kirche, einen konterrevolutionären Coup, der den ökonomischen *Status quo* garantierte. Diese Ausgangskonstellation des Bürgerkrieges, dessen Ergebnis schließlich der „Neue Staat" war, bewirkte zum einen, dass im Franco-Regime neben der dominierenden traditionell-oligarchischen und militärischen Herrschaftsgruppe ein faschistischer Flügel koexistierte, zum anderen, dass die faschistische Fraktion von Anfang an eine untergeordnete Position im Machtkartell des „Neuen Staates" einnahm. Die (im Vergleich zu Deutschland und Italien) rückständige Sozialstruktur Spaniens bewirkte somit eine Art der ‚Machtergreifung', bei der nicht eine faschistische Massenpartei, sondern das Militär der ausschlaggebende Faktor war. Das politische Gewicht der Falange blieb im Machtapparat des Franquismus relativ gering, da sie für den Diktator kein notwendiges Instrument zur Erlangung der Macht gewesen war.

---

32 Vgl. hierzu die detaillierte und faktengesättigte Untersuchung von José Angel Sánchez Asiaín, der deutlich herausarbeitet, dass die Wirtschaftselite (Großgrundbesitzer, Industrielle, Finanziers) seit Beginn der Republik mit allen Mitteln auf deren Abschaffung hinarbeitete. Dementsprechend war diese Elite daher auch – neben der Kirche – ein Hauptprofiteur des franquistischen Sieges. Vgl. Sánchez Asiaín, José Angel: La financiación de la guerra civil española. Una aproximación histórica. Barcelona 2012.

2. „Alter" und „neuer" Faschismus zwischen Bürgerkrieg und Weltkrieg: die Falange

Die Volksfrontwahlen von 1936 stellten den Wendepunkt in der Geschichte der Zweiten Republik dar. Der Sieg der Linken erschütterte bei jenen Kräften, die ihre sozioökonomischen und politischen Interessen bis dahin in der Anwendung ‚legaler' Methoden am besten vertreten sahen, den Glauben an die Möglichkeit, das demokratisch-parlamentarische System weiterhin instrumentalisieren zu können. Die antiparlamentarische Falange erhielt schlagartig enormen Zulauf aus den Reihen der übrigen Rechtsparteien, die Militärs begannen mit der Planung ihres Coups. José Antonio war zwar nicht bereit, sich jedem Militäraufstand bedingungslos anzuschließen; er arbeitete aber von Anfang an darauf hin, an dem geplanten Putsch gegen die Volksfrontregierung mitzuwirken. Die Unterstützung des Militärs durch die Falange ging primär darauf zurück, dass letztere sich über ihre Unfähigkeit im Klaren war, aus eigenen Kräften die von ihr erstrebte „nationalsyndikalistische Revolution" realisieren zu können.[33] Weder für die Falange noch für eine andere politische Gruppierung bestand

---

33 Die falangistische Unterstützung für Franco hat noch eine andere Deutung erfahren: José Antonio soll in Franco eine Art „Wiedergeburt" seines Vaters Miguel Primo de Rivera gesehen haben, der den Geist militärischer Ordnung verkörperte, der das von seinem Vater begonnene Programm fortsetzte und vollendete, die politischen Parteien aufhob, den Weg zu gesteigertem Wohlstand zeigte, politische Unruhen erbte und anschließend Frieden stiftete, schließlich und vor allem die „Integrität Spaniens" trotz starker zentrifugaler Kräfte bewahrte. Vgl. Thomas, H.: „Der Held im leeren Raum". In: Internationaler Faschismus 1920–1945. München 1966, S. 242 (= dt. Buchausgabe des Journal of Contemporary History, Nr. 1. Hg. Walter Laqueur und George L. Mosse).

ein Zweifel daran, dass die entscheidende Rolle im Kampf gegen das republikanische System der Armee zukam. Damit erlangte von Anfang an das Militär eine Bedeutung, die es bei der Zerstörung der Demokratie in Deutschland und Italien nicht gehabt hatte; in keinem der beiden Staaten hatte die Armee bei der ‚Machtergreifung' unmittelbar interveniert. Ihr Übergewicht in Spanien relegierte die Falange machtpolitisch von Anfang an auf den zweiten Rang.

Als der Militäraufstand am 17. Juli 1936 begann, befand sich die Partei – da José Antonio seit März im Gefängnis saß – in einem Zustand innerer Desorganisation. Dass sie auch im weiteren Kriegsverlauf nicht nachdrücklicher auftreten konnte, ist darauf zurückzuführen, dass ein Großteil der verbliebenen falangistischen Elite – einschließlich der vier Führer Primo de Rivera, Ledesma, Redondo und Julio Ruiz de Alda – umkam bzw. erschossen wurde. Die Partei wurde damit führer- und vorübergehend orientierungslos, und die Bestimmung des neuen Vorsitzenden Manuel Hedilla war eher Anlass weiterer parteiinterner Auseinandersetzungen als ein Mittel zur Erhöhung der falangistischen Schlagkraft.

Die Bedingungen des Bürgerkrieges veränderten die politischen Aktionsmöglichkeiten der Falange entscheidend. In den ersten Kriegsmonaten bestand eine ihrer Hauptfunktionen in der Mobilisierung von Frontfreiwilligen und Milizionären für die Etappe.[34] Im Oktober 1936 bereits wurden die Fa-

---

34 Über die Rekrutierung im Bürgerkrieg lässt sich kein genaues Zahlenmaterial beibringen. Payne hat jedoch berechnet, dass Kastilien-Leon, die rurale Mittelschichtregion schlechthin, auf die in früheren Jahren auch ein Großteil der JONS-Anstrengungen konzentriert war, unterdurchschnittlich wenige Freiwillige in den falangistisch-karlistischen Milizen stellte, während Navarra und Aragonien überdurchschnittlich stark vertreten waren. Das Zahlenmaterial muss zwar vorsichtig gedeutet

langefreiwilligen (35.549 von 65.248, somit 54 % aller Milizionäre; der Falange-Anteil an den Milizen stieg bis Januar 1939 auf 72.608, d.h. auf 75 %) in das Feldheer integriert und militärischem Kommando unterstellt.[35] Ist schon die militärische Bedeutung der Falange als hoch, möglicherweise als entscheidend einzuschätzen, so stand dem ihre zivile während des Krieges in nichts nach. Die Falange übernahm vielfältige soziale Aufgaben (zuerst die „Winterhilfe", die später in „Sozialhilfe" umbenannt wurde), sie kontrollierte in der ‚nationalen' Zone nahezu monopolartig Presse und Propaganda, außerdem beteiligte sie sich maßgeblich an allen Entscheidungen in Bezug auf die politische Organisation des „Neuen Staates".

So groß allerdings die Falange-Bedeutung auf diesen Gebieten auch gewesen sein mag, so stellte sich doch sehr schnell heraus, dass die falangistischen Bemühungen weniger Parteizielen als vielmehr den Bestrebungen des „Neuen Staates" dienten. Konnte die Falange anfangs ihr Informationsmonopol noch zur Propagierung der von ihr erstrebten ‚Revolution' einsetzen, so traten später – vor allem, seit Franco im Oktober 1936 in Personalunion militärischer Oberbefehlshaber, Regierungs- und Staatschef geworden war – rein falangistische Ziele immer mehr in den Hintergrund. Nicht mehr von einer falangistisch-nationalsyndikalistischen Revolution war die Rede, sondern vom militärischen Sieg, dem alle Teilinteressen untergeordnet werden müssten, und vom Aufbau des

---

werden; es lässt jedoch den Schluss zu, dass „Klassenzugehörigkeit" für den Eintritt in die Milizen weit weniger ausschlaggebend war als lokale (militärische und politische) Verhältnisse oder (etwa im Falle Navarras) die traditionelle „Kultur" der Provinz. Payne: Social Composition.

35 Casas de la Vega, Rafael: Las milicias nacionales en la Guerra de España. Madrid 1974, S. 84; Ellwood: Prietas las filas, S. 79–80.

neuen, autoritären Staates. Die militärische Führung machte deutlich, dass sie keine Intervention der zivilen Falangisten in Bereichen duldete, die sie als militärische Angelegenheit betrachtete. Andererseits war Franco auf die Kooperation der Falange, die sich zur wichtigsten politischen und paramilitärischen Kraft der ‚nationalen' Zone entwickelt hatte, so lange angewiesen, wie sie ihm nicht unmittelbar unterstellt war. Schon wenige Monate nach Kriegsbeginn entwickelte er daher den Plan, die noch bestehenden Parteien in seiner Zone (Falange, die karlistische *Comunión Tradicionalista*, CEDA, die monarchistische *Renovación Española*) zu einer politischen Organisation unter seiner Führung zusammenzufassen. In den entscheidenden ersten Monaten des Jahres 1937 war die Falange erneut durch innere Auseinandersetzungen um die Person des neuen Vorsitzenden Hedilla geschwächt; entschiedener Widerstand gegen das Vereinigungsdekret vom 20. April 1937, durch das der Zusammenschluss aller politischen Organisationen zu der neuen Einheit *Falange Española Tradicionalista y de las Juntas de Ofensiva Nacional Sindicalista* (FET y de las JONS) unter der Führung Francos verfügt wurde, war daher nicht zu erwarten. Den Vorsitz der neuen Staatspartei übernahm Franco selbst (*jefe nacional*); er degradierte den interimistischen, kurz danach wegen eines angeblichen Putschversuches verurteilten und aus der Partei ausgeschlossenen Führer Hedilla zum Vorsitzenden des neuen politischen Ausschusses (*Junta Política*).[36]

Vom Widerstand Hedillas und einiger weniger Falangisten abgesehen, gab die Partei nach 1936 erstaunlich schnell ihre Unabhängigkeit auf und ordnete sich der Kontrolle des Militärdiktators unter. Mehrere Gründe sprachen für eine derartige Haltung: Zum einen hatte sich die Falange von Anfang

36 Vgl. hierzu ausführlich Thomàs: El gran golpe.

an mit dem Aufstand identifiziert; sie wollte den militärischen Sieg durch Kompetenzgerangel nicht gefährden, ordnete sich daher den militärischen Erfordernissen einer auch politisch zentralisierten Führung unter. Das übergeordnete Ziel blieb der Sieg über die Linke. Zum anderen ging es ihr bei diesem Unterwerfungsakt um ihre politische Zukunft. Was sie auf demokratischem Wege nicht hatte erreichen können – die „Eroberung des Staates"– sollte durch ihre Zwangserhebung in den Rang einer Einheitspartei ermöglicht werden. Das Zusammengehen mit anderen Kräften und die Rolle des Juniorpartners in der ‚Allianz' mit dem Militär waren im Vergleich zu den sich eröffnenden Chancen ein geringer Preis, den die ohnehin opportunistische Partei zu zahlen bereit war. Die realen Kräfteverhältnisse kamen symbolisch in der ‚Kleiderordnung' zum Ausdruck, in der sich Franco während des Krieges bei offiziellen Anlässen präsentierte: die rote Baskenmütze der Karlisten, das Blauhemd der Falangisten, darüber dominierend die Militäruniform – zugleich ein deutlicher Hinweis auf den eklektischen Charakter des neuen Regimes. Schließlich behielt die Falange auch in der zwangsvereinigten Organisation eine herausragende Stellung. Dem Vereinigungsdekret zufolge stellte das Falangeprogramm die „Norm" des neuen Staates dar; die Falange sollte demnach die programmatischen Grundprinzipien des neuen Einparteienstaates liefern. Es entsprach auch dieser hervorgehobenen Position der Falange, dass ihr Name an den Beginn der komplizierten, den Kompromisscharakter der *Unificación* reflektierenden Bezeichnung für die neue Einheitsorganisation gesetzt wurde und diese allenthalben vorerst schlichtweg als „Falange" (unter Weglassung der übrigen Elemente) bezeichnet wurde.

Für Franco wiederum war es in mehrerlei Hinsicht von Vorteil, aus dem Konglomerat an Rechtsgruppierungen gerade die Falange auszuwählen, die der zukünftigen politischen Einheitsorganisation des Staates ihren Namen und ihre

Grundstruktur geben sollte. Der Hauptgrund war die relative Stärke, die sie in den ersten Kriegsmonaten errungen hatte; andererseits ging diese Stärke nicht so weit, dass Franco sie als gleichberechtigten Bundesgenossen in das Machtkartell des ‚nationalen' Spanien hätte aufnehmen müssen. Es reichte, die Falange als Juniorpartner zu integrieren und zugleich durch militärische und traditionalistische Kräfte wirkungsvoll einzurahmen. Ein weiterer Grund dürfte die Überlegung gewesen sein, dass die Falange keine Partei im herkömmlichen Sinne, sondern eine „Bewegung" war, was insofern den Vorstellungen Francos entgegenkam, als dieser den Bürgerkriegs-„Kreuzzug" ja gerade gegen den republikanischen Parteienstaat führte und nicht bereit war, in seinem Regime Parteien zu dulden. Schließlich mag noch ein exogener Faktor eine Rolle gespielt haben: Franco war dringend auf weitere Militärhilfe von Seiten der Achsenmächte angewiesen, und die Erhebung der faschistischen Falange in den Rang der Staatspartei konnte von den faschistischen Staaten als Geste ideologischer Annäherung gedeutet werden.

Trotz aller Bevorzugung der Falange bleibt jedoch festzuhalten, dass die Zwangsvereinigung mit traditionalistischen und monarchistischen Gruppierungen ihr schlagartig zwei der wichtigsten faschistischen Charakteristika nahm: den eigenen Führer und die spezifisch ‚totalitäre' Ideologie. Der „Führer" des Staates war – anders als in Deutschland und Italien – nicht zugleich an der Spitze der Partei, sondern setzte sich erst nach der Zwangsvereinigung an ihre Spitze. Franco hatte seine Herrschaft weit mehr dem Militär und den traditionellen Machteliten, die hinter seinem Putsch standen, als einer faschistischen Massenorganisation zu verdanken. Der spanische Faschismus hat daher nie als Massenpartei ‚von unten' die Macht ergriffen, sondern allenfalls als (eingerahmter) ‚Faschismus von oben' das System zu durchdringen versucht. Da die Falange jedoch ihrer ideologischen Eigen-

und politischen Selbstständigkeit beraubt wurde, musste sie ihre autonome Entwicklungsmöglichkeit aufgeben und sich konservativ-traditionalistischen Kräften anpassen. Die *Unificación* folgte Gründen politischer Strategie und bewies das Übergewicht der militärischen über jede andere Gewalt im Bürgerkrieg. Die erzwungene Akzeptanz der Vereinigung durch die Falange gab Franco eine Initiative, die er nie mehr preisgeben sollte; er war stets der dominierende Partner in diesem Verhältnis. Die neue Einheitspartei zeichnete sich fortan durch drei Charakteristika aus: Unterordnung unter die in Franco personifizierte militärische Macht, interner Pluralismus (vom Karlismus bis hin zum Faschismus), Ausübung vieler Funktionen im Dienste nicht der Partei, sondern des „Neuen Staates".

Hebt man primär auf einzelne phänomenologische Aspekte oder auf die Struktur des politischen Systems ab, so lassen sich im frühen Franquismus viele Affinitäten zu faschistischen Regimen ausmachen: Die politische Organisation des Staates sollte dem deutsch-italienischen Vorbild folgen; Ansätze zum Führerkult waren deutlich erkennbar; ein autoritär-zentralistisches Staatsverständnis dominierte; Massenaufmärsche und faschistische Symbole prägten das Straßenbild; alle Parteien waren verboten, die Einheits-„Partei" versuchte die ganze Gesellschaft zu ‚erfassen' und die Jugend zu mobilisieren; imperialistische Expansionspläne richteten sich auf die gesamte Iberische Halbinsel, auf französische und nordafrikanische Territorien; der staatliche Terror wurde massiv und in äußerst brutaler Form angewandt; als parlamentarisches Surrogat fungierte ein faschistischem Vorbild entlehntes Korporativsystem; die Arbeiterschaft wurde ihrer autonomen Interessenvertretungen beraubt. Selbst in Bereichen, die der Charakterisierung des Regimes als „faschistisch" *prima facie* zu widersprechen schienen, ergibt ein Vergleich mit Italien aufschlussreiche Übereinstimmungen. Diese sind vor allem dort feststellbar, wo das Italien Mussolinis angeblich nicht „ganz faschistisch" war, da die Totalität der nationalsozialistischen Erfassung nicht erreicht wurde: So blieb auch im italienischen Faschismus, ebenso wie im spanischen Franquismus, ein (wenn auch noch so eng begrenzter) politischer ‚Pluralismus' verschiedener Interessengruppen bestehen, der Faschismus konnte den Staat nie in seinem Sinne umformen. In beiden Fällen überlebten auch die präfaschistischen Eliten, mit denen vielfältige Kompromisse geschlossen werden mussten: Die Kirche behielt (oder vergrößerte sogar) ihren Einfluss, der Parteiradikalismus konnte gebremst werden, faschistische bzw. falangistische Syndikate mussten sich den traditionellen Wirtschaftsinteressen unterordnen. Schließlich änderten beide Regime nichts an der bestehenden Wirtschaftsordnung, deren kapitalistische Form sie vielmehr schützten und förderten, was bei den ‚echten' Faschisten in beiden Regimen zu der Klage führte, sie seien um ihre Revolution betrogen worden.

Neben die Übereinstimmungen traten aber von Anfang an die Unterschiede. So muss etwa darauf hingewiesen werden, dass die um die gleichnamige Zeitschrift gescharte politisch-intellektuelle Gruppe *Acción Española* das eigentliche Transmissionsglied des ideologischen und institutionellen Einflusses war, den die ‚gemäßigte' Diktatur Miguel Primo de Riveras auf die ‚harte' Diktatur Francos ausübte.[37] Unter Rückgriff auf reaktionär-spanisches Gedankengut verkündete *Acción Española* eine Staatstheorie, die auf katholischem Integrismus, traditioneller Monarchie und faschistischem Korporatismus gründen sollte. *Acción Española* entfernte sich von den institutionalisierten faschistischen Modellen

37 Morodo, Raúl: Los orígenes ideológicos del franquismo: Acción Española. Madrid 1985.

auch dadurch, dass sie nicht die Bildung einer politischen Partei zur Durchsetzung des von ihr anvisierten korporativen Regimes anstrebte, sondern es vorzog, als „doktrinäres Laboratorium" oder verbindendes Element zur Zusammenfassung aller Organisationen der (extremen) Rechten aufzutreten und damit bereits auf eine Art „Nationale Bewegung" vorauszudeuten, wie sie durch die Zwangsvereinigung von 1937 im franquistischen Lager Realität werden sollte. Zentrale Begriffe der reaktionären Gedankenwelt von *Acción Española* sollten als Legitimation für das *Alzamiento Nacional*, den Bürgerkrieg und den „Neuen Staat" fungieren: militanter Katholizismus, imperialer Messianismus, Kreuzzugsgedanke. Der Nationalkatholizismus, auf den sich das Regime massiv stützte, war – ebenso wie andere Elemente im institutionellen Aufbau des Franquismus – von *Acción Española* bereits vorgezeichnet worden, ihr politisches Credo kann daher als „ideologischer Ursprung" des Franquismus bezeichnet werden.

Die Betonung des Nationalkatholizismus verweist erneut darauf, dass die rebellierenden Militärs von einer breiten Front politisch rechtsstehender Gruppierungen unterstützt wurden, die später die verschiedenen „politischen Familien" des Regimes bildeten. Die Falange war nur eine dieser Gruppierungen, die alle zusammen das *Movimiento* bildeten. In der historischen Literatur über den Franquismus ist immer wieder darauf hingewiesen worden, dass sich die Funktion der Falange seit der Zwangsvereinigung von 1937 darauf beschränkte, Werkzeug eines Regimes zu sein, das aus einem Militäraufstand hervorgegangen war, hinter dem primär die landbesitzende und finanzielle Oligarchie stand. So richtig der Hinweis auf die beschränkte Autonomie der Falange auch ist, so muss andererseits betont werden, dass das Verhältnis zwischen Regime und Partei nicht auf einer einseitigen Instrumentalisierung Letzterer durch Ersteres beruhte, sondern dass eher von einer Wechselbeziehung gesprochen werden muss, von der beide Seiten profitierten. Die Falange akzeptierte es, dass sie im „Neuen Staat“, zu dessen Konsolidierung und Erhalt sie einen enormen Beitrag leistete, keine dominante Rolle spielte; im Gegenzug erhielt sie außerordentliche Privilegien und Garantien. Denn trotz späterer Klagen von Falangisten war – zumindest anfangs – keine andere Organisation so stark wie die Falange in den Machtorganen des Franco-Regimes vertreten; keine andere Organisation konnte ihre Struktur aus der Vorkriegszeit (Aufbau, Bezeichnung, Pressewesen etc.), ihre Symbolik und ihren Gesellschaftsentwurf so relativ intakt bewahren; keine Organisation war im öffentlichen Bewusstsein so allgegenwärtig wie die Falange. Sie hatte fortan keine Finanzprobleme mehr, da sie vom Staatshaushalt getragen wurde; noch 1975 hatte sie Einnahmen in Höhe von neun Milliarden Peseten aus der Staatskasse. Die Stellenvergabepraxis in Staatsorganismen stellte sicher, dass sie auch quantitativ zu einer Massenorganisation wurde.

Es waren im Wesentlichen drei Bereiche, in denen und über die die Falange ihren Einfluss ausüben konnte: die Massenmedien, die syndikalistische Organisation und die Verwaltungsbürokratie auf lokaler, regionaler und nationaler Ebene. Zur eigentlichen Machtdomäne der Falange entwickelten sich die Wirtschaftsorganisationen und die sozialpolitische Kontrolle der Arbeiterschaft durch die „vertikalen Syndikate“; der „Neue Staat“ übernahm das Falangeprogramm am reinsten auf dem Gebiet des Nationalsyndikalismus. In den Falange-Statuten wurde festgehalten, dass die Führung der „Syndikalen Organisation“ nur aus der Falange kommen dürfe; die Struktur der Syndikate müsse „vertikal und hierarchisch“ sein. Das falangistische Konzept eines Wirtschaftsaufbaus nach Berufszweigen sowie der Zusammenfassung von Arbeitern und Unternehmern in einer einheitlichen

Zwangskörperschaft fand im ersten bedeutenden Verfassungstext des nationalistischen Spanien gesetzlichen Ausdruck: im „Grundgesetz der Arbeit“, dem *Fuero del Trabajo* (1938), das Ausgangspunkt und allgemeine Grundlage der falangistischen Arbeitsgesetzgebung war und erst durch die postfranquistisch-demokratische Verfassung von 1978 aufgehoben wurde.[38] Das *Fuero del Trabajo* übertrug der Falange die gesamte Kontrolle über die Organisation und Verwaltung der Syndikate; damit übte sie ein Erfassungsmonopol über die Arbeiterschaft aus. Allerdings bewirkten sowohl die Kräftekonstellation im „Neuen Staat“ als auch Francos unmissverständliche Absicht, keine unkontrollierte Parallelmacht im Staat aufkommen zu lassen, dass sich die Syndikate nicht zu autonomen Institutionen fortentwickeln konnten. So gelang es 1941 den vereinten Anstrengungen der Militärs, der Karlisten sowie der Industrie- und Finanzkreise, den ersten Nationaldelegierten für das Syndikatswesen, Gerardo Salvador Merino, von seinem Posten zu verdrängen, von dem aus er die Syndikate zur wichtigsten zivilen Institution Spaniens machen wollte. Der Sturz Merinos im Juli 1941 bedeutete das Ende der ersten ‚populistischen‘, antibürgerlichen Phase des falangistischen Syndikalismus.[39] Mit der Ernennung von José

---

38 Hierzu Bernecker, Walther L.: „Die Arbeiterbewegung unter dem Franquismus“. In: Waldmann, Peter u. a.: Die geheime Dynamik autoritärer Diktaturen. Vier Studien über sozialen Wandel in der Franco-Ära. München 1982, S. 61–198; vgl. auch Bernecker: Gewerkschaftsbewegung und Staatssyndikalismus, passim.

39 Ellwood: Prietas las filas, S. 125, hat die These aufgestellt, dass der Sturz Merinos weniger auf Bestrebungen der militärischen und konservativen Kräfte als vielmehr auf Animositäten gegen ihn aus den eigenen Falangereihen zurückging, da er als „Neuhemd“ kein legitimer Interpret der falangistischen Ideologie sein konnte. Diese Deutung überzeugt schon deshalb nicht, weil in

Luis Arrese zum Generalsekretär der Falange und von José Antonio Girón de Velasco zum Arbeitsminister endete nicht nur der Versuch, eine unabhängige, revolutionäre Falangepolitik zu betreiben; zugleich orientierte sich das Regime definitiv an einem „autoritären, korporativen und katholischen Syndikalismus“[40] Diese Re-Orientierung war auch auf die relative Schwäche des revolutionär-faschistischen Flügels der Falange nach dem Bürgerkrieg zurückzuführen. In diesem waren über 60 % der falangistischen „Althemden“ gefallen, massiver Zustrom ließ nach 1939 die Ausrichtung der einzig zugelassenen Partei weitgehend diffus erscheinen. Sie entwickelte sich zu einer amorphen, hochbürokratisierten Institution, die kaum Chancen für eine wirkliche Partizipation der Bevölkerung bot.

Die Entledigung von linksfalangistischen Syndikalisten lief parallel zur Zurückdrängung und machtpolitischen Eliminierung anderer „Althemden“. Paradoxerweise waren es diejenigen falangistischen Aktivitäten, die die sozialpolitische Basis des Regimes erweitern sollten, welche in jenen Jahren das größte Misstrauen Francos hervorriefen, etwa die Einrichtung der studentischen Monopol-‚Gewerkschaft‘ *Sindicato Español Universitario* (SEU). Francos Befürchtung ging dahin, dass die Ausweitung des falangistischen Einflussbereiches seine Machtposition gefährden konnte und daher nicht geduldet werden durfte. Der germanophile Innen- und Außenminister Ramón Serrano Súñer wurde als Haupt der

jenen Jahren die „legitimistischen“ *camisas viejas*, die als „Althemden“ eine genuin faschistische Position vertraten, weit eher einflussreiche Posten aufgeben mussten als die später hinzugekommenen „Neuhemden“.

40 Ludevid, Manuel: Cuarenta años de sindicato vertical. Aproximación a la Organización Sindical Española. Barcelona 1977, S. 21.

„expansionistischen“ Falangegruppe betrachtet; zuerst verlor er daher das Innen-, 1942 auch das Außenministerium. Andere Falangisten wiederum (Girón, Arrese, Miguel Primo de Rivera, Agustín Aznar) erhielten Ministerposten und wurden damit in den Machtapparat integriert. Unter dem neuen Falange-Generalsekretär José Luis Arrese begann Ende 1941 außerdem eine Säuberung der Falange. Offiziell sollten die Partei von „unzuverlässigen Elementen“ und Mitläufern gereinigt sowie die „Einheit, Hierarchie und Disziplin“ in der Partei wiederhergestellt werden; faktisch jedoch liefen die Maßnahmen darauf hinaus, radikale, faschistische und schlichtweg nonkonformistische Kräfte loszuwerden und den reaktionären Flügel zu stärken.

Während innenpolitisch zwischen den verschiedenen Fraktionen über die Ausgestaltung bzw. Zurückdrängung der faschistischen Elemente im Staatsaufbau und Wirtschaftssystem gerungen wurde, kam in der Frage eines möglichen Kriegseintritts die wohl wichtigste außenpolitische Entscheidung auf das Regime zu. In dieser Frage zeigte sich am deutlichsten Francos Bestreben, sich weder innen- noch außenpolitisch auf eine bestimmte Machtgruppierung festzulegen. Das Problem sollte zur größten Herausforderung des Regimes in seiner Frühphase werden, der nicht nur außenpolitisch durch eine geschickte Schaukelpolitik, sondern zugleich innenpolitisch durch Austarieren gegensätzlicher Tendenzen begegnet werden musste. Der Diktator bewegte sich zwischen den Gruppen, die den Kriegseintritt wünschten, und denen, die ihn überwiegend ablehnten. Die Befürworter einer spanischen Kriegsteilnahme gehörten einem kleinen Kreis von deutschlandfreundlichen Militärs und Vertretern der Falange an;[41] zu

41 Ruhl, Klaus-Jörg: Spanien im Zweiten Weltkrieg. Franco, die Falange und das „Dritte Reich“. Hamburg 1975, S. 253.

diesen gesellte sich noch eine nicht unbedeutende Gruppierung militanter Linksfalangisten, die über eine Anlehnung an Deutschland doch noch ihren Traum einer nationalsyndikalistischen Revolution in die Tat umzusetzen hofften. Für diese aktivistischen Faschisten, die innenpolitisch damals eine reale Gefahr für Franco darstellten, wurde die ‚Flucht' in die *Blaue Division* nach Russland die zeitgemäße Form des ‚inneren Exils', um die Enttäuschung über die Immobilität der neuen Militärdiktatur zu überwinden.[42] Für Franco wiederum war die Entsendung der *Blauen Division* ein Mittel, durch Ausschaltung einer potentiellen innenpolitischen Opposition sein Regime zu stabilisieren.

So wie Franco sich – stets mit der entscheidenden Rückendeckung des Militärs – außenpolitisch durchsetzen konnte, ließ er auch innenpolitisch keinen Zweifel an seinem Machtanspruch aufkommen. Charakteristisch hierfür ist der Ausgang einer Auseinandersetzung zwischen Falangisten und Karlisten 1942 in Bilbao, die über den lokalen Zwischenfall hinaus Ausdruck des falangistischen Protestes gegen die traditionalistisch-reaktionären Elemente in Francos Regierungssystem war. Trotz vielfältigen falangistischen Drucks ließ Franco die Verantwortlichen verurteilen und hinrichten; der Versuch der Falange, die Machtverhältnisse im Regime einseitig zu ihren Gunsten (und damit zulasten der übrigen politischen Gruppierungen) zu verändern, war damit erneut fehlgeschlagen. Die im gleichen Jahr vorgenommene Entlassung Serrano Súñers bedeutete auch das Ende jener falangistischen Aspirationen, die auf eine unabhängige Position der Falange im neuen Regime hinwirkten.

42 Beyme, Klaus von: Vom Faschismus zur Entwicklungsdiktatur – Machtelite und Opposition in Spanien. München 1971, S. 40.

3. Niedergang des Faschismus als Staatsideologie

Die Entwicklung und Entfaltungsmöglichkeit der faschistischen Partei innerhalb des *Movimiento* hing nicht nur von der Mächtekonstellation im Franquismus ab; in den 1940er Jahren wurde ihr Schicksal weit mehr von der Entwicklung des ‚internationalen' Faschismus bestimmt. Mit der Wende im Weltkrieg (1942/43) und dem allmählichen Niedergang der Achsenmächte büßte der faschistische Flügel innerhalb der Falange zusehends an Einfluss ein. Die ‚Entfaschisierung' der Falange erfolgte im Wesentlichen in drei Schritten:[43] Zuerst wurden die faschistischen Linksfalangisten aus allen Einflusspositionen verdrängt und politisch kaltgestellt; sodann ließ das Regime faschistische Phraseologie („totalitärer Staat") und Symbolik („römischer Gruß") fallen; schließlich verschwand die Falange als Einzelpartei immer mehr hinter der diffusen Kollektivbezeichnung *Movimiento*, Spanien wurde 1945 bereits offiziell zu einem „sozialen und katholischen Staat" erklärt. Es ist keineswegs ausgeschlossen, dass bei einem Sieg der Achsenmächte die faschistische Komponente im franquistischen Herrschaftssystem möglicherweise dominiert hätte; die relative Bedeutung, die der faschistische Falangeflügel in der ersten Hälfte der 1940er Jahre (vor allem im Sozial- und Wirtschaftsbereich) noch spielen konnte, ist nicht nur aus der innenpolitischen Kräftekonstellation Spaniens zu erklären, sondern verweist zentral auf die äußeren Rahmenbedingungen. Diese Außenabhängigkeit besiegelte 1945 auch das Schicksal der Falange als faschistische Organisation; als die „Epoche des Faschismus" international zu Ende ging, bedeutete dies im Wesentlichen auch das Ende der nationalspanischen Variante des Faschismus, war doch

---

43 Vilar, Sergio: La naturaleza del franquismo. Barcelona 1977, S. 188.

innen- wie außenpolitisch seine *Raison d'Être* verschwunden. Der ideologische Kollaps des Falangismus kam auch in der Entfernung seiner führenden Intellektuellen (u. a. Dionisio Ridruejo, Antonio Tovar, Pedro Laín Entralgo, Santiago Montero Díaz) zum Ausdruck.

Allerdings blieben in der Falange stets faschistische Tendenzen bestehen, die sich in den folgenden Jahrzehnten in einer Unmenge kleiner konspirativer Zirkel organisierten, die nationalsyndikalistische Revolution nachzuholen versuchten, selbst vor Attentaten auf den ‚Verräter' Franco nicht zurückschreckten. Diese „Puristen" unter den Falangisten versuchten zuerst, in der Arbeiterschaft Fuß zu fassen; nach dem Fehlschlag dieser Bemühungen orientierten sie in den 1950er Jahren ihre Bemühungen auf die Universitäten, wo sie ein nicht unwichtiges Element der Agitation und der Neubelebung des akademischen Lebens darstellten. Letzten Endes aber agierte diese falangistische Opposition stets im Rahmen des Systems, an dessen Schaffung sie mitgewirkt hatte. Zuletzt ging es dieser „authentischen" Falange – z. B. den *Círculos Doctrinales José Antonio* – nur noch darum, sich von der in das *Movimiento Nacional* integrierten offiziellen Falange abzuheben, den revolutionären Wesensgehalt des nationalsyndikalistischen Gedankenguts zu bewahren und sich selbst als reine *joseantonianos* darzustellen. Diese Linksfalangisten hatten nicht nur gegen die verschiedenen konservativen und traditionalistischen Gruppierungen des Regimes, sondern nicht minder gegen die offizielle Falange anzukämpfen. Diese hatte schon früh, in Anbetracht der tatsächlichen Machtverhältnisse, ihr Schicksal auf Gedeih und Verderb an das des Diktators gekettet. Längst ging es ihren bürokratisierten Repräsentanten nicht mehr um Prinzipien, sondern um die Bewahrung von Pfründen, Einfluss und Macht. Die vollständige Identifizierung der Falange mit dem franquistischen Staat lässt sich an ihrem Verhalten bei allen wichtigen Weichenstellungen des Regimes aufzeigen:

Das gilt zum einen für die Wiedereinführung der Monarchie (1947), für die sich die Parteipresse nachdrücklich einsetzte, obwohl das Gesetz „über die Nachfolge in der Staatsführung“ explizit festlegte, dass das *Movimiento* als politische Basis des Regimes nicht die Domäne einer einzigen Organisation war. Die Vorstellung einer (noch in weiter Ferne befindlichen) Monarchie war für die Falange aber eher akzeptabel als das Risiko, durch offenen Widerstand gegen das Projekt von den übrigen Kräften des Regimes machtpolitisch ausgebootet zu werden.

Das gilt des Weiteren für die Abkommen mit den USA (1953), obwohl sie wirtschaftspolitisch eine Abkehr von falangistischen Autarkievorstellungen und den Beginn der Einbindung Spaniens in das liberalkapitalistische Weltwirtschaftssystem signalisierten. Das ökonomische und politische Überleben des Regimes und die antikommunistische Komponente in der Allianz mit den USA wogen wiederum schwerer als doktrinärer Puritanismus. Die neue Falangistengeneration, die sich im *Sindicato Español Universitario* zusammenfand, bekannte sich primär zu Katholizismus und Antikommunismus; sie verband ihren politischen Konservativismus mit einem sozioökonomischen Liberalismus, der sie von den „Althemden“ der Gründergeneration unterschied. Hauptziel dieser „pragmatisch-reformistischen“ Gruppe war die Bewahrung der Früchte des nationalistischen Sieges von 1939, weniger die formale Struktur des Regimes. Für sie bestand in den 1950er Jahren bereits kein Unterschied mehr zwischen Franquismus und Falangismus: „Die Falange steht zu Franco, und Franco glaubt an Spanien, weil er an die Falange glaubt.“[44]

Dies gilt drittens ebenso für die Verabschiedung (1958) des Verfassungsgesetzes „über die Prinzipien der Nationalen Bewegung“ (*Ley de Principios Fundamentales del Movimiento*), dessen Ausarbeitung zuerst einer falangistischen Equipe unter Generalsekretär José Luis Arrese übertragen worden war. Der von Arrese präsentierte Entwurf zur „Institutionalisierung der Bewegung“ nahm keinerlei Bezug auf die Monarchie, betonte demgegenüber die Rolle der „Bewegung“ und des Generalsekretariats von FET y de las JONS. Entsprechend kritisch wurde der Entwurf von dem engen Franco-Mitarbeiter Luis Carrero Blanco, aber auch von der katholischen Amtskirche und den nicht-falangistischen Ministern aufgenommen. Die maßgeblichen Kräfte des Regimes erstrebten zwar eine Form „ideologischer Kontinuität“, verstanden es aber zu verhindern, dass die Falange selbst zu einer Institution wurde. Das schließlich verabschiedete Gesetz, das auf Grundgedanken des *Opus Dei*-Mitglieds Laureano López Rodó zurückging, betonte den Grundsatz einer „sozialen Monarchie“. Die Rolle der Partei im komplizierten politischen Geflecht des Regimes wurde mit keinem Wort erwähnt. Die gesamte Staatsordnung sollte auf den Prinzipien der Nationalen Bewegung ruhen, die als „Glaubensgemeinschaft aller Spanier in den Idealen, welche den Kreuzzug beseelten“, definiert wurde. Obwohl es der Falange nicht gelang, den neuen „Grundprinzipien“ ihren Stempel aufzudrücken, kettete sie ihr Schicksal erneut, wie in früheren Fällen, an die Entscheidung Francos und identifizierte sich (zumindest offiziell) mit dem Gesetz.

---

44 Zit. nach Ellwood: Prietas las filas, S. 171.

Dasselbe lässt sich schließlich für das „Staatsorgangesetz“ (*Ley Orgánica del Estado*) von 1966 sagen, dessen Hauptzweck (in historischer Perspektive) darin bestand, das Fortbestehen des Regimes auch nach dem Tod des Diktators sicherzustellen. Der „Nationalrat“ der Bewegung fungierte fortan als eine Art zweiter Kammer[45], die Falange wurde jedoch mit keinem einzigen Wort erwähnt. Dessen ungeachtet war es wiederum die Falange, die sich landauf landab für eine Annahme des Verfassungsgesetzes per Volksentscheid einsetzte. Die Partei hatte längst erkannt, dass nur die enge Bindung an das aus dem Bürgerkrieg hervorgegangene Regime ihr Überleben garantierte.

Seit sich das Regime in einer Verbindung von politischer Konvenienz und ökonomischem Pragmatismus in den 1960er Jahren einer „desarrollistischen“, von Technokraten des *Opus Dei* durchgeführten Sozial- und Wirtschaftspolitik verschrieben hatte[46], sank der Einfluss der Falange auch auf diesen Sektoren. Die Autarkiepolitik, die in eine wirtschaftliche Sackgasse geführt hatte, war bereits in den 1950er Jahren aufgegeben worden; „Liberalisierungen“ im Syndikatsbereich beendeten sodann in den 1960er Jahren das Monopol, das die Falange über die Arbeitsbeziehungen gehabt hatte.[47] Der Hintergrund für diese Verschiebungen in den Machtpositionen waren weit mehr die wirtschaftliche Entwicklung und die damit einhergehenden gesellschaftlichen Veränderungen als etwa eine ideologische Reorientierung des Regimes. Franco selbst sprach davon, dass die Falange in

---

45 Zu den einzelnen Bestimmungen des Staatsorgangesetzes vgl. Bernecker, Walther L.: Spaniens Geschichte seit dem Bürgerkrieg. München 1984, S. 181–183.

46 Vgl. hierzu weiter unten Kapitel III, 4.

47 Vgl. hierzu ausführlich Bernecker: Gewerkschaftsbewegung und Staatssyndikalismus.

vielerlei Hinsicht „veraltet" sei. Ihre Bezeichnung wurde in der Öffentlichkeit kaum mehr verwendet; die Rede war nur vom *Movimiento*. Allerdings wurde die Falange auch nie abgeschafft. Gerade ihre unverbrüchliche Treue zum *Caudillo*, unter Preisgabe altfalangistischer Grundsätze, ermöglichte ihr Überleben. Diese totale Identifizierung mit Franco dürfte auch wesentlich mit dafür verantwortlich sein, dass sie nach dessen Tod sehr schnell auseinanderfiel.

Der Bedeutungsrückgang der Falange lässt sich auch an der Mitgliederentwicklung ablesen.[48] Nach 1942 stagnierte ihre Mitgliederzahl bei etwas über 900.000, und ein Gutteil davon gehörte der Organisation lediglich wegen ihrer „bürokratischen Funktion" an. So wurden etwa Armee-Offiziere automatisch Falangemitglieder, und ein beträchtlicher Teil ihrer Anhänger rekrutierte sich aus der expandierenden Regierungsbürokratie. Nicht wenige der *militantes activos* dürften außerdem Karteileichen gewesen sein. Waren 1939 noch 4 % der erwachsenen männlichen Bevölkerung Spaniens Falangisten, so sank deren Anteil in den 60er und 70er Jahren auf unter 3 %. Besonders auffallend ist die Bedeutungseinbuße in der Studentenschaft und der Jugendorganisation. Hatte der falangistische SEU in den 40er Jahren eine Art Monopol an den Hochschulen inne, so gehörten 1962/63 nur noch 4 % der Universitätsstudenten (und auch diese nur auf dem Papier) der Hochschul-‚Gewerkschaft' an; im darauffolgenden Jahrzehnt dürfte der prozentuale Anteil von SEU-Mitgliedern an der Gesamtstudentenschaft weiter zurückgegangen sein. Die Jugendorganisation der FET y de las JONS zählte 1941 immerhin rund 935.000 minderjährige Jungen und Mädchen (ca. 16 % der gesamtspanischen Jugendlichen). Damit erreichte sie zwar bei weitem nicht das

48 Hierzu Payne: Social Composition.

Ausmaß an Jugendmobilisierung wie in Deutschland oder Italien, der Organisationsgrad war unmittelbar nach dem Bürgerkrieg jedoch nicht unerheblich. Bis 1962 war die Anzahl der erfassten Jugendlichen allerdings auf 172.000 (oder ca. 2 % aller nicht Volljährigen) zurückgegangen.

Schließlich lässt sich die untergeordnete Bedeutung der Falange an ihrem prozentualen Anteil an Amtsinhabern erkennen. Mitte der 50er Jahre – zu einem Zeitpunkt also, zu dem die Falange noch relativ einflussreich war – waren zwar immerhin 36 % aller Provinzgouverneure Falangisten, aber nur 24 % der Cortes-Delegierten, nur 18 % der Provinzdeputierten, gerade einmal 16 % der Bürgermeister von Provinzhauptstädten und lediglich 12 % aller Kabinettsmitglieder.[49] Auch in vielen anderen Bereichen lässt sich die Schwäche der Falange dokumentieren: Der Partei gelang es nicht, größere Massen zu mobilisieren; organisatorisch wirkte sie chaotisch; im Bildungs- und Erziehungsbereich musste sie von Anfang an – eine partielle Ausnahme stellte lediglich die Universität dar – wichtige Kompetenzen an andere Institutionen (besonders die Kirche) abtreten; jede Personalunion eines Staats- und eines Parteiamtes diente lediglich zur Unterordnung des letzteren unter das erstere.

Das Fazit der bisher aufgezeigten Entwicklung liegt auf der Hand: Der Faschismus spielte zwar bei der Konstituierung und frühen Entwicklung des Franquismus eine nicht unerhebliche Rolle; die faschistische Bewegung wurde jedoch vom franquistischen Herrschaftssystem schnell und relativ leicht

---

49 Nach Linz, Juan José: „From Falange to Movimiento-Organización: The Spanish Single Party and the Franco Regime, 1936–1968". In: Huntington, Samuel P. / Moore, Clement H. (Hg.): Authoritarian Politics in Modern Societies. New York 1970, S. 128–201.

absorbiert. Die ursprünglich faschistische Programmatik der Falange konnte im Franco-Regime nicht realisiert werden. Mit dieser Schlussfolgerung werden faschistische Elemente im Frühfranquismus keineswegs geleugnet; ganz im Gegenteil. Die Kräftekonstellation während des Bürgerkrieges und die nationale Besonderheit des politischen Kompromisses, den der spanische Faschismus mit den antidemokratischen Kräften der Rechten schließen musste, bewirkten jedoch, dass die faschistische Falange von Anfang an als eine Kraft neben anderen am Machtkartell des Franquismus partizipierte und daher (insbesondere seit der Zwangsvereinigung von 1937) ihre spezifisch faschistisch-totalitären Züge aufzugeben hatte und der Faschisierungsprozess des Systems somit zwangsläufig stagnierte.

III. Militärdiktatur, Nationalkatholizismus, Autoritarismus, Entwicklungsdiktatur: alternative Typologisierungen

1. Der Franquismus: eine Militärdiktatur

Dass Franco im Zuge der „Entfaschisierung" seines Regimes auf die Falange zusehends verzichten konnte, hängt auch damit zusammen, dass er sich primär auf eine andere Institution stützte: das Militär. Die Planung des Aufstandes von 1936, die Führung im Krieg und die Gestaltung der ersten Maßnahmen des „Neuen Staates" befanden sich fest in den Händen hoher Offiziere. Als Franco 1936 zum „Generalissimus" bestimmt wurde, handelte es sich um eine Entscheidung unter Militärs. Die erste Kriegsregierung bestand fast ausschließlich aus Soldaten, und auch als nach 1938 die meisten Ministerposten mit Zivilisten besetzt wurden, behielten Militärs Schlüsselpositionen (vor allem das Innenministerium) in der Regierung. Von den 113 Ministern der Franco-Ära waren immerhin 33 Militärs. Außerdem kontrollierte die Armee weitgehend die Sicherheitskräfte, nahm einen Teil der öffentlichen Verwaltung wahr und übte wichtige Funktionen in öffentlichen Unternehmen aus.[50]

Zweifellos waren die Streitkräfte die wichtigste Stütze Francos; keine andere Institution, nicht einmal die Kirche, unterhielt zum Regime eine vergleichbar entscheidende Beziehung wie die Militärs. Diese besondere Situation führte

---

50 Zur Rolle des Militärs im Franco-System vgl. den Überblick von Mansilla, Hugo C.: „Politik und Militär in Spanien. Wandlungsprozesse im militärischen Bereich." In: Waldmann, Peter (Hg. u. a.): Die geheime Dynamik autoritärer Diktaturen. München 1982, S. 1–59.

dazu, dass der Franquismus als System häufig falsch eingeschätzt, dass die Beziehung zwischen ihm und der Armee als statisch missverstanden wurde, ohne die wichtigen Veränderungen in diesem Verhältnis zu registrieren. Für viele Autoren spielte das Militär eine hegemoniale Rolle im Regime. Sergio Vilar etwa[51], einer der Vertreter der Theorie des spanischen „Militärfaschismus“, meinte bei den herrschenden Klassen eine „militaristische Tendenz“ konstatieren zu können: Jene Klassen seien nicht gewillt gewesen, soziale und politische Konflikte durch friedliche Methoden zu lösen, sondern sie bevorzugten die „bewaffnete Aktion“. Die spanische Bourgeoisie habe „ihr eigenes politisches Vakuum“, d.h. das Fehlen einer großen konservativen Partei, geschaffen und damit den Weg der nackten Gewalt gewählt. Die Entscheidung für den Militärfaschismus sei eine Konsequenz sowohl der „hegemonistischen Unfähigkeit“ der spanischen Bourgeoisie als auch der stärkeren Gesinnung des spanischen Proletariats gewesen.

Die Konzeption vom spanischen Militärfaschismus weist allerdings theoretische Schwächen auf. Sie betont zwar korrekt die untergeordnete Rolle der spanischen Bourgeoisie (im Vergleich zu anderen westeuropäischen Ländern), unterstellt ihr aber zugleich – historisch nicht belegbar – eine fast naturgegebene Bereitschaft zu militaristisch-totalitären Gesellschaftsmodellen. Die schematisierte Konzeption Vilars lässt die spezifischen historischen Umstände außer Acht, die zur militärischen Erhebung von 1936 führten; sie geht auch nicht auf die Komplexität der Siegerkoalition unter Franco ein. Die Konzeption Vilars ist trotz ihrer Mängel aufschlussreich, da sie bemerkenswerte *topoi* vieler ‚linker‘ Studien über die Natur des Franquismus enthält. So geht sie von

---

51 Vilar, Sergio: La naturaleza del franquismo. Barcelona 1977; ders.: Fascismo y militarismo. Barcelona 1968.

der Einheit zwischen Bourgeoisie und Armee aus, die somit als Ausgangspunkt und nicht als Ergebnis der Untersuchung erscheint. Als Beweggrund des Aufstandes von 1936 nimmt sie eine Entscheidung der Bourgeoisie an, der das Verhalten der Streitkräfte untergeordnet gewesen sei – eine Behauptung, die angesichts des spezifisch militärischen Charakters der Rebellion (der sich allerdings bald zivile Gruppierungen anschlossen) empirisch nicht abgesichert ist. Zweifellos hatten die Latifundisten und die Großbourgeoisie massive Interessen, die sie zu Gegnern der Republik machten; aber die Planung des Aufstandes, die Kriegführung und die Politik der ersten Regierungen waren fest in Händen der hohen Offiziere.

Der Bürgerkrieg hatte der Armee erneut ein Gefühl politischer und korporativer Identität verliehen, das seit langem abhandengekommen war. Nach 1939 nahm das Militär eine privilegierte Stellung ein, es war in höchsten Positionen vertreten. Trotz seiner herausragenden Stellung ist jedoch in der weiteren Entwicklung des Franco-Regimes ein auffälliges Phänomen zu konstatieren: Der militärische Anteil am Staatshaushalt blieb nach 1945 konstant niedrig, die Militärs hatten keinen hohen Stellenwert bei der Konzipierung der politischen Leitlinien des Regimes, und selbst das Sozialprestige der Offiziere sank ständig. Der Franquismus zeigte bei seiner Entfaltung sehr bald eine abermalige Bevorzugung der traditionell privilegierten Sektoren. Es lässt sich die These vertreten, dass das aus der militärischen Erhebung von 1936 hervorgegangene Regime allmählich von einer faschistisch inspirierten Militärdiktatur in ein konservativ-autoritäres System umgewandelt wurde, in dem die Streitkräfte eine zunehmend geringere Rolle spielten, vielmehr ‚moderne' und leistungsfähige Eliten eindeutig bevorzugt wurden. Die Identifizierung des Franco-Regimes mit einer monolithischen Militärdiktatur würde die Sicht auf die vielfältige interne Dynamik Spaniens verdecken, die nach 1975 den friedlichen

Übergang in eine parlamentarisch-demokratische Monarchie ermöglicht hat.[52]

Die Blütezeit des Militärs fiel mit der Phase des Bürgerkrieges und des Zweiten Weltkrieges (1936–1945) zusammen. Sowohl die Erfordernisse des Krieges bis 1939 und die anhaltende Gefahr einer Einbeziehung des Landes in den Weltkrieg danach wie die massive innenpolitische Repression im ersten Jahrzehnt nach Kriegsende ließen die zahlenmäßige Stärke, den Verteidigungsanteil am Staatshaushalt und die politische Bedeutung der Armee zunehmen. Die Militärgerichtsbarkeit wurde ausgedehnt, viele Bereiche der öffentlichen Verwaltung unter militärische Aufsicht gestellt; die Armee erhielt mannigfaltige Sicherungsfunktionen übertragen. Das aufgeblähte Feldheer der Kriegsjahre wurde 1939 zwar auf rund 220.000 Mann reduziert, in den folgenden Jahren jedoch – auch wegen des Einsatzes gegen die sehr aktiven Guerillaeinheiten – zusammen mit Marine und Luftwaffe erneut auf rund 380.000 aufgestockt.[53]

Die Militärs genossen unmittelbar nach dem Krieg ein hohes gesellschaftliches Prestige; die Bezüge der Offiziere blieben zwar niedrig, durch bestimmte Sozialleistungen (Sonderverpflegung, Wohnungsvermittlung, Befreiung von Verbrauchssteuern) und eine Welle von Beförderungen wurde die Sonderstellung der ranghöchsten Soldaten in der Gesellschaft jedoch unterstrichen. Das reguläre Offizierskorps wuchs von etwa 15.000 (1940) rapide auf rund 25.000 (1945) an, was vor allem auf die vielfältigen Beförderungen zurückzuführen

---

52 Vgl. Busquets Bragulat, Julio: El militar de carrera en España. Estudio de sociología militar. Barcelona 1971.

53 Ynfante, Jesús: El ejército de Franco y de Juan Carlos. Paris 1976. Payne, Stanley. G.: Los militares y la política en la España contemporánea. Paris 1968.

war. Parallel zu dieser erneuten Aufblähung des Personalbestandes lief ein technischer Rückschritt auf dem Gebiet der Ausrüstung. Schon vor Ende des Zweiten Weltkriegs hätte die spanische Armee von ihrem technischen Ausrüstungsstand her keine internationale Auseinandersetzung bestreiten können. Gelände- und Kampfausbildung wurden vernachlässigt, die finanziellen Zuwendungen zugunsten der Armee eingeschränkt, die fachliche Qualifikation der Offiziere ließ sehr zu wünschen übrig, auch der politische Einfluss der Spitzengeneräle in Regierungsämtern nahm ab; das Regime wandte sich verstärkt den drängenden Wirtschaftsproblemen zu.

Die in nahezu allen Bereichen feststellbare Zurückdrängung des Militärs und seine konsequente Entpolitisierung deuten darauf hin, dass das Regime bereits in den 50er Jahren sich selbst als stabilisiert betrachtete und von außen nicht bedroht fühlte. Die innenpolitischen Repressionsfunktionen, die die Streitkräfte im Jahrzehnt nach dem Bürgerkrieg ausübten, wurden später zumeist von den verschiedenen Polizeikräften und der kasernierten Gendarmerie (*Guardia Civil*) übernommen. Die Sicherheitskräfte umfassten ca. ein Drittel der militärischen Ist-Stärke; sie waren primär für die öffentliche Ordnung zuständig. Für die 40er Jahre liegen keine verlässlichen Zahlenangaben vor; 1971 umfassten sie rund 90.000 Mann. Dazu gehörten die Zivilgarde, Grenz- und bewaffnete Polizei.

Trotz der allmählichen Einfluss-, Macht- und Kompetenzbeschneidung der Militärs hat sich unter ihnen keine organisierte Opposition entwickelt. Finanzielle Privilegien und dekorative Ämter ließen die Offiziere zumeist ihr Schicksal widerspruchslos akzeptieren. Das durch den Bürgerkrieg geschmiedete Zusammengehörigkeitsgefühl, die überragende Stellung Francos als Oberkommandierender und Staatschef sowie die formale Beibehaltung vieler ranghoher Positionen trugen zur weitgehenden Disziplinierung und Entpolitisierung der Armee bei, die zwar weiterhin die wichtigste Stütze des Regimes blieb, in der Praxis aber keine großen Mitentscheidungsrechte genoss. Es ist Franco immer wieder gelungen, Unzufriedenheit und Kritik seitens der Streitkräfte durch geschicktes Ausspielen einer Militärfraktion gegen die andere, durch gezielte Beförderungen bzw. Entlassungen, durch überlegtes Taktieren und Ausmanövrieren unterschiedliche Richtungen zu neutralisieren – zum Beispiel zwischen den deutsch- und alliiertenfreundlichen Offizieren während des Zweiten Weltkrieges oder zwischen den Befürwortern einer Restauration der Monarchie und eher falangefreundlichen Kräften.[54]

Die (soziale und geographische) Herkunft der Offiziere, ihre Selbstrekrutierung, ihr besonderer Lebensstil und ihre weitgehende Isolierung vom Rest der Gesellschaft haben unter ihnen eine besondere Mentalität erhalten oder erzeugt, die das Offizierskorps als katholisch-konservativ, national und autoritätsgebunden erscheinen lässt. In einer Studie über Bedeutung und Einfluss der verschiedenen Offiziersgenerationen auf die Politik Francos hat die Autorin Barbara Könitz die spanischen Streitkräfte nach Generationen unterteilt und damit zugleich herausgearbeitet, welche Unterschiede es zwischen den generationellen Gruppierungen im Militär gab.[55]

„Die Franco am treuesten ergebene Generation ist die der Afrika-Offiziere. Hierunter fallen alle Offiziere, die den 18 Jahre lang währenden Krieg (1909–1927) in Marokko mitgemacht haben (...) Die Offiziere dieses Kolonialheeres waren die verlässlichsten Machtstützen Francos und nahmen

54 Zum Gesamtzusammenhang vgl. Collado Seidel, Carlos: Franco. General-Diktator-Mythos. Stuttgart 2015.

55 Könitz, Barbara: „Die Sozialstruktur der spanischen Streitkräfte“. In: Wehrkunde 8/1975, S. 404–408 und 9/1975, S. 464–469.

wichtige Positionen im militärischen und politischen Leben ein […] Die meisten Generale, die unter Franco Kabinettsposten und andere hohe Stellungen in der Militärhierarchie wie Militärgouverneur, Wehrbereichsbefehlshaber, hohe Verwaltungsposten in den Ministerien erreichten, gehörten der Afrika-Generation an. Viele von ihnen sympathisierten mit Deutschland, was nicht gleichzusetzen war mit Sympathien für den Nationalsozialismus. Einige, besonders die einflussreicheren Monarchisten, waren anglophil, ebenso fast alle Aristokraten unter den Afrika-Offizieren […] Was war die Geisteshaltung dieser Afrika-Kämpfer, die auch die Generation von 1915 genannt wurde? Sie zeichnete sich vor allem durch Loyalität und Ordnung aus […] Die dritte Offiziersgeneration ist mit dem Bürgerkrieg von 1936–1939 eng verbunden. Sie ist bestimmt durch die große Zahl von provisorischen Leutnants (alféreces provisionales), die in die Streitkräfte der Nationalisten aufgenommen wurden. Das Offizierskorps der Nationalisten wurde hauptsächlich von jungen Männern zwischen 20 und 30 Jahren aufgefüllt, die eine Berufsausbildung oder einen dem Abitur vergleichbaren Abschluss haben mussten. In der Praxis bedeutete das, dass die rund 29.000 am Ende des Bürgerkriegs festgestellten Hilfsoffiziere Universitätsstudenten waren oder die mittlere Reife mit Berufsausbildung hatten. Etwa 4.000 der provisorischen Leutnants sind gefallen. Ein großer Teil kehrte nach dem Bürgerkrieg ins Zivilleben zurück, doch bestand Mitte der 60er Jahre noch ungefähr die Hälfte des spanischen aktiven Offizierskorps aus inzwischen in die Streitkräfte aufgenommenen und beförderten ehemaligen Bürgerkriegsleutnants. Diese Generation zeichnet sich durch Nationalismus, Antikommunismus, Antiliberalismus und vor allem starken Dogmatismus aus, wie dies logisch ist bei Leuten, die ihre Ideen jahrelang mit der Waffe in der Hand verteidigt haben […] Anhänger der Nationalisten zu sein, bedeutet gleichzeitig ein Synonym für Religion, Tradition und spanischen Patriotismus."

Die knapp 40 Jahre Franquismus haben jedoch bei zumindest partieller Professionalisierung und weitgehender Entpolitisierung des Militärs ein neues Rollenverständnis der Streitkräfte hervorgebracht, zu dem nicht unbedingt die Identifizierung mit dem Franquismus gehörte. Gerade die Respektierung von Autorität sowie die Entpolitisierung und Disziplinierung der Militärs während des Franquismus sollten zu entscheidenden Voraussetzungen dafür werden, dass die Streitkräfte nach 1975 letzten Endes doch den in legalen Wahlen vorgenommenen politischen Wechsel zu einer demokratischen Staatsform akzeptierten. Für die Frage nach der Typologie des Franco-Regimes wiederum bedeuteten die strukturelle Entwicklung des Militärs und die Einstellung des Offizierskorps, dass das franquistische System nicht vorbehaltlos – bei aller Bedeutung des Militärs – als Militärdiktatur bezeichnet werden kann, da letztlich auch die Institution Militär von Franco primär zur Absicherung seiner Autokratie eingesetzt wurde, das Militär aber nicht als Korporation der eigentliche Machthaber im „Neuen Staat" war.

2. Der Nationalkatholizismus als Wesen des Franco-Regimes

Die rebellierenden Militärs wurden von einer breiten Front politisch rechtsstehender Gruppierungen unterstützt, die später die verschiedenen „politischen Familien" des Regimes bildeten. Eine der Institutionen, die den frühen Franquismus mittrugen, war die katholische Amtskirche, die über 20 Jahre lang zu den wirkungsvollsten Stützen der franquistischen Herrschaft gehörte und deren Legitimationsbeschafferin war. Die Kirche hat sich nach 1939 als eine Märtyrerorganisation des Bürgerkriegs verstanden und für die Leiden und Verluste an Kirchengut und Priestern vom Staat erhebliche Konzessionen im Bereich von Gesellschaft und Erziehung einräumen lassen. Nicht von ungefähr ist der Franquismus eine „klerikalfaschistische" Herrschaftsform genannt worden – eine Bezeichnung, die auf die enge Verflechtung staatlicher und kirchlicher Institutionen hinweist.

Seit Beginn des Bürgerkriegs schon war die katholische Kirche eine tragende Säule des neuen Regimes. Zum Verständnis der späteren Rolle der Kirche im „Neuen Staat" muss deshalb darauf hingewiesen werden, dass der Bürgerkrieg im Selbstverständnis der Kirche und der „nationalen" Seite insgesamt ein „Kreuzzug" war. Am 16. November 1937 erklärte Franco:[56]

„Unser Krieg ist kein Bürgerkrieg, kein Krieg eines *Pronunciamiento*, sondern ein Kreuzzug der Menschen, die an Gott glauben, die an die menschliche Seele glauben, die an das Gute, das Ideal, das Opfer glauben, die gegen die Menschen ohne Glauben, ohne Moral, ohne Edelmut kämpfen [...] Ja, unser Krieg ist ein Religionskrieg. Alle, die wir kämpfen, Christen oder Muslime, sind wir Soldaten Gottes; wir kämpfen nicht gegen andere Menschen, sondern gegen den Atheismus und den Materialismus, gegen all das, was die menschliche Würde erniedrigt, die wir aufrichten, reinigen und veredeln wollen."

Am 1. Juli 1937 hatte der spanische Episkopat (von zwei Ausnahmen abgesehen) jenen berühmt gewordenen gemeinsamen Brief (*Carta Colectiva*) an die Bischöfe der ganzen Welt veröffentlicht, der praktisch eine politische Stellungnahme, eine deutliche Rechtfertigung des Militäraufstandes und dessen theologische Sanktion war. Die Bischöfe sahen im

56 Zit. nach Altaffaylla Kultur Taldea: Navarra 1936. De la esperanza al terror. Bd. 1. Tafalla 1986, S. 412.

Krieg eine Konfrontation zwischen Gut und Böse, des „gesunden Volkes“ gegen die fremde und gottlose Einmischung des Kommunismus; sie stellten damit die unversöhnliche Dualität Spaniens fest, die in moralischen Kategorien begriffen wurde. Die Auseinandersetzung nahm für sie die Form einer fundamentalen metaphysisch-ethischen Konfrontation gegensätzlicher Werte an, wobei die Kirche sich gemäß dieser Vorstellung nur auf die Seite des Guten stellen konnte. Einige aussagekräftige Sätze aus dem Brief:[57]

„Es hat im nationalen Geist eine Reaktion religiöser Art stattgefunden, die der nihilistischen und zerstörenden Aktion der Gottlosen entgegentrat [...] Das Volk war in zwei Richtungen getrennt: die geistige auf der Seite der Aufständischen, die für Ordnung, den sozialen Frieden, für die traditionelle Kultur und für das Vaterland und ein großer Teil sehr offen für die Verteidigung der Religion auftrat; auf der anderen Seite die materialistische, d. h. marxistische, kommunistische oder anarchistische, die die alte Kultur Spaniens mit all ihren Faktoren durch die neueste ‚Zivilisation‘ der russischen Sowjets ersetzen wollte [...] Wir behaupten, dass die bürgerlich-militärische Erhebung im Grunde des Volksgewissens einen zweifachen Grundzug hatte: den vaterländischen Sinn, der darin die einzige Art, Spanien zu erheben und seinen endgültigen Ruin zu vermeiden, sah, und den religiösen Sinn, der den Aufstand als die Gewalt betrachtete, welche die Feinde Gottes entkräften sollte, und als die Garantie für das Fortdauern ihres Glaubens und die Ausübung ihrer Religion. Heutzutage gibt es in Spanien keine andere Hoffnung, um das Recht und den Frieden und die sich daraus ableitenden Güter wieder zu erobern, als den Sieg der nationalen Bewegung.“

57 Rundschreiben der spanischen Bischöfe an die Bischöfe der ganzen Welt über den Bürgerkrieg in Spanien. Graz 1937, S. 20, 22.

In diesem Brief wurden die Begriffe Vaterland und Religion, nationale Tradition und katholischer Glaube vermischt; der andere Teil Spaniens wurde als „antispanisch" und „antichristlich" bezeichnet. Die geistige Zweiteilung Spaniens war keineswegs neu, sie hatte vielmehr Tradition. Francisco Ayala hat die Folgen dieses Manichäismus folgendermaßen beschrieben: „Die Spanier wurden nach einer ideologischen Formel eingeteilt, die davon ausging, dass in Spaniens Schoß ein ungeheuerliches Geschöpf entstanden war, das sogenannte Anti-Spanien, das man unbedingt wie ein bösartiges Gewächs herausschneiden musste [...] Als diese geistige Strömung sich mit dem Traditionalismus verband, der den nationalen Gedanken mit der Sache des Katholizismus identifizierte, gewann der Bürgerkrieg von 1936 auf der rechten Seite einen geradezu religiösen Charakter; der Kampf verwandelte sich in einen Religionskrieg, so wie man von Anfang an gepredigt hatte. Entsprechend ihrer Zugehörigkeit zu der einen oder anderen Seite waren die einen Spanier rein und die anderen verrucht."[58]

Gefestigt wurde das Bündnis zwischen den Mächtigen von Kirche und „Neuem Staat" noch durch die Abwehrhaltung gegen den hasserfüllten Antiklerikalismus, der zu Beginn des Bürgerkrieges zerstörerisch aufbrach. Die Erinnerung an den Krieg als glorreichen Kreuzzug wurde sodann zu einem Dauerthema der spanischen Amtskirche nach 1939. Enrique Pla y Deniel, als Nachfolger von Kardinal Gomá Primas von Spanien, sagte 1948: „Sollten wir nicht auch ‚defensores civitatis' werden – nicht beim Ergreifen der Waffen, wohl aber bei der Ausübung unseres Lehramtes und angesichts des moralischen Gewichts unserer Autorität – zur Rettung der Religion und des Vaterlandes? Eben das haben wir, die spa-

58 Ayala, Francisco: Spanien heute. Darmstadt 1966, S. 34.

nischen Bischöfe, mit unserem Brief von 1937 getan." 1958 führte er weiter aus: „Die Kirche hätte weder einen bloßen Militärputsch noch eine Partei im Bürgerkrieg gesegnet. Sie segnete einen Kreuzzug [...] Jene, die die schwierige Aufgabe unternahmen, die Rechte Gottes und der Kirche in Spanien zu verteidigen."[59]

Rückhaltlose Anerkennung und Unterstützung erfuhr das neue Regime nicht nur von Seiten des spanischen Episkopats; am 15. April 1939 hatte auch Papst Pius XII. in einer Rundfunkbotschaft den Siegern im Bürgerkrieg gratuliert: „Mit größter Freude wenden wir uns an Euch, geliebteste Kinder des katholischen Spanien, um Euch unseren väterlichen Glückwunsch für den Frieden und den Sieg auszusprechen, mit dem Gott gnädigerweise das christliche Heldentum Eures Glaubens und Eurer Barmherzigkeit gekrönt hat, die Ihr in so vielen und großzügigen Leiden unter Beweis gestellt habt [...] Die Absichten der Vorsehung, geliebteste Kinder, haben sich erneut gegenüber dem heldenhaften Spanien gezeigt, der von Gott als wichtigstes Instrument der Evangelisierung der neuen Welt und als uneinnehmbare Festung des katholischen Glaubens auserwählten Nation; der katholische Glaube hat soeben den Anhängern des materialistischen Atheismus unseres Jahrhunderts den erhabensten Beweis dafür geliefert, dass die ewigen Werte der Religion und des Geistes über allem stehen. Es ist nun an Euch, verehrte Brüder im Episkopat, die eine ebenso wie die andere Seite zu beraten, damit alle in ihrer Befriedungspolitik die Prinzipien verfolgen, die von der Kirche gelehrt und mit so viel Edelmut vom Generalissimus verkündet worden sind: Gerechtigkeit gegenüber

59 Zit. nach Arbeloa, Victor Manuel: Aquella España católica. Salamanca 1975, S. 248.

dem Verbrechen und gütige Großzügigkeit gegenüber den Irregeleiteten."[60]

Es ist aufschlussreich, dass diese päpstliche Botschaft im „neuen" Spanien zensiert wurde; jene Abschnitte nämlich, die Menschlichkeit bei der Behandlung der Besiegten forderten, wurden verschwiegen. Auch der Hirtenbrief von Kardinal Gomá „Die Lehren des Krieges und die Pflichten des Friedens" vom 8. August 1939, der einen Aufruf zur Vergebung und Versöhnung sowie eine Verurteilung des Totalitarismus enthielt, durfte nicht veröffentlicht werden.[61] Diese Beispiele deuten darauf hin, dass in den Jahren nach 1939 (dies gilt insbesondere für die Zeit bis 1945) ein Machtkampf zwischen Falange und Kirche um die Ausrichtung und die führenden Positionen des Regimes stattfand. Der anfangs vorherrschende faschistisch-totalitäre Charakter des „Neuen Staates" etwa erfuhr sofort die Gegnerschaft der katholischen Kirche. In einem Brief an den Vatikan charakterisierte, unmittelbar nach Kriegsende, der Erzbischof von Sevilla, Kardinal Pedro Segura, die Falange mit den Worten: „Falange ist der große Feind der spanischen Kirche, der Ort, wo sich alle alten Feinde der Kirche verschanzt haben; und aus diesem Schützengraben, den sie sich gesucht haben und in dem sie sich durch den Staat geschützt sehen, schießen sie aus dem Hinterhalt heraus gegen unsere Heilige Religion."[62]

Andererseits bestand nicht (wie etwa im nationalsozialistischen Fall) eine unüberwindbare weltanschauliche Gegnerschaft zwischen Einheitspartei und Kirche. Erstere hatte vielmehr von den spanischen Traditionalisten des 19. Jahr-

---

60 Zit. nach Altaffayla Kultur Taldea 1986, S. 417.

61 Hierzu Garriga, Ramón: El Cardenal Segura y el Nacional-Catolicismo. Barcelona 1977, S. 267–268.

62 Ebda., S. 273.

hunderts die Vorstellung der Einheit von Staat und Kirche übernommen. Die Forderung eines „neuen Staates" faschistischer Katholizität ist auch bei Ernesto Giménez Caballero, einem der Hauptideologen des spanischen Faschismus (*Genio de España*, 1932), anzutreffen. Der Falangegründer José Antonio Primo de Rivera behauptete ebenfalls die Idee der Katholizität als konstitutives Moment des Selbstverständnisses des zu schaffenden neuen Staates. Dadurch, dass die aufständischen Kräfte von 1936 die Ideologie der Falange zur Grundlage eines Großteils ihrer Staats- und Gesellschaftslehre machten, wurde der neue Staat eine Art praktische Verwirklichung der Vorstellungen spanischer Traditionalisten. Die Einheit und die Katholizität gaben dem staatlichen Gefüge Festigkeit, sie wurden zur Legitimationsinstanz des politischen Regimes. Religionsfreiheit war damit im neuen System nicht möglich.[63]

Erwartungsgemäß erhielt die Kirche im franquistischen Staat all ihre Vorrechte zurück; in dem 1945 verabschiedeten „Grundrechtskatalog" wurde die katholische Religion zur Staatsreligion erhoben: „Das Bekenntnis zur katholischen Religion, die die des spanischen Staates ist, und ihre Ausübung stehen unter staatlichem Schutz. Niemand wird wegen seiner religiösen Überzeugungen und der privaten Durchführung von Kulthandlungen behelligt. Andere öffentliche Zeremonien und Kundgebungen als die der katholischen Religion sind nicht erlaubt." (Grundgesetz der Spanier, Art. 6)

---

63 Zum Verhältnis Katholizismus-Faschismus sowie zum Kampf um Hegemonie im Franco-Regime zwischen Katholiken und Falangisten vgl. die überaus detaillierte und faktengesättigte Studie von Gallego, Ferran: El evangelio fascista. La formación de la cultura política del franquismo (1930–1950). Barcelona 2014.

1946 legten Abkommen zwischen Staat und Kirche fest, dass der Staat die Kirche zu subventionieren habe. Das Eherecht von 1947 erklärte zivile Eheschließungen ebenso wie Scheidungen für ungesetzlich; seit 1950 verfügten Kirchenangehörige über eigene Gerichte. Die Kirche erhielt direktes Repräsentationsrecht in wichtigen Staats- und Regierungsgremien, etwa in den Cortes, im Kron- und Staatsrat. Im gesellschaftlichen Bereich übte sie (vor allem über die Zensurbehörde) eine Sexualrepression aus, von der sich die spanische Gesellschaft erst nach Francos Tod allmählich erholte.[64] Zu den bedeutendsten Rechten und Einflussmöglichkeiten der Kirche gehörte zweifellos die Kontrolle fast des gesamten Bildungswesens – nicht nur in der Schule, sondern auch auf der Universität.[65]

Andererseits band sich auch die Kirche eng an das Regime, von dem sie nicht weniger abhängig war als dieses von ihr. Gemäß dem Abkommen zwischen der spanischen Regierung und dem Heiligen Stuhl vom 7. Juni 1941 wurden die spanischen Bischöfe von Staatschef Franco dem Vatikan zur Ernennung vorgeschlagen, womit die Treue des Episkopats zum Regime sichergestellt war.[66] Seit 1953 mussten die Bischöfe folgenden Treueeid leisten: „Ich schwöre und verspreche

---

64 Vgl. Tejada, Luis Alonso: „La represión sexual en la España de Franco". In: Historia 16, Nr. 9, 1977, S. 29–36.

65 Vgl. Miret Magdalena, Enrique: „La educación nacionalcatólica en nuestra posguerra." In: Tiempo de Historia Nr. 16, 1976, S. 4–21; Cámara Villar, Gregorio: Nacional-Catolicismo y Escuela. La socialización política del franquismo (1936–1951). Jaén 1984.

66 Die ausführlichste Darstellung (mit reichem Dokumententeil) über dieses Abkommen ist von Marquina Barrio, Antonio: La diplomacia vaticana y la España de Franco (1936–1945). Madrid 1983.

vor Gott und den Heiligen Evangelien Treue zum spanischen Staat, wie es einem Bischof gebührt [...] Ich schwöre und verspreche, den spanischen Staatschef und die nach den spanischen Gesetzen eingesetzte Regierung zu respektieren und dafür zu sorgen, dass meine Priester sie respektieren. Ich schwöre und verspreche, an keiner Versammlung teilzunehmen, die dem spanischen Staat und der öffentlichen Ordnung schaden könnte, und dafür zu sorgen, dass meine Priester sich dementsprechend verhalten.“[67]

Neben den staatlichen Veranstaltungen, an denen die Kirche ständig partizipierte, machte sich ihre Omnipräsenz vor allem auf dem gesellschaftlichen Sektor bemerkbar, mit dem der einzelne täglich in Berührung kam. Das konfessionell fixierte System und die ständige Kirchenpräsenz führten zu einer religiösen Ausnahmesituation, deren Charakteristika in den ersten Nachkriegsjahren der intolerante „Nationalkatholizismus“, ein religiöses Ausufern im öffentlichen, häufig auch im privaten Leben, Doktrinarismus und Autoritarismus waren.[68] Dass Franco die liturgisch-kanonischen Ehrenrechte, die früher dem König eingeräumt waren, genoss und stets unter dem von Priestern getragenen Baldachin in die mit großem Pomp veranstalteten Hochämter einzog, wurde als selbstverständlich akzeptiert; auch gegen die Münzaufschrift „Francisco Franco, Caudillo Spaniens von Gottes Gnaden“ erhob sich kirchlicherseits kein Widerstand. Alltäglich wurden im Rundfunk vor dem Abspielen der Nationalhymne die „glorreich für Gott und Vaterland Gefallenen“ angerufen;

---

67 Zit. nach Nodinot, Jean-François: L'Eglise et le pouvoir en Espagne. Paris 1973, S. 85.

68 Vgl. Novoa, Laurentino: Religionsfreiheit in Spanien. Geschichte-Problematik-Zukunftsperspektiven. Frankfurt a. M. 1978.

die Muttergottes erhielt den Rang eines Ehrengenerals der spanischen Armee zugesprochen. Die Volksabstimmungen, durch die Franco sein Regime plebiszitär institutionalisierte, erfuhren die rückhaltlose Unterstützung der Amtskirche.

Die spanischen Bischöfe und die katholische Presse lobten Franco in theologisch-messianischen Tönen als Retter der Nation und Vorkämpfer religiöser und kirchlicher Rechte. Er habe nicht nur die christliche Zivilisation vor dem Untergang bewahrt, sondern sei ein religiös-mythischer Messias, der das Reich Gottes in Spanien wiederherstellt. Dieser Ideologie zufolge war die aus dem Krieg hervorgegangene katholische Restauration die Verwirklichung des Gottesreiches auf Erden; darin lag letztendlich der tiefste Grund, der die Legitimation des Regimes durch die Kirche erklärt.

Das neue politisch-religiöse System der Nachkriegszeit, der Nationalkatholizismus, berief sich einseitig auf die „glorreiche“ Vergangenheit unter Verdrängung und Verleugnung anderer Traditionen, um die einheitliche religiös-politische Ordnung zu legitimieren. Die „Restauration“ im politischen, gesellschaftlichen und religiösen Leben wollte damit die „wahre“ Geschichte Spaniens fortsetzen; die religiöse Praxis hatte sich an einem bestimmten Bild der Vergangenheit als einzig verbindlichem Vorbild eines nationalen Katholizismus zu orientieren. Ein Apologet des Regimes drückte dies folgendermaßen aus: „Die großen Gründungslinien des Regimes sind endgültig, nicht veränderbar. Das gegenwärtige Regime zeichnet sich durch seine Katholizität und durch die Einführung eines sozial-repräsentativen Staates aus. Durch seine Katholizität hat der spanische Staat die Neutralität der modernen Staaten überwunden [...] Dies ist wirklich das wahre Spanien, das große Spanien, würdig seiner besten und glorreichen Traditionen; dies Spanien setzt jenes des großen imperialen und katholischen goldenen Zeitalters fort."[69]

Die gegenreformatorischen und kämpferischen Züge der Vergangenheit wurden wiederbelebt, um das Einheitsideal des Systems reinzuhalten; katholisches Bewusstsein wurde daher auch mit patriotisch-nationalem Sinn identifiziert. Auf Schulen und Universitäten wurden Schüler und Studenten im Geist des Nationalkatholizismus erzogen; auf theologischen Hochschulen wurde der Thomismus nach den scholastischen Methoden gelehrt. Das Universitätsgesetz vom 29. Juli 1943 besagte: „Die Universität ruht auf der katholischen Lehre, die der Tradition spanischer Universitäten wesensverwandt ist; sie wird die universitäre Lehre dem Dogma, der katholischen Moral und den Normen des Kanonischen Rechts anpassen."

Ausbildung und Erziehung der jungen Generationen wurden so von einem ausgesprochen gegenaufklärerischen Geist geprägt. Der neue Nationalkatholizismus, der im Werk von José Pemartín *Qué es lo nuevo?* auf den Begriff gebracht wurde, lässt sich folgendermaßen charakterisieren:[70] Das Wesen der spanischen Nationalität ist der Katholizismus; der Katholizismus als „Wurzel Spaniens" hat sich historisch im 16. Jahrhundert konkretisiert; die Hauptelemente des spanischen Nationalismus werden im Traditionalismus bewahrt. Pemartín zog aus diesen Prinzipien die Konsequenz, dass der spanische Staat notwendigerweise katholisch sein müsse, wenn Spanien national (und faschistisch) sein wollte. Die katholische Konfessionalität des Staates erhielt metaphy-

---

69 Rey, José M. del: Religión y Política. Montevideo 1953, S. 212 und 222.

70 Pemartín, José: Qué es lo nuevo? Madrid 3. Aufl. 1940. Zu Pemartín und dem Nationalkatholizismus vgl. Cuenca Toribio, José Manuel: Nacionalismo, Franquismo y Nacionalcatolicismo. Madrid 2008, S. 112–125.

sischen Charakter zugesprochen, da durch sie Nation und Katholizismus zu „einem Wesen“ verschmolzen wurden.

Übte die weltliche Gewalt (des katholischen Staates) eine politisch-ideologische Kontrolle entsprechend den Prinzipien der „nationalen Bewegung“ aus, so beanspruchte die Kirche die religiös-ideologische Kontrolle über Erziehung und Kultur des Landes.[71] Die nationalkatholische Restauration der Nachkriegszeit eröffnete der Kirche die Möglichkeit, ihren Einfluss in allen Bereichen der Kultur geltend zu machen; die „glorreichen“ Zeiten der katholisch-nationalen Vergangenheit schienen wiederzukehren, Wissenschaft und Kultur hatten sich innerhalb der katholischen Orthodoxie zu bewegen, der Traditionalist Marcelino Menéndez Pelayo galt als „Lehrer und Vorbild für alle spanischen Intellektuellen“.

Als Leitlinien des spanischen Episkopats in der Nachkriegsphase lassen sich zusammenfassend festhalten: Der von der Kirche als Kreuzzug legitimierte Bürgerkrieg prägte zu einem Großteil das Denken der Kirchenhierarchie; die Bischöfe wurden zu Behütern der Kreuzzugsideologie. Sie legitimierten öffentlich das aus dem Bürgerkrieg hervorgegangene Regime; damit stellten sie zugleich ihre privilegierte Stellung und ihren Einfluss in allen Bereichen der Gesellschaft sicher. Der Katholizismus galt nicht nur als Religion des Staates und der Nation, sondern als formende Kraft der spanischen Geschichte. Die katholische Einheit wurde daher in einem religiös-politischen Sinn verstanden. Der Grundgedanke der spanischen Traditionalisten, der katholische Glaube sei konstitutiv für die Geschichte Spaniens und erfordere einen Exklusivitätsanspruch gegenüber allen anderen Religionen

---

71 Iribarren, Jesús (Hg.): Documentos colectivos del Episcopado español (1870–1974). Madrid 1974, S. 243–249, 250–257, 277–285.

und Konfessionen, lässt sich auch in den Institutionen und der späteren Gesetzgebung des franquistischen Regimes deutlich erkennen. Die Grundeinstellung der Amtskirche beharrte auf den Prinzipien des Nationalkatholizismus, die den Geist eines katholischen Spanien wieder erwecken und die „wahre" Tradition Spaniens wiederherstellen sollten. Deswegen stellte die Kirche auch die politische Praxis des Regimes selbst dann nicht infrage, wenn diese Praxis die Grundfreiheiten der Menschen missachtete.

In den 40er und 50er Jahren war die Kirche bemüht, innerhalb des Machtblocks ihre Position zu verbessern und ihre Rivalin, die Falange, möglichst aus den Schaltstellen der Macht zu verdrängen. Hierzu bediente der Episkopat sich der Laienorganisationen, die in den Jahren nach 1939 gewissermaßen als Transmissionsriemen kirchlichen Eingreifens in die politische Sphäre fungierten. Insbesondere wurden die Basisorganisationen „Katholische Aktion" (*Acción Católica*) und „Nationale Katholische Vereinigung von Familienvätern" (*Confederación Católica Nacional de Padres de Familia*) gefördert, um einerseits im Bildungsbereich, andererseits im politisch-syndikalistischen Sektor Positionsgewinne zu erzielen. Die wichtigste Laienorganisation nach 1939 wurde die „Nationale Katholische Vereinigung von Propagandisten" (*Asociación Católica Nacional de Propagandistas*, ACNP). Sie gehörte nach dem Bürgerkrieg zu den wichtigsten Säulen des „Neuen Staates" und leistete zweifellos einen entscheidenden Beitrag zur Institutionalisierung des Franco-Regimes. Die Bedeutung der ACNP wurde durch zwei Faktoren potenziert:[72] Zum einen monopolisierte die Falange – wie

72 Vgl. Montero, José Ramón: „Los Católicos y el Nuevo Estado: Los perfiles ideológicos de la ACNP durante la primera etapa del franquismo". In: Fontana, Josep (Hg.): España bajo el fran-

weiter oben dargelegt – keineswegs den Zugang zur politischen Elite, musste vielmehr viele Parzellen von Macht und Einfluss mit anderen Institutionen teilen (die Kontrolle der Presse und des Bildungsbereichs etwa als Juniorpartner mit der sehr viel einflussreicheren Kirche); eine Gleichschaltung gelang ihr nie. Zum anderen spielte die Kirche als Legitimationsinstanz des neuen Regimes eine weit herausragendere Rolle als etwa die falangistisch-faschistische Ideologie.

Der ACNP ging es in ihrer Strategie, die in enger Anlehnung an die Kirche verfolgt wurde, um die Erarbeitung eines ideologischen Projektes, das eine katholische Ergänzung zum falangistischen darstellte und dessen radikale Tendenzen neutralisierte; außerdem sollte es eine gangbare Alternative für die Kontinuität des franquistischen Regimes bieten. Zum anderen schickte sich die ACNP als wirksames Instrument der Kirche an, die Führungspositionen in der Gesellschaft zu besetzen. Schließlich fädelte die Organisation sich in wichtige Bereiche des „Neuen Staates“, des Bildungs- und Wirtschaftsbereichs ein. Als das Regime bei Beendigung des Zweiten Weltkriegs eine partielle Reorientierung vornehmen musste, um politisch überleben zu können, griff es auf die „katholische Lösung“ der ACNP zurück. Die katholischen Laienorganisationen lieferten dem neuen politischen System die größte Anzahl an Personen mit politischer und Regierungserfahrung (aus der Zeit vor 1936). Die Falange stellte allerdings in der Franco-Ära insgesamt 27,8 % der Inhaber politischer Spitzenpositionen (Minister, Staatssekretäre, Generaldirektoren), die Militärs machten gar 37,7 % aus, während aus katholischen Organisationen nur 12,8 % der politischen Elite

quismo. Barcelona 1986, S. 100–122. Die offiziöse Geschichte der Organisation ist González Ruiz, Nicolás/Martínez, Isidoro: Seglares en la historia de España. Madrid 1968.

rekrutiert wurden. Miguel Jerez Mir weist in seiner Elitestudie zum Franquismus jedoch darauf hin, dass mehr auf die Qualität als auf die Quantität der Amtsinhaber zu achten ist; er betont insbesondere die Kompetenz der „Katholiken" und ihren realen Einflussbereich. Zwischen 1938 und 1945 stellten sie den Erziehungs-, Finanz- und Industrieminister, zwischen 1945 und 1951 den Außen-und Erziehungsminister sowie die Minister für Öffentliche Arbeiten und für das Präsidialamt.[73] Eine Schlüsselfunktion sollte der Staatssekretär (später Minister) im Präsidialamt, Luis Carrero Blanco, einnehmen.

Der Regierungswechsel von 1945 brachte den eigentlichen Machtzuwachs der „Katholiken" auf Regierungsebene; dieses Revirement stellte gewissermaßen die öffentliche Anerkennung der Rolle dar, die die katholische Kirche bei der Konsolidierung des Regimes gespielt hatte. Außerdem verfolgte es eine spezifische strategische Zielsetzung: Im Innern wie nach außen musste das Regime an Glaubwürdigkeit gewinnen, dazu bedurfte es des Abbaus der totalitären und der Förderung der katholischen Elemente als regimelegitimierende Faktoren. Es kommt somit nicht von ungefähr, dass das Außenministerium an das ACNP-Mitglied Alberto Martín Artajo fiel und der Kompetenzbereich des Erziehungsministeriums erheblich erweitert wurde. Noch stärker als zuvor schon kam es jetzt zu einer Fusion von Nationalismus und Katholizismus als Formel von Sozialdisziplinierung und politischer Legitimierung. Die bürgerliche Konterrevolution, die der frühe Franquismus darstellte, bedurfte jener nationalis-

73 Jerez Mir, Miguel: Elites políticas y centros de extracción en España, 1938–1957. Madrid 1982, bes. S. 345–366.

tischen und katholisierenden Ingredienzien, deren Mischung den Nationalkatholizismus der 40er und 50er Jahre ergab.[74]

So überzeugend die bisher vorgebrachten Beispiele dafür sprechen, den Franquismus als Nationalkatholizismus zu charakterisieren, so deutlich muss andererseits darauf hingewiesen werden, dass diese Typologisierung nur für die 40er und einen Teil der 50er Jahre zutreffend ist. Denn schon bald nach dem Bürgerkrieg griff in den Regionen, in denen die soziale Situation der unteren Volksschichten am deprimierendsten war, an der Basis kirchlicher Organisationen ein neues Bewusstsein bezüglich der Rolle von Kirche und Religion in Staat und Gesellschaft um sich; die sozialkritische Haltung vieler junger Priester, die die berechtigten Forderungen der Arbeiter unterstützten, richtete sich nicht nur gegen die herrschenden Klassen und den Staat, sondern (vorerst nur indirekt und vorsichtig) auch gegen die kirchliche Hierarchie, die das System wesentlich mittrug und legitimierte. Ein Teil der Kirche ging allmählich dazu über, von der engen Verflechtung mit dem Staat abzurücken und auf deutliche Distanzierung zum Regime zu setzen. Dieser Prozess beschleunigte sich sodann nach dem (von vielen spanischen Bischöfen abgelehnten) *aggiornamento* der katholischen Kirche auf dem Zweiten Vatikanischen Konzil in den 60er Jahren.

Der allmähliche Bewusstseinswandel bei einem Teil der kirchlichen Basis lässt deutlich werden, dass die Kirche sich anschickte, eine neue Funktion im Staat zu übernehmen. Denn in einem nichtdemokratischen Regime wie dem franquistischen übernehmen religiöse Institutionen stillschwei-

---

74 Zur Bedeutung der „Katholiken“, vor allem nach 1945, für die internationale Aufwertung des Franco-Regimes vgl. Tusell, Javier: Franco y los católicos. La política interior española entre 1945 y 1957. Madrid 1984.

gend einige der Funktionen, die in demokratischen Systemen Parteien oder freie Gewerkschaften innehaben. Ab Ende der 50er Jahre wurde die Kirche zu einem bevorzugten Ort einer reformistisch gesinnten Opposition gegenüber dem Regime. Die politische Funktion, die die Kirche in dieser Zeit hatte, war eher kritischer als legitimierender Art, und es ging nicht nur um die Verteidigung religiöser Interessen gegenüber dem Staat, sondern um die Vertretung politischer und vor allem sozialer Belange breiter Bevölkerungsschichten, die keine direkte Repräsentation im System hatten. Die Kirche wurde zu einer Art ‚Volkstribun', zum Verteidiger von Gruppen, denen die Staatsmacht gesetzliche Formen politischer Meinungsäußerung vorenthielt.[75] Die Stellungnahmen der kirchlichen Hierarchie und der Laienverbände wurden immer weiter gefasst, die Grenze zwischen sozialem Lehramt und politischer Stellungnahme war kaum mehr zu erkennen. Es begann mit Kritik an den sozialen Einrichtungen und Zwängen des Staates, führte zur Forderung nach Anerkennung der Menschenrechte und mündete in stets ‚radikalere' Vorstellungen von grundsätzlicher Revision der politischen Struktur. In der letzten Phase des Regimes war die Kritik der Bischöfe unmissverständlich; engagierte katholische Studenten und Arbeiter, ein bedeutender Teil des jungen Klerus und einige junge Weihbischöfe radikalisierten sie weiter, sodass die Kritik schließlich immer mehr die Form eines fast politischen Programms als Alternative zum bestehenden politisch-sozialen System annahm.[76]

---

75 Zum Konzept des „Volkstribuns" für die Kirche in nichtdemokratischen Regimen vgl. Hermet, Guy: Les Catholiques dans l'Espagne Franquiste. 2 Bde. Paris 1980/1981.

76 Vgl. Bernecker, Walther L.: „Der katholische Klerus und das Franco-Regime". In: Oberdorfer, Bernd/Waldmann, Peter (Hg.): Die Ambivalenz des Religiösen. Religionen als Friedensstifter

Demonstrationen von Priestergruppen und Priesterverhaftungen waren Ende der 60er Jahre an der Tagesordnung, die Konflikte zwischen Staat und Kirche mehrten sich. Im September 1971 fand die erste „Gemeinsame Versammlung von Bischöfen und Priestern" statt, die einen umfangreichen Forderungskatalog an die Regierung verabschiedete (Meinungs-, Versammlungs-, Gewerkschaftsfreiheit, Rechte für ethnische Minderheiten, Abschaffung der Folter etc.). Die Schlusspassage der Resolution erhielt zwar nicht die erforderliche Zweidrittelmehrheit der Stimmen, wurde somit nicht offiziell verabschiedet, stellt jedoch trotzdem die deutlichste kirchliche Distanzierung vom Franco-Regime und das beeindruckendste Schuldbekenntnis der spanischen Kirche wegen ihrer seit 1936 eingeschlagenen Politik dar: „Wir erkennen demütig an und bitten um Verzeihung, dass wir es nicht rechtzeitig verstanden haben, echte Diener der Wiederversöhnung im Schoß unseres durch einen Krieg zwischen Brüdern gespaltenen Volkes zu sein."[77]

In den letzten Jahren des Franco-Regimes ging der Streit in erster Linie um die Frage der ‚Einmischung' der Kirche in die Politik. Während kirchliche Repräsentanten wiederholt erklärten, sie hätten ein Recht und die Pflicht, die bestehenden Zustände im Land aus der Perspektive der kirchlichen Moral- und Soziallehre zu beurteilen, interpretierte der franquistische Staat derartige Äußerungen als unerlaubte Einmischung. Am Ende der Franco-Ära erfüllte die katholische Kirche die erforderlichen Voraussetzungen, um zur Verteidigerin jener Gruppen werden zu können, denen die Staats-

und Gewalterzeuger. Freiburg i. Br. 2008, S. 187–217; Casanova, Julián: La Iglesia de Franco. Madrid 2001.

77 Zit. nach Biescas, José A./Tuñón de Lara, Manuel: España bajo la dictadura franquista (1939–1975). Barcelona 1980, S. 417.

macht die Möglichkeit freier, politischer Meinungsäußerung vorenthielt: Sie verfügte über eine genügend starke Präsenz und Glaubwürdigkeit insbesondere in den Schichten, die sie zu verteidigen sich vorgenommen hatte. Außerdem hatte sie einen gewissen Toleranzspielraum, um ihre Meinungen äußern zu können. Und schließlich konnten die Regierungen sich darauf verlassen, dass die kirchlichen Inhaber der neuen ‚tribunizischen' Rolle die politische Elite des Regimes nicht aus ihren Machtpositionen verdrängen wollten.

Somit kann festgehalten werden: In historischer Perspektive kam der Kirche im nationalkatholischen Spanien Francos zuerst die Rolle des wichtigsten ideologischen Regulators zu, des ‚organischen Intellektuellen' der leitenden Schichten im Sinne Gramscis. Damit übernahm sie Legitimationsfunktionen im Dienste der Erhaltung und Rechtfertigung des diktatorischen Regimes. Ab den 60er Jahren vertrat die Kirche jedoch wieder ein offeneres politisches Modell und schloss sich damit zögerlich westeuropäischen Positionen an. Die Ambivalenz der kirchlichen Haltung lässt sich nicht nur im Hinblick auf Legitimierung des Franquismus bzw. Distanzierung vom politischen System der Diktatur feststellen. Sie betrifft auch die gewaltfördernde, ja selbst gewalttätige Rolle der Kirche im frühen Franquismus, als viele Kleriker zu den eigentlichen Scharfmachern im blutrünstigen Repressionsapparat der Diktatur gehörten, sowie andererseits ihre Delegitimierung des franquistischen Systems, als sie sich in den 60er und 70er Jahren gerade wegen der vom Regime ausgeübten Gewalt immer deutlicher von diesem abwandte, bis sie schließlich (zumindest in Teilen) eher als Sammelbecken der Opposition denn als Unterstützerin der Diktatur gelten konnte.

3. Franquismus als prototypische Form des Autoritarismus

Neben die Charakterisierungen des Franquismus als „totalitär“ bzw. „faschistisch“ oder „nationalkatholisch“ gesellte sich schon früh der Typologisierungsvorschlag „autoritär“. Er wurde von vielen Autoren verwendet, allerdings erst vom deutsch-spanischen Soziologen Juan José Linz systematisch entwickelt und angewandt.[78] Linz ist sich darüber im Klaren, dass sein „Modell“ eine Abstraktion, einen Idealtypus darstellt, der graduelle Unterschiede und einander widersprechende Tendenzen der Realität nicht voll erfasst; es geht ihm jedoch primär um die „unterschiedlichen Weisen, in denen die autoritären Regime Probleme lösen, die es in allen politischen Systemen gibt: die Kontrolle zu behalten und Legitimität zu gewinnen, Eliten zu rekrutieren, Interessen zu artikulieren und zu bündeln, Entscheidungen zu fällen und Beziehungen herzustellen zu verschiedenen institutionellen Bereichen wie den Streitkräften, den religiösen Gruppierungen, der Intelligentsia, der Wirtschaft etc.“[79]

Es handelt sich um eine strukturalistische Vorgehensweise, bei der formale Kriterien dominieren. Dabei wird vor allem der Unterschied zu totalitären Systemen hervorgehoben, in denen eine Ideologie, eine Partei, eine terroristische Geheimpolizei, ein Nachrichten- und Waffenmonopol und eine zentralgelenkte Wirtschaft Ausdruck einer umfassenden Gleichschaltung seien. Demgegenüber weist Linz darauf hin, dass im nichtdemokratischen Regime des Franquismus ein

---

78 Vgl. Linz, Juan J.: Totalitäre und autoritäre Regime. Hg. von Raimund Krämer. Berlin 2003.

79 Linz, Juan J.: „Una teoría del régimen autoritario. El caso de España.” In: Payne, Stanley G. (Hg.): Política y sociedad en la España del siglo XX. Madrid 1978, S. 205–263, Zitat S. 209.

eingeschränkter Pluralismus vorhanden war. Das Fehlen einer einheitlichen Staatsideologie ermöglichte die Bildung und Organisierung einer begrenzten Anzahl pluraler Gruppen innerhalb des vorgegebenen politisch-ideologischen Systems. Diese Gruppen blieben zumeist von der politischen Verantwortung ausgeschlossen; die Macht übte ein Führer, Franco, aus. Charismatische Führereigenschaften waren nicht erforderlich, die Funktionen des Partei- oder Staatsführers hätte auch eine Junta erfüllen können. Die Wahl der Machtträger, welche die verschiedenen Gruppen und Interessen repräsentierten, erfolgte durch das Vertrauen des Führers, weniger durch Druckausübung seitens dieser Gruppen; durch Kooptation wurden die einzelnen Bereiche und Institutionen der Gesellschaft im System vertreten.

Im Gegensatz zu totalitären Regimen, die auf einer Ideologie beruhten, seien in autoritären Systemen verschiedene Mentalitäten vorhanden; daher könne auch nicht von einer umfassenden Kontrolle aller Lebensbereiche durch eine Partei die Rede sein. Ein Beleg für den Mangel an einheitlicher Ideologie ist für Linz Francos Manifest zu Beginn des Bürgerkrieges, in dem der spätere Diktator keinerlei ideologische Perspektiven eröffnete.[80] Neben diesem Fehlen einer geschlossenen Ideologie konstatiert Linz auch das Fehlen extensiver und intensiver politischer Massenmobilisierung; passive Zustimmung und politische Apathie seien in autoritären Regimen viel häufiger anzutreffen als Enthusiasmus und Massenmobilisierung. Im Gegensatz zur totalitären sei die autoritäre Partei keine durchstrukturierte ideologische Organisation gewesen, die das Monopol der Machtelitenre-

80 Vgl. den Text des Manifestes bei Bernecker, Walther L. (Hg.): Der Spanische Bürgerkrieg. Materialien und Quellen. Frankfurt a. M. 1986, S. 61–62.

krutierung ausübte; die Falange – bzw. später das *Movimiento Nacional* – sei vielmehr ideologisch und sozial heterogen gewesen und habe nur *ein* Element im Machtpluralismus dargestellt.

Linz fasst seine Definition eines autoritären Regimes, für das Franco-Spanien gewissermaßen ein Paradebeispiel darstellt, folgendermaßen zusammen: „Autoritäre Regime sind politische Systeme mit begrenztem, nicht-verantwortlichem politischen Pluralismus; ohne ausgearbeitete und leitende Ideologie (allerdings mit einer bestimmten Mentalität); ohne intensive oder extensive politische Mobilisierung (außer zu bestimmten Zeitpunkten ihrer Entwicklung), und in denen ein Führer (oder möglicherweise eine kleine Gruppe) innerhalb formal schlecht definierter, tatsächlich jedoch ziemlich vorhersehbarer Grenzen Macht ausübt."[81]

Bei dieser Definition ist der Unterschied zwischen Ideologie und Mentalität – somit der zwischen einem totalitären und einem autoritären System – von zentraler Bedeutung. Im Zusammenhang der Debatten über Theorie und Typologie nichtdemokratischer Regime ist in den vergangenen Jahrzehnten immer wieder über diesen Unterschied debattiert worden. Als eine Art Minimalkonsens hat sich dabei eine Definition von Ideologie herausgebildet, die – bei einer Verbindung beschreibender und normativer Elemente – darauf abhebt, dass Ideologien eine Erklärung dafür bieten wollen, wie Gesellschaften tatsächlich funktionieren, aber auch, wie sie funktionieren sollten. Ideologien stellen in diesem Sinne ein System politischen Denkens dar, das das Monopol auf Wahrheit für sich beansprucht, das „alles" zu erklären versucht – somit einen totalitären Interpretationsanspruch für sich reklamiert – und andere Ansichten nicht toleriert. Ideolo-

81 Linz: Teoría 1978, S. 212.

gien lassen sich auch als säkulare Religionen bezeichnen, die zu Intoleranz und politischer Repression führen. Sie haben eine dogmatische Basis und verfolgen eine utopische Vision im Hinblick auf eine erwartete und angestrebte Zukunft, in der alle Probleme gelöst sein werden.[82]

Während es bei Ideologien primär um den Inhalt des Denkens geht, stehen Mentalitäten für bestimmte Arten des Denkens und Fühlens; sie sind eher eine Denkhaltung. Mentalitäten sind durch allgemeine Werte wie Patriotismus, soziale Gerechtigkeit, Hierarchie, Gehorsam, Regeln oder Ordnung gekennzeichnet, die für die meisten sozialen Schichten leicht nachvollziehbar sind. Die Wahrscheinlichkeit, dass Mentalitäten mit einer Religion oder Wissenschaft in Konflikt geraten, ist geringer als im Falle von Ideologien; sie eignen sich nicht dazu, die Loyalität der Bürger zu testen. Mentalitäten im Sinne von symbolischen Verweisen sind so etwas wie der kleinste gemeinsame Nenner von Regimen, in denen ein komplexes Gefüge aus Kräften, Interessen, politischen Traditionen und Institutionen vorherrscht; damit sollen der Einfluss der meisten potentiellen Opponenten neutralisiert, bestimmte gesellschaftliche Kreise kooptiert und eine pragmatische Politik betrieben werden können. Da Mentalitäten das utopische Element in der Politik eindämmen, treffen sie sich mit den konservativen Tendenzen autoritärer Regime.

Viele dieser Definitionsmerkmale lassen sich im Franquismus ausmachen. So wurden etwa die politischen Schwerpunkte durch die „politischen Familien“ des Regimes bestimmt, die Interessengruppen und politische Parteien ersetzten. Obwohl diese „politischen Familien“ durchaus unterschiedliche

---

82 Vgl. die Ausführungen zu „totalitärer Ideologie“ bei Balík, Stanislav/Kubát, Michal: Undemokratische Regime. Theoretische Verortung und Fallbeispiele. Opladen 2015, S. 105–107.

Vorstellungen über die politische Orientierung des Regimes hatten und in Konkurrenz zueinander standen, galt die unbedingte Loyalität zu Franco für alle zu den Grundvoraussetzungen für ihre Teilnahme am politischen Geschehen. Sieht man vom linken Flügel der Ur-Falange ab, dann lassen sich diese „Familien“ als konservativ (und zumeist monarchistisch) bezeichnen; sie akzeptierten die „Grundprinzipien der Nationalen Bewegung“, war diese doch gerade ein Raum des autoritär-bürokratischen Regimes zur Gewährung einer gewissen, wenn auch eng begrenzten politischen Partizipation. Von den verschiedenen Mentalitätsvarianten dominierten im Franquismus sicherlich die militaristischen; der Regierungsstil Francos war stark von seiner Armee-Erfahrung und von nationalistischen Haltungen geprägt, die im Militär vorherrschten.

Das Modell von Juan José Linz hat viel für sich, kann es doch in gewisser Weise beanspruchen, eine „überwölbende“ Typologie zu sein, die gewissermaßen Elemente anderer Taxonomieversuche integriert.[83] Viele in der Linzschen Definition von autoritären Regimen auftauchende Merkmale lassen sich dem spanischen Fall zuordnen. Andererseits muss auch auf die Grenzen dieser Typologisierung hingewiesen

---

83 Vgl. hierzu auch den Interpretationsvorschlag von Ismael Saz Campos, der den Franquismus als eine „faschisierte Diktatur par excellence“ (zwischen Faschismus und Autoritarismus, je nach Konvenienz, schwankend) bezeichnet. Saz Campos, Ismael: „El franquismo: régimen autoritario o dictadura fascista?“ In: Tusell, Javier (Hg. u. a.): Congreso Internacional. El Régimen de Franco (1936–1975). Política y Relaciones Exteriores. Comunicaciones. Bd. 1. Madrid 1993, S. 189–201. Einige Jahre später hat Saz seinen Interpretationsvorschlag zu einer umfangreichen Monographie ausgeweitet: Saz, Ismael: Fascismo y franquismo. València 2004.

werden. Zum Ersten ist festzuhalten, dass die Reichweite des „begrenzten Pluralismus“ nicht aufgezeigt wird, dass somit nicht erkennbar wird, welche sozialen Gruppen und Schichten überhaupt Bestandteil dieses begrenzten Pluralismus sein können. Innerhalb des „bürgerlichen“ Lagers war in der Tat ein gewisser „pluraler“ Spielraum vorhanden; nicht eingebettet werden konnten in diesen Spielraum jedoch Organisationen und Bewegungen der Arbeiterschaft, die für sich freie Entfaltungs- und Einflussmöglichkeiten verlangten. In diesem Sinne müsste zumindest von einem klassenspezifisch begrenzten Pluralismus gesprochen werden; schon relativ früh hat Klaus von Beyme[84] von „Elitenpluralismus“ gesprochen; die Konfliktschlichtung bleibe schon deshalb auf die Eliten beschränkt, weil die gesellschaftlichen Gruppen keine unabhängigen Organisationen hatten und bei den Eliten das Einverständnis bestanden habe, dass Konflikte – ohne die Gefahr eines neuen Bürgerkrieges heraufzubeschwören, in dem die Eliten am meisten zu verlieren gehabt hätten – nicht mit aller Konsequenz ausgetragen werden dürften.

Des Weiteren ist darauf hinzuweisen, dass in diesem Modell nahezu ausschließlich von „politischer“, nicht aber von „gesellschaftlicher“ Macht gesprochen wird. Die Frage, wem Machtverhältnisse nützen oder gegen wen sie sich richten, wird nicht gestellt. Der Zusammenhang zwischen politischer Macht und gesellschaftlicher Herrschaft bleibt unklar – ein Aspekt, der zum vollen Verständnis des aus einem Klassenkrieg hervorgegangenen Regimes zentral ist.

Schließlich betont ein abstrakter Idealtyp bestimmte Zustände und Formen, ihm fehlt bis zu einem gewissen Grade die dynamische Komponente, er ist eher statisch angelegt und

84 Beyme, Klaus von: Vom Faschismus zur Entwicklungsdiktatur – Machtelite und Opposition in Spanien. München 1971, S. 30.

daher wenig geeignet, Kräfteverschiebungen zu erfassen. Der Prozess der materiellen Entwicklung bleibt unberücksichtigt, die Entstehungszusammenhänge und Entwicklungsperspektiven kommen zu kurz. Der Ansatz ist sicherlich hilfreich bei der Analyse des franquistischen Funktionsgefüges; er dürfte jedoch nur begrenzt verwendbar sein, wenn es um die Untersuchung der gesellschaftlichen Realität und ihrer Widersprüche geht.

Diese und andere Kritikpunkte an seinem Ansatz waren Linz durchaus bewusst. Im „Vorwort zur deutschen Ausgabe" seines Buches ging der Autor 1999/2003 auf einige der in den vorhergehenden Jahrzehnten geäußerten Kritiken an seinem Totalitarismus- und Autoritarismuskonzept ein. Er sprach auch die politische Deutung von wissenschaftlichen Kategorien an und erwähnte explizit die immer wieder vorgetragene Kritik vieler Interpreten, die die Charakterisierung des Franquismus als „autoritär" als zu beschwichtigend empfanden und auf der Bezeichnung „totalitär" möglicherweise auch deshalb bestanden, weil sie dadurch eine größere moralische Legitimation ihres eigenen Widerstandes gegen Franco empfanden. Demgegenüber führte Linz aus: „Niemals würde ich die totalitären Ambitionen der Falange in Spanien bzw. die totalitären Tendenzen im Franco-Regime in jener Zeit, als die Achsenmächte in Europa dominierten, bezweifeln. Jedoch betone ich trotzdem das Erbe des begrenzten Pluralismus, das Franco seiner persönlichen Macht unterordnete und das die Herausbildung eines wirklichen totalitären Regimes verhinderte."[85] Er räumte auch ein, dass beim Konzept Autoritarismus „die Grenze zum Totalitarismus recht diffus" ist.[86] Ihm gehe es aber bei

85 Linz: Totalitäre und autoritäre Regime, S. V.

86 Ebda., S. 129.

der Definition autoritärer Regime vor allem um zwei Aspekte: um den Grad eines begrenzten politischen Pluralismus und das Ausmaß, in dem solche Regime auf politischer Apathie und Demobilisierung oder einer begrenzten und kontrollierten Mobilisierung beruhen. Und bewusst bekannte er sich dazu, dass der von ihm verwendete Ansatz sich auf die Ausübung und Organisation von politischer Macht konzentriere; er frage danach, wie diese Macht mit der Gesellschaft verknüpft ist, wie die Glaubens-und Wertesysteme, die diese Macht stützen, beschaffen sind und welche Rolle der Bürger im politischen Prozess spielt.

Auch Jahrzehnte nach Beginn der Debatte über die Typologie des Franco-Regimes stellte Linz damit klar, dass nach wie vor große Unterschiede in der Charakterisierung des Franquismus bestanden und eine Annäherung der verschiedenen Positionen nicht zu erwarten war. Sein Hauptinteresse galt der politischen Macht und der Art, wie sie ausgeübt wurde.

4. Die Franco-Ära: ein konservatives Entwicklungsregime

Nicht so sehr um politische Macht, sondern um gesellschaftliche Realität und ihre Widersprüche ging es immer wieder bei der Charakterisierung des Franquismus als Modernisierungs- oder Entwicklungsdiktatur. Ob und inwieweit diese Bezeichnung für die lange Franco-Diktatur zutrifft, kann durch eine Analyse der ‚Modernisierungsleistung' des Regimes herausgefunden werden. Zweifellos war Spanien – unabhängig davon, welche der sozio-ökonomischen oder sozio-kulturellen Modernitätsindikatoren herangezogen werden – in der Schlussphase des Franquismus ein „modernes" Land: Die Demographie des Landes hatte in den vorhergehenden Jahrzehnten immer ausgeprägter die Muster entwickelter Industrienationen angenommen: Erhöhung der Lebenserwartung, Nachlassen der Geburtenhäufigkeit, Anwachsen der älteren Bevölkerung, Rationalisierung des generativen Verhaltens etc.; die Wanderungsbewegungen hatten zu hochgradiger Verdichtung der spanischen Bevölkerung in wenigen Provinzen, zu gewaltigen Verschiebungen im Siedlungsgefüge und in deren Gefolge zu einer hohen Urbanisierungsrate geführt; die Erwerbsstruktur entsprach mit ihrem Übergewicht an Beschäftigten im tertiären und sekundären Bereich gegenüber der Landwirtschaft weitgehend der anderer Industriegesellschaften; die Alphabetisierung hatte inzwischen Quoten erreicht, die entwickelten Industrienationen entsprachen; die Familienstruktur hatte sich immer deutlicher auf die sogenannte Kernfamilie hin entwickelt, die Erwerbsquoten der Frauen waren rasch gestiegen; das Wertesystem (Einstellung zur Ehescheidung, Sexualität, Emanzipation etc.) war fundamentalen Wandlungen unterworfen worden, der reale Säkularisierungsprozess der Bevölkerung war weit fortgeschritten, Leistung und Erfolg zählten längst zu den „positiven“ Werten in der spanischen Gesellschaft. Ganz anders sieht der Befund allerdings im politischen Bereich aus. Zeichnen sich „moderne“ Gesellschaften in politischer Hinsicht „durch ein aufgefächertes Parteien- und Verbandswesen, wirksame Vertretungskörperschaften, ein differenziertes und unabhängiges Medienwesen und die Chancen zu direkter Einwirkung möglichst großer Bevölkerungskreise auf die Zusammensetzung des Parlaments aus“[87], so war Spanien alles andere als ein modernes Land. Der sozio-ökonomische und

87 Steinbach, Peter: „Probleme politischer Partizipation im Modernisierungsprozess“. In: Ders. (Hg.): Probleme politischer Partizipation im Modernisierungsprozess. Stuttgart 1982, S. 7.

der politische Bereich wiesen demnach deutlich unterscheidbare Entwicklungsstufen auf.[88]

Der entscheidende sozio-ökonomische Modernisierungsschub erfolgte (im Vergleich zu anderen hochindustrialisierten europäischen Staaten) verspätet, nämlich erst ab den 1960er Jahren. Zuvor hatte die franquistische Propaganda Liberalismus, Sozialismus, Kommunismus und Freimaurerei – die modernisierungswilligen Kräfte der Zweiten Republik – mit dem ewigen „Anti-Spanien“ gleichgesetzt, die konservative Ideologie vom einmaligen Sonderweg Spaniens und seiner kreuzfahrerischen Mission in der Zeit der Säkularisierung und der Ausbreitung des Sozialismus verkündet und nahezu alle Modernisierungsmaßnahmen des vorangegangenen Jahrzehnts rückgängig gemacht. Franco selbst bezeichnete sein Regime als eine „Rückkehr zu den ureigensten Elementen des spanischen Wesens“, die in den Jahrzehnten des großen weltpolitischen Aufbruchs Spaniens unter den Katholischen Königen die Geschichte bestimmt hatten. Die bewusste „Abkoppelung“ der politischen und ökonomischen Entwicklung Spaniens von den westlichen Gesellschaften und die Betonung spanischer Geschichte und Tradition als Grundlage des „Neuen Staates“ stellten fortan Charakteristika der ideologischen Argumentationsstruktur Francos dar.

Die neue Wirtschaftsordnung trug alle Merkmale eines Amalgams aus unspezifischen Zielvorstellungen der Falange, aus Besitzinteressen, Traditionalismus und Pragmatismus. Staat und Privatunternehmer blieben als Wirtschaftsobjekte nebeneinander bestehen. Der Widerspruch zwischen starken

---

88 Zur ungleichen „diachronischen Entwicklung“ Spaniens auf wirtschaftlichem, sozialem und politischem Sektor vgl. Amodia, José: Franco’s Political Legacy. From Dictatorship to Facade Democracy. London 1977, S. 26–31.

Staatseingriffen auf der einen und der programmierten Respektierung des privaten Unternehmertums auf der anderen Seite blieb kennzeichnend für die Wirtschaftspolitik des Regimes. Im Grunde spiegelt diese ordnungspolitische Ambivalenz die ablehnende Haltung des Regimes gegenüber Kommunismus und Liberalismus wider. Die eigentlichen Gewinner des Bürgerkrieges waren nicht die Falangisten, sondern Großgrundbesitz und Finanzbourgeoisie. Diesen ging es aber um eine Wiedererlangung vorrepublikanischer Macht- und Wirtschaftsverhältnisse, um die Verhinderung jeglicher modernisierenden Reform.

Zwischen 1939 und 1959 betrieb die Regierung eine Autarkiepolitik im Sinne einer radikalen Importsubstitution und der systematischen Verringerung der Weltmarktverflechtungen in allen Bereichen. Die importsubstituierende Industrialisierung sollte das Land von Einfuhren unabhängig machen und die Grundlage für eine verhältnismäßig arbeitsteilige und gegliederte, am inneren Markt ausgerichtete Produktionsstruktur schaffen. In erster Linie war dieses Konzept von den sozialen und wirtschaftlichen Vorstellungen der Falange bestimmt, die davon ausging, dass die Wirtschaft sich der Politik unterzuordnen habe, die Produktion im Dienste des Vaterlandes stehen und die Industrialisierung Ausdruck des nationalen Prestiges sein müsse. Außerdem traf sich diese Politik mit einem übersteigerten Nationalismus als Rechtfertigungsideologie des neuen Regimes.[89]

Um die Politik der Autarkie durchzusetzen, griffen die Behörden in den Wirtschaftsprozess ein. Das Ergebnis dieser

89 Hierzu Anderson, Charles W.: The Political Economy of Modern Spain. Policy-Making in an Authoritarian System. Madison 1970; González, Manuel-Jesús: La economía política del franquismo (1940–1970). Dirigismo, mercado y planificación. Madrid 1979.

Politik der Wirtschaftslenkung war ein Sinken des allgemeinen Lebensstandards, eine laufende Erhöhung der (offiziell inexistenten) Arbeitslosigkeit, Fehlinvestitionen großen Stils, Mängel in der Qualität der Industrieerzeugnisse, Stagnation von Forschung und Entwicklung, ein ungenügendes Niveau von Produktion und Produktivität sowie Untergrabung der Wirtschaftsmoral.[90] 1951 war der Misserfolg eines Jahrzehnts wirtschaftlicher Isolierung offenkundig geworden und hatte im März jenes Jahres zu einem Generalstreik geführt, auf den Franco mit einer Regierungsumbildung unter Ankündigung einer „liberaleren" Wirtschaftspolitik reagierte. Eine definitive Wendung zum Besseren schien aber nur mit ausländischer Hilfe und nach einer gewissen Eingliederung in den Weltmarkt möglich zu sein. Diese ausländische Hilfe erfolgte 1953 durch das Stützpunktabkommen mit den USA. Die Verträge des Jahres 1953 hatten für die Stabilisierung des Regimes allerdings eher politische als wirtschaftliche Bedeutung.[91] Zwar konnten in der ersten Hälfte der 50er Jahre die ärgsten Engpässe in der Rohstoff- und Energieversorgung sowie im Verkehrswesen beseitigt werden; die Landwirtschaft führte Traktoren, Dünge- und Futtermittel ein und vergrößerte Produktion wie Produktivität. Diese Impulse bedeuteten aber noch lange nicht den Eintritt in eine neue Wachstumsphase. Insgesamt blieb die Dominanz der Politik gegenüber der Wirtschaft vorerst bestehen. Nach wie vor ging in dieser Phase der institutionellen Ausgestaltung und

---

90 Zur katastrophalen Wirtschaftssituation in den 40er Jahren und zum Leiden von Millionen Spaniern vgl. Cazorla, Antonio: Miedo y progreso: los españoles de a pie bajo el franquismo. Barcelona 2016.

91 Vgl. Viñas, Angel: Los pactos secretos de Franco con Estados Unidos. Bases, ayuda económica, recortes de soberanía. Barcelona 1981.

politischen Konsolidierung des Regimes die Wirtschaftspolitik von (inzwischen gemäßigten) Autarkievorstellungen und umfangreichen staatlichen Regulierungen aus.

Als 1956/57 das Scheitern der nach wie vor primär autarkistischen Wirtschaftspolitik offenkundig wurde, stand die Regierung vor der entscheidenden Frage, ob sie zur alten, von der Falange vertretenen Linie wirtschaftlicher Isolierung zurückkehren oder diese endgültig aufgeben und sich dem Wirtschaftsliberalismus verschreiben sollte. Die weitreichende Regierungsumbildung des Jahres 1957 ließ bereits die Antwort auf diese Frage erkennen. Wegen seiner grundsätzlichen Bedeutung war das Revirement des Jahres 1957 nicht nur die bedeutendste Regierungsumbildung der Franco-Ära, sondern zugleich der Beginn eines grundlegenden Kurswechsels in der Wirtschaftspolitik, einer Veränderung der Entscheidungs- und Lenkungsmechanismen auf wirtschaftlichem Gebiet und des Erwerbs einer neuen Legitimitätsbasis für das autoritäre Regime. Die wirtschaftspolitisch entscheidenden Ministerien für Handel und Finanzen besetzten Alberto Ullastres bzw. Mariano Navarro Rubio, die beide der Organisation angehörten, die im folgenden Jahrzehnt die Schalthebel der Macht innehaben sollte: dem *Opus Dei*.[92]

Die Männer des *Opus Dei* waren die eigentlichen Exponenten jener „technokratischen" Ideologie, deren Verfechter seit den späten 50er Jahren offen auf eine durchgreifende Modernisierung der antiquierten spanischen Wirtschaftsstruktur

---

92 Zum *Opus Dei* vgl. Artigues, Daniel: El Opus Dei en España, 1928–1962. Su evolución ideológica y política. Paris 1971; Ynfante, Jesús: La prodigiosa aventura del Opus Dei. Génesis y desarrollo de la Santa Mafia. Paris 1970; Le Tourneau, Dominique: Das Opus Dei. Stein am Rhein 1988; Mettner, Matthias: Die katholische Mafia. Kirchliche Geheimbünde greifen nach der Macht. Hamburg 1993.

hinarbeiteten, eine forcierte ökonomische Expansion auf der Grundlage eines selbstständigen, aber vom Staat geförderten Unternehmertums anstrebten und Spanien enger an Europa, vor allem an den Gemeinsamen Markt, heranführen wollten. Wirtschaftstheoretisch förderte das *Opus* den Neoliberalismus, der angesichts der volkswirtschaftlich archaischen Autarkievorstellungen der 40er und 50er Jahre zweifellos innovatorisch wirkte. Das „Gotteswerk" verband ökonomischen Liberalismus mit politischem Konservativismus. Die katholische Laienorganisation war davon überzeugt, Spaniens Entwicklung könne am besten durch die rasche Steigerung des Sozialprodukts gefördert werden, und dieses Ziel sei nur dann zu erreichen, wenn man die Kräfte freier Unternehmerinitiative und kommerzieller Konkurrenz im Rahmen einer modernen Marktwirtschaft möglichst ungehemmt spielen lasse und nicht durch Sozialreformen behindere.

Die *Opus Dei*-Mitglieder zeichnet ein ausgeprägtes Arbeitsethos aus, das auffällige Berührungspunkte mit puritanisch-calvinistischem Geist aufweist. Der Widerspruch zur traditionellen Mentalität des romanisch-lateinischen Katholizismus liegt auf der Hand: Was jene „protestantische Ethik" ausmacht, in der häufig (seit Max Weber) zumindest eine der geschichtlichen Wurzeln des modernen Kapitalismus (und damit letztlich der modernen industriellen Zivilisation) gesehen wird, wird beim *Opus Dei* auf der Grundlage vollständiger Ergebenheit gegenüber der Kirche Roms und ohne Berücksichtigung politischer Rahmenbedingungen nachvollzogen. In diesem Sinne erlangte die *Opus*-Doktrin durch staatliche Betonung des Arbeits- und Pflichtethos große Bedeutung für die Überlagerung vorkapitalistischer Strukturen und Einstellungen durch eine kapitalistische Wirtschaftsgesinnung. Das Handeln der Technokraten wurde von bestimmten Werten und ideologischen Mustern geleitet. Zu den Werten gehörten die besondere Betonung, ja der Kult von Effizienzstreben, von Kompetenz, Produktivität und moderner Technik. Die ideologischen Elemente äußerten sich in der Neigung, dem Wirtschaftswachstum einen eindeutigen Vorrang gegenüber sozialem Fortschritt einzuräumen. Dementsprechend wurde die wirtschaftliche Modernisierung des Landes auf Kosten politischer Demokratie und sozialer Gerechtigkeit forciert.

In ihren frühen Annahmen gingen Modernisierungstheorien davon aus, dass die Demokratie eine geradezu natürliche Folgeerscheinung wirtschaftlichen Wachstums und gesamtgesellschaftlicher Modernisierung sei. Umgekehrt konnte die Demokratie angeblich so lange nicht reifen, wie kein ausreichendes wirtschaftliches Wachstum erzielt worden war. Demokratisierung bestand somit primär in einer Politik wirtschaftlichen Wachstums. Auch im spanischen Fall verführte die wirtschaftspolitische Öffnung Ende der 50er Jahre zu der Fehlannahme, dass ihr über kurz oder lang eine politische Demokratisierung folgen müsse. *Apertura económica* (wirtschaftliche Öffnung) wurde zum Schlüsselwort und erweckte in fortschrittlichen Kreisen die Hoffnung auf eine nachfolgende *apertura política* (politische Öffnung), zumal der Wandel in der Wirtschaftspolitik eine Abkehr von falangistischen Ordnungsvorstellungen und eine neue Balance in der politischen Kräftegruppierung des Regimes implizierte. Zu lange wurde übersehen, dass die Teil-Liberalisierungen der 60er Jahre und die Beschleunigung des wirtschaftlichen Wachstums nicht auf die Überwindung des Autoritarismus, sondern gerade auf seine Stabilisierung zielten.[93]

---

93 Vgl. den instruktiven Beitrag von Maravall, José María: „Modernization, Authoritarianism, and the Growth of Working-Class Dissent. The Case of Spain". In: Government and Opposition 8, 4, 1973, S. 432–454, in dem der Soziologe Maravall treffend auf Ziel und Dilemma von Modernisierungsmaßnahmen in autoritären Regimen eingeht.

Als das *Opus Dei* 1957 zum ersten Mal Regierungsverantwortung übertragen bekam, waren die wirtschaftspolitischen Zielvorstellungen des neuen Kabinetts noch relativ unpräzise; sie gingen kaum über allgemeine Vorstellungen einer Wirtschaftsliberalisierung hinaus. Nur eines war klar: Wollte das Regime Francos fortbestehen, so musste es sich dazu bequemen, 20 Jahre eines aggressiven Nationalismus, akuten Protektionismus und willkürlichen Interventionismus abzuschreiben. In den folgenden Jahren wurde sodann die gesamte wirtschaftspolitische Autarkie-Philosophie der Falange über Bord geworfen. Ende Juni 1959 stellte die spanische Regierung in einem Memorandum an die Organisation für wirtschaftliche Zusammenarbeit und Entwicklung (OECD) und den Internationalen Währungsfonds die geplanten Stabilisierungsmaßnahmen vor. Das „Wirtschaftsstrukturgesetz", das unter der Bezeichnung „Stabilisierungsplan" bekannt wurde, stand unter der Devise „Wachstum und Stabilität". In seinen wesentlichen Grundzügen war das Gesetz von wirtschaftsliberalen Technokraten, Bankiers und Wirtschaftsspezialisten ausgearbeitet worden. Die politische Umsetzung des Gesetzes, seine Verabschiedung im Ministerrat, war sodann Sache des *Opus*, das es geschickt verstand, sich selbst als geistigen Vater des Reformgesetzes darzustellen. Mit dem Gesetz sollten ein gleichgewichtiges Wirtschaftswachstum und größere Integration in die Weltwirtschaft, eine Eindämmung der Inflation und bessere Entfaltungsmöglichkeiten für die Privatwirtschaft erreicht, der internationale Waren- und Dienstleistungsverkehr liberalisiert werden. Mit dieser „wirtschaftlichen Öffnung" verband sich eine grundlegende, am Vorbild der Wirtschaft der westlichen Industriestaaten ausgerichtete Neuorientierung der Wirtschaftspolitik.

Auf den Stabilisierungsplan von 1959 folgte nach 1962 als Phase des wirtschaftlichen „take-off" eine Periode des Aufschwungs mit starker unternehmerischer Konzentration und Zentralisation des Kapitals. Die Maßnahmen im außenwirtschaftlichen Bereich beseitigten die Autarkie und führten zur Eingliederung Spaniens in das internationale kapitalistische System. Die Produktion orientierte sich stärker am Export, der vom Staat intensiv gefördert wurde. Emigrationsabkommen mit europäischen Ländern förderten die Auswanderung der Reservearmee an Arbeitslosen; die Devisen aus den Emigrantenüberweisungen (Rimessen) und der touristischen Invasion wiederum besserten die Zahlungsbilanz auf. Kurzum: Für Spanien hatte das Jahrzehnt des „Wirtschaftswunders" begonnen, das den Anschluss des Landes an entwickelte Industriestaaten als Ergebnis hatte.

Die Strategie des *Opus Dei* ist – vor allem von Guy Hermet – als „konservativ-autoritäre Modernisierung" bezeichnet worden; das Mittel zur Erreichung dieser Modernisierung war eine beschleunigte industrielle Entwicklung klassisch-kapitalistischen Typs, die durch den politisch autoritären Rahmen des Regimes abgesichert wurde. Es ging darum, Spanien im 20. Jahrhundert die Verwirklichung der im 19. Jahrhundert gescheiterten industriellen Revolution zu ermöglichen und auf diese Weise die Entwicklung der als politisch „vernünftig" angesehenen Mittelschichten durch eine solchermaßen legitimierte technokratische Diktatur voranzutreiben. Wirtschaftlich mussten Modernisierungsmaßnahmen ergriffen werden, damit politisch alles beim Alten bleiben konnte.[94]

---

94 Hermet, Guy: L'Espagne de Franco. Paris 1974. Noch 1970 sagte der damalige Leiter des *Instituto de Estudios Políticos*, Legaz Lacambra: „Unsere sozio-ökonomischen Strukturen sind auf dem besten Weg, vollständig europäisch zu werden; unser ideologisches System aber – ein Gut, auf das wir nicht verzichten wollen – ist ehrenhaft spanisch." Zit. nach Martínez Cuadra-

So bestechend der Begriff der „konservativen Modernisierung“ zur Charakterisierung der franquistischen Entwicklungsstrategie seit Ende der 50er Jahre auf den ersten Blick erscheint, so angebracht sind andererseits Zweifel hinsichtlich seiner Anwendbarkeit auf alle Bereiche des gesamtgesellschaftlichen Wandels und zur Typologisierung des Regimes. Der Ausdruck impliziert nämlich, dass der Franquismus (zumindest in seiner technokratischen Epoche) über eine gezielte und bewusst angewandte Strategie verfügte, die Ausdruck der Steuerungskapazität des Regimes war – eine Annahme, die sich angesichts der Sachzwänge, denen das Regime im Vorfeld der „großen Wende“ von 1957/59 ausgesetzt war, kaum aufrechterhalten lässt.[95] Der größte Teil der Veränderungen, die auf die „konservativ-autoritäre Modernisierung“ von 1959 folgten, waren auch nicht-intendierte Wirkungen der wirtschaftlichen Moder-

---

do, Miguel: Cambio Social y Modernización Política. Anuario Político Español 1969. Madrid 1970, S. 26. Nichtdemokratische Regime sind stets bestrebt, die Ziele von Modernisierungsprozessen auf solche Aspekte des Wandels zu beschränken, die systemimmanent erfolgen können. Das Erfordernis autokratischer Regime, den induzierten Wandel politisch zu kontrollieren, betont auch Apter, David E.: The Politics of Modernization. Chicago 1965, S. 256–265.

95 Auch heute noch wird Franco von konservativen Historikern (und der politischen Rechten) als „Modernisierer“ stilisiert, dem es vor allem um die Erneuerung und den Fortschritt Spaniens gegangen sei, zuletzt etwa bei Payne, Stanley G./Palacio, Jesús: Franco, una biografía personal y política. Madrid 2015. Vgl. als Gegendarstellung, unter Betonung der Herrschaftsmechanismen, die kritische Abrechnung von Viñas, Angel: La otra cara del Caudillo. Mitos y realidades en la biografía de Franco. Barcelona 2015.

nisierungsmaßnahmen.[96] So führte etwa die massive Industrialisierungspolitik der 60er Jahre zu einem gewaltigen Anwachsen der Industriearbeiterschaft, zu einer Zunahme oppositioneller Untergrundorganisationen, deren Methoden infolge des arbeitsrepressiven Systems weit radikaler, direkter und gewalttätiger waren als die gemäßigten Strategien der Gewerkschaften in den industrialisierten Demokratien des Westens. Das Hauptziel des *Opus Dei*-Entwicklungsmodells, die Sicherung der sozialen und politischen Stabilität des Regimes, wurde nicht erreicht. Im Gegenteil: Die Unruhen nahmen in den 60er Jahren derart zu, dass die Repression im Arbeitsbereich verstärkt werden musste.

Der wesentliche Grund für die Zunahme des Konfliktpotentials dürfte in der Partialität der Modernisierungsmaßnahmen gelegen haben, die den soziopolitischen Bereich im Wesentlichen aussparten. Es zeigte sich, dass Prozesse der sozialen Mobilisierung und Modernisierung nicht teilbar sind. Die Starrheit des politischen Systems[97] und das Fehlen de-

---

96 Shlomó Ben-Amí vertritt – trotz des irreführenden Titels seines Buches, der eine bewusste Modernisierungsstrategie suggeriert – die Ansicht, dass sich das franquistische Regime „nie sehr freiwillig, aber kontinuierlich an die in der Gesellschaft erfolgten Wandlungsprozesse anpasste." Seine Deutung ist allerdings insofern widersprüchlich, als er andererseits wiederum die gesellschaftlichen Wandlungsprozesse während des Franquismus sowie die nachfranquistische Demokratie als Ergebnis einer ‚Revolution von oben' interpretiert. Vgl. Ben-Amí, Shlomó: La revolución desde arriba. España 1936–1979. Barcelona 1980.

97 Wenn von „Starrheit des politischen Systems" gesprochen wird, soll das nicht heißen, das Herrschaftsgebäude, d.h. die wesentlichen politischen Machtträger, und die Prinzipien, nach denen die Macht ausgeübt wurde, seien bis 1975 unverändert

mokratischer Artikulationsmöglichkeiten dürften ursächlich dafür verantwortlich gewesen sein, dass das wirtschaftliche Wachstum für das franquistische Regime keinen legitimatorischen Effekt hatte. Denn entgegen den Erwartungen der Technokraten ließ sich der spektakuläre Aufschwung der spanischen Wirtschaft in den 60er Jahren nicht in eine wachsende ökonomische Legitimierung des Systems als Entwicklungsdiktatur umsetzen. Die autoritäre Unterdrückung offener Auseinandersetzungen wiederum, das heißt die mangelnde Institutionalisierung von Konflikten sowie das Fehlen einer Vermeidungsstrategie und die ideologische Überbetonung sowie gewaltsame Durchsetzung der „staatlichen Einheit“ heizten in den Wachstumsjahren der Franco-Ära die Feindseligkeiten an und schufen „Fremdgruppen“ (Arbeiter, Regionalisten) in der eigenen Gesellschaft, deren Interessen nicht in das politische System des Franquismus integriert waren. Das Ergebnis der franquistischen Politik widersprach in nahezu jedem Punkt den ursprünglichen Intentionen:

Am Ende der Franco-Herrschaft war die spanische Gesellschaft politisierter, urbanisierter und säkularisierter denn je, die soziale Mobilisierung der Bevölkerung hatte vorher unbekannte Ausmaße angenommen, die Arbeiter und Studenten

---

geblieben. Machtapparat und -strategie des Franquismus waren auch einem gewissen Wandel unterworfen, der sich etwa in den Kräfteverschiebungen erkennen lässt, durch welche verschiedene Fraktionen („politische Familien“) am Herrschaftsbündnis partizipierten. Hierzu Tamames, Ramón: La República. La Era de Franco. Madrid 1979, S. 457–500. Zu den intrasystemischen Veränderungen mit dem Ziel der Systemerhaltung vgl. die Ausführungen zum Problem der politischen Modernisierung Spaniens bei Ramírez Jiménez, Manuel: „Modernización política en España. Hipótesis para su estudio.“ In: Revista de Estudios Sociales 2, 5, 1972, S. 107–131.

waren so aufsässig wie noch nie, die Autonomie- und Selbstständigkeitsbewegungen der Regionen ausgeprägter als zu jedem anderen Zeitpunkt der neueren spanischen Geschichte, Sozialisten und Kommunisten bei den ersten Wahlen nach Francos Tod so erfolgreich wie nie zuvor, die spanische Wirtschaft finanziell und technologisch vom internationalen Kapitalismus geradezu in beängstigendem Ausmaß abhängig, das Regime trotz seiner wirtschaftlichen Erfolge nicht legitimiert; die Jugend hatte sich vom Franquismus ebenso distanziert wie die Kirche. Hatte das Regime (notgedrungen) unter der (jahrzehntelang wiederholten) Devise „Spanien ist anders“ die These der radikalen Inkompatibilität der politischen Institutionen Spaniens und der kulturellen Werte des Landes mit dem restlichen Europa zu einer offiziösen Metaphysik hochstilisiert und die Distanz von wirtschaftlichen wie ideologischen Modellen westlicher Demokratien betont, so war diese bewusste Distanzierung in den 60er Jahren bereits einer deutlichen Annäherung an den Westen auf dem Gebiet der Wirtschaft und der Konsummentalität gewichen; nach dem Tode Francos erfolgte sodann geradezu ein Wettlauf, um sich auch politisch (und militärisch) in das früher so verpönte System des Westens zu integrieren. Nie zuvor in seiner Geschichte dürfte Spanien so „europäisch“ gewesen sein wie im Übergang von der Diktatur zur Demokratie.[98]

Fasst man diese Überlegungen zusammen, so lässt sich festhalten, dass die Anwendung der Modernisierungskategorie auf die gesamte Franco-Ära unmöglich erscheint. Sie ist bezüglich der ersten anderthalb Jahrzehnte des Fran-

---

98 Hierzu sowie allgemein zum Verhältnis Spanien-Europa vgl. Bernecker, Walther L.: „Spanien zwischen Isolation und Integration“. In: Salewski, Michael (Hg.): Nationale Identität und Europäische Einigung. Göttingen 1991, S. 125–168.

quismus schon deshalb problematisch, ja ausgeschlossen, weil die unter „Modernisierungstheorien" subsumierten Theorien – etwa Wachstumstheorien, Theorien des sozialen Wandels etc. – alle von einem Prozess der Nachahmung und der Angleichung „unterentwickelter" Gesellschaften an die „entwickelten" Gesellschaften der westlichen Industrieländer ausgehen. Gerade dieses Ziel aber verfolgte das international vorerst geächtete und isolierte spanische Regime nicht. Ganz im Gegenteil: Es wurde nicht müde, die wirtschaftspolitischen und ideologischen Unterschiede zu den angeblich dekadenten Demokratien in den Mittelpunkt seines Rechtfertigungsmusters zu rücken. Der Modernisierungsaspekt, der später von den Technokraten an den Schalthebeln der politischen Macht zur Legitimierung des Systems bemüht wurde, ist erst relativ spät (etwa seit dem Erfolg des ersten Entwicklungsplans Mitte der 60er Jahre) bejaht und in seinem propagandistischen Nutzen erkannt worden. Das Franco-System kann daher auch nicht mit autoritären Systemen gleichgesetzt werden, die von Anfang an innovatorische Impulse entwickelten, blieben doch die traditionsverhafteten Strukturen vorerst so ausschlaggebend, dass in der ersten Phase des Regimes noch keineswegs von einer Entwicklungs- oder Modernisierungsdiktatur gesprochen werden kann.

Nachdem in den 50er Jahren klar geworden war, dass das falangistische Wirtschaftsmodell der Autarkie in eine Sackgasse geführt hatte und das politische Modell des Franquismus nur durch eine radikale Kursänderung der Wirtschaftspolitik erhalten werden konnte, initiierte und unterstützte die *Opus Dei*-Elite den wirtschaftlichen Modernisierungsprozess nachdrücklich, war außerdem – allerdings erfolglos – äußerst sorgfältig darauf bedacht, Modernisierung und alle damit zusammenhängenden Teilprozesse unter ihrer Kontrolle zu behalten. Die wirtschaftliche Entwicklung und andere Formen der Modernisierung wurden als Mittel zur

Erhaltung und zusätzlichen Legitimierung des politischen Systems eingesetzt. Die Veränderungen im Lebensstandard der gewaltig expandierenden Mittelschichten führten allerdings dazu, dass diese deutlicher als zuvor den Unterschied zwischen ihrem materiellen Status einerseits und ihrer kulturellen bzw. politischen Lage andererseits empfanden. Die Errichtung einer „Mittelstandsgesellschaft" sollte das Land vom Druck extremer sozialer Klassen befreien und damit gleichzeitig zur Stärkung des bestehenden Systems beitragen. Die gesellschaftliche Modernisierung führte jedoch nicht, wie ihre Architekten erhofft hatten, zur Konsolidierung des Franquismus, sondern zur Unterminierung der Diktatur.

IV. Fazit: Der Franquismus – eine chamäleonhafte Diktatur?

Im Einleitungskapitel dieses Essays ist bereits auf die Möglichkeit hingewiesen worden, den Franquismus mit einem Chamäleon zu vergleichen. Manche Merkmale dieses Reptils ähneln denen des politischen Systems des Franquismus. Ein besonderes Merkmal des Chamäleons ist seine ausgeprägte Farbwechselfähigkeit, die keineswegs nur der Tarnung dient, sondern nicht minder – ja, sogar vor allem – der Kommunikation. Der Farbwechsel enthält also eine Botschaft nach außen, und von äußeren Faktoren hängt auch die Färbung ab. Am schnellsten wechseln die Farben in Gefahren- und Kampfsituationen. Außerdem kann das Chamäleon bis zu einem gewissen Grad seine Körperform variieren, weshalb es schwierig ist, bestimmte Chamäleonarten genau zu bestimmen.

Betrachtet man die Veränderungen, die das Franco-Regime im Laufe der Jahrzehnte durchlief, so lassen sich auch einige wichtige Merkmale des Franquismus mit denen eines Chamäleons vergleichen. Auch im Falle des franquistischen Systems kann politisch und ökonomisch von Formveränderungen gesprochen werden, denen sich das Regime unterwarf, um sich seiner politischen Umwelt anzupassen und dank dieser Anpassung an die externen Bedingungen zu überleben. Alle fünf in diesem Band kurz diskutierten Typologisierungsversuche haben – für bestimmte Zeiträume und bis zu einem gewissen Grade – ihre Berechtigung; kein einziger dieser Versuche kann für sich jedoch beanspruchen, das System umfassend und für die gesamte Dauer seiner Existenz zu charakterisieren, denn das fast 40-jährige Regime von General Franco durchlief sehr unterschiedliche Etappen, während derer faschistisch-totalitäre Elemente ebenso wie autoritär-militaristische, organisch-etatistische oder modernisierungsorientierte zum Tragen kamen. Da das Regime nur eine äußerst schwache und späte Institutionalisierung erfuhr – entscheidende Gesetze wurden erst 1958 bzw. 1966 erlassen –, muss zu seiner Charakterisierung eher auf die politische Praxis als auf Ideologeme, Institutionen oder politische Strukturen rekurriert werden. Diese Praxis aber erfuhr vielfältige Wandlungen.

Während anfangs, vor allem in den Bürgerkriegsjahren und in der ersten Hälfte des Zweiten Weltkriegs, im entstehenden „Neuen Staat" viele faschistische Elemente anzutreffen waren, entledigte sich das Regime spätestens seit 1945 eines Großteils dieser faschistischen Merkmale und passte sich – sozusagen chamäleonhaft – seiner konservativen europäischen Umwelt an. Hierzu eignete sich ganz besonders der Nationalkatholizismus, konnte Franco sich doch als Wächter des Abendlandes und Verteidiger konservativantikommunistischer Werte stilisieren, dem es angeblich schon immer um die Bekämpfung von Extremismen gegangen war. Dieses Bild seines Regimes passte besonders gut in die politische Landschaft der Nachkriegszeit; das politischreligiöse System des Nationalkatholizismus ordnete das franquistische Regime in die Geschichte der Gegenreformation und des Traditionalismus ein.

Der Machtzuwachs der „Katholiken" und die Institutionalisierung des Nationalkatholizismus im Franco-Regime erfolgten nicht nur zulasten der faschistischen Falange, sondern auch der Militärs als Institution. Denn obwohl Militärs bei der Erringung der Macht durch Franco ohne Zweifel die entscheidende Rolle spielten, entwickelte sich das Regime nie zu einer Militärdiktatur im klassischen Sinne des Wortes, d. h. zu einem System, in dem das Militär als Institution und Korporation die Macht als Diktatur ausgeübt hätte. Denn trotz der herausragenden Stellung des Militärs im Franquismus wurde ihm nie ein besonders hoher Stellenwert bei der Konzipierung der politischen Leitlinien des Regimes zugestanden. Von einer monolithischen Militärdiktatur kann zur Charakterisierung des Franquismus daher nicht gesprochen werden. Allerdings lässt sich auch nicht die Behauptung vertreten, dass der Nationalkatholizismus einen umfassenden Erklärungs- und Typologisierungsanspruch erheben kann. Denn so penetrant auch nationalkatholische Prinzipien in den Alltag der Spanier und das politische System des Franquismus, vor allem nach 1945, eindrangen, so klar lässt sich andererseits ein Niedergang dieses extrem konservativen Ideariums im Laufe der letzten 15 Jahre des Regimes feststellen. Gegen Ende des Franco-Systems war vom Nationalkatholizismus – außer einer sinnentleerten Hülle – nicht mehr viel übrig.

Über die Wandlungen des Franco-Systems im Laufe der Jahrzehnte und seine kontinuierlichen Anpassungen an seine politisch-ökonomische Umwelt, die ihm letzten Endes das Überleben ermöglichten, waren sich auch die Analysten im Klaren, die eine Typisierung und Typologisierung des Systems vornehmen wollten. Die Charakterisierung des Regimes als „autoritär“ schien sich anzubieten, ließen sich doch viele Merkmale des Franquismus unter den Begriff „Autoritarismus“ subsumieren. In der Tat setzte sich bei vielen Historikern und Politologen – vor allem in der Phase des Kalten Krieges und zur Abgrenzung von totalitären Systemen – der Begriff Autoritarismus zur Kennzeichnung des Franquismus durch; zugleich wurde aber auch immer wieder auf die Schwächen dieses Ansatzes hingewiesen, da einige Merkmale desselben – etwa der „begrenzte Pluralismus“– zu unspezifisch seien, der Charakter des zugrundegelegten Machtkonzepts nicht deutlich genug und die Dynamik der gesellschaftlichen Kräfteverschiebungen nicht ausreichend berücksichtigt werde.

Gerade Letzteres sollte in dem Ansatz berücksichtigt werden, der den Franquismus als konservatives Entwicklungsregime charakterisiert – ein Ansatz, der vor allem auf die Entwicklungs- und Modernisierungsleistungen des Franquismus abhebt. Es handelt sich um eine Typologisierungsvariante, die in vielerlei Hinsicht auf die spätere Phase des Franquismus, ab Beginn der 1960er Jahre, anwendbar ist, die aber bestimmt nicht auf die ersten beiden Jahrzehnte des franquistischen Systems zutrifft, in denen vor allem anti-moderne Elemente dominierten und das westliche Entwicklungsmodell als Abschreckung und nicht als Vorbild fungierte.

Dass es unter Historikern und Sozialwissenschaftlern bis heute keine Übereinstimmung bei der Einordnung des Franquismus in ein System von Regime-Typologien gibt, hängt nicht nur mit den unterschiedlichen disziplinären Ansätzen und Fragestellungen zusammen, die den Analysen zugrunde liegen. Es ist weit mehr auf die chamäleonhafte Veränderungs- und Anpassungsfähigkeit des franquistischen Systems an seine politische Umwelt zurückzuführen – eine Fähigkeit, die ihm im Laufe seiner wechselvollen Geschichte zur Tarnung und vor allem zum Schutz gegen „Gefahren" von außen diente und somit in erheblichem Ausmaß zu seinem politischen Überleben bis zum physischen Tod des Diktators beitrug.

Zugleich muss darauf verwiesen werden, dass die Veränderungen und Machtverschiebungen im franquistischen System keineswegs reibungslos vonstatten gingen. Ganz im Gegenteil lässt die detaillierte Analyse konkreter Entscheidungssituationen klar erkennen, dass die Machteliten im Franquismus viel weniger homogen waren, als es von außen und oberflächlich erscheinen mochte. Die Eliten waren vielmehr ausgesprochen fragmentiert. Viele Untersuchungen der letzten Jahrzehnte ermöglichen es, in den verschiedenen Umbesetzungen und Neuorientierungen des Regimes einen hohen Grad an Konfliktivität zwischen den unterschiedlichen Eliten zu erkennen. Aus einer konterrevolutionären Koalition hervorgegangen, war das Regime zu einer Art Interessenallianz zwischen Gruppen geworden, die selbst in wichtigen Punkten unterschiedlicher Meinung waren. So lassen etwa – um nur abschließend einige wenige Beispiele zu nennen – die kritische Meinung vieler Generäle über Franco im Weltkrieg oder der Wille des katholischen Außenministers Martín Artajo, dass die Falange von der politischen Bühne verschwinde, die Divergenzen deutlich werden. Die Auseinandersetzungen innerhalb des Regimes waren permanenter Art. Die Ergebnisse dieser Auseinandersetzungen beeinflussten das Leben vieler Spanier häufig weit mehr als die Aktionen der Opposition. Die regime-internen Debatten erhalten damit für die Analyse des Systems große Bedeutung; auf diesem Gebiet ist die historische Forschung in den letzten Jahren auch erheblich vorangekommen. In einiger Zeit dürften auch erneute Kontroversen über den Regimetypus zu erwarten sein – schon gar, da seit einigen Jahren revisionistische Deutungen aus francofreundlicher Perspektive eine abermals positive(re) Umdeutung des franquistischen Regimes nach sich ziehen dürften.[99]

Die historischen Auseinandersetzungen über die Machtverschiebungen im Franco-Regime und die internen Machtkämpfe weisen zugleich auf die „Methode“ der Führerschaft Francos hin. Dieser hatte einige politische Grundüberzeugungen, die man aber – selbst bei wohlwollender Betrachtung – kaum als ein politisches Konzept bezeichnen kann. Er war viel vorsichtiger als viele seiner Generalskollegen, allerdings auch weit weniger enthusiastisch als die Falange

99 Zu den heftigen Auseinandersetzungen und Differenzen zwischen verschiedenen Flügeln des Franquismus vgl. Thomàs, Joan Maria: Franquistas contra franquistas. Madrid 2016.

bei der Bewertung der militärischen Siege der Achsenmächte im Weltkrieg. Seine Hauptfunktion im Regime bestand darin, eine Art Schiedsrichterrolle zwischen verschiedenen Tendenzen auszuüben. Die Schiedsrichterkompetenz erlaubte es ihm auch, jederzeit denjenigen vom politischen Feld verweisen zu dürfen, der die von ihm aufgestellten Regeln verletzte. Sein Schiedsrichteramt war zugleich eine Art Moderation, der Wunsch, Zeit verstreichen zu lassen, und der Wille, die Siegerkoalition, die ihn an der Macht hielt, zu bewahren.

Die Funktion beinhaltete aber noch mehr; sie war Ausdruck einer Realität, die man „die Diktatur als Zusammenhalt" nennen könnte. Angesichts der mitunter heftigen Konfrontationen zwischen den verschiedenen politischen Lagern der Siegerkoalition hätte die Gefahr bestehen können, dass einige Sektoren sich vom System abwandten, zu den Dissidenten gingen, möglicherweise gar ein neuer Bürgerkrieg hätte entstehen können. Dass es nicht dazu kam, ist wesentlich darauf mit-zurückzuführen, dass in letzter Instanz immer wieder Franco als Schiedsrichter angerufen und akzeptiert wurde.[100] Möglicherweise wurde die Diktatur nicht als die ideale Regierungsform betrachtet; angesichts der Gefahr eines „Rückfalls" in republikanische Verhältnisse oder gar in einen Bürgerkrieg zog man sie aber immer noch jeder anderen Option vor.

Die paradoxe Folge der Tatsache, dass die Diktatur eine von den „politischen Familien" des Franquismus akzeptierte ‚Situation' war, bestand darin, dass die Institutionen schlichtweg nicht bestanden. Damit soll nicht gesagt werden, dass der Franquismus sich nur langsam institutionalisierte, son-

---

100 Zur allseits akzeptierten Schiedsrichter- und Moderatorenrolle Francos vgl. Preston, Paul: Franco. Barcelona 2015, sowie Cazorla, Antonio: Franco, biografía del mito. Madrid 2015.

dern dass er sich im Grunde gar nicht institutionalisierte, was auch damit zusammenhing, dass niemand im Regime die durchaus vorhandenen Institutionen ernst nahm. Was sollte auch von einem Regime gehalten werden, dessen Diktator äußerte, er würde auch mit der Verfassung von 1876 regieren? Oder in dem der katholische Außenminister Martín Artajo erklärte, dass die vom Falangisten Arrese präsentierten Reformentwürfe der „Grundgesetze" zu einer Situation führen würden, die mit der Sowjetunion vergleichbar sei, „aber mit Pfarrern", während der Falangist den Außenminister einen „gefährlichen Liberalen" schimpfte? Personalistische Diktatur, Inhaltsleere der Institutionen, interne Auseinandersetzungen, stets akzeptierte Schiedsrichterrolle Francos: Das sind einige der Faktoren, die bei der Debatte über die Typologie des Franquismus mit berücksichtigt werden müssen.

Die außenpolitische Anpassungsfähigkeit des Diktators und seine innenpolitische Flexibilität in der Machtkoalition erschweren die wissenschaftlich korrekte taxonomische Erfassung seines Regimes. Eines scheint klar: Unangemessen ist ein statisches Modell, das primär auf das Funktionsgefüge, auf bestimmte Zustände und Institutionen abhebt. Die lange Lebensdauer des Regimes macht es vielmehr erforderlich, die dynamisch-prozesshaften Elemente – vor allem im wirtschaftlichen und gesellschaftlichen Bereich –, die (politischen) Überlappungen und „Mischungsverhältnisse" ins Zentrum der Analyse zu stellen. Erst dann wird es möglich sein, den Franquismus vollständig mit und in seinen Veränderungen, aber auch hinsichtlich seiner konstanten Elemente zu erfassen.

Bibliographie

Altaffaylla Kultur Taldea: Navarra 1936. De la esperanza al terror. Bd. 1. Tafalla 1986.

Alvarez Gutiérrez, Luis: „Ensayo bibliográfico sobre José Antonio Primo de Rivera“. In: Palacio Atard, Vicente (Hg.): Estudios de Historia contemporánea. Bd. 1. Madrid 1976, S. 441–495.

Amodia, José: Franco's Political Legacy. From Dictatorship to Facade Democracy. London 1977.

Anderson, Charles W.: The Political Economy of Modern Spain. Policy-Making in an Authoritarian System. Madison 1970.

Apter, David E.: The Politics of Modernization. Chicago 1965.

Araquistáin, Luis: „The Struggle in Spain". In: Foreign Affairs 3, 1934, S. 458–471.

Arbeloa, Victor Manuel: Aquella España católica. Salamanca 1975.

Artigues, Daniel: El Opus Dei en España, 1928–1962. Su evolución ideológica y política. Paris 1971.

Ayala, Francisco: Spanien heute. Darmstadt 1966.

Balcells, Albert: Crisis económica y agitación social en Cataluña (1930–1936). Barcelona 1971.

Balík, Stanislav/Kubát, Michal: Undemokratische Regime. Theoretische Verortung und Fallbeispiele. Opladen 2015.

Ben-Ami, Shlomo: „The Dictatorship of Primo de Rivera: A Political Reassessment". In: Journal of Contemporary History 12, 1977, S. 65–84.

Ben-Ami, Shlomo: „The Forerunners of Spanish Fascism: Unión Patriótica and Unión Monárquica". In: European Studies Review 9, 1979, S. 49–78.

Ben-Ami, Shlomo: Fascism from Above: The Dictatorship of Primo de Rivera in Spain, 1923–1930. Oxford 1983.

Ben-Amí, Shlomó: La revolución desde arriba. España 1936–1979. Barcelona 1980.

Bernecker, Walther L. (Hg.): Der Spanische Bürgerkrieg. Materialien und Quellen. Frankfurt a.M. 1986.

Bernecker, Walther L. (Hg.): Gewerkschaftsbewegung und Staatssyndikalismus in Spanien. Quellen und Materialien zu den Arbeitsbeziehungen 1936–1980. Frankfurt a.M. 1985.

Bernecker, Walther L.: „Der katholische Klerus und das Franco-Regime". In: Oberdorfer, Bernd/Waldmann, Peter (Hg.): Die Ambivalenz des Religiösen. Religionen als Friedensstifter und Gewalterzeuger. Freiburg i. Br. 2008, S. 187–217.

Bernecker, Walther L.: „Die Arbeiterbewegung unter dem Franquismus". In: Waldmann, Peter u.a.: Die geheime Dynamik autoritärer Diktaturen. Vier Studien über sozialen Wandel in der Franco-Ära. München 1982, S. 61–198.

Bernecker, Walther L.: „Spanien zwischen Isolation und Integration". In: Salewski, Michael (Hg.): Nationale Identität und Europäische Einigung. Göttingen 1991, S. 125–168.

Bernecker, Walther L.: „Spanien". In: Wende, Frank (Hg.): Lexikon zur Geschichte der Parteien in Europa. Stuttgart 1981, S. 647–649.

Bernecker, Walther L.: Anarchismus und Bürgerkrieg. Zur Geschichte der Sozialen Revolution in Spanien 1936–1939. Hamburg 1978, (2., mit einer neuen Einleitung versehene Auflage Nettersheim 2006).

Bernecker, Walther L.: Spaniens Geschichte seit dem Bürgerkrieg. München 1984.

Beyme, Klaus von: Vom Faschismus zur Entwicklungsdiktatur – Machtelite und Opposition in Spanien. München 1971.

Biescas, José A./Tuñón de Lara, Manuel: España bajo la dictadura franquista (1939–1975). Barcelona 1980.

Borrás y Bermejo, T.: Ramiro Ledesma Ramos. Madrid 1971.

Busquets Bragulat, Julio: El militar de carrera en España. Estudio de sociología militar. Barcelona 1971.

Cámara Villar, Gregorio: Nacional-Catolicismo y Escuela. La socialización política del franquismo (1936–1951). Jaén 1984.

Casanova, Julián: La Iglesia de Franco. Madrid 2001.

Casas de la Vega, Rafael: Las milicias nacionales en la Guerra de España. Madrid 1974.

Cazorla, Antonio: Franco, biografía del mito. Madrid 2015.

Cazorla, Antonio: Miedo y progreso: los españoles de a pie bajo el franquismo. Barcelona 2016.

Collado Seidel, Carlos: Franco. General-Diktator-Mythos. Stuttgart 2015.

Coverdale, John F.: Italian Intervention in the Spanish Civil War. Princeton 1975.

Cuenca Toribio, José Manuel: Nacionalismo, Franquismo y Nacionalcatolicismo. Madrid 2008.

Ellwood, Sheelagh: Prietas las filas. Historia de Falange Española, 1933–1983. Barcelona 1984.

Foard, D.W.: Ernesto Giménez Caballero o la revolución del poeta: estudio sobre el nacionalismo cultural hispánico en el siglo XX. Madrid 1975.

Franz, Hans-Werner: Der Frankismus. Zur politischen Herrschaftssoziologie Spaniens während der Franco-Ära. Frankfurt a.M. 1981

Gallego, Ferran: El evangelio fascista. La formación de la cultura política del franquismo (1930–1950). Barcelona 2014.

Garriga, Ramón: El Cardenal Segura y el Nacional-Catolicismo. Barcelona 1977.

Gil Robles, José María: Discursos parlamentarios. Madrid 1971.

Gil-Robles, José María: No fue posible la paz. Barcelona 1968.

González Ruiz, Nicolás/Martínez, Isidoro: Seglares en la historia de España. Madrid 1968.

González, Manuel-Jesús: La economía política del franquismo (1940–1970). Dirigismo, mercado y planificación. Madrid 1979.

Harrison, John: „The Regenerationist Movement in Spain after the Disaster of 1898". In: European Studies Review 9, 1979, S. 1–27.

Hermet, Guy: L'Espagne de Franco. Paris 1974.

Hermet, Guy: Les Catholiques dans l'Espagne Franquiste. 2 Bde. Paris 1980/1981.

Iribarren, Jesús (Hg.): Documentos colectivos del Episcopado español (1870–1974). Madrid 1974.

Jerez Mir, Miguel: Elites políticas y centros de extracción en España, 1938–1957. Madrid 1982.

JONS: Antología y prólogo de Juan Aparicio. Barcelona 1939.

Könitz, Barbara: „Die Sozialstruktur der spanischen Streitkräfte". In: Wehrkunde 8/1975, S. 404–408 und 9/1975, S. 464–469.

Le Tourneau, Dominique: Das Opus Dei. Stein am Rhein 1988.

Ledesma Ramos, Ramiro: Fascismo en España? Barcelona 1968 (Erstveröffentlichung 1935).

Linz, Juan J.: „Una teoría del régimen autoritario. El caso de España." In: Payne, Stanley G. (Hg.): Política y sociedad en la España del siglo XX. Madrid 1978, S. 205–263.

Linz, Juan J.: Totalitäre und autoritäre Regime. Hg. von Raimund Krämer. Berlin 2003.

Linz, Juan José: „From Falange to Movimiento-Organización: The Spanish Single Party and the Franco Regime, 1936–1968". In: Huntington, Samuel P. /Moore, Clement H. (Hg.): Authoritarian Politics in Modern Societies. New York 1970, S. 128–201.

Ludevid, Manuel: Cuarenta años de sindicato vertical. Aproximación a la Organización Sindical Española. Barcelona 1977.

Mansilla, Hugo C.: „Politik und Militär in Spanien. Wandlungsprozesse im militärischen Bereich." In: Waldmann, Peter (Hg. u. a.): Die geheime Dynamik autoritärer Diktaturen. München 1982, S. 1–59.

Maravall, José María: „Modernization, Authoritarianism, and the Growth of Working-Class Dissent. The Case of Spain". In: Government and Opposition 8, 4, 1973, S. 432–454.

Marquina Barrio, Antonio: La diplomacia vaticana y la España de Franco (1936–1945). Madrid 1983.

Martínez Cuadrado, Miguel: Cambio Social y Modernización Política. Anuario Político Español 1969. Madrid 1970.

Mettner, Matthias: Die katholische Mafia. Kirchliche Geheimbünde greifen nach der Macht. Hamburg 1993.

Miret Magdalena, Enrique: „La educación nacional-católica en nuestra posguerra." In: Tiempo de Historia Nr. 16, 1976, S. 4–21.

Montero, José R.: La CEDA: el catolicismo social y político en la II República. 2 Bde. Madrid 1977.

Montero, José Ramón: „Los Católicos y el Nuevo Estado: Los perfiles ideológicos de la ACNP durante la primera etapa del franquismo". In: Fontana, Josep (Hg.): España bajo el franquismo. Barcelona 1986, S. 100–122.

Moreno Hernández, M.: El nacionalsindicalismo de Ramiro Ledesma Ramos. Madrid 1963.

Morodo, Raúl: Los orígenes ideológicos del franquismo: Acción Española. Madrid 1985.

Navarro, Vicenc: El subdesarrollo social de España. Barcelona 2006

Nellessen, Bernd: Die verbotene Revolution. Aufstieg und Niedergang der Falange. Hamburg 1963.

Nodinot, Jean-François: L'Eglise et le pouvoir en Espagne. Paris 1973.

Novoa, Laurentino: Religionsfreiheit in Spanien. Geschichte-Problematik-Zukunftsperspektiven. Frankfurt a.M. 1978.

Pastor, M.: Los orígenes del fascismo en España. Madrid 1975.

Payne, Stanley G./Palacio, Jesús: Franco, una biografía personal y política. Madrid 2015.

Payne, Stanley G.: „Social Composition and Regional Strength of The Spanish Falange". In: Ugelvik Larsen, S. (Hg. u.a.): Who were the Fascists. Social Roots of European Fascism. Bergen 1980, S. 423–434.

Payne, Stanley G.: „Spanish Fascism in Comparative Perspective". In: Turner, Henry A. (Hg.): Reappraisals of Fascism. New York 197.

Payne, Stanley G.: A history of Spanish fascism. Stanford 1961

Payne, Stanley G.: El fascismo. Madrid 1982.

Payne, Stanley G.: Los militares y la política en la España contemporánea. Paris 1968.

Pemartín, José: Qué es lo nuevo? Madrid 3. Aufl. 1940.

Pérez-Ramos, Bárbara: Intelligenz und Politik im Spanischen Bürgerkrieg 1936–1939. Bonn 1982.

Preston, Paul: „Alfonsist Monarchism and the Coming of the Spanish Civil War". In: Journal of Contemporary History 7, 1972, S. 89–114.

Preston, Paul: „The 'Moderate' Right and the Undermining of the Second Republic in Spain 1931–1933". In: European Studies Review 3, 1973, S. 369–394.

Preston, Paul: „La lucha contra el fascismo en España: ‚Leviatán' y las contradicciones de la izquierda socialista, 1934–1936". In: Sistema 34, 1980, S. 71–89.

Preston, Paul: „La Revolución de Octubre en España: La lucha de las derechas por el poder". In: Sistema 14, 1976, S. 95–115.

Preston, Paul: „Spain". In: Woolf, S. J. (Hg.): Fascism in Europe. London 1981, S. 329–351.

Preston, Paul: Franco. Barcelona 2015.

Preston, Paul: La destrucción de la democracia en España. Madrid 1978.

Primo de Rivera, José Antonio: Escritos y discursos. Obras completas. Bd. 1. Madrid 1976.

Prutsch, Ursula: Iberische Diktaturen. Portugal unter Salazar, Spanien unter Franco. Innsbruck 2012.

Ramírez Jiménez, Manuel: „Modernización política en España. Hipótesis para su estudio." In: Revista de Estudios Sociales 2, 5, 1972, S. 107–131.

Redondo y Ortega, Onésimo: Obras completas: edición cronológica. 2 Bde. Madrid 1955.

Redondo y Ortega, Onésimo: Onésimo Redondo: textos políticos. Madrid 1975.

Rees, Philip (Hg.): Fascism and Pre-Fascism in Europe, 1890–1945. A Bibliography of the Extreme Right. Brighton 1984.

Rey, José M. del: Religión y Política. Montevideo 1953.

Robinson, Richard A. H.: The Origins of Franco's Spain. Newton Abbot 1970.

Rodrigo, Javier: La guerra fascista: Italia en la Guerra Civil Española, 1936–1939. Madrid 2016.

Ruhl, Klaus-Jörg: Spanien im Zweiten Weltkrieg. Franco, die Falange und das „Dritte Reich". Hamburg 1975.

Rundschreiben der spanischen Bischöfe an die Bischöfe der ganzen Welt über den Bürgerkrieg in Spanien. Graz 1937.

Sánchez Asiaín, José Angel: La financiación de la guerra civil española. Una aproximación histórica. Barcelona 2012.

Sánchez Diana, J. M.: Ramiro Ledesma Ramos: biografía política. Madrid 1975.

Saz Campos, Ismael: „El franquismo: régimen autoritario o dictadura fascista?" In: Tusell, Javier (Hg. u. a.): Congreso Internacional. El Régimen de Franco (1936–1975). Política y Relaciones Exteriores. Comunicaciones. Bd. 1. Madrid 1993, S. 189–201.

Saz Campos, Ismael: Fascismo y franquismo. València 2004.

Southworth, Herbert.R.: „The Falange: An Analysis of Spain's Fascist Heritage". In: Preston, Paul (Hg.): Spain in

Crisis. The Evolution and Decline of the Franco Régime. Hassocks 1976, S. 1–22.

Southworth, Herbert: Antifalange. Paris 1967.

Steinbach, Peter: (Hg.): Probleme politischer Partizipation im Modernisierungsprozess. Stuttgart 1982.

Tamames, Ramón: La República. La Era de Franco. Madrid 1979.

Tejada, Luis Alonso: „La represión sexual en la España de Franco". In: Historia 16, Nr. 9, 1977, S. 29–36.

Tezanos, José Félix: „Notas para una interpretación sociológica del franquismo". In: Sistema 23, 1978, S. 47–99.

Thamer, Hans-Ulrich/Wippermann, Wolfgang: Faschistische und neofaschistische Bewegungen. Probleme empirischer Faschismusforschung. Darmstadt 1977.

Thomas, H.: „Der Held im leeren Raum". In: Internationaler Faschismus 1920–1945. München 1966 (= dt. Buchausgabe des Journal of Contemporary History, Nr. 1. Hg. Walter Laqueur und George L. Mosse).

Thomàs, Joan Maria: El gran golpe. (El ‚caso Hedilla' o cómo Franco se quedó con Falange.) Barcelona 2014.

Thomàs, Joan Maria: Franquistas contra franquistas. Madrid 2016.

Tusell, Javier: Franco y los católicos. La política interior española entre 1945 y 1957. Madrid 1984.

Vilar, Sergio: Fascismo y militarismo. Barcelona 1968.

Vilar, Sergio: La naturaleza del franquismo. Barcelona 1977.

Vilar, Sergio: La naturaleza del franquismo. Barcelona 1977.

Viñas, Angel: La Alemania nazi y el 18 de julio. Madrid 1977.

Viñas, Angel: La otra cara del Caudillo. Mitos y realidades en la biografía de Franco. Barcelona 2015.

Viñas, Angel: Los pactos secretos de Franco con Estados Unidos. Bases, ayuda económica, recortes de soberanía. Barcelona 1981.

Ynfante, Jesús: El ejército de Franco y de Juan Carlos. Paris 1976.

Ynfante, Jesús: La prodigiosa aventura del Opus Dei. Génesis y desarrollo de la Santa Mafia. Paris 1970.